MW00527484

# EMPIRE WORLD

# EMPIRE WORLD

## HOW BRITISH IMPERIALISM SHAPED THE GLOBE

## SATHNAM SANGHERA

**PUBLIC**AFFAIRS

New York

Copyright © 2024 by Sathnam Sanghera

Cover design by Pete Garceau

Cover images © iStock/Getty Images

Cover copyright © 2024 by Hachette Book Group, Inc.

Hachette Book Group supports the right to free expression and the value of copyright. The purpose of copyright is to encourage writers and artists to produce the creative works that enrich our culture.

The scanning, uploading, and distribution of this book without permission is a theft of the author's intellectual property. If you would like permission to use material from the book (other than for review purposes), please contact permissions@hbgusa.com. Thank you for your support of the author's rights.

PublicAffairs
Hachette Book Group
1290 Avenue of the Americas, New York, NY 10104
www.publicaffairsbooks.com
@Public_Affairs

Printed in the United States of America

Originally published in 2024 by Viking in the United Kingdom

First US Edition: May 2024

Published by PublicAffairs, an imprint of Hachette Book Group, Inc. The PublicAffairs name and logo is a registered trademark of the Hachette Book Group.

Lyrics on pages 112–13 from 'Do They Know It's Christmas?' by Bob Geldof and Midge Ure

The Hachette Speakers Bureau provides a wide range of authors for speaking events. To find out more, go to hachettespeakersbureau.com or email HachetteSpeakers@hbgusa.com.

PublicAffairs books may be purchased in bulk for business, educational, or promotional use. For more information, please contact your local bookseller or the Hachette Book Group Special Markets Department at special.markets@hbgusa.com.

The publisher is not responsible for websites (or their content) that are not owned by the publisher.

Print book interior design by Jouve (UK), Milton Keynes.

Library of Congress Control Number: 2024932495

ISBNs: 9781541704978 (hardcover), 9781541705074 (ebook)

LSC-C

Printing 1, 2024

For Noor

Until lions have their own historians, tales of the hunt will always glorify the hunter.

African proverb

# Contents

# Acknowledgements

*Empireland* came about for a host of reasons, but mainly because I wanted to plug large gaps in my knowledge. It has been a surprise and a thrill therefore to see the book resonate with so many other people: to see it being embraced as a teaching resource in hundreds of schools; to have students cite it as the reason they decided to read history at university; to find myself discussing it with ministers, former prime ministers and eminent historians; to have, surreally, been elected a fellow of the Royal Historical Society.

It has also been disorientating to have been dragged, despite intense efforts to provide nuance, into an enervating culture war on the theme of British empire. A culture war which compels me to establish, right at the beginning of this sequel, that it is not intended to be a salvo in the battle. It was not researched with a view to painting British empire in an overall positive or an overall negative light, or written in response to other books which maintain that British empire was, on balance, uniquely/relatively evil or uniquely/relatively enlightened. The 'balance sheet' view of British empire does not, as I've argued at length in *Empireland* and elsewhere, lead to understanding, and, besides, my travels across former British territories have taught me that the world has different concerns when it comes to the legacies of imperialism.

My mission here is to explain, as accessibly as I can, with the guidance of expert imperial historians who have spent their professional lives studying these themes, how British empire has shaped the world we live in today, to interrogate, along the way, some of the common claims and controversies about British imperial influence, and to explore the gap between Britain's sense of its imperial history and the world's experience of it. It's a gap that can at times feel unnavigable – there are an infinite number of routes that could be taken, and the course I've chosen is, in the end, idiosyncratic. In short, I've dwelt on issues not covered in *Empireland* – topics, and complex themes, that kept cropping up in discussions which made my understanding feel incomplete.

You don't need to read that book to make sense of this one, but it does explain a lot that flummoxed me when I was new to this history. Also, the definitions provided there for concepts such as 'race' and 'Britain', and the labels used for events such as the Indian Uprising of 1857, apply here. As do the qualifications I proffer there about Ireland's relationship to Britain, and the complex nature of historical legacies. Some further qualifications: I'll be using the term 'South African War' rather than 'Boer War' because of the extensive involvement of black people as well as Britons and Boers; and I'll be employing both the colonial and post-colonial names of places around the former British empire, the variation being a useful way to indicate which era is in discussion. I'm not, however, editing quotations that feature words or phrases that vary from these rules, or censoring racial epithets. The original language reveals important things about its social context.

This book would have been impossible to write without the colossal number of history books and articles I consulted during my research, and the generous help of historians who provided detailed feedback. I hope readers will consult the plethora of sources cited, and explore the Bibliography for further reading. A sliver of material may have originally appeared in different form under my byline in various newspapers, or in international editions of *Empireland*. Any errors are, as ever, all my own, but I'm grateful for the many people who have helped with research and travel. Particular thanks to Emily Baughan, Duncan Bell, Kate Bernstock, Ben Biggs, Seyi Bolarin, Rishy Bukoree, Jessica Bullock, Sarah Chalfant, William Dalrymple, Elizabeth Day, Corinne Fowler, Thomas Harding, Hafeez Hassam, Shazia Hassam, Molly Ker Hawn, Kieran Hazzard, Anne Irfan, Peter James, Shyam Kumar, Alan Lester, Thierry Macquet, Nesrine Malik, Olivia Mead, Lottie Moggach, José Moirt, Mary Mount, Vikram Mugon, Mark Nesbitt, Matthew Parker, Catherine Phipps, Alex Renton, Angela Saini, Michael Taylor, Kate Teltscher, Kim A. Wagner and Giles Yeo.

# Introduction: Spot the Colonial Inheritance

There is nowhere on earth that crackles with the atmosphere of British empire like New Delhi. The British may have fled the subcontinent many decades ago, but you can still feel the influence of the largest empire in human history in the city which was designated India's capital by the British, in the place of Calcutta (now Kolkata), in 1931.[1] You can sense it in the streets, the uptight diagonals and preternaturally tidy but scorched patches of lawn sitting in contrast to the chaos of Old Delhi, with its winding, narrow roads, some accessible only on foot. You can divine it in Parliament House which, designed by the British architects Edwin Lutyens and Herbert Baker in the classical style, mostly ignores Indian architecture, except for the occasional nod to its context in its decoration. You can almost smell it around the bungalows that Indians invented as a form but the British embraced as a colonial ideal, scattering them on tree-lined roads in what is known as the Lutyens Bungalow Zone.[2] It's a 7,000-acre area originally established to house government officials, the colonnaded verandas offering imperial administrators somewhere to cool down, somewhere to take refreshments and somewhere to maintain, in the paranoid colonial way, surveillance.[3]

The mood even seeps into Old Delhi, where the Maidens Hotel,[4] my home for half a week in the middle of a series of international research trips tracing the legacies of British imperialism, doesn't seem to have got the memo that empire ended at all. Established in 1903 by an Englishman, but now run by the Indian Oberoi chain of luxury properties, its website talks proudly about how it 'offers a journey back in time'.[5] The welcome letter in my room waxes lyrical about how the hotel retains its 'original 19th century colonial charm and architecture' (I've seen British colonialism described in all sorts of ways, but never 'charming'). One of the hotel restaurants is called the Curzon Room, after one of the viceroys who exercised authority in India on behalf of the British sovereign. And it all goes down curiously well with a clientele that consists of a mix of Indian and European guests, one of its many rave online reviews declaring that it is 'one of the nicest hotels . . . Brings you back to the colonial British time.'

It's a surreal place to base myself for my tour examining the international influence of British empire, not least because there are also few places on earth, in the twenty-first century, more committed to the task of decolonization than New and Old Delhi, or what, when combined, India calls its National Capital Territory.[6] I'm not just thinking here of Coronation Park, the 52-acre plot which was once the site of the grandest imperial spectacles, including the Delhi Durbars[7] but has in recent decades become the dumping ground for the unwanted statues of British imperialists, and now, having been cleaned up, is home to only a handful of viceroys and monarchs.[8] I'm thinking of Hindu nationalist Prime Minister Narendra Modi's claim in 2014 that India had been troubled by '1200 years of slave mentality' (he combined British rule with preceding periods of Mughal/Muslim rule in his definition of colonialism),[9] and of his efforts to delete all things colonial since.[10] These decolonization efforts have included redeveloping the capital's Parliament in a $1.8 billion initiative, replacing the building opened by the British in 1927 with one dreamed up by Indian architect Bimal Patel. The two Parliament buildings face each other, but on the day I visit the smog caused by Delhi's intense pollution is such that you can barely make out the edges of one building when standing next to the other. New Parliament House is not quite complete, but there has already been an opening ceremony, when Modi unveiled a 28-foot-tall statue of the militant Indian independence figure Subhas Chandra Bose, near the India Gate memorial – where the statue of the British monarch George V once stood. Bose, who was popularly known as Netaji, and whose defiance of British empire extended to seeking alliances with Nazi Germany and Imperial Japan, is something of an obsession for Modi's governing, Hindu nationalist party, the BJP. I'm in Delhi on the very holiday Modi created in tribute to Bose's birthday: so-called Bravery Day, also known as Parakram Diwas,[11] which is being marked by, among other things, a terrifying fly-past of fighter jets that makes this part of the world feel like it's being invaded all over again.

As a tribute to Bose, Modi – who is reportedly keen to rename India 'Bharat' (the Hindi name for the country) on anti-colonial grounds – has also rebranded three islands of the Andaman and Nicobar archipelago, previously named after imperial figures and once serving as a colonial penal colony,[12] and this impulse to relabel things in the name of decolonization is hardly new. Since independence, the cities of Bombay, Bangalore and Calcutta have been given more indigenous names – Mumbai, Bengaluru and Kolkata respectively.★[13] But efforts have intensified. The ceremonial avenue that links the two Secretariat buildings in central New Delhi was once called Kingsway (and, in translation, as Rajpath), but is now known as Kartavya Path (the Hindi word for 'duty'), the Prime Minister's website declaring that the renaming displays a 'shift to public ownership and empowerment'. Elsewhere, Modi has unveiled a new ensign for the Indian Navy in place of the St George's Cross (described casually in news reports as 'a sign of slavery');[14] the hymn 'Abide With Me', traditionally played to conclude Republic Day celebrations, has been replaced with the patriotic song 'Aye Mere Watan Ke Logon'; Indian musical instruments including the sitar and tabla have been introduced for Independence Day ceremonies; and the government launched the 'Har Ghar Tiranga' campaign in 2022, to mark seventy-five years of India's independence, encouraging Indians to put up the national flag (the Tiranga, meaning 'three-coloured') in celebration. A campaign which means that, as I walk around in 2023, there appear to be more national flags per square foot of the capital than there are posters featuring Modi's face.

The government has also declared war on the English language, colonial use of English having, in the words of Robert Young, 'alienated colonized

---

★ The names of Cawnpore and Jubblepore have also changed (to Kanpur and Jabalpur) to convey indigenous pronunciations and there are campaigns across the former empire to restore the names of other landmarks, villages, towns and cities. In February 2021, South Africa changed the names of several cities, including Port Elizabeth, named after a nineteenth-century governor's wife, to their previous names in Xhosa (Port Elizabeth now being known as Gqeberha). There was a failed campaign in Malaysia to change the name of George Town, the capital of the state of Penang, back to Tanjong Penaga. In 2012, Tasmania formally recognized thirteen traditional place names, including Kunanyi for Hobart's Mount Wellington and recently approved fifteen new dual names including Kennaook for Cape Grim, the site of an 1828 massacre in which thirty Aboriginal people died, and Taneneryouer for Suicide Bay. In 2017 Queensland's government in Australia renamed seven places that featured the word 'nigger', and in the south-eastern region of that state there are efforts to relabel places where massacres of Aboriginal people occurred. In Canada the Ogimaa Mikana Project is campaigning to restore indigenous 'Anishinaabemowin place-names to the streets, avenues, roads, paths, and trails of Gichi Kiiwenging (Toronto)'.

people from themselves' by devaluing their own languages.[15] In October 2022, officials in BJP-ruled Maharashtra were forbidden to say 'hello' when greeting the public[16] – they were instructed to say 'Vande Mataram' instead or 'I bow to thee, oh motherland'.[17] And, following a 2020 move to allow practitioners of ayurveda, the traditional Indian system of medicine, to perform surgery (to the dismay of many medics), the Madhya Pradesh state government has declared its intention to offer medical degrees in Hindi. Speaking to the *Guardian*, Dr Rajan Sharma, former head of the Indian Medical Council, described the move as 'regressive, backward-looking, pathetic, deplorable'. He continued: 'Where are the Hindi speaking teachers to teach medicine? I am not even going to talk about how good the translations are going to be because that implies one accepts the policy which I don't. The policy will be a failure.'[18]

Sharma's fury echoes through my mind as I continue to walk around India's capital, Googling information within the confines of my international roaming data allocation. I understand why he objects and can see why other people might also have problems with this aspect of India's decolonization project. After all, there are factors besides British colonialism which make English today the world's most spoken language, with approximately 1.5 billion speaking it as a first or second language:[19] the enduring popularity of *Friends*, the dominance of English on the internet, American English in general. Also, what happens amid this decolonization to the many English words, not least 'bungalow' and 'veranda', which derive from Indian languages?[20] And what about the practical challenge of removing English from a society which sprinkles it in almost every advert, every TV/Bollywood script, every other conversation, and provides linguistic common ground for India's speakers of at least 121 languages?[21] To see it through, India would need to disown writers like Rohinton Mistry and Arundhati Roy, who happen to be among the best on the planet at writing in English. It would need to take on the popularity of English-language books across India: walk or drive around long enough and someone will try to flog you a pirated copy of Harry Potter or Malcolm Gladwell. It would need to undo its intensely competitive English-language newspaper market,*[22] in which the *Times of India* enjoys a readership of some

---

* The British empire helped spread newspapers around the world, but as the printed word began to undermine imperialism it also spread censorship. John M. MacKenzie

15 million, and the *Hindu* has some 6 million readers.[23] It would need somehow to erase the fondness across India for classic writers such as Dickens and Shakespeare,[24] and then it would have to ban the intense study of English literature, which, as Gauri Viswanathan has pointed out, has a longer academic history in India than in Britain.[25]

But Sharma, and other critics of the Indian decolonization mission, need to pace their anger. For if Modi continues with or even accelerates his initiative, which seems to have proved popular so far, there will be bigger things to get exercised about. Such was the depth and length of British imperial involvement in the Indian subcontinent that ongoing decolonization could reshape India in profound ways. Not least, the nation's built infrastructure would have to be rethought. Banning new Western-style apartments and office blocks might be relatively achievable and even admirable; it turns out they're not particularly suited to the climate, *Time* reporting recently that 'many Indian architects [have] abandoned the vernacular traditions' – such as 'the earthen walls and shady verandas of the humid south, and the thick insulating walls and intricate window shades of the hot dry northwest' – only to find that Western-style buildings struggle to cope so well 'with the weather extremes of different regions' in India.[26] But removing other colonial features of the built environment could be rather more disruptive. Take, for instance, the wide streets that would have to go because British colonialists introduced them for reasons of public health (to 'ventilate the towns and blow away smells and disease'), temperature regulation (though if anything they 'proved to be environmentally unsuited to hot climates') and security (to 'preserve colonial power through surveillance').[27] Digging them up would be quite a task, as would be removing Delhi's postboxes and the associated system of mail, the empire having introduced the imperial postal service to India in 1854. However, electronic communication has probably done for them anyway, and it was very much Indians who made it work, in a country

---

explains: 'Initially, it seemed to the rulers of empire that the printing press and its products could be a valuable handmaiden of imperialism by transmitting information, laying down regulations, as well as propagating the dominant language and ideas of European civilisation. But . . . the press ultimately overwhelmed imperial rule by stimulating forces menacing its very existence . . . By the 1830s, the genie was truly out of the bottle and a prolific Indian-language press was in existence, the first indigenous, non-English press in the empire.'

where few towns even had street names and a dozen different languages might be spoken in one town.[28]

In turn, even these challenges would be dwarfed by the task of curing India of its obsession with cricket, a palpably imperial spectacle which, in India, is only marginally less popular than breathing. As Brian Stoddart explains, 'cricket was considered the main vehicle for transferring the appropriate British moral code from the messengers of empire to the local populations. Colonial governors were especially important in emphasising cricket as a ritual demonstration of British behaviour, standards, and moral codes both public and private.'[29] Imperialists were so successful that the Bollywood film industry plans its releases around the cricketing calendar;[30] gambling on cricket makes up the vast majority of sports betting in the country; India's national cricket team has many of the world's top players; and the Indian Premier League is the most lucrative domestic league on the planet.

And as if that wasn't enough imperial heritage to face up to, Modi could, if he wanted, take on the popularity of other sports introduced by the British, from horse racing ('the sport of kings, as it was known widely, was inevitably among the first of sporting activities to be introduced to new colonial situations, partly because of the availability of horses, partly because of its traditional association with the English landed gentry, and partly because of its established gambling tradition')[31] to croquet ('genteel games like croquet were to be found in most outposts of empire along with indoor activities such as billiards, board games, and different forms of card playing'),[33] tennis (the Colonial Secretary Lord Milner once came to visit Palestine and, after taking tea with the Governor of Hebron and his guests, played tennis with them; the ball boys were two Arab convicts who had been excused from prison for the occasion, but had to fulfil their duties on court while in leg-irons)[34] and football (Sir Richard Turnbull, a governor of Aden, once remarked that 'when the British empire finally sank beneath the waves of history, it would leave behind it only two monuments: one was the game of Association Football, the other was the expression "Fuck off" ').*[35]

---

* 'Britons were directly involved in the beginnings of football in about 60 per cent (well over 100 of them) of the world's countries, and indirectly involved in the spread of football to the rest of the world's countries,' claim Stuart Laycock and Philip Laycock in *How Britain Brought Football to the World*.

Let's face it, Modi would have less on his hands if he attempted to delete dal, or honking in traffic, or religion, from Indian culture. But the ultimate point I'm making here is not that decolonization is futile. Some of these initiatives, and those elsewhere around the globe, are crucial steps in restoring the self-respect and agency of the formerly colonized. In India, they clearly mean a great deal to lots of people: outside New Parliament House, I'm approached by a homeless man who I assume is going to request money, but he instead enquires where I come from and then asks, with pride, 'Do you have anything like this in your country?', indicating the new Parliament. I have to admit that we probably don't: while the Indians have rapidly put up this building, plans to refurbish the disintegrating Houses of Parliament in London are the subject of interminable argument. My ultimate point is that decolonization, which is growing in popularity as an idea across India, across the former British empire and in Britain itself, can only ever be tokenistic. Having spent years tracing the legacies of British imperialism in Britain, and having now spent several more years tracing the legacies of imperialism across the globe, I realize that the British empire's influence upon the quarter of the planet it occupied, and its gravitational influence upon the world outside it, has been profound. British imperialism is baked into our world and, frankly, it would be easier to take the ghee out of the masala omelettes I've become addicted to eating for breakfast in India.

Not convinced? Well, to demonstrate what I mean, let's play a game on my journey back from New Delhi to my home in London, noting down every imperial legacy we happen across, and imagining a decolonized world without it. The list can begin on my autorickshaw ride back to the hotel from what was once Viceroy's House (and is now the official residence of India's President, known as Rashtrapati Bhavan)[36] with the direction of traffic: if about one in three of the world's population drives on the left side of the road it's because of British empire.[37] And if you've ever thought Indian traffic couldn't get any more chaotic, just imagine what it would be like if this rule changed in the name of decolonization. Pulling up at the hotel, there's another imperial legacy in the jackets and ties sported by the hotel desk staff, the popularity of Western dress having been sowed in large parts of the world during British empire when, as Timothy Parsons explains, 'in most territories, missionaries and administrators dressed as gentlemen. This made Western clothes into symbols of affluence, education, and social status.'*[38] In a world set free from British imperial influence, people in all sorts of places would be getting ready for school and work in very different ways.

The cultural legacy of empire is further evident in the music and theatre listings printed in the newspapers available in the hotel lobby: as Caroline Ritter notes, British culture was pushed through imperial bodies such as the Empire Press Union and the Imperial Relations Trust.[39] Meanwhile, my hotel TV, tuned into BBC World News, alerts me to the fact that the BBC would need to be disconnected in our decolonialized world, given that it once distributed imperial Christmas messages from the royal family and programming about Empire Day; indeed the World Service used to be called the British Empire Service.[40] As Simon J. Potter has reported, the BBC considered the overseas projection of 'Britishness' an element of its public-service remit, and worked to connect the white people of the British empire together.[41] The cup of sweet tea I imbibe as I wait for my airport transfer is, of course, one of the most famous British imperial legacies of all, the British not only developing a taste for the beverage, but setting up tea and sugar plantations across the planet to cater for demand, and then shipping in enslaved people and indentured labourers to work on them. The world's agriculture would have developed differently without the British empire: entire one-crop economies based on commodities required by the imperial machine wouldn't have become monocultural economies, and the Indian diaspora would look very different too.

And there's no respite from the legacies of British colonization at the airport. The tour guides getting out of taxis and making their way to Arrivals are a reminder that some travel firms have their roots in empire, not least one of the poshest, Cox and Kings, the upmarket travel agent with over 260 years of experience, which was originally founded in 1758 by Richard Cox, assistant to the British Army's Commander in Chief, 'to supply British troops as they plundered the subcontinent'

---

* 'Colonial peoples who aspired to British respectability also used Western-style clothing to subvert the imperial order,' continues Parsons. 'In the early decades of the twentieth century, a form of popular dance known as Beni spread throughout East Africa. Beni consisted of competing troupes of dancers who satirized European popular culture and military brass bands by affecting elaborate and often outrageous Western styles of dress.'

with goods such as uniforms as well as services such as banking. It became 'an important cog in Britain's imperial war machine', and also carried back to Britain loot taken by the East India Company.[42] The sniffer dogs placed at strategic points around Departures serve to remind us that the British empire was one of the largest drug-trading enterprises of all time, with imperialists smuggling opium grown in India into China (to help pay for the tea they needed before they learned to grow it themselves) and then going to war with China to insist it accepted its imports of the drug.*[43] The first attempts to police the international drug trade came as a consequence of that imperial trade in opium,[44] and the emerging international trade in cocaine was influenced, indirectly, by British imperial policies.[45] Without the British empire, people would be getting their kicks in all sorts of different ways. And at the check-in and immigration desks there's another imperial legacy in the form of the maddening paperwork required for entering and leaving India. Ironically, a large number of academic papers have been published analysing the prominent role that paper bureaucracy played in British empire,[46] paper and wood being described as 'the key material foundations of the colonial state'.[47]

Meanwhile, the airport shops are packed with produce that remind us of British empire's commercial drive. There's a good chance that any diamonds in the jewellery on sale will be from De Beers, which is majority-owned by the miner Anglo American, both companies having deep imperial roots in South Africa.[48] If you're shopping for more prosaic fare and pick up some, say, Vaseline, or Lux soap or Sure deodorant, you'll be providing custom to Unilever, the British multinational, which is one of the largest consumer goods companies in the world, and has its roots firmly in British empire, having merged with the company that descended from the Royal Niger Company, the nineteenth-century British mercantile enterprise which pioneered the British colonization of Nigeria.[49] The cigarettes in duty-free serve as a reminder that the tobacco trade had been intrinsic to British empire from its earliest days,

---

* Thomas Manuel maintains that 'at its peak, opium was the third-highest source of revenue for the British in India, after land and salt. This makes the Honourable East India Company a drug cartel masquerading as a joint stock corporation masquerading as a government. The British Raj in the nineteenth century was a narco-state – a country sustained by trade in an illegal drug.'

various people having been proposed as the first to bring tobacco to England, including crew members on John Hawkins' pioneering slave-trading voyage in 1562,[50] and imperialists proceeding to make a fortune from farming it, often with the use of enslaved labour. Some academics argue that tobacco companies continue to function in imperial ways today, the Tobacco Control Research Group at the University of Bath arguing that 'there is a line of heritage and practice that runs from 17th century slave-trading merchants [of British empire] to modern-day tobacco companies', which still have a 'colonial mindset', using bribes when necessary in Africa, engaging in corruption, exploiting cheap labour, often interfering in the governance of post-colonial regions, making widespread use of unlawful child labour, using predatory marketing to target black customers, while still preaching racial justice.[51] The booze in duty-free is a reminder that British imperialists tried to control the production of local spirits in all sorts of places, as the revenue generated from imported alcohol was so lucrative for them,[52] alternating profiteering with bouts of alcohol prohibition, often under the influence of missionaries. The sight of travellers drinking enthusiastically before their night-time flights is a reminder of the fact that British imperialists spread drunkenness across the planet, most notably among indigenous Americans.★[53] And the mention of 'curry' on numerous menus serves to remind us how British empire shaped modern cuisine.[54]

Walking up to the airport destination and arrival boards, the names of all sorts of cities and countries alert us to the fact that navigating the

---

★ A medical paper published in 2000 maintained that the extraordinary barrage of inducements to drink heavily in the first years after European contact should be taken into account in order to understand the rise of 'native drinking cultures'. 'Alcohol has a disproportionately negative impact on Native Americans; their age-adjusted alcoholism mortality rate for the period 1992–1994 is around six times that of the US population as a whole in 1993 . . . In areas north of Arizona and New Mexico there were no significant traditions of fermented or distilled beverages before European contact, and alcohol's effects were largely unknown through much of North America.' Several historians have shown evidence of the early Americans' conscious and planned exploitation of alcohol as a highly lucrative trading product. 'Alcohol was also used as a tool of "diplomacy" in official dealings between authorities and natives, which later evolved into a de facto policy of using alcohol as a bargaining chip in the appropriation of traditional land holdings.'

planet would be a very different experience without British imperial influence. The British claim to have founded the Indian cities of Calcutta, Madras and Bombay (in their modern forms, as they were then known).[55] Modern Singapore was established in the nineteenth century by imperialist Sir Thomas Stamford Raffles, at a time when the British empire was looking for somewhere to base its merchant fleet.[56] Nairobi was established by colonial authorities in 1899 as a rail depot on the Uganda–Kenya Railway.[57] Sierra Leone, and its capital, Freetown, were created and shaped by British imperialists.[58] Hong Kong became the global capital it is today after being developed by the British. Not only was the modern nation of Nigeria created by the British, but the story goes that it was a writer on *The Times* who came up with the name, rather putting my career achievements on the newspaper into context.★[59] And then, flickering across the destination and arrival boards, there is the presence of the nation that India increasingly wants to see itself on terms with: the United States of America. Which would have to go too. One of the biggest lies America tells itself is that it rejects everything the awful empire ever stood for. In accordance with this version of events, the American Revolution gave birth to a brand-new country dedicated to the ideals of Life, Liberty and the Pursuit of Happiness when the Thirteen Colonies faced off against the British Crown over the issue of local taxation. However, the Thirteen Colonies in themselves, and most of the settlers involved, represented a unique phase of British empire. The US was a British imperial creation.

I'll admit that the deletion of entire superpowers makes me doubt the wisdom of continuing with this game in decolonization. If nothing else, the counterfactuality it inspires is silly. Imagining alternative narratives in world history occasionally makes for diverting novels and films, but it's an inane way of viewing history. Who is to say that if the Puritans, members of that reform movement that arose within the

★ 'The name "Nigeria" was a consciously invented one, first appearing in an article of the London *Times* on 8 January 1897, at the beginning of the year in which Queen Victoria celebrated her Diamond Jubilee,' asserts Kwasi Kwarteng. 'Flora Shaw, a journalist and commentator on colonial affairs, suggested the name, which she thought would be a good title for the "agglomeration of pagan and Mohammedan states which have been brought . . . within the confines of a British protectorate".'

Church of England in the sixteenth century, had not set up a successful society in a specific part of North America, someone else would not have? Or that if British imperialists had not got into the tea trade, other people wouldn't have done so, or that if the British had not built railways in India and Africa, the indigenous would not have got around to it, or that if the British hadn't insisted on driving on the left, the Indians wouldn't have decided to drive on the left anyway. But the book I happen to be reading, *I Didn't Do It for You: How the World Used and Abused a Small African Nation*, provides unexpected encouragement when its author, Michela Wrong, reveals that others play a version of the game. 'Those who travel around Africa will be familiar with the mental game of "Spot the Colonial Inheritance",' she says.

> Is that Angolan secretary's failure to process your paperwork the result of Mediterranean inertia, fostered by the Portuguese, or a symptom of the bureaucratic obfuscation cultivated by a Marxist government? Is the bombast of a West African leader a legacy of a French love of words, or a modern version of the traditional African village palaver? Which colonial master left the deeper psychological mark: Britain, France, Portugal, or Belgium? There are places where the colonial past seems to have left only the most cosmetic of traces on a resilient local culture, and places where the wounds inflicted seem beyond repair.[60]

So, I carry on and I'm afraid that the sight of 'Melbourne' on the departures board, a city named after the one-time British Prime Minister William Lamb, 2nd Viscount Melbourne, alerts me to the fact that decolonization would require the renaming of thousands of places. For it's a curious fact that after long, difficult, dangerous journeys colonists often named the new places they had 'discovered' after the places they had just left, or after British monarchs and aristocrats whom they had just escaped. Various online sources used in combination reveal[61] that there are at least thirty-five places called York in the world, there are at least eighteen places named Birmingham,[62] there are more than eighty named Victoria[63] (in Mauritius, a couple of days before I arrive in India, I find myself driving through a village called Queen Victoria – the colonists in that case not even bothering to delete the royal title), there are at least fifty-three Plymouths,[64] and there are at least forty-one places in the world named Jamestown (I'm not sure if it's flattery or an insult that no one has named anything anywhere after my hometown of Wolverhampton). Elsewhere, there are at least seventy-six Kingstons or Kingstowns outside the UK, at least fifty places called Georgetown, including the capital of Guyana, and at least fifty-one places named after Queen Elizabeth II, including two sets of Elizabeth Islands, a national park in Uganda and an old, abandoned mine in Australia. Indeed, a Twitter user informed me recently that their regular drive from Allentown, Pennsylvania, to Baltimore, Maryland, would take them through, in order, Reading, Lancaster, York, Shrewsbury and Hereford, places all named after British counterparts.[65]

I encounter adverts for HSBC on the walk to the plane – the Hongkong and Shanghai Banking Corporation having been established in 1865 to facilitate British imperial trade. And upon boarding, I spot a BP truck refuelling another aircraft on the tarmac, and remember that BP grew out of the Anglo-Persian Oil Company, which was founded by the British when oil was discovered in Iran.[66] So the thousands of BP operations across the planet might have to go. I'm flying with an Indian airline, but there are more than a few British Airways planes on the tarmac, an airline which would have to go as it was formed from a combination of the British Overseas Airways Corporation (BOAC), British European Airways (BEA) and Imperial Airways, which offered routes to imperial territories.[67] And once we're in the air, the darkness is not enough to stop the identification of potential imperial legacies. If that's a freight ship lit up on the ocean below, there's roughly a one-in-three chance that it's run by DP World, which operates five terminals in India,[68] and which not long ago acquired P&O Ferries,[69] the 'O' in P&O standing for 'Oriental' and coming from the success the company had navigating new journeys to and from the empire.[70] If that is Cyprus lit up in the distance, then British empire can take some of the credit, the British colonial government having launched an island-wide electrification scheme after the Second World War in order to counter a 'legitimacy crisis' over its continued rule.[71]

It'll be a shame to plunge places like these back into darkness. Just as it will be unfortunate to dig up or erase all the things that might or might not be passing below, including the nations with unnatural, arbitrary borders drawn by colonists,[*][72] the cities laid out by British imperialists in rectilinear or grid-iron form (a feature of imperial cities beyond New Delhi – not least Brisbane, 'a striking example of the failure of the rectangular plan in undulating or hilly country, sometimes generating road gradients as steep as 1 in 3'),[73] the thousands of public squares (British imperialists, having admired what was done by 'the London aristocratic estates', spread them across the empire, from the North American colony of New Haven[74] to Savannah, 'the Ulster plantation towns' and Charleston in 1680),[75] the shanty towns and informal settlements which are 'perhaps the most serious legacy of the colonial city' (such informal building being 'a feature of colonial urban development from its outset, with patterns of informal settlement on the edge of the city which the colonial authorities had little interest in controlling or managing'),[76] the hundreds of miles of canal (the British having doubled the area under irrigation in India between 1891 and 1938),[77] the 'water supply and sewerage systems, electricity, streetcars, hospitals, railways, telephones, paved roads, and other amenities' installed elsewhere,[78] the 'mines [which] brought the outside world into central Africa', the 'harbours, shipping lines, and the telegraph [which] linked the tropical lands to the rest of the world', the 'irrigation works, telecommunications networks, and botanical research stations',[79] the freight railways in Africa,[80] the bridges,[81] the modern port in the Israeli Haifa,[82] the treaty ports built outside empire in places like Shanghai and packed with Western buildings,[83] the hill stations like Simla, Ootacamund and Penang Hill built to offer the British 'an escape from discomfort, illness and homesickness',[84] the libraries, museums, public parks, botanic gardens, zoos, art galleries, universities and hospitals,[85] the general post offices,[86] the cathedrals, churches and cemeteries,[87] the Freemasons' lodges, and the new towns that spread across empire even as the

---

* Academics sometimes label countries with political borders which are not aligned with how their citizens wish to be distributed as 'artificial states'. Alberto Alesina et al. elaborate on the phenomenon: 'Former colonizers or post-war agreements among major powers regarding borders have often created monstrosities in which ethnic, religious or linguistic groups were thrown together or separated without any respect for those groups' aspirations. Eighty percent of African borders follow latitudinal and longitudinal lines, and many scholars believe that such artificial (unnatural) borders, which create ethnically fragmented countries or, conversely, separate the same people into bordering countries, are at the root of Africa's economic tragedy.'

imperial project began to dissolve,[88] the population growth and political chaos it inspired creating the need for them in India, Israel, Malaysia and elsewhere.★[89]

There comes the inevitable moment when I succumb to the onboard entertainment, and you've guessed it, there's no respite here from British imperial legacies. If the Indian content is dominated by light-skinned actors and models, it's partly because the British empire was one of the enterprises that pushed light skin as an ideal. It's sometimes claimed that such attitudes in India are a consequence of globalization – or of the economic liberalization of the late 1980s, which exposed the nation to Western influence. But Mobeen Hussain has shown that this colourism began to take root in India in the colonial age, through the sale and advertising of products such as Hazeline creams and Pond's Vanishing Cream.[90] If most actors and models, across all of the onboard content, are relentlessly skinny, then it's a consequence of French and British imperial attitudes, Sabrina Strings arguing that 'at the same time that gluttony and fatness were becoming associated with African women in scientific racial literature, the values of delicacy, discipline, and a slimmer physique were becoming associated with English women by the arbiters of taste and the purveyors of morality'.†[91] And if a striking number of Hollywood films feature the

---

★ Any reflection upon the incredible built legacies of British empire needs to take in the fact that British imperialists were also enthusiastic demolishers. The wide street that was developed into the primary physical feature of the colonial urban landscape was frequently imposed at great social cost by destroying densely populated areas, as was the case in Indian cities following the Rebellion of 1857 and in port cities during the early twentieth-century plague epidemics. 'Entire villages and sections of Calcutta and Bombay were pulled down for reasons of security,' writes MacKenzie. The fortresses of Indian rulers were reduced to make sure they could not be used against the British. 'After the second Anglo-Burmese War in the 1850s, the British destroyed the indigenous town on the banks of the Yangon River and set about building the new capital of Rangoon. In the third Anglo-Burmese War, the British demolished parts of Mandalay . . . In Africa, the great Abyssinian fortress of Maqdala was totally razed to the ground after the British invasion in 1867–68. Part of the city of Kumasi and the then royal palace were destroyed by the British during the third Anglo-Asante War in 1874. In 1897, the city of Benin was seriously damaged in the British campaign . . . In many parts of the world, villages were destroyed as acts of war or of revenge and punishment.'

† Strings states earlier that 'it is not surprising that the French and British were at the helm of eighteenth-century racial scientific discourse marking black people as

modern Hollywood phenomenon of the British baddie, in the form of Alan Rickman, for instance, taking on the role of a sinister Sheriff of Nottingham opposite Kevin Costner in *Robin Hood: Prince of Thieves*, or Christopher Lee playing Count Dracula, Frankenstein's monster and the gruesome Kharis in *The Mummy*, I reckon it's because of British empire. Let's face it, Hollywood has a history of favouring British actors when casting villains, even when those villains are actually German Nazis.[92] Film enthusiasts offer a variety of explanations for this phenomenon, including the British stage tradition and the relative affordability of British actors, but in my opinion British imperialism explains it entirely. Having famously fought the British empire, America finds it natural to equate Britishness with 'evil', even though it is itself a creation of the 'evil' enterprise in question.

I fall in and out of sleep while watching Ralph Fiennes do a half-decent job of making Lord Voldemort appear forbidding, his appearance merging in my half-dreams with the noseless abandoned imperial statues I'd encountered earlier that day in Delhi's Coronation Park. It'll be a shame to get a non-Brit to play him in the name of decolonization. Just as it will be a shame to get rid of the other imperial motifs I spot on the remainder of my journey home, not least the green belt which I spot bordering English cities visible below me in the light of dawn (it might be a planning concept closely associated with England but the concept of the 'physical separation of town and country by a building-free zone, usually encircling the town', was there in early colonial plantations, such as Ulster and Philadelphia, which reserved a common for sheep pasturing, and was extended to all sorts of imperial developments including Adelaide)[93] and the pet dogs being walked around my neighbourhood (academics have argued that

---

"gluttonous." The growing codification of black people as greedy eaters developed against the backdrop of the accelerating slave trade among these two colonial powers of the eighteenth century. This, together with the exigencies of reasoned self-management in the context of the High Enlightenment, transformed the act of eating from personal to political. Indulging in food, once deemed by philosophers to be a lowbrow predilection of slow-witted persons, became evidence of actual low breeding . . . Such behaviour was deemed wholly uncharacteristic of the rational thinkers sitting atop the new racial hierarchy . . . The tail end of the eighteenth century would mark the dawn of a new era. In an attempt to rationalize even aesthetic values, the beauty of the plump feminine form was reconsidered.'

thinking and processes involved in the creation of modern breeds were influenced by imperial notions of race).★[94]

Yes, even your resident floof would get it in this fully decolonized world, though not even imagining my life without Betty, Renée and Fluffy has me finally quitting this game. If I eventually give up, or at least take one day off, it's because of the pile of unread newspapers waiting for me at home in my study. For the endless news stories they contain with imperial explanations demonstrate that full decolonization is ultimately impossible not only because of the sheer volume of imperial legacies (truly, to understand the modern world, you need to understand British empire), but because many of the legacies are contradictory. For instance, just as imperialists both put up and pulled down buildings, just as the spread of newspapers across empire led to the spread of press censorship, and just as British colonialism both introduced people to alcohol and kept them away from it, a news item about an impending election in New Zealand reminds me that British empire spread democracy to large parts of the world, as another news story, about violence in the former British Mandate of Palestine repression in Myanmar, reminds me that the imperial enterprise also sowed discord in ways that still destabilize many other regions of the planet. A story about tea workers being exploited in Kenya reminds me that the British empire both dehumanized millions of Indian labourers across its plantations through indenture and laid the foundations of international labour laws, which have protected millions of others.

On it goes. The British empire both spread malaria and other diseases to millions and helped millions survive them. The British empire was an incubator and propagator of white supremacy, as well as a forum in which humanitarians founded campaigns that liberated people from crude ethnic classification. The British empire spread anti-gay repressive legislation which continues to delimit lives, but in other places it

---

★ Dog breeds were essential to Charles Darwin's early thinking on species, and just a glance at W. Gordon Stables' 1877 book *The Practical Kennel Guide* shows how dogs were racialized in imperial ways. Stables writes: 'it is . . . a strange fact, that the more highly civilised a nation is, the greater is its care and culture of the canine race, and the more highly bred are its dogs. Look at China, for example, or even native India – whose semi-civilisation seems to have been crystallised in the bud many, many hundreds of years ago – look at these nations, and look at their dogs – mongrel, gaunt, and thievish, and only half reclaimed from the wild state.'

encouraged fair treatment through the establishment of the rule of law. The British empire at times facilitated the smooth delivery of justice and at others set up colonial police forces which brutalized their own people, and some descendent police forces continue to do so into the twenty-first century. The British empire played a formative role in identifying hunger as a blight to combat across the globe, but colonial policies also caused deadly famines and imperialists used claims of charity as a cover for cynical exploitation. British empire drove some animal species to the point of extinction and was a pioneer in inflicting man-made climate change upon the planet, but then created ways to protect both animals and the environment. It brought communities together by giving them the common ground of the English language and alienated people from their own culture and traditions by insisting on the use of English. It supercharged education in Nigeria and allowed illiteracy to thrive in Iraq out of total self-interest. It displaced and unmoored millions, and gave millions of others work and shelter. The British empire was both haphazard and planned. It was involved intensely in slavery and in the mission of anti-slavery. It resisted dissent with brutal violence and was also innately auto-critical. It transported the human race into a world of instant global communication, yet propagated prejudices that meant millions closed their hearts to, and sometimes raised their fists at, their own neighbours. Not only would fully decolonizing the planet of British empire be more difficult than, as I said earlier, getting the ghee out of a breakfast-time masala omelette, it would also involve putting the ghee back in. And then repeating the impossible process over and over and over and over again.

# 1.   The Civilized Island

The beach holiday is a British institution. A report published by a travel firm a few years ago found that the majority of Brits regard their fortnight in the sun as so essential that they'd even cut down on their beloved booze to be able to afford it. But despite considering myself as British as a moan and a queue, the beach holiday has been an institution I've struggled with. Mainly due to a lack of practice: as with relationships, you need good examples to holiday well, and Indian immigrant parents are not known for their familiarity with the concepts of 'leisure' and 'holidays'. The businessman who hired me to work during the summer at his sewing factory occasionally organized trips to Blackpool for the workers; however, these were somewhat tainted by the fact that he was employing me illegally as a child labourer and paying me such abusively low wages that I could barely afford a chip butty once I got there.

Then there was the one-off family day trip by coach to Weston-super-Mare when I was eight, which gave me my first bewildering experience of sea and sand, and left me with the memorable and (at the time) mortifying image of my Punjabi mother producing a five-course Indian meal amid a crowd of sunbathing locals. It was not until my thirties that I had my first proper foreign beach holiday of the kind most Britons aspire to. To be frank, it was better than my own wildest aspirations, given it was a PR freebie, through my work on a newspaper, to a luxury resort in Egypt that I could not have afforded myself, and where my then girlfriend and I got put up in our own private mini-villa, with its own private mini-pool. An experience we rather spoiled by spending it breaking up. It's possible that, like many children of immigrants, I've just never learned how to be at leisure. But it's amazing how a global pandemic can change your perspective.

Let's face it, by the start of 2022, even the most unrelenting workaholic was desperate for a holiday, and I had the added exhaustion of having spent the pandemic embroiled in the culture wars after writing a book examining the legacies of British imperialism in Britain. It was an experience which had exposed me to thousands of abusive tweets and letters (e.g. 'It's not your nation, Baboo. You're another third world shitholian leeching off another nation's luxuries . . . Keep it up and all you street-shitting goat fuckers will be sent back home to Sisterfuckistan'), hundreds of suggestions that I leave the country if I couldn't learn to love British history ('I'm sure India would be glad to welcome home a son of such high calibre') and repeated shouty accusations from persistent men in their seventies, in letters, in emails and at literary events, that I was a disgrace for not being more respectful towards British imperial history (one of my regular correspondents has, to date, complained – that I'm not nice enough about empire – at several online and offline literary events, in multiple reviews for Amazon and Goodreads, on multiple social media platforms, in letters to *The Times*, in comment form at the end of several articles and even in a letter of response to a TV review of my documentary in the *Financial Times*).*

So when my partner, Noor, mentioned the possibility of a generic beach holiday, I leaped at the idea. As soon as it was suggested, the need for a week of catching up with prize-winning novels in the winter sun, dozing off at 5 p.m. due to daytime drinking and generally avoiding thinking about colonialism, felt like a biological necessity. And the subsequent holiday was, in many ways, a success. I logged off social media and was not told to get back where I came from for a disorientating seven days. At one point I managed not to think about covid for sixteen hours. I probably relaxed on holiday for the first time, I think, in my entire life. The only problem was that, in ending up in Barbados, described variously as 'for so long the leading sugar colony and the jewel in the crown of England's western empire'[1] and 'the most systematically violent, brutal and racially inhumane society of modernity',[2] we had not exactly escaped the topic of British empire.

It was not entirely my fault: Noor had picked the location, in coordination with a travel agent friend, and the options, amid global covid restrictions, were limited. And it's only polite to learn *something* about the history of your holiday location, even if this education doesn't go beyond reading the relevant Wikipedia page. In my case though this polite education extended beyond the internet into *The Sugar Barons*, an acclaimed book about Britain's West Indian Empire by Matthew Parker, and two books (*Britain's Black Debt* and *The First Black Slave Society*) by

* Hello again.

Sir Hilary McD. Beckles, the Barbadian historian. And while I did manage to lose myself in a fog of daytime drinking, prize-winning novels and viral TV, part of my head remained in imperial history. I found myself interspersing Maggie O'Farrell's spectacular novel *Hamnet*, for instance, with the story of how Barbados became a sugar colony as a result of the focus of individuals like James Drax. Drax was an Englishman who in the 1640s mastered, through trial and error, the processes of sugar production, processes considerably more complex than cotton or tobacco production, and imported from the Dutch Republic 'the Model of a Sugar Mill' for crushing the canes to extract the juice. In doing so he produced a sugar crop which, when it hit the London market, turned out to be vastly more profitable than any other commodity from the Americas, and which led to him becoming so rich that an initial £300 investment eventually enabled him to buy 'an estate in England worth £10,000 a year'. He was also rich enough to be able to afford the highly unusual habit in Barbados of serving beef at his home, and the use of slaves for entertainment.[3]

More than a decade after the rest of the planet, I got into *Breaking Bad*, bingeing on successive series in the hot evenings, but episodes depicting Walter White's attempts to master the process of producing methamphetamine were interspersed with learning how British colonizers had made a success out of sugar production as a result of exploiting enslaved Africans. They weren't the first to get into the transatlantic slave trade: the Portuguese got there first, it generally being accepted that the Africans enslaved to toil on the sugar plantations of São Tomé, back in the early sixteenth century, were the first victims of a murderous business[4] which was unlike any form of slavery that preceded it.[*][5]

---

[*] As Alan Lester explains, transatlantic slavery was unique in its scale (12.5 million Africans were trafficked across the Atlantic, more even than the figures estimated for the Arab slave trade), in its racialized nature ('only Black people could be enslaved in the modern plantation system, and they were owned overwhelmingly, though not exclusively, by White people'), in its transformation of three continents ('the entire demography of the Americas was changed as Indigenous people were decimated and replaced by an enslaved population trafficked from a third continent') and in its connection to industrial modernity ('the enslaved workforce was forced to produce . . . commercial crops for European consumption on an industrial scale. This in turn accelerated industrial capitalism through new sources of capital, new techniques of production and new consumer tastes').

Black people were not the first labour force on Barbados: over 24,000 individuals had arrived on the island by 1645, with around three-quarters of them being white and many of them being or having been indentured servants.[6] And the British weren't solely responsible for the wiping out of the native people of the Caribbean: it had been European settlers in general who decimated indigenous Taíno populations across the region through 'overwork, malnutrition and epidemic disease'.*[7] But they were the first to integrate black slavery so successfully with a plantation system, becoming 'the masters of industrial processes and the ruthlessly ambitious leaders of a newly created system of global maritime commerce'.[8] Between 1627 and 1808, around 600,000 enslaved men, women and children were transported to the island.[9]

And in between negronis and falling asleep in the afternoon sun, I collected a bunch of facts about our holiday destination which had almost certainly not been considered for our resort's cheerful blog on 'Incredible Things Barbados Is Known For'. Not least there was the fact that Barbados' colonizers became so successful that they were involved in setting up South Carolina as another imperial territory, a so-called 'Colony of a Colony'.[10] That white women were active participants in black slavery on the island, twenty-seven of them being listed as owning over fifty enslaved Africans on their sugar plantations in 1834,[11] poor unmarried white women even managing brothels and slave-rental services and selling the infants of enslaved prostitutes when weaned.[12] That within the enslaved African community, a few people secured personal liberty and ownership of property and sometimes even possessed the enslaved, though their priority seems to have been to buy members of their family in order to then free them.[13] That white enslavers were so paranoid that they blamed the low fertility rate among slaves on

* 'When Europeans started settling in the Caribbean, it was only a matter of time before the viruses and bacteria that had evolved in the Old World in the wake of the Neolithic Revolution made the jump across the Atlantic,' writes Jonathan Kennedy. 'The Taíno had never before been exposed to these pathogens and so hadn't developed resistance. They were obliterated by wave after wave of virgin-soil epidemics. First came illnesses like common colds and stomach bugs that had relatively mild symptoms for Europeans but were devastating for the immunologically naive indigenous inhabitants of Hispaniola. Then smallpox hit in 1518, killing between a third and half of the population. And over the next few years came a plethora of other infectious diseases. These devastating epidemics made the conquest of the New World possible.'

female slaves somehow imposing 'restraints on their [own] fertility'.[14] That the owner of the most enslaved people on Barbados in the 1780s, when the slave economy was at its zenith, was the Rector of St John's parish church, the Reverend John Brathwaite.[15]

Perhaps inevitably, this immersion in history had me wondering if these facts and events had legacies in modern-day Barbados. Or, to put it another way, while I should have been relaxing, I was still working, doing what had become a professional habit at home, tracing the historical in the contemporary. Some connections and parallels were more obvious than others, such as the way modern-day and colonial Barbados both have a reputation for luxury. In the twenty-first century, the island's most famous resort is the Sandy Lane Hotel, where double rooms will cost you £1,000 a night even off-season, and the island generally has a reputation for indulgence – even our relatively modest all-inclusive resort with its creatively miniature meals, and its vagueness when it came to defining things like 'champagne', felt sumptuous. This was in keeping with a history where the naval surgeon John Atkins observed in the 1720s that Barbados men had a 'magnificent way of living', even though 'the crops of late years have very much failed'.[16] I was being offered a piña colada by a poolside at 11 a.m. when I read about a visitor in 1747 remarking that 'There are some good Fellows here, who, 'tis said, will drink five or six Bottles of Madera Wine . . . every Day, for which they find sweating the best Relief.'[17] I was standing in the shallow end of one of the resort pools, not doing a particularly good job of concealing the fact that I can't really swim, when I read how 'towards the end of the century sea bathing . . . became fashionable' and how dancing was almost compulsory. In fact, William Hillary, a respected doctor who studied disease in Barbados, even cautioned: 'Dancing is too violent an Exercise in this hot Climate, and many do greatly injure their Health by it, and I have known it fatal to some . . . But most of the Ladies are so excessive fond of it, that say what I will they will dance on.'[18] And I was somewhere between my third and fourth (tiny-portioned) meal of the day when I read about how one feast at the home of James Drax not only involved beef, 'the greatest rarity in the Island', but also 'pork prepared in three different ways, chickens, turkey, duck, veal and shoulder of young goat, all cooked in a variety of fruit, spices, herbs and wines', followed by 'bacon, fish roe, pickled oysters, caviar and anchovies, together with olives, fruits and pies', then puddings and more fruit, including a 'magnificent pineapple, "worth all that went before"', all washed down with gallons of 'perino, English beer, French, Spanish and Madeira wines, together with sherry and brandy'.

Then there was the distinctly British air of both historical and contemporary Barbados. In the twenty-first century this Britishness can be felt through the language, the driving on the left, its first-past-the-post electoral system and the omnipresence of British tourists, British accents and even British pubs (there's one inside our resort). Colonial-era Barbados was considered so much more British than its Caribbean equivalents that it was dubbed 'Little England'[19] for its churches, rolling countryside, manor houses and bright red postboxes.[20] Barbados also had another, frankly racist, label – 'the civilised island' – which could be explained by Barbados' 'proportionally larger white population' (there were roughly four black people for every white person in Barbados, a ratio that made it possible for the whites to form a class-driven society like the one in England. In comparison, Antigua had roughly eighteen black people to every white person, and Jamaica ten to one), by the early arrival of the Sugar Revolution in Barbados (which meant that by the mid-eighteenth century some English families had resided on the island for as many as five generations, and might even describe themselves as Barbadian/Bajan),[21] by the relatively early arrival of African slavery (up to half of the black population were Creole),* by the entrenchment of the people controlling the slaves and benefiting from their toil (rather than opportunists coming over from Europe to make their fortunes, most of those who ran the plantations were born on the island, and even schooled their children there), and by the planters' need to be present (the early and intense development destroyed the island's soil, and led to falling yields, meaning that as a rule only those planters who were hands-on and physically present could keep their estates going. Only a privileged few could afford to retire to England).

And then, of course, there was the racial divide that has long afflicted the island. There's no ignoring the fact that, with a few exceptions, such

---

* 'Creole' seems to mean different things in different places. In Barbados it refers to someone born in the West Indies rather than arriving from elsewhere. They could be white, black or mixed, but it usually refers to people of African origin born into slavery in the Caribbean.

as the white Barbadian who has the onerous task of giving me my first ever pedicure, and the local black couple who are married on the beach on our final day, almost all the guests at our resort are white and almost all the staff are black. Parker notes this historical echo, saying that 'tourism, for its part, has, for some, awkward resonances with the region's history. In the large plantation-house-style hotels, the tourists are almost all white, the waiters, the cleaners, the gardeners, the servants are all black.'[22] And this racial divide has been a fact of life at least since the first comprehensive legal codes for the governance of enslaved Africans were passed in the second half of the seventeenth century. Among other things, these codes provided that Africans, described in legislation as 'brutish' and 'a dangerous kind of people', could in various parts of the Caribbean be branded with hot irons, be dismembered and have their noses slit if they committed crimes. They decreed that Africans were not allowed to give evidence in court against persons defined as 'white' (it took until the nineteenth century for this law to change). If a slave died while being 'lawfully' punished by his master, there were no consequences. In Barbados, a master would only be fined £15 for wilfully killing his own slave, and if a man killed another master's slave, he would compensate the owner to twice the value of the slave, and be fined £25. It was only in 1805 that the murder of an enslaved person by a white person became a capital crime.[23]

Enslaved people had no entitlements to family life, religious practice or leisure time, and could be executed just for threatening a white person or stealing their livestock, with Beckles adding that 'under these laws, Africans were gibbeted [hung in chains on a gibbet until they starved to death], castrated, branded with hot irons, dismembered and locked in dungeons for unlimited periods as punishment for insubordination'.[24] This was an island where, according to Parker, one of your first sights might be a gibbeted slave, with some bread placed just out of his reach, sometimes reduced to gnawing the flesh from his own shoulders.[25] An island where visitors might be taken aback by the sight of the severed heads of the enslaved, skewered on stakes, or unburied corpses left to be picked apart by vultures or dogs, where one Lieutenant Edward Thompson was once 'deeply shocked to see . . . a young slave girl tortured to death for some trivial domestic error',[26] where 'a habit of cruelty to the enslaved population was taken in almost with the mother's milk',[27] with a visitor reporting he had 'seen children as young as five or six "knocking the poor Negroes about the cheeks with . . . passion and . . . cruelty"'.[28] The English captain of the slave ship *Hannibal* in 1693 said the enslaved had 'a more dreadful apprehension of Barbados than we have of hell'.[29]

Reading about the violence had me wondering, not for the first time, how historians themselves cope with analysing such accounts on a sometimes daily basis. The trauma of other professionals encountering such material is widely acknowledged: studies have found that lawyers, journalists, psychotherapists and mental health professionals dealing with violent crime suffer from 'secondary' or 'vicarious' trauma. But what about historians? I texted Kim Wagner, the one expert in colonial violence I know, asking how he handled it, and he replied that one of his concerns was actually becoming inured to the violence rather than being unmoored by it. 'Dealing with extreme violence, including photographs of atrocities, I worry that I will not be able to convey the experience of suffering in a sufficiently empathetic way,' he said. 'This is especially the case when you're "tallying the butcher's bill" and spend a lot of time trying to find the evidence for the number of men, women and children killed in a massacre.' He referred me to an article on the theme by James Robins, who lost the ability to fall comfortably to sleep during the five years he spent studying the Armenian genocide, and has, in his research, uncovered a 'reservoir of pain' among scholars of such events, with symptoms including:

> insomnia, rapid weight gain or loss, abuse of booze or pills, unexplainable anger or fear, paralyzing anxieties. Some reactions are more subtle: the sudden unwillingness to watch a particular film or read graphic news reports; claustrophobia in a crowd. Traditionally, we've supposed that these kinds of reactions would afflict only firsthand witnesses to violence: the victims, the bystanders, maybe the journalists . . . Historians, by contrast, have neither seen nor heard the catastrophes they study – they've reached them through imagination and immersion.[30]

I've mainly encountered such material in recent years in secondary sources, but having been immersed in it for a few years I nevertheless identified with the loneliness that Elena Gallina, a researcher of sexual violence in wartime, cited as a side effect of her work in the article. 'The extent to which my research is "dark" and therefore not polite dinner conversation means I'm repeatedly isolated in piecing through the material,' she told Robins. She added that the nature of the research, 'sitting with the facts and figures . . . is made heavier by societal distaste for these things',[31] and I understood what she meant as I tried not to let my reading affect our rare holiday. But it was there, in my head, most of the time. As an expert black masseur pummelled my back, the indulgence of the experience made me contrast it with how one visitor to Barbados reported he'd seen 'terrible Whippings . . . for no other Reason, but to satisfy the brutish Pleasure of an Overseer'. When I went up for my gluttonous third serving of the hotel buffet breakfast, I couldn't help but recall that, while white planters feasted, black slaves lived on a dish known as loblolly, a grain mush which they loathed especially,[32] with the occasional addition of low-quality imported salted fish. When I saw a white American tearing a black member of staff off a strip in reception for some minor oversight, I was staggered at his lack of self-awareness. Did he not realize what this looked like, in the context of the island's brutal history?

In retrospect, I was probably going too far. I know that sometimes I need to take a day off with the colonial parallels – it's one of the reasons why I was on holiday in the first place. But it didn't feel right not to spend some of the trip acknowledging the history, and when I suggested visiting some of the former slave plantations, my long-suffering girlfriend conceded it was a good idea. She had glanced at the books and, besides, the steel drum renditions of 'Yesterday' were becoming claustrophobic. So we signed and initialled the bewildering sixteen-page contract required to book a taxi out of the resort and headed off to the first of three stops – the Drax Hall plantation, where as many as 30,000 of the enslaved are estimated to have lived and died between the 1620s and the abolition of slavery in 1834,[33] and which not only still produces sugar but has also remained in the same family since it was built more than 350 years ago.★[34]

---

★ One of the richest people in the House of Commons is Richard Grosvenor Plunkett-Ernle-Erle-Drax, the Conservative MP for South Dorset, whose estimated £150 million of wealth comes from the Drax plantation in Barbados, who owns 22.5 square miles of Dorset. He is anti-immigration and has spoken out against BLM protests. Voting to increase curbs in 2013, he said: 'I believe, as do many of my constituents, that this country is full.' And if the name Drax reminds you of a Bond villain, that's because

The journey through the technicolour of Barbados' countryside felt oddly familiar, perhaps because I had imagined it as I read about how rapidly colonizers had stripped the whole island and shaped it into iden-tikit sugar plantations, razing its original geographical character.[35] Or perhaps the minibus journey through the fields of sugar cane was rem-iniscent of the bullock-cart journeys of my childhood in the Punjab. My farming family's crop of choice in the 1980s was sugar cane – every visitor who returned from the homeland came back with raw samples and, for inner-city children, we became remarkably adept at sucking the sweet deliciousness out of the woody stalks. Its growth had been made possible, in part, by the British empire's irrigation of the land in that part of India, and realizing that gave me a short, sharp electrical shock of insight into the sheer size and reach of the enterprise. Two dis-tant points on planet earth shaped by my tiny home nation, the legacies still influencing my life in the twentieth and twenty-first centuries. Comments on Google's entry for the Drax plantation had suggested the possibility of a visitor centre or a museum, but not only did these not transpire, a line of tape strung between oil drums sitting at the estate entrance provided firm instructions not to enter. The driver obeyed, but we jumped out, risked a walk down the driveway and came across a decommissioned windmill. Apparently, the sugar cane is now processed elsewhere, but this mill, a Dutch design with heavy rollers, was the first one on the island built for crushing sugar cane, capable of processing eight tons a day,[36] was working until 1937[37] and began a process which allows Barbados' government website to boast today that Barbados once had the second highest number of windmills per square mile in the world, second only to Holland.[38] It was one of the few mechanized parts of an otherwise painfully laborious process, where enslaved Afri-cans would, under a merciless sun, be required first to strip the ground of its abundant vegetation before planting, tending and harvesting the sugar cane, and, once it had been crushed in the mill, to extract its syrup for crystallizing in a boiling house.★[39]

---

Drax's grandfather, Reginald Drax (or, more properly, Sir Reginald Aylmer Ranfurly Plunkett-Ernle-Erle-Drax), provided Ian Fleming with the name of the villain in *Moonraker*: Sir Hugo Drax.

★ Molasses, the residue left over after sugar has crystallized from sugar-cane juice, enabled the creation of a famous alcoholic spirit. 'Barbadians invented rum,' declares

Around the corner, in the middle of the fields which extended, according to Parker, 'almost exactly' as far as Sir James Drax directed in the 1650s, there stood a dark, tall house built in the Jacobean style. It was forbidding enough on its own, resembling something that might now house a severe boarding school in Scotland, and became even more so when our appearance set off the guard dogs behind the gates around the house, which, in turn, sparked the attention of the overseer I'd read about.[40] The barking and the glaring didn't make us want to hang around for a chat, but I got a photograph and had a moment to reflect upon the significance of the plantation. This is where the British, through merciless drive, became the world leaders in maritime trade and new industrial processes, where Barbados began a journey which led to it becoming one of the richest and most brutal places in the Americas,[41] where a substance was manufactured that transformed the British and West Indian diet (it's not a coincidence that the Caribbean, where a staple crop for centuries was sugar, has extremely high rates of diabetes), where a British elite established fortunes so large that their descendants in the twenty-first century would still be living off the profits made through the industrialized exploitation, torture and murder of Africans.

The next plantation, St Nicholas Abbey, centred around another Jacobean manor house in the north of the island, which, similar to Drax Hall, was built out of coral bricks and plaster in the mid-seventeenth century,[42] and which in common with mansions constructed at that time in England had a Dutch air, was rather a contrast in terms of welcome. Indeed, given that the latest owners, a Barbadian architect named Larry Warren and his wife, Anna, have essentially turned it into the rum equivalent of Alton Towers,[43] you could even say they could afford to be less welcoming. The attractions packed on to the site included not only a house tour, a museum and a café but a steam railway and a

---

Jordan Buchanan Smith in a PhD thesis on the topic; '. . . no single group of residents was singlehandedly responsible for this invention. Continental European, British, African, and Amerindian inhabitants all brought experiences of alcohol production and consumption with them. Once in place, these men and women encountered new recipes, new ingredients, and new pieces of equipment and adjusted how they made alcohol.' Slaves were brought from Africa and sometimes swapped for molasses in the West Indies. In the American colonies, molasses was converted into rum in New England, which was then sometimes traded in Africa for slaves.

water-powered mill which uses cane juice to produce forty barrels of rum annually.[44] There was strikingly little information, though, about the slavery that had sustained the estate for so long. The printed guide talked euphemistically of the 'colourful history' of the plantation and apologized for not offering more slavery-related exhibits, but it insisted there were 'future plans ... to professionally upgrade the House Museum to correct' what it admitted was a lack of information about the enslaved, and suggested to visitors that they 'please take a moment to also reflect on the enslaved who toiled within the plantation system supporting the production and expansion of the sugar industry in Barbados and the West Indies'. Yet there was no sign of any such desire for reflection among the gaggle of visitors we entered with. Our black guide struggled even to get them interested in the antiques furnishing the house. 'I know y'all here for the rum tour,' she laughed after repeated attempts at audience participation fell flat.*

I've encountered such amnesia about slavery while touring plantation homes in the Deep South, and at certain British stately homes established and sustained by slave planters' wealth, but it was shocking to come across it in the Caribbean. Given that slavery explains so much about Barbados, I thought they'd be better at it. And when such elision also turned out to be a feature of our third location, the Sunbury Plantation House, I cracked. Our 23-year-old black Barbados-born guide talked us through 'the great house', showing us the planter's office, where the chair and the desk were original to the plantation, the living-room furniture, made of Barbadian mahogany, the Sun Room, where the 'lady of the house came to have tea or entertain guests', without mentioning slavery once. It was not just that slavery was not emphasised or elaborated on, it felt as if the topic was being deliberately sidestepped. We were given the name of the white man who 'built the house', for instance, without the mention of the indentured/enslaved workers who did the actual building. We were shown a cellarette with the explanation that it was locked so that 'workers' couldn't steal their

---

* Matthew Parker tells me that when he was last there, quite a few years ago, there was a display of slave registers from the 1820s, 'those heartbreaking and sick-making lists of enslaved people – names, ages, short descriptions'. There was also a portrait of one of the many owners, a Cumberbatch, ancestor of the actor Benedict Cumberbatch who acknowledged this when he acted in the 2013 movie *12 Years a Slave*.

contents, without it being mentioned that the workers in question were in fact slaves. We were told that the upstairs bathroom was not plumbed with running water because 'it was considered an unnecessary expense', without it being explained that it was probably considered an unnecessary expense because the owners had slaves to do the water-carrying.

The elision echoed the absence of the black and enslaved in nineteen-year-old George Washington's diary, which he kept when he visited Barbados for seven weeks in 1751[45] and which I had read about in *The Sugar Barons*. The future first President of the United States had ended up in the Caribbean because Barbados had a reputation for healthy air that eased respiratory diseases, and his elder half-brother, Lawrence, was suffering from tuberculosis. It was the only time he left North America, and while his diary describes lodging in a Bridgetown tavern, being 'perfectly enraptured' by the beauty of Barbados, riding around the island, where he carefully noted the intensive plantation agriculture, enjoying the hospitality of the local elite at leisurely afternoon dinners, touring the island's fortifications, taking interest in military matters and having what seems to have been his first experience of theatre, there was hardly any reference in his diary to the enslaved Africans who made up three-quarters of the island's population, beyond a comment on how the young white ladies of the island were 'Generally very agreeable, but by ill custom . . . affect the Negro Style'.

It transpired, however, that our guide, Pryje – who chooses not to use his surname because 'it is the name of whoever it was that enslaved my ancestors', preferring his first or 'middle' name 'Ashaki' ('it means "beautiful" [in West Africa] – a name my father looked for') – was working hard at keeping his own, more significant anger at bay. A musician, he began working at the plantation during the covid-induced downturn and was about to start a master's in cultural studies. He told us he had taken the job because he was keen to learn about what life was like for slaves on the plantation, only to discover that the pamphlet he was given to crib from contained 'nothing . . . as it relates to the enslaved'. Moreover, it turned out that tourists, '95 per cent of whom are white', and the majority of whom are British, didn't care. 'The people who do come here, they are marvelling at the accomplishments of their ancestors,' he said in what was becoming my favourite accent in the world. 'They say – "this is a magnificent house, this is so beautiful, imagine what it would have been like to live here".' They're not thinking about the slavery that sustained it? 'No. Honestly. Since I started working here, a month now, I've had three persons ask about that other side of history. The funny thing is that when I came here as a young person, I was able to see shackles that were used for slavery. But none of it is here any more. It all clicked for me yesterday. Back then it was struggling to stay open because the people who came here didn't want to see shackles, it reminded them of what happened. So you white-wash it, and you turn it into something more palatable. People who come here come as part of a package. They come on cruise ships. Yesterday we had some persons come here for a house tour and by the time they got here . . . they didn't even care about the tour, they just wanted to get some food.'

I told him that some Britons had similar attitudes towards National Trust houses in Britain: they were more interested in a cream tea than in encountering history, especially colonial history, and had come together to lobby the National Trust against even conducting research. He responded that his own curiosity had led to him looking into the history of the bell house on the estate, used for storage in modern times: he was convinced it was once a church for the enslaved. I asked if slavery, in his view, had modern legacies in Barbados. '*Yes!*' came the quick reply. If the tone was slightly mocking, I deserved it. 'So, for example, integration. Black people and white people mixing? That doesn't happen at all. We don't work with white people, we work *for* them. You know, we have apartheid in Barbados. Me, as a black person, I'm not going to go in certain parts of the white community . . . we police ourselves. Which in my opinion is even worse. Cos it is you limiting yourself, you putting yourself in a box.' He offered healthcare as another example of an imperial legacy, seeded when slaves were not offered even the most basic medical care. 'We have universal healthcare. You can go to the hospital. But you'll have to wait twelve hours to see someone. White people just call a doctor. Or go to some private clinic. Clinics that we don't even know exist.'

We continued talking about the legacies of slavery, I took his details out of professional habit, he encouraged me to use his remarks if I ever wrote on the topic and the conversation stayed with me for weeks afterwards. More than anything else, it left me with a powerful sense of the enormous gap between what British people think empire did to the world and what the world knows empire did to the world. And also of the gap between a post-colonial world that wants to discuss these issues and a nation that doesn't want to listen and, if forced to do so, would rather focus on abolition or the myopic, crusty old debate over whether British empire was 'good' or 'bad'. Furthermore, it made me realize that, despite my intense self-education in recent years, there was still lots I didn't know about the British empire, not least the extent of the legacies of the transatlantic slave trade. I had learned via *White Debt* — a book in which Thomas Harding explores how his ancestors, through trade in tobacco and other commodities grown on plantations in Guyana, had benefited from slavery — that the legacies in British Guiana included 'the highest suicide rate in the world', an epidemic of domestic violence against women, a housing crisis and the poor working conditions and health outcomes of men working on modern sugar plantations.[46]

Meanwhile, through reading *Blood Legacy*, in which Alex Renton traces how his aristocratic family participated in the transatlantic slave trade, I'd learned that he blames slavery for everything from murder rates ('the origins of the violence are in the deeper traumas that derive from history') to poverty ('exacerbated by the failure to develop the economy during the British colonial period, along with the usual Caribbean brain-drain that sees so many leave for the UK, Canada or United States'), the legacy of colourism/light-skin bias within the Caribbean (because under slavery the paler-skinned black people got the better jobs), absent fathers (sociologists and psychologists believe that 'the normal role of a father was destroyed in the plantation system. A male was only there for breeding: all the other jobs of fatherhood, like protecting and providing for family, were deleted. Generations of that experience must leave a mark'),[47] dire healthcare in the Caribbean ('despite a crackdown on visas for academics and others, Jamaican health and education professionals continue to migrate as they have since independence, much to the despair of those services in the country'), poor education ('British schools pay six times what a teacher can earn in Jamaica and many, especially science and maths teachers, leave for the UK and North America ... Underfunding education in Jamaica is a story that starts at emancipation') and mental health problems (he mentions the historian Timothy Snyder who has argued that all African American descendants from the enslaved have an inherited post-traumatic stress disorder, and the psychologist Professor

Frederick Hickling, who believes slavery could ultimately explain why serious mental health problems occur far more frequently in those of African-Caribbean origin resident in the UK than in those in the Caribbean. Hickling raised the possibility that black people are becoming ill because of the impossible stress of trying to fit into a British society that has rejected them).[48]

But I had only patchy knowledge of the campaign waged since 2013 by the CARICOM group of Caribbean countries – a collection of twenty countries, stretching from the Bahamas in the north to Suriname and Guyana in South America[49] – for reparations from European powers including Britain, France and the Netherlands for the damage they inflicted upon them through slavery. My close reading of the relevant website, when I got home from Barbados, informed me that the CARICOM Reparations Commission – chaired by Hilary Beckles, one of my literary guides to Barbados – had, in a process which they hope echoes the ambition of the Marshall Plan to rebuild western Europe after the Second World War, come up with a ten-point reparation plan which included requests for everything from debt cancellation to a full formal apology to money for those people who want to be 'repatriated' to Africa. CARICOM, whose reparations commission is reportedly seeking $33 trillion in compensation from European governments ($19.6 trillion from Britain, $6.3 trillion from Spain and $6.5 trillion from France),[50] had also identified legacies including a 'genocide upon the native Caribbean population' ('a community of over 3,000,000 in 1700 has been reduced to less than 30,000 in 2000. Survivors remain traumatized, landless, and are the most marginalized social group within the region'), a 'public health crisis' ('the African descended population in the Caribbean has the highest incidence in the world of chronic diseases in the forms of hypertension and type two diabetes. This pandemic is the direct result of the nutritional experience, physical and emotional brutality, and overall stress profiles associated with slavery, genocide, and apartheid'), illiteracy ('some 70 percent of black people in British colonies were functionally illiterate in the 1960s when nation states began to appear . . . Widespread illiteracy has subverted the development efforts of these nation states'), psychological distress ('for over 400 years, Africans and their descendants were classified in law as non-human, chattel, property . . . This history has inflicted massive psychological trauma upon African descendant populations') and a lack of technological development ('the trade and production policies of Europe could be summed up in the British slogan: "not a nail is to be made in the colonies". The Caribbean was denied participation in Europe's industrialization process, and was confined to the role of producer and exporter of raw materials . . . The effectiveness of this policy meant that the Caribbean entered its nation building phase as a technologically and scientifically ill-equipped backward space within the postmodern world economy').[51]

Nevertheless, becoming aware of all this was not actually the point at which I committed to extending my examination of British imperial legacies beyond Britain. If anything, the holiday had made me realize that the quarrelling, trolling and racism that had become part of my life had taken its toll. I remember receiving just one racist email during my first ten years of working as a journalist, when I was at the *Financial Times*. My manager was so outraged on my behalf that he called the chairman of the company where the emailer worked to ask what the hell was going to be done about them. This was before I started writing about empire, after which racist abuse ingrained itself into my daily existence, becoming as commonplace as my morning bowl of porridge. Even though I've a fairly thick skin, and social media companies are getting better at quickly removing abuse once it has been reported, there were still instances when it was painful. Such as when William Dalrymple, the acclaimed historian of India, observed in the *Guardian* that he had not received a single piece of similar hate mail from a British person in decades of similar writing. 'It's a direct result of his ethnicity and skin colour,' he said. 'You can't really draw any distinction between what Sathnam's writing and what I've written. And my books have got a free pass. There's a very serious distinction to be drawn between what he's gone through writing what he has on empire, and me as a Caucasian writing the same thing.'[52] And such as when I woke up one morning and discovered a load of empire-related racist abuse had been posted online in response to some whimsical remarks I had made in a column about . . . wind farms. Getting the abuse deleted, then discussing the problem with a colleague who thought the repeat offender should be banned from the website, took up more than an hour of my morning. Toni Morrison was right when she famously stated that 'the function, the very serious function of racism is distraction. It keeps you from doing your work. It keeps you explaining, over and over again, your reason for being.'[53] Female and Jewish colleagues know what I'm talking about, because they get a version of it too, and the black historian David Olusoga gets a much more intense version of it, to such a degree that he has had to employ a bodyguard.[54] However, my white male co-workers don't have to spend a portion of their working hours either responding to or attempting to ignore this nonsense. They also don't have it suggested to them every time they write or say something even remotely critical about any aspect of British life or history that they should be more 'grateful' for everything Britain has given them or move to another country.

It felt like time to move on from it all, to do something else. Besides, I also had doubts about the legitimacy of some of the things that are commonly identified as legacies of slavery and empire. Alex Renton is frank about the fact that he encountered similar scepticism as he went around the Caribbean, from actual Caribbeans themselves, not least from the historian Susan Craig-James, whom he interviewed while visiting the site of a family plantation in Tobago. 'There is such variation in all these people descended from slavery,' she told him. 'Some go one way, some people another. We have to explain that rather than lazily say that everything negative comes from slavery. Are we going to blame everything on slavery for ever?' Meanwhile, a Trinidadian academic told him: 'The narrative of Tobagonians is that they are oppressed by Trinidad far more than by slavery or by Britain.'[55] A guide in Jamaica he calls Mike, a young farmer and a tour guide at what Renton told me was a 'TripAdvisor-leading ex-slavery plantation tourist site' who was 'keen to play down any unsavoury past', even said: 'slavery is what God meant to be. I have to ask, where would I be without [it]? Back in Africa squeezing mud to get water?'[56] There is also intense debate among economists about the role that the arguments made by the Caribbean historian and politician Eric Williams play in the quest for reparations.[57] Specifically, his disputed claim that Britain's economic growth in the nineteenth century was down to the huge financial benefits of the trans-atlantic slave trade and the business of plantation slavery, and that the reason slavery was abolished was because British industry no longer required it.*[58]

* The argument rages on, with the recent publication of an important book on the theme, *Slavery, Capitalism and the Industrial Revolution* by Maxine Berg and Pat Hudson,

Meanwhile, there is controversy and scepticism about the role that epigenetics plays in some claims made about the legacies of slavery. Epigenetics, a term meaning 'above genes', is a fascinating new area of scientific research that apparently shows how people can suffer from the effects of trauma inflicted on ancestors generations before – as demonstrated by the discovery that the effects of famine on human development lasted up to two generations after the Dutch Hunger Winter, or Hongerwinter, of 1944. In *The Gene: An Intimate History*, Siddhartha Mukherjee explains that when, 'amid the most vengeful phase of World War II', German troops occupying the Netherlands blocked food supplies, 'food intake fell to about four hundred calories a day – the equivalent of three potatoes'. Many thousands died as a result of famine, millions survived, with child survivors subsequently suffering from chronic health problems including depression, anxiety and heart disease. And 'when the children born to women who were pregnant during the famine grew up, they too had higher rates of obesity and heart disease'. Later, in the 1990s, it was found, to great surprise, that the grandchildren of men and women who experienced the famine also had greater rates of obesity and heart disease (some of these health issues are still being evaluated). 'Some heritable factor, or factors, must have been imprinted into the genomes of the starving men and women and crossed at least two generations. The Hongerwinter had etched itself into national memory, but it had penetrated genetic memory as well.'[59]

Mukherjee and other geneticists have warned that epigenetics is 'one of the most controversial arenas in the history of the gene' and we should be careful about drawing wider conclusions from the science, but it has nevertheless been a factor in claims that black people in the modern age can suffer, psychologically, perhaps even physiologically, from the effects of slavery many many decades after its abolition. In the USA this idea, combined with other assumptions and concepts, has helped fuel the notions that slavery can explain problems in the twenty-first century including workaholicism ('on any given day, an enslaved person would have to work from sunup to sundown. If they appeared fatigued or unproductive, they would be called lazy and would be

---

and researchers Stephan Heblich, Stephen Redding and Hans-Joachim Voth arguing that Britain's involvement with slavery did make an important contribution to its industrial development.

beaten . . . the trauma from those experiences is embedded in our DNA')
and the downplaying of achievements in public ('during slavery a parent
would downplay their child's intelligence or strength to protect them
from being seen as valuable and sold on the auction block').[60] For what
it's worth, I buy into the general contention that this history wasn't
actually that long ago and still shapes modern lives. I mean, the last
person to die who was born enslaved in the USA was Peter Mills who
didn't pass away until 1972, and Beckles argues in his 2013 book that
slavery in the Caribbean 'is still within living memory. It was abolished
in the different Caribbean islands at various times in the nineteenth century. Even when the British state abolished chattel slavery in its own
colonies . . . its citizens continued to invest in slavery in the Spanish
colonies until the 1880s. Some persons living in the Caribbean today
had grandparents and great-grandparents who were enslaved.'[61] But it
should be remembered that geneticists have warned against unsound
and false conclusions in the new field of epigenetics, with geneticist and
author Giles Yeo pointing out to me in an email exchange that epigenetic changes cannot be passed on indefinitely for multiple generations.
'There has to be genetic material around to be exposed to the environment; so with the Hongerwinter example the mother would have been
exposed to the fasting environment, the foetus clearly, and depending
on how far developed the foetus, then the ovaries of the foetus itself. So
the mother, child and eventual grandchild would have experienced the
epigenetic effects of the Hongerwinter, but no further. Plus, these
effects get smaller from grandmother through to grandchild.'[62]

  Three things, however, eventually persuaded me to continue my
work exploring the legacies of empire beyond Britain, the first of which
was that the Caribbean's claims for reparations got louder and louder. In
a surreal echo of my initial efforts to trace the legacies of empire in Britain, when my niche concerns suddenly became popular ones with the
emergence of the Black Lives Matter movement, the issues that occupied me in Barbados suddenly became major themes in international
relations. In the months after my holiday to Barbados, British newspapers started reporting that the government of the island was considering
plans to make MP Richard Drax 'the first individual to pay reparations
for his ancestor's pivotal role in slavery'.[63] It subsequently transpired
that Jamaica, where the Drax family had other plantation interests, was
planning something similar with the country's National Council on

Reparations looking at the case for pursuing Drax for damages,[64] and that Barbados was also considering pursuing the royal family, Lloyd's of London, Oxford University and the Royal Bank of Scotland for reparations.[65] The *Daily Telegraph*, which claimed that Drax is the subject of a 'vitriolic, abusive hate campaign over the deeds of his ancestors', quoted David Comissiong, Barbados' Ambassador to the Caribbean Community and Deputy Chairman of the island's National Commission on Reparations, saying: 'We are just beginning.'[66]

The second thing that renewed my investigations: after returning from holiday, I read widely and deepened my understanding of what happened in the Caribbean in the age of slavery. It made me appreciate that you don't, frankly, need to buy into complex science or contested post-colonial theories to see how British involvement in slavery has permanently and clearly disadvantaged nations in the Caribbean. All you need are the facts. Just look at what actually happened after abolition. It's relatively well known now that Britain compensated slave owners rather than the enslaved, dishing out £20 million, around 40 per cent of the gross national spending for the year, to people who were already wealthy.[67] But slave owners were enriched beyond this: rather than being freed at once, the enslaved were subjected to 'apprenticeships', a scheme which enabled owners to continue to benefit from free labour, and which was supposed to run for six years to 1840, but was abolished after four years in 1838.[68] From 1 August 1834, all enslaved people over the age of the six were required to work for sixty hours a week, up to forty-five of which were for the benefit of their enslavers.*[69] Eighteen-year-old James Williams gave an account of the apprenticeship system in 1837 in which he recorded repeated occasions on which he was punished for 'insolence', 'indolence', 'vagrancy',

---

* The number of hours varied: 45 hours in Barbados; 40.5 hours in Jamaica. According to Kris Manjapra, between 1834 and 1838 the apprenticeship system earned slave owners at least £27 million (more than £200 billion in today's money) in forced labour from black labourers. Apprentices were not allowed to purchase land, look for other jobs or relocate within the colony. When the apprenticeship system was abolished in 1838, black people throughout the plantation colonies celebrated. Manjapra adds: 'In the years after 1838, black people enacted collective redress for themselves by disobeying the planters, running away from plantations, and creating their own free villages. Some 40 per cent of the black population was on the move in just the first two years after final emancipation.'

working too slowly, not working for long enough, 'not taking orders' and 'talking back'. 'Apprentices get a great deal more punishment now than they did when they [were] slaves,' he continued. 'The master . . . [does] all he can to hurt them before freedom [comes].'[70] Enslaved children under six were unconditionally free, which meant that the cost of rearing them, previously met by the enslavers, was now the responsibility of their parents. In Barbados, many of the 14,000 children under six freed became destitute.

The colonists could see the point of religious education when it came to black people, as it might help to 'improve their morality and character, and to create a docile labour force', but secular education that encouraged the accumulation of knowledge and free-thinking could only cause trouble.[71] In spite of an ever increasing thirst for education from the black population, the imperial education grant for blacks issued in 1834 was cancelled in 1845. In 1846, a derisory £750 was allotted to educate all of the colony's 'poor' over a period of three years.[72] Between 1838 and 1850, policing in Bridgetown swallowed between 50 and 60 per cent of all government revenue; education, health and poor relief got less than 10 per cent.[73]

Public health for black people was also not considered important: an expansion of slums around Bridgetown in the 1840s brought with it epidemics of diseases including dysentery and yellow fever and a rising death rate. In 1854, cholera killed more than 20,000 people, around 15 per cent of the population,[74] and Bridgetown was designated the most insanitary town in the Caribbean. Meanwhile, property and land ownership largely remained out of the grasp of black people: in 1838, there were 297 major sugar plantations in Barbados, and only three of them were owned by non-white people;[75] the planters, who had an effective monopoly over land ownership (441 of the 508 estates in Barbados in 1842 controlled 81 per cent of the land), had a policy not to sell land to black people; and the government, both local and imperial, did not want the slaves to become landowners and thus threaten their sugar production, either through competition or through worker shortages. Some black people did manage to buy small pockets of land and become peasant workers, but not enough to pose a threat to the economy. Laws were written giving the police great powers over black people: under the guise of combating vagrancy they were allowed to arrest black people in transit and throw them into prison. They could also break up any gathering of black people.[76]

In 1838, the slave laws had been replaced by the Masters and Servants Act, otherwise known as the Contract Law. Among other things, the law dictated how workers should behave during non-labouring hours. If they were deemed to be insubordinate by their employer, they could be thrown off the plantation without compensation and punished in other ways. They could also be punished if found to be using bad language, gambling or taking part in unauthorized gatherings. The planters were permitted to employ private policemen for their estates to ensure compliance. As they did during slavery, employers differentiated between their workers: there were 'good' black people who were compliant and 'bad' black people who wanted to rebel. Given all this, it wasn't a surprise when there was a rebellion in Barbados in 1876. On 24 June, *The Times* of London listed the causes as: 'low and falling wages, insufficient education and social relief, oppression, taxation, stark poverty, rising vagrancy and destitution, high and rising infant mortality rates, social suffering, spiralling crime and the general cruelty associated with the contract laws'.[77]

There was a similar situation in Jamaica. Alex Renton, who believes that every European tourist to Jamaica should be lectured on the history before being allowed to collect their bags,[78] an idea I fear would only fuel the culture war over colonialism in the West,* points out that the underfunding of education after abolition was such that in 1943 not even 1 per cent of black people in Jamaica attended secondary school, while the figure for mixed-race people was 9 per cent (in Britain in 1951, almost half of children did). He also reports that Joseph Chamberlain, Secretary of State for the Colonies, once described the Caribbean colonies as 'the Empire's darkest slum' and swore to take action to alleviate their poverty. Renton continues: 'The British government's failings in Jamaica and other colonies after 1838 – the true date of the end of slavery in the British Caribbean [rather than 1807, when the slave trade in the British Empire was formally abolished] – are perhaps the least told story of all. The history of Britain's Caribbean colonies after emancipation is a story of decades of gross neglect, careless and deliberate. It is not the benevolent imperialism about which we were taught.'[79] The plight of the British Caribbean, which had between 1713 and 1792

---

* We should not fuel the culture-war myth that exploring this history is about inciting white guilt, when it's about promoting understanding.

accounted for a quarter of imports into Britain,[80] was exacerbated by the decline of the sugar markets.[81] Things started to deteriorate from the mid-nineteenth century, after the British stopped giving preference through duties to Caribbean sugar and allowed cheaper sugars from outside empire to enter their market;[82] Caribbean sugar also faced the challenge of cheaper European beet sugar.[83] At the height of the Jamaican sugar industry's success in 1805, exports reached 100,000 tons; that figure declined to 20,000 for most of the remainder of the century, and by 1913 had fallen to just 5,000. Although England didn't lose its taste for sugar and consumption continued to rise, little of the money made its way back to Jamaica. Several Caribbean islands attempted to shift to other crops, ending their sugar monoculture, but for most their efforts were too late.[84] At the start of the twentieth century, Barbados, an island roughly the size of the Isle of Wight, which at one stage was worth more in trade than all of England's colonies combined,[85] was in such a wretched state, economically and socially, that in some parts of the island infant mortality was close to 50 per cent.[86]

It was an economic, moral, social, humanitarian and political catastrophe. Having put them there, having exploited them in the most brutal and inhuman ways, having played a major role in the greatest human calamity the continent of Africa has seen★[87] and having benefited as a nation from their toil,[88] we abandoned them. Which brings me to the third and ultimate thing that persuaded me to extend my journey into the legacies of British empire. The gap that our guide Pryje had originally highlighted for me, between Britain's sense of its imperial history and the world's actual experience of British imperialism, kept coming up. It came up when Adam Stewart, the white Executive Chairman of the resort we'd stayed at, deleted a tweet he had sent celebrating the sixtieth anniversary of Jamaica's independence ('as a sixth generation Jamaican, I couldn't be prouder to celebrate our beautiful and iconic island'),[89] after Twitter users pointed out that those six generations meant he was 'a direct descendant of SLAVERS?!' and had 'better cough up reparations for Black & indigenous Jamaicans'.[90] It came up during the Conservative Party leadership election campaign of

---

★ 'Over the long term, the impacts of slavery on Africa were catastrophic,' reports Peter Frankopan. 'By 1800, the population of the continent was half of what it would have been had the slave trade not existed.'

2022 when one candidate, Penny Mordaunt, claimed that she first understood how this 'country stood up to bullies'[91] when she watched Royal Navy warships leave Portsmouth harbour for the Falklands, seemingly oblivious to the fact that large parts of the world have less warm memories of Britons arriving in warships. It came up after half a dozen people forwarded to me a viral meme on Instagram, where 'England in English history book' is portrayed as a cheerful Thomas the Tank Engine or a cute Gremlin, and 'England in other Countries' history book' is correspondingly portrayed as a demonic ghost train or Gremlin monster.[92] And it was dramatized vividly by the two biggest royal news stories of the year: Prince William and his wife Kate's disastrous eight-day tour of the Caribbean, Belize, Jamaica and the Bahamas, to mark the Queen's Platinum Jubilee, just a few weeks after our visit; and the death of Queen Elizabeth II.

In many ways the royal tour was just another royal tour, like dozens before it.[93] The couple, who were then styled the Duke and Duchess of Cambridge, looked uncomfortably warm in clothes that were visibly ill-suited for the climate. They appeared mortified when encouraged to dance to local music in front of the world's media. They struggled to look interested as they were given endless guards of honour and regaled with the national anthem dozens of times. The whole thing had an imperial air, as royal tours traditionally have done.[94] The only difference was that everyone suddenly noticed these things, and suddenly the royal couple couldn't do anything right. Before they had even arrived in the Caribbean, the couple cancelled their first engagement, at a cacao farm in Belize, when a dispute over indigenous land rights led to protests, with locals brandishing 'Prince William leave our land' signs. Awkwardly, the Jamaican Prime Minister Andrew Holness stated during a meeting broadcast on live TV that Jamaica was planning, as Barbados had already done, to ditch the monarchy – using a phrase, 'moving on', which Prime Minister David Cameron had used during a 2015 visit, as he deflected questions about slavery reparations.[95] They faced demonstrations by groups such as the human rights initiative the Advocates Network, which demanded compensation from the royal family for slavery. They participated in awkward photo opportunities with unfortunate colonial connotations, where they played bongos, greeted children who had arms outstretched through a wire fence and were driven standing in the back of a Land Rover used by the

Queen and the Duke of Edinburgh on tour in 1962.[96] At one point William expressed his 'profound sorrow' over slavery, adding that it 'forever stains our history', but it was not enough to save the trip. There was consensus, even in the monarchist press, that the trip had been a disaster.[97] Meanwhile, I T V News reported that there would be a new 'Cambridge way' for Prince William and Kate's future royal tours,[98] with the young royals reportedly keen to address 'how colonial powers behaved in places like the Caribbean and how that impacts on relations today'.[99]

Then we had the death of Queen Elizabeth II. It seems to have been accepted during the extended mourning period, in both Britain and abroad, that the late monarch, daughter of the last Emperor of India, owner of the Koh-i-Noor diamond, who learned that she would inherit the crown while in Kenya, had been a symbol of British empire. But while her work on the imperial front was painted, in Britain, as constructive and unifying (one liberal magazine even bore the claim in a headline that HM had 'made us feel less embarrassed about Britishness and empire'),[100] the world sometimes had a different view. In South Africa, the Economic Freedom Fighters political party declared that it would not grieve the British queen's death because 'to us her death is a reminder of a very tragic period in this country and Africa's history'.[101] In Dublin, an anti-monarchy protest march culminated in a coffin marked with 'RIP British Empire' being dumped in the River Liffey by Anti Imperialist Action Ireland, who said they were recreating an event from 1897, when the Irish republican James Connolly protested during a visit to the city by Queen Victoria.[102] Australian anti-monarchy protesters covered themselves in fake blood and chopped up the Australian flag on the country's designated day of mourning for the Queen, while over in Melbourne the Warriors of the Aboriginal Resistance led a huge rally, declaring that they stood 'against racist colonial imperialism and its ongoing effects on us as Aboriginal people'.[103] CNN brought its viewers the news that 'Queen Elizabeth was not universally loved in Africa' with a 'live report on colonialism, fairy tales and the Africans who refuse to mourn her death'.[104] The *Guardian* reported from Asia that 'the somewhat muted response to the Queen's death in India reflects her complex position in a nation where the British monarchy is still seen as a lasting symbol of colonial rule'.[105] Writing in the *New York Times* Maya Jasanoff said 'the queen helped obscure a bloody history of decolonization whose proportions and legacies have yet to be adequately acknowledged'.[106]

There were unpleasant scenes when these British and international views clashed. The *New York Times* found itself being subjected to vicious criticism online from Britons who were keen to enforce reverence for the late Queen ('Ignore the nasty, malevolent attacks on the Queen, the British Monarchy, and Great Britain, from the New York Times and the liberal elite US media,' complained a former aide to Margaret Thatcher).[107] And I had a taste of the vitriol when, after the funeral was over, I went on *Channel 4 News* and remarked, quite gingerly, respectfully and tentatively (I thought), that while Elizabeth II did some good work on post-colonialism, making an apology for British imperial policy of the 1860s when she visited New Zealand in 1995, and expressing the 'regrettable reality' of British relations with Ireland, she conspired with the British establishment to act like empire had never really happened. When empire ended, British imperialists had resorted to destroying files systematically, to prevent incriminating information ending up in the wrong hands,[108] and the Queen had participated in this silencing by going straight from talking about empire in her speeches to talking about the vacuous Commonwealth, helping the nation pretend that urgent work was not necessary to help everyone come to terms with what had happened. Urgent work that both the nation and the royal family needed to do.

For the royal family doesn't just have a deep imperial history, it also has a deep association with the slave trade. This involvement included Elizabeth I being the patron of early English slave-trading expeditions led by John Hawkins in the 1560s; King Charles II granting a 1,000-year royal monopoly to 'The Company of Royal Adventurers Trading into Africa' in order to trade in Africans on the coast of Gambia*[109] (a company in which his younger brother the Duke of York took a governing role), ensuring the security of the royal investment by holding weekly board meetings in his apartment at Whitehall Palace,[110] while the Africans delivered to Barbados were branded with the initials 'DY',

---

\* When, in 1663, 'King Charles II chartered the Royal Adventurers of England Trading into Africa and placed it in charge of his younger brother, James . . . [t]he British Crown commemorated the occasion with the minting of a new denomination of coinage, the guinea, named after Britain's term for the West African slave coast.'

representing the Duke of York, or 'RACE', representing the Royal Africa Company of England;[111] Queen Anne, in 1712, establishing exclusive rights for Britain to provide enslaved Africans to the Spanish West Indies;[112] and mid-eighteenth-century British slavers representing themselves as licensed agents of King George III.[113] Of course, some royals, such as Prince Albert, expressed anti-slavery sentiments, in his case in the form of risk-free sympathy after abolition and emancipation, but they were outnumbered by those who supported the slave trade and the West Indian plantations; a debate on abolition in the House of Lords saw seven royal dukes vote in favour of slavery with just one against. The Duke of Clarence, who became William IV, was presented with a gift of fine silver dinnerware by the Jamaican assembly in thanks for his efforts fighting the abolition lobby; the gift is still among the royal family's possessions.[114] Our national connection to slavery in the Caribbean is so strong that fewer Scots go by the surname Campbell than do Jamaicans, whose families were often given slave owners' names.[115] And royalty's connection to the slave trade is so strong that when Elizabeth II visited Barbados in 1966 she was hosted by her first cousin Lord Harewood, whose family became wildly wealthy through Caribbean sugar plantations, the money funding their grand family seat, Harewood House,[116] and their name still being carried by many of the descendants of the people they enslaved, not least the actor David Harewood.★[117]

Two perceptive commentators drew attention to the enormous gap, at this time, between the discussion of empire in Britain and the

---

★ Not long ago I met David Harewood, who told me he had, for a documentary, recently visited Viscount Lascelles at Harewood House. 'I'd met him before, but in the light of Black Lives Matter and George Floyd, it was odd,' he said. 'I drove on to the Harewood Estate and you're looking at the name Harewood everywhere, and staying in Harewood Cottage. It's a beautiful place, and he's actually a nice guy. At least he's been the first incumbent of Harewood who has acknowledged where the money came from, and he's been honest about it. He's got bursaries trying to help your young inner-city kids, and he's got rooms dedicated to black art; the library's got books on slavery . . . he showed me a picture of the 2nd Earl of Harewood, the man who owned my great-great-great-great-grandfather . . . He enslaved them, beat them, raped them and all that malarkey. And I remember sitting in this room full of gold and fine art and beautiful cutlery and gilt-edged paintings, and I just thought, "The whole thing's disgusting, because nowhere, nowhere is there a single mention or picture of the people who worked all day to fund it. It's like we're invisible."'

discussion of it elsewhere. In an outtake posted on social media, Trevor Noah, the South African former television host of the satirical news programme *The Daily Show*, confessed to being 'shocked' that people mourning the Queen expected 'others, who were under the British empire, to share the same level of mourning. Why would they? All over Africa, all over India, there's so many places in the world where people go "Yeah, but do you know what the British empire did to us?" '[118] Then there was the historian David Olusoga who made an appearance on the *Empire* podcast to discuss the passing of the Queen and observed that the debates we have in Britain about empire are actually 'monologues'.[119]

> As if we on these islands can sit around among ourselves and decide whether the empire was good or bad. As if the conversation doesn't necessitate it being a dialogue with the 2.6bn people around the world who are the inhabitants of former British colonies (more if you add the US). That urge to have a monologue about empire is something that is absolutely breaking down. It was always a dialogue, we just didn't listen to the other side.

Anti-slavery is a dominant theme within this British monologue. Within our enervating national conversation about whether British empire was a force for good or a force for bad, as if lengthy, deeply complex history can be reduced to the level of football fandom, to the question of whether you support team 'imperialism' or not, is our obsession with abolition. For too many Britons, the fact that we abolished slavery, and then urged other nations to abolish it too, cancels out the need to talk about anything else, from the fact that we dominated the transatlantic slave trade for large periods, to the claims that Caribbean countries make about its complex modern legacies, to the fact that 'freedom' for many of the formerly enslaved involved intense repression, to the fact that abolition itself has unstraightforward modern legacies of its own. Complex legacies that, not least, include other kinds of political activism[120] (including working-class activism,[121] the suffragettes and white feminism in general),*[122] the establishment of

* Anti-slavery campaigns provided British women with their first chance to become political activists, with Jenny S. Martinez observing that 'the movement for women's

major campaigning organizations that continue to lobby today (several NGOs have their roots in abolition, including Anti-Slavery International),[123] the development of international human rights law[124] and international law itself.[125] Meanwhile, imperial historians have written about how abolition led to more imperialism, as it created the notion that there was something intrinsically good about the British variety of colonialism,[126] and how abolition, itself afflicted by racist attitudes,★[127] led to an intensification in imperial racism, Richard Huzzey describing a process where 'the complicity of African chieftains in slave trading, the failure of West Indian laborers to conform to free-labor expectations, and the pervasive presence of slavery among African societies all reinforced racist attitudes'.[128]

---

suffrage' grew out of 'the abolition effort, as activists who had learned organizing techniques in the context of abolitionism turned to other issues'. It has been argued that white feminism more generally grew out of British imperialism, with early twentieth-century British feminists embracing all sorts of imperial causes: Florence Nightingale, for example, described India as 'a home issue' and a 'vital and moral question'; Mary Carpenter visited India and then promoted the cause of Hindu female education; and Josephine Butler campaigned against the Contagious Diseases Act in India. The academic Antoinette Burton famously argued in 1990 that, in taking up the cause of brown women in this way, white feminists were actually trying to boost their own cause. Butler's campaign against the Contagious Diseases Act in India, for instance, came after many years of campaigning to get similar legislation, which regulated prostitution and saw women suffering as a consequence of enforced medical examinations, repealed in Britain. Burton coined the phrase 'white woman's burden' to describe the phenomenon, contending that due to imperial attitudes Indian women were seen not as equals but rather as unfortunates who needed the help of their British feminist sisters. Butler and her followers had almost no contact with Indian women, although they claimed to understand and know their Indian counterparts.

★ Thomas Macaulay despised what he called the 'lazy, ungrateful negroes' of the Caribbean; George Stephen didn't care about the fate of 'half-castes' after abolition; and even Wilberforce put the people of colour who attended a dinner for the African & Asiatic Society behind a screen. The eighteenth-century reference work *Universal Modern History* attacked the slave trade but was according to one analysis 'almost hysterical' in its 'Negrophobia', while the historian Catherine Hall explains that 'the famous anti-slavery slogans, "Am I not a man and a brother? Am I not a woman and a sister?", and the icon of the kneeling slave seeking British help' exhibited 'the cultural racism of the anti-slavery movement'. For they contained within them the 'paradoxical conviction that slaves were brothers and sisters, all God's children, but younger brothers and sisters who must be educated and led by their older white siblings'.

Turning our national monologue into a dialogue would expose us to these fascinating complexities, because this is the complex way the world actually experienced the British empire. This dialogue would allow us to live in an infinitely more sophisticated, more interesting world where even something like abolition could be allowed to have nuanced legacies and areas of grey, where seemingly opposite things, such as our deep involvement in slavery and our earnest efforts to wipe out slavery, could be true at once. And when I returned from holiday, I realized I owed it to people like Pryje, to the tourists who explore the Caribbean in wilful ignorance and to the many proud Britons I've met in recent years who want their nation to have a sane relationship with the rest of the world, to try to encourage it. It felt like an intimidating task, possibly an impossible one, but I had to look at Britain's imperial history from a broader perspective than I had done so far. I had to work out how British empire had really shaped, and continues to really shape, the modern world.

## 2. Useful Plants

A couple of months later, I'm somewhere even hotter than the Caribbean. Somewhere so hot, in fact, that my glasses have steamed up and I've had to take them off. Somewhere so hot that there's sweat trickling off my brow on to the floor. Somewhere so hot that a session of Bikram yoga would actually provide an opportunity to cool off. Though, as two teenagers on the 24 bus once reminded me during a London heatwave, in one of the best things I've ever overheard on public transport, 'It's the humility [sic] that kills you.' The sky is clear but the air is thick with moisture and water drips from the trees around us like rain. Frankly, I feel faint as my expert guide, Kate Teltscher, informs me that the plant I've just identified as a palm is in fact a cycad that is some 250 years old. And the claustrophobia increases as we make our way between a set of trees that do actually turn out to be palms, and she tells me that Queen Victoria visited this location three times in less than six weeks in 1848.

This royal fact (Queen Victoria famously never left Europe) may betray that I'm not, as I expected to be when I decided to explore the international legacies of British empire, abroad, in the rainforests of, say, Kenya or Malaysia. I'm just a dozen tube stops from my home in London, touring the Grade I-listed glass and iron Palm House at the centre of Kew Gardens, which has, for more than 170 years, been kept at a temperature and at a humidity level that mimics a rainforest. And why am I in Britain when I could be in, say, Tasmania, Ireland or South Africa instead? Well, it turns out that Kew Gardens deserves more than the footnote I've dedicated to it so far during my journey into the history of British empire. It has been a challenging thing to comprehend, for someone who associates flora mainly with interior design, but the British empire transformed large parts of the planet through . . . plants. And Kew Gardens, working with botanical gardens scattered across the empire, was at the centre of this transforming process.

I admit that, until my reading about empire guided me here, thinking about British imperialism through the prism of plants no more occurred to me than viewing the Tudors through the prism of, say, shoe buckles or fish. To be honest, until now I've not even considered Kew in terms of plants: I last visited because my mum was in town and she is notoriously difficult to entertain and I couldn't think of a single other thing to do. But it was as a result of its manipulation of plants that British imperialists, among many other things, enabled the colonization of large parts of Africa, established new markets in new commodities, enabled global communications, ended up fighting a vicious war in Malaya which involved mass murder, spread/cured various catastrophic human/plant diseases, engaged in international espionage which involved bizarre disguises and incidents of torture and introduced into global cuisine 'unknown names such as Demerara, Assam, Darjeeling and many more, from obscure corners of the globe'.[1] It was also through plants that they caused massive environmental destruction, triggered ecological and climate disaster, inspired far-reaching conservation measures and intense environmentalism in turn, established plantations and one-crop economies which changed the shape of the planet, provided employment for millions and led to the displacement and exploitation of millions of others. It's wild! And Kew Gardens, an organization which I'd classed alongside sleepy garden centres and regarded as the leisure manifestation of a cuddly edition of *Gardeners' Question Time*, played a central role within it all![2] Those surprising botanists.

It's not the classic histories of British empire that bring this home to me: in general, they rarely dedicate more than a few hundred words to plants and botany. It's reading about Barbados that finally makes me appreciate the significance of Kew in the international imperial story in particular, and botany in general. After all, it was an act of plant transfer that inspired the idea of sugar plantations in the Caribbean in the first place: more specifically, Christopher Columbus transplanting sugar-cane seedlings from La Gomera in the Canaries to the New World on his second voyage in 1493.[3] It was an agricultural process that people like Drax had to master in order to make plantations thrive: the enslaved workforce had to be taught to clear areas for planting, to plant or weed sugar cane, to harvest it at a precise moment and to extract the juice as quickly as possible before it spoiled. Then, after the sugar monoculture had sapped the island's soil of life and increased the frequency of crop diseases, and after felling the island's forests had created a shortage of material from which to build things,★⁴ heat homes and fuel the boiling houses on plantations, the solutions sought were often botanical. Lumber was imported from New England (and coal from England). Ever increasing amounts of manuring and replanting were necessary to produce the same amount of sugar. At one point soil was even brought in from Suriname, though this was a failure: wood ants damaged the hull of the ship and the project was abandoned.⁵

Finally, it was botanists in general, and Kew in particular, who came to the rescue when the island, and the Caribbean at large, struggled after the collapse of the sugar market⁶ in the late nineteenth and early twentieth centuries. Sugar cane had been a bedrock of the Caribbean economy ever since its introduction in Barbados in the mid-seventeenth century, and the crisis, caused by disease in sugar cane, the depletion of soil after centuries of nutrition-intensive sugar cultivation, the removal of tariffs on imports into Britain of cheaper sugars and competition from the sugar-beet industry in Europe, hit hard, leading to a glut on the international market and a downward spiralling in price. Whereas in 1850 sugar cane had provided 90 per cent of the world's sugar, by 1900 that figure had plummeted to 32 per cent.⁷ It was the propagation of fresh varieties of sugar cane that turned things around: work led by one John Redman Bovell, a scientist and agronomist in Barbados, with the assistance of Kew.⁸ His efforts paid off spectacularly: official figures show that between the early 1880s and the 1930s, the annual sugar production in Barbados increased by 76 per cent, and Bovell himself concluded that by the 1920s his varieties of sugar cane had increased planters' revenues by approximately $2 million per annum, despite occupying just over half of the available cane fields.⁹

It was in this way that Kew, the centre of a network of around one hundred botanic gardens across empire during the Victorian era, from Fiji, St Helena, Burma, Trinidad and Tobago, to Mauritius, the Cameroons, Tanganyika and Jamaica,¹⁰ was less the bland, pretty garden that I had long viewed it as and more like an extension of the East India

★ A report from 1667 emphasized the island's almost total loss of woods. In Barbados, it was said that 'all the trees are gone, thus they are compelled to send for wood to England in order to boyle their sugar'. The same document continued by saying that, compared to Barbados, Tobago's natural resources were untouched and wild.

Company or the Colonial Office. It's a point that Kate Teltscher, the author of the intensely readable *Palace of Palms*, which tells the gripping tale of what she calls 'the finest surviving Victorian glass and iron building in the world',[11] brings home to me as she continues my tour of the Palm House. After informing me, as even my shins begin to sweat, that the magnificent structure is composed of some 16,000 glass panes and was built using techniques developed in shipyards, that while the building is now painted white, and its glass is clear, the glass and paint scheme were originally green (it was literally a green house) and that the Palm House is home to what might be the oldest pot plant in existence (not actually a palm but a cycad, collected by Kew's Francis Masson in South Africa in 1773). She takes me up the spiral staircase that offers a view over the canopy of trees and tells me that, when it was opened in 1848, the Palm House was seen as offering a window into British empire. Literally, for the majority of the plants came from the Calcutta Botanic Garden, but also more impressionistically as it offered the Victorian public an immersive journey into the exotic vegetation and humidity of the colonies. The *London Journal* compared the temperature inside to 'the heat of India' and the *Quarterly Review* fretted that 'a tiger might start out from among tree-ferns, a boa-constrictor might be climbing the trunk of that cocoa-nut palm'.[12]

Around the same time, the artist Marianne North, whose work is celebrated at Kew,*[13] was painting the landscapes of British empire, and the palm was becoming a symbol of imperialism in Britain,[14] a reflection

---

* The Marianne North Gallery is another Victorian nod to empire at Kew. North was an intrepid female artist who, after inheriting a fortune from her father, rejected the small, domestic life expected of her and chose instead to roam the world, recording the landscapes, plants and people she encountered. In 1879, in an act, frankly, of intense solipsism, she informed Kew's Director Joseph Hooker that she would fund a new gallery at the gardens – on condition that it would display her oeuvre. Walking around the gallery today, I'm glad North got her way. Her more than 800 sometimes garish paintings provide an illustration of how the Victorians saw, fetishized and attempted to classify the natural world of the empire. The building is designed to resemble, in part, an Indian bungalow, which, as we heard earlier, was embraced by colonial Brits around the world as a residential form. The paintings are displayed under headings including 'Jamaica', 'Ceylon' and 'Sacred Plants of the Hindus'. There are rare taxidermied animals on display and, in one case, a photograph of North in Sri Lanka dressed as a 'native'.

of the fact that the Victorians saw the palm as a wonder plant in terms of usefulness – as Teltscher explains to me, 'the trees produced everything from wood, to wax, oil, fibre, starch, alcohol and sugar'. The production of palm oil, the edible vegetable oil that derives from the fruit growing on the African oil palm tree, may be seen as an evil in the modern age,[15] as it often requires the cutting down of acres of rainforest, leading to a loss of animal habitat for endangered species and considerable carbon emissions, but it was embraced enthusiastically in the nineteenth century. In just fifteen years, between 1840 and 1854, the amount of palm oil imported to Britain from West Africa more than doubled as it became indispensable in industry,[16] serving as a lubricant for machines and railways, and becoming an ingredient in soap,[17] candles and margarine. The need for palm products was a factor in Britain's colonization of West Africa and the creation of the modern nation that is Nigeria, its prevalence in West Africa leading to palm oil being pitched as a 'legitimate trade' that would help wipe out slavery. Some candlemakers paraded their anti-slavery credentials in advertising, prompting one writer to joke that 'Every candle of 'em that's burnt helps to put out a slave.'[18] The palm oil business, though, often used the feral, violent ship crews who had worked in the slave trade, crews known as 'palm oil ruffians', notorious for mistreating anyone they could get away with mistreating.[19]

In turn, the continued existence of the Palm House today serves as a more general reminder of the fact that Kew, from its very origins as a royal hobby in the eighteenth century to its development into a national institution 'aiding the Mother Country in everything that is useful in the vegetable kingdom', was from 1841 onwards in the business of 'economic botany', exploiting the natural resources of empire for the benefit of empire.[20] It's probably a relationship that younger people struggle with more than older people, given that school textbooks, at the height of empire, often stressed how Britain benefited from the natural resources of empire,[21] but botany and colonialism were often inseparable. For instance, the botanist Joseph Banks,[22] who, like Marianne North, had inherited a fortune from his father[23] and used it to further his knowledge of the natural world of the empire, and who, as King George III's adviser for the Royal Botanic Gardens, was the closest thing Kew then had to an official director, accompanied Captain James Cook on his journey to the South Pacific on board HMS *Endeavour*,[24] a venture that sparked British colonization of the region.*[25] Indeed, 'Botany Bay', the name James Cook gave to the site of the first landing of *Endeavour* on the land mass of Australia, really should have provided me with a clue to the influence of the discipline.[26]

Using his high-level connections, Banks pushed the idea that horticulture could help British empire get ahead of the French and Dutch, if it became 'a great botanical exchange house',[27] and he associated himself with the cause. The East India Company enlisted him to find gardeners to test growing Chinese hemp in Britain; the government asked him to find a suitable botanist to join a voyage to Africa and assess horticultural possibilities as they scouted for locations for a new penal colony; Banks lobbied the government to choose Australia's Botany Bay as a location for warehousing British criminals and undesirables, as its plant life and climate made it ideal for a self-sustaining settlement – while its 'extremely cowardly' natives, he noted, were unlikely to cause trouble.[28] He also famously became an advocate for the breadfruit tree, which he had come across in Tahiti, as an efficient solution to the challenge of feeding large numbers of enslaved workers in the Caribbean.[29] The way he saw it, it was not cost-effective to rely on supplies imported from the North American colonies, and neither was he keen on encouraging slaves to grow their own food on allotments, as this might make them dangerously self-reliant and cut into the time they spent cultivating sugar cane. It took Banks a while to see his breadfruit plan through, after his first attempt had been scuppered by the Mutiny on the *Bounty*, a tale you'll be familiar with if you have watched one of the five feature films on the subject,[30] but by the end of 1793 no fewer than 679 trees were ensconced in botanic gardens in St Vincent and Jamaica. What he

---

* The huge collection of plants and animals Banks amassed included over 1,000 that were previously unknown in Europe and now feature in the collection of the Natural History Museum. He also somehow found the time while doing it to establish the merino wool industry in Australia. Andrew Wulf tells us that 'as a Lincolnshire landowner and sheep farmer, Banks had suffered from the closure of the American market during the war and had investigated ways of improving Britain's wool production in order to target the European clothiers, who preferred the finer wool from the Spanish Merino. Smuggling sheep out of Spain, he had cross-bred them with British species, producing a breed that would become the Australian Merino. These sheep, when dispatched to Australia years later by Banks, formed the basis of the Antipodean wool industry which would bolster the British economy over the next century.'

hadn't considered, however, was whether the enslaved actually wanted to eat his breadfruit. As it happens, they didn't: they saw the stuff as fit only for feeding pigs.★[31]

Later, Joseph Hooker, the younger half of the father–son duo who were Kew's founding directors when it became a state body in 1840, was at one point sent on a trip to India (on a trip engineered and financed by his father) with combined botanical and colonial aims.[32] There he gathered around 7,000 specimens of Himalayan plants to bring home, including rhododendrons whose descendants today still flourish in Southern England and Scotland, and at the same time created maps that would later be used by the British Army.[33] Meanwhile, his father William Hooker, Kew's first official Director, did most for so-called economic botany when he formalized and promoted the garden's imperial function by opening up the Museum of Economic Botany in 1847.[34] Located initially on the site of an old fruit store, the museum, which subsequently spread into three other buildings, was pioneering in its highlighting of the practical use of plants. William Hooker argued that investment in home-grown innovation was much needed: after all, in 1853, according to the Department of Liverpool Customs, 'articles of vegetable origin' comprised at least three-quarters of the total value of British imports.[35]

I return to Kew a fortnight after my Bikram botany session with Kate Teltscher to talk to Mark Nesbitt, the enthusiastic 61-year-old expert who now looks after this aspect of Kew's work in the twenty-first century.[36] He informs me that the museum was such a success in its early years that it inspired copycat museums of economic botany as far afield as Missouri, Adelaide, Edinburgh and Hamburg.[37] That the curators of the time liked to display the useful material with examples of items that had been fashioned out of it – a palm, for instance, alongside a walking stick that had been carved out of its timber.[38] That the museum eventually fell out of favour with the public in the twentieth century and was closed in stages, until it was completely gone by 1987. That the collection of nearly 100,000 objects remains, however, stored in a building named after Joseph Banks. Like the Palm House, it's kept at a fixed temperature

---

★ Breadfruit is now a part of the Jamaican diet, which raises the possibility that its rejection back then, when it was pushed as 'slave-food', was not about taste but, as B. W. Higman puts it, about 'resistance to the will of the slave-owning class'.

and humidity, albeit a rather more bearable 17°C and 45 per cent humidity.[39] And after explaining he was not a particular fan of the phrase 'economic botany', preferring 'useful plants' (people sometimes complain that his talks feature no actual economics), Nesbitt shows me some of the specimens, beginning with the South American cinchona tree,[40] a plant I've never heard of but which saved millions of lives and enabled the European colonization of large parts of the planet. In fact, it turns out that in the mid-nineteenth century cinchona was the most sought-after economic crop in the world. This was because the bark of the cinchona tree was known to contain quinine, a chemical compound understood to prevent fever caused by malaria, which is reported to have killed more people than all other diseases and wars on earth combined,[41] and which was both spread by colonists and an impediment to them.

In *The Making of a Tropical Disease: A Short History of Malaria*, Randall M. Packard explains how colonists may have spread malaria.[42] In the nineteenth century, the British built embankments in western Bengal, for example, which helped to protect the area from flooding. In order to increase rice production, landowners dammed rivers and streams at the same time. These 'swamp-like conditions' created the perfect environment for the introduction of new anopheline mosquito species.[43] Although the science behind what happened is unclear, early English settlers are understood to have brought malaria with them to North America from London and the eastern counties of Kent and Essex, where the disease was endemic in the sixteenth and seventeenth centuries.[44] It's also known that colonial economic policies often led to overcrowding in slums, in cities like Bombay, which became habitats for mosquitoes carrying malaria.[45] Meanwhile, Jonathan Kennedy, who teaches global public health at Queen Mary University of London, explains how malaria blocked the colonization of large parts of Africa: in the early nineteenth century, a European in Mali, facing both malaria and yellow fever, could expect to survive for only one-third of a year, the region having the staggering annual mortality rate of 300 per cent.[46] This was one of the main reasons why by 1870 only 10 per cent of Africa's land mass was controlled by European powers. If this figure hit more than 90 per cent by the early twentieth century, it was not just because of the emergence of the steamship and the Maxim gun, but because of quinine, which didn't prevent people from getting very ill but often saved them from death.

Colonists in affected regions such as Africa, India and South-east Asia were instructed to ingest a daily dose of powdered quinine, often mixed with alcohol to take the edge off its bitter taste – though the common claim, which I've repeated many times, that imperialists took their quinine through the great British gin and tonic is, to my surprise, not precisely accurate, according to Nesbitt.★[47] Of course, as their empires spread, the British and the Dutch were keen to take this natural prophylactic from its original home in South America and cultivate it in their own colonies – and embarked upon what Luke Keogh has called 'one of the most infamous acts of biological espionage in world history'.[48] The intensity of the effort is reflected in the fact that, among its 100,000 economic botany specimens, Kew keeps around 1,000 bunches of cinchona bark, dating from the period between the 1780s and the 1930s, and when I'm shown a sample from the 1850s I'm reminded of the sticks that relatives from India would often have packed in their luggage. More specifically it reminds me of a visit, in my teenage years, from an elderly Indian aunt. Rather than clean her teeth with a brush at a bathroom sink, she sparked amusement among her British Asian nephews and nieces by heading into our garden early in the morning, and brushing her teeth with a stick, a 'dattan', that Punjabis traditionally use for dental hygiene. Nesbitt tells me that such daily encounters with plants might have been the process by which indigenous people in South

---

★ There is little evidence that gin and tonics were ever consumed medicinally. What seems to have happened is that tonic water, and quinine (in other kinds of alcohol), emerged, separately, as health drinks. And then one Erasmus Bond, a London businessman, brought the two together. The use of quinine as a preventative antimalarial in the British Army did not begin until the 1850s, when it was administered daily, explain Kim Walker and Mark Nesbitt in *Just the Tonic*. It would have taken a concentration of quinine five to ten times higher than that found in a modern tonic to have any preventative effect from a standard drink of gin and tonic. The writers were unable to locate any advice for drinking gin and tonic as a preventative in historical medical texts. 'There is nothing to suggest a medical purpose in [the] consumption [of gin and tonic], rather it is the refreshing properties of gin and tonic in the tropics that come to the fore,' they continue. 'The medicinal properties of quinine are, however, relevant to the origins of gin and tonic. The long history of quinine as a tonic for general health surely inspired Bond to develop his tonic water and encouraged a ready market for the product. Equally, the long history of quinine in alcoholic drinks, whether in tonic wine or in spirits, must have suggested to the first consumers of gin and tonic that the combination was a plausible one.'

America worked out that this cinchona bark material was a cure for malaria. Historians now point to the likely role of traditional healers in the Andes.

British imperialists faced massive hurdles in trying to harness the antimalarial chemicals within quinine. These included the challenge of transporting plants across the world, which may be easy now but was then a major logistical challenge. One of the key developments that helped on this front was the invention of the Wardian case. Nesbitt has one sitting on the floor, in the corner of the warehouse he shows me around. A wooden box, with a lid that allowed light in through slits and glass, it has Kew's address inscribed on one side, together with a warning on another side to 'Keep under awning on deck'. Its story has recently been told beautifully in a book by Luke Keogh, in which he reminds us that on a long sea or land journey there were all sorts of ways, back in the day, to destroy a delicate seedling: extreme temperatures, rough handling, the salt from ocean spray. The Wardian case changed everything, and, like many breakthroughs, it was invented by accident. In 1829, the amateur naturalist Nathaniel Bagshaw Ward experimented with placing the pupa of a moth with soil and dried leaves in a sealed glass container and leaving it for a while. He expected the moth to hatch, but also observed, to his surprise, that a fern and grass had sprouted from the soil. It appeared that plants sealed in glass containers could survive for a long time without watering. The discovery led Ward to design portable glazed cases for transporting plants, which he tested successfully on a voyage from London to Sydney in 1833, and which then revolutionized the logistics of international plant transportation.

Thanks to the Wardian case, which appeared at the Great Exhibition in 1851, and has been described by historian Lynn Barber as 'probably one of the best investments the British government has ever made',[49] scientists could send cinchona plants across the planet. But they still faced other challenges, not least the inconsistency in quinine yield between tree species. Not only were there no fewer than twenty-five different species of cinchona tree, and not only did they all look similar, but each yielded different amounts of quinine and all sorts of environmental factors, from the amount of rain and sun, to the nature of the elevation and soil, influenced quinine yield, as did the part of the tree the bark was taken from. And it was these maddening subtleties that scuppered the first significant effort by the Dutch. Using a pseudonym, botanist Justus Karl Hasskarl travelled to South America and roamed the Andes, collecting enough cinchona plants to fill twenty-one Wardian cases, and in 1854 transported them, plus a load of seeds, to Java. Initially, the mission appeared to be a success. The transplanted plants survived and by 1860 there were nearly 1 million cinchona plants of the species *Cinchona pahudiana* flourishing on plantations in Java. But it was then discovered that the bark of this particular species of cinchona contained virtually no quinine. A failure which must be classed, alongside the Beagle 2 mission to Mars and the finale to *Game of Thrones*, as one of the most agonizing project failures of all time. For the Dutch, the humiliation was profound.

A few years after this disaster, the British tried their luck, in a major mission led by Clements Markham and funded by the India Office. In his application letter for the role, Markham proposed an ambitious plan to prospect for eight valuable species of cinchona in four separate areas of the Andes, and reminded the government of the need for a secure supply as it was currently costing £53,000 a year to purchase quinine just for India. In 1859 the project got officially under way: a 'halfway greenhouse' was constructed at Kew to propagate the plants en route;[50] thirty flat-pack Wardian cases were sent ahead to ports in South America, to be picked up by collectors; a plantation in Madras was cleared and prepared for the plants. Around this time, other parts of the empire which had also become home to experimental cinchona plantations, established with the cooperation of Kew Gardens and botanic gardens across empire, included Fiji, St Helena, Burma, Trinidad, Mauritius and Jamaica. Markham himself travelled to Bolivia with his wife, while two other collectors, Richard Spruce and Robert Cross, went to Ecuador and Peru.[51] There was another painfully long wait: the medicinal value of the bark could not be ascertained until the trees became established after some fifteen years of growth.[52] Which probably puts into perspective any difficulties you've faced with keeping houseplants alive.

Meanwhile, the Dutch, while still mortified, hadn't given up on cinchona. An entrepreneurial British trader who lived in Peru procured thirty-five pounds of high-quality cinchona seeds from his local friend Manuel Incra Mamani and sold them on to the Dutch Consul General in London. The trader then asked Mamani to get hold of some more, but this time his friend was apprehended by the authorities. Mamani was thrown in jail and beaten, later dying from his injuries. Neverthe-less, Mamani's first shipment of seeds made it to Java, and 12,000 were planted in a nursery. The resulting plant was designated a new species, *Cinchona ledgeriana*, and its bark was found to contain a very high per-centage of quinine – 13 per cent. Most commercial quinine barks contained between 3 and 5 per cent quinine, so this was deemed an extraordinary development.[53] The discovery led to the Dutch dominat-ing the quinine market, and by the 1930s they were exporting 2 million pounds of bark a year and controlling nearly 90 per cent of the trade, which they carried on doing until Japan took Java during the Second World War.

But while the Dutch Java plantations ended up dominating the world market, the British did not fail. You see, as Arjo Roersch van der Hoogte and Toine Pieters explain, the two empires had different aims:[54] the Dutch cultivated *Cinchona ledgeriana* in Java for its rich content of the main quinine alkaloid, aimed at the export market, whereas the British in India concentrated on varieties suitable for local consumption, and which contained lots of specific 'quinoline alkaloids' that proved to be as effective as quinine. There is considerable debate among historians about whether British imperialists succeeded in providing Indians with meaningful access to the medicine. Significant efforts were made by national and state governments to get quinine into villages by means as diverse as post offices, district officers, schoolteachers, village headmen and Junior Red Cross Brigades, but, even at the time, these were recog-nized as insufficient, with a variety of practical and financial factors (including racialized healthcare, with brown people receiving much inferior care) obstructing efforts and imperial administrators at the time expressing strong discontent with the results.[55]

Together, the Dutch and British empires wiped out the South Ameri-can trade. The transfer had consequences for the world beyond the fact that it made the European colonization of large parts of Africa possible, in the so-called Scramble for Africa, until then a graveyard for Euro-peans. While trying to synthesize quinine, a scientist accidentally invented one of the first synthetic dyes – Perkin's mauve.[56] It transpires that European imperialists may have invented the concept of 'greenwash' while justifying the theft of cinchona.[57] And while quinine has long been superseded by synthetic, pharmaceutical treatments for malaria, the World Health Organization still recommends its use as a last resort for sufferers resistant to the synthetic drugs.[58] It's amazing that a single plant could have changed so much, though it was equalled by Kew's other great econo-botanical success story, rubber.[59] It's a tale that surprises me for many reasons, not least that I had no idea that rubber can be a naturally occurring material. Learning that Playstations grow on trees would have been only marginally more surprising than hearing that natural rubber starts life as a sticky white sap called latex, or caoutchouc, derived from certain trees. Yet more staggering was the news from Nesbitt that the liquid excreted by dandelions when you break off stems is also rubber, and that during the Second World War Russia started a huge rubber industry based on dandelion cultivation. However, the mid-nineteenth-century sample of latex he shows me comes from the Brazilian rubber tree or Pará, *Hevea brasiliensis*. I want to touch it and squeeze it to see if it feels like the stress toy it vaguely resembles, but it's in a jar, pickled in a highly poisonous mixture of formaldehyde and alcohol.

Long used by indigenous peoples in the Amazon, for items such as shoes, rubber proved useful even before the emergence of the motorcar, featuring in industrial machinery, hoses and waterproof clothes. Thomas Goodyear's invention of vulcanization in 1839, where treatment with sulphur made rubber more stable, supercharged its popularity and, as demand rocketed, the species of trees in South America, Africa and Asia that yielded it became intensely sought after. The demand for rubber from the United States and Europe sparked a boom in the Amazon regions of South America, which resulted in an estimated 30,000 indigenous South Americans being murdered, enslaved or tortured. In some places, 90 per cent of the Indian population was eliminated by atrocities and disease linked to the rubber boom, and many of today's uncontacted Indians are the descendants of survivors, who fled into remote areas to escape a similar fate.[60] One of the people who lobbied Kew to help the British empire to get into the trade was the rubber manufacturer Thomas Hancock, who in 1855 suggested to William Hooker that the East and West Indies would be suitable for rubber cultivation.

The botanists at Kew, however, once again faced considerable challenges, dwarfing even the agony I've faced over the years trying to make chilli plants grow from the seeds that the Wahaca restaurant chain used to give away with meals. First of all, the South Americans had a monopoly and were not keen to share their trees, seeds or production secrets. Second, rubber seeds are 'recalcitrant', which means they die if permitted to dry out, which made them hard to transport over long distances. Third, the trees took a long time to grow, which meant it could, once again, be decades before botanists knew if their transplants had worked. Regardless, several men took these challenges on, including Henry Alexander Wickham, a British plant collector who managed a plantation in the Amazon basin. He was offered £10 per thousand seeds by Kew's Joseph Hooker and began the job in early 1876. Another botanist called Robert Cross was also collecting seeds in the Amazon and transporting them back to Britain, and then, once sprouted, taking them on to Ceylon. Between them, the men managed to break into the wild rubber industry, despite yet more problems emerging – not least that on one voyage a ship loaded with a cargo of Cross' plants hit a reef near the Jamaican coast, and that some planters turned out to dislike growing the rubber trees. At one point Ceylon botanical gardens sent 2,000 seeds back to Kew as a result of the lack of enthusiasm.[61]

Botanic gardens in India, Burma and Singapore received shipments of rubber plants from Kew. In an example of scientific cooperation between colonial powers, a batch was even conveyed to the Dutch Buitenzorg Gardens in Java.[62] All in all, there were more than two decades of trial and error, including yet another one of those long waits for the trees to mature, before imperial plantation rubber was unleashed upon the world market. When Ceylon's rubber industry finally got properly going in the early twentieth century, plantations there even supplied rubber plants back to Brazil, where rubber crops had become blighted by disease and the industry was struggling. In the end, though, it was in Singapore where things really took off: when the price of coffee fell in 1896, plantations on the Malay Peninsula turned instead to rubber, planting 12,000 acres of trees over five years. The emergence of the automobile had made rubber crucial to the West; add in the world wars, and the West consumed almost all of the total crude rubber output in the first half of the twentieth century. By 1913, Britain was supplying all of its own rubber needs and then some. Crude rubber also became Britain's top re-export, and rubber eventually became a multi-billion-dollar industry. Incredibly, the whole thing came about as a result of a few hundred seedlings that made it from Brazil to Kew. Some of the brands flourishing then still exist today, such as Dunlop, the British tyre firm, which was one of several companies with its own plantations in Malaya.[63]

The global market for rubber is nowadays divided between synthetic and natural versions – around two-thirds of the total is produced synthetically.[64] And in the twentieth century the rubber industry in British Malaya – which comprised the island of Singapore and a number of states on the Malay Peninsula that came under British control between the late eighteenth and the mid-twentieth century – became so significant that Malaya, though one of Britain's smaller colonies, turned into its most profitable. In an echo of the wild success that British planters had in Barbados, a territory once focused on the export of sea products, timber and tin, and trading mainly with China, suddenly became the world's leading supplier of rubber. By 1929, GDP per head in British Malaya was the highest in all Asia – including Japan.[65] Those canny enough to have shares in rubber companies could see dividends of over 200 per cent – 5 per cent would be considered a decent yield from a British commodity company nowadays – and, subject to the fluctuations in world rubber prices, the industry continued to grow. Britain didn't want to give up on its star money-making colony, and in 1948, when its interests in British Malaya were threatened by the communist fighters of the Malayan National Liberation Army, it was ruthless in its response.

The Malayan Emergency, also known as the Anti-British National Liberation War,* was a guerrilla war that pitted the British empire's military against those who wanted independence to establish a socialist state in the region. The spark was the killing of three British rubber-plantation managers, in the context of plummeting rubber prices, labour unrest and the mistreatment of workers.[66] The British then declared a state of emergency, and in response the leaders of the Malaya Communist Party disappeared into the jungle and re-emerged as the new MNLA, dedicated to liberating the region from colonial rule. To defeat the insurgents, the British resorted to extremes, attempting to starve them by limiting food, massacring livestock and destroying crops by dropping herbicides – including Agent Orange – from the air. Caroline Elkins points out in *Legacy of Violence: A History of British Empire* that

---

* It was apparently called an 'emergency' because plantation owners and miners would not have been compensated by insurers if it had been classed as a 'war'.

even as Britain helped draft the European Convention on Human Rights its representatives in Malaya were introducing emergency regulations which allowed them to 'impose bans, curfews, and collective punishments together with the death sentence for a range of offenses, which included the possession of firearms and consorting with terrorists', arresting and detaining entire villages 'for the smallest infractions, including providing food and intelligence to the Malayan National Liberation Army', opening fire with live ammunition in detention camps and torturing detainees*[67] by starvation, locking them up in cages beneath the hot sun for days at a time, force-feeding them soapy water and kicking/punching/beating them.[68] There was also straightforward mass murder, the most infamous incident of the war occurring on 12 December 1948 when a unit of Scots Guards killed twenty-four unarmed villagers on a rubber estate at Sunga Rimoh near the town of Batang Kali – a massacre often labelled as 'Britain's Mỹ Lai', in reference to the murders of villagers by US forces in Vietnam. In 2012 the *Observer* newspaper reported the existence of papers which showed that, following the killings, the British hastened to pass a regulation with retrospective power that gave troops in British Malaya the right to use 'lethal force' to prevent escape attempts.[69] Historians sometimes marvel at how Kew Gardens, working with the India Office, managed to launch a whole new plantation industry with literal 'seed money' of just £1,505.[70] They are right to be astonished: it's remarkable how such a modest imperial initiative is largely the reason why the Asia-Pacific region dominates the natural rubber market in the twenty-first century.[71] But if you're talking about the legacies of British imperialism across the modern world, it's only right to include the deportations, the torture and the deaths.

* Chen Yung-liang, a detainee, described what happened after he had been arrested under suspicion of carrying messages for Malayan communists: 'After taking me to the police station, the detectives stripped me of all my clothes and said to me: "Your body is not made of steel. Now speak and be quick!" When I simply replied that I knew nothing, their fists rained upon my head and body. In the evening they again forced me to take off my clothes, shut me in a bathroom and poured water on me with a hose for several hours. They then dried me with an electric fan. This process was repeated again and again until I was stiffened with cold. Afterwards I was tortured with all sorts of cruel methods, such as forcing sharp bamboo sticks into my fingertips.'

Having said that British perspectives on empire need to be tallied with international perspectives, I find it almost impossible to plug the gap between this violent history and the rarefied, painfully polite, English atmosphere of Kew Gardens' café, whenever I head there for tea and cake between meetings with Nesbitt and Teltscher. Just as I struggle to tally the twee, middle-class vibe of the Gardens, where the middle-aged exchange and pick up gardening tips, with the racism of influential botanists (Carl Linnaeus, the eighteenth-century Swedish naturalist who created the modern system of classifying plants and organisms, including human beings, identified Europeans as 'acute, inventive . . . Governed by laws' but Africans as 'crafty, indolent, negligent . . . Governed by caprice') and the racism of common plant names (names still in use in 1991 included 'Niggerhead', 'Niggerfinger', 'Nigger-toes', 'Jew Bush' and 'Kaffir Plums').[72] But the tea rooms do bring us to a British imperial botanic initiative that perhaps has even more significant modern legacies than those cited so far – the creation of tea plantations across India and then across British empire more generally.[73]

I don't ask Mark Nesbitt to show me any of the 350 samples of tea that sit in the archives of the Museum of Economic Botany, because while Kew was involved to a small degree, and while Kew's Joseph Banks had been the one to make the initial suggestion that the oriental tea plant might be cultivated in British colonies,[74] Kew didn't play a central role. Also, for once, I actually know something about the transplantation. Indeed, the familiarity of tea, after the novelty of cinchona and rubber, and the wild, unfamiliar, intricate stories involved in their cultivation, makes me feel that I am once again on dry, level ground after a period in space. Not only is botany an entire world I've not considered before, it feels as if botanists almost literally speak another language (with all those Latin plant names). However, the tale of how British imperialists got into the business of cultivating it is familiar. It's possible you think you know about it too. The famous story goes that in 1848 the East India Company hired Robert Fortune, a plant collector with knowledge of China, to steal Chinese tea plants and transfer them to India. Arriving in China, where Europeans were forbidden and the tea industry was guarded carefully, Fortune decided that the mission required a disguise and so roamed the country clad in full traditional costume, including a shaven head. Travelling from plantation to plantation, he collected tea varieties, packed them in Wardian cases and sent them off to India. He used a method of planting tea seeds at the foot of mulberry trees, under an inch of soil, so that they were sprouting by the time they arrived after the long voyage. He spent years in the country and finally, in 1851, accompanied the last fourteen Wardian cases, containing tens of thousands of seedlings, to Assam, via the new British port of Hong Kong. In 1853, Fortune returned to China, on a second mission for the EIC. By now, he had made lots of local contacts, and he used them to acquire the exact seeds he wanted. To begin with he shipped thirty Wardian cases to India, and then in the following two years dispatched a further 131 – at the time, one of the largest shipments of cases ever.[75]

This story has created the popular idea that British India's tea-plantation industry, beginning in the foothills of the Himalayas, was seeded by one adventurous spy, but I discover via Nesbitt, and via the reading he provides, that things were, in reality, much more complicated, are in fact still incompletely understood, and it's not long before I once again feel like I'm in orbit around Mars. It's true that the East India Company had real motivation for creating a tea industry in India: its outlay on Chinese tea was as much as £9 million a year.[76] It's true that following the Opium War of 1839–42, British botanists took advantage of China's defeat to procure plants from the country.[77] It's true, to use Nesbitt's words, that 'Fortune's teas contributed to the Chinese stock that still forms the basis of tea cultivation in Darjeeling today.'[78] But Fortune was not the only person involved: at about the same time, G. J. Gordon was given the responsibility by the Calcutta Botanic Garden to smuggle tea seeds out of China.[79] And the majority of the tea plants in India allocated to the tea industry are actually native to India. You see, it was long known that tea grew in India: back in the 1780s, a colonel in the Bengal Infantry had cultivated tea in his Calcutta garden; in the early 1800s, the plant was reported to be growing in the garden of the Kathmandu Palace; and, while engaged in the 1824–6 Anglo-Burmese War, British soldiers encountered tea in local use in Assam.[80] But if the East India Company ignored, overlooked, sat on this knowledge, it was partly because it had no incentive to develop the Indian tea industry: after all, it held the monopoly on Chinese tea. However, the 1830s saw a turning point when that monopoly was abolished by the British government, and China threatened to cut off Britain's supply. Suddenly, there was competition in the trade from America (where tea had, of course, played a role in inspiring the revolution against British empire, in the form of the Boston Tea Party), for tea that had been cultivated by the Dutch in Java, and the EIC realized that growing tea in India could help them fight back.[81] The East India Company also took an age to wake up to the merits of native tea plants in India, because of the disparaging, borderline-racist attitudes it had adopted towards the people and produce of the area.[82]

Fortune's real contribution was bringing Chinese tea-growing expertise to India – initially nine Chinese tea makers who could instruct on the manufacturing process – as well as vital tools such as stone slabs, drying baskets, mats and sieves. The British had a lot to learn: their tea knowledge was so basic that it was only in 1845 that Fortune realized that green and black teas were the product not of two different plants but rather of the same one processed differently. They got there in the end, however, and by the second half of the nineteenth century the North Indian tea industry was thriving, with Darjeeling – an area now in the Company's possession – at its centre. In 1844, there had been 70 acres of tea plantations in the Garhwal Himalaya region; by 1880, there were more than 10,000.[83] At the very start of the nineteenth century, when the British middle and upper classes went crazy for tea, the Company sold around £20 million of costly Chinese tea per year to England; but by 1888 Indian tea, predominantly from Assam, had outstripped that from China, and accounted for a 57 per cent share of the market.[84] Nowadays, while China is still world leader, three of the four largest tea producers in the world (India, Kenya and Sri Lanka) are all former regions of the British empire, tea having been introduced to Kenya by the British in 1903.[85]

The modern legacies go beyond these huge plantations, the associated industry and even the Forrest-Gump-style role played by tea in permanently reshaping Britain's relationship with the two superpowers of the USA and China. The British played a significant role in turning tea into a mass-market drink in India, with the India Tea Association, set up by producers in the late nineteenth century, running adverts for the beverage, demonstrating how to brew tea in village bazaars, setting up tea services on Indian railways and sending pamphlets on 'How to Prepare Tea' to high-school students.[86] Tea drinking has almost become a religion in Britain, the imperial crop being credited with improving Britons morally (the 'drunken nurses and bibulous coachmen' of Charles

Dickens' day would be replaced by a citizenry that was civilized and free from the curse of British 'manliness', according to A. E. Duchesne in the early twentieth century), and, according to George Orwell in 1946, increasing our wisdom, bravery and optimism (Orwell added that it functioned as 'one of the mainstays of civilisation in this country, as well as in Eire, Australia and New Zealand').[87] In *A Thirst for Empire: How Tea Shaped the Modern World*, Erika Rappaport identifies yet more legacies, including the imperative to Buy British (for their latest offering, Assamese tea, the East India Company sought endorsements from British aristocrats, merchants and royalty in 1838);[88] the 'farm to table' movement ('pure food activists, retailers, and Indian tea growers asserted that Chinese teas were adulterated with dangerous chemicals and bore the residue of sweaty and dirty Chinese laborers');[89] and slick corporate marketing ('the Planter Raj invented many of the advertising and marketing techniques that similar industries still use today').[90]

When it comes to plants, the archives of the Museum of Economic Botany reveal hundreds of other imperial legacies. Not least, there's the global communications that were established as a result of the discovery of a certain tree most often found in Malaysia and Indonesia – the gutta-percha, of the genus *Palaquium* in the family Sapotaceae. A natural thermoplastic, gutta-percha became a vital component of underwater telegraph cables, the undersea infrastructure which enabled rapid international communication and speedy news reporting,[91] and which remains the foundation of modern international communication systems, with today's higher-tech cables following the same routes.[92] It's also still used in dentistry today as a filler, but this led to an ecological disaster as it was harvested unsustainably.*[93] There's the sisal-fibre industry seeded in East Africa because of research published by Kew. The tough fibre of sisal, a useful plant found in the south of Mexico, can be turned into products such as carpets, ropes, shoes and dartboards, and European colonizers became aware of its possibilities after Kew

* John Tully explains that 'gutta-percha is all but forgotten today', but 'during the Victorian era it was a household word. Ironically, the high-tech Victorian telegraph industry was served by a primitive cottage industry. The gum was extracted by killing wild trees in the forests of Southeast Asia, and the scale of demand ensured that many millions of trees were destroyed. This industry brought about a Victorian ecological disaster that presaged the greater destruction of tropical rain forests occurring today.'

published a series of articles about it in the *Kew Bulletin of Miscellaneous Information*.[94] The catalogues at Kew also tell us that, at various points, tobacco and cinchona were sent to St Helena, Liberian coffee to the East and West Indies, tea seeds and plants to Jamaica, mahogany, ipecac and papyrus to India, cork oaks to the Punjab, plantation crops to Africa and pineapples to the Straits Settlement. In 1941, on Kew's one-hundredth anniversary as a public botanic garden, the *Bulletin* reported it had been involved in transfers to 'the Dominions and Colonies' of coffee, oranges, bananas, pineapples, mangosteen, almonds, tung oil seeds, cochineal cactus, chaulmoogra, ipecacuanha, *Artemisia*, *Pyrethrum*, *Lonchocarpus* and mahogany.[95] Just as soldiers and bureaucrats travelled back and forth between the hubs of the empire, these plants and their seeds followed the same paths, seeking the most fertile terrain.

While marvelling at the ingenuity behind all this enterprise, it's important to acknowledge the role that the indigenous, the colonized and/or the enslaved have played in imperial transplantations. In most of the cases we've covered so far, imperialists did not make botanical 'discoveries' so much as find out that the indigenous, colonized or enslaved had already discovered things. Gutta-percha was being used in Malaya for canes and handles for tools and knives centuries before Westerners 'discovered' it. The Singpho people are thought to have been India's first drinkers of tea, mainly for medicinal reasons, yet the British labelled them as 'tribal' nomads with no sovereignty over the territory they inhabited, and overlooked for years the usefulness of native Indian tea plants. When it came to rubber, it was indigenous people in South America who first spotted its usefulness, creating objects from it. Mark Nesbitt shows me a water bottle in Kew's collection, obtained in 1817, made by indigenous peoples of the Amazon and thought to be the oldest rubber item in the world. The so-called New World Indians also used other plant species of rubber for balls, torches, jars, containers, syringes, toys, breastplates and quivers, for raincapes and shoes, for the heads of drumsticks, for applying feather decorations and for treating cuts, bruises and haemorrhaging.[96] The multiple applications for palm products in the West were developed only after Europeans saw Africans make use of the tree. As for quinine, Lucile Brockway poses the question whether Spanish colonizers learned about the medical properties of the bark from indigenous peoples. There is little hard evidence available, but after weighing it up she concludes that the answer 'must surely be yes . . . Plant-based medicine was more highly developed among the Indians of the New World than it was in Europe at that time.'★[97]

Indeed, while imperialists played a large role in the development of global food variety, the role and influence of indigenous peoples, the colonized and the enslaved, is too often erased. Read *The Columbian Exchange* by Alfred W. Crosby and you'll learn how essential crops such as maize, potato, tomato, chilli peppers and sweet potatoes were initially cultivated by indigenous peoples before being introduced to Europe.[98] Enslaved Africans made important contributions to world cuisine. Judith A. Carney and Richard Rosomoff reveal in *In the Shadow of Slavery: Africa's Botanical Legacy in the Atlantic World* how the enslaved were experts in cultivating plant staples including vegetables such as okra and pigeon peas and cereals such as sorghum, millet and African rice;[99] they also brought with them horticultural methods such as multi-storey garden plots, in which one type of plant is used to give shade to another.[100] The West rarely appreciates the fact that many foods it relies upon – from millet to okra and watermelon – are actually African. Western products like Coca-Cola and Worcestershire sauce depend on African plants that were transported to the Americas on slave ships 'as provisions, medicines, cordage, and bedding'.[101]

Another thing that you can miss when you focus on the ingenuity of some of the transplantations is that failure was more common than success. It's a point that Nesbitt is keen to make to me before I depart Kew. 'I talk about this as, primarily, a museum of failure,' he elaborates, 'in that most of the plants in here were never commercialized. So – purely viewed through Victorian eyes – it's a museum of failure because they

---

★ It's not always the West which diminishes the role of indigenous people. Founded in 1881, the Indian Tea Association (ITA), which claims to be 'the premier and oldest Association of tea producers in India', asserts that 'the credit for creating India's vast tea empire goes to the British, who discovered tea in India and cultivated and consumed it in enormous quantities between the early 1800s and India's independence from Great Britain in 1947'. This ignores the fact that tea plants were native to India and were cultivated by indigenous people long before the Brits came around. Erika Rappaport is right to complain that 'all too often, Assam has served merely as a backdrop for the adventures of soldiers and naturalists, who struggled to nurse China plants or courageously explore dangerous jungles in search of tea. In reality, several nationalities and people of mixed-race descent transformed the political economy of these northeast borderlands.'

didn't make money out of it.' The final item he shows me, a sample of Jamaican lacebark, illustrates his point. This extraordinary object lives up to its name: a length of standard tree trunk that abruptly turns into something that looks just like lace. It's as if a doll in a skirt was emerging from a tree branch. No wonder that those lovers of frills and novelty, the Victorians, couldn't get enough of it. If this stuff was available in garden centres, I'd be going all the time. The lacebark tree usually grows to between 13 and 30 feet tall and thrives in the rocky crevices of Jamaica's mountains. Eighteenth-century records show that local people used it to make hard-wearing clothing; the planters meanwhile found it just the thing for whips. But it was also used to make doilies and fans (Nesbitt shows me some), Charles II is said to have been sent a suit made out of it, and it was presented as a wonder material at the Great Exhibition of 1851. But it was already being harvested to death. 'The problem is it took off when tourists arrived on the banana boats coming from Boston at the turn of the century,' explains Nesbitt, as I put on my coat. 'Within ten years, you start to see newspaper reports that it's becoming hard to find the tree: it's a really good example of overharvesting.'[102] This mention of bananas serves as a reminder of the fact that, after colonialists had failed to revive Jamaica's post-slavery economy through the introduction of cinchona and plant fibres,[103] the Jamaican Botanical Department did nothing to promote bananas, the crop that did finally prosper.[104]

In the weeks that follow, as I tackle the reading recommended to me by Teltscher and Nesbitt, I trace imperial botanical legacies outside the realm of industry, not least the huge number of garden plants that came into Britain and America from the colonies and beyond, and which sometimes went back out to the colonies again. Plants had been imported for many centuries, of course – the Romans gave Britain the grapevine, rosemary was introduced in the fourteenth century and trees that are now ubiquitous such as firs, planes and pines came here in the six-teenth.[105] But the process accelerated with empire. In the eighteenth century there was a vibrant plant trade between Britain and North America when the latter was still part of the empire, in which Philadel-phian farmer and collector John Bartram was a key player, dispatching shipments of seeds and hardy plants to a contact in London, Peter Collinson. The two came up with a subscription scheme for 'Bartram's boxes'; each crate would cost five guineas and contain around a hundred varieties of seeds and dried plant specimens. Through the scheme,

Bartram introduced common garden plants to Britain which have remained popular to this day, such as magnolias, rhododendrons, mountain laurels, azaleas, sugar maples and sumacs.[106] At the more exclusive end, Roderick Floud has found that rich Britons were willing to pay extraordinary prices for rare species from empire.[107]

Then there were ferns. The Wardian case's very first journey, in 1833, involved the transporting of two cases of ferns, grasses and mosses from the British capital to Sydney. For the return journey, the cases were filled with Australian plants, including a species of fern not found in Britain.[108] Both legs of the voyage were a success. In the mid-nineteenth century Britain succumbed to 'fern mania', and it became fashionable to display ferns in a domestic Wardian case. There were downsides to this activity. The social historian David Allen lambasted the Victorian fern craze, for instance, as 'the greatest and ultimately most destructive natural history fashion of all'.[109] All over the world, forests were being trampled in the rush to uproot new fern varieties and send them to Britain to furnish the drawing rooms of the middle classes.

In *The Wardian Case*, Luke Keogh tells how the live plant trade, in its many variations, was to blame for sending pests around the globe along with the plants, with serious ecological and economic ramifications.[110] It's believed that more than a third of invasive arthropods in Europe were introduced by the live plant trade, and that in Britain nearly 90 per cent of invertebrate pests first arrived on live plants. In the US, imported live plants are responsible for almost 70 per cent of the insects and pathogens that harmed forests between 1860 and 2006.[111] In the words of the biologist Richard Mack, the results of the nineteenth-century nursery trade 'have been both beautiful and disastrous'. Disease and pests threatened the very agricultural economies that the cases had introduced across the world. As Keogh puts it: 'We had become very good at moving environments – too good.'[112] One particularly damaging fungus was coffee rust, which devastated coffee plantations in Ceylon in 1869, causing losses of up to £2 million per year. Live coffee plants from British Guiana, Cuba, Jamaica, Java or Liberia were thought to have introduced the fungus. There were similar crises in the East Indian plantations, and by the 1880s, just two decades after coffee had started to be intensively cultivated in South Asia, the industry was on its knees. Planters turned to other crops such as tea, rubber, cacao and cinchona. The agricultural monocultures introduced by the British were intrinsically susceptible to disease. The ecologist Rob Dunn explains: 'economically planting just one crop is a simple way to turn a profit, but biologically it causes problems'.[113] Another cautionary tale involved the prickly pear,[114] a cactus found in Mexico and the southern states of America, which was introduced to Australia in 1788 by the first intake of British colonists. Prickly-pear fruit is edible and can also be used as an ornamental plant and for cattle feed.[115] However, when it was introduced to Australia and South Africa it spread alarmingly quickly, swamping farmland reserved for different crops. All efforts to curb its progress failed, and by 1925 it had carpeted more than 60 million acres, resulting in some farmers just abandoning land. The Intergovernmental Science-Policy Platform on Biodiversity and Ecosystem Services recently estimated that plants and animals that have moved beyond their native habitats as a result of human activity cause some $423 billion in damage around the world each year.[116] In this case, the problem was eventually solved with the ingenious introduction of the cactoblastis moth, which one Australian government website says is 'regarded as the world's most monumental example of successful pest plant repression by biological means'.[117] It's a slightly strange thing to boast about: it would have probably been better if the pest had never taken hold in the first place.

British colonialism was also largely responsible for the environmental destruction of the South Atlantic island of St Helena, with all its native plants having declined or become extinct as a result of three waves of destructive colonial activity. Like many isolated islands, St Helena possessed a large number of plants which only grow in one particular place. But these endemic species were particularly vulnerable to habitat loss. The first invader was the *Capra hircus*, introduced in 1502 by Portuguese imperialists, shortly after they had 'discovered' the island. The animal – street name goat – was responsible for thinning vegetation to the point of leaving the soil on slopes vulnerable to drastic sheet and gully erosion. Next, in 1659, came human residents, courtesy of the East India Company, who set about felling the island's trees for cooking, heating and the distillation of booze. Finally, sealing its ecological fate, the nineteenth and twentieth centuries saw deliberate alien-plant introduction to the island by British imperialists, many of which became invasive and highly destructive to the native ecosystem.[118] Such environmental destruction, echoed also in the stories of gutta-percha and lacebark, generally followed colonialism of all varieties. But the damage wreaked upon the planet by British imperialism in particular is staggering.

Among other things, there was the disastrous decision taken by the British in the late eighteenth century to end the indigenous tradition of controlled burning in southern Australia, which had been practised for centuries in order to reduce the range of wild fires and benefit biodiversity: in the northern areas of the country where the practice continued, wildfires inflicted far less damage on the environment.[119] British imperialists oversaw the cutting down of oak forests, which were resistant to wildfires, in India's western Himalayan regions in the late 1800s and replaced them with large-scale pine plantations for procuring resin: the dry pine needles became a cause of massive wildfires.[120] Barbados, as we've heard, was brought to its knees by British plantation agriculture, but the deforestation of vast swathes of the Americas and rainforests in Guyana and the West Indies, in order to pave the way for yet more sugar-cane plantations, led to severe soil erosion elsewhere.[121] It's estimated that British colonialism resulted in present-day New Zealand losing at least 60 per cent of its forests. The demand for mahogany furniture and doors which were fashionable from the eighteenth century to the mid-nineteenth, and that visitors to National Trust houses coo over in the twenty-first century, led to near extinction of the trees in the West Indies.[122] There was also widespread deforestation of the Ganges and Indus river basins, and of regions around Calcutta, Madras and Bombay.[123]

The correlation between colonialism and environmental destruction was noted during empire and has been picked up by numerous historians since. In 1995 Richard H. Grove was pointing out that 'it may even be appropriate to argue that [East India] Company expansionism was normally associated with timber shortage',[124] adding that environmental destruction may be one of colonialism's most lasting legacies. It's only relatively recently, however, that the correlation has been acknowledged in the mainstream. Shozab Raza, a postdoctoral associate at Yale University, has recently claimed in the *Guardian* that the catastrophic flooding in Pakistan which killed more than 1,100 people in 2022 was down to empire.[125] *Disaster Trade*, a recent report by academics at Royal Holloway, University of London, has found that landslides in Sri Lanka and elsewhere are being caused by tea plantations introduced by the

British,[126] not least because the deep root systems of trees have been replaced by the shallow root systems of tea plants.[127] We've also had a Greenpeace UK report, in the boiling hot summer of 2022,[128] proclaiming that 'the environmental emergency is the legacy of colonialism'. It argued that 'the outcomes of the environmental emergency cannot be understood without reference to the history of British and European colonialism, which set in motion a global model for racialised resource extraction from people of colour'.

Meanwhile, colonialism's role in climate change, as well as environmental destruction, is being highlighted. Prizewinning author Amitav Ghosh is a notable proponent of the argument, maintaining in *The Nutmeg's Curse*[129] that 'pillaging of lands and killing of indigenous people laid the foundation for the climate emergency' in parts of India, such as the Sundarbans, a group of islands in the Bay of Bengal which are vulnerable to rising sea levels and extreme weather.[130] More significantly, the recent sixth report from the UN's influential Intergovernmental Panel on Climate Change (IPCC) detailed the impact of global warming and, for the first time in over three decades of observation and analysis, acknowledged that colonialism had compounded the effects of climate change.[131] And before anyone is tempted to dismiss these conclusions as the fevered suggestions of the derangedly woke, it should be noted that the correlation between colonialism and climate change was acknowledged by some people as British imperialism was still spreading. The sophistication of some of the insights from this time takes you aback. In a footnote in an 1849 paper Edward Balfour, Assistant Surgeon in Madras, suggested that a 1770 famine in India could have been a direct result of British rule and its revenue policies, which led to a reduction in forest cover.[132] The origins of the contemporary 'greenhouse' discourse can be seen in the work of one J. Spotswood Wilson, who in 1858 penned a paper for the British Association for the Advancement of Science entitled 'On the general and gradual desiccation of the earth and atmosphere', in which he wrote that the 'destruction of forests and waste by irrigation' was not solely to blame for climate change; rather, he thought the main factor was the changing ratios of oxygen and carbonic acid in the atmosphere, and that the ratios were related to how successfully the 'animal and vegetable kingdom' produced and absorbed them.[133] Man-made climate change even concerned the Founding Fathers of the United States, with Benjamin Franklin fretting out loud in the 1760s that 'When a Country is clear'd of Woods, the Sun acts more strongly on the Face of the Earth.' The heat of the sun 'melts great Snows sooner than they could be melted if they were shaded by the Trees'. He asserted that while a 'regular and steady Course of Observations' would be required over the years, the climate was changing, and human beings were changing it.[134] When, in the twenty-first century, the IPCC, Greenpeace and other campaigners observe that colonialism caused environmental destruction[135] and contributed to climate change, they are participating in something that is, in itself, an imperial tradition.

It should be noted that the 'colonialism' being discussed in this context is almost always that by multiple European powers, not just Britain, though examples from British empire, the largest in human history, are prominent. It should also be noted that different people often mean different things when they talk about 'environmental colonialism' or 'ecological imperialism' or 'green colonialism', and the conversation can quickly become confusing. Sometimes they're not referring to the destruction of environments by the French, Dutch and British empires in the eighteenth, nineteenth and twentieth centuries. Sometimes they mean that small states are being punished for the actions of large states in the West, such as when the *Guardian* recently pointed out that 'the entire continent of Africa is responsible for less than four percent of historic global emissions, yet African people are bearing the brunt of the climate crisis'.[136] Sometimes they mean that international climate policies and initiatives do not take indigenous populations into account, despite the fact that these people often experience the worst of extreme weather events and rising sea levels. Sometimes they're referring to 'waste colonialism', whereby countries in the global North offload their hazardous waste on to poorer nations in the global South (for example, Britain sending waste to be processed in Vietnam). Sometimes they mean that 'natural disasters' such as floods, droughts and landslides are an intensifying risk for millions in the global South and are connected to processes originating in Britain – examples include the manufacture of clothes in Cambodia and bricks in South Asia.[137] But they're usually observing that colonialism of all kinds has disrupted and destroyed environments of all kinds around the world.

Which brings us to perhaps the most surreal imperial legacy of all from the field of plants and botany: environmentalism. In another encounter with the paradoxical nature of British imperial legacies, an echo of the paradoxical legacies of abolition, an experience which I'll eventually get very used to, my reading informs me that the environmental destruction of empire gave birth to conservation initiatives and environmentalism. 'It is now clear that modern environmentalism, rather than being exclusively a product of European or North American predicaments and philosophies, emerged as a direct response to the destructive social and ecological conditions of colonial rule,' explains Grove, citing multiple kinds of colonialism pioneered by multiple colonial powers.[138] Pointing out that some of the earliest systematic initiatives for soil and forest preservation in the colonies began in the battered environment of St Helena, which set the tone for later East India Company land-use policies, he adds: 'The global environmental consciousness . . . can now be observed to have arisen virtually simultaneously with the trade and territorial expansion of the Venetian, Dutch, English and French maritime powers.'[139] Colonial conservation initiatives within the British empire included the establishment of the Bombay Forest Conservancy in 1847;[140] as Peter Frankopan observes, 'protecting forests and indeed replanting trees became a central part of British colonial policy – starting with India and the Charter of Indian Forestry, which annexed all forests that were not privately owned and declared them to be state property'.[141] Authorities in Australia, Canada and Africa soon adopted similar measures, though the reasons for taking over forests had little to do with conservation: what mattered to them was maintaining control over timber. Frankopan notes that the implications were catastrophic for populations that had spent generations living in the forests but were suddenly caught up in industrialized deforestation. Painfully, the story usually employed to justify change was that local communities were woeful stewards of the environment and practised primitive agriculture, and that the creation of new landscapes was not only advantageous to them but beyond their capacity.

Colonial administrations frequently asserted – and often had the assumption codified in law – that in places like India all uncultivated land belonged to the state. This, too, was a component of the commonly held belief that native peoples were irresponsible and were destroying forests. Imperial Brits saw themselves as environmental stewards defending the natural world from human beings who had sometimes lived in that natural world for millennia. Over time, concepts like these developed further, leading to the taking over of land as well as the forced eviction of inhabitants: the 1870s and 1880s saw the establishment of national parks in Yellowstone in the United States, Banff in Australia, and Tongariro in New Zealand. These parks were founded on the notion that, in order to safeguard nature, humans ought to be removed, forcibly if necessary. A series of conferences entitled 'Our Land, Our Nature', dedicated to 'Discuss[ing] How to Decolonize Conservation', and Guillaume Blanc, the French author of an enlightening book entitled *The Invention of Green Colonialism*, have recently taken up the theme. Blanc argues that the Africa we imagine in the West – of 'Virgin forests, majestic mountains surrounded by savanna, vast plains punctuated with the rhythms of animal life where lions, elephants and giraffes reign as lords of nature, far from civilization' – has always been a fiction. There is a correlation between the damage we inflict on our natural environments in the West and the way we romanticize the ones in Africa. We tell ourselves that the African nature reserves and national parks are the precious last enclaves of wild, virgin nature, and vow to preserve them. As a result of this conviction, the World Wide Fund for Nature (WWF), UNESCO and other organizations are responsible for turning huge swathes of the African continent into parks and reserves, at great cost to the people who have lived there for generations. Local people have been violently evicted from their homes and prevented from farming their land or grazing their livestock.[142]

I find it astonishing that mere, literal seeds should have given birth to these massive contemporary controversies. I'm still in the early stages of my international journey, though, and I quickly happen upon another imperial legacy that is linked to, and possibly even overshadows, botany: the too often elided role that the physical labour of the colonized, enslaved, imprisoned and indigenous played in botanical transplantations.[143] The human consequences of meddling with crops and agriculture around the world were often enormous: when the land used in Burma to cultivate rice, for instance, increased by twelve times, the population of the Irrawaddy Delta grew from 1.5 million to more than 4 million between 1852 and 1900.[144] Meanwhile, the hard work involved in moving and cultivating plants was almost always not done by the cerebral botanists themselves: when it came to cinchona plantations in India, convicts cleared the land;[145] when Clements Markham collected his haul of cinchona plants, he reportedly sent fifteen Wardian cases to

Madras where the cases, weighing around 150 kilos each, were carried by Indian labourers to the mountainous plantation;[146] one plantation overseer, William McIvor, used children aged between twelve and fourteen to transport the heavy cargo, many of whom 'were not even tall enough to lift the cases from the ground' – they were witnessed 'lying by them completely exhausted'.[147] Also, human beings were moved across the planet in their millions to work on the plantations. These people included the enslaved, who we've already heard about, but also more than 1 million indentured labourers from India, whose descendants shape, influence and define large parts of the planet today.

# 3. Phenomenal People Exporters

Even by the standards of social media, the accounts run by Mauritian entrepreneur Arvind Veerapen* project an image of unrelenting consumption and success. They show him pictured at award ceremonies and parties around the world next to, among others, British comedians, Australian actors and American sports stars. We see him photographed, in his tailored suits and bespoke shirts, at locations including the Royal Enclosure at Ascot and the Cannes Film Festival. We see him riding a Harley, displaying luxury watches, smoking expensive cigars, posing next to an array of beautiful women. In one post, one of the straps of these watches is used, for reasons that aren't immediately apparent, to hold a bunch of his cigars.

The bling is almost as blinding in real life. I drive from my chaotic three-star hotel across the island of Mauritius to meet him for lunch at a sumptuous five-star resort of his choosing. He greets me sporting aviator shades and what turns out to be a solid-gold watch worth 42,000 euros (I ask). We engage in small talk about the replacement car he's driving as his own car is being fixed: an electric BMW so swish that you can control the screens by seemingly swiping bits of the wood panelling (which makes me more than a little self-conscious about the four door handles of my nearby hire car, which are kept in place with gaffer tape). His elegant sister, Jaya, sporting an orange sindoor, joins us for food at a beachside restaurant, and during more small talk about a recent event in London that made global headlines it transpires she had actually attended, in her capacity as a senior diplomat. Even Hugo Lambert, the man who has been kind enough to arrange this meeting, is as swanky as hell. Describing himself as an entrepreneur, media expert and philanthropist, he is a member of the Franco-Mauritian community which makes up just 2 per cent of the Mauritian population[1] and owns over a third of the island's land.[2] He has residences, in addition to one in Mauritius, in London and the Balearic Islands, he has a habit of awkwardly

* The names of the guests at this lunch have been changed, at their request.

offering the fact that he descends from a slave trader who moved to the island and died with his human cargo when one of his slave ships sank, and he gives interviews to luxury magazines where he says things like: 'If you don't get your suit tailored, you're doing it wrong.'

When combined with the disorientation of jet lag, new surroundings (Indians in an African country speaking French!) and the strangeness of visiting a beach holiday destination for work when you've only recently learned how to have beach holidays (the staff at the chaotic hotel simply do not accept I'm visiting for work and every morning ask me how I'm enjoying my vacation), it could all, frankly, be a bit much. But the meeting is a lesson in not jumping to conclusions about people as a result of first impressions. Lambert works in the field of luxury goods and they often talk like that about what they wear. He also turns out to have thought deeply about the complex history of his island, which had no indigenous population, was visited by explorers from the Arab world from at least the tenth century and then by the Portuguese 500 years later. The Dutch were the first Europeans to settle in the seventeenth century, establishing plantation slavery, which was enthusiastically embraced by subsequent colonizers. Mauritius was governed between 1721 and 1810 by the French (initially by the French East India Company, which rechristened the island Île de France, and then, from 1767, by the French Crown) before being taken over by the British, who had no problem running it as a slave colony from 1810 despite having abolished the slave trade in 1807–8.[3] It turns out that the money his family made from slavery is long gone, having been squandered by an 'alcoholic grandfather'; his family is not among the small number of Franco-Mauritian families who are rich in land ownership, and he talks intelligently about the need for reparations. 'You need to give back,' he says, sounding as French as his name. 'I'm always fighting for the Creole community here. I'm totally for it.'

As for Arvind Veerapen, he's certainly not shy, but many of his social media posts appear as a result of his work. He has a business relationship with the watch brand he is sporting. And while his sister's job illustrates the fact that Indo-Mauritians, who account for an estimated two-thirds of the island's population of 1.26 million, are nowadays the largest and most politically powerful ethnic group on the island,[4] accounting for all but one of its post-independence prime ministers,[5] the family are also an example of the most remarkable social mobility the planet has ever

seen. Trust me, you might also be parading your success if, like the Veer-
apens, and like 70 per cent of the residents of Mauritius,[6] you had
descended from the lowly, impoverished Indian labourers, or so-called
'coolies', recruited by the British en masse in the nineteenth century.
The workers were shipped over from cities such as Madras and Calcutta
to make up the shortfall of labour after slavery was abolished on British
plantations of sugar, tea, coffee, rubber and cinchona.

It's sometimes said when someone is poor that 'they didn't even have
a penny to their name', but when some Indian indentured labourers
arrived, they often didn't even have a name: there's a family on Mauritius which goes by the moniker of 'City of Palaces' because their
ancestor was bestowed with the name of the ship he came on[7] (the
phrase refers to Calcutta, with its colonial mansions).[8] When Veerapen's
ancestor arrived in Mauritius in 1866, aged twenty-seven, he wasn't registered with a surname: their family name was the single moniker he
was given. As for the job title of 'coolie', which derives from 'kuli',
meaning 'hire' or 'wages' in the Tamil language,[9] it's unlikely to be a
label that he or many of the other labourers would have chosen for
themselves. It was often taken as a racial slur when the British used it.
The racist common plant names that we happened across at Kew, still in
use in 1991, included 'Coolie's Cap'.[10] My guide to Aapravasi Ghat, the
museum based on the remains of the immigration depot where Mauritius' indentured labourers were received, tells me he refuses to use the
word, and points out that labourers sang songs of protest against the
label, including one originating from British Guiana, which asked:
'Why should we be called coolies? / We who were born in the clans and
families of seers and saints.'[11]

Arvind picks up his phone (encased in monogrammed leather) and,
talking with pride about how far his family has come, shows me a
photograph of his entrepreneurial father and great-uncle appearing at
high-society events and visiting dignitaries around Europe. 'I'm the
third generation to wear a top hat at Ascot,' he says, pointing to his
father's dress.[12] He forwards me a WhatsApp message from a relative he
had recently shared the photograph with, along with other family
photographs. 'Somebody told me I should write the memoirs of our
family!' it begins. 'I told them the pictures speak for themselves. Our
labourer hippie-looking ancestor, great-grandfather coming from backward Bihar, and then Papa, Uncle meeting up with kings and queens!

Our grandfather sitting under a mango tree eating his lunch could never have imagined what his descendants would have achieved in such a short time. We should be truly proud of our heritage.'

The story is an intense version of one that has been repeated by many families on Mauritius and across the globe: Veerapen was one of more than 1 million Indian nationals who travelled to British colonies during some eighty-odd years of contracted migration. The first colony to introduce Indian indentured labour was Mauritius, in 1834, quickly followed by British Guiana (1838) and Trinidad and Jamaica (1845). In the 1850s, some smaller colonies in the West Indies followed suit, including Grenada, St Lucia, St Kitts and St Vincent. Natal joined them in 1860, and Fiji in 1879.[13] The salient factor of the system was that workers had to commit in advance to a fixed term of labour at their destination – usually five years – by signing a contract, or 'girmit' (a Hindi and Bhojpuri form of the English word 'agreement'). Typically, the 'girmit' laid out working hours, pay and the type of labour to be undertaken, alongside details about accommodation, food rations and healthcare. At the end of the five-year term, migrants would be offered return passage to India at their own expense – or, if they agreed to stay on and commit to *another* five-year term of work, they'd be rewarded with a free return voyage home after that.[14]

Academics have put forward numerous explanations for why planters decided indentured labourers were necessary after the abolition of slavery, when they could have employed the formerly enslaved, who were required anyway to be 'apprentices' for a number of years.[15] It's true that the formerly enslaved did not, in general, want to work on the plantations, given that they had only narrowly survived mass murder, torture and rape: as one analyst puts it, 'in Barbados and some of the small islands, it was physically impossible for them to quit the plantations. But where there was any alternative, the newly-freed Blacks departed . . . Whenever possible, the Creole Black, whether in the Caribbean or in the Mascarenes [the group of volcanic islands in the Indian Ocean consisting of the islands of Réunion, Mauritius and Rodrigues], took himself away from the plantation forever.'[16] Also, many of the enslaved wanted to leave to be reunited with family members who had been sold off to different plantations. But it also seems that planters had simply become addicted to exploiting cheap labour on their own terms, and lavish 'compensation' paid out by the British government to owners of the enslaved meant they could afford the upfront costs of indenture. As Madhavi Kale explains, 'evidence from planters' own documents as well as from other sources strongly suggests that planters had to negotiate wages, hours, and benefits with their former slaves, and that they objected to their recently diminished authority'.[17] As an illustration, Kale uses the example of British merchant-planter John Gladstone, whose son William, the future Liberal Prime Minister, grew up in a castle in Aberdeenshire that had been bought with the profits from the family's sugar plantations in British Guiana.[18] When John Gladstone first came up with the idea of replacing slaves in the Caribbean with indentured Indians, he did not wait to see how emancipated slaves would react before he began to import indentured labourers from the subcontinent: 'he took this initiative after only one full season under apprenticeship'.[19]

Meanwhile, Indians ended up as indentured labourers for all sorts of reasons. Among other things they were fleeing famine (in the last quarter of the nineteenth century alone, India endured twenty-four separate famines),[20] the economic policies of empire (the British flooded India with factory-made textiles from England, for instance, plunging weavers into unemployment and poverty),[21] the crackdown on rebels following the Indian Uprising of 1857 (serious thought was put into the idea of sending defeated sepoys to the Caribbean as exiled or convict labour, but in the end those found guilty of mutiny and homicide were thrown into prison on the Andaman Islands, while the others were dispersed elsewhere),[22] penury, displacement, family troubles, social disrepute, unpayable tax bills and rent increases. And more ended up in Mauritius than anywhere else: nearly half a million.[23] 'Mirchias' – Mauritius-bound – became a generic term for indenture in India as so many went there.[24] Preferences changed over time but the island's proximity to India and its history of trade links to the subcontinent[25] worked in its favour and the island thrived as a result. This is starkly illustrated by the fact that before slavery was abolished in Mauritius in 1835 it was producing only half as much sugar as Jamaica, but twenty years later was producing five times more, and had become Britain's leading sugar-producing colony. A chart on display at Aapravasi Ghat, where you still can walk up the steps that every single indentured labourer encountered at the end of their journey, points out that at one stage in the nineteenth century Mauritius produced 7 per cent of the world's sugar. Today, sugar remains one of the island's most important exports.[26]

The movement of indentured labour from India became one of the greatest migrations in the history of the planet despite the fact that travelling across the seas was considered taboo by many Hindus, the offence of crossing the *kala pani* ('black water'), known as 'Samudrolanghana' or 'Sagarollanghana', and resulting in the loss of social respectability and caste.[27] These labourers, who included Muslims, were the first large groups of Indians abroad, the pioneers of what would become the colossal Indian diaspora, one of the main reasons why you see Indians almost wherever you go in the world, and an echo, within British empire, of the mass emigration of British people which prompted Eric Richards to opine that the British 'pioneered mass migration' and 'have been phenomenal people exporters'. It should be noted, though, that indentured labour was not limited to British empire, or limited to Indians, nor was it something that existed only as a replacement for slavery. If you recall, the first labourers on Barbados' sugar plantations were a mixture of 'free colonists, indentured servants, and occasionally enslaved Africans and Amerindians': the 'indentured servants, largely young males from England, Scotland, Ireland, and Wales (that is the British Isles)'.[28] There was a certain amount of indentured labour in places that eventually received large numbers of Indian labourers before the end of slavery: for instance, around 4,600 Indian and Chinese workers landed on Mauritius and Réunion in the later 1820s.[29] Also, indentured Chinese, African, Indian, Japanese and Melanesian labourers were sent to Dutch, French and Spanish colonies in the Caribbean, South Africa, the south-west Indian Ocean and the South Pacific,[30] and some decades later Indians moved within India on an indentured basis, to work on, for example, Assam's tea plantations on one of the edges of British India.[31]

It's important, I think, to put indentured labour in the context of the British empire's colossal influence upon the human geography of the planet. Let's not forget that the Atlantic slave trade from 1500 to 1866 saw 12,521,000 human beings transplanted overall[32] – the British responsible for around 3 million of them. An estimated 1 million people died during the famine in Ireland under British rule in the late 1840s, and many more were uprooted and resettled abroad. Over the course of 150 years, between 1789 and 1939, Britain offloaded well over 100,000 Indian, Chinese, Burmese and Malay criminals to penal colonies on the Andaman Islands and elsewhere in the Indian Ocean, as well as to prisons in mainland India. The majority of these had been convicted of offences including murder, gang robbery and rebellion.[33] A number of the Indian criminals initially sent to Mauritius were reconvicted and transported to the Australian penal settlement, Van Diemen's Land (now Tasmania), and to the Cape's Robben Island.[34] Elsewhere, the South African War saw 27,927 Boers, mostly children, perishing in the British-run concentration camps – 14.5 per cent of the entire Boer population. These camps killed more adult Boers than died from direct military involvement. Adding to this horrific tally are the 14,000 of 115,700 black internees – 81 per cent of them children – whose lives ended in other camps.[*][35] Three historians, working together, have estimated that in total the British were responsible for the deaths of over a million people between 1838 and 1880, during the First Afghan War, the First Opium War, the Indian Uprising, the Second Opium War, the Second Afghan War and the 1878–80 wars in South Africa.[36] The Briggs Plan, a military initiative during the Malayan Emergency which involved the relocation of 573,000 Chinese squatters on the fringes of jungle into New Villages to starve communist guerrillas of 'material support and much-needed information',[37] saw the British move nearly 10 per cent of the population[38] and was, according to Caroline Elkins, 'the British empire's largest forced migration since the era of trade in enslaved people'.[39] In turn, Elkins also informs us that in Kenya, by the end of 1955, 'the British colonial government had managed ... to detain nearly the entire Kikuyu population', an ethnic group native to central Kenya, 'a feat that was unprecedented in the empire save for the Chinese population in Malaya'.[40] Although Mauritius attained independence in 1968, Britain kept ownership of the nearby Chagos archipelago, effectively paying

---

* Concentration camps were a product of the late nineteenth-century colonial wars, conceived as a way of containing hostile forces and were used by the Spanish during the Cuban uprising (1895), by the Americans in the Philippines (1898) and, infamously, by the British during the South African War (1900–1902). As Robert Home explains, General Kitchener gave the go-ahead for the establishment of 'concentration camps' in South Africa in order to segregate the families of Boer commandos and therefore cut off a source of comfort, food and supplies. Tens of thousands Afrikaner women and children perished in these despised camps thanks to poor hygiene and inadequate access to water, and there were large numbers of deaths among black Africans in similar camps, which had lower rations, poorer sanitation and fewer medical facilities than the white camps, while imposing enforced work for the British military and mines.

Mauritius more than £4 million for the islands. Between 1,500 and 2,000 people were forcibly removed in the early 1970s so that the US could lease the main island, Diego Garcia, for use as an airbase, and they were never permitted to return.[41] Meanwhile, some 15 million people were displaced as a consequence of the Partition of India, and between 200,000 and 2 million people died.[42]

Some might argue that such estimates are so broad they stop being useful. And it's true that some such estimates can vary hugely: you'll see it claimed in all sorts of places, for instance, that some 10 million Bengalis, one-third of the population, died in the Great Bengal Famine of 1770, but some analysts say that even 5 million might be an exaggeration.[43] It's also the case that some estimates can be controversial: such as Shashi Tharoor's recent claim that Britain caused the deaths of 35 million Indians 'in totally unnecessary famines caused by British policy';[44] and a recent estimate in a paper for the journal *World Development* that around 100 million people died prematurely 'under the aegis of British colonialism during the period from 1891 to 1920'.[45] But variations in estimates sometimes tell a story in themselves: they convey how little the British cared about 'uncivilized' enemy casualties, whereas British losses were almost always counted with care and precision and mourned accordingly. It says a lot about the chaos and horror and bloodshed of Partition that, even in the twentieth century, the margin of error for estimated deaths could be 1.8 million lives. And the uncertainty when it comes to estimating the numbers of indigenous peoples of North America and Australia who died as a result of encountering white settlers also tells a harrowing tale.

Recent research has revealed that over 140 years in Australia there were at least 270 organized massacres of First Nations people[46] as a consequence of which the First Nations community was decimated, falling from around 1–1.5 million to less than 100,000 by the start of the twentieth century.*[47] You might recall from *Empireland* that in a notorious

---

\* June 2023 saw the 185th anniversary of one of the more notorious killings, the Myall Creek Massacre, in which British colonists murdered at least twenty-eight Aboriginal people in New South Wales. With the Myall Creek Station manager away, a dozen men led by John Henry Fleming brutally murdered Wirrayaraay women, children and elderly people. 'In several editorials published before, during and after two Sydney trials in late 1838 relating to the massacre, the Herald essentially campaigned for the 11

act of genocide the Tasmanian Aborigines, a hunter-gatherer people, whose population numbered around 7,000 in 1803, were down to just a small group of survivors on Flinders Island by 1835.[48] There was the wiping out of the indigenous people of the Caribbean, referred to variously as 'Indians', 'Caribs', 'Arawaks' and 'Kalinagos',[49] by a variety of European powers including Britain, in what was once 'one of the most densely populated regions in the New World',[50] with the native population of the Lesser Antilles collapsing by as much as 90 per cent between 1492 and 1730.[51] In the territory that would become British North America, the Native American population had stood at around 560,000 in the year 1500. By 1700, there existed less than half that number. Overall, in 1500, the land that is now the United States was home to around 2 million indigenous people. By 1700 there were just 750,000 left, and by 1820 a mere 325,000. 'Massacres were the order of the day,' states Niall Ferguson: 'of the Powhatan in 1623 and 1644, of the Pequots in 1637, of the Doegs and Susquehannocks in 1675, of the Wampanoag in 1676–7.'[52]

Jonathan Kennedy points out that it was disease, rather than violence, that was the biggest factor in the decimation of indigenous populations encountering European colonialism. He argues that early attempts to colonize the American mainland would probably have been unsuccessful had it not been for the diseases the Europeans brought along as hand luggage, in an inversion of the phenomenon that saw malaria and yellow fever felling European imperialists in large numbers in West Africa. 'Why did the Pilgrims succeed where others failed?' he asks rhetorically. They weren't better prepared or a more formidable force. But between 1616 and 1619 the Massachusetts Bay area was ravaged by a deadly epidemic – probably smallpox or viral hepatitis – which killed as many as 90 per cent of the people who lived there.[53] Another smallpox epidemic – again, almost certainly courtesy of the foreigners – came in 1630, killing off a further half of the surviving indigenous people. It was these epidemics, and the ones that followed over the

---

accused mass murderers to escape prosecution,' said the *Sydney Morning Herald* in a recent apology. 'It also opposed the death sentence eventually handed to seven of the men.' This apology did not mention that, aside from this one case, its campaign succeeded. Settler rage over the hanging of seven white perpetrators discouraged governors from seeking justice in future cases.

ensuing decades, that made it possible for the English Puritans to settle
in North America. Like the conquistadors of the fifteenth and sixteenth
centuries, who established the Portuguese and Spanish empires, the Pilgrims saw the eradication of the Native American community as a sign
from God upholding the righteousness of their mission. In 1634, John
Winthrop, the inaugural Governor of the Massachusetts Bay Colony,
claimed: 'For the natives, they are neere all dead of small Poxe, so as the
Lord hathe cleared our title to what we possess.'*⁵⁴

Nonetheless, within all of this movement of humans, growth in
humans and erasure of humans, indentured labour was significant and is
not particularly well understood, even within the Indian diaspora, and
even among the descendants of the indentured. Every single person
I interview on Mauritius tells me they weren't taught much about the
history of indenture at school, with Vikram Mugon, the 44-year-old
Heritage and Tradition Manager at Aapravasi Ghat, informing me that
people on the island do not generally distinguish between slavery and
indenture. 'They identify indentured labourers as being slaves, even the
descendants do,' he says, talking to me at the museum, which is an
impressive institution, despite the motorway built right next to it in the
1980s not long after it had been officially declared a national monument.
'They say "they came as slaves". Sometimes, even when you ask people

---

* Kennedy maintains it was disease that ultimately led to the creation of one of the
biggest British imperial legacies of all: white Americans and their distinct culture.
'The 21,000 settlers that came in the twenty years after the foundation of Plymouth
Colony were the only significant influx of people into New England until Irish Catholic immigration began in the 1840s. [The English] Puritans were the "breeding stock
of America's Yankee population" and by the end of the twentieth century had multi-
plied to 16 million people. Their influence goes well beyond numbers. In contrast to
the fortune-seeking conquistadors [of Spain/Portugal], the Puritans travelled to the
New World to build a new godly society where they could raise their families free
from persecution. They brought with them institutions that encouraged the emergence of capitalism, most notably a legal system that placed a strong emphasis on
property rights and checks against abuse of government power. The North American
colonies were better off than back home because of the absence of a powerful landed
aristocracy – many of whom had controlled their vast estates since the Norman invasion of England in 1066. The political and economic system created by settlers on the
north-east coast persisted after independence and helps to explain why the USA has
developed into one of the most individualistic and wealthy societies the world has
ever seen.'

"Why are we commemorating 2nd November, which marks the Arrival of Indentured Labourers?" they will tell you, "Oh, it's the arrival of the slaves, of Indian slaves." And for us at Aapravasi Ghat Trust Fund, we've tried to [highlight] the difference, because our value stands on the fact that this was a new system.' Not that this ignorance makes me feel better about the mortifying fact that I wrote several essays on the work of Trinidad's Nobel Laureate Sir V. S. Naipaul at university, and also interviewed the man for a magazine, without fully understanding how his family's experience of indenture had enabled him to write with such authority about what it is to be colonized.[55] And that I read the work of the Nobel Prize-winning poet Derek Walcott without fully comprehending how the indentured labourers of St Lucia had inspired him.[56] Too often immigrants, and the children of immigrants, think their experience is *the* definitive experience of migration.

What's more, as Kay Saunders has made clear in an essay collection she has edited on the theme, indenture operated in different ways across the British empire.[57] Just as there are endless variations on migration within British empire, there were variations on indenture. Unlike Mauritius, Jamaica's demographics, economy and history were not, for example, fundamentally altered by indentured labour: an estimated 37,000 Indian indentured workers came to Jamaica between 1845 and 1917, but Jamaican planters weren't happy with their work, seeing them as inferior to the Creoles and Africans, and their economic influence was limited.★[58] Unlike many other sugar colonies, Trinidad, known by some Indians as 'Chinitat', gave labourers a stake in the colony when their contract was over: in 1869 a land grant was offered to any Indian who had been in the colony for ten years. Towards the end of the indenture period this helped to make it the most popular destination for

---

★ Their cultural influence was, however, substantial. Just as the Cornish pasty was imported into Jamaica by Cornish sailors and evolved into the Jamaican Patty, and just as the Jamaican spiced bun came about through Britain's introduction of spiced buns and hot cross buns to the island, the one-pot dishes favoured by the Jamaican Maroons, Africans who had escaped slavery, developed into curries after the arrival of Indian indentured labourers. Nowadays, of course, curry goat and rotis are as closely associated with Jamaica as . . . cannabis. And it turns out that cannabis plants were also introduced by indentured labourers from India in the 1850s – the influence being reflected in the fact that 'Ganja', the popular moniker for cannabis in Jamaica, comes from Hindi.

Indian migrants, as Mauritius became the least favourite place to go.[59] In Malaya, Chinese, Indian and Javanese indentured workers arrived after early and unsuccessful experiments with African slave labour. In Fiji, planters did something similar for similar reasons: Indian migration to Fiji began in 1879 and lasted until 1916, during which period 60,965 workers landed there. In South Africa, indentured labour was used in the Transvaal not just for agriculture but for mining, especially gold mining. The main workforce was Chinese, not Indian, though Gandhi was involved in aiding the Indians.[60] In Queensland, now a state in Australia, it was not the end of slavery but the end of penal transportation in the late 1830s which created the desire for cheap indentured labour. The work was not just in agriculture but in mining too, and the indentured included Chinese and, mostly, Pacific Islanders as well as Indians.[61] They were discouraged from settling: by the late 1890s, there was a growing political movement to make Australia a 'white' nation.

All this people movement has left all sorts of legacies, beyond the enormous Indian diaspora. In Fiji, some of the descendants of Indian indentured labourers are still working as cane cutters.[62] In a parallel to various claims made about the legacies of abolition, the academic Rachel Sturman has argued that many of the ideas and policies that inform international labour rights today were born out of the need to regulate indentured labour.[63] In turn, it's frequently claimed that indenture was itself a legacy of slavery. 'Slavery under a different name' is how indentured labour was described by the British and Foreign Anti-Slavery Society in 1839.[64] Mahatma Gandhi, who became famous for dressing in the way that some of the indentured would have done, called indenture 'semi-slavery'. Meanwhile, 1974 saw the publication of Hugh Tinker's *A New System of Slavery* which, via a thorough review of emigration from rural India, argued that Indian indentured labour included many of the worst features of slavery.[65] And slavery is what keeps coming to mind when I start to read about the workings of indenture.

First, there was the recruitment, which didn't quite involve the violent kidnapping endured by the enslaved but frequently depended on deception. The recruiters were notoriously dodgy: often local villains in trouble with the authorities, or in debt, they would hang about markets, railway stations, temples, telling potential recruits, for example, that the government was looking for gardeners to work in an area near Calcutta which was only reachable by boat; or they would get them drunk and give them dinner before ferrying them off in covered carts lest their friends spotted them. Recruiters were also known to use prostitutes to lure men and trick women into depots by giving them false directions if they asked for help getting somewhere.[66] If the targeted got cold feet during the process, the recruiter might exert pressure by presenting a bill they couldn't afford for the travel that had already been undertaken.[67] Some recruits were misled about what they were getting into until they stepped off the boat. Tinker proffers a story about a man called Boodishoosho who had been told he was going to Mauritius to become a physician, and who had been encouraged to bring his medicine case with him, only to discover eventually that he and his wife were heading into a life of labour, in the district of Mauritius where I, as it happens, am staying for the week. On becoming aware of the deception, he poisoned his wife and tried to commit suicide, to save them both from their fate.[68]

Then there was the journey. When delivered into the hands of a licensed recruiting agent, before travelling to the port of embarkation, the recruit was often put up in a house or warehouse where diseases like cholera were common. When the day arrived for them to head off to the port, recruits in the early days of indenture were often made to travel by foot for hundreds of miles. In order to put the emigrants at ease, decoys were often placed among them to gush about the new life awaiting them and to discourage plans to escape. On one journey, five of the fourteen supposed emigrants en route to Calcutta were actually employees of the recruiters. While slave journeys from West Africa to the Caribbean would take four to six weeks, Indians shipped to the Caribbean were at sea for three to four months, with the journey from Calcutta to the Caribbean in one case lasting some 188 days.[69] As Gaiutra Bahadur observes, the conditions on board could sometimes be brutal: passengers' 'stomachs often churned from unfamiliar, religiously forbidden or spoiled food. The ship reports refer to putrefying pumpkins, potatoes past their prime, milk that curdled, tins of mutton gone bad, dal infiltrated by dirt and drinking water laced with rust and cement.'[70] In 1858 the *Salsette*, sailing from Calcutta to Trinidad, had a mortality rate of over 38 per cent.[71]

The parallels to slavery are also unavoidable when it comes to the living conditions endured by the indentured, as they were often put up in the former quarters of the enslaved. Bahadur tells us how in British

Guiana new arrivals were housed in the 'nigger yard', where 2,600 immigrants, including 800 children, lived in 'logies' previously occupied by the enslaved. The one-storey barracks were composed of small rooms, each holding a number of single men or one family, and were divided by partitions that offered no soundproofing. Furniture might simply consist of a charpoy, the most basic Indian rope bed. There was usually no running water and only the most rudimentary toilet facilities.[72] Floors were generally clay or mud, and the roofs made of metal, which made the rooms hideously hot under the unrelenting sun (one planter in Trinidad called Robert Guppy said that his metal roofs insured against his workers idling in their rooms: 'These people ought to be in the field all day long').[73] Disease was rife as a result and an inspector who visited a plantation in Fiji in 1881 said he was 'dissatisfied with nearly everything'. On the food being served, he added: 'I can only stigmatise it as filth not even good enough for a superior class of poultry.'[74] A 1902 report on estate hospitals in Mauritius showed that a total estate population of 91,924 people was looked after by fifteen doctors, three of whom were responsible for 11,000 people each.[75]

Contributing to the misery was the fact that a conventional family life was difficult to sustain due to the low numbers of female migrants. The imbalance is noticeable at the Aapravasi Ghat museum where the remains of four bathrooms for new male arrivals correspond to only one bathroom for women, and sure enough Tinker tells us that even after efforts were made to increase the numbers of female workers, in 1873, there were still only around forty women for every hundred men on Mauritius estates.[76] An annual report in 1901 in Mauritius indicated that a female population of 116,781 gave birth to just 9,905 babies (768 of them stillborn). Few children went to school, because there were barely any schools on estates: they would join a weeding gang aged ten, and then become indentured when the law allowed it. The relative rarity of women meant the normal Indian dowry system was reversed and fathers began demanding a bride-price for their daughters, provoking the claim from some outsiders that families were selling their children. Moreover, a custom emerged of polyandry, where one woman would cook for and have relations with several men, which led to vicious disputes.[77] There are many reports from the sugar colonies concerning quarrels over women, often resulting in fatal violence. The problem was such that in 1871 the Colonial Office felt compelled to commission a study, which uncovered the disturbing fact that such murders were up to 142 times more common in the colony of British Guiana than in India's North-Western Provinces and Oudh.[78] As a result, colonies like Natal enacted special laws in an effort to stop husbands killing their wives.[79]

Finally, there was the work. In Mauritius this could involve waking up at 4 a.m. to weed or to move volcanic boulders, in heat which I find difficult to endure for more than five minutes when walking around on modern pavements as a visitor.[80] As in slavery, planters used indentured labourers for work such as ploughing and hauling heavy goods which would have been better done by animals. The women would often have to combine this work with cooking for the family – waking up at 3.30 in the morning.*[81] The newly arrived were often in no fit state to work, their distress being both physical and psychological: the voyage, and the strange food, often left them unfit and distraught. Whereas the recently enslaved were often allowed a 'seasoning' period in which they learned about their work, indentured labourers, being the planter's property for a limited time, weren't allowed to acclimatize.[82] In particular, the new indentured labourers found it difficult to adjust to the 'task' way of working, whereby they wouldn't get paid at all if they failed to complete a task supposedly based on one day's labour, as defined by an employer.[83]

The indenture system was penal – meaning there were criminal rather than civil penalties for breaking labour contracts – and more than a fifth of the emigrant workers were convicted for labour violations which often sprang from the unproven accusations of unscrupulous overseers.[84] In the majority of the sugar colonies, the indentured and even ex-indentured Indians were compelled to carry an ID document called a livret, and absence from the estate without one was a fineable or imprisonable offence.[85] In Fiji, the penal system was so all-encompassing that a free migrant visiting his still indentured wife on an estate without

---

* Totaram Sanadhya, who returned from indenture in Fiji in 1914, told his story to an Indian nationalist anti-indenture campaigner. He was quoted saying: 'When women return from work, there is corpse-like shading to their faces. One is so sad to see the dirtiness of their faces at that time it is indescribable. These women who had never been out of their village in India, who didn't know that there was a country outside of their district, who are soft and tender by nature, who never did hard work at home, these women today, having gone thousands of miles away, in Fiji, Jamaica, Cuba, Honduras, Guyana and so forth have to do hard labour.'

permission was fined.[86] In Malaya, as well as having to repay the cost of their passage, workers faced disproportionate punishment for even the smallest infringement of their contracts, and could be imprisoned with hard labour 'not only for fraud, not only for deception, but for negligence, for carelessness and . . . for even an impertinent word or gesture to the manager or his overseers'.[87] And if workers were in a group, they could all sometimes be held liable for the crimes of a single person. In British Guiana, Alan Adamson writes, 'it was a well-known boast of the planters that every immigrant ought to be either in the fields at work, in hospital or in jail'.[88] One immigrant who turned up to court in British Guiana's capital, having been ordered to appear as a witness against his employer, was subsequently jailed for the crime of leaving his estate without permission.[89]

As in slavery, the planter could administer beatings and floggings for offences. According to Tinker, punishment on plantations continued to include beating or whipping well into the twentieth century: the cattle whip was the weapon of choice in the West Indies; the cane took precedence in Malaya; in Natal it was the sjambok, a 'rawhide cattle lash'.[90] In 1840, the Anti-Slavery Society was so concerned that indenture was repeating the outrages of slavery that they sent a team to British Guiana, where John Gladstone had a plantation, to investigate. They discovered very long working hours, appalling housing conditions, bad health and floggings. Over a hundred Indians had died during their first year of indenture. A number of witnesses were interviewed, including the formerly enslaved Elizabeth Caesar, who claimed that the indentured workers 'were locked up in the sickhouse and next morning they were flogged with cat-o'-nine-tails. The manager was in the house, and they flogged the people under his house. They were tied to the post of the gallery of the manager's house. I cannot tell how many licks; he gave them enough. I saw blood. When they were flogged at the manager's house, they rubbed salt pickle on their backs.'[91]

Meanwhile, the wages were sometimes non-existent. Some of the planters did everything they could to avoid paying their workers.[92] In Trinidad between 1899 and 1904, the average daily earnings of an indentured labourer on task work was just over 18 cents, although 25 cents was the official minimum wage.[93] There was a custom of keeping back the pay of workers for at least one month and often two or three months. The most powerful method for avoiding paying workers in Mauritius was the 'double cut' system: anyone who was absent for a day, for any reason whatsoever, forfeited his pay for two days.[94] In British Guiana, foodstuffs (for example, flour, rice, dried fish, salt pork) were taxed, whereas the more luxurious goods consumed by the planter class were duty free (fresh fish, meat and vegetables – and diamonds). Immigrants were also taxed for things such as Poor Rates, which supported non-Indian native residents of Mauritius (Indian paupers were sent back to India); and tax revenue was used to bolster the sugar industry.[95]

All these factors, in combination, made plantations sustained with indentured labour sites of despair. An investigation undertaken in 1882 found that some potential migrants in the north of India viewed foreign indenture as a form of punishment. They described penal settlements and plantation work synonymously as *kala pani* and asked what crime they had committed to be condemned to such a fate. Some of them also thought indentured labourers who had returned home were actually convicts released from the Andaman Islands.[96] Such was the lack of awareness of what indenture involved that rumours abounded elsewhere that workers lured to the colonies were having their skulls crushed to extract oil.[97] Amid the misery, the indentured sought escape in all forms available. Workers often got drunk to the point of oblivion,[98] and the planters continued to profit from their misery: in Mauritius, 'grog shops' on the plantations sold overpriced rum to the workers and encouraged credit.[99] Suicide was common – on Mauritius, between 1860 and 1866, there were thirteen times more known and suspected suicides among Indians than in the rest of the population,[100] and the suicide rate in the sugar colonies was far greater than that in India.[101] And then there are the pitiful accounts of attempted escape in places like British Guiana, desperate workers hoping it would somehow be possible to find a walking route from South America back to India.[102]

But, having reported all this, the routine comparison to slavery, which, as we heard earlier, persists today even among the descendants of the indentured, doesn't feel right. There were all sorts of ways in which indenture was clearly not like slavery, not least in terms of the voyage out. It's true the journey for the indentured could be brutal, but it was not the Middle Passage, which involved the enslaved being chained to one another, stacked up in tiers, unable to get up or stretch except maybe to be' hosed down' occasionally or to be 'made to dance in their chains to preserve their physique',[103] excrement piling up in barrels around them, many being raped and dying from disease, suicide and murder before the journey was over. At Aapravasi Ghat, where a section of a boat used to transport the indentured is reconstructed for visitors, my guide points out that the migrants had more freedom to move around than the enslaved had, while Ashutosh Kumar claims that 'the hazards were ultimately no greater for Indian emigrants than they were for the Englishmen'. They would likely have experienced the same risk of disease if they had remained at home.[104] Indeed, detailed study by the academics David Eltis and David Northrup has revealed that the indentured-labour passenger ships were far less packed than those used as African slave ships,[105] and that indentured passengers enjoyed a better state of health. Elsewhere, Ralph Shlomowitz and John McDonald observe that the mortality rates of indentured workers were far lower than those of the victims of the transatlantic slave trade.[106]

Second, there was generally some medical care available to indentured labourers, on plantations and on the journeys to the plantations and before they embarked. Illness had often been caused by the system of indenture, of course: for instance, indentured servants employed to work on the sugar estates in Malaya during the nineteenth and early twentieth centuries were exposed to malaria and, coming from South India, where malaria was seasonal, they lacked adequate immunity.[107] And admittedly the doctors who had the responsibility of delivering them alive at the end of voyages would be in a rush and under pressure to fill the ship: the examination took place three or four days before sailing, so it was all done quickly, with 400–600 Indians being paraded before them; and, often, as long as a person was not suffering from an obvious malformation or disease, he would pass the examination.[108] Furthermore, the kind of person who was attracted to becoming a surgeon superintendent in charge of the health of the emigrants was 'often the loner, the unconventional, the misfit',[109] and sometimes truly loathsome: Dr J. R. Brown was taken off the Mauritius voyages for drunken behaviour and for violating female emigrants.\*[110] But there were principled men too: in 1901, the surgeon travelling onboard the *Main*,

---

\* Dr William Johnston kept a diary of his voyage to Trinidad in 1873, and noted the deaths on board in this callous fashion:

*26 October 1873:* Another coolie whelp skedaddled to kingdom come . . .

*29 October:* Another coolie infant vermosed . . .

one Dr Oliver, wielded his revolver while trying to protect the female passengers and only just avoided a crew mutiny.[111] Needless to say, there was generally much more medical care available to the indentured than to the enslaved.

There was another meaningful difference: indentured labour came after abolition, and it was analysed, critiqued, monitored, closely examined and criticized from its very earliest days, not least by those who had campaigned successfully against slavery. Indian nationalists embraced it as a cause. The British and Foreign Anti-Slavery Society was a constant source of pressure, petitions and memos to colonial secretaries.[112] In some places, there was a system of twice-yearly visits to plantations by the Inspectors of Immigrants.[113] Between 1837 and 1915, numerous government officials and Parliamentary committees were instructed to investigate conditions in the sugar colonies and other aspects of indentured migration from India.[114] It made a difference. The Calcutta–Caribbean mortality rate, which we heard earlier hit 38 per cent in 1858, fell to 'only' 5 per cent by 1861–2; medics may have let almost every applicant on to the boats at one stage, but in 1894 the Protector of Calcutta noted that, out of 26,707 registered emigrants, only 14,865 actually boarded the boat.[115] The fear that indentured labour was a new form of slavery led in 1840 to the suspension of Gladstone's indenture scheme in British Guiana.[116] In Mauritius, incoming labour was halted in 1839, although it resumed again in 1842.[117] More generally, regulations changed greatly over time, and ultimately, with Indian nationalists applying intense pressure, all existing indenture contracts expired in 1919.[118]

There were other ways in which the indentured often had it better than the enslaved. Their agony was not permanent – a point that Tinker himself concedes, writing that before the day of freedom arrived 'some were dead and others were crippled by disease, while some were so in debt or otherwise ensnared by the system that they could not extricate themselves. But for some – for most – a day would come when the indenture was cancelled and the master no longer had a hold over him.'[119] The indentured managed to retain much more of their indigenous culture and identity than the enslaved, largely because the colonists allowed them to: on the voyage out, they were permitted to practise their beliefs and express their customs in the forms of worship, food,

---

*7 November:* One of the coolies jumped overboard [the third] assigning as a reason that he had not enough grub. This amusement is getting rather too common . . .

clothing and entertainment, up to and including the occasional puff of opium, hukka or ganja.[120] This culture very much survives today in Mauritius: many Hindu festivals are designated public holidays; a couple of days after we meet, Arvind posts a message on Instagram celebrating the Hindu festival of Makar Sankranti; most of the radio stations available on my battered hire-car radio are playing Bollywood tunes; shops offering pani puri seem as common as coffee outlets. Furthermore, I end up in Mauritius rather than Guyana because the reporter helping me in the latter country was, in the end, too busy organizing Diwali events.

In addition, a portion of the indentured managed to find social and economic liberation through indenture in a way that the enslaved generally did not. Many of the indentured chose to stay after their contracts expired: it's thought that only one-quarter of indentured workers who travelled to the West Indies ever returned home,[121] while some returned to India and then came back. Admittedly, some of those who came back did so only because they were rejected at home: returning workers were known to risk ostracism in their villages for having traversed the 'black water' and for having consorted with other castes and religions. If they had managed to save up some money overseas, they might have been robbed or cheated out of it, in punishment for supposed transgressions.[122] But returnees were significant enough in numbers for imperialists to gloat about them.[123] Also, for all the trauma of the voyage out, many of the Jahajibhai (shipmates) developed relationships as important as family.[124] Indenture allowed many lower-caste individuals to escape the tyranny of the caste system, and it offered opportunities to some women, who had been punished by Indian society for, say, marrying out of caste, or just becoming widowed.* There's plenty of academic research on this theme, showing how indentured women could be both punished and emancipated by indenture, seeing the eradication of dowries as either crushing or liberating, but no one does a better job of conveying the complex position of women than Gaiutra Bahadur. Her book, *Coolie Woman:*

---

* Young widowhood was widespread since arranged weddings frequently took place extremely early in a woman's life, often before she had reached puberty. These widows were typically forbidden to remarry and were often considered a burden on families and society.

*The Odyssey of Indenture,* is a powerful attempt by the American journalist to trace the story of her great-grandmother over three continents, nothing less than the single most compelling treatise on indenture and one of the most important books written on the British empire. The diligence of the research, even when it doesn't generate clear answers, and perhaps particularly when it *doesn't* produce precise explanations, makes you appreciate just how lowly the indentured were within the British imperial system. And, like all great literature, it offers nuance: Bahadur illustrates how a female indentured labourer could be at once a victim and use her sexuality and gender as 'leverage' within a perilous and unjust system.[125]

The other thing that sheds light on the comparative severity of the two systems is that the descendants of the indentured seem to have been held back less by the legacies of their system than the descendants of the enslaved. I say 'seem' because I've not found hard evidence, and I'm not sure that it would be possible to conduct a comparative study, given that slavery and indenture were so different: they happened at different times, lasted for different periods, involved different numbers of people and occurred in different geographies under varying jurisdictions. The Dutch and the French were largely responsible for the slavery in Mauritius,★[126] for example, and the British alone introduced indenture there, whereas in places like Jamaica the British were largely responsible for both. According to Pier Larson, the historian of slavery, between the 1720s and 1820s some 200,000 enslaved people were shipped from East Africa and Malagasy to Mauritius and Réunion Island,[127] less than half the number of indentured labourers who would migrate there. Also, how do you trace such legacies when the groups have intermixed to a certain degree, and when we do not know the precise size of its ethnic communities – Mauritius doesn't categorize its population on ethnic grounds in the national census?[128]

Nevertheless, the relative fortunes of the enslaved and indentured are striking when you visit Mauritius, which received the largest number of indentured labourers in British empire, and which saw Indians displacing Creoles even before the latter were fully liberated from slavery.[129] While Indians occupy almost every important

---

★ At the time of emancipation, Mauritius had one of the largest populations of enslaved people in the British empire.

position on the island, and dominate several industries, the Creoles, who are the descendants of the 66,613 slaves present on Mauritius on the eve of the abolition of slavery, and who account for around a quarter of the population,[130] appear sidelined. On Mauritius Air, the Bollywood offering vastly outweighs the African offering on the inflight entertainment system. There's a museum for slavery next door to Aapravasi Ghat, its entrance emblazoned with the words 'a site of conscience', but it's home only to temporary exhibitions and is closed when I visit. Lots of people get in touch with me to offer advice on what Indian food and culture to experience when they see from Instagram that I'm in Mauritius, but when I ask for Creole equivalents, there's silence. I suspect most holidaymakers are as unaware of, and as indifferent to, this racial stratification as they are in Barbados: I finally understand now that, while on a beach holiday the locals may provide service, holidaymakers are almost discouraged from thinking too deeply about them. Most European visitors to Mauritius are probably not even entirely sure whether the island is Indian or African (it's an African country). But it bothers me enough for me to investigate.

I resist the urge to lie on the beach and repeatedly leave my hotel, which is so unused to hosting business travellers that one night, eating alone, and eating late to avoid the hordes of children at the buffet, my table is surrounded by dancers who perform around me, and only for me, for five whole mortifying minutes. I visit a monument to the slave route, a UNESCO World Heritage site, located at the foot of Le Morne mountain, in view of caves where it's said that runaway slaves took refuge.[131] Strapped into my dilapidated hire car, I crisscross a country which is supposedly one of the most densely populated places on the planet[132] but still somehow feels like it's dominated by fields of sugar cane and roundabouts, to talk to lawyers, politicians, diplomats and journalists, often at the same table of the same hotel in Mauritius' capital, Port Louis. I walk around the Port Louis neighbourhood of Cité Martial, which has a significant Creole population. I raise the issue in every conversation with every Indo-Mauritian and Franco-Mauritian I meet and I read the incredibly dense report produced by the independent Truth and Justice Commission of Mauritius, established in 2009 to investigate racial problems on the island. And make no mistake, the island does, despite the curious claim from the

Prime Minister's Office in 2017 that racism didn't exist on the island,[133] have racial problems.

Indeed, racial tension might be the most striking modern global legacy of indenture, a system which pitted Indian labourers against the formerly enslaved. As Alan Adamson puts it in relation to British Guiana: 'Immigration destroyed the temporary power which free black workers had enjoyed immediately after 1838; and it gradually restored to the estate proprietors the command of the labour market which they had possessed under slavery.'[134] The seeds of racial tension began, arguably, to be planted even before Indian immigrants arrived, with black people often not being allowed to work on ships carrying indentured workers on account of 'their generally incorrigible addictedness to sexual intercourse', according to Jamaica's protector of immigrants writing in 1891. On two occasions, ship surgeons passed resolutions at their conferences stating that 'the employment of Negroes and Mulattos in any capacity on board coolie ships is most undesirable'.[135] Tinker explains that European planters aggravated tensions between Creoles and Indians by labelling the former lazy and irresponsible, and the latter docile and hardworking.[136] V. S. Naipaul's biographer asserts that the black population of Trinidad was feared by the newly arrived East Indians, as they looked and acted tough and had the dark colouring associated with Hinduism's lower castes.[137] In Guyana, the indentured labourers were kept isolated on the estates, having little to no contact with the local Creoles, resulting in mistrust on both sides.[138] Segregation was encouraged by the planters, 'divide and rule' giving them greater control. The Truth and Justice Commission in Mauritius has noted that instilling division among the working classes was a tactic of the elite throughout the nineteenth century. Religion became another divide, as one group heavily adopted Christianity while the other maintained its Hindu and Muslim beliefs. There were also two conflicting forces when independence was granted: the Creoles sided with anti-independence while the Indo-Mauritians supported independence. The Mauritius Truth and Justice Commission also observed that 'this episode has embittered relations between the two groups since'. Decades of division have, in many places, only calcified in more recent times, the *Economist* reporting in a perceptive survey that 'the Indo-Guyanese and Indo-Trinidadians have plenty of racist terms for their compatriots of African origin'. Apparently, in the French Caribbean and Fiji, 'z'Indiens' are stereotyped as money-obsessed, and common expressions include 'faib con an coolie' ('weak as a coolie' in Creole). Sakeasi Butadroka, a Fijian politician, stated publicly in the 1970s that 'people of Indian origin' should be 'repatriated', and in 2014 the Zulu band AmaCde had a hit song containing the message that black South Africans should stand up to the Indians and 'send them home'.[139]

Most of the people I meet in Mauritius bear witness to this tension. Rishy Bukoree, a Mauritian diplomat, recalls that while he was blind to race as a schoolchild, racial awareness kicked in with age, and he felt Franco-Mauritian parents didn't generally want their children to mix with other groups. He conveys a common sentiment on the island, that it was unfair for the French to end up with so much land in the way they did. 'Mauritius was not inhabited, and when the British took over, they allowed the French to have so many portions of land everywhere, but the people of Indian origin, they had to buy [it], you know? There should have been a better mechanism.' Hugo Lambert talks about being the subject of racial abuse from Mauritians of colour, as a white, French Mauritian. 'Most of the time, they think I'm a tourist, and I get "Fuck off, go back to your country."' Veerapen tells me that his family faced resistance from Franco-Mauritian companies when they investigated entering the tourism sector. Then there is José Moirt, a 58-year-old former mayor turned lawyer, of Creole background (though he rejects all such labels), who in 2018 was involved in the launch of Affirmative Action, a pressure group campaigning to fight back against the racism that Creoles face from the Indo-Mauritian majority.

At my regular spot in the foyer of the Labourdonnais Hotel, named after one of the founders of French colonialism in the Indian Ocean, I meet Moirt, not looking at all like the one-time champion weightlifter that he once was, and not resembling the official portrait either that graces the autobiography that he hands over (in a reversal of convention, he's much thinner).[140] He alerts me to the fact that in the run-up to the Mauritian declaration of independence on 12 March 1968 there were ten days of riots in Port Louis, arising from tensions between the largely Christian Creoles and the Muslim population over the country's political future. That 1999 saw further nationwide protests after a well-loved 'seggae' musician called Joseph Réginald Topize, nicknamed 'Kaya', died while in police custody.[141] That there has been tension in recent decades over the education system, which is ostensibly free and available to all, but intense competition means that extra private tuition is deemed necessary to access higher education, which takes the poorer, often Creole population out of the running. That there is friction over rising Hindu militancy, over housing, over ethnic patronage for jobs,[142] especially in government, over ethnic representation in government.[143] 'The Creole community work hard, they do the hardest jobs,' he observes. 'In construction, in the hotel industry. The civil service, it's out of bounds, civilian institutions, out of bounds. Yes, you get one here, one there, but it's token. They want to maintain that Hindu supremacy.'

He pushes a copy of a 2021 report produced by Affirmative Action across the coffee table between us.[144] Among other things, it alleges that 'scientific communalism' (which is a term given to the widespread practice of pairing electoral candidates as far as possible with constituents of the same caste and ethnic profile) has led to racist voting patterns and contributes to the perpetuation of racism in Mauritian society.[145] Furthermore, it claims that in order to ensure the supremacy of Indo-Mauritians, a clandestine contract was made between the main Hindu majority party and the British colonial authorities to design 'the final shape' of the country's electoral system, evidenced by the fact that in the fifty-two years since Mauritius gained its independence six of its prime ministers have come from two dynasties, the Ramgoolam and the Jugnauth families, both of which are part of the minority Vaish caste. In conclusion it asserts that 'the Mauritian electoral system is an illusion of democracy because the racial outcome is predetermined. The short parenthesis of two years (from 2003 to 2005) where a non-Hindu became Prime Minister . . . is the exception that confirms the rule.'

In person, he claims that the reason the Mauritian state has not published official data on the ethnic makeup of the nation since 1972 is to 'maintain this Hindu supremacy'. I struggle to believe that this lack of measurement can be true, but sure enough, when I get in touch with the relevant government department, an official emails to tell me that 'data on community was last collected in the 1972 Census, and no data was collected in 1983, 1990, 2000, 2011 and 2022'. In a recent report, the UN's Committee for the Elimination of Racial Discrimination concluded that 'hierarchical structures along ethnic and caste lines linger' in Mauritius, that Creoles face 'de facto discrimination in all walks of life', and urged the government to drop its opposition to gathering statistics broken down by ethnicity so the extent of the problem can be fathomed.[146] Meanwhile, that dense Truth and Justice report asserted that the descendants of the enslaved endure, as consequences of historic exploitation, poor housing,[147] poor literacy,[148] over-concentration of employment in hard manual work, poor representation,[149] anti-African prejudices,[150] 'disjointed' family relationships,[151] violence[152] and racial prejudice.[153]

It's revealing that everyone I talk to agrees that the descendants of the enslaved have been held back more than the descendants of the indentured, because the system of slavery was so much more brutal. 'After the abolition of slavery, many slaves went into hiding,' says Rishy Bukoree. 'Many people from the Creole community, they were so scared of the white masters, they were depressed, they were traumatized, they didn't want to have anything to do with the whites, whereas the indentured, when they came, they could work for the whites.' Hugo Lambert adds: 'The Creoles had their identity, their religion, their culture, taken from them. They are the only community in Mauritius that don't really have a true culture. You also have that issue that while they were freed, they were given nothing else.' He points out that, in contrast, it helped the Indians that they moved from a British colony to another British colony: it gave them some sense of familiarity. This continues. The Hindu elite of modern-day Mauritius is highly Anglicized, keen on attending British private schools and universities, Arvind and his sister Jaya among them. Before I leave, Jaya adds: 'The mindset of indentured labourers and the enslaved was different. They [the Creoles] were traumatized, broken by what happened.'

Although I have gone out of my way to make the point that slavery was worse than indenture, it doesn't feel like the right note to end on. Indentured labour was still a system of brutal exploitation, and the fact is that some of the descendants of the indentured are still struggling to escape from the burden of the history. In a recent survey of post-indenture, the *Economist* observed that 'indentured workers' descendants have done least well where their ancestors could not own land, as in Fiji'. And sure enough Minority Rights Group International, a London-based international NGO with an international governing council, reports that while Indo-Fijians constitute the second largest ethnic community in the country with over 90 per cent of them descended from indentured labourers, and while 'a small number of Indo-Fijians can be defined as wealthy or engaged in business enterprises', 'the majority of Indo-Fijians are workers and peasant farmers, and also include the poorest of the poor in the country . . . Indo-Fijians remain marginalized in most spheres.'[154] Meanwhile, a Malaysian news outlet recently reported that those who are descended from the country's Indian plantation community are now deeply impoverished, an underclass beset by issues such as crime, addiction, violence, gangs, broken families and a pervasive sense of hopelessness, with scant opportunities to improve their lot. Systemic racism and oppression are to blame. The report draws comparisons with the African American underclass in the US.[155]

Furthermore, in *Coolie Woman*, Gaiutra Bahadur, echoing the work of the CARICOM countries in relation to the legacies of slavery, blames indenture for a host of negative features in contemporary Guyana, including domestic violence and 'an alarming rate of intimate partner homicide' ('4.07 per 100,000 women, four times the rate in the United States in 2007 and thirteen times the rates in the United Kingdom and Canada that year'), the frequently gruesome methods of partner homicide ('most households in Guyana's villages possess a cutlass. It's still the tool to chop cane, and it's still an instrument to dismember women'), the lack of justice in these instances of homicide ('no one was held responsible in more than half the cases in which women were killed in 2010 and their partners credibly implicated . . . [there is] a deep-seated acceptance of domestic violence among police'), high rates of alcoholism ('rum comes from cane. It's a by-product of sugar, made by fermenting molasses or cane juice . . . The spirit was introduced to coolies at the outset of their journeys west. At the emigration depots in Calcutta, the British issued recruits rum as medicine') and the poor socio-economic outcomes for women ('for their first ten years in the colony, Indian immigrants who kept their boys out of school would be spared fines for breaking the law. But no Indian, immigrant or native-born, no matter their tenure in the colony, would ever incur penalties for keeping their girl children home. The edict stayed in effect for three decades, and Indian girls suffered the consequences of illiteracy and limited opportunity for far longer').*[156]

---

* Some of the phenomena which Bahadur cites as legacies of indenture in Guyana are also cited as legacies of slavery in Guyana by Thomas Harding in *White Debt*. This

Even in Mauritius, that 2009 Truth and Justice report pointed out that while up to a third of the indentured acquired land, a key to the accumulation of their wealth, the majority after indenture 'lead a precarious life as labourers on sugar estates or as unemployed'.[157] Also, 'the inside story of Indian immigrants and of their descendants continued to be marred by caste prejudice', and there is a popular view that the descendants of the 'sirdars' in the indentured system (the men who acted as foremen, recruiters, labour leaders and intermediaries between white and brown)[158] have generally done better in the modern age than the descendants of lowly labourers (Arvind and Jaya have sirdars in their ancestry). Meanwhile, the Veerapen siblings observe that some of the descendants of the indentured in Mauritius still lead brutal working lives in ways that echo the brutal history. Arvind recalls working in one of his family's retail outlets as a young man in the 1990s when an old Indian man, a farm labourer, came in saying he was having trouble with his eyes in the harsh sunlight and needed drops. 'I said, "Why don't you wear sunglasses?"' Arvind has switched back to English, having in the casual Mauritian way, been switching between Creole and French over lunch. 'He said, "No, I could never do that, the master would never allow it." Ill-treatment is still there. Even now.'

'Don't come here, stand there,' says Jaya, recalling the way that an Indian labourer was spoken to in a sugar field in her presence. Behind us, the waves of the Indian Ocean lap upon the beach, and someone somewhere opens a bottle of champagne.

'Even today, some people will be frightened to approach the white boss with a simple request,' adds Arvind.

Their observations echo the argument of Kamala Kempadoo, who maintains that rather than engage in a 'hierarchisation of oppression' between slavery and indenture, it's more productive to consider parallels and connections between indenture and conditions of modern slavery and 'unfree' labour today.[159] South Asians occupy some of the highest positions in the world outside India, from the offices of the British Prime Minister to the Irish Taoiseach, to the CEO positions at Google, Microsoft and Starbucks. But it also remains the case that labourers from South Asia continue to be exploited all around the

reveals the difficulty of separating slavery and indenture, and also the sometimes unscientific nature of tracing imperial legacies.

world. In Britain, it was recently reported by the *Guardian* that Nepali fruit pickers who took on thousands of pounds of debt to come and work on UK farms, expecting six months' employment, were forced to return much sooner and so left deep in debt.[160] At the 2022 World Cup in Qatar, Amnesty International warned that migrant workers from Bangladesh, India and Nepal were being exploited in all sorts of ways that echoed the nineteenth century: they had to pay for the privilege to work, paying dodgy recruitment agents anything from US$500 to US$4,300; once in Qatar they found themselves unable to change jobs or leave the country; they often had to wait months to get paid, only to discover they had been lied to about salary levels; they endured terrible living conditions, threats and intimidation.[161]

Moreover, the exploitation of Indian labourers is often happening in exactly the same places and in exactly the same industries which exploited Indian indentured labour in the nineteenth century.\*[162] Serious labour rights abuses on Assam tea plantations financed by the World Bank were uncovered by an internal investigation in 2016 – Assam being a part of India where in the nineteenth and early twentieth centuries indentured labourers arrived and worked and were exploited pretty much as they were exploited in territories abroad.[163] In 2009, protests were held at a tea estate in West Bengal after the collapse of a pregnant worker, while in 2010 another 25-year-old worker collapsed and died allegedly after being exposed to pesticides, resulting in protests at which two people were killed.[164] More than a century beforehand, death rates for newly indentured labourers were as high as 30 per cent in some areas of Assam,[165] where 95 per cent of the labour was imported. Because

---

\* Professor Genevieve LeBaron from the University of Sheffield has reported that 25 million men, women and children across the world, including many tea workers who lack access to 'basic necessities like water, toilets, housing, and sufficient food', are affected by forced labour. 'Instead of the picturesque, serene and happy environments we consumers like to envisage, for many workers tea plantations are harsh and difficult places to work. It's not uncommon for workers to pick 80kg of leaves a day – that's the weight of 25,600 teabags – in order for them to make around 140 rupees, which is about £1.50.' Meanwhile, in 2015 a BBC investigation found dangerous and degrading living and working conditions at tea estates which supply 'several of Britain's biggest tea brands, including PG Tips, Tetleys and Twinings', reporting that workers and their families receive pitiful wages and suffer malnutrition and illness due to their terrible living and working conditions.

there were no hospitals or medical facilities available in the tea gardens, workers' injuries sometimes went untreated, resulting in horrific scars from beatings.[166]

The Chief Commissioner for Assam, Sir Henry Cotton, once conceded that the region's tea planters were slave drivers,*[167] and a scandalous court case in the early twentieth century, involving one W. A. Bain, demonstrated exactly that behaviour. The young planter was sent to prison by a European jury for six months for beating a coolie to death in the region of Cachar – a sentence so light that a judge increased it to 'prevent similar punishments of natives'.[168]

In another case, a beating led to the man's death, but the examining doctor claimed that the actual cause lay in his pre-existing health conditions. Similarly, when a boy on the Rangliting Tea Estate was flogged by his manager in 1899 and died three days later, an official doctor testified that the flogging did not cause the death, and the manager was let off with a fine. Meanwhile, colonists provided chilling advice on how to maintain discipline. The Chairman of the Assam division of the Indian Tea Association, one J. Buckingham, stated that 'the whole matter of coolie treatment' had to be considered in light of 'the enormous difficulties of a planter's position', which he likened to that of the captain of a ship far from land and conventional law enforcement, trying to contain disorderly men 'always ready to hatch disturbances'. 'What is he to do?' Buckingham asked rhetorically. 'Coolies certainly need a strong hand.' The best approach, he suggested, was first to contain the ringleader, perhaps by giving him a 'thrashing', and then to lecture the other men who, having witnessed their leader capitulate, will blame him for encouraging their disobedience, perhaps give him a kicking themselves, apologize and return to work peaceably the next morning. 'No doubt the planter has broken the letter of the law, but he has quelled a disturbance, which might have cost the garden thousands of rupees.'[169]

This is grim, unsettling history. But if your response, as a British person, is to feel guilt and shame, or to feel that guilt and shame are

---

* Henry Cotton was vocal in exposing the brutal and unjust treatment of indentured labourers on tea plantations in a 1900 *Annual Labour Report* on Assam. Cotton was attacked by the planter community and praised by Indian nationalists. The Viceroy, Lord Curzon, withdrew his support and Cotton resigned.

somehow being solicited, you're missing the point. History does not care about anyone's feelings. There are other good reasons for Britons to understand this imperial history, and other imperial histories we've touched upon so far. When it comes to India, we need to appreciate its version of events because it's a burgeoning superpower that will shape our future in all sorts of ways, and we can't assume, as we've tended to, that they're nostalgic for a time they're actually trying to decolonize out of their system. When it comes to Barbados, we need to understand their version of events because they've been pleading for us to understand for decades now, and because the international conversation on reparations is leaving us behind: we will look increasingly irrelevant and ignorant if we continue not to engage. As for Mauritius, it does not seem to be interested in decolonization like India, it's not requesting reparations like Barbados, and it doesn't even seem to be asking Britain to care about the history. All it seems to want, officially at least, is for Britons to continue visiting, which I plan to do, next time hopefully through the prism of child-free five-star hotels of the kind that Arvind frequents and hire cars that aren't disintegrating. But with Britain exiting the European Union, and Brexiteers explicitly talking up trade with Mauritius, and other nations like it[170] where we already have good economic relationships,[171] it's simply in our own interest to show up knowing what we were responsible for the last time we turned up.

## 4.  White Saviours

I can't say 'Do They Know It's Christmas?', written by Bob Geldof and Midge Ure, has ever been my favourite Christmas song. If anything, I've always slightly resented it for preventing the actual best Christmas song of all time, 'Last Christmas' by Wham!, from getting to number one in the 1980s. But like many kids of my generation I still could tell you, off the top of my head, which pop stars sing which bits and in which order, I'm a sucker for trivia related to it (for example, George Michael telling Paul Weller during the recording: 'Don't be a wanker all your life. Have a day off'),[1] and it has been distressing to watch it age so badly.

It's hard to identify the most dated or misjudged bit as so much of it is dated and misjudged, but Bono screeching 'Well, tonight thank God it's them, instead of you' is a low point: apart from being an oddly self-centred remark for a charity record, it's a decidedly unseasonal sentiment for a Christmas song (Bono reportedly hated singing the lyrics and had to be persuaded to do so). Then there is Boy George (and others) claiming that 'there won't be snow in Africa this Christmas time', suggesting, vaguely, that Africa might be one country, and obscuring the fact that there will almost certainly be snow on Kilimanjaro at Christmas. We also have the ludicrous insinuation that in Ethiopia/Africa we have a land 'where nothing ever grows, no rain nor rivers flow', and the absurd question at the heart of it all – 'Do they know it's Christmas time at all?' Of course they know it's Christmas. Not least because, as a casual glance at Christian faith in Africa, or even at black faith in Britain,[2] will reveal, decades of colonial missionary activity from the West have helped turn Africa into a continent of fervent Christian belief.★[3]

---

★ 'The influence of Islam and Christianity dates back long before colonization, but colonial rule opened new spaces to Catholic and Protestant missionaries,' explains Frederick Cooper. 'Less obvious is the fact that colonization, despite the intentions of the colonizers, also resulted in a large-scale extension of Islam; something like a third of sub-Saharan Africa's population are now Muslims.' Max Siollun explains how the initial efforts of Christian missionaries actually led to the flourishing of Islam in West

But atrocious lyrics are the least serious of the criticisms to have been levelled at Band Aid's organizers, and the organizers of the initiatives it inspired, including Live Aid. In the decades that have followed the charity record and the global live event, they have been accused, among other things, of: perpetuating negative stereotypes of Africans; underplaying the role that armed conflict and politics played in creating famine in Ethiopia and instead focusing on drought; enabling food aid to conceal structural inequality; depriving African victims of a voice, by prioritizing the voices of camp workers and white aid workers in broadcast coverage; depicting the Ethiopian people as entirely helpless without British assistance and, worst of all, of acting in an imperialistic manner.[4] These are criticisms that came up repeatedly when the Band Aid song was re-recorded in 2014 to help with the Ebola crisis. The lyrics had been changed (Bob Geldof removed references to Africa's 'burning sun' as well as the assertion that it's somewhere 'no rain nor rivers flow'), but Jessica Howard-Johnston still complained online that 'Band Aid 30 fulfils some kind of colonial "them" and "us" fantasy, where we are waiting to sweep in and help a continent filled with suffering victims,'[5] and Bim Adewunmi still protested in the *Guardian* that 'there exists a paternalistic way of thinking about Africa, likely exacerbated by the original (and the second, and the third) Band Aid singles, in which it must be "saved", and usually from itself'.[6]

It's a criticism that has been levelled at other British charitable initiatives in recent years,[7] not least Comic Relief, which announced in 2020 that it would cease sending celebrities like the TV presenter Stacey Dooley to film appeals in Africa after criticism of 'white saviour' stereotypes.[8] This highlights a striking legacy of the British empire: the large number of international charities in Britain, which continue to exercise considerable influence across the world. This sector of international non-governmental organizations (INGOs) grew out of empire, has

---

Africa. In the first fifty years of British rule, more West Africans converted to Islam than had done in the entire millennium before, leading to a doubling of the Muslim population. He argues this was because conversion to Islam was less complicated than conversion to Christianity; because of a feeling that Islam was more indigenous to West Africa (both religions originated from abroad, but Christians who converted seemed to model themselves after their colonizers, speaking English, adopting Anglo-Christian names and dressing in Western fashion) and because Islam did not 'require polygamous people to destroy their family lives by divorcing'.

been deeply influenced by it, has a history of imposing dysfunctional, imperialistic solutions upon the planet, and, in the twenty-first century, continues to do so in a way that risks the future of all Western international charity work. Though, as with Kew, I don't expect to uncover such a dark, global history in something so seemingly benign when I get started (first they came for the houseplants, and then they came for the standing orders . . .). My research only begins after the discovery, as a result of my visit to Barbados, that some modern NGOs like Anti-Slavery International, and Britain's humanitarianism in general, grew out of the abolition movement. It intensifies after my visit to Kew, as a consequence of which I learn that British NGOs are prominent among those accused by critics like Guillaume Blanc of turning huge swathes of Africa into parks and reserves, at great cost to the people who have lived there for generations. These include WWF, originally established in London after 'a series of articles in a UK newspaper . . . about the destruction of habitat and wildlife in East Africa',[9] and Britain's Fauna & Flora International (FFI), 'the world's first international wildlife conservation organisation', known for creating protected areas including the Kruger and Serengeti National Parks,[10] and founded by, among others, British conservationist and Liberal Party politician Edward North Buxton.[11] Then, as a result of my visit to Mauritius, I notice it's Amnesty International, a campaigning organization founded in London, which warned that migrant workers from Bangladesh, India and Nepal were being exploited at the last World Cup in Qatar, and that it's another British NGO, Minority Rights, that warned of the marginalization of Indo-Fijians in Fijian society.

The intense involvement of British charities in such international issues shouldn't come as a surprise, as we have a disproportionate number of them, including outfits like Oxfam, Save the Children, Christian Aid, Action Aid, Tearfund and CAFOD (the Catholic Agency for Overseas Development). How big is our sector overall? In a 2019 paper, academics from the University of Manchester Development Institute reported that 'it is generally recognised that the UK's development NGO sector is among the most remarkable in the world', that 'international activities' are 'the one area in which the UK's third sector was significantly larger than that of any other country in the world'.[12] They then calculated the size of the sector, concluding that 'in 2015, Britain's development NGO sector spent nearly £7 billion, equivalent to over half the UK government's official development assistance that year', and that 'the funds spent by British-based development NGOs exceed many other individual countries' recorded expenditure by an order of magnitude'. Meanwhile, the 2014 report *Fast Forward: The Changing Role of UK-Based INGOs* from Bond, 'the UK network for organisations working in international development', claimed that 'the UK has one of the most developed and diverse INGO sectors', and that Bond was, as a reflection of this, 'by far the biggest membership body for international development organisations in the world, far bigger than its equivalent in the US and other European countries of comparable size, such as France, Germany and Italy'.[13] The report proceeded to compare the 'ecosystem' of British INGOs to Silicon Valley in California – calling the network of organizations focused on humanitarian work from Cambridge to Brighton, Bristol, London and Oxford a 'golden triangle', which supports some 40,000 jobs in the UK. It added: 'there is little doubt the UK sector punches well above its weight internationally with 5 out of the 11 largest INGOs having their origins in the UK. Why this should be the case is perhaps the subject of a whole other report.' In the absence of this 'other report', I'm happy to offer an explanation: the British empire.

Britain's disproportionate desire to get involved in other nations' business in the modern age in the name of humanitarianism can be explained by the fact that we have a very long history of interfering in other nations' business, often in the name of humanitarianism. Indeed, various British humanitarian bodies were a factor in imperial expansion: alongside the influence of missionary organizations around the empire, British colonization of Australia and New Zealand was 'heavily influenced' by the Aborigines' Protection Society, 'an early-nineteenth-century example of an NGO which had lobbied the government under the guise of concern for indigenous populations'.[14] More generally, Britain's INGO sector is a legacy of the 'civilizing mission' which was for many imperialists of the nineteenth and twentieth centuries central to the British imperial mission. Colonization, in imperial eyes, involved spreading Western values, such as Enlightenment ideals, Christianity, liberalism, democracy and abhorrence of slavery, as well as establishing British laws, language, education and customs. And the obvious racism of the belief, which put people into racial hierarchies and was captured most memorably by Rudyard Kipling in his poem 'The White Man's

Burden',[15] is one of the reasons why I was, at the start of this journey, hoping to dodge it. Besides, the 'civilizing mission' remains popular with adherents of the hoary old balance-sheet view of imperial history, who want to demonstrate that the 'good' of British empire outweighed the 'bad', in part by highlighting how suppressing the 'savage' practices in India of, say, female infanticide, or thagi (the assassin-priest cult which was rumoured to strangle unsuspecting travellers on Indian roadways),\*[16] or sati (the act of Hindu widows burning themselves alive on their husbands' funeral pyres),[17] somehow made up for famines, massacres and other kinds of violence and exploitation. I realize now, however, that the topic is undodgeable, and that there are scholars out there who manage to evaluate the success imperialists had in eliminating 'savage' customs such as thagi or female infanticide/sati†[18] without

---

\* Contemporary academics question many of the more sensational claims made by imperialists, with even Niall Ferguson, one of the great defenders of the 'civilizing mission', himself conceding that when it comes to 'thagi . . . modern scholars have suggested that much of [the phenomenon] was a figment of the over-heated expatriate imagination'. Historian Kim Wagner takes on the history in more detail in a forthcoming Oxford World's Classics edition of Philip Meadows Taylor's Anglo-Indian novel *Confessions of a Thug* (1839). The East India Company administration of the second half of the 1820s was guided by a new sense of evangelical zeal and responsibility towards their subjects. 'To the British, the different gangs of bandits, mendicants, and petty thieves who periodically indulged in murder and robbery all appeared as the regional variations of the same evil, namely "Thuggee".' By dramatizing and exaggerating the threat that thugs posed and bringing it to the government's notice, the official William Henry Sleeman launched his career. He was later given control of the operations to subdue the thugs. If captured, thugs often testified against their companions in the hope they would receive a pardon. They openly admitted to being thugs, which was not necessarily a misnomer considering it was one of their nicknames. 'Yet it is clear that the British misconstrued the practice of the bandits, based on preconceived and Orientalist notions of caste, religion, and Indian criminality,' continues Wagner. 'The erstwhile bandit-retainers were thus stripped of their socio-economic motivations and recast as Thugs: hereditary criminals who murdered for religious purposes alone.'

† The fact that female infanticide remains a problem in India says something about how much success the British had on this front, while the consensus among academics on the subject of sati, as presented by Arvind Sharma in an essay collection, is that British imperial missionaries deserve some credit for helping to eradicate the practice in India, though the claims made about the extent of their work and success have been exaggerated. The British were not alone in taking against it: Portuguese colonizers,

descending into crude racism. And I can see that some of our most famous charities have their roots in this mission, not least Save the Children, Britain's biggest INGO.[19]

The organization's past was recently interrogated in book form by the historian Emily Baughan, who took on the subject after official archives first became available to researchers in 2019 (she was able to look at records going up to 1972). In *Saving the Children*, Baughan explains that the charity did not begin with explicitly imperial roots. It was founded in 1919 by the aristocratic activist Dorothy Buxton[20] as a reaction to the post-war policies of the Allied countries and started off by giving grants to emergency feeding centres in Austria and Germany organized by British Quakers. Initially the fund was run by a mix of feminists, Quakers, socialists and liberals, who were considered left-wing and 'unpatriotic' by other British relief operations. So much so that some conservative leaders even started a rival charity, the Imperial War Relief Fund, to do similar work to Save the Children in war-stricken Europe, collaborating only with aid organizations from British territories. But things changed after Buxton's sister, Eglantyne Jebb, took the helm.

In common with many other humanitarian organizations of the era, and in another illustration of how British women boosted their position in society through imperial causes, Save the Children was led by women, continuing the domination by women of Protestant missionary activity.[21] Also, in common with many other 'international thinkers' of the time, Jebb believed in empire's 'civilizing' mission, imagined imperial unity as a shining example of global collaboration and wrote letters to

---

Sikh Gurus, the Tantrics, certain Hindu scholars, certain Hindu government officials, the Mughal Emperor Akbar and some Maratha chiefs also railed against it. Indeed, Afonso de Albuquerque, the Viceroy of Portuguese India from 1509 to 1515, abolished it in Goa in 1510. Also, the activity was not as widespread as is often suggested, being limited to certain Hindu groups. Furthermore, the motivations of British missionaries were not as pure as is often implied: 'it is not that they were not moved by compassion for the victims of sati but that the desire to demonstrate the superiority of Christianity to Hinduism was there . . . and this was before the abolition of slavery in the modern world', writes M. N. Srinivas in the Foreword. Sharma adds: 'It became necessary for British writers to SENSATIONALIZE sati on the one hand and for British historians to MONOPOLIZE the credit for having abolished it on the other.'

the *Express* saying things like it was 'a matter of national pride . . . to carry British standards of welfare into foreign land'. Under her leadership, Save the Children became both Britain's largest international humanitarian organization[22] and the most imperial one – the fund not just providing relief but aiming to 'rehabilitate' or 'develop' the communities it worked in. This meant that beneficiaries of aid were typically required to adapt their methods of providing for, clothing and educating their children to reflect British practice – an approach which sometimes resulted in the subjects of charity rebelling, with 'children disrupting notions of innocence by giving fascist salutes or going on strike at humanitarian "work schools", and mothers pouring donated milk on the ground or throwing stones at aid workers' white jeeps'.[23]

In 1928 Save the Children's press secretary Edward Fuller, trying to interest donors in Africa, reprinted reports on African child welfare from missionaries. These relied on imperial tropes which described Africa as one homogeneous place in the manner of Band Aid/Live Aid, and made salacious mention of 'tribal customs', 'native taboos' and 'savage' African practices. If funds didn't pour in, it was partly due to the Depression of the 1930s. Dorothy's sister-in-law Victoria de Bunsen, who was also involved with Save the Children, proposed a different strategy: with the support of the Colonial Office, she assembled a meeting of experts to determine the best course of action for 'the African child'. And in 1931 Save the Children hosted a Conference on the African Child at Lake Geneva, which makes Band Aid's lyrics feel highly sophisticated. The fact that it was arranged with the help of Britain's Colonial Office and held in Switzerland, which meant that only very rich Africans could travel over from the continent, was not even the most colonial aspect of it.*[24] Missionaries made up half of those attending. The majority of the European delegates were British: an organizer claimed this was because of the essentially humanitarian nature of British imperialism. The 'expertise' of European delegates was considered more important than the experience of Africans. Those attending were encouraged 'never to forget the baffling pace at which civilisation has sprung upon Africans'. The economic development of Africa was presented as essential for the prosperity of the West. The discourse was

---

* Out of 200 delegates there were five Africans, one West Indian and one African American.

infected with racist notions about the 'fundamentally different capabilities' of African children.[25] The infant mortality rate in Africa was attributed to a variety of factors including alleged poor hygiene, malnutrition, neglect, disease and supposed practices such as exposure, where children were 'being placed in the bush to be eaten alive by vultures and other kinds of . . . creatures'.[26]

The African American communist James Ford, representing the International Trade Union Council of Negro Workers, was a rare dissenting voice, arguing that the Fund's interest in the continent was motivated by profit rather than altruism, that the 'chief pride' of European educators was to 'furnish white contractors with a staff of fit workmen'. Here, Lord Noel-Buxton, Dorothy's brother-in-law, labelling all the conference's black attendees, including this African American, as 'African', reminded the 'African delegates inclined to criticize European efforts' that 'there would be no schools in Africa were it not for the missionaries'.[27] When Ford continued, railing against racism and colonialism, a white male missionary hauled him off the stage and Buxton pronounced that the conference 'had not been convened to discuss political questions'. Ford's incredible speech retains its power today and is worth looking at. 'You have done everything to keep us from speaking,' he said.

> You claim to be saving the Children of Africa. But, if we examine the board of patrons and organizers of the Conference, we find them to be the same people who are associated with plundering and exploiting the African colonies; they are members of the highest nobility, high colonial officers, industrialists . . . bishops, generals, and diplomats. [At this point Lord Noel-Buxton yelled at him to stop speaking, but Ford continued.] You explain that the time has come to Save the Children of Africa, but this is a hypocritical gesture invented because you fear that the African population that produces huge profits may die out and endanger the income of the imperialist coupon-clippers . . . It is imperialist barbarism in the colonies, and in particular Africa, that is the immediate cause of the terrible death rate among [African] children.[28]

In the years that followed, a succession of the charity's leaders had colonial connections. In 1949 its President, Lord Noel-Buxton, was replaced by Edwina, Lady Mountbatten, the last vicereine of India. Also joining Save the Children in 1952 was Lady Alexandra Metcalfe, daughter of the famous imperialist Lord Curzon, former Viceroy of India. This new leadership argued that Save the Children should leave 'international' issues to UNICEF and focus on the more 'natural' territory in the empire. As Baughan puts it, 'the empire was a space in which the Fund could retreat from the complexities and competition of American-led international aid, playing a more insular, imperial role'.[29] She also observes that at times the charity 'drew upon eugenics and colonial racial "science" to determine the relative value of children'. These episodes included: Lady Cynthia Mosley,* as head of one of the charity's subcommittees in the 1920s, remarking that 'cripples' or 'halfwits' shouldn't receive preferential treatment; the charity working alongside organizations which were keen to reduce the birth rate of 'lower' social classes to improve the balance of 'British stock'; Lord Noel-Buxton, already the Fund's British President, being 'cautiously optimistic' in the 1930s about 'the emergence of fascism in Europe' because 'Mussolini's Italy and Hitler's Germany pursued pro-natalist policies that placed the production and health of children at the centre of society, highlighting their value as future soldiers and the bearers of the purity of the race'; and, in the 1950s, the charity's experts regarding juvenile delinquency in Africa as 'a racial failure to adapt to modernity, rather than a symptom of the colonial economy failing to provide security for African youth'.[30]

Sometimes the charity's work took it into areas of huge imperial tension, where it acted as an unapologetic agent of British rule. One such project was the Serendah Boys School in Malaya, which became a model for a delinquent-child centre in Essex called Hill House, between the years 1946 and 1958. As you will recall from our trip to Kew, Malaya was a British colony which had become a cash cow for the British as a result of its rubber plantations, but when it rebelled, Britain responded brutally with deportations, torture and murder. In an illustration of how the British used education as a tool of imperialism, and in yet another illustration of how British charities became inextricably involved in the imperial project, the school aimed to teach poor Malayan boys British values and was run like an elite public school, with boarding houses named after stars of the British empire like Mountbatten and Milner,

---

* The politician Oswald Mosley's first wife, in his pre-fascist, socialist days, and also an elder sister of the aforementioned Lady Alexandra Metcalfe.

timetabled games of rugby and cricket, a prefects system and caning. The boys were also taught skills such as farming, cobbling and sewing, to set them up for later life and the school benefited financially from this training – the colonial government bought handmade Union Jacks from the pupils. Save the Children General Secretary Tony Boyce claimed that helping the teenage boys of Malaya turn their backs on communism and become self-sufficient was crucial for 'the stabilization of Malaya and the re-establishment of British rule'.[31]

Similar projects funded by the charity were set up in Somaliland, with the aim of preventing youth crime, which was often synonymous with anti-colonial resistance. The boys' home established in Hargeisa in Somaliland was different to the one in Malaya – more like a ramshackle work camp where the pupils were effectively imprisoned. Save the Children's John Watling told the Fund's council that they shouldn't expect too much of the boys who knew nothing of 'civilisation' or Western ideas, who saw begging as normal and who were experienced only at the 'raiding of water holes, and the carrying off of women'.[32] Save the Children was also in Kenya during the Mau Mau uprising in the 1950s, another brutal period of imperial violence, in the course of which the British inflicted torture, beatings, murder, castration and sexual abuse upon Africans, and for which the British government was forced to pay £20 million compensation in 2013.[33] Here it became embroiled in what Baughan calls 'explicitly punitive work', running a camp for 300 youths called Ujana Park, and providing funding and staff to Wamumu Approved School, home to nearly 2,000 boys. 'Both the camp and the school were prisons in all but name,' explains Baughan. 'The camps met minor infractions with harsh discipline, such as beatings or solitary confinement . . . in Kenya, humanitarianism's collusion enabled colonial brutality.'[34]

The British Red Cross has a parallel history of getting involved in colonial repression: in 1948, the charity transferred a number of its workers from Europe to Malaya during another colonial 'emergency', its nurses working to win the 'hearts and minds' of Malayans through education and sanitation initiatives. Such work, in Kenya and Malaya, was a part of a larger shift for the British Red Cross and Save the Children from post-war Europe to the decolonizing British empire, where they used their legitimacy as 'international' agents to deflect criticism from colonial barbarity. Red Cross homecraft officers expected a cordial welcome in Kenya based on their perceived accomplishments in Malaya, but were shocked by the so-called 'Mau Mau infected women', who, despite the offers of gifts including 'brightly coloured threads' and 'used Christmas cards', were 'sullen and uncooperative'. Kikuyu women did not see the Red Cross as separate from the state because British soldiers always escorted them. The parent body, the International Committee of the Red Cross (the ICRC, based in Geneva), considered the Kenyan emergency a civil war, and wanted to see the camps where Mau Mau suspects were held. The British Red Cross was upset by this approach and said it was a rebellion, not a war, and that the 1949 Geneva Convention did not apply. Baughan finds in a research paper that 'for the latter organisation, patriotism trumped humanitarian internationalism. The British Red Cross . . . sided with the British government rather than its own international parent body, both covering up colonial brutality and acting against criticisms of its own work.' According to the ICRC, Lady Limerick, the President of the British Red Cross, was either unaware of the extent of colonial violence and misery in Kenya, which was 'unpardonable', or she was aware of the extent of suffering but was 'hushing things up (equally unpardonable)'. The international parent body came to the conclusion that the British Red Cross 'did NOT do its duty' in Kenya.[35]

As the empire crumbled in the early 1960s, Save the Children expanded and was invited by post-colonial governments with limited resources to establish social and welfare programmes.[36] It established itself as 'the aid organization of the establishment' and when in 1966 the Biafran conflict ignited in West Africa, resulting in the deaths of hundreds of thousands and the displacement of some half a million people,*[37] Save the Children stepped in. Seeing the crisis as an

---

* The Biafran War (now usually called the Nigerian Civil War, but the name is a vexed issue), which took place from 1967 to 1970, was a conflict between the Nigerian federal government and the rebel state of Biafra. Following the country's independence, two coups and turmoil led to between 1 million and 2 million Igbos returning to the south-east of Nigeria. The Republic of Biafra, in the predominantly Igbo-populated eastern region, seceded with 33-year-old military officer Chukwuemeka Odumegwu Ojukwu in charge. The breakaway territory was rich in oil, and the Nigerian federal government would not agree to its secession. A merciless war ensued, and the superior might of the government devastated Biafra's civilian population, who suffered massacres and famines. In January 1970 the coup leaders surrendered, and the

opportunity to evade the 'Nigerianization' of its staffing (the post-colonial Nigerian government had sought to place a cap on the number of white, Western staff NGOs could employ and make employing Nigerians mandatory), it requested the help of a number of British expats who, it was stated, would be 'easier to control' than local employees. This new young cohort, many of them the children of colonial officers, were actually not that easy to control: after difficult days in the field they had parties and some of the men had local 'girlfriends'. The young British women workers were, however, kept away from the Nigerian male staff, 'invoking classically colonial, racialised discourses of sexual danger to segregate British and Nigerian staff'. One Nigerian nurse working for Save the Children complained that a doctor employed by the charity had addressed her like 'a master speaking to a servant . . . which I am not'.[38] Furthermore, the Nigerian staff didn't feature in publicity about Save the Children's efforts in the country, which instead focused on their young British heroes – particularly young white nurses in miniskirts. Save the Children assisted in the evacuation of thousands of Biafran children to Gabon and the Ivory Coast, and many were never reunited with their parents.

In conversation, I drag Baughan, who is now researching a completely different subject,[39] down memory lane. With a little effort she recalls originally embarking on the Save the Children project after realizing that she had been 'mis-sold' the dream of British humanitarianism; she tells me that academics have been opining on 'the neocolonial character of international aid since the 1960s'[40] and that what is true of our largest INGOs is probably true of many other smaller organisations. 'I don't think it's possible to practise Western humanitarianism outside of a colonial inheritance, because it *is* Western liberalism,' she says, adding that many other international intergovernmental organizations

---

Republic of Biafra was no more. Hundreds of thousands of people died as a result of the conflict, mostly from starvation, despite intense international relief efforts from organizations including the Red Cross and Save the Children. The attention infuriated the Nigerian government, which felt that the Western press had exaggerated Biafra's suffering and didn't understand the internal politics and conditions in Africa; they also, notably, in another illustration of how the work of INGOs can go awry, condemned the 'neo-imperialist and self-righteous attitude of the international charitable organisations' and pointed out that the Red Cross – and indeed the Pope – had not spoken out against Hitler's outrages.

are known to have recruited former colonialists, not least the UN, which during the 1960s recruited over a third of its development officials from European colonial powers. In one study, more than half (53 per cent) of the British colonial officers polled went on to work for international agencies, most notably the World Bank (17 per cent) and the Food and Agriculture Organization of the United Nations (14 per cent). According to a different study, in the 1950s nearly one-third of all UN development experts were hired from European colonial nations.[41] Charlotte Lydia Riley has observed that, for many relatively ordinary British people, opportunities at new institutions such as Oxfam, Voluntary Services Overseas (VSO), the Food and Agriculture Organization of the United Nations (FAO) and the UN had 'extended the opportunities once offered by empire for work, travel and adventure',[42] and it was true for many colonial administrators too, who walked straight into prestigious NGO jobs when empires collapsed. Baughan continues: 'As I wrote the book, I realized we are inflicting imperial ideas on people in incredibly vulnerable moments. I don't think it's just that empire has left us a form of humanitarianism that has colonial legacies. I truly think that without imperialism we have no modern aid sector.'

In their teasingly entitled paper 'The Missionary Position: NGOs and Development in Africa', Firoze Manji and Carl O'Coill echo the sentiment, noting that the language of modern development reflects the language of imperialism,[43] observing that 'there has been an explosive growth in the presence of Western as well as local non-governmental organizations (NGOs) in Africa', and suggesting that 'their role in "development" represents a continuity of the work of their precursors, the missionaries and voluntary organizations that cooperated in Europe's colonization and control of Africa'. They add: 'Africa's decline contributes to the continued justification for their work. NGOs will "do better the less stable the world becomes . . . [because] finance will become increasingly available to agencies who can deliver 'stabilising' social services".'[44] Meanwhile, the US academic Gregory Mann suggests that NGOs represent a new type of colonialism: with NGOs fulfilling basic functions usually provided by the state, housing, sanitation and so on, in his view they deprive people of meaningful citizenship rights: 'in less than a generation . . . the people living in the West African Sahel . . . that long, thin band of arable land lining the Sahara' found themselves becoming 'the subjects of human rights campaigns and humanitarian interventions'.[45] (It should be noted though that while Mann does glancingly address the curious role of British INGO Amnesty International in the former British colony of Ghana,[46] his focus is specifically on the legacies of French empire in Africa.) There's an emerging fashion for 'decolonizing the endowment' or 'decolonizing philanthropy', which has seen charitable funding entirely reimagined by some charities in North America and by one large charitable foundation with an endowment of £130 million in Britain.[47] And there's even a long-standing critique of development as repackaged colonialism that provides the context for such studies – post-development theory.

People seeking further, less abstract evidence could look at Christian Aid, eighth in a recent list of Britain's largest INGOs. You might assume that this charity emerged as a direct consequence of the tens of thousands of British Christians who headed out into British empire to convert 'unenlightened' natives and who have direct philanthropic legacies such as the thousands of educational establishments they founded across the planet which still educate and shape young lives,[48] and the even more numerous churches which are scattered across the globe. But, like Save the Children, Christian Aid did not actually have explicitly imperial origins. It was never officially a missionary organization: the humanitarian arm of the ecumenical British Council of Churches, which had various incarnations before settling on its present name in 1964, the charity was started in order to help with post-war reconstruction in Europe, with a focus on refugees, and saw itself very much in global, internationalist terms.[49] Indeed, none of our large INGOs were founded by imperial missionaries. Even CAFOD was born well after British empire peaked, when, according to its own website, a team led by Jacquie Stuyt responded to 'an appeal from the people of the Caribbean island of Dominica where children were starving to help raise funds for a mother-and-baby clinic'.[50]

There were, however, many looser links between many of our faith-inspired charities and imperial missionaries and, as academics Manji and O'Coill put it, 'Christian Aid evolved out of a network of such [missionary] bodies'.[51] Or as INGO trade body Bond puts it, while citing the examples of Christian Aid, World Vision, Tearfund and CAFOD, 'faith communities have a long tradition of supporting international development'.[52] Meanwhile, Anna Bocking-Welch's lively examination of

Christian Aid in *British Civic Society at the End of Empire* provides an illustration of how this worked in practice. Even if it didn't have clear imperial origins, Christian Aid didn't shy away from identifying with imperial missionaries, possibly as a marketing strategy. A Christian Aid pamphlet from 1965 told how missionary societies had worked for 250 years with the aim that 'schools, hospitals and agricultural projects were part of the "new life" promised in the gospel'. The charity's lists of recommended speakers in the mid-1960s included many members of missionary networks. Bocking-Welch reports that 'on a practical level, many of the missionaries forced to leave their posts at the end of empire moved into the humanitarian sector and became part of Christian Aid's network of organisers'.[53]

By the mid-1960s, Christian Aid's expenditure was heavily concentrated on the former British colonies, particularly in Africa, and its focus shifted from refugee work to development projects. In 1962, over half of its expenditure benefited agricultural schemes in the former British imperial territories such as Uganda, Northern and Southern Rhodesia, Nigeria, Pakistan and India.[54] And some felt Christian Aid continued, even in the mid-twentieth century, to see the world through the prism of the old missionary mindset, as demonstrated by many annual broadcasts on the BBC Home Service for Christian Aid Week, during which representatives of the charity spoke about the cause.[55] As an example, Bocking-Welch presents a cringe-inducing 1963 BBC item on parish life, which gives an account of Christian Aid packed full of tropes worthy of the nineteenth century and makes most sense when you imagine it voiced by Lord Mountbatten:

English people find it astonishingly difficult to see beyond the Parish pump and so we try to look outward at the big world. We have visiting speakers to talk about outlandish places that I can't find on the map. We have a display at the back of our church: photographs of hospitals in unpronounceable parts of Africa, and of black doctors in white coats peering into highly technical microscopes. It is all very humdrum but occasionally we have our moments. Inter-Church Aid sent us a black priest from Africa for a month. He was supposed to learn from us but really we learned from him. This calm and courteous fellow Christian with frizzy hair that one wanted to stroke. This man of God one jump from the stone age, whose friends had just been murdered in a tribal massacre . . . I can hear his voice, smooth as black velvet, struggling with our outlandish English.[56]

Bocking-Welch also brings attention to how the Freedom from Hunger Campaign of the 1960s and the post-war charitable work of the Women's Institute and the British Rotary Club had an imperial flavour.[57] In these cases the colonial behaviour was almost unconscious – the result of sheer force of habit. As with Christian Aid and Save the Children, none of these initiatives had explicitly imperial roots. When the Women's Institute was established in Britain in 1915, it aimed to revitalize rural communities and encourage women to produce food for the war effort, and up to the 1960s the organization remained the definition of provincial;*[58] the Rotary Club, founded in 1905, was intended to be a global movement, connecting men across the world, but was focused on advancing the interests of its businessman members. Meanwhile, the Freedom from Hunger Campaign was a United Nations initiative, by far the largest humanitarian undertaking of its time, with over a hundred UN member states participating, its express aim being to 'awaken the conscience of the world to the continuing problem of hunger and malnutrition in many lands'. Nevertheless, each of these projects somehow developed an imperial tone in the way British people interacted with them.

The WI and the Rotary Club, non-activist organizations with a predominantly white, middle-class membership, both got involved with World Refugee Year in 1959–60, and with the Freedom from Hunger and Save the Children campaigns. And in tackling them, members of the WI and Rotary resorted to old imperial tropes, including: perpetuating the idea that developing nations weren't ready to stand unaided (both organizations closely monitored their donations by hiring British experts to assess the outcomes of their efforts, rather than relying on feedback from the beneficiaries themselves); not valuing feedback from non-white people (they were never presented as experts); exoticizing new friends from the former colonies (three guests from Nigeria, the Caribbean and Vietnam attended Greysouthen's WI meeting and

* A record of the monthly meetings at the Burythorpe WI in Yorkshire provides a flavour:
March 1952: Competition for the best darn in a sock heel.
June 1952: Miss Seaton gave a demonstration on salads.
July 1954: Demonstration on butter icing.
June 1959: Presentation on the Hoovermatic Washing Machine.
August 1960: Competition for the best necklace made from garden produce.
June 1961: Presentation on soft slippers.

'delighted the audience with some of their native songs', while Stepney
Rotary Club put on a night for foreign nurses working in local hospitals, and asked them to come dressed in their national costumes for a
'wonderfully colourful occasion'); using racially offensive language (a
contest for the best verse of a brand-new Beatles song with 'an oriental
slant' was advertised by the WI's magazine *Home and Country* when the
Beatles were on tour in Japan. Entries included: 'she's a cutie, my slant-
eyed girl' and 'baby be my little geisha, be my fragrant lotus bloom');
and perpetuating racial stereotypes (when giving advice on hosting foreign guests, WI hosts were told that 'life for inhabitants of the Asian
and African countries is leisurely. All time belongs to them').

Meanwhile, the UN's Freedom from Hunger Campaign (FFHC)
seized the British public's imagination. In the first five years of the campaign, the public raised almost £7 million. But some initiatives were
better judged than others,*[59] and empire was never far from the mind.
Many former colonial administrators worked on the campaign – not
least the chairman, Earl De La Warr, who had had a lengthy career in
colonial administration and spent four years chairing the Royal Commonwealth Society. When finding a replacement for the retiring Vice
Chairman, Warr stated he sought 'the right type of retired colonial governor or diplomat'. The successful candidate was Sir Gilbert Rennie,
former Governor of Northern Rhodesia.[60] In another continuation of
colonialism there was the fact that the projects funded by the British
FFHC were almost all located in the countries of the empire-
Commonwealth (the French and Spanish also concentrated their efforts
on their former colonies). Given the number of former colonial officials
who sought employment with charities at the time of decolonization, it
has been argued that NGOs 'were conduits for the transfer of expertise
at the end of empire'.[61]

Why does any of this matter? A sceptic might say these events were a
long time ago. The charities in question have still, surely, made the
world a better place and are doing good now. The fact that imperfect

---

* A group of businessmen's 'Hunger Lunch' led to a sarcastic letter to the *Guardian*
from one Mrs G. V. Thompson in 1963: 'Only melon, veal, peas, potatoes, fresh fruit
and coffee! And only one wine! . . . One is filled with sympathy for them in such an
ordeal and for their courage in undertaking it.'

humanitarianism exists must be better than if it didn't. Reflecting on this, I'm reminded of the TV producer who made a programme criticizing the kind of food aid favoured by Live Aid and who took a close look at the manner in which such charities hide structural inequality. He was reported remarking: 'I made the programme, but I still sent a donation.'[62] For what it's worth, I've not cancelled my standing order to Save the Children. Besides, many of the INGOs I've talked about here (inadvertently) propounded anti-colonialism even as they propounded colonial attitudes, the bodies not being immune to the intrinsically autocritical nature of the British empire. There were, for instance, anti-colonial activists at Save the Children's African Child Conference, such as James Ford, representing the International Trade Union Council of Negro Workers, and the conference inspired subsequent activism.[63] Moreover, the British INGO sector, despite the criticisms levelled at it, is by definition packed with empathetic people and has made sincere efforts to decolonize itself. Anxieties about the imperial tendencies of British NGOs in the post-war period were such that in 1968, as Charlotte Lydia Riley reports, 'activists working across several British humanitarian organisations, including Youth Against Hunger, Christian Aid, the Overseas Development Institute and perhaps most notably Oxfam, gathered in the small Surrey town of Haslemere to share their frustrations about the way that humanitarian action replicated many of the tropes of imperialism'.[64] Across the sector there have been efforts to blend local care traditions into emergency responses, to put decision making into the hands of the local communities and to unshackle Western donations from the expectation of Western cultural norms. Comic Relief has not just stopped sending white celebrities to Africa, but now hires local filmmakers and photographers for a 'more authentic perspective'.[65] NGOs like Action Aid and the Agency for Cooperation and Research in Development (ACORD) have moved their headquarters from London to African cities,[66] while Oxfam's attempts to address its use of colonial language have recently earned it mockery on the front page of the *Daily Mail*.[67]

From the 1960s, Save the Children started to employ local experts in the Caribbean who began to criticize its approach to raising children; in the 1990s, as a consequence of the Rwandan genocide, Save the Children shifted its stance towards family reunification, preventing international adoption agencies swooping on supposed orphans.[68] The charity no longer evades 'Nigerianization': it has been compelled by the Nigerian government to ensure that at least 50 per cent of its staff in the country is hired locally. The INGO has also begun to review its past. In a remarkable incident, Save the Children hired the renowned left-wing director Ken Loach to create a documentary about its operations in 1969. Loach was well known at the time for directing social realist movies like *Cathy Come Home* and *Kes*. The film did not turn out how Save the Children had hoped: it criticized the charity's neo-colonial attitudes and practices. In a panic, Save the Children took legal action to have the film suppressed. The documentary was eventually screened in 2011 after languishing for more than forty years in the archives of the British Film Institute. At the screening, the then CEO of Save the Children confessed that the charity's response to the documentary had been wrong and that from the 1960s to 1980s 'aid did more harm than good'.[69] Meanwhile, Emily Baughan informs me that Save the Children responded constructively to her revelations: it has a department called Humanitarian Affairs which encourages the charity to think critically about its past work. 'They unpack what they might have done differently in particular crises, and one of the things that I did was kind of write a history course, essentially, for people coming into the organization to understand some of the imperial origins of international aid. The fact they hosted a centenary conference and aired their past dirty laundry publicly is even more remarkable – and they've left most of it sitting unedited on the official website.'

Furthermore, in *Hunger: A Modern History* James Vernon suggests two ways in which empire shaped modern humanitarianism constructively: through nutritional science and influencing how hunger is understood.[70] Nutrition was seen by imperialists as a tool to improve the health of their subjects, and so create a more productive workforce, and also to improve the health of the British imperial race of the future. There was widespread dismay in Britain at the poor condition of the young men volunteering to serve in the South African wars of the late nineteenth century, and, like missionaries, British nutritionists were sent across the empire to educate and enlighten, supposedly disabusing colonial subjects of their ignorance about food and studying the effects of an insufficient diet. The research was sometimes ropey as hell,★[71] and resulted in the colonized being led away from eating and feeding habits which were actually healthy; but discoveries made by imperial nutritionists were used for some worthy ends (such as informing international food programmes in the League of Nations and the UN, as well as UK policies like the Colonial Development and Welfare Acts of the 1940s), and research on deficiency diseases in Africa and South Asia changed the way the world viewed the lack of adequate food. Vernon explains that imperial Britain played nothing less than 'a formative role' in changing the meaning of hunger and 'the systems for redressing it in the modern era'.[72] These days, hunger, in its many forms, from famine to families forced to rely on foodbanks in Britain, to children going hungry during the school day, is deemed newsworthy. However, it was not always this way: it took until the middle of the nineteenth century for starvation to elicit sympathy and action from the British people. Before then, it was seen as a form of population control: 'a natural basis for the moral order, in forcing the indigent to work and preventing unsustainable overpopulation'.[73] Back then, when the word first emerged, to call someone a 'humanitarian' was insulting: the connotation was that the person was excessively, even dangerously, humane. The abolitionists of the 1820s and 1830s were derided as 'philanthropists', and 'philanthropy' itself was thought to be

---

★ On the question of ropiness, a special mention must go to the work of Robert McCarrison at the Pasteur Institute in Coonor, who decided in the 1930s that the best way to study and categorize the diverse 'races' of India was to feed rats with a range of regional Indian diets and chart the results. The rats fed a 'northern diet', based on wheat and meat, fared better than those condemned to the 'southern' menu of rice or vegetables. McCarrison concluded that the northern Sikhs, and the 'manly, stalwart and resolute races of the north', were the ones to emulate, not the 'poorly developed, toneless and supine people of the east and south'. Whereas many of the diets studied risked malnutrition and the development of 'a wide variety of ailments', the Sikh diet bestowed a 'remarkable freedom from disease', and even compared most favourably to the eating habits of the British working classes, who were 'prone to pulmonary and gastro-intestinal disease'. The results apparently revealed psychological benefits, too: rodents fed the Sikh way 'lived happily together', whereas those forced to consume the typical menu of a 'poor Britisher' were nervy and stunted, 'lived unhappily together and . . . began to kill and eat the weaker ones amongst them'. This would have been of great interest to my mother in the 1980s, as she pleaded for us to value Punjabi cuisine over the fast food and freezer fare we preferred, but perhaps to no one else.

an anti-British pursuit.[74] Attitudes started changing when the New
Poor Law of 1834 prompted a campaign in *The Times*. Labelling the
measures 'the Starvation Act', the press used vivid, emotive first-hand
reporting to bring home the reality of those condemned to terminal
hunger – particularly the women and children – and their lack of cul-
pability for it. This 'human interest' approach to the poorest in society
led to a seismic shift in public attitudes. The famine in Ireland under
British rule in the late 1840s, described by Fintan O'Toole as the first
media famine,[75] saw more publications adopting the techniques. First-
hand accounts in the form of letters from those at the scene – be they
travellers or philanthropists – were extremely effective in drumming
up sympathy for the afflicted.[76]

But, having said this in defence of British I N G O s, if our international
charities have imperialism in their blood, and if they are unthinking
about how imperialism has shaped them and continues to do so, they risk
imposing unsuitable, hectoring, colonially minded solutions on the
world, in the manner of Live Aid, Comic Relief, Save the Children, the
British Red Cross and so on. If this results in scepticism among donors,
not only could it lead to a fall in donations, but in an echo of what happened when, after abolition, some British people began to despair out
loud that the enslaved were 'too primitive' to benefit from emancipation,
it could also lead to an intensification in the racism identified as a surprising legacy of Britain's anti-slavery movement. There was a long tradition
within empire of disillusion setting in when colonized people refused to
conform to the behaviours that sympathetic Westerners expected. At
worst, allegations of colonial behaviour, the belief that charities are still
dressing up exploitation as charitable help, could undermine the entire
international charitable sector. This would be a calamity in a world
where Western humanitarian initiatives stand accused, increasingly, of
doing the work of Western governments; and where humanitarian
interventions are facing more accountability than ever, with Oxfam, for
example, experiencing months of negative publicity after it was revealed
that staff paid Haiti earthquake survivors for sex, and Save the Children
being the subject of similar negative press after allegations of inappropri-
ate sexual behaviour among senior managers (an episode which had
Baughan cancelling her direct debit donation).

Even today, charities like Save the Children can stumble unthinkingly into neo-colonial attitudes. For example, at Save the Children's

centenary conference in 2019 there were about as few black delegates in attendance as there had been at its 1931 Conference on the African Child – many of those who attempted to travel from Africa or the Middle East had been prevented from entering the country by the Foreign Office.[77] And Save the Children's Australian branch recently became involved with the offshore detention of children by the Australian government, a policy with all sorts of colonial connotations.[78] Australia has been renowned for operating one of the world's strictest immigration regimes for decades, right back to the days of its 1901 Immigration Restriction Act, or 'White Australia policy', drafted by its white colonial settlers to restrict non-British migration to Australia.[79] The spirit of this policy lives on today in the country's sending of asylum seekers to the remote Papua New Guinean island of Manus and the tiny Pacific republic of Nauru, under a system of 'offshore processing', first introduced in 2001, arguably imperial in inspiration[80] and influential in its own right.★[81] Save the Children worked with children on Manus Island between November 2012 and June 2013, and on Nauru from July 2013 until October 2015. Among other things, it offered services for education and child protection, to begin with mainly to families and later to people without children as well. The 'Nauru Files', a leaked dossier of 2,116 incident reports from offshore custody between May 2013 and October 2015, were published by the *Guardian* in August 2016 and exposed a harrowing catalogue of abuse:[82] children were involved in more than half of the episodes, including thirty instances of

---

★ It has inspired severe policies in other countries, not least in Britain, which has been attempting to develop an offshoring policy which holds asylum seekers in locations such as barges and then sends them to Rwanda. Reportedly, one of the islands considered as an offshoring destination by Britain's Home Office was St Helena, which has a painful imperial history of its own related to the enforced movement of people around the world. In 2012, an archaeological dig on St Helena unearthed the mass graves of around 5,000 enslaved people who had been liberated by the British navy but had subsequently died in their custody. The modern idea of using fines to deter the movement of migrants is not new either. Today, migrants to Britain are subject to charges for healthcare, and those deemed to be working illegally can have their wages confiscated. The 1905 Aliens Act allowed the Home Office to charge shipping companies for the cost of removing migrants. In another curious colonial parallel, there have been reports that the company supplying the Home Office with barges has roots in the transatlantic slave trade.

child self-harm, fifty-nine reports of child assault and seven instances of child sexual assault. The 'Nauru Files' disclosures did not involve any Save the Children Australia employees, but the violence and suffering raised concerns about whether Save the Children Australia had spoken out loudly enough about what was happening. To have a charity built on humanitarian principles implement this system, even just partially or momentarily, was controversial to say the least.[83] An investigation discovered weaknesses in the Nauruan authorities' ability to look into abuse or assault claims. The Australian government and Save the Children Australia got into a bitter dispute, with the latter eventually winning out, but not quickly enough for many.

Elsewhere, British charities have been accused of colonial attitudes and habits, whether it's draining local talent through the offer of higher salaries and better perks[84] or, in the case of Uganda, having its textile industry killed off with charitable donations.[85] Colonial influence gets harder to deny as some INGOs find themselves working closely with the British government,[86] as the gap between development and business becomes indistinguishable (the government recently turned the Commonwealth Development Corporation into British International Investment,[87] leading to twelve NGOs, from Global Justice Now to CAFOD, accusing the government of 'chasing colonial . . . fantasies'),[88] and as the fighting of so-called 'humanitarian wars' in places like Afghanistan and Iraq has blurred boundaries more generally between aid, government and colonialism in Britain, the US and beyond.[89] In short, with the British it's sometimes difficult to tell where humanitarianism and neo-colonial exploitation begin or end, just as it was difficult to tell during the age of empire.

It's not just humanitarian-focused INGOs which have blurred these boundaries, Britain's ever popular animal conservation charities have done so too. In fact, no charities are as popular as animal charities in Britain: more than a quarter of the population of the UK, or an estimated 15 million people, donated money to animal charities in 2021, with an average monthly payment of more than £20. According to statistics from the Charities Aid Foundation, this makes animal welfare the most popular cause for donations.[90] Among these charities are various NGOs which aim to protect threatened species and wild animals, a tradition that goes way back to empire when British natural history organizations such as the Society for the Preservation of the Fauna of the Empire (another British charitable body that exists today, campaigning in the twenty-first century as Fauna & Flora International) convened international conferences, created game reserves in British colonies, funded like-minded alliances and pushed for new laws to protect wild animals. In turn, over time, these preservation efforts mutated into acts of conservation in a way that reflects what happened with imperial environmental preservation initiatives – with the establishment of national parks and tourism taking the place of hunting. Plans for parks in East Africa had been formulated in the 1930s and, having been put on hold during the war, were completed immediately after it. These imperial parks paved the way for similar initiatives back home, with the 1949 National Parks Act providing for the opening up of conservation areas in Britain.[91]

An uncomplicated achievement of the British empire? Not necessarily. In an echo of what happened with imperial initiatives to conserve forests, where nature was conserved only so that British imperialists could have exclusive access to destroy it further, these organizations were driven and dominated by . . . hunters! Who not only wanted to conserve animals to shoot them, but had pushed these animals to the point of extinction in the first place! It's a surreal tale told in *The Empire of Nature: Hunting, Conservation and British Imperialism* by John M. MacKenzie, who begins by explaining that hunting, which he describes as both a cult and a craze, became as intrinsic to the imperial enterprise as booze. It was seen as perfect training for imperial domination over other lands and races: controlling wild animals was akin to controlling native people. Apparently, in the early days of colonial rule in Africa, prospective governors were judged on their hunting skills,[92] a host of imperial officials treated their posts as opportunities to hunt (with a little administration on the side), and a staggering proportion of senior imperialists hunted. In some places, hunting even financed imperialism, the meat and ivory produced sustaining colonialists as they explored and colonized, providing income and allowing them to pay 'native people' for assistance.

MacKenzie reports that between 1840 and 1875, the game population of the Orange Free State in southern Africa, the Boer republic that was under British suzerainty during the latter half of the nineteenth century, was decimated by hunters. By 1850, a profitable skin trade was firmly established there. Conversely, the collapse of the ivory trade in the Cape Colony – located in what is now South Africa, and which was under British control between 1795 and 1910, albeit with a four-year break in 1802–6 – was a reflection of the fact that elephants in the region had been slaughtered en masse. In 1875 the trade was estimated to be worth over £60,000, yet ten years later it was valued at not much more than £2,000. Meanwhile, two southern African species, the quagga and the blaubok, were wiped out completely. 'The game was simply worked out, like a mineral seam,' adds MacKenzie. Resorting to the excuse of 'crop protection', elephants were killed in southern India, Ceylon, Assam, the western Ghats and Chittagon – this was despite the fact that the ivory from Indian elephants wasn't prized commercially, and that by the 1870s there was growing concern about the shrinking elephant population in India, as the animals were historically used in domestic settings. By the 1930s, the tiger was an endangered species in India. The disquiet of official conservationists can be felt through papers that the Natural History wing of the British Museum provided to the Foreign Office on the subject of species extermination.[93] In one of these, from 1900, the Director of the Museum described the dire situation in southern Africa: he was worried not just about the blaubok and the quagga becoming extinct, but also about the hugely reduced populations of bontebok and white-tailed gnu. Furthermore, there was the destruction of elephants across the whole continent, with only a few white rhino left in Mashonaland, and similar concerns for the hangul stag in Kashmir and the colobus monkey in the Gold Coast.★[94]

---

★ It required eight elephant tusks to manufacture a single set of the ivory balls that graced many of the billiard tables in upper-class English homes. Peter Frankopan explains that hunting was partly driven by such consumer demand for animal products. 'In the late 1870s, British and Boer hunters advanced north into modern Zimbabwe, northern Botswana and eastern Zambia in search of elephants,' he writes. 'Export figures show the shocking scale of slaughter, with thousands of elephants killed each year in the second half of the nineteenth century. Ivory was highly desirable in Victorian-era Britain and the United States, as well as elsewhere, used for fashion accessories ranging from collar studs, hairbrushes and vanity sets to sewing cases, toothpicks and napkin rings.' As pianos gained popularity in working-class pubs and music halls and also became status symbols for the expanding middle classes, whether in British houses or in recently settled farming villages on the Great Plains of North America, piano manufacturers saw significant demand for ivory keys. Beavers

The people who raised the alarm? Hunters! The very hunters who had mindlessly slaughtered these animals to the point of near extinction in the name of 'sport' in the first place.[95] How mindless had this hunting been? Very. MacKenzie consults many of the hunting memoirs that were popular in the nineteenth century, books which sometimes outsold even Charles Dickens,[96] and brings us news of individuals like 'hunter and administrator' Robert Coryndon, who in 1893 destroyed what were then believed to be the last two white rhinoceros in Mashonaland. Their remains were subsequently mounted and sold at appropriately high prices, given their rarity, to Cape Town and to Lionel Rothschild, for his famous collection at Tring. There was also Captain (later Major Sir) William Cornwallis Harris (1807–48), who in the service of the East India Company played a part in the near extinction of the lion population in Gujarat – he boasted that he had shot them all before they reached maturity – as well as travelling by elephant to kill bucks and tigers. When in southern Africa, he bemoaned the fact that there was barely any game left to shoot in the Cape Colony, and blamed African hunters for this sorry state of affairs. Nonetheless, he managed to find and kill large numbers of rhino, hippos, impala, wildebeest, hartebeest, water buck and quagga, before landing on the big prizes: elephants and giraffes. Their size made them hard to kill – it took fifty shots with a muzzle-loading firearm to bring down a bull elephant, and seventeen for a giraffe. He particularly enjoyed his first time killing a giraffe, which he saw as the 'summit of hunting ambition': it gave him a 'tingling excitement'.[97]

In the imperial age, it was men like these who protested most loudly about the decimation of wild animal populations and pushed for preservation measures to prevent species extinction – to ensure, more than anything else, that they had plenty more animals to kill. Many supporters of 'preservation' societies were not only passionate hunters but held positions of status and authority, such as senior colonial officers, governors, rich landowners and aristocrats – and as a result they often got things changed.[98] Although the way events developed varied throughout the empire, MacKenzie explains that there was a general

---

were captured in large numbers not only for their fur but also for the castoreum that could be extracted from their anal scent glands and was used in common treatments for fever, headaches, spasms, epilepsy and mental illness.

pattern, which began with unbridled economic exploitation of wild-life, led to a stage when game was preserved in order to be more successfully hunted by the elite, and then concluded with non-violent tourism and conservation.[99] And this could be spun positively. You could emphasize that British empire is responsible for: a whole load of conservation and preservation legislation around the world; the development of a whole load of game reserves around the world, which then turned into national parks; a whole load of conservation and preservation pressure groups and charities; and, ultimately, the transformation of hunting across empire into tourism, where people pointed cameras at wild animals rather than weapons. It's all true, but *the opposite is also true.* Namely, that it was imperial hunters who had hunted these beautiful animals to the point of extinction in the first place, that it was indigenous people who were then blamed for animal depletion, and that it was indigenous people who were kept away from animals in 'preservation' projects.[100] When laws were passed to preserve African wildlife, their main aim was to eradicate hunting by Africans. In the process, Africans not only lost a source of food, exchange and ceremony, they had to live in a world where animals and humans were largely segregated. Moreover, as species began to become extinct, the problem was intensified by the rush by museums to procure specimens.[101]

The British are not responsible for all animal extinction across the planet: other imperialists partook in mindless hunting in the name of 'sport' too (not least the Germans), and there have been multiple factors behind extinctions. But they were pioneers in extinction, and it's an important thing to acknowledge within our national obsession for animal conservation and protection. If we forget it, as we do, we risk looking cynical and hypocritical as we go about lecturing the planet and even intervening at times. And no institution is a better illustration of how our ignorance can make us look silly than the royal family, which was heavily involved in imperial hunting, before advocating for animal preservation and conservation in the modern age. I'd half noticed, some time ago, that the social class who hunted exotic animals during British empire were the same social class who are nowadays most into animal conservation and preservation. That the ruling class which slaughtered wild animals en masse in Africa and India in the nineteenth century was the same social class who, in the twenty-first century, run and chair many animal charities,[102] and who, in the case of the wife of one-time British Prime Minister Boris Johnson, lobbied the government to evacuate animals from Afghanistan even as we left behind to die human beings who had risked their lives for us.[103] But I didn't realize that often literally the same families, such as the Windsors, were involved in both.

The first setpiece delivered by William, the new Prince of Wales, after the death of Queen Elizabeth II, was about the campaign to end the illegal wildlife trade. Among other things, he spoke of the 'war going on' between rangers and poachers in Africa as lives are destroyed because of the 'heinous crime' of illegal wildlife trading.[104] Prince Harry and his grandfather the late Duke of Edinburgh were involved in similar animal conservation campaigns.[105] All of them were seemingly oblivious to the fact that their ancestors (and, in the case of the late Duke of Edinburgh, the man himself) were at the forefront of destroying some of these animal species in the first place. In 1860, Prince Alfred, Queen Victoria's then sixteen-year-old second son, was treated to 'a drive of game' during a visit to the Orange Free State. An estimated 25,000-strong herd of game was corralled by native people, of which many thousands were slaughtered (several men were trampled and killed by a stampede of terrified zebras). His brother the Prince of Wales hunted on a trip to India and Ceylon in 1875–6, and the future George V proved himself an adept shot during his own visit to the country; later, at his coronation Durbar in 1911, he was awarded a dedication in a hunting book. And so it went on. The future Edward VIII shot his first tiger in Nepal, and George VI and Queen Elizabeth spent their honeymoon in 1924–5 on a shooting safari in East Africa. Even as late as 1961, Prince Philip, the late Duke of Edinburgh, shot a tiger while on a royal visit to India. 'There was world-wide outrage and the British press suggested that the Queen's presence had indicated her approval,' reports MacKenzie.

> The royal couple moved on to Nepal where the King had set up the tiger shoot of the century. The ground had been carefully prepared, the tigers marked down, the elephants marshalled. But the Duke arrived with an allegedly infected trigger finger so that he could not participate. Lord Home, the accompanying secretary of state, was to shoot the tiger. He failed and it was eventually despatched by a member of the Duke's staff.

Newspaper opinion was again hostile and although the event was filmed, the BBC declined to transmit it.[106]

I have said that personal guilt has no role to play in the response to difficult history like this, and that no living Briton needs to feel responsible for what was done, but there are caveats. A national sense of responsibility is not the same thing as personal guilt: a bunch of former imperial powers are, in the twenty-first century, looking back at what they did during their empires and, quite admirably, deciding that they need to make amends. Equally, if your lavish life is still being financed from the proceeds of slavery and/or exploitative colonialism, you might well feel the need to make amends: various foreign royal families are talking about making reparations for their involvement in slavery; a great many private collectors have been returning imperial loot, while the Heirs of Slavery, an association of aristocratic British families whose lives have been partly supported by the proceeds of slavery, have decided that they do bear some responsibility for the actions of their ancestors and have volunteered to get involved in processes of 'apology, dialogue, reconciliation and reparative justice'.[107] Also, if you're a member of the royal family, you're part of an institution as well as a member of a family, and institutions can and do bear responsibility for what they did in the past. In relation to this tiger shooting, it would have done the royal family, and Britain, the nation it represents, a massive favour if the BBC had aired the footage of a member of the royal staff killing a tiger. Not just because it might have subsequently exposed the institution's hypocrisy, and our wider national hypocrisy, when it comes to animal conservation (and what is the point of a constitutional monarchy, after all, if not to dramatize and work through our national anxieties?). It might also have highlighted their and our partial responsibility for a problem that we're now trying to remedy around the world.

As it happens, I sense the penny might be slowly dropping with Prince William and his father. It was reported in 2014 that the former wanted all the ivory in the royal collection at Buckingham Palace to be removed and destroyed, while his father asked for all ivory objects at two of his homes to be removed from sight.[108] If they had gone further, if they had discussed the destructive behaviour of their ancestors during empire, if they had gone beyond ivory to talk about the devastation represented by the animal skins and mahogany in royal buildings and collections, and responded to the inevitable questions that came as a result, their frankness could have endowed their modern-day pleas for conservation and preservation with real power. The personalized argument of complicated human beings, from a family of flawed human beings set up to represent a flawed nation, would be infinitely more persuasive than a depersonalized lecture delivered from on high.

# 5.  A Rational and Intelligible System of Law

There were scenes of jubilation across the subcontinent when in 2018 the Supreme Court of India decriminalized consensual sexual conduct between adults of the same sex, overturning a 2013 judgment that upheld the country's section 377 law, under which gay sex was categorized as 'against the order of nature'. In Delhi, staff at a gay-friendly nightclub in the Lalit Hotel danced in the lobby. In Bangalore people proudly waved the LGBT flag and set off celebratory balloons.[1] Men and women who hadn't even come out to their families hugged their same-sex partners in front of newspaper photographers. And when India's Parliament passed a bill to protect transgender rights in 2019,[2] it appeared to confirm that the nation was heading in a liberal direction.

But a couple of years later, thirty-year-old Kiran, a trans woman who chooses not to use her surname and works at the Naz Foundation,[3] a campaigning organization which played an important role in the multi-decade battle to get rid of section 377, struggles to feel cheerful. 'The law has changed and we are very grateful,' she says, talking to me at Naz's Delhi offices, which serve as an administrative facility, a care home for around twenty children with HIV and a base for several mental health/LGBT support groups. 'We can hold our partners' hands in public places, we can express our sexuality, but attitudes are still the same. The attitudes I faced in my schooldays.' Assigned male at birth and growing up in the former imperial penal colony that is the Andaman Islands, Kiran faced such intense bullying as a child for not conforming to stereotypical male behaviour that she contemplated suicide. She eventually left home for Delhi before her education had concluded. 'I thought the mindset of the people might be more accepting in the metropolis.' But it wasn't: she had travelled some 1,500 miles but found hearts and minds were just as closed to LGBT people in India's capital. She applied for jobs, and frequently got through to the interview stage, only for interviewers to ask crude questions about her appearance and sexual orientation. 'They judged me for my appearance, not for my talent or qualifications.'

Fortunately she visited the Naz Foundation, where she discovered enlightened attitudes, like-minded people and potentially life-saving advice on safe sex. She now works for them, helping to train Delhi police, schools and workplaces in what the Foundation calls 'LGBT-QIA+ rights and sensitisation'. She still comes up against intense prejudice in this work, despite the change in the law, prejudice that will intensify not long after we meet, when India's top court refuses to recognize same-sex marriage in law. 'They think homosexuality is against morality, not natural.' There's a pause during which I notice that her fingernails have been painted a beautiful shade of turquoise. She, like everyone in the building except for me, is in a thick sweater, Indians overreacting to winter temperatures below 25°C in the way Britons overreact to spring temperatures above 14°C. Kiran adds that LGBT people still get blackmailed by the police and are targeted with abuse and violence on gay dating sites. 'Gay and LGBT people still don't have marriage rights. Gay students are still killing themselves as a result of bullying.[4] It would be wrong to say we have full acceptance – 30 per cent acceptance maybe. There is a lot of anxiety and trauma.'

What has any of this got to do with British empire? It turns out it was British imperialists who introduced the homophobic legislation to India and elsewhere. That is not to suggest that section 377 is the only legal legacy of empire. As you may have picked up from the revelations that abolition sowed the seeds of international law and that the regulation of indentured labour evolved into a framework of international laws and codes to regulate labour rights, just as the UK's Judicial Committee of the Privy Council remains the highest court in Mauritius (meaning that when litigation goes through the Mauritian legal system, the final arbiter is not a Mauritian court but a panel of British judges sitting in London),[5] British empire shaped law in profound ways across the planet. Indeed, it helped establish order through the rule of law in some places where there had been disorder, it failed to impose the rule of law in other places, failing on its own terms, and it produced legislation which continues to influence lives in all sorts of ways all around the world today. What forms does such legislation take? There is English common law that according to one definition is 'the part of English law that is derived from custom and judicial precedent rather than statutes'; it has been developing since the twelfth century and was applied in numerous direct colonial holdings.[6] There is also the British colonial legal concept of *terra nullius*, which made the occupation of some of the territories we've come across legal in British eyes. The Latin phrase means 'land belonging to no one' and it has been used as a get-out when it comes to indigenous rights to territory and dispossessing millions, especially in Australia.*[7] Then there are the constitutions that British empire supplied to nations across the planet (in 1884, when the British empire was peaking, Woodrow Wilson, the future US President who was at the time a doctoral student, stated that the Westminster model had become the 'world's fashion'), the aforementioned British imperial courts that still, in the twenty-first century, have legal authority over some Commonwealth countries (the Judicial Committee of the Privy Council, which is based in Parliament Square and shares a building and some judges with the UK Supreme Court, acts as the final court of appeal for twenty-six jurisdictions in addition to Mauritius),[8] and the 1,500-odd other archaic Indian laws that date back to the British Raj and which Indian decolonizers have declared war on (laws that range from 'equating kites with aircraft so that anyone wanting to fly a kite needs a licence' to a requirement for car inspectors to have 'well-brushed' teeth).[9]

But the imperial legacy of homophobia is something that regularly inspires headlines around the world, as activists battle in the twenty-first century to get the legislation repealed. Concerned that British colonial administrators and soldiers would, as a result of absent wives, resort to sodomy, British colonial lawmakers began from around 1860 to spread homophobic legislation across large parts of the planet in the form of legal codes and common law. The law that had the biggest

---

* John Locke, who as well as being a profoundly influential Enlightenment philosopher was also Secretary to the Lords Proprietors of Carolina and heavily invested in slavery, provided a definition of sorts when he stated that a man's ownership of land was dependent on whether he 'mixed his Labour with [it] and joyned it to something that is his own'. In other words, only land that was already enclosed and farmed was off-limits; the rest was there for the taking. *Terra nullius* is an idea that is being challenged in the modern day. In 1835, the Governor of New South Wales, Richard Bourke, adopted the principle of *terra nullius* to justify British settlement in Australia – about half a century after the arrival of the First Fleet. It was overturned only in 1992, when the High Court of Australia acknowledged and restored the continuous rights to land of the Aboriginal and Torres Strait Islander people. This ruling is known as the Mabo decision, named after the leader of the group of Torres Strait Islanders who lodged a claim for legal ownership of the island.

effect was section 377 of the Indian Penal Code, which maintained that 'Whoever voluntarily has carnal intercourse against the order of nature with any man, woman or animal shall be punished with imprisonment for life, or with imprisonment . . . for a term which may extend to ten years, and shall be liable to a fine.'[10] A bunch of post-colonial nations inherited identical or mildly altered versions of India's section 377, including Pakistan, Bangladesh, Uganda, Kenya, Singapore, Malaysia, Brunei, Burma, Tanzania, Kenya, Uganda, Malawi and Zambia.[11] As Enze Han and Joseph O'Mahoney explain in their authoritative 2019 survey *British Colonialism and the Criminalization of Homosexuality*, 'the link between British colonialism and currently having anti-gay laws is strong. Of the 72 countries with such a law in 2018, at least 38 of them were once subject to some sort of British colonial rule.'*[12] The academics also concluded, after intense data analysis, that 'British colonies are much more likely to have laws that criminalize homosexual conduct than other colonies or other states in general.'[13]

This homophobia is a real contrast to the legacies of French empire. Enlightenment thinking, and developing notions of 'rights' as a result of the French Revolution, led to the French penal code of 1791 actually *decriminalizing* sodomy between consenting adults in private.[14] This relatively liberal code subsequently spread across French colonies, Douglas Sanders concluding that 'of the great colonial powers of Western Europe – Britain, France, Germany, the Netherlands, Portugal and Spain – only Britain left this legacy [of homophobia]'.[15] When it came to sexuality and gender, British actions also stood in sharp contrast to the tolerance that often existed in pre-colonial societies, and in colonial communities outside the empire's immediate influence. Homosexuality had existed openly across pre-colonial India,[16] for example, with stories

---

* The numbers keep changing, with countries lining up in recent years to decriminalize homosexuality. The High Court in Barbados struck out laws that criminalized gay sex in December 2022, making the island the third Caribbean nation to make similar reforms that year. There has also been change in Singapore, though sex between males continued to be criminalized after the decriminalization of oral and anal sex between a man and a woman, though not between two men. In September 2022 the *Wall Street Journal* reported: 'Prime Minister Lee Hsien Loong said the government will repeal a law that criminalizes sex between men, which isn't enforced but that rights advocates say stigmatizes homosexuality. At the same time, he said, the government would move to safeguard its definition of marriage as between a man and a woman.'

spread through oral tradition often portraying homosexuality positively. Meanwhile, historians of India have traced back through centuries
the existence of so-called *hijra*, people who might today describe themselves as eunuchs, intersex or transgender. They appear in the *Kama
Sutra* and the *Mahabharata*, and during the Mughal empire they even
worked as servants, advisers and military commanders. Meanwhile, in
what is now Nigeria, pre-colonial Igbo communities ran a flexible
gender system, with gender-neutral pronouns and male roles open to
certain women through the phenomena of *nhanye* ('male daughters')
and *igba ohu* ('female husbands').[17] And in the goldmines near Johannes-
burg at the end of the nineteenth century, there were so-called mine
marriages in colonial mining communities between older and younger
African men.[18] Under this system, young workers called 'wife' were
often proposed to by more senior workers ('boss boys') and courted
with gifts. Marc Epprecht estimates that 70–80 per cent of men at these
mines took male sexual partners.[19] Apparently, these mine marriages
allowed young men to save, and thus afford more conventional marriages with women. Sex between men was socially accepted and not
considered a hindrance to marriage with a woman: it was possible for
sexuality to be fluid.

This history might come as a surprise to modern-day conservatives
in post-colonial states who like to portray homosexuality, gender fluidity and the battle for LGBT rights as Western phenomena. Kiran
tells me that the police officers she trains often claim that homosexuality 'is against morality, is not natural, and doesn't exist in Indian
culture. I tell them, no, this has existed since long time.' She shakes
her head, exhausted for a moment by the challenge of her work.
Through her office window I see a TV flickering in another room, a
TV which turns out to have been donated by pop star Lady Gaga on
a recent visit to the charity. 'In Indian mythology, in Mughal empire,
this is nothing new.' Nevertheless, in 2013 Rajnath Singh, the President of the Hindu Nationalist BJP, claimed that homosexuality was
an 'unnatural act', and his view was subsequently echoed by party
spokesperson Mukhtar Abbas Naqvi, who portrayed homosexuality
as part of 'Western culture'.[20] Meanwhile, it's not uncommon in post-
colonial Africa to come across the claim that homosexuality is a
Western disease which is intrinsically 'unAfrican'. But it was actually
formalized homophobia which British colonialism left as a legacy

across empire, not homosexuality.[21] The British and Dutch made gay sex punishable by death in nineteenth-century South Africa, and into the twentieth century gay people faced a hundred lashes or fifteen years in prison for their 'crime'.[22] From 1871 British officials in India targeted the *hijra* community who traditionally earned an income by singing and performing to mark births and marriages. Dismissing them as 'habitual sodomites' and 'unnatural prostitutes', British imperialists banned them from performing and compiled a register of *hijra* individuals with a view to eventually eliminating them.[23] After missionaries complained about the behaviour of those aforementioned men working in South African goldmines, the cricketer and colonial administrator Henry Taberer filed a report examining the 'loathsome' same-sex relationships among them. More generally, gender binaries and strict heteronormativity were forcibly imposed by imperialists who had fixed ideas of what was 'correct' in relation to sexuality and gender.

Having said that, we should resist the idea, which is widespread, that British empire deliberately spread homophobia in a logical and deliberate way. As ever with the British imperial project, things were more complicated on the ground. Some colonized states gained homophobic legislation not through the imposition of penal codes, for example, but through common law (law based on court decisions rather than statutes and codes); versions of Britain's homophobic Offences against the Person Act, which was passed in 1861,[24] held sway in the Australian colony of New South Wales, Jamaica, Hong Kong, Sierra Leone, Swaziland, Trinidad and Tobago, the Bahamas, Antigua and Barbuda, St Kitts and Nevis.[25] In some cases, the influence of British empire upon the development of homophobic legislation was informal: as Han and O'Mahoney explain, this was where laws were 'borrowed from British exemplars. This is seemingly the case in so-called protected states, like Bhutan, where British control extended only to external affairs and not to domestic politics or legislation. This is similarly the case . . . in the primarily white settler colonies of Canada, Australia, and New Zealand.' There were also instances of indirect British influence in the international spread of homophobic legislation: 'the history of several other modern states has included very close relations with the British empire, or at least its representatives, without it being reasonable to attribute their adoption of a law criminalizing homosexuality to direct

British influence. For example, Tonga . . .'[26] Moreover, many of Britain's most famous imperialists, like Rhodes and Mountbatten, were rumoured to be gay and attracted to empire for the relative sexual freedom it provided.*[27]

There are other qualifications to be made. We should not project 'noble savage' notions on to pre-colonial societies when it comes to gender and homosexuality, implying they were idyllic societies (for Western liberals) of open sexuality and gender fluidity: it's hard to define what homosexuality actually was and was not in that era, or to know how things worked precisely. Second, we should interrogate the clichéd claim that British Victorians spread prudery across empire. They arguably legislated and intervened on these topics because they were *obsessed* with sex. The Victorians didn't outlaw homosexuality because they were prudish, but because they were fanatical about controlling sex and using sexual practices as proof of 'civilization'. Third, if countries still have homophobic legislation, you can't blame it entirely on the British empire: empire may have instilled homophobia but these nations could have got rid of the legislation on independence. Indeed, when I speak to Kiran, she notably doesn't blame British imperialists. 'I don't think the LGBT community [in India] blames the British empire for section 377,' she says. 'Because India got rid of empire a long time ago and this law is still there.' Fourth, in some cases the British colonial law has combined with local law to produce homophobic legislation, and locals should share the responsibility: colonial law combining with sharia law in places like Kuwait, Qatar and the United Arab Emirates, for instance. Fifth, while the British judiciary acted against homosexuality

---

* Ronald Hyam's controversial book *Empire and Sexuality* began with the claim that 'sexual dynamics crucially underpinned the whole operation of British empire and Victorian expansion. Without the easy range of sexual opportunities which imperial systems provided, the long-term administration and exploitation of tropical territories, in nineteenth-century conditions, might well have been impossible.' At the same time, some imperialists went the other way and attempted to drive homosexuality out of the societies they ruled over. Lord Curzon compiled a list of Indian princes who had homosexual preferences, attributing the phenomenon to early marriage. 'A boy gets tired of his wife, or of women, at an early age, and wants the stimulus of some more novel or exciting sensation,' he claimed. The Viceroy tried to 'turn' one gay prince by sending him to Cadet Corps, hoping self-discipline would do the job, but then he fretted that his presence might 'corrupt' other young men.

in the colonies, they also often turned a blind eye to that practised by Britons themselves – there were double standards for white British and local colonized 'offenders'. Finally, the evidence supporting the assertion that British imperialism fundamentally 'poisoned' cultures against homosexuality is, according to Han and O'Mahoney, inconclusive. 'The speed of decriminalization of homosexual conduct for those colonies with such a law is not systematically slower for British colonies compared to colonies of other European states.'[28]

Unfortunately, crude simplification is common on this theme and there was a disappointing example in a recent documentary from the BBC, *Tom Daley: Illegal to be Me*. The Olympic gold medallist and double world champion diver did admirable work in the film – timed to coincide with the Commonwealth Games – highlighting the colonial roots of the discrimination and persecution faced by many gay athletes across the Commonwealth. But the documentary also featured an interview with Carla Moore, introduced as a university lecturer specializing in race and sexuality, in which she suggested that one of the reasons for homophobia in the West Indies was 'buck breaking', the apparently common and ritualized 'anal rape of enslaved men' by slave owners, in front of their family and friends. She argued that, as a result, attitudes to same-sex sexuality were tied to a 'complicated history of sexual trauma that went on for, like, 300 years' and that 'if the representation you have of queerness is plantation owners sexually assaulting men, you get the idea that it's a white people thing, it's a thing white people do to black people to harm them. The end result is the homophobia we see today.'[29]

It's certainly true, despite the fact that women were by some distance the greater victims of sexual assault and rape on British plantations, that enslaved men were sexually assaulted. Common punishments like flogging and whipping were sometimes carried out in ways that felt sexual, and especially degrading and humiliating as a result. As Thomas Foster puts it, 'masters and overseers would often strip men nude, contributing to the sexually abusive and invasive nature of the punishment'.[30] Enslaved men and women were also forced to reproduce, with this compulsory reproduction being a kind of secondary sexual assault, given that these men and women were compelled to engage in sex against their will. Meanwhile, abolitionists widely translated and reprinted an account by Joseph LaVallée about an enslaved man, Itanoko, raped by a white slaver named

Urban. Itanoko describes Urban as a 'ravisher' who did 'violate, what is most sacred among men'.[31] Abolitionist literature often contained passages about masters sexually abusing enslaved people: the episodes were used to create sympathy and outrage at the abusive and violent treatment towards enslaved men. But I cannot find any serious historical study of the practice of 'buck breaking'. All the mentions I find online are on popular-culture websites like urbandictionary or appear as a result of the recent film *Buck Breaking* ('a documentary film about the historic sexual exploitation of Black people globally'), and many modern depictions of it seem to be rooted in homophobia. Thomas Foster, talking about the frequent depictions of gay male sexual assault of the enslaved, argues that they are likely to have emerged as a consequence of modern fictional imaginations of slavery where sexual violence is often used as a way to 'underscore the particular depravity of slavery in America'.[32] He cites a 1968 novel by William Styron, *The Confessions of Nat Turner*, where Turner endures groping and comments about his 'unusual big pecker' and the enslaver tries to 'ravish' him.[33] And Quentin Tarantino's *Django Unchained* has a scene in which the main character is whipped naked and hanging by his wrists – the character whipping him seeming to take sexual satisfaction from it.[34] In short, such sexual violence has become a cheap way to use homophobia to project the horrors of slavery.

Furthermore, there's a danger when focusing on imperial legal legacies more generally that one creates the impression that British empire imposed legal structures across its empire from London in a neat, simple, uniform and considered way. But as Lauren Benton and Lisa Ford show in *Rage for Order*, while the influence of British empire upon law around the world was profound – they argue that it shaped nothing less than the origins of international law itself – it was also an incredibly messy process. Their argument goes that in the nineteenth century it wasn't that top-ranking British imperialists laid down the law in the colonies. Rather, laws evolved haphazardly as a consequence of crises and incidents, and were enacted by middle-ranking officials in colonial administration. This so-called 'middle power' was encouraged by reformers who wanted to take on imperial despotism and tyranny, preventing, for example, imperial strongmen from wreaking havoc by taking unilateral decisions. Separately, the British empire also saw the creation of multiple 'commissions of inquiry' sent by the Colonial

Office – often prompted by a local scandal – to find out exactly how things were run in the colonies and to propose reforms, such as, say, fairer trials. In other words, things only got flagged when something went wrong. Moreover, British imperialists found themselves getting involved in legal reform across the planet when encouraged by specific groups of people in the colonies to provide 'protection' (against both internal despotism and external attack), when campaigning against piracy on the seas, when fighting to shut down the international slave trade and when attempting to trade internationally with nations that weren't actually part of the empire.

I must confess that it took multiple re-readings of Benton and Ford to get my head around this messy process, and it has proved even more difficult to explain it to others. I've found it sometimes helps to introduce an analogy I use when trying to explain the British empire to children: school. Not that British empire was structured anything like a normal school, with the classes representing colonies, the children representing colonized subjects, the head/governors symbolizing the British government, the teachers acting as imperial administrators and the school rules standing in for what was law. It's more that British empire *rarely* functioned like a normal school. For one thing, classes in this school-that-is-British-empire differed enormously in size: some tiny, some huge. Each class had a different sense of belonging to the school, some being very much part of the enterprise, others detached to the extent of almost considering themselves schools in their own right. Some classes were fairly peaceful, some out of control and violent. There was no national curriculum (constitution) and, although there was a head teacher, they rarely got directly involved, not least because, before Federal Express, the internet and telephones, it could take months to get a message to a classroom. Instead the various classes did different things in different ways. Some of these teachers knew what they were doing but others really didn't. Some were nice, but others were cruel. Some teachers were so lazy that they forced pupils to do all the work for them on pain of death, while taking all the payment and credit. But within this analogy the most confusing thing is how the school rules (that is, law) worked in empire.

It wasn't that the headmaster and governors came up with a list of regulations and then imposed them uniformly on each class. Quite often the class already had its own rules before the head had taken charge, and

those rules continued to apply to varying degrees, and merged to varying degrees, and arbitrarily, with new rules. It was not unusual for the
head to begin thinking about how the rules should be reformed in a particular class only after they had heard about a scandal occurring in a
classroom. Then the head might send out commissioners to observe
what was happening in the classroom and ask for advice on what might
be needed.* Or those in charge would respond to pleas from pupils in
the classes to be protected against internal despotism and/or external
attack, and get people of middling authority to make legal reforms.† As
for the way British empire developed international law while combating
piracy and the slave trade and engaging in trade, I suppose the analogy
within the school analogy would be a headmaster turning up at random
homes, shopping centres and parks and attempting to impose discipline
there. It's an idea that doesn't seem so outlandish when you remember
how most headteachers, who spend their working lives telling people
what to do, develop a tendency to become hectoring.

Perhaps it would be more helpful if I give up on the comparison to
school entirely and just cite some of the crises and scandals that Benton
and Ford say prompted 'worries about petty despotism and arbitrary
justice' and then led to legal reform across empire.[35] One of them was
the 1808 Rum Rebellion in Australia, when the Governor of New South
Wales, William Bligh, the victim of the notorious mutiny on the *Bounty*
(which we came across when at Kew), was overthrown in an uprising
organized by the New South Wales Corps. The rebels' main grievance
was Bligh's curbing of the colony's illicit rum trade.[36] Another crisis
involved Governor Thomas Picton, the first British Governor of Trinidad, who was known for his cruelty towards those he had enslaved and
anyone else who crossed him. One poor victim was a fourteen-year-old
free 'mulatto' girl called Luisa Calderón, who had been accused of stealing. He sentenced her to the 'picket', an agonizing form of torture in

---

* If you're still following this, I guess the commissioners in this scenario would basic-
ally be inspectors from Ofsted.
† The deputy head? The head of year? Or maybe this is the equivalent of a British
headmaster haranguing other headmasters at a conference? I'll admit it's getting hard
to stretch the analogy now, leaving aside the fact that a historian friend suggests the
whole thing doesn't work anyway because schools don't exist to make money like
empire did.

which she was hung up by her wrist, so that her body was supported by just a wooden peg, for nearly an hour. In 1803 he was ordered to London to stand trial for the act, and was subsequently also accused of decapitating and burning alive enslaved people who were suspected of sorcery and witchcraft (he was found guilty of the charges, but the verdict was then overturned).[37] Yet another crisis was inspired by notoriously brutal slave owner Edward Huggins on the Caribbean island of Nevis, who ordered the flogging of a group of enslaved people; some of them received over 200 lashes, and a woman called Fanny died. In 1810 Huggins was tried for cruelty, but acquitted.[38] And then there was the scandal of Arthur Hodge, another sadist who around 1792 inherited the Belle Vue estate in Tortola, and was accused of ordering boiling water to be poured down the throats of two enslaved women called Else and Margaret, who then died. Another enslaved man called Prosper was accused of stealing a mango and flogged so hard that he, too, died. Hodge, however, did not escape punishment for these heinous acts, and became the first British slave owner in the West Indies to be hanged for the murder of an enslaved person.[39]

Each of these crises resulted in legal reform across the empire, as explained by Benton and Ford. For example, in New South Wales, the spectacular deposition of Governor Bligh in 1808 set the stage for a decade-long discussion about the administration of justice that led to the reconstitution of the colony's courts in 1823. In the case of the degenerate Hodge, the execution of a well-known planter served as an example of the advantages of giving governors in autonomous colonies more control over judicial processes. Hodge's lengthy history of abuse also served to highlight how frequently West Indian magistrates failed to exercise their limited authority over masters. Additionally, Benton and Ford note that a local incident involving the public punishment of slaves on the island of Nevis was used first to defend Crown autocracy in Trinidad, before serving as the impetus for a significant project of inquiry into Caribbean legal procedures. More generally, it was not centralized efforts but 'the cruelties of slave owners, the indifference of captains to the suffering of captives and sailors, the perversion of justice by despotic governors, the unnecessary violence of rogue officials on the margins of empire' which 'filled colonial correspondence, official and otherwise . . . peppered the headlines and letter columns of newspapers in England' and became 'fodder for reformers and critics'.[40]

As for the role that 'protection' played in shaping colonial law, which in school terms was probably the imperial equivalent of grassing up a bullying teacher to the head and governors, or putting a school in special measures, Benton and Ford make a useful comparison to the modern world. It was essentially a version of the justification Vladimir Putin has provided for military interventions in places like the Crimea and Ukraine. In claiming to protect ethnic Russians in these nations Putin has been invoking 'an older imperial notion of protection; unlike human rights talk, the appeal to protection contained within it the seeds of authoritarian meddling and permanent annexation'.[41] Throughout imperial history, various groups of colonized people appealed to the Crown to protect them, or the British Crown/campaigners took it upon themselves to protect certain groups, with sustained efforts, for example, among a group of campaigners around Thomas Hodgkin (the prominent physician who, as a Quaker, supported the abolition of slavery) and Thomas Fowell Buxton (leader of the Parliamentary anti-slavery campaign after William Wilberforce retired) to protect the Aboriginal people of Australia and New Zealand.[42] The 'protection' of the Crown, then, could mean protection for those colonial subjects in need of it, as well as protection against the abuse of arbitrary power, even when that power was wielded by those under the authority of the Crown. Sometimes the language and idea of 'protection' were employed as an excuse for taking over independent kingdoms, as in 1815, when the British occupied the Kingdom of Kandy, the central highland region of Ceylon. The British were already in possession of Ceylon's coastal strip, with its rich cinnamon plantations and strategic ports, won from the Dutch during the Napoleonic Wars, but the Kingdom of Kandy remained independent. To consolidate their control over the whole island, the British invaded Kandy and deposed the King. As a pretext, they claimed that they were intervening on behalf of the Buddhist Sinhalese population, to protect them from their despotic ruler, who was a Hindu of Malabar (South Indian Tamil) descent. To appeal to the Sinhalese, the British even styled themselves as protectors of Buddhism.[43]

Then there were the imperial commissions. Again, there's a useful comparison to be made with the modern world, more specifically with modern British governments, with their predilection for making difficult policies the subject of inquiries, as a way of kicking a problem into the long grass or testing appetite. As I write, in Britain we have inquiries looking at everything from cryptocurrencies to nuclear power,[44] and things have long been this way. In 2006 *Public* magazine complained that Britain was essentially being governed by inquiry,[45] with Kate Barker at the time employed to look at planning for housing, Lord Leitch looking at the nation's skills mix for 2020, Sir Rod Eddington examining transport and productivity, Andrew Gowers looking at intellectual property, Sir Nicholas Stern reporting on the economics of climate change, Sir Michael Lyons investigating council finance, Sir George Cox examining creativity, Sir David Cooksey reporting on health research funding. Something similar happened during empire with 'commissions of inquiry', which were generally led by lawyers and were intended to investigate colonial issues and disputes, with some degree of impartiality, and testimony at their heart.[46]

Although informal commissions of this sort had existed in the early centuries of British imperialism, it was in 1802 that they assumed a central role in the reform of the empire, when a commission of inquiry requested that Trinidad compile a 'report . . . of the actual Civil, Naval and Military State of the Island' with a view to 'improving its resources and providing for its permanent Security and Protection'.[47] There have been examples of commissions in the stories we've covered so far, not least in the multiple commissions of inquiry into various aspects of indenture. At other times lawyers leading commissions of inquiry examined the state, laws and constitution of New South Wales, eighteen West Indian colonies (where the disposal of the enslaved freed under the 1833 Abolition Act was also examined), the Cape Colony, Ceylon, Mauritius and India. Malta had the distinction of being the most examined colony in the British empire: commissions of inquiry were tasked with drawing up a constitution and establishing a judicial system and legal code on the island in 1824, 1831–2, 1835 and 1836. Following a rebellion in Canada in 1838, a commission of inquiry there led by Lord Durham went so far as to recommend that British North America should become self-governed.[48]

In this way, British empire's shaping of law around the world, although profound, was also untidy, driven not by imperialists with grand visions and almighty authority in London, but, in the words of Benton and Ford, by 'the slaves who organized the protest on Edward Huggins's estate, the freed woman who testified against Arthur Hodge, the slaves in Mauritius who flooded the protector's court . . . the Kandyan elites who

argued for, then turned against, British intervention [in Ceylon] . . .'. Or
to put it another way, it was 'the continual autocriticism of empire', the
self-criticizing nature of the British imperial project, combined with the
complaints, protests and resistance of those whom Britons colonized,
which dictated empire's legal direction. Yes, British empire shaped the
origins of international law itself but did so chaotically – 'porous and
malleable, coopted and coopting, this lost empire of law constituted a
distinctive, formative phase in the legal history of the world'. And this
messiness, which has been observed as a feature of British empire more
generally,[49] makes imperial law an impossible area to navigate for those
concerned only with establishing whether British empire was good or
bad, or whether it was relatively good or relatively bad. As Benton and
Ford put it, 'alternative stories of good and evil are rarely satisfying.
They too often flatten history by turning it into a morality play.'[50]

When it comes to imperial law, though, there is a long tradition of
people trying to flatten the complex history to turn it into a morality
play. Here we have Niall Ferguson saying of British empire that 'no
organization has done more to impose Western norms of law, order and
governance around the world'.[51] Here, in an otherwise nuanced and
admirable book on the geopolitical legacies of empire, we have Kwasi
Kwarteng asserting that 'the empire stood for order and the rule of law',
without providing convincing evidence for the claim.[52] It's a claim that
emerges regularly when Hong Kong rule under the British is compared
to what China offers the former British colony now. 'One of the legacies of British colonialism is a judicial system that is impartial, clean,
independent, and guarantees basic human rights, such as access to a
lawyer, clear limits to periods of detention, and decent detention in custody,' as one recent report put it in *The Times*. 'The Chinese authorities,
by contrast, are frequently accused of arbitrary arrest, prolonged and
abusive periods of detention, and of maintaining courts which are susceptible to corruption and political pressure from the communist
party.'[53] Further back, we had Winston Churchill asking rhetorically in
1899 what could be more 'noble and more profitable' than 'to administer justice where all was violence?'[54] John M. MacKenzie suggests that
the 'generally impressive law courts' that the British built across empire
were an expression of its imperialists' insistence that 'the rule of law was
inherent in the nature of their power'.[55] And in 1844 we had the Bombay
Supreme Court puisne judge Erskine Perry gloating that 'one of the

most valuable boons, which it lies within the competence of Government to confer upon this vast country, consists in the establishment of a rational and intelligible system of Law'.[56]

Leaving aside the common but questionable implication in these claims that the quarter of the planet colonized by Britain didn't already have versions of the legal concepts introduced by the British,[57] there is no doubt that the British empire did introduce 'a rational and intelligible system of Law' to some territories. The withdrawal of these legal norms has led to the mass emigration of the Hong Kong Chinese in the twenty-first century. There is also no doubt that some imperialists worked earnestly to introduce concepts such as the rule of law (meaning, in the most basic terms, that 'nobody is above the law') to parts of the British empire. These efforts saw the launching of the extraordinary seven-year impeachment proceedings against Warren Hastings, the first Governor-General of Bengal and co-founder of British rule in India, and the prosecution of Governor Eyre for his brutal suppression of rebellion in Jamaica. Then there was Sir James Stephen, the grandfather of Virginia Woolf, and the son of a famous abolitionist, who oversaw the rule of law in British colonial territories in the first half of the nineteenth century.[58] A man known as 'Mr. Mothercountry', he administered the British empire 'almost singlehandedly' for about three decades while serving as Under Secretary of the Colonies. From 1813 to 1847, he acted as legal counsel before resigning to become a history professor at Cambridge. During that time, he outlasted twenty secretaries of state and issued hundreds of rulings regarding laws made in the colonies.[59] Almost every colony-passed law found its way to his desk, including those issuing tariffs on goods, regulations governing immigration and migration, plans for planting bamboo or aloe, levies to promote hygiene or confine pets, and laws governing migration and immigration. As Keally McBride tells us, Stephen, the son of 'a particularly fiery abolitionist', was so devout that he only deviated from his Sabbath observance once (to write the legislation that ended slavery in the British empire) and was so puritanical that the one time he smoked a cigar, he liked it and therefore threw it away and never smoked another.[60] He also paid close attention to indigenous legal customs, tried to stop colonial administrators and settlers from abusing their power and believed that the rule of law could be a force for good in the face of what he called 'the cruel wrongs' that the British had committed against the rest of the world. 'Stephen's personal morality led him to embrace the principle of the rule of law to a highly unusual degree.'[61]

If his work seems to challenge the idea that Britain's imposition of law across its empire was haphazard, it's because it does. But, as we keep discovering, the imperial project was full of contradictions. And in the school analogy, he was not the founder or governor or even the head-master in charge of the educational enterprise, but rather a sort of head-of-department who worked for a limited period of British empire. He represented one attempt to impose order amid general disorder which saw that within the Colonial Office 'colonial despatches went unanswered, colonial governors reported crises, complained of their wrongs, and even died, without the minister seeming aware of the fact'.[62] And, however earnest his intentions, and however good a man, the success he had in actually spreading the rule of law is highly debat-able. Indeed, Keally McBride concludes that Stephen's work reveals that the imposition of the rule of law across empire was 'historically bound, contextually contingent, and invariably messy'. She adds that his experience shows that 'the rule of law could never be achieved definitively; it can only be a specter in an ongoing struggle to reconcile ideals with particular situations', and that while Stephen 'truly believed that the law could be used as a force for good and equity . . . whether he was successful in using it as such is another question entirely'.[63]

The point that the rule of law is not absolute is important. The fact that it's called a 'rule' may imply that it's something nations either pos-sess or do not possess, but it can only be achieved to a degree, if at all. If it's true that, in McBride's words, 'the rule of law is supposed to provide a boundary for normative politics by establishing frameworks of behav-ior for all citizens, and those who govern them',[64] how can it exist within a colonial system where, by definition, one group of people ultimately governs another through the threat or application of vio-lence? Indeed, McBride concludes clearly that 'colonialism is no way to deliver justice'.[65] Even in modern Western nations which boast about valuing the rule of law and attempt to encourage it elsewhere, there are always people who, as a result of historical precedent, power, influence, luck, conceit, connections or money, are more or less equal before the law than others. One of these, under the doctrine of sovereign immun-ity, is the British monarch, who as head of state is not litigated against, in criminal or civil law. It was recently reported, a few months before her passing, that personalized exemptions for the late Queen Elizabeth II had been baked into more than 160 laws since 1967, giving her immunity from reams of British law, including aspects of workers' rights.[66] Moreover, if law governs the behaviour of officials, which officials get to choose how these laws are enforced upon them? And how can anyone ensure laws are enforced in an equal way upon the highest and lowest in society?

I do not share the absolute certainty of Ferguson et al. in diagnosing the positive presence of the rule of law across the British empire, and nor does McBride. She tells us that Stephen was 'wracked by doubts' about his success in spreading the rule of law and reports that he ultimately considered himself unsuccessful. She herself adds that 'his vision failed and the realities of colonial domination resisted the incursion of grand idealism', that 'the British empire failed miserably to live up to its own rhetoric' and that 'it is not a surprise that scholars, practitioners, colonial subjects, and even some British colonial administrators viewed the proclamations about the rule of law within practices of British colonization with cynicism'. It's undeniable that some British imperialists like Stephen held up the rule of law as an ideal. It was idealism which led to the rule of law being made central to the mission of Sierra Leone, a nation founded by the British after it had been colonized by freed slaves arriving from England, Nova Scotia and Jamaica, and which inspired the prosecution of imperialists like Warren Hastings and Governor Eyre.[67] But both defendants were found not guilty of the most serious charges they faced, and while something resembling the rule of law was achieved in some places at some times, its spread was curtailed by the other great imperial ideal, white supremacy, which demanded that white people be treated preferentially in colonial law.[68]

This preference was evident in the highly racialized nature of colonial policing, where, as David Anderson and David Killingray explain, 'gazetted officers were for the most part white'[69] and quite often Irish,[*][70]

---

[*] British empire's colonial police forces had a distinctly Irish flavour. Several former Royal Irish Constabulary (RIC) officers joined the Indian and colonial police forces after Ireland gained its independence as a dominion in 1921. They were valued for their training, their experience in the challenging conditions of Ireland and their reputation for discipline. As David Anderson and David Killingray explain: 'RIC men

and the 'African, Asian and West Indian constables' who made up the rank and file 'tended to work in a world where those with white skins generally policed themselves: it was a bold "native" constable indeed who would, of his own initiative, have sought to police a member of the white ruling class'.[71] And for all the success imperialists may have had in extending the rule of law elsewhere, in India, the largest colony, and the most common illustration of imperial legal reform, Britain famously failed on its own terms, when the British Whig politician and historian Thomas Babington Macaulay couldn't get his fellow imperialists to buy into the idea that Indians should have equality before the law – the whole thing beginning as a result of one of the commissions mentioned a few pages ago.

In 1834, Macaulay led a commission of inquiry to codify Indian civil and criminal law. He was a proud and committed imperialist, believing that Britain had a duty to ensure the 'diffusion of European civilisation amongst the vast population of the East'[72] and that absolute power was the only way to achieve this. He also famously asserted, despite not being able to read or speak any Asian language, that a 'single shelf of good European literature' was worth the entire 'native literature of India and Arabia'.[73] At the time of the inquiry, in 1834, the British saw it as a fact that the Indian justice system was in dire need of reform, believing that Hindu and Mughal rulers had left it in chaos. Macaulay thought that putting together a new code of law would be straightforward, thanks to Britain's grip on the country. A 'quiet knot of veteran jurists', with none of the internal factions, deep-rooted disputes or need for

---

"stiffened" the ranks of many colonial forces during the 1920s, but their most notable (although perhaps also notorious) contribution was made in Palestine. With the independence of India and the relinquishing of the Palestine mandate in 1947–8, a second wave of "migratory" police officers found their way from these territories to Malaya, Nyasaland and to West Africa, where [they made a] contribution to counter-subversion and anti-terrorist operations.' However, historians have also advised wariness of broad generalizations about the influence of the Irish policing model, one noting that 'no colonial constabulary was ever an exact replica of the RIC'. Another has emphasized that some colonial forces claimed to be structured according to English patterns and others were hybrid. Sir Charles May founded Hong Kong's first police force in the 1840s, which was modelled on the Metropolitan Police. Indian policing drew strongly on the style and methodology of both the Met and the RIC with centrally controlled officers who operated primarily in rural regions.

public accountability that plagued a 'large popular assembly', would swiftly get the job done.[74] The 'quiet knot' assigned to the task was, unsurprisingly, led by Macaulay himself, keen to replace India's existing religion-based Hindu and Muslim laws with a more 'rational' legal code.

To conduct his inquiry Macaulay spent three years in India, during which time he rarely strayed outside the fortified palace in which he lived. He viewed the country as chaotic, corrupt and threatening – 'we are strangers here', he said – and thought that engaging with it might challenge his authority and direction. According to the historian Jon Wilson, the rules he drafted during his solitary exile were examples of 'detached rationalist abstraction. His Code of Criminal Law was a body of jurisprudence written for everyone and no one, which had no relationship to previous Indian laws or any other form of government at all.'[75] In a move that suggested he had hidden depths, he was keen on the law treating brown and white fairly. 'Unless . . . we mean to leave the natives exposed to the tyranny and insolence of every profligate adventurer who may visit the east, we must place the European under the same power which legislates for the Hindoo . . . India has suffered enough already from the distinctions of caste and from the deeply rooted prejudices which those distinctions have engendered.'[76] However, although Macaulay and his three fellow law commissioners finished their Code of Penal Law in 1837,[77] it remained unimplemented for twenty-four years. There were numerous factors behind the delay, not least the fact that his fellow British colonialists were not keen on the idea of racial equality before the law: in fact, some were so enraged by what they saw as a threat to their rights that they hinted Macaulay deserved to be lynched.[78]

Things eventually came to a head with the Ilbert Bill crisis of the 1880s – when new legislation sought to permit Indian magistrates to judge British defendants on trial in India.[79] Previously, Indian magistrates were not able to preside over the trials of white defendants in criminal cases. The Viceroy, the Marquess of Ripon, who took office in 1880, thought this unjustifiable, and requested a bill to change it. The subsequent legislation, drafted by Sir Courtenay Peregrine Ilbert, stated that suitably qualified Indians would be allowed to try defendants of any skin tone. The British community in India saw this as an outrageous attack on their God-given superior status. Several thousand protested outside the Calcutta Town Hall, listening to speeches such as one by

J. J. Keswick, a senior partner in the tea and trading company Jardine Skinner & Co., who said that even the best-trained Indian was simply incapable of fairly judging a European: 'these men are not fit to rule over us . . . they cannot judge us . . . we will not be judged by them'. Ripon was ambushed by the hostile response, admitting that he hadn't realized 'the true feeling of the average Anglo-Indian toward the natives' and that 'the knowledge gives me a feeling akin to despair as to the future of this country'.[80]

Having dropped the bombshell, both Ripon and Ilbert left Calcutta to spend the summer in Simla, hoping that the controversy would die down. Instead, consternation only fermented during the hot, febrile summer months, until it reached the point of a 'White Mutiny'. One of the supposed fears of the protesters was that the Bill would let Indians take advantage of white women. This claim – that equality before the law would encourage interracial rape – illustrates the sexual insecurity prevalent in the empire at the time. An effigy of Ilbert was burned, and on his return to Calcutta Ripon was jeered by protesters. A weak man, he conceded a major compromise – that should a white defendant be put before an Indian magistrate in a criminal case, they had the right to request a jury, of which half the members must be English or American. The subsequent counter-outrage resulted in all sorts of races and classes across India becoming united in purpose. Unintentionally, Ripon had, as Niall Ferguson says, 'brought into being a genuine Indian national consciousness'. Eighteen-eighty-five saw the inaugural meeting of the Indian National Congress, known colloquially as the Congress Party, which would become the 'crucible of modern Indian nationalism' and remains a powerful force in Indian politics to this day.[81] Founder members included the lawyer Motilal Nehru, whose son Jawaharlal would become the first Prime Minister of an independent India.

The Britons of India had been given a chance to demonstrate a belief in the rule of law, and had rejected it for the comfort of crude racism. Whatever they achieved elsewhere in terms of legal fairness is overshadowed by this episode, the grim consequences of their decision made apparent by Elizabeth Kolsky, whose revelatory book *Colonial Justice in British India* surveys and analyses over 150 years of violent crime in colonial India and exposes nothing less than an epidemic of white violence.[82] She reports, for instance, that in four years between 1901 and 1905, a period of violent unrest in Assam, twenty-seven cases of fatal assaults on Indians committed by Europeans ended up in the colonial courts, along with twelve such assaults on Europeans by Indians. Out of those twenty-seven European attacks, over half were judged to be the result of an accident following a minor assault (in most cases, the cause of death was a ruptured spleen), two of the cases saw successful pleas of self-defence from the European defendants, and, overall, two-thirds of the accused Europeans literally got away with murder. In stark contrast, of the twelve fatal assaults by Indians on Europeans brought to trial, eleven (92 per cent) resulted in murder convictions. Kolsky also reproduces research that illustrates how, in spite of imperial law reform, colonial justice did not improve over time: in colonial Calcutta, the number of Europeans charged with serious crimes and convicted actually declined as the nineteenth century went on.[83] And then there's the fact that in the last two decades of the nineteenth century eighty-one 'shooting accidents' were reported in which Europeans shot Indians but claimed in their defence to have mistaken their victims for hunting prey such as birds, monkeys or buffaloes. The newspaper *Samvad Purnachandrodaya* complained that 'shooting natives has become something like a disease' with Brits, adding that 'they are tried by their own countrymen, so they are generally acquitted after shooting natives'.[84]

Kolsky further brings the inequality before the law alive by examining the fine details of the cases hitting the colonial courts at the time. To read about them is to experience a cumulative horror. The fact that so many involve sexual violence makes them particularly difficult to read, reminding me that when it comes to the trauma endured by historians there is no more harrowing illustration than that of Iris Chang, author of the award-winning *The Rape of Nanking: The Forgotten Holocaust of World War II*, a book published in 1997 packed with detailed descriptions of some of the most heinous sexual crimes (and murders) ever committed, detailing the savagery the Japanese Imperial Army inflicted on Chinese citizens during its march across China in 1937. A wife and a mother aged just thirty-six, Chang was working on a new book in which she was compiling the testimonies of Americans and Filipinos who had endured the 1942 Bataan Death March, another Japanese war atrocity, when she shot herself.[85] The work for which she suffered is a powerful legacy, as is Kolsky's, and it feels important to bear witness to the details of the cases, however difficult they are to read. They include the rape, in April 1899, of an elderly Burmese woman by thirty soldiers of the West Kent Regiment in Rangoon, for which the men faced no punishment whatsoever.[86]

The incident took place in broad daylight when a woman named Ma Gun was grabbed by a soldier and dragged screaming to where several other soldiers were waiting. Holding Ma Gun down, the soldiers took turns raping her before hauling her into a ditch out of sight of passers-by, whom soldiers armed with daggers and dogs warned to keep away. As four police officers arrived on the scene, they discovered Ma Gun surrounded by men, with Private Benjamin Edward Horricks on top of her. In Burmese, she shouted out, 'If you can save me, save me.' Horricks was detained by the police 'as he was rising from the woman', and he was tried in Rangoon the following month. Eighteen witnesses were called by the prosecution, many of whom attested to witnessing the gang rape. One claimed to have seen Horricks' erect penis as he was taken off Ma Gun, and police inspector James Hewitt testified that he arrived on the scene to find Horricks smeared in dirt, with his trousers falling down. An inquiry by the police into 'the history of Ma Gun' revealed a woman 'of weak intellect but of respectable character'. The Europeans in the courtroom laughed during her jumbled testimony and the defence called soldiers from Horricks' regiment, who claimed that Ma Gun acted like a prostitute, beckoning them for a 'jig-jig' (sex). Many admitted to having sex with her, but all claimed it was for money and without force. Horricks was unanimously acquitted by a jury of nine European men. In the following months, other soldiers present at the attack were charged with rape. The same witnesses were called to testify at each of their trials, and all of them were acquitted. Ma Gun died the following year, without seeing the British empire deliver its famed justice.

Kolsky presents us with dozens of similar cases from the era, and another theme that emerges from them is the violent abuse of servants. In March 1903, an English official shot a palanquin bearer for being too slow, and then pleaded insanity to escape prosecution. Sent home to England, he spent a whole two days in an asylum before moving to Switzerland, where he wrote to British imperial authorities demanding compensation for his treatment from the Government of India. In 1893, Alfred Webb MP asked the Secretary of State to reassess the case of Private John Rigby, who was fined just 100 rupees for kicking to death a punkhawallah (a servant who operated a fan, usually functioning through a pulley system) after claiming the servant had fallen asleep at his post. The Secretary of State demurred, saying, 'The medical evidence showed that the cause of death was rupture of the spleen, which was in such a state that the slightest blow might have broken it, and there were no external marks of violence.' An 'enlarged spleen' was often cited as the cause of Indian deaths in this era, with the bizarre racial 'science' so popular with British imperialists asserting that Indians were particularly prone to the affliction. A 1904 Royal Engineers handbook advised that 'natives should never be struck, as a very large number suffer from enlarged spleens and other complaints, and a blow, or sometimes even a shove, can be fatal'.[87]

Of course, the real reason for so many fatalities was widespread and brutal white violence. Writing about yet another case when a soldier kicked a punkhawallah to death, the newspaper *Banganivasi* reported sarcastically: 'The writer has as yet got no information about the size of the coolie's spleen and whether his death was due to a sudden bursting of it.'[88] And British soldiers did not reserve their abuse for their own servants or underlings; all Indian labour was seen as fair game. In the years after the Indian Uprising of 1857, polite notices posted on the walls of colonial hotels openly reminded white patrons that 'Gentlemen are earnestly requested not to strike the servants.'*[89] A newly arrived British private recalled seeing an 'old soldier' punching a sweeper while yelling: 'You black soor [a derogatory Anglo-Indian word meaning 'pig' or 'worthless person'], when I order you to do a thing I expect it to be done at once.' The 'old soldier' continued: 'The blasted natives are getting cheekier every day. Not so many years ago I would have half killed that native, and if he had made a complaint and had marks to show, any decent Commanding Officer would have laughed at him and told him to clear off. Since old Curzon has been Viceroy things are different, you see.'[90] Indians were also seen as innately unreliable witnesses.

---

* Fae Dussart points out that much of the violence meted out by Britons against Indians, and subsequently unpunished, was by masters and mistresses against household servants. 'Physical chastisement of Indian servants was seen as more legitimate than that of British servants precisely because they were Indian. The opinion expressed in *The Pioneer* newspaper that "cuffs and stripes, and all kinds of corporeal mistreatment, are recognised in India by Indians as well as Europeans, as more in accordance with the natural order of things than such phenomena would be thought in Europe" was not unique among Anglo-Indians.'

Thomas Macaulay may have wanted to ensure that the European and the Indian were equal before the law in his codification, but he also maintained that 'what the horns are to the buffalo, what the paw is to the tiger, what the sting is to the bee, what beauty, according to the Old Greek song, is to woman, deceit is to the Bengali'. In 1831, Richard Clarke, Registrar at the Sadr Diwani Adalat (Court of Appeal) in Madras, informed a Parliamentary select committee that perjury prosecutions were quite frequent in Madras: 'A native will in general give his evidence rather with reference to the consequences of what he may say to his own interest, than from any regard to its truth or falsehood.' At the turn of the twentieth century, a belief in Indian mendacity was as strong as ever. As Charles Johnston observed in 1911 in the *Atlantic Monthly*: 'The dusky folk of Lower Bengal make imaginative witnesses.'[91]

The justification for the racism of Indian law changed over time: at one point it was posited as a demand for legal distinctions based on the constitutional rights of freeborn Englishmen; it was then replaced by an argument based on the assertion, essentially, that Indians didn't 'do' equality. But it's obvious what this was all about – it was all about white supremacy. Systemic, institutional racism. In 1907, the Indian nationalist Bal Gangadhar Tilak stated, 'The goddess of British Justice, though blind, is able to distinguish unmistakably black from white.' Indeed, white violence was regularly accompanied by base racial abuse. One Private Frank Richards recorded in his memoir that when the barracks' punkhawallah took a momentary break from pulling the fan, a soldier would shout, 'you black bastard, or I'll come out and kick hell out of you.' It was common for the British in the years following the 1857 Rebellion, whatever their class, to call Indians 'blacks' and 'niggers'. In 1874, the *Hindoo Patriot* carried a report of the trial of a planter called George Meares – who had tied a postal runner to a post and beaten him to death – bearing the headline 'The Saheb and the Nigger'. The Viceroy Lord Ripon himself declared that one of the main problems facing the government was the ever expanding population of Europeans in India, with their unassailable sense of superiority over the natives and their ' "damned nigger" style of conversation'.[92]

Racial discrimination before the law was repeatedly and consistently observed as a fact of life by Indian newspapers at the time. An editorial in the *Vrittanta Chintamony* in July 1892 asked what was so special about this much extolled system of British justice, as 'Englishmen now grind down the natives in the same way as the Brahmins did the other classes in former days. If Englishmen commit any crimes, their deeds are not regarded as criminal, while the same deeds performed by others become serious crimes.' A decade later, things hadn't improved: in March 1903, a European soldier who killed an Indian police constable at the Delhi Durbar, through stoning, was punished with just nine weeks of imprisonment, but then appealed and his sentence was quashed altogether. Reporting on the case, the Bangalore newspaper *Surodaya Prakasika* remarked acerbically: 'Really it seems to be no crime to kill a Hindu.' In 1893, *The Record of Criminal Cases as Between Europeans and Natives for the Last Sixty Years* was published at the urging of the recently formed Indian National Congress. The report's author, Ram Gopal Sanyal, had gathered 'cart-loads of newspaper writing' during research for what he originally pictured as a ten-volume series on the subject.[93] Yet, as even the Viceroy Lord Curzon remarked, the 'cart-loads' of newspaper reports Sanyal looked through for his book did not reflect the true scale of incidents of white violence in India.

Many white Britons also remarked upon the racial inequality of Indian justice. In 1894, the MP William Caine made a statement to the Commons about how 'the Administration of Criminal Justice in India is such as to bring it into contempt and render it a terror to Law-abiding people'. A pamphlet published in 1913 entitled *British Justice and Honesty: Addressed to the People of England and India* by Sir Walter Strickland opened with the line: 'The English in India and elsewhere boast of their even-handed justice . . . my personal experience is that this boast has no foundation whatever.' There followed examples of European atrocities such as: 'an Irish private soldier murdered a beautiful Burmese girl whom he was "in love" with and her mother, and then raped one or both of the still warm bodies'. In response, the British government banned the pamphlet. Meanwhile, in 1904, the former Assam Chief Commissioner Henry Cotton condemned the trials of British people accused of killing Indians as 'a judicial scandal',[94] and, in 1876, the Viceroy Lord Lytton had observed that 'Our greatest danger in India is from the whites, who with far less justification for it, have all the arrogance of the Jamaica Planters, or American Southerners, and, claiming absolute liberty to outrage in every way the feelings of a vast alien population, resent the slightest control on the part either of the Government at home or the Government in India.'[95]

Defenders of the British imperial legal mission might offer, in response to all this depressing evidence, examples of Indians obtaining justice under the British, when British people weren't involved. They might even, if they extended the canvas to the whole of empire, be able to produce some examples of non-white imperial subjects being treated equally before the law when white people were involved. But there is no getting over the fact that, when it came to Britain's largest colony, Indians were institutionally disadvantaged before the law compared to white people. And even if you acknowledge that the rule of law is impossible to achieve in an absolute way, British imperial law is revealed to be a catastrophe by the fact that the British tried so hard to introduce it in India and failed on their own terms. Men like Stephen would have been mortified to see how it all ended up. Indeed, many analysts trace not benign legal legacies in modern India to the British empire but legal inequality and dysfunction, from discriminatory treatment of the poor to extra-judicial executions.[96]

Furthermore, Pulitzer prize-winner Caroline Elkins asserts that the main political legacies of the British include emergency provisions which they pushed through on the eve of independence that could revoke the rule of law. 'As the 1950s progressed, the exceptional and temporary became the rule. Legally enabled emergency conditions beset colony after colony, where statutory martial law created police states aimed at quashing dissent and installing politically acceptable regimes that would facilitate Britain's interests.'[97] Intensifying these problems has been the fact that many post-colonial states such as India inherited colonial policing systems, which continued enforcing the law (or not) in colonial ways. 'It is hard to see that any significant change in police methods and attitudes occurred after independence,' write David Anderson and David Killingray.[98] 'Faced with a series of crises that threatened the unity and viability of the new nation-state . . . governments in New Delhi and the provinces shelved indefinitely any possibility of a radical overhaul of the police organisation they had inherited from the British.'*[99]

---

* Keally McBride makes an explicit connection between the brutality of colonial Indian police forces and the East India Company's efforts to raise ever more revenue, which perhaps provides an antecedent explanation for the dysfunction of India's modern-day policing. 'At the start of the nineteenth century, trade was decreasing,

In general, British people find it easy to look at former colonies and observe the existence of corruption and injustice. They find it harder to connect it to the dysfunction and unfairness that British imperialists baked into colonial legislation.[100] But there's a clear illustration of how dysfunction in the colonial era led to dysfunction in the modern age in the way the homophobia of section 377 has been enforced and policed badly in India from its implementation in the nineteenth-century empire right into the twenty-first century. In the nineteenth century there were different interpretations of what gay sex actually amounted to – the phrase 'carnal intercourse against the order of nature' being decidedly vague, and it proved almost impossible to catch people engaging in such 'carnal intercourse'.[101] Surreally, in one 1884 case the police cited the 'distortion of the orifice of the anus into the shape of a trumpet' as evidence. After independence, in the twentieth century, the Indian police, unable to bring about successful prosecutions, became known for blackmailing gay men for money or sexual favours and employing crude entrapment techniques.

In 2001, local police raided Kiran's employer, the Naz Foundation (its Lucknow branch), and arrested activists under section 377, claiming that they were 'promoting homosexuality'. Incredibly, they were held in custody for nearly fifty days. In 2006, also in Lucknow, Indian police put up fake profiles on gay dating websites and arrested four people under section 377. The resulting press coverage, which identified the men and even published the name of the wife of one of them (and identified where she worked), led to one man being fired as a school administrator and another having to leave the city. In 2018, when gay sex was decriminalized, another LGBT group, the Humsafar Trust, reported that its crisis team in Mumbai had attended to eighteen cases in two years of gay men who were being blackmailed by people, including the police.[102] I see for myself, during my visit to Naz, and through

---

and the administrative needs of the Company were increasing,' she writes. 'Revenue needed to be raised from the peasant population, the equivalent of drawing blood from a stone. Physical coercion was the surest way of accomplishing this . . . The only lining in this storm cloud is that the methods of torture for revenue extraction were more mild than those used in extracting confessions. After all, the future working and tax-paying capacity of the peasant needed to be secured, not jeopardized.' In the House of Lords on 14 April 1856, the Earl of Albemarle expressed horror at the methods of torture that had been detailed in a report.

conversations with its employees, what fearing the law and its enforcers can do to your sense of security and self-esteem. And the 2021 World Justice Project (WJP) Rule of Law Index, an annual series measuring the rule of law based on the experiences and perceptions of the general public and in-country legal practitioners and experts worldwide, suggests Naz are not alone. It put India at 79th out of 139 countries, ranking it poorly in terms of corruption (ranked 95th out of 139), fundamental rights (93rd), order and security (121st), civil justice (110th) and criminal justice (86th).[103] Frankly, citing Indian justice as a great imperial legacy, and suggesting it's symptomatic of wider imperial achievements, is a pretty weak boast.

# 6. The Colour Line

The enervating culture war on empire in Britain has created the idea that decolonizing curriculums will, by definition, involve the erasure of the great texts of Western culture; but, as I tried to explain in relation to Delhi, decolonization can only ever be tokenistic, and it needn't require all the classics to be withdrawn. The history class I would have loved, putting the work of V. S. Naipaul and Derek Walcott into the context of indentured labour, need have taken only a morning or two at university, and a broader course about empire could have been spread over a term of weekly classes. And, trust me, a dozen classes on Chaucer or John Milton could have been sacrificed from my three-year degree course without damaging the sense it left with me of the traditional English literary canon. Equally, space could easily have been made ear-

lucation, perhaps at the expense of the fortnight we
e Ten Commandments by heart, or those hundreds of
irs of hymn practice, to boost our self-esteem as non-
d teach us something about the complicated history of
turalism and race through the achievements of notable
of colour.

ves, there was a week or two of Martin Luther King in history (racism being presented as something that happened in America, even though one-time local MP Enoch Powell had lived about 100 yards from our school gates). There was some time spent on slavery and abolition (although slavery, like racism, was presented as essentially a US phenomenon, with millions of nameless enslaved victims, and the remarkable former black slaves who helped achieve abolition didn't get a look-in). But otherwise, on top of the complete absence of teachers of colour during my entire education, the author of every book we read, every historical figure we came across, was white. I wish we had been taught about Ira Aldridge, the remarkable African American actor, playwright and theatre manager who found international fame playing Shakespearean roles in the early nineteenth century. I wish I'd been told about the black Georgian, Francis Barber, Dr Johnson's servant and heir.[1] Born enslaved on a Jamaican sugar plantation and brought to England by his owner, Barber was ten years old when he first joined Samuel Johnson's household in 1752, and in later years acted as Johnson's assistant in revising his famous *Dictionary of the English Language*. When Barber married a white woman, Elizabeth, she too joined the house (the couple had four children) and on Johnson's death, in 1784, Barber was bequeathed the great man's books and papers, and a gold watch; moreover, to the astonishment of London society, Johnson had made him his residual heir. Barber moved from London to Johnson's native city of Lichfield, attempted to set up a school there – he was possibly the first black schoolmaster in Britain – and remained a subject of curiosity until his death in 1801.*[2]

And, more than anything else, I wish I'd been made aware of W. E. B. Du Bois, a man not well known outside academic circles. The great-great-grandson of an enslaved person born in West Africa in the eighteenth century, Du Bois became an American sociologist, historian, editor, novelist and civil rights activist. He was a man who, according to the *Encyclopaedia Britannica*,[3] ultimately became 'the most important Black protest leader in the United States during the first half of the 20th century', who penned a collection of essays, *The Souls of Black Folk* (1903), which became a 'landmark of African American literature', and who was a key figure in Pan Africanism, 'the belief that all people of African descent had common interests and should work together in the struggle for their freedom'. At Harvard, where he paid his way through four years of study with money from summer jobs, an inheritance, fellowships and loans from friends, Du Bois became, in 1895, the first African American to earn a doctorate. He was one of the founders of the National Association for the Advancement of Colored People (NAACP), the civil rights organization established in 1909 that still fights the fight today. He founded and edited *The Crisis*, the NAACP's

---

* In 1787, there was much excitement when the newspapers announced the publication of a biography of Johnson by Francis Barber – finally, the famous companion reveals all! However, it turned out that a crucial comma had been omitted from the advertisement – on purpose – and it should have read *Francis, Barber*. The book was actually written by Johnson's barber, who was also called Francis, and offered little more than fifty pages of scatological jokes.

pioneering magazine, from 1910 to 1934.*[4] Concerned that the text-books used by African American children ignored black culture and undermined African self-esteem, he wrote the first English-language general history of black Africans, *The Negro*, and created a monthly children's magazine called *The Brownies' Book*. This was all more than a century before Black Lives Matter. But even extraordinary lives must come to an end and in 1963, while living in Ghana, where he was working on a proposed *Encyclopedia of the Negro*, an overview of the African diaspora, Du Bois died at the age of ninety-five. At the request of Kwame Nkrumah, the first President of Ghana, he was given a state funeral.

Learning about W. E. B. Du Bois' work might have helped us – a racially diverse student body in Wolverhampton, itself a racially diverse part of Britain sometimes compared in the national press to Harlem for its racial tensions – comprehend the prejudice around us. For he made countless original observations about race, some of which explain how racism worked in the British empire, and the most important of which came when he spoke at the First Pan-African Conference, held in London in July 1900.[5] The event, which took place at Westminster Town Hall, was organized by the Trinidadian barrister Henry Sylvester Williams and was attended by a small number of delegates from Africa, the West Indies, the US and the UK. These included the mixed-race composer Samuel Coleridge-Taylor[6] and Dadabhai Naoroji, the Indian scholar and politician who was one of the founder members of the Indian National Congress and the first Asian to become an MP (representing Finsbury Central in 1892–5). Du Bois' speech, 'To the Nations of the World', was addressed to European leaders, entreating them to repel racism and to grant self-governance to colonies in Africa and the West Indies. The address included Du Bois' observation that 'the problem of the twentieth century is the problem of the colour line'.[7]

Du Bois returned to the theme of the 'colour line' repeatedly, not

---

* The debut issue cited a letter printed in the *Baltimore Sun* in which the writer opined upon the humiliation of having to live next door to a black person and, in his editorials, Du Bois did not pull his punches, such as when describing the 'lynching barbecue' of a black man in Pennsylvania in 1911, where white men and women poured out of churches, 'poked the ashes' and shouted gleefully when they discovered 'a blackened tooth or mere portions of unrecognizable bones'.

least when, in his incendiary essay collection *The Souls of Black Folk*, he defined it as 'the relation of the darker to the lighter races of men in Asia and Africa, in America and the islands of the sea' and described the condition of the African American in terms of 'his two-ness – an American, a Negro; two souls, two thoughts, two unreconciled strivings'.[8] A few years later he explained that the 'colour line' was a consequence of the 'tendency of the great nations' to 'territorial, political and economic expansion', which invariably 'brought them into contact with darker peoples' and as a consequence of which the 'Negro problem in America is but a local phase of a world problem'.[9] Then, in an article published in the New York journal the *Independent*, entitled 'The Souls of White Folk', he observed a change sweeping the planet – 'the world, in a sudden emotional conversion, has discovered that it is white, and, by that token, wonderful!' Whiteness, he elaborated, involved 'the ownership of the earth forever and ever, Amen . . .'

> The discovery of personal whiteness among the world's peoples is a very modern thing, a nineteenth and twentieth century matter, indeed. The ancient world would have laughed at such a distinction. The middle ages regarded skin color with mild curiosity, and even up into the eighteenth century we were hammering our national manikins into one great Universal Man with fine frenzy which ignored color and race even more than birth. Today we have changed all that.[10]

What Du Bois was addressing here was the emergence of white supremacy as an international phenomenon. And in doing so he was making nothing less than one of the most important observations of the twentieth century – something the writer and civil rights activist St Clair Drake picked up on when he observed that 'it is hard for us, across the vast expanse of years, to appreciate the significance of those words or the courage it took to fling them forth'.[11] It raises an important question: how much can the British empire, in relation to which Du Bois, incidentally, had a complicated and changing position,*[12] be held

---

* Du Bois maintained in the early years of the century that the British were significantly better at resolving the issue of the 'colour line' than other Western nations, despite the obvious harms they imposed on their colonies in Africa and India. He wrote: 'Say what you will of England's rapacity and injustice, (and much can be said)

responsible for the spread of racism, the perpetuation of the colour line, across the planet? The colour line is a theme I've already tripped across in relation to every topic considered so far, whether in the form of the racism that came about as a result of the belief that abolition had failed,[13] the racially offensive common names given to plants, the East India Company taking an age to wake up to the merits of native tea plants in India because of disparaging attitudes it had adopted towards Indians, the imperial hunters for whom controlling wild animals was akin to controlling 'natives', the indentured labourers of Indian/Chinese/Pacific Island origin who were discouraged from settling in 'White Australia', European planters aggravating tensions between Creoles and Indians in Mauritius by labelling the former as lazy and irresponsible and the latter as docile and hardworking, African American James Ford being dragged off the stage by a white missionary at the Conference on the African Child for daring to criticize colonialism, and, of course, the deep institutional racism of the legal system in British India. It's no more possible to talk about the British empire without mentioning racism than it's possible to listen to Taylor Swift without being made to think about relationships.[14]

But looking at the theme more closely, after reading revelatory books and essays by academics including Alan Lester, Paul Gilroy, Marilyn Lake, Henry Reynolds and Duncan Bell,[15] I've a more precise answer to the question of what role British empire played in the spread of racism. Racism varies around the planet and often has explanations that are

---

the plain fact remains that no other European nation – and America least of all – has governed its alien subjects with half the wisdom and justice that England has.' He hoped the British would triumph in South Africa in 1900, saying that this would be 'a step towards the solution of the greater Negro problem'. He also admired the Brits' rule over Egypt. Our 'brown cousins' had been 'rescued from war and rapine, slavery and centuries of misrule', and they were 'to-day enjoying stable government under England and rapid industrial advancement'. But as the twentieth century progressed, Du Bois took against British exceptionalism. He eventually came to believe that the British empire was a model of European aggressiveness, created to subdue and exploit the 'darker nations' of the planet. Du Bois was a supporter of Japanese imperialism, which means that his legacy today is regarded very differently in parts of the world that suffered under Japanese rule, as opposed to the US, where he is now canonized, at least in academic circles.

specific to the locale, explanations which interact in all sorts of complex ways; and racism came in many different forms, from pseudo-scientific biological determinism to the 'civilizing mission' of philanthropists.[16] But the British empire was the single most significant incubator, refiner and propagator of white supremacy in the history of the planet. If anything, Dr Hilary Beckles understated Britain's role in the spread of racism when in relation to the slave plantations of Barbados he observed 'the moral descent of the British mind into the darkest pit of racial hatred', declared that 'the English actions . . . had the greatest impact upon the black race' and asserted that 'the English justification of slave trading was a large-scale literary and intellectual project'.[17] Most British imperialists were proudly racist and, as British imperialism peaked, prominent journalists and authors throughout British empire corresponded and conspired to spread ideas of white supremacy across the planet. Many of the proudly white supremacist politicians, thinkers and diplomats of British empire coalesced around various international racial 'crises' in the late nineteenth and early twentieth centuries, such as the South African War, Japan's bid to have a clause on racial equality featured in the Treaty of Versailles after the First World War and the question of what to do about the millions of Asians who ended up in 'white men's countries' as a result of indentured labour. In short, there was a concerted, direct, demonstrable effort by the elites of the British empire in the nineteenth and twentieth centuries to ensure that white people dominated people of colour all around the globe. To sustain the colour line.

Even so, I find myself hesitating to expand upon these points and very much wish this wasn't the story of race in British empire. Why? Because I know from bitter experience that Britain is not ready to acknowledge the racism of its imperial machine, let alone ready to accept that it incubated and propagated many of the racist notions that persist across the West into the twenty-first century. Do I really want to be the person who tells defensive Britons this news? The most intense anger I've encountered when talking about British empire has been when I observe the simple fact of imperial racism. The fact that Britain took on and beat the evil racist Germans in the Second World War, and the fact that we abolished slavery and then went around the world to ensure it was abolished elsewhere too, and, more recently, the fact that the Conservative Party has managed to appoint a brown person as Prime Minister, seem to have created the popular view that we are, and have always been, as a nation, beyond racism. It extends to not being able to accept that racism was as central to British imperialism, at least in the nineteenth and twentieth centuries, as blowing your horn is to Indian traffic. One Indian commentator surveying instances of racial violence may have remarked in the early twentieth century that 'Europeans have no regard for the lives of the Indians. They rank them with the beasts,'[18] the historian Catherine Hall may have observed that 'even if there were shifts and slippages between the cultural and biological connotations inherent in the concept of the colonial master race, the salience of race itself never slipped away',[19] the Calcutta barrister H. A. Branson may have warned fellow whites during the Ilbert Bill controversy of 1883 that 'we who have read history know what happened when the niggers of the Southern States of America got privileges over their white brethren',[20] Winston Churchill may have had several notorious outbursts of imperial racism when discussing colonial issues,*[21] race may have been so central to the British imperial mission that it even came up as a factor when deciding who could look after lighthouses in Ceylon,[22] and even the historians most nostalgic for British empire (from Niall Ferguson to Jan Morris) may record the vicious racism as fact, but God help you if you observe this fact in the 2020s. And God help you if, as Trevor Noah discovered recently, you make the observation and have the temerity to be foreign.[23]

So, before I explain how British empire spread racism across the planet, I feel the need to pre-empt some of the angry objections that will inevitably arise, in the tone they usually arise for me at events and on social media. The first furious objection being: IT WAS COLONIALISM *IN GENERAL*, AND NOT BRITISH EMPIRE *IN PARTICULAR*, THAT SAW WHITE PEOPLE INTERACTING WITH BROWN PEOPLE IN SIGNIFICANT NUMBERS AND DEVELOPING WHITE SUPREMACIST IDEAS. This is true. In a 1915 essay, Du Bois blamed the colour line on the international,

* 'I do not admit that the dog in the manger has the final right to the manger, even though he may have lain there for a very long time,' said Churchill in a testimony before the Peel Commission on Palestine, in 1937. 'I do not admit that right. I do not admit, for instance, that a great wrong has been done to the Red Indians of America, or the black people of Australia. I do not admit that a wrong has been done to those people by the fact that a stronger race, a higher grade race, or, at any rate, a more worldly-wise race, to put it that way, has come in and taken their place.'

multi-imperial Scramble for Africa, which saw multiple Western European powers invading, annexing, colonizing large parts of Africa between 1881 and 1914;[24] and Sean Elias observes in the entry for 'colour line' in 2015's *The Wiley Blackwell Encyclopedia of Race, Ethnicity, and Nationalism* that Du Bois documented how:

> an international colour line emerged with the advent of *European* colonialism [my emphasis] across the globe and formation of the global North–global South divide ('first world–third world') . . . the global colour line developed through whites' actions of exploiting, oppressing, and 'othering' (excluding and segregating) people of colour across the globe. British colonization of Indians and plundering of India, Belgians' oppression of the Congolese and exploitation of the Congo, Spanish and Portuguese decimation of inhabitants of southern America and appropriation of lands in present-day South and Central America, and Dutch conquest of South African peoples and land shaped the global colour line.[25]

But accepting that white supremacy was a consequence of European colonialism in general doesn't eliminate the disproportionate influence of the British empire. Given that the British empire became the largest empire in human history at a time when it was also at its most racist, and given that, in the words of Benedict Anderson, 'no one in their right mind would deny' the racist nature of the British empire,[26] it's entirely logical that British imperialism had disproportionate influence in shaping the way racial prejudice emerged across the planet. The British were not exempt as a result of others also being involved.

Another inevitable angry objection: 'RACE' AND 'RACISM' MEANT DIFFERENT THINGS IN THE PAST. This is also true. As Nancy Stepan explains in *The Idea of Race in Science*, the word 'race' had a large range of connotations in the eighteenth, nineteenth, twentieth centuries, referring to everything from cultural to religious, linguistic, ethnic and geographical groupings. 'At one time or another, the "Jews", the "Celts", the "Irish", the "Negro", the "Hottentots", the "Border-Scots", the "Chinese", the "Anglo-Saxons", the "Europeans", the "Mediterraneans", the "Teutons", the "Aryans", and the "Spanish Americans" were all "races" according to scientists . . . Even today [by which she meant 1982] scientists are not agreed on the meaning or usefulness of the term.'[27] This can make navigating historic discussion of 'race' difficult for citizens of the twenty-first century. The past is a world where 'Liberals' were often not liberal, where the 'Enlightened' were not enlightened, where abolitionists could be deeply racist,[28] where people in favour of slavery could be kind to individual black people,[29] and where a notorious imperialist like Lionel Curtis, who became known for pronouncing on colonial matters during the first half of the twentieth century, could condemn 'racialism' and do so apparently referring to divisions within the white population of South Africa.[30] But just because the meaning of 'race' was less fixed then, it doesn't mean racist behaviour didn't occur in the past in the way that we understand racist behaviour now.

A third inevitable objection/complaint: the late nineteenth and early twentieth centuries were a time when the U S A was becoming increasingly influential and its problems with race, even more profound than its problems with race in the present day, were what really shaped global racism. Or: IT'S AMERICA'S FAULT. And there's no doubt that America was even more screwed up about race a century or so ago than it is today. Part of what makes Du Bois so interesting was the brutally racist context of his life. It was a time of lynching: in 1916 *The Crisis* published a table of the 2,843 lynchings that occurred between 1885 and 1916.[31] Among the victims, in 1899, was one Sam Hose, who was tortured and killed by a mob of whites; when walking through Atlanta to discuss the lynching with newspaper editor Joel Chandler Harris, Du Bois heard that Hose's burned knuckles were on display in a grocery store window.[32] It was a time when blacks were excluded from employment at many federal agencies, barred from officer ranks in the army and generally discouraged from making the U S A their home. People of African ancestry did not have much joy with the immigration service.[33] It was a time of disenfranchisement: in the South, states passed new laws to strip voting rights from the majority of African Americans, an exclusion that was not remedied until the 1960s. It was an era of cruel racist stereotypes and race riots, such as those which broke out during the so-called Red Summer of 1919, in which over 300 African Americans were killed in more than thirty cities (it included a vicious attack in Elaine, Arkansas, in which at least 200 blacks were murdered).[34] And it was a time when, in 1915, *Birth of the Nation*, celebrating the Ku Klux Klan, was given a special screening at the White House, after which President Woodrow Wilson is said to have endorsed it with the words

'It's like writing history with lightning. My only regret is that it is all so terribly true.'[35]

Yet the widespread idea that racism is an American phenomenon which is always at risk of being imported into racism-free Britain is a myth.*[36] We must also keep in mind that the USA, as I've already argued, was an outgrowth of the British empire, and that racism in the USA was in many ways inextricably linked to racism in the British empire. Although the War of Independence is often perceived as an open rejection of colonialism which led to the creation of a fresh new nation, the Thirteen Colonies were in fact a clear stage of British imperialism. While it's true that the Puritans fled religious persecution in England for the New World, the institutions they established to advance capitalism, safeguard property rights, prevent the abuse of government power and so on were English. In Tom Holland's words from a recent edition of *The Rest Is History* podcast: 'The fascination both for English people and for Americans about the relationship between Britain and America is that America in a way is taking a path that Britain might have taken and vice versa. In so many ways the War of Independence is a Civil War.'[37] In truth, as the imperial historian Alan Lester explains, the British empire and the United States did follow the same course: the settler colonization of Australia, New Zealand, South Africa and, in particular, Canada echoed the westward expansion of the United States; the destiny of Native Americans, Aboriginal people, First Nations and others were intertwined, all of them persecuted by British colonists; all

* Concerns were expressed about how US troops might impose their segregationist practices when they first began to arrive in Britain during the Second World War in 1942. Oliver Harvey, Anthony Eden's personal secretary, submitted a letter after a War Cabinet meeting in which it was suggested that restrictions should apply on the entry of black troops into Britain. It said: 'It is rather a scandal that the Americans should export their internal [racial] problem. We don't want to see lynching begin in England. I can't bear the typical southern attitude towards the negroes. It is a great ulcer on the American civilisation and makes nonsense of half their claims.' The episode is regularly recounted by people keen to emphasize Britain's relative racial enlightenment, but, as Gary Younge observes, a colour bar existed across British empire *at the very same time.* Moreover, as Charlotte Lydia Riley explains, some British businesses went along with US segregation to keep white custom, a restaurant in an English port city barred African American troops, and a vicar's wife in Weston-super-Mare produced a six-point plan to avoid black GIs, including the suggestion that women cross the pavement to avoid them.

of them were subjected to the same residential school systems and reserve confinement, while the entire expansion effort was funded by networks and commodities transactions that linked the United States, settler colonies and Britain.[38]

In this way and others, the racism of British empire and America were inextricable. As George M. Fredrickson points out, the word 'segregation' spread across both South Africa and the American South around the same time, in the first decade of the twentieth century. It's possible that the term was appropriated by South African white nationalists from their American counterparts.[39] Fredrickson stresses that 'the two modes of legalized discrimination reveal some major differences in how they worked and in the functions they performed. Both, of course, were necessarily based on separatism; but the specific kinds of separation that were stressed and regarded as crucial for maintaining white privilege and furthering white interests were not the same.'[40] It's important, he adds at another point, that we do not simplify how ideas of white supremacy spread across and between these territories.

> I have not . . . found it possible to treat 'white supremacy' as a kind of seed planted by the first settlers that was destined to grow at a steady rate into a particular kind of tree. On the contrary, I have found it more plausible to regard it as a fluid, variable, and open-ended process. Major shifts in both societies in the forms of white dominance and the modes of consciousness associated with them bely any notion of a fixed set of attitudes and relationships. What justifies comparison, therefore, is not a primordial and predetermined aptitude for 'racism' common to American and South African whites, but rather the emergence of long-term, historically conditioned tendencies leading to more self-conscious and rigorously enforced forms of racial domination – trends that were similar in general direction but surprisingly variable in rate of development, ideological expression and institutional embodiment.[41]

It needs to be noted not only that the Enlightenment ideals which, counterintuitively, permitted the development of racism were a transatlantic phenomenon,[42] but also that the slavery in North America was supported by Britain, even after abolition. It's true that Britain finally abandoned the slave trade, with some northern English manufacturing employees even refusing to process cotton harvested by slaves,[43] but for centuries the UK and USA worked together to exploit black slaves. Consider Liverpool, which in the nineteenth century acquired 95 per cent of the raw materials at its docks from US plantations and was described by Karl Marx as 'waxed fat on the slave trade',[44] and which sided with the Confederates in the American Civil War (three of the city's four local newspapers were pro-Southern, and in 1864 a Confederate bazaar held there to support Southern prisoners of war was celebrated by the Liverpool *Daily Courier* as a 'triumphant success' for raising some £20,000).[45] When Manchester was the largest processor of cotton in the world, the American slave-holding South was its most significant supplier, as the world's largest producer of cotton,[46] the *Economist* estimating in 1861 that nearly 4 million out of 29 million British people in the north were dependent on the cotton trade 'for their daily bread',[47] and the African American abolitionist Sarah Parker Remond observing in 1859: 'When I walk through the streets of Manchester and meet load after load of cotton, I think of those 8,000 cotton plantations on which was grown, the 125 millions of dollars' worth of cotton which supply your market, and I remember that not one cent of that money ever reached the hands of the labourers.'[48] Moreover, Britain's racist imperialism inspired America's own racist imperialism. Kipling's famous poem 'The White Man's Burden' was penned as an exhortation to America to embrace the burden of empire as it took control of the Philippine Islands, just as Britain had colonized other parts of the world, while the future President Theodore Roosevelt remarked in a letter to a friend in 1899 that 'I believe in the expansion of great nations.' India had done lots for 'the English character. If we do our work well in the Philippines and the West Indies, it will do a great deal for our character.'[49]

More than a century later, we have the British Professor of Black Studies Kehinde Andrews arguing that:

> in the new age of empire, the United States has become the centre of modern colonial power. The country likes to present itself as a victim of British colonialism, which freed itself from tyranny and now looks to do the same for the rest of the world. But this is a delusional fantasy. The United States is in fact the most extreme expression of the racist world order. Not only does the United States have its own history (and present) of colonial possession but its entire existence is based on the logic of Western empire.[50]

Indeed, as Duncan Bell reports, between the end of the nineteenth century and the First World War, a transatlantic elite of influential scholars, journalists, politicians, businessmen and writers fantasized about the integration of the British empire and the United States, but non-white people were not included in the plans. 'People excluded from the embrace of whiteness were largely absent from the unionist discourse, except when they were figured as a problem or threat,' he writes. 'African Americans rarely appeared in fantasies of a future Anglo-racial polity, their supposed inferiority and political subordination accepted as a given. The indigenous populations of North America and the Pacific were assumed to be either irrelevant due to their relatively small numbers – or heading for eventual extinction, and thus not worth sustained discussion.'[51]

A fourth and final inevitable objection: British empire WAS OFFICIALLY NON-RACIST. This incontrovertible and admittedly disorientating attribute is reflected in the fact that when the leaders of Canada, the Cape Colony, Queensland, Tasmania, South Australia, New Zealand and other colonies gathered at the London Colonial Conference of 1897 to address 'certain Imperial questions',[52] Joseph Chamberlain, as Secretary of State for the Colonies, asked his audience to keep in mind the 'traditions of the Empire, which make no distinction in favour of, or against, race or colour'. It's reflected in the fact that during the later stages of the South African War at the turn of the century, which the British fought with the aim of uniting the British South African territories of Natal and the Cape Colony with the Boer-controlled republics, the British government condemned the discriminatory policies of the Boers.[53] It's reflected in the fact that when the British finally won this war (with the aid of controversial strategies such as putting civilians into concentration camps), and a few years later when the House of Commons debated the new Union of South Africa, a model devised solely by white South African politicians which had segregationist policies that laid the foundations for apartheid,[54] the Liberal MP Ellis Ellis-Griffith proclaimed that the proposed colour bar was 'contrary to all the proceedings and all the traditions of the Empire'.[55] And it's reflected in the fact that, as a young man, no less an individual than Mahatma Gandhi believed in some of the bombastic claims we heard being made in the last chapter about the legal equality of British imperial subjects.[56] Between 1893 and 1914, Gandhi lived and worked in South Africa (and is thought to have served in the disastrous Battle of

Spion Kop as a British stretcher bearer), campaigning for the rights of the country's Indian population, and was a fervent advocate of the British empire and the common law, believing that the British legal system was blind when it came to matters of race.

However, most of us, even those of us who left school with poor knowledge of British imperial history, know that Gandhi's views changed on a whole bunch of issues during his lifetime, to such a degree that he eventually became the British empire's single most effective opponent. And there are countless other illustrations of how British empire became white supremacist. There was the racial violence. The way the empire became divided between 'white men's countries' and brown people's. The way white colonies were allowed to pursue racist policies towards the end of the nineteenth century when it came to issues such as immigration and civil rights. The way the Colonial Office used tactics of 'delay and duplicity' in order to permit racist policies in 'white men's colonies'.[57] There was also the betrayal of Africans when, despite the alarm of Liberal politicians such as Ellis-Griffith, Britain allowed segregationist policies in the Union of South Africa, the last Prime Minister of the Cape Colony J. X. Merriman observing that the imperial authorities had managed 'to reconcile the whites over the body of the blacks'.[58]

The racism was evident in the way Sir Edward Grey, the Liberal MP and long-serving Foreign Secretary, and the colonial bigwig Lord Elgin[59] privately expressed their feelings that the 'doctrine of the equality of man' could not apply to matters of empire. It was evident in the way those who spoke out in favour of racial equality were referred to derogatorily as 'sentimentalists'. It was evident in the way the Secretary of State for India, John Morley, in 1907 confided to Austen Chamberlain (son of Joseph Chamberlain, the Colonial Secretary, and half-brother to the more famous Neville) that he didn't believe Indians should occupy the senior levels of the Indian civil service, a sentiment Chamberlain agreed with, believing the Raj's status in India relied on the English being seen as the ruling race ('We could not admit equality'). It was evident in the claim, following the anti-immigration Vancouver riots of the early twentieth century, uttered by the colonial administrator Alfred Milner before an audience in Ottawa that although he was against race discrimination he was nonetheless a 'British Race Patriot', who believed in the 'fundamental . . .

importance of the racial bond'.[60] And it was evident in the French government asking the British Foreign Office in 1902 how the Japanese should be classified when it came to race – as white or non-white? The answer was non-white, which Japan considered a terrible injustice.[61]

If this were any other theme, and any other argument, I'd normally consider all of this to be enough evidence. But given that I am bombarded every few weeks with a stream of messages on social media suggesting I am, for some reason, making up this history of racism, and given that, at the time of writing, the British book charts are graced with a book which mitigates and minimizes the racism of British empire,[62] I feel the need to continue. And there's more proof to be found in the way white supremacist politicians, colonies and institutions across British empire (and the USA, which I include for its inextricability from British imperialism) corresponded and rallied over pan-imperial racial 'crises'. Some of this correspondence took place in plain sight through newspapers. Publications across the empire propounded racist ideas in the way newspapers today might lobby for policies like Brexit or tax reform. So, in yet another illustration of how abolition fuelled an increase in racism, we had a Liverpool correspondent for the *Sydney Morning Herald* in 1835 excitedly informing the colonists in what was then New South Wales that abolition had not worked out: that West Indian former slaves were not bothering to work at all since the constraints on their freedom had been 'removed', and West Indies goods were, as a result, no longer available in Britain.[63] We had Wellington's *Evening Post* in New Zealand complaining in 1905, after the Canadian province of British Columbia had been blocked by Canada's capital, Ottawa, from implementing immigration restrictions,[64] that 'British Columbia is not to be allowed to shape its destiny as a white man's country, because the exigencies of British policy in the Far East demand that the white man and the yellow man shall lie down together on equal terms.'[65] When a debate erupted in the USA about the possibility of deporting black slaves, one Australian newspaper opined about the USA's 'race problem', writing, 'whether the white man and the negro can live in harmony under conditions of equality may be doubted', while Melbourne's the *Age* proclaimed in 1890: 'The latest solution of the race problem has been propounded ... They would remove the Blacks to Africa, which was provided for the negro as certainly as the Garden of Eden was prepared for Adam and Eve.'[66]

The nineteenth century also saw the emergence of new settler presses publishing newspapers on the edges of empire, which made it their mission to take on the humanitarian movement that had triumphed as a consequence of abolition (and would later have influence on the demise of indenture) and to propound white supremacy. By the mid-1830s, newspapers could be sent between Britain and the colonies exempt from postage duty, and the colonial papers freely printed extracts from each other as well as from the major urban publications. Readers in Britain could subscribe directly to colonial papers, and established organs such as *The Times* often ran stories from these small settler papers, as well as providing them with a source of content. Settler newspapers joined missionaries' reports, Parliamentary debates and commissions of inquiry as 'a channel through which the metropolitan reading public created an imagined geography of empire'. This new interest caught the eye of the *Sydney Morning Herald*, which saw the colonial newspapers as indicative of a phenomenon: a distinctly British middle-class culture being manufactured on the outskirts of the ever expanding empire. Its editor wrote in March 1838: 'A few years ago scarcely a newspaper was to be seen in the Southern hemisphere: now they abound, as in Europe.'★[67]

White supremacists also propagated racism through books, published across, and discussed within, the British empire. British historians who were widely read across empire in the middle of the nineteenth century were prone to viewing history through a racial lens, with the likes of Thomas Arnold, E. A. Freeman and Thomas Carlyle asserting that the Anglo-Saxons were destined to rule the world.†[68] And then there was

---

★ The frequently racist tone of these newspapers is captured in an item in an 1863 edition of the New Zealand paper the *Southern Cross*, which complained that 'we have conceded them [Maoris] rights and privileges which nature has refused to ratify . . . and we now experience their hatred of intelligence and order . . . The [native] is now known to us as what he is, and not as missionaries and philanthropists were willing to believe him . . . a man ignorant and savage, loving darkness and anarchy; hating light and order; a man of fierce, and ungoverned passions, bloodthirsty, cruel, ungrateful, treacherous.' Elsewhere, we have the *Sydney Morning Herald* proclaiming – on the treatment of Xhosa in the Cape in January 1838 – that 'the only question at issue was the extermination (should it be found necessary) of murderous savages, and the protection of British subjects, to whom inducements to settle had been held out'.

† Freeman wrote about feeling that he belonged in America but couldn't extend warmth to people of colour. 'The really queer thing is the niggers who swarm here;

the British historian (and prominent jurist, politician and statesman, who served in the Cabinet and also as Ambassador to Washington) James Bryce, whose three-volume survey of US political and social institutions, *The American Commonwealth*, first published in 1888, was instrumental in 'educating' English-speaking readers across the world about what he saw as the 'negro problem' that resulted from Radical Reconstruction, the failed attempt at multiracial democracy following the Civil War.[69] He continued, throughout his life, to proclaim on the supposed lessons of this ill-fated episode in history, referring to 'the risks a democracy runs when the suffrage is granted to a large mass of half-civilized men', and *The American Commonwealth*, which counted Theodore Roosevelt among its proofreaders, began to be treated as a work of 'Biblical authority'.[70] In later revised editions of the book, Bryce's assessment of the 'problem' darkened further, his sympathy deepening for the white southerners having to deal with it. The negro was akin to a child: 'His intelligence is rather quick than solid, and though not wanting in a sort of shrewdness, he shows the childishness as well as lack of self-control which belongs to primitive peoples.'[71] And when, in the 1880s, there was debate over whether black Americans should be kicked out of the country altogether, Bryce joined in, describing them as 'an alien element, unabsorbed and unabsorbable'.[72] Leaning on 'science' to argue that races deemed to be less than fully evolved could not expect to have full rights in a democracy, Bryce laid the template for an argument that echoed in academic and popular literature for decades.[73] On the subject of 'retransportation', he highlighted two 'fatal objections' to the scheme: 'One is that they will not go; the other is that the whites cannot afford to let them go.'[74] After all, who else would do the dirty, low-paid work?

Then there was Charles Pearson, a Liberal politician in the

---

my Aryan prejudices go against them, specially when they rebuke one and order one about. And the women and children are yet stranger than the men. Are you sure they are men? I find it hard to feel that they are men acting seriously: tis . . . easier to believe that they are big monkeys dressed up for a game.' Freeman also came across Indians while in the US ('less repulsive than niggers, but dumpy figures with dull faces') and noted the demand on the West Coast for immigration restrictions on the Chinese – 'Only the natural instinct of any decent nation to get rid of filthy strangers.'

south-eastern Australian colony of Victoria who in 1893 published a book called *National Life and Character: A Forecast* which predicted that:

> The day will come, and perhaps is not far distant, when the European observer will look round to see the globe girdled with a continuous zone of the black and yellow races, no longer too weak for aggression or under tutelage, but independent, or practically so, in government, monopolising the trade of their own regions, and circumscribing the industry of the Europeans . . . represented by fleets in the European seas, invited to international conferences and welcomed as allies in the quarrels of the civilised world . . . We shall wake to find ourselves elbowed and hustled, and perhaps even thrust aside by peoples whom we looked down upon as servile and thought of as bound always to minister to our needs. The solitary consolation will be that the changes have been inevitable.[75]

In short, Pearson predicted, perceptively, the end of colonialism and imagined a new world that would emerge from its ruins, a world in which the white man would no longer dominate. Colonized people would take control of their lives and their countries, mastering trade, commerce and defence to become equal and respected players on the international stage. Written at the greatest possible distance from Europe, Pearson's book challenged the prevailing imperial line, and while it became an international bestseller and made its author famous, it incensed many, including the Melbourne writer W. H. Fitchett, who, in the Australian edition of the *Review of Reviews*, labelled Pearson a traitor to his race. He ridiculed the 'dyspeptic melancholy' Englishman who refused to admit the 'superiority' of the Anglo-Saxon. Having overlooked his 'pride of race', Pearson expected his fellow white men, fumed Fitchett, 'to vanish before a procession of coffee-coloured, yellow-tinted or black-skinned races'.[76]

Imperial white supremacy also found an expression through those Anglo-world fantasies that hoped for a union between Britain and the United States of America. As Duncan Bell informs us, the discourse of Anglo-Saxonism, imagining Britain, the US and the settler colonies as composed largely of a single superior racial group, was widespread.[77] At the same time, in the period between the late nineteenth century and the First World War, the idea of *formal* union between Britain and the

US was taken up by a transatlantic group of the great and the good, such as the likes of the Scottish-American industrialist and philanthropist Andrew Carnegie, the British editor and journalist W. T. Stead, the colonialist Cecil J. Rhodes and the writer H. G. Wells, who pressed for unification of the two powers. Overcoming what Bell calls 'the inconvenient fact that the United States had waged a war of independence against British rule' and that 'Anglophobia was a prominent feature of American political culture throughout the nineteenth century',[78] these fantasies saw the likes of Theodore Roosevelt proclaiming to his friends and followers that he approved of the idea of consolidating the relationship between the two nations he considered the principal residences of the most 'civilized' race on earth. 'It must always be kept in mind', he wrote in *The Naval War of 1812*, his first book, published at the age of twenty-three, nineteen years before he was elected President, 'that the Americans and the British are two substantially similar branches of the great English race, which both before and after their separation have assimilated and made Englishmen of many other peoples.' The Sherlock Holmes author Arthur Conan Doyle dedicated his 1891 novel *The White Company* to the 'hope of the future, the reunion of the English-speaking races',[79] and, writing to W. T. Stead in 1898, further expanded on the theme, saying that he wanted 'a restoration of racial patriotism, a reunion of sympathies, an earnest endeavour to clear away prejudices and to see things from a common point of view'.[80]

In Benjamin Rush Davenport's 1898 novel entitled *Anglo-Saxons Onward!* the US headed a 'semi-alliance' of the Anglo-Saxon nations which first destroyed the Spanish empire and then took over the world, while Stanley Waterloo's *Armageddon: A Tale of Love, War, and Invention*, published the same year, similarly imagined America winning a war with Spain before the nineteenth century 'flickered out in something like racial warfare'. Amid all the international violence, the Americans and the British realized their kinship: 'the idea of an Anglo-Saxon alliance had grown and broadened'.[81] And then there was H. G. Wells, who fantasized about the merging of the British colonial empire with that of the United States. 'A great federation of white English-speaking peoples', he claimed in 1901, was both likely and desirable during the coming decades.[82] On the face of it, to people from the twenty-first century, this vision doesn't seem to be a racial one: Wells, in an explicit and fervent rejection of racial theorizing that was unusual at the time, openly condemned the era's racial conjecture, expressing unease in 1905 over the 'delirium about race and the racial struggle' that he saw in public discourse. A couple of years later, he wrote: 'I am convinced myself that there is no more evil thing in this present world than Race Prejudice; none at all.' But, in one of those contradictions that make you want to lie down in exhaustion when you first happen across them, because you know so much work will be required to make sense of them, he didn't let this apparent anti-racism get in the way of eugenicist tendencies.[83] In his bestselling non-fiction work *Anticipations of the Reaction of Mechanical and Scientific Progress upon Human Life and Thought*, better known as *Anticipations* (1901), which contained his ideas of what the world would be like a hundred years later, in the year 2000, he asserted that 'whole masses of human population are, as a whole, inferior in their claim upon the future to other masses'. For the good of society – and themselves – these inferiors should be eradicated. Although ostensibly this 'social hygiene' was not racialized, in practice it would be: Wells predicted that while some 'white and yellow people' would be among those killed, the majority would be from 'the black and brown races'. In the most bewildering paradox in this field of paradoxes, even as Wells positions himself as an anti-racist, he seemingly advocates the wiping out of 'inferior' races, prompting Duncan Bell to observe that 'even as he denied the validity of group classification, Wells rearticulated a politics of racial domination'.[84]

Finally, and most importantly, white supremacists in British empire and beyond, into America, also rallied around particular racial 'crises', in a way that is not dissimilar to how they coalesce around international racial crises today, such as the killing of George Floyd, or Prince Harry's accusations of racism within the British royal family (which he has since withdrawn). We might think of the twenty-first century as being a time when we are uniquely obsessed with race, and a time when social media enables racists from across the planet to confer with one another, but trans-imperial conversations about race were regularly triggered by controversies in the nineteenth and twentieth centuries. White supremacists came together, for instance, around the emergence of the literacy test as a way of keeping brown people out of 'white countries'.[85] Mississippi led the way in 1890, South Africa's Cape Colony copied the policy two years later, Joseph Chamberlain, as Colonial Secretary, promoted it as an instrument by which to effect racial exclusion in the colonies in 1897,

Australia proposed to require all immigrants to pass a dictation test in a 'European language' in 1901, and New Zealand introduced a dictation test of a hundred words in English in 1907. The 'Liberals' of the age were also at it: in 1892, J. X. Merriman, the leader of the Cape Colony in South Africa, wrote to the writer James Bryce: 'I have just been reading your article in the *North American Review* on the position of the Negro in the United States . . . The best solution of the difficulties will probably be found in the same remedy that you suggest for the Southern States – viz by an educational test . . . My object in troubling you is to ask you where I can find out how the plan works.'[86]

The white supremacists of empire also colluded and coalesced over the 'problem' of Asian immigration into 'white men's' countries. The admittance of Indian indentured labour to Mauritius, Fiji, Natal and parts of the Caribbean, Chinese and Japanese migration to Britain's colonies in the Pacific, the movement of Melanesian workers to Queensland, had turned the race 'question' into a global one. In the United States, American miners responded with vigilante action to repel the intruders,[87] and in 1896 the South African city of Durban took on the alien onslaught, in this case Indian indentured workers for sugar plantations rather than Chinese goldminers, with the establishment of the European Protection Association[88] whose objective was to 'take all steps that may be found advisable for limiting the number of Indians introduced into the colony'. It explicitly aimed to 'have the Australian laws on immigration made applicable to Natal' and then, a few weeks later, the Colonial Patriotic Union was formed in the city with the goal of halting 'the further influx of free Asiatics into the country'; again, the organization looked to Australia as an example, arguing in a petition that 'the older and richer British colonies of Australia and New Zealand have found that this class of immigrant is detrimental to the best interests of the inhabitants and have passed laws [which have] as . . . their object the total exclusion of Asiatics'. Meanwhile, Canada followed New Zealand in 1923, with the Canadian politician A. W. Neill spending a good chunk of a Parliamentary speech reporting on New Zealand's proudly racist immigration legislation which had been designed, according to one politician, to keep both white and Asian races 'pure' and which was described by one commentator as 'one of the most arbitrary and reactionary measures ever introduced in a British community'.[89]

White supremacists across empire and beyond also rallied and colluded when Japan requested, and very nearly succeeded in getting, a clause included in the 1919 Treaty of Versailles that asserted the equality of all nations, regardless of race.[90] We spent a whole term at school studying the Treaty, but, needless to say, we were not introduced to one of the most fascinating aspects of it. Namely, the efforts made by Japan to consolidate its power in the wake of its success in the 1905 Russo-Japanese War and participation with the Allies during the First World War, by seeking to insert a statement about racial equality into the treaty's preamble. In doing so, Japan was not gunning for universal suffrage, nor was it interested in, say, improving the lot of black Americans; rather, it wished for Japanese immigrants to the US to be on equal terms with white European immigrants. But this was too much for Australia. The White Australia Policy, established by the British dominion in 1901, curtailed non-white immigration, and in Paris in 1919 the Australian Prime Minister William 'Billy' Hughes pressed any participants who would listen into opposing the proposed addition to the treaty. The British delegation, headed by Lord Robert Cecil and A. J. Balfour, followed suit, and between them the white men of the UK, US, Australia, New Zealand, South Africa and Canada blocked Japan's attempt to include a racial equality clause in the treaty. Justifying his stance, Balfour declared that he did not agree with the notion that 'all men are created equal'.[91] Meanwhile, 'Billy' Hughes, an unabashed white supremacist, delightedly addressed the federal Parliament: 'White Australia is yours . . . Here it is, at least as safe as it was on the day when it was first adopted by this Parliament.'[92]

I could go on, and in the face of inevitable resistance, and President Biden's recent pronouncement that white supremacy is 'the most dangerous terrorist threat to our homeland',[93] and the British Post Office's recent admission that a racist term from the British colonial era – 'negroid types' – was directed at suspects in a scandal in which more than 700 former Post Office staff were wrongly prosecuted for theft and false accounting,[94] will do so for a little longer. White supremacists across empire also rallied, colluded and conspired over the issue of White New Zealand and over the South African War. They provided support for one another on the occasion of various 'race riots', which almost always seemed to involve a brown community being attacked first. There was outspoken collusion at international conferences, over U S President Roosevelt's attempt to intimidate Japan by sending the United States fleet on a tour of the Pacific Ocean ('It is delightful to us to say', wrote an Australian journalist, W. R. Charlton, 'whether it be delusion, half-truth or the truth-absolute – that the Americans are our kinsmen, blood of our blood, bone of our bone, and one with us in our ideals of the brotherhood of man'),[95] and when people worried out loud that the British were losing influence when it came to white men★[96] (the *Wellington Post* declared the United States to be 'the champion of white ascendancy in the Pacific' as it acted in support of 'the ideals of Australia and New Zealand far better than Britain').[97] And as all of this was happening, it needs to be remembered that the British were coming up with all sorts of absurd racial theories about martial and non-martial races,[98] which persist in the twenty-first century even among the groups who were theorized about, and all sorts of race science was emerging.[99] Race science of a distinctly British flavour. As Nancy Stepan explains, 'American racial science was largely derivative of British science.'[100] Many of the scientific hypotheses influencing the study of race, not least eugenics and those bastardizing Darwin's theory of evolution (Darwin himself was avowedly anti-slavery and anti-racist), began in Britain and underwent significant development there.

These eugenic theories would eventually be discredited, not least because of their grotesque implementation in Nazi Germany. But also because of another global legacy of British imperialism: anti-racism. British empire played a leading role in spreading racism across the planet, but it also inspired a massive international movement in anti-racism. Just as slavery inspired the campaign for abolition, which, in turn, laid the groundwork for a bunch of progressive movements in Britain including trade unionism and Chartism, trans-imperial racism was fought at every stage. Take the White Australia policy. As Lake and

---

★ In his 1908 paper 'Suggestions as to Coloured Immigration into the Self-Governing Dominions', prepared for the Colonial Office, Charles Lucas observed that this was 'a question second to none in difficulty and importance' for the empire. 'There is also to my mind a constant and serious danger that, if we do not take the initiative, the United States may stand out on and through this question as the leaders of the English-speaking peoples in the Pacific as against the coloured races. This is not my own view alone.'

Reynolds explain, it might have had wide support across party and gender lines, but it was also opposed across party and gender lines: by men and women, white and non-white, left-wing and right-wing.[101] Every writer propounding white supremacy seems to have faced criticism, not least the politician-historian James Bryce, who, after he had endorsed segregation, attracted these words in a letter from Wendell Phillips Garrison, the prominent American author and editor (and member of a famous radical/abolitionist/anti-imperialist family): 'I fear you will comfort both our Imperialists and the lynchers, for the latter have caste for their stronghold, and it seems to me you justify caste.'[102]

Anti-Asian policies everywhere, whether it was governments discriminating against the Indian, the Chinese or the Japanese, were furiously opposed wherever they emerged. The Canadian publication the *Free Hindusthan*[103] complained after the Vancouver riots in 1908, for instance, that 'We are treated worse than cats and dogs of Englishmen in the British Colonies. The gate of the Commonwealth of Australia, a British colony is barred against the natives of India. We are getting worse treatment in the South African colonies than we used to get from the hands of the Boer republics.'[104] In the early twentieth century British intelligence got wind of the activities of the secretive, ultra-nationalist Black Dragon Society in Japan and its publication *The General Outlook in Asia*, which championed 'an uncompromisingly hostile attitude towards the white races'.[105] Some academics maintain that Japanese anger about the way they were classified racially ultimately led to Pearl Harbor.[106] And as we heard earlier, the white supremacy of the settler press was actually a reaction to the humanitarianism that had emerged from the successful campaign to abolish slavery around the planet.[107] The new newspapers were an attempt to take on the humanitarianism propounded by the missionary press and the Parliamentary Select Committee on Aborigines, which warned in 1837 that the redemption that the British had earned by abolishing slavery was now at risk thanks to their seizing of indigenous people's land and property. 'Too often their territory has been usurped; their property seized; their numbers diminished; their character debased.'[108]

There was also the intense resistance by black people to white supremacy or what Du Bois called the 'religion of whiteness'.[109] One of the most formidable critics of racial ideology was T. Thomas Fortune, a writer, editor and founder of the short-lived Afro American League

(1887–9), who published diatribes against white supremacy. The campaigner and philosopher Anna Julia Cooper, in her 1892 book *A Voice from the South: By a Black Woman of the South*, argued for the vital role of African American women in the campaign of racial emancipation: because they had so much experience of oppression, she declared, they had particular insights into how to confront it. One of the most illustrious black journalists of the time, John Edward Bruce, who wrote under the pen-name 'Bruce Grit', delivered a famous speech in 1883 in Washington entitled 'Is This Our Country?' in which he declared: 'Our Country! Oh, what a mockery, what a farce! What a delusion! What a lie! . . . It will never be our country until every living being of every race and nationality within its vast borders is secure in his or her civil and political rights.'[110]

Meanwhile, Theophilus E. Samuel Scholes, a black Jamaican physician, Christian minister, author and Baptist missionary to the Congo and the Gold Coast, advocated complete social and political equality between Europeans and Africans. In the splendidly titled *Glimpses of the Ages, or the 'Superior' and 'Inferior' Races, So-Called, Discussed in the Light of Science and History* (1905–8), he debunked the idea that there were any biological differences between black and white people. He demonstrated his point with the ever growing list of eminent black intellectuals in the US, who showed that non-white people made progress even under extremely adverse conditions, and challenged a central ideology of racial supremacy, claiming that it was actually the black Africans of ancient Egypt who founded Western civilization rather than the Greeks or Romans. Du Bois employed this argument about Egypt too, and thinking about him again, and his foresight not only in observing the international nature of white supremacy, but in spotting that the 'religion of whiteness' would be crushed by the weight of its intellectual and political failings ('the magic of the word "white" is already broken', he wrote, arguing that its currency would decline after the Japanese defeated the Russians in 1905), I realize that presenting him as a potential role model is to underplay his vision and significance.

It's true that Du Bois was a hero for a surprisingly wide range of people in his lifetime, not least the Indian social reformer and civil rights activist B. R. Ambedkar, who corresponded with Du Bois in the 1940s.[111] And it's true there's a fashion at the moment, especially in children's books, for promoting historical figures of colour, unfairly elided in the past, to boost the self-esteem and ambitions of communities of colour.[112] But Du Bois was more than an example. Like every great historical figure, he was complicated: as a communist and a supporter of Japanese imperialism, who backed Japan's invasion of Manchuria and didn't speak out about Japan's colonization of Korea, he had, and continues to have, detractors. But he was also, when it came to race, a prophet. Study his work closely enough and it provides, for both black and white people, liberation from imperial notions of race that still delimit lives today. The story of 'the colour line', as Du Bois explained it, should be studied everywhere, alongside abolition and the Magna Carta. Meanwhile, if Britons accepted, even to a small degree, that the British empire played a role in spreading racist ideas across the planet, if we realized that the world doesn't always see us as we see ourselves when it comes to the colour line, then we might get a step closer to confronting the racism that afflicts our society and earn the right to pontificate upon racism elsewhere.

# 7.   Reaping the Chaos

It could, in some ways, be a tour of any public school in England. The college, occupying some 10 acres of land, has many of the standard features: day and boarding options; flats for teachers known as masters; buildings more than a century old. The boys are sporting the compulsory impractical uniform – in this case, of spotless white shirts and white trousers, offset with dark-blue blazers. The school has an official crest (designed by the College of Heralds in London)[1] and a school motto in Latin (*Spero lucem*, 'I hope for light'). The student body is organized, in part by house (the house system having been established in 1920),[2] there is a school magazine with pretensions (the *Mermaid*), there are tributes around the place to the school's old boys (who include a Nobel Laureate) and there's a school song with lyrics that plug into British imperialist ideals ('Playing up and striving each to do his best / This shall be our watch word, "Always play the game!" ').

There are a number of details, however, which betray the fact that I'm not at home in Britain. The Principal's online biography, for instance, features some of the hyperbole that makes the English language in this part of the world such a delight (among other things, it describes him as 'a teacher per excellence, a father, a role model, peacemaker, motivator, a great thinker with an excellent personality' and a 'highly unassuming bundle of experience'). I spot a member of staff wielding a cane in a way that hasn't happened in Britain for decades now (I don't see him use it, but the severe school rules, which warn of the college having 'no room for morally bankrupt children', make it possible to imagine). Meanwhile, the school's fundraising campaigns are focused not on building a new swimming pool or a flash new drama hall as they usually are at home, but on basic upkeep ('the College physical infrastructure is suffering from old age . . . particularly at the annex where the sewage system poses serious challenge').

For I am not in the British countryside, but at the boys-only King's College in Lagos, the first government secondary school in Nigeria,[3] a country which was so central to the British imperial mission that when it became independent in 1960 the number of independent citizens in Africa doubled instantly, and the British empire lost over half of its territory. Based in a coastal region favoured by the British for its plentiful production of palm oil, extracted for a long period through the Royal Niger Company,[4] it describes itself online as 'the nation's numero uno in post-primary education' and compares itself favourably to Eton College and Harrow.[5] It also marked a recent centenary with the publication of a book which boasted about the 'weird and wonderful public schools customs' that the school inherited from their 'immense' counterparts in Britain,[6] referred admiringly to 'the doughty men of the Colonial Office' who set up the school, and echoed the sentiments of imperialists by opining on how the cricket played at the school 'was not only "a gentleman's game"' but 'a symbol of fair play and justice and a great builder of character, which could reform society'.[7] The book and the school's website also quote Sir Frederick Lugard, a former governor-general of the region[8] who was inclined to generalize about Africans pseudo-scientifically, maintaining that education made Africans 'less fertile, more susceptible to lung trouble and to other diseases, and to defective dentition', and complaining bitterly in his diary that 'the self-assurance and importance of these anglicised blacks is beyond calculation'.[9]

I'd read about the existence of intense imperial nostalgia in Nigeria before my trip in Max Siollun's superlative *What Britain Did to Nigeria*.[10] I'd experienced it along with other British voters through the Conservative minister Kemi Badenoch, who spent parts of her childhood living in Lagos and has defended the British empire on the basis of what she learned in Nigeria.[11] And my British Nigerian fixer in Lagos suggests that the ease with which I walk into King's College and get a tour is another example of it: she'd spent months trying but failing to get permission for me, the ease of my entry reflecting, she says, the bias too many Nigerians have for foreigners with British accents. But it still takes me aback. Visiting King's College makes me appreciate that I might have underestimated the role that education played in the British imperial mission, despite having previously confronted the way a traditional British education may have shaped my own thinking, and that of the British establishment, in colonial ways. I didn't appreciate then the sheer extent to which British imperial propaganda helped establish British education, with its colonial attitudes, as a gold standard all over the globe: some of it through schools like King's College and Mayo in India. British education united an entire generation of post-colonial leaders, even as they won independence from empire, revealing the paradox of how, even in independence, parts of the post-colonial world continued to be shaped by British empire.*[12] Indeed, the influence of British education on world leaders persists, with UK institutions having educated one or more rulers in a total of fifty-three countries in 2023, giving it influence over a quarter of the world,[13] and with British education with a colonial flavour remaining a force in parts of the former empire, like Nigeria, even as it fades in the mother country.

British education came to Nigeria, which was conquered by the British extremely slowly, over some seven decades, in two ways: through missionaries, and then, belatedly and somewhat reluctantly, via the colonial government.[14] I say reluctantly because colonial administrators fretted that education would encourage Nigerians to consider themselves equal to whites, and aim beyond their lowly position in the colonial hierarchy, not least at clerical positions, and thus deprive colonists of essential indigenous labour.[15] Apparently, it was only when the colonial government realized that it would be more cost-effective to educate and employ literate Nigerians, rather than import Europeans or other Africans to fill positions in their offices, that they changed their position.[16] There were also intense differences between how the north and south of the country, one of the defining divisions of Britain's colonization of the region,[17] responded to the education on offer in this ethnically diverse region of Africa.

The British occupation turned the prevailing educational norms of Nigeria upside down. Pre-colonization, the predominantly Muslim north – home to ethnic groups such as the Fulani and Hausa – was far

---

* Oxbridge has produced four of India's post-independence prime ministers, starting with Jawaharlal Nehru (Trinity College, Cambridge, 1907–10) and the next two generations of his family, daughter Indira Gandhi (Somerville College, Oxford, 1937–40) and her son, Rajiv Gandhi (Trinity College, Cambridge, 1961–4). India's thirteenth Prime Minister, Manmohan Singh, was an alumnus of St John's College, Cambridge. It is notable that India's Hindu nationalist Prime Minister, Modi, recently urged Indians to remove 'any vestiges of colonialism . . . in our hearts', in a reference to the idea that being ruled by Western-educated leaders like Nehru was little better than being governed by the British or the Mughal emperors. The ruling party claims that Modi's accession to power marked the start of India's real independence.

more educationally developed than the south of the country, home to ethnic groups such as the Igbo and Yoruba. With the arrival of colonizers, the Muslims in the north resisted Western education in part for its association with Christianity, while southerners embraced both, having realized that education and Christianity could protect them from being exploited by colonialists and could boost their socio-economic mobility. By the close of 1914, when the Southern Nigerian Protectorate formally merged with the Northern Nigeria Protectorate to form a single colony, almost all (95 per cent) of Nigeria's schools could be found in the south, and almost all (over 97 per cent) of students enrolled into these schools were southerners. The approach of independence saw a wave of people from the south, largely Igbos, relocated to the north to take up jobs that less educated northerners could not access. Not surprisingly, this movement led to friction, and was one of the factors that led to an outburst of violence in 1966 and the subsequent Nigerian Civil War, also known as the Biafran War.[18]

Colonial education intensified the great divide between the north of Nigeria and the south, the former being twice the size of the latter,[19] helping to create deep religious discord,*[20] and the bloody Biafran War was only one manifestation of the subsequent tensions between regions. There have been many north–south eruptions, such as one sparked by the annulment of the presidential election of June 1993, and an emergency over sharia law more recently.[21] And geopolitical instability is the ultimate reason I'm in West Africa. For the country is a useful

---

* I'm seated next to an elderly Nigerian woman on my flight out to Lagos who reads the Bible for three hours of our six-hour flight, and she's an illustration of the success Christian missionaries eventually had in West Africa. Their success at conversion was boosted by the fact that the missionaries were associated by many with colonial authorities, who held the power in the country, and who also earned the trust of communities through their command of medicine. Nowadays, around half of Nigeria's population is Muslim, and about 46 per cent is Christian, and the communities have a history of clashing. The Muslim-majority north has seen much religious violence and, since 1999, has been under sharia law. The World Index of Christian Persecution estimates that 89 per cent of all the world's murders of Christians occur in Nigeria, while, in 2002, an inflammatory article in a Lagos newspaper suggested that the Prophet Muhammad would look favourably upon a Miss World pageant that was mooted to be held in Nigeria, leading to four days of violence in the northern capital, Kaduna, which left 200 dead and many religious buildings destroyed.

introduction to two of the most commonly cited, and conflicting, modern legacies of the British imperial project: chaos and/or democratic stability. Here in 2002 we have the then Foreign Secretary Jack Straw arguing that many global problems were the legacy of Britain's colonial past.[22] And here in 2011, in *Ghosts of Empire: Britain's Legacies in the Modern World*, we have the then recently elected Conservative MP Kwasi Kwarteng arguing that 'much of the instability in the world is a product of its legacy of individualism and haphazard policymaking' and that 'individualism . . . with very little strategic direction from London, often led to contradictory and self-defeating policies, which in turn brought disaster to millions'. Notably, for a man who eventually became a member of a government which embarked upon a culture war propounding the idea that being proud of British empire is a patriotic act, he claimed in *Ghosts of Empire* to be sidestepping the 'sterile debate' over whether 'empire was a good thing or a bad thing'.[23]

Kwarteng traces the legacies of empire in various former British colonies he considers unstable (Iraq, Kashmir, Burma, Sudan, Nigeria and Hong Kong), before reaching this conclusion, and I opt for Nigeria from the list, as it feels like the safest to visit, as a journalist from the West. It turns out that the problem with visiting countries that have reputations for being unstable is that they sometimes feel somewhat unstable. A glance at the Foreign, Commonwealth & Development Office website informs me that 'there is a high threat of criminal and terrorist kidnap throughout Nigeria' and that 'those engaged in tourism, humanitarian aid work, journalism or business are viewed as legitimate targets'. The website also informs me that there are heightened levels of violence around elections, and I'm booked to travel just before a major national election. The US State Department is more forceful, telling US citizens to 'reconsider travel to Nigeria due to crime, terrorism, civil unrest, kidnapping, and maritime crime', with kidnapping gangs stopping victims on interstate roads. Meanwhile, a friend who was born in Nigeria urges me to reconsider the trip: he has a friend who was shot while being driven to his hotel from the airport, he has never felt the country was safe enough for his mixed-race children to visit, and he frets that non-Nigerians are targets. News reports corroborate this picture, the *Sunday Times* informing me that while Nigeria is 'a booming country of 200 million people', it is 'sick, its long list of ailments enough to make the heart skip'. A third of adults are unemployed; Nigeria's most valuable export, oil, is constantly being stolen or wasted, with hundreds of millions of barrels lost each year; and annual inflation has reached 21 per cent.[24] The *Financial Times*, meanwhile, reports that the problems Nigeria faces in the months before the election include: low levels of tax collection; low degrees of power generation; high levels of poverty; worsening security; and an epidemic of kidnapping.[25] According to a security agency, in the year to June 2022, a total of 3,420 people were abducted, with some 564 others killed in incidents related to abduction.

I solicit further advice and, frankly, it's not entirely helpful: Nigerians may be the one group of people on earth more fissiparous and argumentative than Punjabis. Some think I'm unwise to travel at all, others that it's ridiculous to take any precautions at all. In the end, I proceed, but cautiously, the half-empty plane to Lagos, and the incredulity of a fellow passenger travelling only because of a family emergency, suggesting it's unwise. I'd heard so much about the vibrant arts scene and the nightlife of Lagos, the theatre of the street life, the infectious hustle of young entrepreneurs, the similarities to Indian culture, with the instinctive respect shown to elders, but the painful truth is that I don't get to experience a huge amount of it. I'm advised against getting Ubers as there have been reports in recent years of taxi drivers kidnapping passengers, or passing on passengers to kidnappers.[26] My fixer is nervous about trains because, a few weeks before my visit, gunmen armed with AK-47 rifles abducted more than thirty people from a train station in Nigeria's Edo state.[27] And travelling on motorways is not recommended because motorists using them have been the target of violent criminals for years.[28] I'm left with some sense of Lagos as a charismatic city, its ill-served people irrepressible, its cuisine the only cuisine I've encountered that is naturally spicy enough for my battered taste buds, but while I'd flitted around Mauritius at will, my movements in Nigeria are restricted. I mainly hop between secure compounds in the company of a driver known to my fixer and me, in a permanent cloud of the insect spray I apply a little too liberally to make up for not taking anti-malarial medication, with little wandering around in public in between. I get to visit one public park in Lagos, Freedom Park, formerly Her Majesty's Broad Street Prison,[29] but even this requires payment to enter and has walls around it, and it turns out there are reasons for this atomization, beyond the security situation:

many households and institutions have to set themselves up as discrete, self-sufficient entities in the absence of a properly functioning state.[30]

Max Siollun spots the influence of British empire here, arguing that aspects of this way of living, at least for the middle classes and above, go back to a time when the British resided in spacious houses within compounds in exclusive districts called Government Reservation Areas (GRA), believing that prolonged contact with Nigerians was bad for their health. Their local servants lived separately in the 'boys' quarters', more modest accommodation elsewhere within the compound. This atomized and segregated set-up has endured as a living model and today many middle-class and upper-middle-class Nigerians aspire to live in a big house, with their coterie of cleaners, nannies, drivers and so on squirrelled away in the 'boys' quarters', all of them within a walled compound.[31] One Nigerian I meet recalls that this compound life made storming off difficult when he was a petulant teen: all he could do was ask a servant to turn off the lights over the swimming pool and try to escape his parents by hiding in the dark. And, as frustrating a way as it is to see a country, it's a neat introduction to the idea, propounded by Siollun and other academics, that many of Nigeria's problems were created by the British empire.

Not least of these is something we've already alluded to: the disastrous merging of very different ethnic groups into one political structure. Tensions between ethnic groups in Nigeria are numerous, accentuated in the early years of independence by the fact that each region had its own ethnically based political party, the consequent instability becoming, in Kwarteng's words, 'the perfect recipe for "ethnic combat"'.[32] Siollun insists we can overplay the idea that the instability of Nigeria is caused by imperialists putting together ethnic groups who previously had no co-history: he points out that plenty of pre-colonial kingdoms were multi-ethnic, many groups of people had trading and business history with one another.[33] However, because of colonialism's centralizing effects, large 'super tribes' were formed from individuals who had not previously identified as belonging to the same ethnic groups.[34] Also, while 'British colonialism did not introduce Nigeria's ethnic groups to each other', it, 'without their consent, amalgamated them within a single political system for the first time'. There seems to be some popular awareness in the West of the fact that the borders imposed on Africa by Westerners often make no sense on the ground, as reflected in the fact that 44 per cent of Africa's borders are straight lines, rather than along natural phenomena.[35] But the composition of Nigeria was particularly crude: the amalgamated regions had, by Lugard's own account, 'totally different traditions and peoples' (while he was an expert in governing the north of the country, he confessed to knowing next to nothing about the Igbo);[36] and George Goldie, whose 'aggressive imperialism' was so key to the establishment of the country that it was once mooted that it be called 'Goldesia', stated that they were 'as widely separated in laws, government, customs, and general ideas about life, both in this world and the next, as England is from China'.[37] The ultimate reason for the amalgamation was as mundane as the story behind the selection of the country's name:*[38] it was a way for Britain to save money. 'The colonial government's priority was not to create a new nation with a common ethos,' reports Siollun. Rather, to please the British taxpayer they wanted to maximize revenue, cut down on bureaucracy and reduce the cost of running the country.[39]

The issue of 'ethnic combat' leads us to another imperial legacy: violence. The influence of the transatlantic slave trade upon this region of Africa is reflected in the fact that it was for a sustained period known as the Slave Coast,†[40] and this violent trade resulted in the import of a huge

---

* Siollun queries the story, repeated by Kwarteng, that the journalist Flora Shaw came up with the name in 1897 in an article for *The Times*. He insists that the 'origin of the name "Nigeria" remains opaque . . . even before . . . this article, the terms "Nigeria" and "Nigerians" had been used informally for decades to refer to the territories and people in the River Niger area. By the time Shaw wrote her article, "Nigeria" had already crept into casual, albeit imprecise and irregular, use. However, credit cannot completely be withdrawn from Shaw. While she is definitely not the inventor of the name, she may take credit for being the first to suggest using it as an official territorial name for part of the lands that would eventually become Nigeria . . .'

† We've heard about how Maxim guns, quinine and steamships accelerated the colonization of Africa, but it was the slave trade that made this part of the world vulnerable to colonization in the first place. In 1759's *The Theory of Moral Sentiments*, Adam Smith put the relative lack of African economic development down to the 'continual danger' that faced the continent's citizens, and Max Siollun takes up the theme. 'The slave trade disrupted West Africa in a manner that made it vulnerable to conquest by Britain. The fear of being captured and sold into slavery made some Africans voluntary prisoners of their own villages and cities. Venturing too far from home carried a risk of being captured by slave hunters. This inhibited inter-community and inter-ethnic alliances and cooperation. This lack of African inter-ethnic patriotism later came back

number of weapons, which led to yet more violence and instability. As Daron Acemoglu and James A. Robinson explain in *Why Nations Fail*, war was intrinsic to the slave trade. Europeans brought over vast quantities of arms and ammunition, which they exchanged for slaves; the enslaved themselves were often war captives. In 1730, on the West African coast, around 180,000 guns were being imported every year and this number rose to 394,000 from the British alone by the early nineteenth century. Around the same period, the British sold an estimated 22,000 tons of gunpowder to West Africa. 'All this warfare and conflict not only caused major loss of life and human suffering but also put in motion a particular path of institutional development in Africa . . . Warring and slaving ultimately destroyed whatever order and legitimate state authority existed in sub-Saharan Africa.'[41] As I learned at Kew, imperialists celebrated when 'legitimate commerce' in products such as ivory, rubber, peanuts and palm oil replaced slavery in this part of Africa, but this trade often used the violent ship crews who had worked in the slave trade; these 'palm oil ruffians' were infamous for their dishonesty, violence, callousness and willingness to mistreat natives.[42]

Contributing to this legacy of violence was the brutality of colonial conquest. The first phase came under the Royal Niger Company, which, says Siollun, 'operated in part like a government',[43] at times 'resembled a Mafia protection racket'[44] and at others seemed to be an exercise in 'corporate terrorism'.[45] There are many horrific examples of its behaviour, not least its kidnapping in 1885 of three young village boys in the Niger Delta. Despite being ordered to release them by a British consul, it kept them hostage for seven months.[46] Meanwhile, the company's own constabulary force was known for brutal attacks in the name of law and order, such as making an entire village liable for the misdemeanours of a single resident and retaliating by razing the village to the ground, killing livestock and destroying livelihoods. The misdemeanour could be slight: in 1890 the Igbo town of Aguleri was obliterated after one of its men used his knife to puncture an RNC palm oil barrel.[47] Ultimately, the British state opted for a formal colonial takeover of the region. The annexing of the south-east of the country cost

---

to haunt Africans and contributed to their inability to form a united coalition to oppose British invasion and rule. Slavery also drained the population of its able-bodied adult population, leaving behind the elderly and young children.'

the lives of over 10,000 people, the British discharging more than 54,000 cannon shells and 350,000 rounds of bullets.[48] This high-tech violence had a profound effect on the region,[49] not least creating a long-standing belief that violence is a legitimate tool for politics and governance. 'Those in power have achieved that power through violence and have used violence to maintain their control of state power,' claims Nigerian historian Toyin Falola. 'The police and the army are not agencies of development or progress but instruments of state terrorism.'[50]

Which brings us to another imperial legacy that British colonists bestowed upon Nigeria, an echo of the problems faced by India's police forces and recounted in the previous chapter: popular distrust in the country's law enforcement and security agencies. I'd noted the *Financial Times'* remark, in relation to kidnapping in Nigeria, that 'families see little point in contacting police and many negotiate directly with kidnappers, paying in total hundreds of millions of naira in ransom'.[51] The reality of this lack of faith in the security forces is brought home to me when I have to establish, on advice, a 'proof of life' protocol with my loved ones – prearranged questions and answers that will be put to those who have taken me hostage, to prove it's not a hoax and that I'm still alive. The threat of violence overshadows daily life in much of the country. One of Nigeria's biggest social media movements in recent times has been #EndSARS, referring to a famously brutal unit of the Nigerian police force, the Special Anti-Robbery Squad.[52] Then there's the Boko Haram insurgency in the north-east, a recent separatist movement in the south-east, and endemic kidnapping almost everywhere else (or 'banditry', as many Nigerian newspapers call it, in their lively way), all of it resulting in a boom in private guard services for those who can afford them.[53] And if there is so little faith in Nigeria's army and police, which predate the creation of the country itself, it's partly because of the way they were established by the British. Echoing what the British did in India with the Sikhs and with other ethnicities in other parts of the world, the British in Nigeria developed a racialized military recruitment process, labelling a certain ethnic group – here, the Hausas – a martial race. Both Siollun and Falola argue that such stereotyping affected the stability of the country.[54] The so-called Hausa Militia were subsequently favoured by the British not only for their supposed superior physical and mental qualities but also because, when the British first came to Nigeria, many of their military campaigns pitted them against non-Hausa ethnic groups. The Hausas, it was felt, would feel no compunction about taking on these other communities. Soon the British designated the Hausa language – just one of many spoken in West Africa – as the one the army would use to command its men.

While British officers were impressed by the fighting prowess of their Hausa warriors, their names suggest that not all of them were Hausas or even Muslim by ethnicity. Other colonial paramilitary armed groups later combined with the Hausa Constabulary, one of the foundational units of the Nigerian police,[55] and Siollun maintains that although the army's decision to use Hausa men to vanquish other ethnic groups worked well for the British during their years of occupation, it left a toxic legacy. By the time of Nigeria's independence in 1960, the army was firmly divided along racial lines, with northerners making up around three-quarters of the fighting troops on the ground, and southerners taking the majority of the technical and support positions. This division led to internal conflict within the army, escalating to several military coups and a devastating civil war.[56] Furthermore, for many Nigerians the army is forever compromised by the fact that it was a creation of the British in the colonial era, and that Nigerian soldiers assisted the British in occupying the country and subjugating their fellow countrymen.[57]

Beyond the infrastructure of Nigeria and into its culture, British imperialists also had something to do with the corruption and bribery that Nigeria is notorious for. Lagos airport is plastered with posters declaring that bribery and corruption will not be tolerated, with WhatsApp numbers advertised to submit complaints to, but it's a sign of how pervasive the problems are that I'm nevertheless solicited for bribes in the airport by a police officer and a security officer scanning my bag (it's done so quietly and politely that I don't mind: I've met more aggressive charity fundraisers). The country's reputation though probably causes as many problems as the corruption itself. I don't risk logging on to a load of public wifi services, which I normally would do, because it feels risky to do so in Nigeria; it's a struggle to pay with international credit cards, with my bank seemingly assuming that any transactions in Nigeria must, by definition, be fraudulent; I assume the hotel has defrauded me when I get double charged, as does the enraged gentleman in the queue behind me, who is charged five times for the same booking, but it turns out to be genuine human error in both cases. Of course, corruption in Nigeria gets more serious than this: a large steel mill in Ajaokuta is incomplete and largely abandoned, despite costing some $8 billion.[58]

The imperial connection to this? The gifts and money that British traders gave to local chiefs, in exchange for permission to conduct business in their territories. These gifts were known as 'comey' or 'dash', and established a form of payment which the chiefs or 'Big Men' came to regard as their entitlement. In other words, the British made tipping and the taking of commission an intrinsic part of doing business in colonial West Africa in the nineteenth century. 'In the late 20th century, these ex-gratia payments acquired new names: bribery and corruption,' writes Siollun. 'When English law was transplanted to West African society, legitimate trade payments that had existed for centuries were suddenly transformed into illegal financial transactions. Nigeria's modern-day bribery is at least partially a descendant of this elaborate system of payments.'[59] Nigeria's modern '419' scams – when a victim is contacted out of the blue and asked to help move a vast sum of money from one foreign country to another – oh, and pay a small admin fee – on the promise that they will then be given a percentage of the cash – had an imperial precursor in scams where 'fraudsters deployed British motifs to intimidate their victims'. Apparently, some dishonest Nigerians exploited their countrymen's fear of the all-powerful white man in order to extort from them. A fraudster might put on a soldier's uniform and march into a poor village claiming to be working for the British. He would demand money or items from the villagers, saying that otherwise the British would destroy the village. The terrified villagers were often illiterate and had no way of verifying his claims.[60]

You may have come across the most famous Nigerian email scam of all, which involves a 'Nigerian prince' offering a once-in-a-lifetime, and completely non-existent, money-making opportunity,[61] which brings us to another imperial legacy: Nigerian 'Big Men'.[62] If in modern Nigeria there are legions of men who claim they are the 'traditional rulers' of 'kingdoms', and as such expect to be addressed as HRH, 'his royal majesty' and 'royal father', or local titles such as 'obi' or 'igwe', it's because British empire created a whole new social elite while in charge of the country, to sit alongside legitimate kings and rulers. Before the British landed in the south-east and the Niger Delta, the power structure of the region, which we last encountered when happening across its notably flexible gender system, with gender-neutral pronouns and male roles open to certain categories of women,[63] was such that various people and groups held positions of high authority rather than one autocratic leader. On their arrival, the British got rid of some of the most powerful of these individual rulers, including the Jaja of Opobo, the Oba of Benin and Nana Olomu. But then, in need of people to run things for them, they had to reappoint chiefs, and where they couldn't find someone with credentials for the role, they'd choose a man who *seemed* like he'd be a good leader. This newly minted leader would be given a red cap 'warrant' certificate – which literally involved recipients often donning a red cap[64] – and such men were called 'warrant chiefs'.

The selection process for these chiefs was sometimes bizarre: in one case, a town crier was appointed as a warrant chief because villagers responded to his call to attend gatherings; for the British, this showed he was a man of power and influence. The system of warrant chiefs, Siollun says, threw south-eastern Nigeria 'into political turmoil from which it may not yet have recovered'. In south-eastern Nigeria, new forms of extortion and fraud emerged thanks to the enormous power warrant chiefs possessed. In addition to enforcing the law as judges, they had the power to levy taxes and compel people to work for the colonial government.[65] Essentially, the British created thousands of new, government-endorsed rulers. According to Femi Adegbulu, 'by the 1920s, the Warrant Chief institution had, in many places, become synonymous with greed, avarice and corruption, and British adminis-trative officers were increasingly aware of this'.[66] By the late 1980s, almost three decades after independence, there were 820 traditional rulers in Igboland alone, and most of these positions had not existed before colonialism. And an administrative position created under Brit-ish rule has evolved into a hereditary title, with many of today's chiefs in Nigeria having descended from warrant chiefs, and some claiming to be 'royalty'.[67]

I find myself discussing the legacies of this system with a British Niger-ian journalist in Lagos, who maintains that some common generalizations about Igbo political culture are not true[68] and observes that 'Nigeria almost always gets flattened into two dimensions when written about in the West.' He's right: things are so much more complex on the ground than they seem in print. But like all good historians, Siollun seeks out complexity and nuance. He concludes, for instance, that although the way Western education was introduced sowed division between north and south, it transformed the country: it provided a new common language, enabling communication between different groups,★[69] a new religion that was taken up by half of the country and 'a new cultural and societal ethos for advancement'.[70] Some societal changes have been profound and positive: whereas in 1952 over 90 per cent of the population could not read or write in English, by 2010 some 76 per cent of Nigerians aged 15–24 were literate. Less than seventy years after the British left Nigeria, there are now greater numbers of English-speakers and English-literate people there than there are in Britain. Moreover, Siollun credits imperialists for being the founders of the 'Union Igbo' language commonly spoken today in Nigeria's cities. More specifically, he points to translations undertaken by missionaries in the country, namely one Thomas John Dennis. Wishing the Word to reach as many of the Igbo people as possible, the Anglican clergyman decided to translate the book into 'Union Igbo', a version of the language that would be understood by all of those living in what is now called Igboland.[71] Siollun also tells us how another British missionary, the Scottish Presbyterian Mary Slessor, played an important role in ending the tradition of twin abandonment in parts of Efik and Igboland, which existed as a consequence of the belief that twin births were a sign of evil. Although he reminds us that British accounts from the time overstated the savagery of pre-colonial Nigeria and although imperialists generally claim too much of the credit for turning things around,[72] he credits Slessor for helping to wipe out a practice which sometimes saw whole communities being evacuated on the birth of twins.[73]

When, on my final day in Lagos, I venture out of the compound

---

★ The BBC recently reported that Nigeria wants to put less of an emphasis on English. 'More than 60 years after independence from Britain, English remains Nigeria's official language, and is used in public settings such as schools, universities, government and many work places. But the political tide appears to be turning. In November [2022], Education Minister Adamu Adamu announced the National Language Policy which stipulates that the first six years of primary education should be taught in the children's mother tongue . . . Currently, primary school children are taught in English, with teachers in certain communities mixing local languages with English for ease of comprehension. However, it is unclear how the new policy will be rolled out because – in a country where government estimates say 625 different languages are spoken . . . – many Nigerian children live in areas where their mother tongue is not the dominant local language.'

which is my hotel and travel down George V Road, which is another legacy of British empire,[74] in the company of that trusted driver employed as a defence against kidnapping (which is surely yet another legacy of empire)[75] and meet Lawon Adams, I'm reminded that what is or is not an imperial legacy is sometimes subjective. 'It's easy to [blame the British], because it starts from there,' says the smoothly dressed 54-year-old, rejecting many of the imperial legacies I've identified as imperial legacies. Adams is an oil executive doing pioneering work in developing Lagos' nascent tourism scene, and a draught from the air-conditioning unit in his office alerts me to the fact that I might have overdone the Jungle Formula again. 'India probably had a rougher time than we did, and they found a way to pick themselves up. So how do we stop focusing on what the British did, pick ourselves up and say, "Eh, look, you've got mineral resources, you've got the human resources, you've got this young population, and you've got a future ahead of you." You want to step out and stop crying and get on with your lives. Everything looks good for us in the heart of Africa, we've got all the things that we need.'

Siollun makes a persuasive case when I put this argument to him via email, but a version of Adams' point gets made wherever you go in the world to trace the legacies of British empire. It's a point that gets made to Alex Renton by the historian Susan Craig-James and a tour guide in relation to the legacies of slavery in the Caribbean. It's a point Kiran at the Naz Foundation makes about India's homophobia. It's a point that invariably gets made whenever I present a list of suggested imperial legacies to Nigerians on my trip. And it's a point always worth keeping in mind. The links to the British empire are clear and direct with some phenomena, such as the religious, geopolitical and ethnic makeup of Nigeria. But enough time has passed since colonialism to make it at least debatable about who exactly is responsible for, say, the violence in Nigeria, or the bribery in Nigeria, or the distrust of security forces in Nigeria, or the kidnapping in Nigeria. Some Nigerians, like Adams, would blame many of these problems, or bestow responsibility for sorting them out, on post-independence Nigerians. But, having proffered this caveat, if even half the things which academics identify as imperial legacies are direct imperial legacies in Nigeria, and across other parts of the former empire, then that's a startling quantity.

It's bewildering to consider that I could have visited, in theory if not in practice, a dozen other countries and discovered a similar array of imperial legacies in each case, not to mention a corresponding array of creative ways in which British imperialists sowed geopolitical instability. The newspaper and magazine articles I read on my phone on the long journey home from Lagos to London throw up numerous examples. A news story about the brutal nature of the violence in Kashmir, for instance, serves to remind me that the roots of the region's instability lie in the mid-nineteenth century, when British imperialists sold the majority-Muslim state to a tyrannical Hindu monarch.*[76] Thus came about the sometimes bizarre 1846 Treaty of Amritsar, which stipulated that, along with the money, Gulab Singh would also provide annually 'one horse, twelve goats (six male and six female) and three pairs of shawls'.[77] A news feature about a cemetery in Iraq reminds me not only of how the 2003 invasion, led by the USA with support from the UK, sowed instability through human rights abuses and destruction, but of how the British empire played a major role in provoking volatility a century or so beforehand. A time when it cynically exploited the country's vast resources of oil and installed a disastrous Hashemite monarchy, thus creating the conditions for a series of revolutionary governments, one of which eventually included Saddam Hussein's.[78] British imperialists also sowed discord in Myanmar, the nation formerly known as Burma, which is in the news in early 2023 as the result of the imposition of new EU sanctions.[79] Kwasi Kwarteng has argued that the nation's current predicament of civil war, authoritarian military regimes and poverty can be blamed on the British, whose annexation of the country led to Japan occupying it in the Second World War, which resulted in a power vacuum that allowed a military junta to seize control.†[80] Meanwhile, other analysts maintain that British colonial control 'helped set the stage' for later atrocities, such as the genocide of the

---

* Kashmir is rare in being a place where a modern British prime minister has actually accepted national responsibility for discord, David Cameron remarking in 2011 that he didn't want to mediate because 'I don't want to try to insert Britain in some leading role where, as with so many of the world's problems, we are responsible for the issue in the first place.'

† Henry Richard, MP for Merthyr Tydfil, got there first when he remarked in Parliament at the time, in 1886, that the 'summary annexation' of Burma 'was an act of high-handed violence for which there is no adequate justification'. Not only was it unjust but it was also 'an act of flagrant folly. By suddenly overthrowing the existing

Rohingya in Myanmar and discrimination against other minorities based on their ethnicity. Alexandra Green, curator for South-east Asia at the British Museum, recently explained that this happened because 'British ideas of ethnicity and making links between ethnicity and territory . . . were very new in Myanmar; ethnicity, historically, was quite flexible but it became quite rigidified and associated with territory.'[81] Marja-Leena Heikkilä-Horn added that censuses conducted by British imperialists divided 'British Burma into arbitrary ethnic, geographic and administrative units. These categories remain a major obstacle for peace and for the unity of independent Burma.'[82]

The British empire is not, of course, the only empire to have sowed instability – according to Jeffrey Mankoff, the fall of China's, Iran's, Russia's and Turkey's geographical empires has left these states uneasily intertwined with the regions and populations on their periphery.[83] But no other empire sowed chaos so far and wide. And on it goes. The 'greater Sudan' region of Africa is unstable for a host of reasons,[84] but more than anything else for the bitter tensions between the north and south, which resulted in some twenty years of civil war and South Sudan gaining independence from Sudan in 2011.[85] 'Post-independence conflicts in Sudan were largely caused by ethnic divisions created by the British colonial administration between 1899 and 1956,' writes Kim Searcy.[86] ' "Divide and rule" policies pursued by the British continue to haunt contemporary Sudan, both north and south. During most of the colonial period . . . Sudan was ruled as two Sudans. The British separated the predominantly Muslim and Arabic-speaking north from the multi-religious, multi-ethnic, and multilingual south.' In *I Didn't Do It for You* Michela Wrong reports on how, during the Second World War, after the British had driven the Italians from power, British imperialists are estimated, during 'an eight-month looting spree', to have removed 80 per cent of Ethiopia's Italian assets, including whole factories, a radio transmitting station, road-making equipment and medical stores, 'without paying a penny in compensation' to Ethiopia.[87] In doing so, the British broke international law concerning enemy property.[88] (Yet more context that would have been useful for viewers of Live Aid.) Wrong also reports that during the ten years that Britain ran a neighbouring country, Eritrea, after quashing the occupying

government, it looks as though we [have] consigned the country to . . . a prolonged anarchy.'

Italian army there in 1941, the British did something similar, stripping the country of many of the assets introduced by Italy, from railway tracks to oil-surveying equipment. In 1947, the Eritrean Chamber of Commerce estimated total lost assets at '1,700m East African shillings, the equivalent of £1.85 billion today [2005] – a tidy sum for such a small territory'.[89]

Then there is Palestine, the site of the world's single most intractable conflict. I sense a reluctance among the great surveyors of British imperial history to opine upon one of the world's most contentious issues. But having read multiple accounts from multiple perspectives,[90] it strikes me that British empire's seminal role in sowing chaos in the roughly thirty years, 1917–48, that it ruled Palestine, as the result of a mandate conferred upon it by the League of Nations, is simple. As part of the more general surreptitious double-dealing that took place between the British and French after the First World War,[91] when the two imperial powers created several new countries in the region and decided upon their destinies, the British simultaneously offered Palestine to two groups of people. As Tom Segev puts it:

> Before setting out to war in Palestine, the British had gotten themselves tangled up in an evasive and amateurish correspondence with the Arabs, who believed that in exchange for supporting the British against the Turks, they would receive Palestine. [Then came the Balfour Declaration, in which] for all practical purposes, the British had promised the Zionists that they would establish a Jewish state in Palestine. The Promised Land had, by the stroke of a pen, become twice-promised . . . The British pretended, and perhaps some of them even believed, that the establishment of a national home for the Jews could be carried out without hurting the Arabs. But, of course, that was impossible . . . From the start there were then only two possibilities: that the Arabs defeat the Zionists or that the Zionists defeat the Arabs. War between the two was inevitable.★[92]

The British empire also permanently altered relationships between states that were never part of the enterprise. In her magisterial book on

---

★ The late British author and journalist Arthur Koestler summarized it thus: 'One nation solemnly promised to a second nation the country of a third.'

the Opium Wars between Britain and China,[93] Julia Lovell argues that Sino-Western relations, in general, have been influenced for nearly 200 years by the Opium Wars and their repercussions, with both sides manipulating history to suit their own agendas. The Opium Wars saw the creation of stereotypes about the Chinese that still haunt political and cultural relations – not least the 'stereotype of the obtusely anti-foreign Chinese' in the West,[94] and the racist idea that the Chinese were inclined to 'vice, violence and mutiny' and were 'a secretive, alien, xenophobic community that refused to integrate with Anglo-Saxon society'.[95] Meanwhile, the Opium Wars have become a totemic episode in China's nationalist history, exemplifying the evils of Western imperialism and representing the beginning of China's 'century of humiliation' at the hands of the bullying West between 1842 and 1949. It is, says the Chinese Communist Party, emblematic of all that was bad about the 'old society'; under the Party's leadership, China will right the wrongs.[96]

More generally, beyond the examples of individual nations, the double standards which the West exhibits when embarking on military action around the world, and which incite such bitterness, anger and retaliation, were arguably laid down by British imperialists. Decades before we started classifying our enemies as 'unlawful combatants' in the so-called War on Terror, and before we started treating our enemies in ways we wouldn't want our own soldiers to be treated (by imprisoning them in Guantanamo Bay, for instance), the British empire was insisting that its enemies in the colonies had to be seen differently to themselves. Racialized double standards, sometimes referred to as 'the rule of colonial difference', were a defining feature of the Hague Convention of 1899, which explicitly did not apply to so-called 'uncivilized' people. Kim Wagner has shown that British imperialists only began doubting the suitability of expanding dum-dum bullets – designed to splinter inside the body, so as to inflict maximum damage – which they had used to control indigenous people in Africa and Asia, when the ammunition was used against one of their own men serving on the North West frontier.[97] With the exception of Luxembourg, Britain was the only country that did not sign the Hague Convention's ban on the use of such bullets. The British government found itself in the unprecedented position, at the dawn of the twentieth century, of urging the deployment of two distinct types of bullet for its colonial armies:

the older, non-expanding Mark II for use against 'civilized' foes, and the expanding Mark IV/Mark V for use against 'savages'.*[98]

There seems to have been little awareness among imperialists of the problems they were creating. In Eritrea, official British accounts of the time would ignore the way empire had stripped the nation of assets and instead commend Britain for bringing freedom to the people, by reforming the political system, improving education and establishing a free press.[99] As for Nigeria, colonial administrators there similarly believed that they had introduced peace and order in the country, as Lugard's secretary insisted: 'We have, admittedly by force, given the people good government in place of tyranny, we have abolished human sacrifice and slavery, and we have secured for the country a material prosperity which could never have been realized under the chaotic conditions that previously existed.'[100] Meanwhile, A. H. Poynton of the Colonial Office told the United Nations in 1947: 'the fundamental objectives in Africa are to foster the emergence of large-scale societies, integrated for self-government by effective and democratic political and economic institutions both national and local, inspired by a common faith in progress and Western values and equipped with efficient techniques of production and betterment'.[101] This mention of democracy is not unusual: it's frequently cited as a legacy of British empire and was made boldly by Niall Ferguson in *Empire: How the British Made the World* in 2003: 'Without the influence of British imperial rule, it is hard to believe that the institutions of parliamentary democracy would have been adopted by the majority of states in the world, as they are today.'[102] It's possible to take issue with the precise validity of this statement in the 2020s, two decades after it was published, but it brings us to the greatest contradiction of all when it comes to facing up to the legacies of British empire: it both instilled chaos *and* spread democracy.

It's interesting that you rarely, if ever, see these points being made

---

* Major General Sir John Charles Ardagh attempted to justify use of dum-dum bullets by arguing: 'In civilized war a soldier penetrated by a small projectile is wounded, withdraws to the ambulance, and doesn't advance any further. It is very different with a savage. Even though pierced two or three times, he doesn't cease to march forward, doesn't call upon the hospital attendants, but continues on, and before anyone has time to explain to him that he is flagrantly violating the decision of the Hague Conference, he cuts off your head. For this reason the English delegate demands the liberty of employing projectiles of sufficient efficacy against savage races.'

together. I'm not sure why. Perhaps it's because the historians researching the democratizing effects of British empire, or the instability-instilling effects of British empire, have enough on their hands: they're both massive subjects in their own right and the historians don't have the capacity to address both. Perhaps it's because historians like to present arguments, and are not in the business of undermining their own case. Perhaps it's the influence of culture wars, which reward the unnuanced. But it seems irrefutable that while British empire did instil chaos in some parts of the world, it instilled democracy elsewhere, and given that absolute democracy is no more possible to achieve than an absolute rule of law, sometimes it instilled both chaos and democracy *in the same place at the same time.* Despite the large number of studies which have found that colonialism *in general* has been bad for democracy,[103] finding, variously, that colonialism is associated with underdevelopment and 'high levels of ethnic and religious fractionalization', many other studies have found that the longer a country was administered by the British, the more likely it is to have sustained democracy once it became independent. In short, British rule helped democracy to flourish.[104] Multiple studies over multiple decades have noted the phenomenon,[105] Michael Bernhard et al. concluding in 2004 that while 'a colonial past *generally* diminishes a democracy's prospects for survival', and while 'the advantages that the literature attributes to the British colonial legacy have been overstated in certain regards . . . specifically, former Spanish colonies have performed better historically in terms of democratic survival . . . British colonialism had constructive effects for post-colonial democracies in terms of the relationship between the state and civil society compared to other forms of colonialism.'[106]

How did this instillation of democracy work? The dominant explanation, as summarized by Nicholas Owen, is that the British established important 'democratic innovations' before they departed.[107] 'Power was transferred to elites used to elections and [with] experience of "training ground" legislatures. Britain left locally recruited, trained bureaucracies, independent judiciaries, military forces under civilian control, and constitutions that established the parliamentary rather than presidential system of government, with its propensity for a broadly based, negotiated politics.'[108] And of these factors, the easiest to elaborate upon is the influence of Britain's Westminster constitution, which has been adopted by a striking number of former British colonies that developed into democracies. The widespread adoption illustrates an imperial paradox that should be familiar by now: that even in their new-found independence, many post-colonial nations continued being shaped by British imperialism. Indeed, ninety-two constitutional instruments for territories all over the world were prepared by the Colonial Office in the brief period between June 1959 and June 1960 alone, according to Sir James McPetrie, a legal adviser to the Colonial Office.[109] The countries that are most famous for adopting the Westminster constitution, and that are cited most routinely as illustrations of positive imperial guidance, are the 'self-governing dominions' of Canada, Australia, New Zealand and South Africa – where 'dominions' refers to 'British-settled, white-ruled, self-governing colonies that were autonomous but, notwithstanding, recognized the sovereignty of the British monarch'.★[110] These were, in the words of Rhodes et al.,[111] 'all white, British autonomous polities . . . four relatively rich settler societies, all of which ruled over the original indigenous inhabitants or other "coloured" races who were largely disenfranchised, in South Africa's case until 1994. Each of these settler societies consciously (and in many respects unquestioningly) adopted the Westminster system of government between 1848 and 1910, understood at the time as British governmental traditions.' Though there were variations in the adoption, Rhodes et al. stress that 'it is at best a half-truth to claim that Britain developed the conventions

---

★ The British used an astonishing variety of terms to describe imperial territories, from 'colonies' to 'protectorates', 'condominiums', 'mandates', 'dependencies', 'treaty ports' and 'subordinate empires'. But 'dominion' is the most bewildering, R. A. W. Rhodes, John Wanna and Patrick Weller describing the term as being 'devoid of logic'. 'It had at least three meanings. Its earliest British usage dates from the mid-seventeenth century when it was applied to selective American colonies recognizing their loyalty to the Crown (for example, New England and Virginia often still nicknamed the "old dominion"). Second, it gradually occurred in the King's title where it referred to all British territories and possessions overseas (the King's dominions overseas). From the mid-nineteenth to early twentieth centuries, it was then used to refer specifically to the colonies such as Australia, Canada, New Zealand, and South Africa, which had achieved a measure of self-government. Except in Canada, the term did not become part of the formal name of the country; the preferred use was elsewhere the Commonwealth of Australia and the Union of South Africa . . . It was also driven "by a racial instinct . . . to erect a compartment between the white man's empire, and that of lesser breeds".'

of responsible government and then the dominions replicated the system when granted self-government. When colonial administrations began to rule themselves they selectively adopted components of Westminster that suited them. They adapted these as they considered appropriate, and added other elements as they saw fit. So, all systems were hybrids and all systems, including the UK, had evolving conventions.'[112]

Elsewhere, Harshan Kumarasingham complains that Asia's embrace of the Westminster model often gets overlooked by academics.[113] Countries in this part of the world ended up with the Westminster model by different routes.[114] Apparently, the 1935 Government of India Act, which holds the record for the British Parliament's longest piece of legislation, was the model for the constitutions of India and Pakistan when they became independent: 'almost two-thirds of the Republic of India's 1950 constitution's articles consciously and acquiescently transferred provisions from the Government of India Act, which, of course, was initiated, debated, scrutinised and assented to without any real Indian involvement'.[115] Meanwhile, Ceylon didn't even have an act passed to mark its independence in 1948; King George VI instead just promulgated its constitution through an Order in Council. When it came to Malayan independence in 1957, local rulers and the British Crown joined forces to consult a group of Commonwealth notables on the new constitution – but neglected to ask anyone else from Malaya itself. And while Nepal was never officially colonized by the British, the small country was umbilically connected to the fortunes and travails of its vast neighbour India. 'The elite-led constitutions that flowed through the Himalayan kingdom bore the debris of British and Indian influence.'[116]

The Englishman Professor Sir Ivor Jennings frequently acted as a consultant in constitution-making,[117] a consultant easily more powerful than anyone who has graduated from McKinsey or Bain, given that he advised on nothing less than the founding constitutions of many countries, including Pakistan, Nepal, Singapore, Malaya, Malta, Ghana, the Maldives, Eritrea and Guyana.[118] In this way, the constitutions of many post-colonial states influenced one another, Kumarasingham citing the example of Malaya's which, thanks to Jennings, included clauses informed by the experiences and constitutions of Canada, Australia, New Zealand, Ireland, India, Pakistan, Ceylon, Burma, Ghana, South

Africa and Newfoundland.[119] When Kumarasingham tries to make sense of this process of inter-influencing, he cites the fact that many Asian post-colonial leaders had British educations as a factor: nine of the twelve prime ministers who led India, Ceylon, Malaysia, Singapore and Pakistan in their first decade of independence went to Oxbridge.[120] Increasingly it feels as if education may be the most profound and consequential British imperial legacy of all.

It would be an understatement to say that these Asian countries have had varying success with these constitutions. In Nepal, in December 1960, King Mahendra carried out a 'royal coup' by suspending the constitution ratified just a year earlier and getting rid of the ruling party.[121] The political scientist Chandra Bhatta points out that since the late 1940s Nepal has gone through seven constitutions and no elected prime minister has stayed in office for a full term.[122] Asanga Welikala observes mournfully that while 'the moment of independence held so much promise' for Ceylon – in Sir Oliver Goonetilleke's words, it was 'the best bet in Asia' – things have not worked out well.[123] Renamed Sri Lanka in 1972, the island has been ravaged by a seemingly endless civil war between the Sinhalese majority and the Tamil minority, as well as beset by chronic political and economic mismanagement and corruption.[124] Elsewhere, Tahir Kamran tells us that democracy in Pakistan has 'right from the outset' been 'hobbled because of the self-aggrandisement of the ruling elite . . . Most of its leaders in West Pakistan belonged to landed aristocracy, therefore distant from the masses.'[125] Pakistan has gone through a number of constitutions, and has seen democracy suspended repeatedly.

Which brings us to the complicating fact that while British empire evidently instilled stable democracy to a significant degree in some places like Australia, Canada and New Zealand,* it didn't do so everywhere, even in places that adopted the Westminster constitution. Moreover, in an inversion of Lawon Adams' point about blame having to be shared

---

* I say 'to a significant degree' because, crucially, these settler colonies did not generally extend the democratic franchise to the indigenous. Indeed, Australia held a Voice to Parliament referendum on 14 October 2023, which could have changed the nation's constitution for the first time in forty-six years, creating a body for Aboriginal and Torres Strait Islander people to advise the state on policies influencing their communities. But the nation voted 'no'.

when it comes to instability, sometimes you have to give the people involved in building independent nations the credit for developing democracy, not the imperialists. Moreover, there were evidently cases where the British actively worked against democracy. Certainly, the British didn't have democracy in mind when they encouraged the sale of Kashmir to one deeply flawed man who suited their purposes, and whose family then ruled the roost for the next century.[126] The British did not have democracy in mind when, under the constitution they introduced in Iraq, political parties in the words of Martin Walker 'could be banned at will, a power used ruthlessly in times of crisis to prevent parliament from falling into opposition hands. If parliament threatened to become difficult, the prime minister could be replaced, allowing new coalitions to form, or the whole parliament could be dismissed and new elections called.'[127] The British did not have democracy in mind when, in 1866, in the wake of the Morant Bay Rebellion, a group of plantation owners and landowners in Jamaica decided they would no longer govern the island, instead choosing colonial rule from London, because self-governance risked making them answerable to the expanding local black electorate.[128] Herbert Thirkell White, the Lieutenant Governor of Burma between 1905 and 1910, did not have democracy in mind when he declared that it was pointless 'to impose representative institutions on people who neither demand nor understand them'.[129]

It's true that real nostalgia for British empire has emerged in Hong Kong in recent years as the former colony succumbs to Chinese authority, with the Communist Party exerting political pressure, squashing dissent and influencing the courts.[130] It's also true that the twenty-first Governor of Hong Kong, Sir Mark Young, attempted to introduce democratic reforms in the 1940s and that, in the late stages of governing Hong Kong, the British also suddenly rediscovered an enthusiasm for democracy. But, as Kwarteng explains, the efforts of Chris Patten, the final Governor, to consolidate democracy 'baffled and surprised' the Chinese, and he was viewed by the Foreign Office establishment as 'a nuisance and, at worst, a grave threat to Sino-British relations'.[131] It was only Sir Mark Young who, in the entire century and a half of British administration, made a serious attempt at expanding democracy in the colony, and his efforts were thwarted by his successor.[132] The fact is that democracy was never a serious prospect in Hong Kong,[133] Kwarteng adding that 'the British Empire had nothing to do with liberal democracy, and, particularly in Hong Kong, was administered along lines much closer to the ideals of Confucius than to the vivid, impassioned rhetoric of Sir Winston Churchill'.[134]

Often the British became enthusiastic about democracy only when they were sure how the issue would play out, such as in the Sudan, where they knew that free Sudanese citizens would vote for independence rather than for becoming part of Egypt. But if it was looking like the colonized electorate might not veer the 'right' way – for instance, when it looked like the populations of Borneo and Sarawak might not vote to be absorbed back into Malaya, or black voters in Nyasaland or Northern Rhodesia might not wish to be part of the Central African Federation – elections were dodged, and voters were instead offered non-binding 'consultations'.[135] Even in India, the world's largest democracy, and frequently the ultimate illustration of British empire's benevolent democratic tendencies, democracy was not freely offered. When, in 1935, the British ceded full control of the provinces, and two years later Indians were put in charge of the major portfolios of government, this ostensible 'democratic innovation' wasn't quite what it seemed. The Viceroy and his people still sat at the centre of things, and had the power to rule without Indian input if so desired. Furthermore, measures were put in place to prevent the emergence of majorities which might push for total independence from Britain.[136]

Numerous Indian intellectuals have rejected the idea that democracy was bestowed upon them by the British, not least the Nobel Laureate Amartya Sen.[137] Frankly, as with British empire's patchy record with the rule of law, I'm not sure how much of an accomplishment it is to claim to have introduced democracy to India anyway given that, in assessing the degrees of democracy present around the world today, the country is hardly excelling, recently being ranked 46th in the *Economist*'s global democracy index out of 167 countries and being labelled a 'flawed democracy'.[138] And then, of course, there is Nigeria, Africa's biggest democracy, with 93 million eligible voters, which will surpass the United States in population by 2050, making it the second-largest democracy in the world,[139] and which, on paper, is another of British empire's democratic successes. But Kwarteng makes it more than clear that democracy was never the intention of its colonial architects: 'The whole tenor of British rule in Nigeria, as in other places, had been elitist and aristocratic . . . the whole premise of indirect rule in Nigeria had been "unashamedly elitist"; indeed it was the very nature of British rule that had encouraged the elitism in the first place . . . Democracy, even without tribal conflict, never really stood a chance in Nigeria.'[140]

Depressingly, Kwarteng's bleak verdict from 2011 may still be valid. Between 2019 and 2022, an estimated fifty armed attacks have been aimed at disrupting Nigeria's election process.[141] Allegations of votes being illegally traded are rife,[142] and it's common to see party officials doling out bribes to voters outside polling stations.[143] And the democracy I witness being tested in the run-up to a national election is very much on the ropes. An electoral commission centre in south-east Nigeria is attacked by armed men, who destroy 800 ballot boxes.[144] There are open suggestions from the ruling politicians that cash and fuel shortages afflicting the nation have somehow been manufactured to undermine their chances.[145] I listen to a journalist with an American broadcaster wondering out loud if it's safe enough to attend a rally in Lagos, given that opponents are known to employ thugs to disrupt such events. Voter intimidation, theft of ballot boxes and outbreaks of violence mar polling day, which also sees problems emerge with new digital vote-counting technology.[146] The ultimate result which, in the words of *The Times*, sees 'Africa's most populous country and largest economy' replace 'Muhammadu Buhari, an ailing northern septuagenarian Muslim with a reputation for financial propriety, with an ailing southern septuagenarian Muslim with a reputation for lavish spending and corruption', is disputed in the wake of electoral irregularities.[147]

In *Ghosts of Empire* Kwarteng extends his grim verdict to other parts of the world when he states that Britain's empire 'openly repudiated ideas of human equality and put power and responsibility into the hands of a chosen elite, drawn from a tiny proportion of the population in Britain. The British empire was not merely undemocratic; it was anti-democratic.'[148] It feels strange to defend the British empire from the criticisms of a one-time Conservative minister, whose government has had a knee-jerk policy of defending imperialists and imperialism, but Kwarteng goes too far here. What he says is true for many of the nations he focuses on in his book – Iraq, Kashmir, Burma, Sudan and so on – but it doesn't apply to nations like Australia, Canada and New Zealand, former settler colonies where imperialists, in the eyes of the West at least, helped usher in democracy and stability to a substantial degree. It seems to me that claims made about the democratic and non-democratic influence of the British empire are routinely overgeneralized and nuance-free. Democratization studies which turn this complex history into data points and classify any former British territory which has any sort of democracy as a 'success', or academics who classify any nation which has adopted the Westminster constitution as 'stable', miss the huge variations in outcomes around the world. Furthermore, too many analysts miss the fact that in geopolitics, and in life, opposite things can be true at once. It's true both that British empire sowed discord and chaos across the planet and that it gave birth to democracy in all sorts of places. British empire didn't always sow discord nor did it always plant the seeds of democracy. Similarly, democracy in former imperial states hasn't always led to stability, instability hasn't always stopped the subsequent development of democracy, and there are places like Nigeria and India where British empire can be credited/blamed for both the democracy *and* the instability.

In the days that follow my trip to Lagos, the final leg of my journey into Britain's international imperial history, I find myself dwelling on how bewildered the 'balance sheet' crew, the vocal and furious individuals who forever need to put the achievements of the British empire into inane 'good' and 'bad' categories to come to an overall conclusion, will be by this intense complexity. The next time one starts shouting at me at a literary festival, I'm going to ask them how many 'free' votes cast in Nigerian elections since independence make up for the hundreds of thousands of deaths that have come about as a result of Britain amalgamating the country in such a crude way. Furthermore, at which precise point did the prosperity introduced by imperial capitalists to North America begin to balance out the deaths of millions of indigenous people through disease and settler violence? How many animals saved in the national parks set up in Africa by British imperialists make up for the damage caused by the prickly-pear invasion of Australia? This view of British imperial history, where our national history is forever being given an overall rating, as if complex history were a phone-case purchase being rated on Amazon, where apples are forever being balanced against pears, where human lives somehow get balanced against claims of technological development, feels more absurd than ever. Yet it persists.

Writing it down, I wonder whether I need to go further in my professed commitment to rejecting such corrosive balancing. After all, have I not participated in a micro form of balance-sheet thinking myself –

when I've said that the anti-racism that came about in reaction to the racism of empire, as discussed in the last chapter, did not make up for it, or when I thought that the conservation initiatives that followed the environmental destruction of empire did not compensate for the damage Brits caused? I'm not doing it to come to an overall positive or negative conclusion about British empire like the balance-sheeters do, but I'm still making qualitative judgements, on a smaller scale, and is it not problematic in its own way? Furthermore, when I've suggested in recent years that abolition was simply 'good', in comparison to the 'bad' of slavery, am I not ignoring the complicating fact that some money generated by slavery was used to fund abolitionist initiatives,*[149] and justifying, in a small way, the racism which underpinned many abolitionist arguments and the racism that came about when it was felt that abolition had failed? When I've praised British people who took on British imperialism as it happened, implying that all anti-colonial resistance was simply 'good', have I not unthinkingly supported the violence that resistance may have involved, excessive or not? Unfortunately, there's no guidebook to consult on imperial balance-sheet thinking – these are emerging dilemmas. But the question bothers me enough to consult the imperial historians Alan Lester and Kim Wagner, who have together probably considered the issue of the 'balance sheet' more than anyone else.[150] And talking to them makes me conclude that this kind of balance-sheeting on a thematic level is often unacceptable too, even if it involves comparing things in the same units.

Take, for instance, the theme of slavery. It might feel acceptable to say that abolition did not make up for Britain's active role in the trans-atlantic slave trade. After all, the British transported more than 3 million Africans across the Atlantic[151] and then, on abolition, liberated only 800,000 people.[152] But this is an argument that could be countered on the grounds that, by passing the 1833 Emancipation Act, Britain

* The Wills family tobacco business in Bristol, which eventually merged with other companies to become Imperial Tobacco, bought tobacco cultivated by the enslaved, via brokers in London and Bristol. The Fry family, also based in Bristol, used cacao and sugar produced by the enslaved in the Caribbean and on São Tomé to manufacture its chocolate products. But as Quakers both families were supporters of abolition and made contributions, financial and personal, to the cause. (The Frys were significantly more committed than the Wills: in 1850, J. S. Fry's second son embarked on a three-month tour of Europe promoting the cause.)

saved innumerable millions from being enslaved over subsequent centuries, so the number of 800,000 should be inflated by tens of millions. It might also feel superficially logical to say that the animal- and nature-preservation/conservation efforts that British imperialists eventually embarked upon did not make up for the destruction of animals and nature that they instigated in the first place. But this could be countered on the grounds that, over subsequent centuries, the number of animals and the amount of nature imperialists conserved through, say, the building of national parks and reservations, far outweighs any damage they may have originally caused. These kinds of arguments are both hypothetical in the extreme and far from illuminating. Much better to simply accept slavery, anti-slavery, destruction/preservation of animals/nature as phenomena in their own right and attempt to understand their complicated stories. Much better to try, at every possible stage, to seek nuance than to come to some kind of generalized ethical-mathematical conclusion.

Wagner is right when he argues that 'balance' is not actually something that is useful in history: it's more important to seek out 'nuance', 'complexity' and 'a multiplicity of perspectives'. 'The so-called balance-sheet approach is not, and never was, a genuine tool for historical analysis,' he adds.

> Instead, it was always intended as a way to deflect critique and redeem the Empire. The flip-side to this narrative, namely the insistence that the Empire was simply 'bad' rather than 'good', or that the British today should feel 'shame' rather than 'pride', is by the same token not conducive to a deeper historical understanding either. This critique simply tallies the balance-sheet differently, with imperialism coming up short, but doesn't ultimately challenge the basic premise of historical judgement.

He adds that he has as little time for, say, Niall Ferguson as he does for Shashi Tharoor, two writers who have respectively talked up the 'achievements' and the 'crimes' of empire. 'Both locate the key drivers of historical change exclusively with the British, while reducing Indians [and other indigenous peoples] to passive colonial subjects who are merely acted upon.'

Lester adds that the important thing when it comes to tracing the modern legacies of empire is to follow links in chains, rather than come to judgement about whether the good outweighed the bad, even on a local level. British empire was ultimately a mass of contradictions, and its legacies are contradictory too. 'To me the empire is something that consists of trillions, infinite numbers of interactions between people, between groups,' Lester says over email.

> The same person in British empire might be impacted negatively by colonialism on one day and positively the next. They could find themselves humiliated in the street by a white man or woman one day, and the next day call on the colonial police to sort out a dispute. People could be imprisoned or elevated in status at different stages of their lives. People like Gandhi and Solomon Plaatje* benefited from British educations and professional qualifications and supported the empire at a certain stage of their lives and then came deeply to resent its racial exclusions at another and campaigned against it. So weighing up a balance sheet, even for just one individual, is impossible, let alone for millions of people over hundreds of years over 25 per cent of the world's surface. It's a fruitless exercise. It's better I think to just trace causative connections.

I find the idea that you can identify contradictory legacies, without having to weigh them up even on a local level, liberating. Obviously, there is complexity within this complexity: it only goes so far. There are certain facts about empire which are incontrovertibly uncomplex. When it comes to an institution like the royal family, it's perfectly possible to observe that their involvement in slavery far outweighs their involvement in abolition. But when it comes to generalizing about British empire as a whole, whatever you say about the British empire, the opposite is almost always true to a certain degree. To how much of a degree? It's often unknowable. And accepting anything else will eventually tie you into intellectual knots. Anyone approaching this history with an open mind, and looking at it for long enough, will eventually come to the conclusion that the legacies are contradictory and complex. And there's no better example of what I mean than Jan Morris, who wrote a deeply nostalgic and hugely influential trilogy on the British

* The South African journalist and politician who was the first General Secretary of the South African Native National Congress, which became the African National Congress.

empire, only to remark, in an act of insight towards the end of her life, that she was 'ashamed' of the work.[153]

Asking whether British empire was good or bad is as inane and pointless as asking whether the world's weather has been good or bad over the last 350 years. The history resists simplistic explanations. The British empire spread the rule of law, for example, but also institutionalized legal inequality in a way which means that millions of people still can't bank on justice today. The British empire was a propagator of racism, but also witnessed a spread of anti-racism in reaction to it and sometimes took on settlers for their extreme racism. The British empire both destroyed and saved large swathes of the global environment, spread the free press and press censorship, saw the mass destruction and construction of buildings, both combated and propagated hunger, encouraged both education and wilful ignorance.

However, seeing British empire as an incredibly complex mass of contradictions doesn't prevent us from saying it's absurd to maintain, as too many people do, that the achievements of abolition mean that our national involvement in slavery should not be explored. Nor does it stop us observing that historians have for too long approached this history from the point of view of the colonizers and ignored the colonized; that imperialists made concerted efforts to repress evidence of what had happened; that there is now an organized, well-funded campaign to shut down discussion of slavery and empire in Britain; that anyone who attempts to talk about imperial history with real nuance is shouted down by culture warriors of various stripes keen on basic views of history; and that we need to pay more attention to what nations formerly in the empire are trying to tell us about how the British empire shaped their development.

If it helps some people to deal with the subsequent conversation, and I know some do struggle with it, for deeply felt reasons, quite often feeling personally attacked by new emphases in imperial history, I would remind them that history is rewritten all the time (it's literally what historians do), and that it's human nature to be exercised about the injurious but to accept the constructive as part of the furniture of life. In Britain, we're more likely to be cross about, say, how the Germans bombed the hell out of places like Coventry in the Second World War than we are to sit around thanking the Romans for all the roads they built. It's entirely natural that the residents of, say, Jamaica, would be exercised about Britain leaving its population impoverished after slavery, even while they benefit from another imperial legacy such as, say, the introduction of cricket. It's time to abandon this monochromatic way of seeing our imperial history once and for all. It's time to seek nuance wherever it's available. It's time for everyone, even those of us who think we know a lot, to challenge what we thought we knew and to be, like Jan Morris, open to changing our minds sometimes. Most importantly, it's finally time to turn Britain's hoary old monologue on the British empire into a real dialogue.

# Conclusion: An Evolutionary Outgrowth

I don't expect to have fun at the opening ceremony of the Commonwealth Games, and the journey to the stadium lowers expectations further. The habitually lousy public transport connections between London and Birmingham are, somehow, the worst they've ever been: cancellations mean it takes seven hours to travel by train to Britain's second city. Once in Birmingham, the walk between the main station and the stadium shuttle bus involves navigating chaotic building work, despite some £778 million having been spent on the games.[1] This is a maddening but age-old problem with Birmingham: it's forever trying to be the city of the future and, as a result, it's forever a building site. Even the arrival of an international games event cannot seemingly make a difference.*[2]

Compounding my downheartedness is the date and its significance. It's ten years almost to the day that we had the opening ceremony of the 2012 London Olympics – a confident, triumphant celebration of London's creativity and diversity which some of us are convinced annoyed some on the right so much that it sparked the war on the 'woke' that has cursed our politics ever since.[3] Will this ceremony, in one of Britain's most diverse cities, in my home county, provoke a similar reaction? It's too depressing to contemplate. Then there's the melancholy issue of what the hell the Commonwealth Games are for anyway. Nowadays, it's often a struggle to get cities to put them on,[4] while comedian John Oliver has labelled them an 'off-Broadway Olympics' and a 'historic display of a once-mighty nation gathering together the countries it lost and finding a way to lose to them once more'.[5] Which leads to another awkward question: what the hell is the Commonwealth about

---

* The Brummie comedian Joe Lycett, one of the hosts of the opening ceremony, noticed it too and tweeted: 'To those visiting Birmingham for the first time and wondering why much of it is still a building site, we kindly ask you to refrain from commenting. Construction delays, road works and diversions are actually an integral part of our culture.'

anyway? A basic query that has been answered in a staggering number of ways since its inception in 1931.[6]

The late Queen, as head of the Commonwealth, described it variously as 'an entirely new conception, built on the highest qualities of the spirit of man: friendship, loyalty, and the desire for freedom and peace',[7] a 'family of nations'[8] and, in a statement that made me fret about her tech skills, 'the original world wide web'.[9] In 1962 one member of the Royal Commonwealth Society, which now identifies itself as 'a network of individuals and organisations committed to improving the lives and prospects of Commonwealth citizens across the world',[10] bewilderingly described the Commonwealth as 'an epic in which the idealism of explorers, doctors, missionaries, magistrates and scientists is interwoven with the expediency of soldiers, merchants, engineers and farmers'.[11]

More formal attempts at definition aren't necessarily any more helpful. The *Encyclopaedia Britannica* calls the Commonwealth 'an evolutionary outgrowth of the British empire',[12] but then the official website for the Commonwealth forces one to qualify the definition immediately, telling us that while 'the Commonwealth's roots go back to the British empire . . . today any country can join the modern Commonwealth'.[13] The last two countries to join were Gabon and Togo in 2022, which were never part of the British empire. The royal family website tells us that a 'Commonwealth Realm' is a country which has the King as its monarch, but given that the Commonwealth has fifty-six members, and there are only fourteen 'Commonwealth Realms' in addition to the UK, this clearly cannot be a defining factor of membership. When India joined the Commonwealth in 1947, it did so without the Queen as monarch, and a bunch of Commonwealth countries have recently become, or plan to become, republics, including Barbados and Jamaica.[14] As for the idea that crops up sometimes when you ask people to define the Commonwealth, that it may offer its citizens some kind of common citizenship, just take a look at what happened to Commonwealth citizens in the Windrush Scandal. They found themselves facing deportation to countries they barely knew. Immigration legislation in post-war Britain has progressively hacked away at the right of Commonwealth citizens to live in Britain.[15]

Nevertheless, by reading several sources alongside one another, it's possible to get the gist. The Commonwealth is essentially a voluntary association of fifty-six independent countries, home to 2.5 billion people and including both advanced economies and developing countries. The member governments agree on shared goals like development, democracy, peace and 'values and principles' as expressed in the Commonwealth Charter. It emerged as an idea in the nineteenth century when 'white' dominions like Canada, Australia, New Zealand, South Africa and Ireland developed degrees of sovereignty outside empire.[16] In 1884, the Liberal peer and staunch imperialist Lord Rosebery spoke of the empire as 'a Commonwealth of Nations'[17] and the concept was formalized at the Imperial Conference of 1926, with a declaration that such territories should be seen as 'autonomous communities within the British empire, equal in status . . . united by a common allegiance to the Crown, and freely associated as members of the British Commonwealth of Nations'. In 1931, the Statute of Westminster marked the official formation of the body.

Various roles have been proposed for the Commonwealth in its history. It has been talked up by some as a cultural body, offering public funding for projects in the 1960s that aimed to 're-insert the Commonwealth into the national imagination'.[18] But the two largest state-endorsed cultural projects, the Commonwealth Institute (formerly the Imperial Institute) in Kensington and the Commonwealth Arts Festival are long gone.[19] Some have suggested more recently that the Commonwealth could become a platform to tackle climate change, but even those who have suggested it have conceded that the superpowers (India) and small island nations (Nauru) that are members have wildly different priorities. It has been proposed that the Commonwealth could counteract the power and influence of China, Roger Boyes and Jane Flanagan arguing that the body could be a trade-and-culture soft-power platform to give China 'a run for its money' in terms of global influence, though they conceded in the same piece that the Commonwealth can't compete in terms of actual finances.[20] And there has been no shortage of efforts to talk up its economic potential: initially in the form of 'the Sterling Area arrangement', which saw many Commonwealth countries peg their exchange rates to the British pound and hold their reserves in the Bank of England, and more recently as a trading bloc alternative to the European Union. The former, however, is no more, and the latter simply has not emerged, despite the wishful thinking of Brexiteers (a few days after the 2016 referendum result, the *Daily Telegraph* carried an article by Lord Howell, chairman of the Royal Commonwealth Society, entitled 'A bright future awaits Britain post-Brexit in the Commonwealth markets').[21]

Perhaps the clearest thing you can say about the Commonwealth is that it lacks a clear mission. Writing anonymously in *The Times* in 1964, Enoch Powell described the Commonwealth as a 'gigantic farce'. Around the same time John Chadwick, the first Director of the Commonwealth Foundation, alleged that the Commonwealth had reached a 'nadir of disillusion' and was 'an international idea rather than an organization', while the writer Guy Arnold pronounced that the Commonwealth was a body with which Britain appeared 'to have little idea what to do'.[22] India's first Prime Minister, Jawaharlal Nehru, thought the Commonwealth meant very little for independent India, telling his chief ministers in 1952 that India's association with the Commonwealth posed no threat to the country's independence because 'it is completely informal and there are no commitments'.[23] Meanwhile, in 1968, Arnold Smith, Commonwealth Secretary General, explained, not particularly helpfully, that 'the Commonwealth is what we think it is. It can be what we make it.'[24]

The cause was not helped by the fact that, in the late 1950s and early 1960s, Commonwealth Day, a replacement for the once-popular Empire Day, did not grab the public's imagination,[25] and that it became the responsibility of the retired and eccentric Air Marshal Sir Victor Goddard. Anna Bocking-Welch calls him 'enthusiastic but misguided', as she recalls that he penned a surreal sequence of barely coherent Commonwealth Day messages to schools.[26] The 1960 message, for instance, began: 'Rial Real Royal Realm / Regal Regular Rule / Region Regiment Rector Rex / Regina Ream & Reign'. It concluded with the words: 'The Royal Road to true understanding of Man and Commonwealth runs through a Realm of Realness. There is nothing more really Real than the Commonwealth of Man: but it needs to be known – to be experienced – to be Realized. That is not just an idea: it is a Universal Truth: it is the road to Commonwealth.'[27] By 2003 Niall Ferguson was calling the Commonwealth 'little more than a subset of the United

Nations or the International Olympic Committee, its only obvious merit being that it saves money on professional translators'.[28] Writing in spring 2022, Ben Macintyre compared the Commonwealth to a gentleman's club, albeit one that faced 'changing membership, altered rules, cashflow problems, and accusations of obsolescence'.[29]

Meanwhile, in the wry and illuminating *The Empire's New Clothes*, Philip Murphy finds dozens of entertaining ways to restate his main argument which is 'essentially, that the Commonwealth has lost almost all of the limited significance it once possessed, and has become something of a mirage in the field of British foreign policy'.[30] Among other things, he asks himself the rhetorical question: what does the Commonwealth mean to me? And he suggests that for himself, as the one-time Director of the Institute of Commonwealth Studies, it meant 'lots of drinks receptions in the hollowed-out citadels of Britain's former imperial power' and 'endless well-meaning conferences exploring how the Commonwealth could achieve its "true potential"'.[31] Devastatingly, he recalls that when the Royal Commonwealth Society issued a poll of opinions from across its member states in 2010, just half of those surveyed were aware that the Queen was the head of the Commonwealth. A tenth of South Africans and Indians believed it to be the former UN Secretary General Kofi Annan, while a quarter of Jamaicans believed it to be US President Barack Obama.[32]

Reading this on a heavily delayed train to the opening ceremony doesn't exactly put a spring in my step. And weighing me down further, more than anything else in fact, is the ultimate purpose of my trip. You see, the Commonwealth Games, once known as the British Empire Games, the British Empire and Commonwealth Games and the British Commonwealth Games,[33] are meant to give me an avenue into discussing how British empire has shaped many different aspects of our tangible and intangible international infrastructure, and then allow me to bring my multi-year efforts to trace the modern legacies of British empire to a neat conclusion. But it's becoming apparent that there will be no neat conclusion. It's true, as I said at the start of the international leg of my journey into Britain's imperial history, that to understand the modern world, you need to understand British empire. But it's probably impossible to ever fully understand either, and this is reflected in the fact that the global legacies of the British empire feel endless. For when it comes to infrastructure alone, it has been argued that British empire helped invent the Western corporation and bestow it with power;[34] helps explain the power dynamics of big tech;[35] explains the now defunct gold standard monetary system;[36] helped to corral numerous nations into a global system of time zones;[37] aided, through colonial science, the emergence of meteorology and, later, climatology;[38] explains, in part, the United Nations;[39] and explains, in part, the shape and flavour of global tax avoidance.[40] Then there are the imperial legacies which do not fit neatly into the broad themes I've identified for this book, not least the contemporary paranoia about the severing of the undersea cables that enable modern telecommunications;[41] the concept of corporate lobbying;[42] the emergence of tropical medicine;[43] the creation of Britain's controversial 'non-dom' status;[44] Britain's emergence as a nuclear power[45] and patterns of violence in India.[46] Beyond these, there are the broad themes, when it comes to imperial legacies, that I've not tackled because others have done such a comprehensive job: there's not much anyone could add to Caroline Elkins' comprehensive *Legacy of Violence*, for instance, or *The Hungry Empire: How Britain's Quest for Food Shaped the Modern World*, by Lizzie Collingham. There are themes that I've not taken on because I've not got anything fresh to say on them: the British empire's legacy in terms of 'free' media and taxation, for instance.[47] And even among the topics I've tackled at length, such as the legacies of slavery, there are threads that keep emerging and could be teased out further: the intriguing possibility, implied by the Truth and Justice Commission of Mauritius, for instance, that the descendants of the enslaved may have ended up in entertainment in disproportionate numbers because of the way clowning around saved some of the enslaved from the wrath of their masters.★[48]

In short, my mission will be incomplete, however much time I devote to the task, and I will soon have devoted half a decade to it. Taking my seat in the Alexander Stadium, the realization sits more heavily upon

---

★ 'Playing the clown saved slaves from feeling the wrath of their masters,' the Truth and Justice Commission of Mauritius reported. 'Being entertaining was a coveted status because, from nothingness, slaves could emerge in the master's favour. It appears that this identification process is still ongoing, to a great extent, through comedy or entertainment rather than in the intellectual sphere.' The idea that black humour in the US developed as a form of resistance to slavery has been explored extensively.

my shoulders than the roadside curry I've just scoffed sits in my gut. But then there is movement in the royal box as the dignitaries arrive, the lights go out, the show starts and . . . guess what.

I love it.

I clap.

I jump.

I high-five volunteers (at their suggestion, I'm British after all).

And I admit I also cry my eyes out.

The trigger is, in part, just the sight of thousands of local volunteers being so proud of their much maligned, endlessly self-deprecating city. People in the West Midlands don't big up their home towns like they do in Wales and Yorkshire. If anything, we compete to tell mocking stories. And to see, for the first time in my life, this part of the world, forever ridiculed for its architecture and its accent, forever beating itself up about its traffic and roadworks, finally take pride in itself is moving. Especially when one of the things they're taking pride in is racial diversity. Throughout my life, the multiculturalism of my home region has been a stick with which people have beaten it. If anything, this tendency has increased in recent years, with the media amplifying ludicrous claims that parts of Brum are no-go areas for white people.[49] Sure, there have been racial tensions at times, but it has long been drowned out by harmony and productivity. Where else could interracial bands like the Specials and UB40 have emerged but the West Midlands? Which other region could have produced the balti curry? This is the first time I've seen any of it celebrated on the international stage and it's an emotional experience.

Then there's the poignancy of seeing young people perform. As the athletes walk in, the adolescent male and female cheerleaders placed opposite our seats attempt to sustain our enthusiasm and applause, and if you cease to be moved by the sight of a young person working so hard at something, and then excelling, you're a harder person than me. You're also a harder person than me if you can keep it together when your own life story plays a small part in such proceedings. For it turns out that the ceremony includes a literary segment, featuring local authors like Kit de Waal and . . . me. And I challenge anyone out there, who had a father who couldn't read or write, who couldn't speak English when they started school, whose household didn't possess a book until they won a book token at school, not to shed tears when their memoir is turned into a costume, and the young person in that costume then dances their heart out in front of a stadium full of their own people. I have to lean back in my chair so my brother doesn't see me weep at the sight of *The Boy with the Topknot* in costumed, dancing form. Once I start, though, and as my phone fills up with messages from friends who have seen my life story bopping around on TV, I can't stop. And as I make my way to the Gents to compose myself, I have a moment of clarity about how and why I've ended up here. My working life has often felt disconnected: you don't generally make it as a writer if you produce a memoir, then a novel, then a book about history, and intersperse it all with business and magazine journalism. You find one thing you're good at, keep at it and become known for it. But I can see now that everything has been connected after all: the memoir was an attempt to make sense of my family history, the novel an effort to make sense of British Asian history, and *Empireland* a project to make sense of my nation's history. Perhaps I've been a historian of some sort for some time, without knowing it.

Furthermore, it suddenly makes sense that my journey into the history of British empire would end here, at this event, at this time, in this region. In 1600, the East India Company was born to make the most of the potential of trade with Asia. The Company, through a combination of enterprise, overreach, duplicity, greed, innovation, accident, repression, violence, looting, opportunism and improvisation on the ground, turned into the Raj. The Raj and the empire would die, but when the mother country needed help during world wars and in the economic crises that followed them, it would call upon the citizens of empire, my family among them. Ultimately, if this part of Britain is so racially diverse, it's because British empire was racially diverse, and the histories of both are inextricable. If Queen Elizabeth I had not blessed the East India Company centuries ago, we wouldn't be here. And, in this moment at least, it feels as if the Commonwealth has meaning. After all, the relative applause directed at the athletes emerging into the stadium, nation by nation, is informed by real knowledge and experience. If the Pakistani contingent gets loud cheers from the crowd at the back, for instance, it's because the crowd at the back includes a fair few British Pakistanis. If the Barbados delegation gets whooped around us, it's because everyone in the West Midlands knows at least one Barbadian family. The ethnic diversity of the stadium of athletes, once they've all filed in, echoes the ethnic diversity of the region's primary school sports days.

Despite my expectations, for this moment at least, the Commonwealth feels like a tangible thing. Which, in turn, inspires an idea: we should revive the Commonwealth as an institution, by establishing it as a forum for post-imperial discussion, a place where we can all face up to the consequences of the British empire. It's obvious, once you think about it: on one side, we have debates about the legacies of empire among a bunch of nation states, united largely by their experience of British empire, that just won't go away; on the other we have an organization struggling for purpose, headed by a monarch struggling to navigate the debates. A monarch who also has the job of uniting a multicultural nation, which is multicultural mainly because of the British empire. There's also the gap between how the world sees Britain through the prism of its imperial history, and how we fail to see ourselves through the prism of that history. What better organization to find a path through it all, to finally turn the monologue into a dialogue, than one whose isolated successes have almost all been related to decolonization? Take, for example, the Commonwealth's 1961 ruling that its members must practise respect for racial equality, which led to South Africa immediately withdrawing its application for membership. The mid-1960s witnessed the organization focusing its energy on the apartheid policies of South Africa and Rhodesia. The Commonwealth also played a role in achieving independence for Namibia, and in pushing for debt relief for poor countries in the 1990s.[50] It's natural that in the new millennium it would, among other things, become a forum through which many of the CARICOM countries, Britain and other nations face up to the consequences of imperial indenture, imperial slavery, imperial environmental exploitation, imperial species destruction, imperial racism, imperial legislation, imperial geopolitical instability and imperial humanitarianism.

It's such a good idea, in fact, that other people have also had it. The chairman of the Royal Commonwealth Society Council, John Hope, touched upon it when he wrote a letter to *The Times* in April 1964 claiming that the Commonwealth could 'become a unique instrument of racial cooperation over the whole field of human endeavour'.[51] The think tank Demos suggested it in 2002,[52] its Director imagining the Queen going on a world tour to apologise for the 'past sins of the

British empire'.[53] In that piece cited earlier, Roger Boyes and Jane Flanagan wrote that 'the transformational gesture that Britain could make in the post-Elizabethan age is to lead (or listen, follow and help shape) a cross-Commonwealth reappraisal of the impact of slavery on its former colonies'.[54] Philip Murphy, meanwhile, has wondered out loud whether:

> the Commonwealth might yet come to the rescue of Britain, which currently seems to find it so difficult to have a sensible debate about its Empire. In many ways, the Commonwealth is the ideal forum for a debate at the highest levels about the impacts and legacies of colonialism. All of its members have been profoundly shaped by that history – from the UK as colonial hegemon to the tiniest of colonial dependencies; from countries shaped by British imperialism over centuries to those where its direct impact lasted little more than a generation ... The Commonwealth has a rare 'competitive advantage' in its ability to air and possibly help to reconcile wildly conflicting points of view.[55]

Too right.

I must confess though that, in the light of day, some twelve hours later, and under the influence of coffee rather than beer, some problems with the plan do become apparent. Not least, it seems from recent pronouncements that King Charles is doing his very best to resist the obvious. In the summer of 2022, while he was still the Prince of Wales, it was reported that he had been in contact with experts and world leaders on the topic of slavery, 'and that he hoped that a charitable organisation would take on the mantle in order to better educate and inform',[56] seemingly oblivious to the rather large organization, headed by his mother, that could do the job. More recently he was hoping out loud that the Commonwealth could play an 'indispensable role' in 'the most pressing issues of our time', mentioning everything from climate change to biodiversity loss, opportunities for young people, global health and economic cooperation, except for the one issue, British imperialism, which has exercised him and many Commonwealth nations more than any other in recent times.[57] Moreover, some might say that the Commonwealth, which includes many of the Caribbean countries that have formally requested reparations through CARI-COM, is precisely the wrong organization given its closeness to British empire. As with many British international charities in the post-war period, the Commonwealth and affiliated bodies recruited straight from empire: the Royal Commonwealth Society, for instance, appointed Alan Lennox-Boyd as Chairman in 1961, a man who had been Secretary of State for the Colonies in the Conservative government between 1954 and 1959, and who had thought it unwise, for economic reasons, to grant colonies independence before they were ready.[58] Early in his book Philip Murphy remarks that during his doctoral research in the late 1980s/early 1990s he 'became familiar with the idea of the Commonwealth as a great, soothing comfort blanket for the [Conservative] party's dwindling band of post-war imperial enthusiasts'[59] and adds later that 'Commonwealth gatherings' could in certain lights 'seem less like family reunions and more like support groups for the victims of a particularly brutal kidnapper'.*[60]

At the same time, it could be argued that the symbol of the monarch, and the associated symbolism of the royal family, are so linked to the imperial project that King Charles wouldn't have the distance required to help resolve these issues through the Commonwealth. After all, Queen Elizabeth I sponsored early slaving missions and honoured the slave trader John Hawkins by giving him a coat of arms that featured a chained African.[61] The Royal African Company was run from royal palaces and sent more enslaved African women, men and children to the Americas than any other single institution during the transatlantic slave trade's entire history.[62] The East India Company loaned vast amounts of money to Charles II (in the late 1670s, these transfers became gifts to royalty, which didn't need to be repaid).[63] George III defended the transatlantic slave trade and opposed abolition during his reign.[64] Prince William, the third son of George III and future William IV, supported the slave lobby throughout the late eighteenth and early nineteenth

---

* 'Until recently, there has been a tendency by those representing former colonies at the Commonwealth to uphold a collective amnesia,' continues Philip Murphy. 'Many of those who had posed for group photos with the Queen at Commonwealth premiers' meetings in the 1960s and '70s had previously been detained in her name. At [a] farewell lunch, Prince Charles recalled "asking the wrong question to [Kenyan] President Jomo Kenyatta, 47 years ago, about whether he had ever visited Lake Rudolf, now Lake Turkana (where I had just been), only to be met by an ominous silence until he let out a roar of laughter and said, 'Yes I was a guest of your mother there for some time!' " '

centuries, and delivered a pro-slavery speech in the House of Lords.[65] The Windsors have ancestors who were directors of the East India Company and received enormous sums in 'compensation' on abolition.[66] Places like Upper Burma were annexed in the name of the royal family.[67] The 'three pairs of shawls' cited in the peculiar 1846 Treaty of Amritsar, which handed over Kashmir to a tyrant king, were presented to the British monarch.[68] Queen Victoria used royal tours to display approval for imperial policies.[69] The royals were routinely given a share of the loot when the British state pillaged places like Benin[70] and the Imperial Summer Palace at Peking: the Pekingese dog found there and taken back as a gift to Queen Victoria was christened 'Looty' and even had its portrait painted.[71] The royal family did not rise above the racism of empire, even in the twentieth century. According to Hilary Sapire, a 1947 tour of South Africa was 'soaked' in racial segregation★[72] and, until at least the late 1960s, the Queen's courtiers prohibited 'coloured immigrants or foreigners' from working in clerical positions in the royal household[73] (not long after the time the Queen had pledged to 'give myself, heart and soul' to the 'new conception of an equal partnership of nations and races').[74]

But these experiences are precisely why the Commonwealth, headed by King Charles, could function so well as a Truth and Reconciliation body.[75] He and his family have been tiptoeing awkwardly around the subject for years anyway. I'm not just thinking here of what happened during that disastrous visit to the Caribbean. Or Prince Harry's observations in a recent Netflix documentary about the royal family's historic

---

★ Hilary Sapire explains: 'State banquets, civic balls, and garden parties at government houses were all-white affairs, while separate events were organized for coloured, Indian, and African publics in "native reserves", selected city squares and open spaces, a mission school, segregated townships, and in a miners' compound. Whereas the princesses danced with members of the public at the "white" civic ball in Cape Town, at its coloured counterpart, they were placed high on a balcony to watch the dazzling array of dancers and a Malay wedding enactment. No opportunities were created for presenting leaders from the Indian and African congresses to the royal family, and to the chagrin of many Africans, it was presumed that the presentation to the royal family of the (white) native representatives who sat in parliament and the senate would suffice. Even where provision was made for all "races" to line city streets, separate areas of the pavements were allocated to "Europeans" and "non-Europeans" to prevent racially mixed crowds.'

involvement in slavery. I'm thinking of the dozens of times they have issued words of regret – usually falling short of an outright apology – for colonial catastrophes. Charles, when still Prince of Wales, said in Barbados in 2021 for instance that 'the appalling atrocity of slavery for ever stains our history'. The Queen remarked, in 2011, on the 'regrettable reality' of British relations with Ireland and, in 1995, put her signature to a fulsome apology to a Maori community in New Zealand for killings and land theft committed during the time of Queen Victoria.[76] Two years later, at the Jallianwala Bagh memorial to the Amritsar Massacre of 1919, she declared that 'history cannot be rewritten, however much we might sometimes wish otherwise. It has its moments of sadness, as well as gladness.'[77]

Besides, King Charles just can't escape the planet's keen desire to snap Britain out of its monologue and begin a real dialogue. As I write, the nation has just witnessed the new monarch's lavish coronation, the lavishness in itself being an imperial legacy,[78] and throughout which the royal household did its best not to get embroiled in yet more controversies of an imperial flavour. Not least, it was decided early on that Queen Camilla was not to wear a crown set with the Koh-i-Noor diamond, taken by the East India Company after its victory in the Second Anglo-Sikh War of 1849 and now claimed by India (among other countries).[79] Yet it turned out that the Queen *would* be wearing a crown adorned with one of the Cullinan diamonds, which are imperial in origin and contentious in themselves.[80] A South African trade unionist named Zwelinzima Vavi, whose father worked in the mines during apartheid, remarked that if the diamond was sported by the Queen it would 'be like spitting in the face of South Africans . . . We remain in deep, shameful poverty, we remain with mass unemployment and rising levels of crime due to the oppression and devastation caused by her and her forefathers.'[81]

Official efforts to defuse tension around the crown jewels were further undermined when the *Guardian* reported that the India Office, the government agency once in charge of Britain's rule over the subcontinent, had kept a lengthy document in its archives exposing the frequently bloody origins of a number of other crown jewels.[82] At the same time, a blizzard of headlines in the run-up to the coronation drew attention to the royal family's involvement in slavery as Britain built the largest empire in human history. They were inspired, among other things, by a letter from twelve countries' republican and reparations activists requesting that the new monarch begin the process of 'a formal apology and for reparatory justice to commence',[83] the Prime Minister of St Kitts and Nevis in the Caribbean declaring that his country was 'not totally free' while King Charles remained its head of state,[84] and a senior Jamaican government minister announcing that the coronation had accelerated the nation's plans to become a republic.[85] The coverage was so relentless that King Charles went further than any British royal has ever done and expressed public support for an independent research project exploring the involvement of the British monarchy in the trans-atlantic slave trade.[86] For some, though, this research is too little too late, because it involves nothing more than supporting the work of a single PhD researcher who may or may not report by 2026.

The awkwardness has been palpable, and should the Common-wealth's new imagined mission in decolonization begin to feel too difficult for those involved, I suggest they remember that dissent against colonialism is in itself an imperial legacy. Show me any event or contro-versy during British empire and I'll find some Britons who opposed it at the time. These days, you can't move for modern British politicians arguing that you're not patriotic if you're not 'proud' of British imper-ial history. But, as we've learned, there were Britons who resisted imperialism at the time, *as it happened*. Furthermore, this tradition has been baked into the Commonwealth, dissent being one of the most striking features of the opening ceremony of the Commonwealth Games. The International Olympic Committee may ban political gestures, but the Commonwealth Games Federation, the organization controlling the Games, has introduced rules supporting athletes' right to protest on social issues. So we had the diver Tom Daley making a show of support for LGBTQ+ rights, continuing his work highlight-ing the fact that many Commonwealth countries still criminalize same-sex relationships.[87] We had the opening ceremony alluding to dark episodes in imperial history, with the depiction of enslaved people in chains pulling a giant bull into the stadium[88] (these chains having been manufactured in places like my home town). The website for the CGF also features a reference to the British empire's 'historical injust-ice'.[89] These are not empty gestures: one of the people I speak to before the ceremony, in the half-hour queue for that heavy-going curry, is a gay telecoms order manager, who tells me that Daley's stance is one of the things that made him book tickets. 'It needs to be called out, and the Commonwealth Games allow it.'

Besides, global interest in the legacies of colonialism just keeps increasing – in part, I suspect, because new information keeps emerging, empires like Britain's having done their best to suppress bad news at the time.★[90] In the Netherlands, the Dutch Prime Minister has issued a formal apology on behalf of the Dutch state for the national historical involvement in the slave trade, saying that slavery must be recognized in 'the clearest terms' as a crime against humanity, and King Willem-Alexander has followed suit,[91] having commissioned research into the role of the royal family in the nation's colonial past.[92] The Belgian Parliament launched a Special Parliamentary Commission in 2020 to examine Belgium's colonial past and reparations,[93] while the return of tens of thousands of artefacts, including human skulls, is now a topic of intense discussion between Belgium and the Democratic Republic of the Congo, Rwanda and Burundi, with a significant diplomatic and national effort being made to address the origins of 84,000 items.[94] Portugal's President Marcelo Rebelo de Sousa has said his country should apologize for its role in the transatlantic slave trade, which saw the country forcibly trafficking 6 million Africans, primarily to Brazil.[95] The European Union has suggested that reparations may be required for what it referred to as a 'crime against humanity' in which millions of people were subjected to 'untold suffering' due to Europe's participation in the slave trade.[96] The Pope recently revealed that discussions were afoot to return artefacts in the Vatican Museum that had been looted from indigenous peoples in Canada and expressed an interest in giving back other colonial objects.[97] Meanwhile, a fifteen-member

---

★ I had heard of Operation Legacy, a project run by the British Colonial Office (eventually merged with the Foreign Office) to hide or destroy documents so they wouldn't be passed on to the country's former colonies. Across the world, diplomatic missions had bonfires lit as part of the cleansing. I was also aware of the open document burning that occurred in New Delhi in 1947 and was reported on by Indian news sources. But I did not know that in places like Nigeria information was suppressed even as imperialism was happening. Max Siollun tells us of 'massive gaps in historical accounts regarding the time [the Royal Niger Company] was most influential (between 1885 and 1900). The gaps exist because the company's founder made a concerted effort to obscure the history of that era and to prevent its story from ever being told . . . This lacuna in Nigeria's history is due to the actions of one man, Sir George Goldie.'

delegation of African royals recently travelled to Jamaica and consulted the CARICOM Reparations Commission.[98]

In general, the British remain allergic to confronting this history, the *Economist* reporting recently, in an article bearing the headline 'Two centuries of forgetting', that Britons 'show little interest in re-assessing it',[99] and there being a largely indifferent response to claims from a leading judge at the International Court of Justice that the UK is likely to owe more than £18 trillion in reparations for its historic role in transatlantic slavery.[100] But there are signs that attitudes are very slowly shifting. A poll published in the spring of 2023 found that 44 per cent of Britons thought that the royal family should pay reparations of some sort for their role in the slave trade.[101] The Church of England has given £100 million to a compensation fund to 'address past wrongs' brought about by its involvement in the slave trade.[102] Trinity College, Cambridge is looking into the allegation that it benefited from slavery.[103] The family of William Gladstone, one of Britain's most famous prime ministers, have recently travelled to the Caribbean to apologize for its historical role in slavery, and offered reparations.[104] Rishi Sunak, who has remarked in Parliament that 'trying to unpick our history is . . . not something that we will focus our energies on', is being urged by some MPs to start talks with Caribbean leaders on making amends for Britain's involvement in slavery.[105] After the coronation renewed concerns about the monarchy's historical involvement in slavery, Ed Davey, the leader of the Liberal Democrats, called for a national discussion on the role we played in the trade. The trust that owns the *Guardian* newspaper has expressed regret for the involvement of its Mancunian founders in the slave trade and promised millions of pounds to 'descendant communities connected to the Guardian's 19th-century founders'.[106] Professor Verene A. Shepherd, the Chair of the UN Committee on the Elimination of Racial Discrimination and Director of the Centre for Reparation Research at the University of the West Indies, has encouraged the British state and monarchy to follow the newspaper's example and investigate their own historical links to transatlantic slavery.[107] And finally, the Australian Foreign Minister Penny Wong has said that Britain must be ready to confront the unsettling reality of its colonial past in the contemporary Indo-Pacific area. Malaysian-born Wong drew on her own family's history with British colonialism to argue that nations like Britain would struggle to establish common ground in the area if they remained 'sheltered in narrower versions' of their past. 'Such stories can sometimes feel uncomfortable – for those whose stories they are, and for those who hear them. But understanding the past enables us to better share the present and the future.'[108]

Well expressed. It's no longer an option for the British to sit around wondering, self-indulgently, whether their empire was 'good' or 'bad'. The world has other questions on its mind. More specifically, Britain cannot hope to have healthy relations with Caribbean nations without confronting the deep social, economic, educational, environmental and psychological disadvantage it sowed in the region. Our royals cannot campaign on the issues of preservation and conservation without facing up to what their predecessors did to the environment and animals all over Africa and Asia during the age of empire. We cannot, post-Brexit, endeavour to establish new trading relationships with Malaysia, India, Mauritius, Guyana, Nigeria, without reflecting upon what we did to these places during colonization. We cannot lecture nations about homophobia, like we often do, without accepting that we determinedly enforced homophobia upon large parts of the world. We cannot negotiate climate-change treaties, and lobby the developing world on the subject, without acknowledging that we were pioneers in inflicting man-made climate change upon the planet. We cannot judge the USA for its problems on race, as we tend to, when we helped spread and establish many of those racist ideas in the first place. We cannot proffer solutions to the world's greatest geopolitical problems without acknowledging that we helped to create a bunch of them, not least in Palestine. We cannot lead humanitarian projects, let alone get involved in 'humanitarian wars', without facing up to the damage we caused in the name of humanitarianism over hundreds of years. Or, to put it all more simply: Britain cannot hope to have a productive future in the world without acknowledging what it did to the world in the first place.

# Bibliography

'"A form of colonialism": Activists demand climate reparations', *Al Jazeera*, 25/09/2022, https://www.aljazeera.com/news/2022/9/25/why-are-climate-activists-calling-for-reparations

Abadi, Mark, and Gal, Shayanne, 'Only about 30% of the world's population drives on the left side of the road', *Insider*, 19/10/2018, https://www.businessinsider.com/which-countries-drive-on-left-2018-10?r=US&IR=T

Abdulrahman, Suberu Ochi, and Gyang Mang, Henry, 'The Nigerian Army as a Product of its Colonial History: Problems of Re-building Cohesion for an Army in Transition', *International Affairs and Global Strategy* 2017, 53, pp. 21–31

'About International Telecommunication Union (ITU)', ITU, accessed 04/07/2023, https://www.itu.int/en/about/Pages/default.aspx

Abu-Lughod, Lila, *Do Muslim Women Need Saving?*, Harvard University Press, 2013

Acemoglu, Daron, and Robinson, James A., *Why Nations Fail: The Origins of Power, Prosperity and Poverty*, Profile Books, 2012

Adams, Matthew, 'Book review: Erika Rappaport's *A Thirst for Empire: How Tea Shaped the Modern World*', *Arts & Culture*, 05/08/2017, https://www.thenational-news.com/arts-culture/books/book-review-erika-rappaport-s-a-thirst-for-empire-how-tea-shaped-the-modern-world-1.617022

Adamson, Alan H., 'The Impact of Indentured Immigration on the Political Economy of British Guiana', in Kay Saunders (ed.), *Indentured Labour in the British Empire: 1834–1920*, Routledge, 1984, pp. 42–56

Adebowale, Oludamola, 'Jaja of Opobo: The Slave Boy Who Became King', *Guardian: Life*, 25/08/2019, https://guardian.ng/life/jaja-of-opobo-the-slave-boy-who-became-king/

Adegbulu, Femi, 'From Warrant Chiefs to Ezeship: A Distortion of Traditional Institutions in Igboland?', *Afro Asian Journal of Social Sciences* 2011, 2:2.2, pp. 1–25

Adeoye, Aanu, 'Bola Tinubu leads disputed Nigerian vote as opposition calls for election rerun', *Financial Times*, 28/02/2023, https://www.ft.com/content/64724f5c-a6b5-45cb-8fa6-96e1531a98f8

Adewunmi, Bim, 'Band Aid 30: clumsy, patronising and wrong in so many ways', *Guardian*, 11/11/2014, https://www.theguardian.com/world/2014/nov/11/band-aid-30-patronising-bob-geldof-ebola-do-they-know-its-christmas

Afigbo, A. E., *The Warrant Chiefs: Indirect Rule in Southeastern Nigeria, 1891–1929*, Longman, 1972

AFP, 'Cash and fuel shortages crank up Nigeria election tensions', *Eyewitness News*, 03/02/2023, https://ewn.co.za/2023/02/03/cash-and-fuel-shortages-cranks-up-nige ria-election-tensions

'African royalty touchdown in Jamaica to discuss reparations', *The Voice*, 02/03/2023, https://www.voice-online.co.uk/news/world-news/2023/03/02/african-royalty-touchdown-in-jamaica-to-discuss-reparations/

Agarwal, Anil, and Narain, Sunita, 'Global Warming in an Unequal World: A Case of Environmental Colonialism', in Navroz K. Dubash (ed.), *India in a Warming World: Integrating Climate Change and Development*, Oxford University Press, 2019, pp. 81–91

Agbo, George, 'Omu and the red cap controversy in Okpanam', *[Re-]Entanglements*, https://re-entanglements.net/omu-of-okpanam/

Agency, 'Archaeologists find graves containing bodies of 5,000 slaves on remote island', *Guardian*, 08/03/2012, https://www.theguardian.com/world/2012/mar/08/slave-mass-graves-st-helena-island

Agency staff, ' "Leftie multicultural crap": Blundering Tory MP Aidan Burley insists London 2012 opening ceremony swipe was "misunderstood" ', *Mirror*, 28/07/2012, https://www.mirror.co.uk/news/uk-news/london-2012-tory-mp-aidan-1178770

Ahmad, Rizwan, 'Renaming India: Saffronisation of public spaces', *Al Jazeera*, 12/10/2018, https://www.aljazeera.com/opinions/2018/10/12/renaming-india-saffronisation-of-public-spaces

Aidoo, Lamonte, *Slavery Unseen: Sex, Power and Violence in Brazilian History*, Duke University Press, 2018

Ajith Kumar, P. K., 'Commonwealth Games: Relic of a lost empire', *Sportstar*, 21/07/2021, https://sportstar.thehindu.com/magazine/commonwealth-games-relic-of-a-lost-empire-british-empire-games/article65661962.ece

Akalu, Haile Muluken, 'The British and Ethiopian Disposal of Italian Property in Ethiopia, 1941–1956: A Historical Review of the Theory and Practice of the Custodianship of Enemy Property', *Canadian Social Science* 2019, 15:2, pp. 22–33

Akinwotu, Emmanuel, 'Gunmen destroy 800 ballot boxes in Nigeria, the latest in a series of attacks', *NPR*, 02/02/2023, https://www.npr.org/2023/02/02/1153753025/nigeria-election-ballot-boxes-destroyed

Akpan, Ntienyong, *Epitaph to Indirect Rule*, Frank Cass, 1967

Akumu, Patience, 'Charity at heart of "white saviour" row speaks out', *Guardian*, 03/03/2019, https://www.theguardian.com/tv-and-radio/2019/mar/03/we-need-to-talk-about-race-no-white-saviours-tells-stacey-dooley-comic-relief

Akyeampong, Emmanuel, 'Threats to Empire: Illicit Distillation, Venereal Diseases, and Colonial Disorder in British West Africa, 1930–1948', in Jessica Pliley, Robert Kramm and Harald Fischer-Tiné (eds.), *Global Anti-Vice Activism, 1890–1950: Fighting Drinks, Drugs, and 'Immorality'*, Cambridge University Press, 2016, pp. 152–78

Akyeampong, Emmanuel, 'What's in a Drink? Class Struggle, Popular Culture and the Politics of Akpeteshie (Local Gin) in Ghana, 1930–67', *Journal of African History* 1996, 37:2, pp. 215–36

Alam, M. S., 'Colonialism, Decolonisation and Growth Rates: Theory and Empirical Evidence', *Cambridge Journal of Economics* 1994, 18:3, pp. 235–57

Aldrich, Robert, *Colonialism and Homosexuality*, Taylor & Francis, 2002

Alesina, Alberto, Easterly, William, and Matuszeski, Janina, 'Artificial States', February 2006, https://williameasterly.files.wordpress.com/2010/08/59_easterly_alesina_matuszeski_artificialstates_prp.pdf

Alesina, Alberto, and Spolaore, Enrico, 'Conflict, Defense Spending, and the Number of Nations', *European Economic Review* 2006, 50:1, pp. 91–120

Alesina, Alberto, and Spolaore, Enrico, *The Size of Nations*, The MIT Press, 2005

Alibhai, Zaina, 'Equalities minister Kemi Badenoch says British Empire achieved "good things" throughout rule', *Independent*, 21/03/2022, https://www.independent.co.uk/news/uk/politics/kemi-badenoch-british-empire-colonialism-b2040002.html

Allam, Lorena, and Evershed, Nick, 'Almost half the massacres of Aboriginal people were by police or other government forces, research finds', *Guardian*, 15/03/2022, https://www.theguardian.com/australia-news/2022/mar/16/almost-half-the-massacres-of-aboriginal-people-were-by-police-research-finds

Allbrook, Malcolm, *Henry Prinsep's Empire: Framing a Distant Colony*, Australian National University Press, 2014

Allen, Richard B., 'Asian Indentured Labor in the 19th and Early 20th Century Colonial Plantation World', *Asian History*, 29/03/2017, https://oxfordre.com/asianhistory/display/10.1093/acrefore/9780190277727.001.0001/acrefore-9780190277727-e-33#acrefore-9780190277727-e-33-note-3

Allen, Richard B., 'Re-conceptualizing the "new system of slavery"', *Man in India* 2012, 92:2, pp. 225–45

Allen, Richard B., 'Slaves, Convicts, Abolitionism and the Global Origins of the Post-Emancipation Indentured Labor System', *Slavery and Abolition* 2014, 35:2, pp. 328–48

Allen, Richard B., *Slaves, Freedmen and Indentured Laborers in Colonial Mauritius*, Cambridge University Press, 1999

Ambler, Charles, 'Alcohol, Racial Segregation and Popular Politics in Northern Rhodesia', *Journal of African History* 1990, 31:2, pp. 295–313

Ames, Jonathan, and Baksi, Catherine, 'Lawyer condemns British court as colonialist relic', *The Times*, 09/06/2022, https://www.thetimes.co.uk/article/802fbe26-e74a-11ec-aa87-2eea7c6e5b01?shareToken=b7e9eb6df701848be465236d027a1dbb

Anderson, Clare, 'Convicts and Coolies: Rethinking Indentured Labour in the Nineteenth Century', *Slavery and Abolition* 2009, 30:1, 93–109

Anderson, Clare (ed.), *A Global History of Convicts and Penal Colonies*, Bloomsbury, 2020

Anderson, David M., and Killingray, David, *Policing and Decolonisation: Politics, Nationalism, and the Police, 1917–65*, Manchester University Press, 1992

Anderson, David M., and Killingray, David (eds.), *Policing the Empire: Government, Authority, and Control, 1830–1940*, Manchester University Press, 1991

Anderson, Robert S., Grove, Richard H., and Hiebert, Karis, *Islands, Forests and Gardens in the Caribbean: Conservation and Conflict in Environmental History*, Macmillan Caribbean, 2006

Andrews, Kehinde, 'Blood Money', *Fabian Society*, 25/06/2021, https://fabians.org.uk/blood-money/

Andrews, Kehinde, *The New Age of Empire: How Racism and Colonialism Still Rule the World*, Allen Lane, 2021

Anene, I. C., *Southern Nigeria in Transition, 1885–1906*, Cambridge Press University, 1966

Anstey, Roger, *The Atlantic Slave Trade and British Abolition, 1760–1810*, Macmillan, 1975

Antonelli, Alexandre, 'Indigenous knowledge is key to sustainable food systems', *Nature* 2023, 613, pp. 239–42, https://www.nature.com/articles/d41586-023-00021-4

Aribisala, Femi, 'Bigmanism in Nigeria', *Vanguard*, 01/10/2013, https://www.vanguardngr.com/2013/10/bigmanism-nigeria/

Arnold, David, *Colonizing the Body: State Medicine and Epidemic Disease in Nineteenth-Century India*, University of California Press, 1993

Arnold, Edwin T., 'Across the Road from the Barbecue House', *Mississippi Quarterly* 2008, 61:1/2, Special Issue on Lynching and American Culture, pp. 267–92

Arora, Pallavi, and Thapliyal, Sukanya, 'Digital Colonialism and the World Trade Organisation', *TWAIL Review*, https://twailr.com/digital-colonialism-and-the-world-trade-organization/

'Arthur Hodge', *Centre for the Study of the Legacies of British Slavery*, accessed 31/01/2023, https://www.ucl.ac.uk/lbs/person/view/2146650163

'Arthur William Hodge', *National Portrait Gallery*, accessed 31/01/2023, https://www.npg.org.uk/collections/search/portrait/mw14993/Arthur-William-Hodge?LinkID=mp14472&role=sit&rNo=0

Ashby Wilson, Richard, and Brown, Richard D. (eds.), *Humanitarianism and Suffering: The Mobilization of Empathy*, Cambridge University Press, 2009

Assheton, Richard, 'Nigeria election 2023: opposition demands cancellation of "sham" vote', *The Times*, 27/02/2023, https://www.thetimes.co.uk/article/f53d0046-b5fa-11ed-a513-158bcb2665eb?shareToken=9f85359135067ab84c4a37aea6662aab

Assheton, Richard, 'Nigeria presidential election: Bola Tinubu claims victory as rivals demand rerun', *The Times*, 01/03/2023, https://www.thetimes.co.uk/article/nigeria-presidential-election-bola-tinubu-claims-victory-as-rivals-demand-rerun-n07228v57

Assheton, Richard, 'Nigeria's advertising regulator recently banned the use of foreign models and voiceover artists', *The Times*, 26/08/2022, https://www.thetimes.co.uk/article/nigeria-becomes-first-country-to-ban-foreign-models-in-adverts-3xv8klvp7

Assheton, Richard, 'Peter Obi, the 61-year-old "youngster" who wants to clean up Nigeria', *Sunday Times*, 07/01/2023, https://www.thetimes.co.uk/article/538d8d6e-8e00-11ed-a303-61858d68dcd6?shareToken=d9715f67849647111dc08285cf02161c

Aster, Natalie, 'Natural vs. Synthetic Rubber: Key Market Trends & Statistics', *Market Publishers*, 31/07/2018, https://marketpublishers.com/lists/23821/news.html

Atkinson, Anthony B., Backus, Peter G., Micklewright, John, Pharoah, Cathy, and Schnepf, Sylke V., 'Charitable giving for overseas development: UK trends over a quarter century', *Journal of the Royal Statistical Society: Series A (Statistics in Society)* 2012, 175:1, pp. 167–90

Atkinson, Emily, 'Prince Charles "wants slave trade to be taught as widely as Holocaust"', *Independent*, 26/06/2022, https://www.independent.co.uk/news/uk/home-news/prince-charles-slave-trade-holocaust-b2109517.html

Aubrey, Lisa, *The Politics of Development Co-operation: NGOs, Gender and Partnership in Kenya*, Routledge, 1997

Axelrod, Josh, 'A Century Later: The Treaty of Versailles and its Rejection of Racial Equality', *NPR*, 11/08/2019, https://www.npr.org/sections/codeswitch/2019/08/11/742293305/a-century-later-the-treaty-of-versailles-and-its-rejection-of-racial-equality?t=1654014119173

Azim, Firdous, *The Colonial Rise of the Novel: From Aphra Behn to Charlotte Brontë*, Routledge, 1993

Backhouse, Fid, et al., 'Nigerian Civil War', *Britannica*, accessed 21/03/2023, https://www.britannica.com/topic/Nigerian-civil-war

Bahadur, Gaiutra, *Coolie Woman: The Odyssey of Indenture*, Hurst, 2013

Baio, Ariana, 'Tom Daley enters Commonwealth Games surrounded by Pride Flags to make powerful statement', *indy100*, 28/07/2022, https://www.indy100.com/sport/commonwealth-games-tom-daley-opening-ceremony

Bakaari, Farah, Benlloch, Vincent, and Driscoll, Barry, 'Political scientists talk about African "Big Men" inconsistently', *London School of Economics*, 22/03/2021, https://blogs.lse.ac.uk/africaatlse/2021/03/22/political-science-talk-about-african-big-men-governance-patronage-inconsistently/

Bakar, Faima, 'How History Still Weighs Heavy on South Asian Bodies Today', *Huffington Post*, 14/03/2022, https://www.huffingtonpost.co.uk/entry/south-asian-health-colonial-history_uk_620e74fee4b055057aac0e9f

Bakht, Shayma, and Dowell, Anna, 'Britain vies with America to educate the world's leaders', *The Times*, 22/08/2023, https://www.thetimes.co.uk/article/0527fd6e-4069-11ee-8b31-3c9c533abb75?shareToken=28cf9540f551a71741dac13146d854a5

Balasegaram, Mangai, 'Special Report: Different Class: The Marginalisation of Indians in Malaysia', *Between the Lines*, accessed 13/03/2023, https://betweenthelines.my/malaysias-indians-marginalised-over-a-century/

Baldwin, Norman C., *Imperial Airways (and Subsidiary Companies): A History and Priced Check List of the Empire Air Mails*, Francis J. Field, 1950

Banks, Nicola, and Brockington, Dan, 'Mapping the UK's development NGOs: income, geography and contributions to international development: GDI Working Paper', GDI Working Paper 2019-035, University of Manchester, 2019, https://hummedia.manchester.ac.uk/institutes/gdi/publications/workingpapers/GDI/GDI-working-paper-2019035-banks-brockington.pdf

Baptist, Edward E., *The Half Has Never Been Told: Slavery and the Making of American Capitalism*, Basic Books, 2014

Baral, Maitree, ' "The school has killed me": Arvey Malhotra's mother recalls his suicide note and elaborates on the bullying that led to her son's death; awaits justice even after 4 months', *Times of India*, 07/07/2022, https://timesofindia.indiatimes.com/life-style/parenting/moments/the-school-has-killed-me-arvey-malhotras-mother-recalls-his-suicide-note-and-elaborates-on-the-bullying-that-led-to-her-sons-death-awaits-justice-even-after-4-months/articleshow/92721354.cms

'Barbados – Home of Many Windmills', *Barbados.org*, accessed 19/01/2023, https://barbados.org/windmill.htm#.YtlVjHbMKUk

'Barbados PM hails "loss and damage" addition to climate agenda at Cop27 – video', *Guardian*, 08/11/2022, https://www.theguardian.com/environment/video/2022/nov/08/barbados-pm-hails-loss-damage-addition-climate-agenda-cop27-video?utm_term=Autofeed&CMP=twt_b-gdnnews&utm_medium=Social&utm_source=Twitter#Echobox=1667931135

Barber Wellington, David, 'The Queen says sorry to wronged Maoris', *Independent*, 02/11/1995, https://www.independent.co.uk/news/world/the-queen-says-sorry-to-wronged-maoris-1536901.html

Barnes, Leonard, *Empire or Democracy? A Study of the Colonial Question*, Routledge, 1998

Barnett, Michael, *Empire of Humanity: A History of Humanitarianism*, Cornell University Press, 2011

Barratt Brown, Michael, *After Imperialism*, Heinemann, 1963

Barrett, David, 'Channel migrants should be deported to processing centres on South Atlantic islands if an agreement with France fails, report suggests', *Daily Mail*, 16/02/2022, https://www.dailymail.co.uk/news/article-10517365/Channel-migrants-deported-processing-centres-South-Atlantic-islands.html

Barton, Patricia, ' "The Great Quinine Fraud": Legality Issues in the "Non-Narcotic" Drug Trade in British India', *Social History of Alcohol and Drugs* 2007, 22:1, pp. 6–25

Bass, Gary J., *Freedom's Battle: The Origins of Humanitarian Intervention*, The Knopf Doubleday Publishing Group, 2008

Bates, Crispin, and Carter, Marina, 'Sirdars as Intermediaries in Nineteenth-Century Indian Ocean Indentured Labour Migration', *Modern Asian Studies* 2017, 51:2, pp. 462–84

Baughan, Emily, 'Humanitarianism and History: A Century of Save the Children', in Juliano Fiori, Fernando Espada, Andrea Rigon, Bertrand Taithe and Rafia Zakaria (eds.), *Amidst the Debris: Humanitarianism and the End of Liberal Order*, Routledge, 2021, pp. 21–34

Baughan, Emily, 'Rehabilitating an Empire: Humanitarian Collusion with the Colonial State during the Kenyan Emergency, ca. 1954–1960', *Journal of British Studies* 2020, 59:1, pp. 57–79

Baughan, Emily, *Saving the Children: Humanitarianism, Internationalism, and Empire*, University of California Press, 2021

Bayly, Christopher, A., *Empire and Information: Intelligence Gathering and Social Communication in India, 1780–1870*, Cambridge University Press, 2009

Bayly, Christopher, A., *Imperial Meridian: The British Empire and the World, 1780–1830*, Cambridge University Press, 1989

Bayly, Christopher A., Beckert, Sven, Connelly, Matthew, Hofmeyr, Isabel, Kozol, Wendy, and Seed, Patricia, 'A H R Conversation: On Transnational History', *American Historical Review* 2006, 111:5, pp. 1441–64

Beckles, Hilary McD., *Britain's Black Debt: Reparations for Caribbean Slavery and Native Genocide*, University of the West Indies Press, 2013

Beckles, Hilary McD., *The First Black Slave Society: Britain's 'Barbarity Time' in Barbados, 1636–1876*, University of the West Indies Press, 2016

Beckles, Hilary McD., *Great House Rules: Landless Emancipation and Workers' Protest 1838–1938*, Ian Randle Publishers, 2004

Behal, Rana P., 'Coolie Drivers or Benevolent Paternalists? British Tea Planters in Assam and the Indenture Labour System', *Modern Asian Studies* 2010, 44:1, pp. 29–51

Belich, James, *The New Zealand Wars and the Victorian Interpretation of Racial Conflict*, Auckland University Press, 1986

Belich, James, *Replenishing the Earth: The Settler Revolution and the Rise of the Anglo-World, 1783–1939*, Oxford University Press, 2011

Bell, Duncan, 'The Anglosphere: new enthusiasm for an old dream', *Prospect Magazine*, 19/01/2017, https://www.prospectmagazine.co.uk/magazine/anglosphere-old-dream-brexit-role-in-the-world

Bell, Duncan, *Dreamworlds of Race: Empire and the Utopian Destiny of Anglo-America*, Princeton University Press, 2020

Benbow, Mark E., 'Birth of a Quotation: Woodrow Wilson and "Like Writing History with Lightning"', *Journal of the Gilded Age and Progressive Era* 2010, 9:4, pp. 509–33

Bentley, Tom, and Wilsdon, James, 'The new monarchists', in Tom Bentley and James Wilsdon (eds.), *Monarchies*, Demos Collection 17, 2002, https://demos.co.uk/wp-content/uploads/files/monarchies.pdf

Benton, Lauren, *Law and Colonial Cultures: Legal Regimes in World History, 1400–1900*, Cambridge University Press, 2002

Benton, Lauren, 'This Melancholy Labyrinth: The Trial of Arthur Hodge and the Boundaries of Imperial Law', *Alabama Law Review* 2012, 64:1, pp. 91–122

Benton, Lauren, and Ford, Lisa, *Rage for Order: The British Empire and the Origins of International Law, 1800–1850*, Harvard University Press, 2016

Berg, Maxine, and Hudson, Pat, *Slavery, Capitalism and the Industrial Revolution*, Polity, 2023

Bernhard, Michael, Reenock, Christopher, and Nordstrom, Timothy, 'The Legacy of Western Overseas Colonialism on Democratic Survival', *International Studies Quarterly* 2004, 48:1, pp. 225–50

'Beyond the Binary: Gender, Sexuality, Power', *Pitt Rivers Museum*, 01/06/2021, https://www.prm.ox.ac.uk/event/beyond-the-binary

Bhambra, Gurminder K., and McClure, Julia (eds.), *Imperial Inequalities: The Politics of Economic Governance across European Empires*, Manchester University Press, 2022

Bhatta, Chandra D., 'Nepal's political and economic transition', *Observer Research Foundation*, 15/06/2022, https://www.orfonline.org/expert-speak/nepals-political-and-economic-transition/

Bhattacharya, Sanjoy, Harrison, Mark, and Worboys, Michael, *Fractured States: Smallpox, Public Health and Vaccination Policy in British India, 1800–1947*, Orient Blackswan, 2005

Bhowmick, Nilanjana, 'India's Opposition BJP Calls Homosexuality Unnatural', *Time*, 16/12/2013, https://world.time.com/2013/12/16/indias-opposition-bjp-calls-homosexuality-unnatural/

Bhugra, Dinesh, and Littlewood, Roland (eds.), *Colonialism and Psychiatry*, Oxford University Press, 2001

Bibler, Michael P., *Cotton's Queer Relations: Same-Sex Intimacy and the Literature of the Southern Plantation, 1936–1968*, University of Virginia Press, 2009

Biggar, Nigel, *Colonialism: A Moral Reckoning*, William Collins, 2023

'Birmingham (disambiguation)', *Wikipedia*, accessed 20/03/2023, https://en.wikipedia.org/wiki/Birmingham_(disambiguation)

Biswas, Shampa, *Nuclear Desire: Power and the Postcolonial Nuclear Order*, University of Minnesota Press, 2014

Biswas, Soutik, 'Forced to Undergo Genital Exams in Colonial India', *BBC News*, 18/10/2020, https://www.bbc.co.uk/news/world-asia-india-54528868

Blackmon, Douglas A., *Slavery by Another Name: The Re-Enslavement of Black Americans from the Civil War to World War II*, Anchor Books, 2009

Blake, Elly, 'King Charles "wants Camilla to wear the Queen Mother's crown with Koh-i-Noor diamond at the Coronation, like his grandmother" but critics warn Palace it would be "a massive diplomatic grenade", royal author says', *Mail Online*,

13/10/2022, https://www.dailymail.co.uk/news/article-11311031/King-Charles-wants-Camilla-wear-Koh-Noor-diamond-Coronation-like-grandmother.html

Blanc, Guillaume, *The Invention of Green Colonialism*, Wiley, 2022

Bleasdale, John, 'Things Britain Does Better than America | Top 5 Best British Baddies', *Hotcorn.com*, 18/10/2020, https://hotcorn.com/en/movies/news/top-5-best-british-villains-movies/

Blondel, Jean, *Comparing Political Systems*, Praeger, 1972

Bocking-Welch, Anna, *British Civic Society at the End of the Empire: Decolonisation, Globalisation and International Responsibility*, Manchester University Press, 2018

Bocking-Welch, Anna, 'The British Public in a Shrinking World: Civic Engagement with the Declining Empire, 1960–1970', PhD thesis, University of York, 2012

Bocking-Welch, Anna, 'Whose Commonwealth? Negotiating Commonwealth Day in the 1950s and 1960s', in Saul Dubow and Richard Drayton (eds.), *Commonwealth History in the Twenty-First Century*, Palgrave Macmillan, 2020, pp. 291–309

Bollen, K. A., and Jackman, R. W., 'Economic and Noneconomic Determinants of Political Democracy in the 1960s', *Research in Political Sociology* 1985, 1, pp. 27–48

Bolt, David, Independent Chief Inspector of Borders and Immigration, 'An inspection of the Home Office's approach to Illegal Working', August–December 2018, https://shorturl.at/jCJM6

Boswell, Rosabelle, 'The Immeasurability of Racial and Mixed Identity in Mauritius', in Zarine L. Rocha and Peter J. Aspinall (eds.), *The Palgrave International Handbook of Mixed Racial and Ethnic Classification*, Palgrave Macmillan, 2020, pp. 457–78

Bourke, Joanna, *What It Means to Be Human: Reflections from 1791 to the Present*, Virago Press, 2011

Boyes, Roger, and Flanagan, Jane, 'How revitalised Commonwealth can be a bulwark against Beijing', *The Times*, 17/06/2022, https://www.thetimes.co.uk/article/533d9990-ee4f-11ec-b47a-cf598c451bbb?shareToken=0e59d173a4c585bb77fb23be06cff025

Boyle, Tristan, 'The Modern Myth of the British Empire with Kim A. Wagner – Modern Myth – Episode 20', *Archaeology Podcast Network*, 05/05/2021, https://www.archaeologypodcastnetwork.com/anarchaeologist/mm20-empire

Bradley, Kaleigh, 'What's in a Name? Place Names, History, and Colonialism', *Active History*, 02/02/2015, http://activehistory.ca/2015/02/whats-in-a-name-place-names-history-and-colonialism/

Bremner, G. A., 'Stones of Empire: Monuments, Memorials, and Manifest Authority', in G. A. Bremner (ed.), *Architecture and Urbanism in the British Empire*, Oxford University Press, 2016

Brennan, Emily, Harris, Lori-Ann, and Nesbitt, Mark, 'Jamaican Lace-Bark: Its History and Uncertain Future', *Textile History* 2013, 44:2, pp. 235–53

Bretschneider, Emil, *History of European Botanical Discoveries in China*, Marston, 1898

Briggs, Laura, McCormick, Gladys, and Way, J. T., 'Transnationalism: A Category of Analysis', *American Quarterly* 2008, 60:3, pp. 625–48

Brion Davis, David, *The Problem of Slavery in the Age of Revolution, 1770–1823*, Cornell University Press, 1975

Brion Davis, David, *The Problem of Slavery in Western Culture*, Cornell University Press, 1966

'Britain is responsible for deaths of 35 million Indians, says acclaimed author Shashi Tharoor', *Independent*, 13/03/2017, https://www.independent.co.uk/news/world/asia/india-35-million-deaths-britain-shashi-tharoor-british-empire-a7627041.html

'The British Empire on Trial', *BBC History Magazine* 2008, 9:1

Brockway, Lucile H., *Science and Colonial Expansion: The Role of the British Royal Botanic Gardens*, Yale University Press, 2002

Brooks, Richard, 'A relic of empire that created a tax economy', *Financial Times*, 20/02/2015, https://www.ft.com/content/6b83be28-b863-11e4-b6a5-00144fe ab7de

Brown, Christopher L., *Moral Capital: Foundations of British Abolitionism*, University of North Carolina Press, 2006

Bruce, Charles A., *Report on the Manufacture of Tea, and on the Extent and Produce of the Tea Plantations in Assam*, Bishop's College Press, 1839

Bruun, Kettil, Pan, Lynn, and Rexed, Ingemar, *The Gentlemen's Club: International Control of Drugs and Alcohol*, University of Chicago Press, 1975

Buchan, Ursula, 'Has Kew Gardens Really Climbed Down after Criticism over its "Decolonisation of Science" Policy?', *History Reclaimed*, 03/02/2022, https://histo ryreclaimed.co.uk/has-kew-gardens-really-climbed-down-after-criticism-over-its-decolonisation-of-science-policy/

Buchanan Smith, Jordan, 'The Invention of Rum', PhD thesis, Georgetown University, 2018, https://repository.library.georgetown.edu/handle/10822/1050790

Buckner, Phillip, 'The Royal Tour of 1901 and the Construction of an Imperial Identity in South Africa', *South African Historical Journal* 1999, 41:1, pp. 324–48, https://doi.org/10.1080/02582479908671897

Bull, Andy, 'Can radical changes restore sagging prestige of Commonwealth Games?', *Guardian*, 23/07/2022, https://www.theguardian.com/sport/blog/2022/jul/23/can-radical-changes-restore-sagging-prestige-of-commonwealth-games

Bullough, Oliver, *Butler to the World*, Profile Books, 2022

Bundock, Michael, *The Fortunes of Francis Barber: The True Story of the Jamaican Slave Who Became Samuel Johnson's Heir*, Yale University Press, 2015

Burger, John, 'Backgrounder: Why is there so much Christian persecution in Nigeria?', *Aleteia*, 24/01/2023, https://aleteia.org/2023/01/24/backgrounder-why-is-there-so-much-christian-persecution-in-nigeria/

Burnard, Trevor, 'As a historian of slavery, I know just how much the royal family has to answer for in Jamaica', *Guardian*, 25/03/2022, https://www.theguardian.com/commentisfree/2022/mar/25/slavery-royal-family-jamaica-ducke-duchess-cambridge-caribbean-slave-trade

Burton, Antoinette M., *Burdens of History: British Feminists, Indian Women, and Imperial Culture, 1865–1915*, University of North Carolina Press, 1994

Burton, Antoinette M., 'The White Woman's Burden: British Feminists and the Indian Woman, 1865–1915', *Women's Studies International Forum* 1990, 13:4, pp. 295–308

Butler, Josh, 'Commonwealth Indigenous leaders demand apology from the king for effects of colonialism', *Guardian*, 04/05/2023, https://www.theguardian.com/uk-news/2023/may/04/commonwealth-indigenous-leaders-demand-apology-from-the-king-for-effects-of-colonisation

Butler, Kathleen M., *The Economics of Emancipation: Jamaica & Barbados, 1823–1843*, University of North Carolina Press, 1995

Butler, Patrick, 'UK charity foundation to abolish itself and give away £130m', *Guardian*, 11/07/2023, https://www.theguardian.com/society/2023/jul/11/uk-charity-foundation-to-abolish-itself-and-give-away-130m?CMP=share_btn_tw

Byers, David, 'What is non-domicile status? How it's earned and why it cuts tax', *The Times*, 08/04/2022, https://www.thetimes.co.uk/article/what-is-non-domicile-status-how-its-earned-and-why-it-cuts-tax-7tlx5g538

Calver, Tom, Clover, Jack, Keith, Michael, and Menzies, Venetia, 'The ties that bind: how we rely on a fragile network of undersea cables', *Sunday Times*, 30/10/2022

Campbell, Craig, 'Untold lives blog: The forgotten Prince of Burma', *British Library*, 09/07/2020, https://www.britishcouncil.org/sites/default/files/3603_bc_essays_commonwealth.pdf

Capurro, Daniel, 'We are not trashing history, says Kew chief Daniel Capurro', *Telegraph*, 14/01/2022, https://www.telegraph.co.uk/news/2022/01/14/kew-gardens-change-wont-decolonising/

Carayol, Tumaini, 'Athletic feats at Commonwealth Games cannot distract from Britain's colonial sins', *Guardian*, 28/07/2022, https://www.theguardian.com/sport/2022/jul/28/athletic-feats-at-commonwealth-games-cannot-distract-from-britains-colonial-sins

Carney, Judith A., and Rosomoff, Richard, *In the Shadow of Slavery: Africa's Botanical Legacy in the Atlantic World*, University of California Press, 2011

Carrell, Severin, Evans, Rob, Pegg, David, and Savarese, Mario, 'Revealed: Queen's sweeping immunity from more than 160 laws', *Guardian*, 14/07/2022, https://www.theguardian.com/uk-news/2022/jul/14/queen-immunity-british-laws-private-property

Carter, Marina, *Lakshmi's Legacy: The Testimonies of Indian Women in 19th Century Mauritius*, Éditions de l'Océan Indien, 1994

Carter, Marina, *Servants, Sirdars and Settlers: Indians in Mauritius, 1834–1874*, Oxford University Press, 1995

Carter, Marina, *Voices from Indenture: Experiences of Indian Migrants in the British Empire*, Leicester University Press, 1996

Cartwright, Mark, 'The Portuguese Colonization of São Tomé and Principe', *World History Encyclopedia*, 28/05/2021, https://www.worldhistory.org/article/1763/the-portuguese-colonization-of-sao-tome-and-princi/

Chakrabarti, Pratik, *Medicine and Empire: 1600–1960*, Palgrave Macmillan, 2014

Chakravorty, Sanjoy, 'Viewpoint: How the British reshaped India's caste system', *BBC News*, https://www.bbc.co.uk/news/world-asia-india-48619734

Chamberlain, Phil, Karreman, Nancy, and Laurence, Louis, 'Racism and the Tobacco Industry', *Tobacco Tactics*, 10/02/2021, https://tobaccotactics.org/wiki/racism-and-the-tobacco-industry/

Chan, Bernice, and Reinfrank, Alkira, 'The history of egg tarts: from savoury to sweet, from medieval England to Hong Kong, from short crust to flaky pastry', *South China Morning Post*, 25/09/2020, https://www.scmp.com/lifestyle/food-drink/article/3102712/history-egg-tarts-savoury-sweet-england-canton-short-crust

Chatterjee, Nandini, *Negotiating Mughal Law: A Family of Landlords across Three Indian Empires*, Cambridge University Press, 2020

Chatterjee, Nandini, 'Reflections on Religious Difference and Permissive Inclusion in Mughal Law', *Journal of Law and Religion* 2014, 29:3, pp. 396–415

Cheang, Sarah, 'Women, Pets, and Imperialism: The British Pekingese Dog and Nostalgia for Old China', *Journal of British Studies* 2006, 45, pp. 359–87, https://www.cambridge.org/core/journals/journal-of-british-studies/article/abs/women-pets-and-imperialism-the-british-pekingese-dog-and-nostalgia-for-old-china/DE527C14F5805999402ACC870519FE91

Chhachhi, Amrita, and Herrera, Linda, 'Empire, Geopolitics and Development', *Development and Change* 2007, 38:6, pp. 1021–40

Chhina, Man Aman Singh, 'PM Narendra Modi unveils new naval ensign, here's why it is significant', *Indian Express*, 02/09/2022, https://indianexpress.com/article/explained/explained-what-naval-ensign-why-indian-navy-set-new-8121252/

Chikoweo, Moses, 'Subalternating Currents: Electrification and Power Politics in Bulawayo, Colonial Zimbabwe, 1894–1939', *Journal of Southern African Studies* 2007, 33:2, pp. 287–306

Chiles, Adrian, 'Adrian Chiles: Birmingham's brilliant – we'd just rather not show off', *The Times*, 24/07/2022, https://www.thetimes.co.uk/article/adrian-chiles-birminghams-brilliant-wed-just-rather-not-show-off-0dr2zbcbh

China – Hai guan zong shui wu si shu, *Opium in China*, Statistical Department of the Inspectorate General, 1881–8

Choudhry, Sabah, 'Jamaica: King's coronation accelerates plans for Jamaican republic – with referendum "as early as 2024"', *Sky News*, 04/05/2023, https://news.sky.com/story/jamaica-kings-coronation-accelerates-plans-for-jamaican-republic-with-referendum-as-early-as-2024-12872453

Chukwujama, Uduegbunam, 'Violent Attacks: Nigeria's 10 Most Dangerous Highways This Season', *Prime Business*, accessed 04/07/2023, https://www.primebusiness.africa/violent-attacks-nigerias-10-most-dangerous-highways-this-season/

Churchill, Winston, *The River War: An Historical Account of the Reconquest of the Soudan*, Dover Publications, 2007

Clary, Christopher, *The Difficult Politics of Peace: Rivalry in Modern South Asia*, Oxford University Press, 2022

Clemons, Jacquelyn, 'Black Families Have Inherited Trauma, But We Can Change That', *Healthline*, 26/08/2020, https://www.healthline.com/health/parenting/epigenetics-and-the-black-experience

'Climate Colonialism', *Oxford Talks*, 25/01/2021, https://talks.ox.ac.uk/talks/id/48b2c915-3965-496e-8dc0-ade137f218cb/

Clowes, William, and Olurounbi, Ruth, 'Bright Side of Nigeria's Cash Shortage: Vote Buying Declines', *Yahoo Movies*, https://uk.movies.yahoo.com/bright-side-nigeria-cash-shortage-131553672.html?guccounter=1&guce_referrer=aHR0cHM6Ly93d3cuZ29vZ2xlLmNvbVS8&guce_referrer_sig=AQAAADUf1GBGkvmo3pn8SQJhoGhDfRWBziayj8NUFHvRf6hCPulCtCin5JcwLhJpgUCeev_HkuFGfqKmx9ourlfblGHBkK8WwhVFE2jbjzSecxGPGwuwVi63fJGrsEFWHRtokqbPFMzRcx2A8DfNPndJSiDm5OQCskJqmmoCqoKiQQKh

Cobain, Ian, 'Revealed: the bonfire of papers at the end of Empire', *Guardian*, 29/11/2013, https://www.theguardian.com/uk-news/2013/nov/29/revealed-bonfire-papers-empire

Cole, Teju, 'The White-Savior Industrial Complex', *The Atlantic*, 21/03/2012, https://www.theatlantic.com/international/archive/2012/03/the-white-savior-industrial-complex/254843/

Collen, Lindsey, 'Another Side of Paradise', *New Internationalist*, 02/05/2009, https://newint.org/features/2009/05/01/mauritius-class

Colligan, Colette, 'Anti-Abolition Writes Obscenity: The English Vice, Transatlantic Slavery, and England's Obscene Print Culture', in Lisa Z. Sigel (ed.), *International Exposure: Perspectives on Modern European Pornography, 1800–2000*, Rutgers University Press, 2005

Collingham, Lizzie, *The Hungry Empire*, Penguin Books, 2017

Collyer, Michael, and Shahani, Uttara, 'Offshoring Refugees: Colonial Echoes of the UK–Rwanda Migration and Economic Development Partnership', *Social Sciences* 2023, 12:451

'Colonial Frontier Massacres, Australia, 1788 to 1930', The University of Newcastle, Australia, accessed 17/03/2023, https://c21ch.newcastle.edu.au/colonialmassacres/map.php

'Comic Relief to stop sending celebrities to Africa after "white saviour" criticism', *Sky News*, 28/10/2020, https://news.sky.com/story/comic-relief-to-stop-sending-celebrities-to-africa-after-white-saviour-criticism-12116723

'The Commonwealth: A Network for Now', *British Council*, June 2018, https://www.britishcouncil.org/sites/default/files/3603_bc_essays_commonwealth.pdf

'Commonwealth: association of sovereign states', *Britannica*, accessed 22/03/2023, https://www.britannica.com/topic/Commonwealth-association-of-states

Condos, Mark, ' "Fanaticism" and the Politics of Resistance along the North-West Frontier of British India', *Comparative Studies in Society and History* 2016, 58:3, pp. 717–45

'Conference of San Remo', *Britannica*, 13/04/2023, https://www.britannica.com/event/Conference-of-San-Remo

Conn, David, Mohdin, Aamna, and Wolfe-Robinson, Maya, 'King Charles signals first explicit support for research into monarchy's slavery ties', *Guardian*, 06/04/2023, https://www.theguardian.com/world/2023/apr/06/king-charles-signals-first-explicit-support-for-research-into-monarchys-slavery-ties

Cookson, Clive, 'Biodiversity body warns of $423bn annual hit from "invasive alien species"', *Financial Times*, 04/09/2023, https://shorturl.at/fBM37

Cooper, Frederick, *Africa since 1940: The Past of the Present*, Cambridge University Press, 2002

Cooper Owens, Deirdre, *Medical Bondage: Race, Gender, and the Origins of American Gynecology*, University of Georgia Press, 2017

'COP 26: What is climate colonialism?', *BBC My World*, 20/11/2021, https://www.youtube.com/watch?v=irzoFqkn82M

Cornish, Caroline, 'Curating Science in an Age of Empire: Kew's Museum of Economic Botany', PhD thesis, Royal Holloway, University of London, 2013, https://pure.royalholloway.ac.uk/en/publications/curating-science-in-an-age-of-empire-kews-museum-of-economic-bota

Cornish, Caroline, Gasson, Peter, and Nesbitt, Mark, 'The Wood Collection (Xylarium) of the Royal Botanic Gardens', *IAWA Journal* 2014, 35:1, pp. 85–104

'Coronation Park: Where the Statues of the Raj Rest in Ruins', *Outlook India*, accessed 20/03/2023, https://www.outlookindia.com/national/coronation-park-where-the-statues-of-the-raj-rest-in-ruins-photos-82480

Cotterell, Paul, *The Railways of Palestine and Israel*, Tourret Publishing, 1984

Cotterill, Joseph, 'Reforms in Mauritius hint at discontent over ethnic representation', *Financial Times*, 30/10/2018, https://www.ft.com/content/cd36800a-cb1b-11e8-8d0b-a6539b949662

'Cotton Capital: How slavery changed the Guardian, Britain and the world', *Guardian* [no date], https://www.theguardian.com/news/series/cotton-capital

Couacaud, Leo, Sheena Sookrajowa, Sheetal, and Narsoo, Jason, 'The Vicious Circle that is Mauritian Politics: The Legacy of Mauritius's Electoral Boundaries', *Ethnopolitics* 2022, 21:1, pp. 48–79

Coupland, Robin, and Loye, Dominique, *The 1899 Hague Declaration Concerning Expanding Bullets: A Treaty Effective for More than 100 Years Faces Complex Contemporary Issues*, Cambridge University Press, 2011

Cowen, Michael P., and Shenton, Robert W., *Doctrines of Development*, Routledge, 1996

Cowie, Helen, 'Michael Worboys, Julie-Marie Strange, and Neil Pemberton, *The Invention of the Modern Dog: Breed and Blood in Victorian Britain*', *American Historical Review* 2021, 126:2, pp. 855–6

Cronk, Quentin, 'The Past and Present Vegetation of St Helena', *Journal of Biogeography* 1989, 16:1, pp. 47–64

Crosby, Alfred W., *The Columbian Exchange: Biological and Cultural Consequences of 1492*, Praeger, 2003

Crozier, Anna, *Practising Colonial Medicine: The Colonial Medical Service in British East Africa*, Bloomsbury Publishing, 2007

Currier, Charles, 'A Plan of the Town of New Haven with All the Buildings in 1748 Taken by the Hon Gen. Wadsworth of Durham to Which are Added the Names and Professions of the Inhabitants at That Period – Also the Location of Lots to Many of the First Grantees . . .', *Rare Maps*, accessed 20/03/2023, https://www.raremaps.com/gallery/detail/20308/a-plan-of-the-town-of-new-haven-with-all-the-buildings-in-1-currier

Daley Olmert, Meg, 'Genes unleashed: how the Victorians engineered our dogs', *Nature*, 16/10/2018, https://www.nature.com/articles/d41586-018-07039-z

Dalrymple, William, 'The East India Company Invented Corporate Lobbying', *JSTOR Daily*, https://daily.jstor.org/the-east-india-company-invented-corporate-lobbying/

Dalrymple, William, and Anand, Anita, 'Queen Elizabeth II & Empire (with David Olusoga)', *Empire* podcast, 13/09/2022, https://open.spotify.com/episode/5fvidV68X1ddQrNLfdJOaz?si=879ddc1fb23f4c18&nd=1

Dalrymple, William, and Anand, Anita, 'Royal African Company: Slavery Inc', *Empire* podcast, 06/06/2023, https://open.spotify.com/episode/3Ya8NXoDAXZkQ62dOyLRDM?si=0e0f295e32334b7c

Damilola John, Micah, 'Public Perception of Police Activities in Okada, Edo State Nigeria', *Covenant Journal of Business & Social Sciences* 2017, 8:1, pp. 29–42

Das, Subhadra, and Lowe, Miranda, 'Nature Read in Black and White: Decolonial Approaches to Interpreting Natural History Collections', *Journal of Natural Science Collections* 2018, 6, pp. 4–14

Daunton, Michael, and Halpern, Rick (eds.), *Empire and Others: British Encounters with Indigenous Peoples, 1600–1850*, Routledge, 2020

Davey, Eleanor, 'The conscience of the island? The NGO moment in Australian off-shore detention', in Juliano Fiori, Fernando Espada, Andrea Rigon, Bertrand Taithe and Rafia Zakaria (eds.), *Amidst the Debris: Humanitarianism and the End of Liberal Order*, Routledge, 2021, pp. 83–106

Davies, Lizzy, 'UK accused of abandoning world's poor as aid turned into "colonial" investment', *Guardian*, 21/12/2021, https://www.theguardian.com/global-development/2021/dec/21/uk-accused-of-abandoning-worlds-poor-as-aid-turned-into-colonial-investment

Davis, Barney, 'Comic Relief to stop sending celebrities to Africa following "white saviour" criticism', *Evening Standard*, 28/10/2020, https://www.standard.co.uk/showbiz/comic-relief-drops-white-savior-trips-africa-stacey-dooley-lenny-henry-a4573203.html

'De Beers S.A.', *Britannica*, accessed 20/03/2023, https://www.britannica.com/topic/De-Beers-SA

Debnath, Angela, 'British Perceptions of the East Pakistan Crisis 1971: "Hideous Atrocities on Both Sides"?', *Journal of Genocide Research* 2011, 13:4, pp. 421–50

DeGruy, Joy, *Post Traumatic Slave Syndrome: America's Legacy of Enduring Injury and Healing*, Joy DeGruy Publications, 2017

Demony, Catarina, 'Portugal Should Apologise, Confront Past Role in Slavery, Says President', Reuters, 25/04/2023, https://www.usnews.com/news/world/articles/2023-04-25/portugal-should-apologise-confront-past-role-in-slavery-says-president

Demony, Catarina, and Carreño, Belén, 'EU says slavery inflicted "untold suffering", hints at reparations', Reuters, 18/07/2023, https://shorturl.at/dgHL7

Desai, Manan, 'What B. R. Ambedkar Wrote to W. E. B. Du Bois', *SAADA*, 22/04/2014, https://www.saada.org/tides/article/ambedkar-du-bois

Desai, Miki, and Desai, Madhavi, 'The colonial bungalow in India', *The Newsletter: International Institute for Asian Studies*, Summer 2011, https://www.iias.asia/sites/iias/files/nwl_article/2019-05/IIAS_NL57_2627.pdf

Destrooper, Tine, 'Belgium's "Truth Commission" on its overseas colonial legacy: An expressivist analysis of transitional justice in consolidated democracies', *Journal of Human Rights* 2023, 22:2, pp.158–73

Devlin, Hannah, 'Industrial Revolution iron method "was taken from Jamaica by Briton"', 05/07/2023, *Guardian*, https://www.theguardian.com/science/2023/jul/05/industrial-revolution-iron-method-taken-from-jamaica-briton?CMP=Share_Android App_Other&s=03

DeVotta, Neil, 'Behind the crisis in Sri Lanka – how political and economic mismanagement combined to plunge nation into turmoil', *The Conversation*, 18/07/2022,https://theconversation.com/behind-the-crisis-in-sri-lanka-how-political-and-economic-mismanagement-combined-to-plunge-nation-into-turmoil-187137

Dhillon, Amrit, 'Don't say hello, it's too western, Indian civil servants told', *The Times*, 03/10/2022, https://www.thetimes.co.uk/article/1df7bc02-4269-11ed-abc9-d0d53e948d21?shareToken=9cfc72be6c540ab1b0d8e8e2a9c5c69e

Dhillon, Amrit, 'Indian army on the march to erase its colonial past', *The Times*, 21/9/2022, https://shorturl.at/zF256

Dhillon, Amrit, 'Indian minister calls for abolition of 1,500 laws dating back to Raj', *Guardian*, 25/10/2022, https://www.theguardian.com/world/2022/oct/25/indian-minister-calls-for-abolition-of-1500-laws-dating-back-to-raj

Dhillon, Amrit, 'Modi employs new tool in India's war against the English language: Hindi medical degrees', *Guardian*, 22/10/2022, https://www.theguardian.com/world/2022/oct/22/modi-employs-new-tool-in-indias-war-against-the-english-language-hindi-medical-degrees

Diamond, Larry, 'Introduction', in Larry Diamond, Juan Linz and Seymour Martin Lipset (eds.), *Democracy in Developing Countries*, vol. 2: *Africa*, Lynne Rienner, 1988, pp. 1–32

Dirks, Nicholas B., *The Scandal of Empire: India and the Creation of Imperial Britain*, Belknap Press of Harvard University Press, 2006

'Do They Know It's Christmas?', *Song Facts*, accessed 01/02/2023, https://www.song-facts.com/facts/band-aid/do-they-know-its-christmas

Doherty, Ben, ' "Stop the Boats": Sunak's anti-asylum slogan echoes Australia's harsh policy', *Guardian*, 08/03/2023, https://www.theguardian.com/uk-news/2023/mar/08/stop-the-boats-sunaks-anti-asylum-slogan-echoes-australia-harsh-policy

Donald, Caroline, 'Why the Palm House at Kew is still a palace of exotic wonders after all these years', *Telegraph*, 25/07/2020, https://www.telegraph.co.uk/gardening/gardens-to-visit/palm-house-kew-still-palace-exotic-wonders-years/

Donnington, Kate, *The Bonds of Family: Slavery, Commerce and Culture in the British Atlantic World*, Manchester University Press, 2019

Dorn, Nathan, 'New Acquisition: *The Trial of Governor Picton* – A Case of Torture in Trinidad', *Library of Congress blogs*, 10/03/2021, https://blogs.loc.gov/law/2021/03/new-acquisition-the-trial-of-governor-picton-a-case-of-torture-in-trinidad/

Douglas, Roy, *Liquidation of Empire: The Decline of the British Empire*, Palgrave, 2002

Douzinas, Costas, *Human Rights and Empire: The Political Philosophy of Cosmopolitanism*, Routledge-Cavendish, 2007

Downer, Alexander, 'The threat to Britain's undersea cables', *Spectator*, 29/10/2022, https://www.spectator.co.uk/article/the-threat-to-britains-undersea-cables

Drayton, Richard, *Nature's Government: Science, Imperial Britain, and the Improvement of the World*, Yale University Press, 2000

Drescher, Seymour, *Econocide: British Slavery in the Era of Abolition*, University of Pittsburgh Press, 1977

Driesen, David M., 'Review: Colonialism's Climate?', *International Studies Review* 2007, 9:3, pp. 369–84

Driver, Felix, *Geography Militant: Cultures of Exploration in the Age of Empire*, Blackwell Publishing, 2001

Du Bois, W. E. B., 'The Souls of White Folk', *Library of America,* accessed 10/02/2023, https://www.loa.org/news-and-views/1681-web-du-bois-the-souls-of-white-folk

Du Bois, W. E. B., 'Strivings of the Negro People', *The Atlantic*, August 1897, https://www.theatlantic.com/magazine/archive/1897/08/strivings-of-the-negro-people/305446/

Dubow, Saul, *Racial Segregation and the Origins of Apartheid in South Africa, 1919–36*, Palgrave Macmillan, 1989

Durgahee, Reshaad, 'The Indentured Archipelago: Experiences of Indian Indentured Labour in Mauritius and Fiji, 1871–1916', PhD thesis, University of Nottingham, 2017, https://eprints.nottingham.ac.uk/44058/ (published as *The Indentured Archipelago: Experiences of Indian Labour in Mauritius and Fiji, 1871–1916*, Cambridge University Press, 2021)

Dussart, Fae, *In the Service of Empire: Domestic Service and Mastery in Metropole and Colony*, Bloomsbury, 2022

Dussart, Fae, ' "Strictly Legal Means": Assault, Abuse and the Limits of Acceptable Behaviour in the Servant–Employer Relationship in Metropole and Colony 1850–1890', in Claire Lowrie and Victoria K. Haskins (eds.), *Colonization and Domestic Service: Historical and Contemporary Perspectives*, Taylor & Francis, 2014, pp. 153–71.

Dyikuk, Justine John, ' "Scores of Christians killed, others displaced" – Nigerian think tank builds "atrocities database" ', *The Pillar*, 14/02/2023, https://www.pillarcatholic.com/scores-of-christians-killed-others-displaced-nigerian-think-tank-builds-atrocities-database/

Dyson, Tim, *A Population History of India: From the First Modern People to the Present Day*, Oxford University Press, 2018

Easterly, William, *The White Man's Burden: Why the West's Efforts to Aid the Rest Have Done So Much Ill and So Little Good*, Oxford University Press, 2007

Edkins, Jenny, *Whose Hunger? Concepts of Famine, Practices of Aid*, University of Minnesota Press, 2000

'Edward Huggins Sr.', *Centre for the Study of the Legacies of British Slavery*, accessed 16/02/2023, https://www.ucl.ac.uk/lbs/person/view/2146635234

Edwards, Adam, 'In praise of the British baddie', *Daily Express*, 23/04/2010, https://www.express.co.uk/expressyourself/170852/In-praise-of-the-British-baddie

Eichengreen, Barry, *Globalizing Capital: A History of the International Monetary System*, Princeton University Press, 2019

Eissa, Salih Omar, 'Diversity and Transformation: African Americans and African Immigration to the United States', Immigration Policy Center, https://www.

americanimmigrationcouncil.org/sites/default/files/research/Diversity and Transformation March 2005.pdf

Elbourne, Elizabeth, *Blood Ground: Colonialism, Missions, and the Contest for Christianity in the Cape Colony and Britain, 1799–1853*, McGill-Queen's University Press, 2002

Elbourne, Elizabeth, 'The Sin of the Settler: The 1835–36 Select Committee on Aborigines and Debates over Virtue and Conquest in the Early Nineteenth-Century British White Settler Empire', *Journal of Colonialism and Colonial History* 2003, 4:3, pp. 1–33

Elias, André J. P., ' "Vande Mataram!": Constructions of Gender and Music in Indian Nationalism', *Asian Music* 2017, 48:2, pp. 90–110

Elias, Sean, 'Colour Line', *The Wiley Blackwell Encyclopaedia of Race, Ethnicity, and Nationalism*, Wiley Blackwell, 2015, https://www.researchgate.net/publication/315772103_Colour_Line/link/6079cf6a907dcf667ba44372/download

Elkins, Caroline, *Imperial Reckoning: The Untold Story of Britain's Gulag in Kenya*, Henry Holt, 2005

Elkins, Caroline, *Legacy of Violence: A History of the British Empire*, Bodley Head, 2022

Ellis-Petersen, Hannah, 'Amitav Ghosh: European colonialism helped create a planet in crisis, Indian author says', *Guardian*, 14/01/2022, https://www.theguardian.com/books/2022/jan/14/amitav-ghosh-european-colonialism-helped-create-a-planet-in-crisis

Ellis-Petersen, Hannah, ' "There hasn't been closure": India mourns Queen but awaits apology', *Guardian*, 14/09/2022, https://www.theguardian.com/world/2022/sep/14/india-mourns-queen-elizabeth-apology-commonwealth

Elson, Peter R., Lefèvre, Sylvain A., and Fontan, Jean-Marc (eds.), *Philanthropic Foundations in Canada: Landscapes, Indigenous Perspectives and Pathways to Change*, PhiLab, 2020

Eltis, David, 'Free and Coerced Transatlantic Migrations: Some Comparisons', *American Historical Review* 1983, 88:2, pp. 251–80

Endersby, Jim, *Imperial Science: Joseph Hooker and the Practices of Victorian Science*, University of Chicago Press, 2008

Epprecht, Marc, ' "Unnatural Vice" in South Africa: The 1907 Commission of Enquiry', *International Journal of African Historical Studies* 2001, 34:1, pp. 121–40

Erakat, Noura, *Justice for Some: Law and the Question of Palestine*, Stanford University Press, 2019

Erlanger, Steven, 'A Global Outpouring of Grief Mixes with Criticism of the Monarchy', *New York Times*, 8/9/2022, https://www.nytimes.com/2022/09/08/world/europe/queen-elizabeth-reaction.html

Etherington, Norman (ed.), *Missions and Empire*, Oxford University Press, 2005

Everill, Bronwen, 'Review of *Humanitarianism* and *Humanitarian Intervention*', *Reviews in History*, October 2011, https://reviews.history.ac.uk/review/1141

'Everything You Ever Wanted to Know About Rubber', *Bouncing Balls*, accessed 16/01/2023, http://www.bouncing-balls.com

'Evil Brit', *TVtropes.org*, accessed 20/03/2023, https://tvtropes.org/pmwiki/pmwiki.php/Main/EvilBrit

'The Exploitation of Tea Plantation Workers in Sri Lanka', *The Borgen Project*, 22/08/2021, https://borgenproject.org/tea-plantation-workers-in-sri-lanka/

'Exploited and marginalized, Bangladeshi tea workers speak up for their rights', *UN News*, 21/03/2021, https://news.un.org/en/story/2021/03/1087622

Falola, Toyin, *Colonialism and Violence in Nigeria*, Indiana University Press, 2009

Falola, Toyin O., et al., 'Nigerian Civil War', *Britannica*, accessed 29/07/2023, https://www.britannica.com/topic/Nigerian-civil-war

Faloyin, Dipo, *Africa Is Not a Country: Breaking Stereotypes of Modern Africa*, Penguin Books, 2022

Farrell, Paul, Evershed, Nick, and Davidson, Helen, 'The Nauru files: cache of 2,000 leaked reports reveal scale of abuse of children in Australian offshore detention', *Guardian*, 10/08/2016, https://www.theguardian.com/australia-news/2016/aug/10/the-nauru-files-2000-leaked-reports-reveal-scale-of-abuse-of-children-in-australian-offshore-detention

'Fast Forward', *Bond*, 01/07/2014, https://www.bond.org.uk/resources/fast-forward/

Ferguson, Jane M., 'Who's Counting? Ethnicity, Belonging, and the National Census in Burma/Myanmar', *Bijdragen tot de Taal-, Land- en Volkenkunde* 2015, 171:1, pp. 1–28, https://www.jstor.org/stable/43819166

Ferguson, Moira, *Subject to Others: British Women Writers and Colonial Slavery, 1670–1834*, Routledge, 1992

Ferguson, Niall, *Empire: How Britain Made the Modern World*, Penguin Books, 2004

Fettweis, Christopher J., *The Pursuit of Dominance: 2000 Years of Superpower Grand Strategy*, Oxford University Press, 2022

'Fibre optic cable sabotage causes global internet slowdown', *Brussels Times*, 25/10/2022, https://www.brusselstimes.com/311704/fibre-optic-cable-sabotage-causes-global-internet-slowdown

Flanagan, Jane, 'Return to Sender: designer upcycles British hand-me-downs to reboot Ugandan textile industry', *The Times*, 29/04/2022, https://www.thetimes.co.uk/article/return-to-sender-designer-upcycles-british-hand-me-downs-to-reboot-ugandan-textile-industry-b8sdfkkzx

Flanagan, Jane, 'Tribes win payout from South African tea industry over rights to rooibos', *The Times*, 14/07/2022, https://www.thetimes.co.uk/article/tribes-win-payout-from-south-african-tea-industry-over-rights-to-rooibos-2zlcsmw96

Flood, Alison, ' "Imperially nostalgic racists" target Empireland author with hate mail', *Guardian*, 12/03/2021, https://www.theguardian.com/books/2021/mar/12/imperially-nostalgic-racists-target-empireland-author-with-hate-mail

Flood, Vincent, 'Hollywood, and the enduring British villain', *Screen Robot*, 09/07/2019, https://screenrobot.com/hollywood-enduring-british-villain/

Floud, Roderick, *An Economic History of the English Garden*, Penguin Books, 2020

Floyd, Troy S., *The Columbian Dynasty in the Caribbean, 1492–1526*, University of New Mexico Press, 1973

Fong, Fernando, 'Georgetown Won't Be Renamed Tanjong Penaga', *T R P*, 15/03/2022, https://www.therakyatpost.com/news/malaysia/2022/03/15/georgetown-wont-be-renamed-tanjong-penaga/

Foreign, Commonwealth & Development Office and The Rt Hon. Dominic Raab M P, 'U K Official Development Assistance (O D A) allocations 2021 to 2022: written ministerial statement', *GOV. UK*, 21/04/2021, https://www.gov.uk/government/speeches/uk-official-development-assistance-oda-allocations-2021-to-2022-written-ministerial-statement

Forrest, Adam, 'End S A R S protests: U K government admits it did train and supply equipment to Nigeria's "brutal" police unit', *Independent*, 30/10/20, https://www.independent.co.uk/news/uk/politics/sars-nigeria-police-protests-uk-government-training-equipment-b1424447.html

Foster, Thomas A., *Rethinking Rufus: Sexual Violations of Enslaved Men*, University of Georgia Press, 2019

Foucault, Michel, *The History of Sexuality*, vol. 1: *The Will to Knowledge*, Random House, 1978

Fowler, Corinne, *Green Unpleasant Land: Creative Responses to Rural England's Colonial Connections*, Peepal Tree Press, 2020

Frank, John W., Moore, Roland S., and Ames, Genevieve M., 'Public Health Then and Now: Historical and Cultural Roots of Drinking Problems among American Indians', *American Journal of Public Health* 2000, 90:3, pp. 344–51

Frankopan, Peter, *The Earth Transformed: An Untold Story*, Bloomsbury, 2023

Frankopan, Peter, 'West's reckless lack of expertise on China will cost us dear', *The Times*, 18/02/2023, https://www.thetimes.co.uk/article/d006ad54-af9c-11ed-bdeo-64a2adofcf88?shareToken=bb15e644b80e5368ab5e24c708ae1a78

Fredrickson, George M., *White Supremacy: A Comparative Study*, Oxford University Press, 1981

'Freetown', *Britannica*, https://www.britannica.com/place/Freetown

'Freetown, Sierra Leone, 1792–', *Blackpast*, 20/04/2011, https://www.blackpast.org/global-african-history/places-global-african-history/freetown-sierra-leone-1792/

French, Patrick, *The World Is What It Is: The Authorized Biography of V. S. Naipaul*, Picador, 2008

Freyre, Gilberto, *The Masters and the Slaves: A Study in the Development of Brazilian Civilization*, trans. Samuel Putnam, abridged from the revised edn, Alfred A. Knopf, 1946

Friar, Danny, 'History of Jamaican Food', *Mas Media: Leeds Carnival Blog*, 28/02/2018, https://leedsmasmedia.wordpress.com/2018/02/28/history-of-jamaican-food/

Friedland, Martin L., 'Codification in the Commonwealth: Earlier Efforts', *Commonwealth Law Bulletin* 1992, 18:3, pp. 1172–80

'Friedrich Wilhelm Keyl, *Looty*', *Royal Collection Trust*, https://www.rct.uk/collection/406974/looty

Frost, Mark R., 'Pandora's Post Box: Empire and Information in India, 1854–1914', *English Historical Review* 2016, 131:552, pp. 1043–73

Funes, Yessenia, 'Yes, Colonialism Caused Climate Change, IPCC Reports', *Atmos*, 04/04/2022, https://atmos.earth/ipcc-report-colonialism-climate-change/

Galloway, J. H., 'Botany in the Service of Empire: The Barbados Cane-Breeding Program and the Revival of the Caribbean Sugar Industry, 1880s–1930s', *Annals of the Association of American Geographers* 1996, 86:4, pp. 682–706

Gardner, Kyle J., *The Frontier Complex: Geopolitics and the Making of the India–China Border, 1846–1962*, Cambridge University Press, 2021

Gasiorowski, Mark J., 'The 1953 *Coup d'État* in Iran', *International Journal of Middle East Studies* 1987, 19:3, pp. 261–86

Gately, Iain, *Tobacco: A Cultural History of How an Exotic Plant Seduced Civilization*, Grove Books, 2007

Gayle, Damien, 'Climate emergency is a legacy of colonialism, says Greenpeace UK', *Guardian*, 21/07/2022, https://www.theguardian.com/environment/2022/jul/21/climate-emergency-is-a-legacy-of-colonialism-says-greenpeace-uk

Gbadamosi, T. G. O., Alo, Olugbolahan Abisogun, and Osisanya-Olumuyiwa, Wale (eds.), *Floreat Collegium: 100 Years of King's College, Lagos*, Third Millennium Publishing, 2014

Genovese, Eugene D., *The Political Economy of Slavery: Studies in the Economy and Society of the Slave South*, Pantheon Books, 1965

'George Washington House', *Barbados.org*, accessed 19/01/2023, https://barbados.org/george_washington.htm#.YtGJR3bMKUk

GHFP, 'Trauma of slavery and epigenetics', *Healing the Wounds of Slavery*, 15/10/2018, https://shorturl.at/KMOS2

Ghose, Indira, 'The Memsahib Myth: Englishwomen in Colonial India', in Celia R. Daileader, Rhoda E. Johnson and Amilcar Shabazz (eds.), *Women & Others: Perspectives on Race, Gender & Empire*, Palgrave Macmillan, 2007, pp. 107–28

Ghosh, Amitav, *The Nutmeg's Curse: Parables for a Planet in Crisis*, University of Chicago Press, 2021

Gilbert, Helen, and Tiffin, Chris (eds.), *Burden or Benefit? Imperial Benevolence and its Legacies*, Indiana University Press, 2008

Gilbert, Jason, 'Empire and Excise: Drugs and Drink Revenue and the Fate of States in South Asia', in James H. Mills and Patricia Barton (eds.), *Drugs and Empire: Essays in Modern Imperialism and Intoxication, c. 1500–c.1930*, Palgrave Macmillan, 2007

Gilroy, Paul, *The Black Atlantic*, Harvard University Press, 1995

Global Industry Analysts, 'Global Industry Analysts Predicts the World Industrial Rubber Products Market to Reach $136.5 Billion by 2026', *CISION PR Newswire*, 23/03/2022, https://shorturl.at/ovLQ2

Godden, Lee C., and Casinader, Niranjan, 'The Kandyan Convention 1815: Consolidating the British Empire in Colonial Ceylon', *Comparative Legal History* 2013, 1:2, pp. 211–42

Godden, Richard, and Polk, Noel, 'Reading the Ledgers', *Mississippi Quarterly* 2002, 55:3, pp. 301–59

Godwin, Richard, 'Roll with the rum punches in Barbados', *The Times*, 15/01/2022, https://www.thetimes.co.uk/article/roll-with-the-rum-punches-in-barbados-m333dxb6g

Goetz, Nathaniel H., 'Humanitarian Issues in the Biafra Conflict', *New Issues in Refugee Research* 2001, 36, https://www.unhcr.org/uk/3af66b8b4.pdf

Gopnik, Adam, 'Finest hours: The making of Winston Churchill', *New Yorker*, 23/08/2010, https://www.newyorker.com/magazine/2010/08/30/finest-hours

Gorman, Daniel, *Imperial Citizenship: Empire and the Question of Belonging*, Manchester University Press, 2006

Graboyes, Melissa, *The Experiment Must Continue: Medical Research and Ethics in East Africa, 1940–2014*, Ohio University Press, 2014

Grant, Kevin, *A Civilised Savagery: Britain and the New Slaveries in Africa, 1884–1926*, Routledge, 2005

Grant, Kevin, Levine, Philippa, and Trentmann, Frank, *Beyond Sovereignty: Britain, Empire and Transnationalism, c. 1860–1950*, Palgrave Macmillan, 2007

Graves, Adrian, *Cane and Labour: The Political Economy of the Queensland Sugar Industry*, Edinburgh University Press, 1993

Green, Elliott, 'On the Size and Shape of African States', *International Studies Quarterly* 2012, 56:2, pp. 229–44

Greenlee, James G., *Education and Imperial Unity, 1901–1926*, Routledge, 2016

Greenwood, Anna, 'The Art of Medicine: Diagnosing the Medical History of British Imperialism', *Lancet*, 03/09/2022, 400, pp. 726–7

Greenwood, Anna, *Practising Colonial Medicine: The Colonial Medical Service in East Africa*, I.B. Tauris, 2007

Grey, Becky, 'Commonwealth Games: Birmingham puts on captivating opening ceremony', *BBC Sport*, 28/07/2022, https://www.bbc.co.uk/sport/commonwealth-games/62340186

Griffiths, Ieuan, 'The Scramble for Africa: Inherited Political Boundaries', *Geographical Journal* 1986, 152:2, pp. 204–16

Grove, Richard H., *Green Imperialism: Colonial Expansion, Tropical Island Edens and the Origins of Environmentalism, 1600–1860*, Cambridge University Press, 1995

Guha, Amalendu, *Planter-Raj to Swaraj: Freedom Struggle and Electoral Politics in Assam, 1826–1947*, Indian Council of Historical Research, 1977

Gurney, Christabel, ' "A Great Cause": The Origins of the Anti-Apartheid Movement, June 1959–March 1960', *Journal of Southern African Studies* 2000, 26:1, pp. 123–44

Hadenius, Axel, *Development and Democracy*, Cambridge University Press, 2009

Hagan, James, and Wells, Andrew, 'The British and rubber in Malaya, c1890–1940', *University of Wollongong Faculty of Arts*, 2005, https://ro.uow.edu.au/cgi/viewcon tent.cgi?referer=&httpsredir=1&article=2648&context=artspapers

Hall, Catherine, 'Missionary Stories: Gender and Ethnicity in England in the 1830s and 1840s', in Catherine Hall, *White, Male and Middle Class: Explorations in Feminism and History*, Polity Press, 2013, pp. 205–54

Hall, Matthew, 'Anglo American's history in South Africa', *Mining Technology*, 03/02/2021,https://www.mining-technology.com/analysis/anglo-americans-history-in-south-africa/#:~:text=Anglo%20American%20has%20its%20roots,American%20to%20 the%20company%20name

Han, Enze, and O'Mahoney, Joseph, *British Colonialism and the Criminalization of Homosexuality: Queens, Crime and Empire*, Routledge, 2019

Han, Enze, and O'Mahoney, Joseph, 'British colonialism and the criminalization of homosexuality', *Cambridge Review of International Affairs* 2014, 27:2, pp. 268–88

Handler, Jerome S., and Reilly, Matthew C., 'Contesting "White Slavery" in the Caribbean: Enslaved Africans and European Indentured Servants in Seventeenth-Century Barbados', *BRILL: New West Indian Guide*, 01/01/2017, https://brill.com/view/journals/nwig/91/1-2/article-p30_2.xml?language=en

Harding, Thomas, *White Debt: The Demerara Uprising and Britain's Legacy of Slavery*, Weidenfeld & Nicolson, 2022

Hardt, Michael, and Negri, Antonio, *Empire*, Harvard University Press, 2000

Hardwick, Joseph, *Prayer, Providence and Empire: Special Worship in the British World, 1783–1919*, Manchester University Press, 2021

Harman, Kristyn, 'Explainer: the evidence for the Tasmanian genocide', *The Conversation*, 17/01/2018, https://theconversation.com/explainer-the-evidence-for-the-tasmanian-genocide-86828

Harris, Rob, 'Penny Wong tells Britain to confront its colonial past', *The Age*, 01/02/2023,https://www.theage.com.au/politics/federal/penny-wong-tells-britain-to-confront-its-colonial-past-20230131-p5cgvw.html?ref=rss

Haskell, Thomas L., 'Capitalism and the Origins of the Humanitarian Sensibility, Part 1', *American Historical Review* 1985, 90:2, pp. 339–61

Haskell, Thomas L., 'Capitalism and the Origins of the Humanitarian Sensibility, Part 2', *American Historical Review* 1985, 90:3, pp. 547–66

Hawkins, Amy, 'Is the British Empire to blame?', *Foreign Policy*, 13/08/2019, https://foreignpolicy.com/2019/08/13/the-world-is-reaping-the-chaos-the-british-empire-sowed/

Haynes, Douglas M., *Imperial Medicine: Patrick Manson and the Conquest of Tropical Disease*, University of Pennsylvania Press, 2001

Hays, Jo N., *Epidemics and Pandemics: Their Impacts on Human History*, ABC Clio, 2005

Head, Matilda, 'Cambridge's Trinity College to examine its links to slavery', *Independent*, 18/03/2023, https://www.independent.co.uk/news/uk/trinity-college-university-of-cambridge-africa-b2303546.html

Headrick, Daniel R., *The Tentacles of Progress: Technology Transfer in the Age of Imperialism, 1850–1940*, Oxford University Press, 1988

Headrick, Daniel R., *The Tools of Empire: Technology and European Imperialism in the Nineteenth Century*, Oxford University Press, 1981

Heard, Danielle, 'Comedy', *Oxford African American Studies Center*, https://doi.org/10.1093/acref/9780195301731.013.50279

Heartfield, James, *The Aborigines' Protection Society: Humanitarian Imperialism in Australia, New Zealand, Fiji, Canada, South Africa, and the Congo, 1837–1909*, Hurst, 2011

Heblich, Stephan, Redding, Stephen J., and Voth, Hans-Joachim, 'Slavery and the British Industrial Revolution', Working Paper 30451, National Bureau of Economic Research, Cambridge, Mass., 2022, http://www.nber.org/papers/w30451

Heikkilä-Horn, Marja-Leena, 'Imagining "Burma": a historical overview', *Asian Ethnicity* 2009, 10:2, pp. 145–54, https://doi.org/10.1080/14631360902906839

Henderson, Janice, and Osborne, Daphne J., 'The oil palm in all our lives: how this came about', *Endeavour* 2000, 24:2, pp. 63–8

Herman, Arthur, *Gandhi and Churchill: The Rivalry That Destroyed an Empire and Forged our Age*, Random House, 2010

Hewison, Hope H., *Hedge of Wild Almonds: South Africa, the Pro-Boers & the Quaker Conscience, 1890–1910*, James Currey, 1989

Heyningen, Elizabeth van, *The Concentration Camps of the Anglo-Boer War: A Social History*, Jacana, 2013

Higman, B. W., *Jamaican Food: History, Biology, Culture*, University of the West Indies Press, 2008

Hill, Richard, 'Policing Ireland, Policing Colonies: The Royal Irish Constabulary "Model"', in Angela McCarthy (ed.), *Ireland in the World: Comparative, Transnational and Personal Perspectives*, Routledge, 2015, pp. 61–80

Hilton, Matthew, 'Charity and the End of Empire: British Non-governmental Organizations, Africa, and International Development in the 1960s', *American Historical Review* 2018, 123:2, pp. 493–517

Hilton, Matthew, 'Ken Loach and the Save the Children Film: Humanitarianism, Imperialism, and the Changing Role of Charity in Postwar Britain', *Journal of Modern History* 2015, 87:2, pp. 357–94

Hilton, Matthew, McKay, James, Crowson, Nicholas, and Mouhot, Jean-François, *The Politics of Expertise: How NGOs Shaped Modern Britain*, Oxford University Press, 2013

Hinchy, Jessica, *Governing Gender and Sexuality in Colonial India: The Hijra, c.1850–1900*, Cambridge University Press, 2019

Hirshfield, Claire, 'Liberal Women's Organizations and the War against the Boers, 1899–1902', *Albion: A Quarterly Journal Concerned with British Studies* 1982 14:1, pp. 27–49

'History and curation of economic botany collections', *Royal Botanic Gardens Kew*, accessed 20/01/2023, https://www.kew.org/science/our-science/projects/history-curation-economic-botany-collections

'History of Indian Tea', *Indian Tea Association*, accessed 01/02/2023, https://www.indiatea.org/history_of_indian_tea

Hoefte, Rosemarijn, *In Place of Slavery: A Social History of British Indian and Javanese Laborers in Suriname*, University Press of Florida, 1998

Holland, Tom, and Sandbrook, Dominic, 'The Enlightenment', *The Rest is History* podcast, episode 86, 16/08/2021, https://open.spotify.com/episode/3Lu92A3BRBL3uYQ15wwmSS?si=OSGGDLDITA2OnPzMCUl5Cg&dl_branch=1

Holland, Tom, and Sandbrook, Dominic, 'USA vs England: The 200-Year Rivalry', *The Rest Is History* podcast, episode 263, 25/11/2022, https://open.spotify.com/episode/1fmP92v1fZeUWdXVFZTDFB?si=e21eed1527e54a6b

Holligan, Anna, 'Netherlands slavery: Saying sorry leaves Dutch divided', *BBC News*, 19/12/2022, https://www.bbc.co.uk/news/world-europe-63993283.amp

Holmes, Oliver, 'After 130 years of obscurity, Myanmar's forgotten royals make a comeback', *Guardian*, 30/12/2016, https://www.theguardian.com/world/2016/dec/30/myanmar-burma-royal-family-monarchy-king-thibaw-comeback

Holt, Thomas C., *The Problem of Freedom: Race, Labor and Politics in Jamaica and Britain, 1832–1938*, Johns Hopkins University Press, 1992

Home, Robert, *Of Planting and Planning: The Making of British Colonial Cities*, E. & F. N. Spon, 1997

Hooker, J. R., 'The Pan-African Conference 1900', *Transition* 1974, 46, pp. 20–24

Howard-Johnston, Jessica, 'Band Aid 30: A neo-colonial controversy?', *Pi Media*, 04/12/2014, https://uclpimedia.com/online/band-aid-30-a-neo-colonial-controversy

'How did CAFOD begin: your questions answered', *CAFOD*, 25/07/2018, https://cafod.org.uk/About-us/Our-history-Q-A

'How many places are named Birmingham?', *geotargit.com*, accessed 20/03/2023, https://geotargit.com/called.php?qcity=Birmingham

'How Sam Hose's lynching became an awakening for W. E. B. Du Bois', *The official blog of The Library of America*, 18/03/2011, http://blog.loa.org/2011/03/how-sam-hose-lynching-became-awakening.html

Huff, W. G., 'The Development of the Rubber Market in Pre-World War II Singapore', *Journal of Southeast Asian Studies* 1993, 24:2, pp. 285–306

Hui, Neha, and Kambhampati, Uma, 'The Political Economy of Indian Indentured Labour in the 19th Century', *University of Reading*, accessed 10/03/2023, https://www.reading.ac.uk/web/FILES/economics/emdp202016.pdf

Hull, Matthew, *Government of Paper: The Materiality of Bureaucracy in Urban Pakistan*, University of California Press, 2012

'Humanitarian Emergency Response Review', *Department for International Development (UK)*, 2011, https://assets.publishing.service.gov.uk/government/uploads/system/uploads/attachment_data/file/67579/HERR.pdf

Humphreys, Josephine, 'History and Mystery on Nevis', *New York Times Style Magazine*, 12/11/1995, https://www.nytimes.com/1995/11/12/t-magazine/history-and-mystery-on-nevis.html

Hunt, Lynn, *Inventing Human Rights: A History*, W. W. Norton, 2007

Hunt, Nancy Rose, *A Colonial Lexicon of Birth Ritual, Medicalization, and Mobility in the Congo*, Duke University Press, 1999

Hunter, Melvin, 'Racist Relics: An Ugly Blight on our Botanical Nomenclature', *Scientist*, 24/11/1991, https://www.the-scientist.com/opinion-old/racist-relics-an-ugly-blight-on-our-botanical-nomenclature-60358

Huntington, S., *The Third Wave: Democratization in the Late Twentieth Century*, Oklahoma University Press, 1991

Huntington, S., 'Will More Countries Become Democratic?', *Political Science Quarterly* 1984, 99, pp. 192–218

Hussain, Mobeen, 'Combining Global Expertise with Local Knowledge in Colonial India: Selling Ideals of Beauty and Health in Commodity Advertising (c. 1900–1949)', *South Asia: Journal of South Asian Studies* 2021, 44:5, pp. 926–47

Huxtable, Amy, 'A cuppa reality: The truth behind your brew', *University of Sheffield*, https://www.sheffield.ac.uk/research/forced-labour

Huzzey, Richard, *Freedom Burning: Anti-Slavery and Empire in Victorian Britain*, Cornell University Press, 2012

Hyam, Ronald, *Empire and Sexuality: The British Experience*, Manchester University Press, 1990

Ihejirika, Chidera, 'Fuck your gender norms: how Western colonisation brought unwanted binaries to Igbo culture', *gal-dem*, 19/02/2020, https://gal-dem.com/colonialism-nigeria-gender-norms-lgbtq-igbo/

'Ilbert Bill', *Britannica*, 18/01/2023, https://www.britannica.com/event/Ilbert-Bill

'Inclusive Language Guide', *Oxfam*, 13/03/2023, https://policy-practice.oxfam.org/resources/inclusive-language-guide-621487/

'Indigenous American Words in the English Language', *Day Translations Blog*, 01/11/2022, https://www.daytranslations.com/blog/indigenous-words-english/#:~:text=the%20dirty%20water.-,',wigwam%20and%20powwow%20are%20examples

'Indo-Fijians', *Minority Rights*, accessed 10/03/2023, https://minorityrights.org/minorities/indo-fijians/

Ingram, Edward, *Empire-Building and Empire-Builders: Twelve Studies*, Routledge, 2016

'The Intersection: English is an Indian language', *Mint*, 27/03/2023, https://www.nitinpai.in/2023/02/27/english-is-an-indian-language

Irfan, Anne, 'Israel: unpopular judicial reform involves repeal of law set up under British colonial rule in Palestine – here's what that tells us', *The Conversation*, 26/07/2023, https://theconversation.com/israel-unpopular-judicial-reform-involves-repeal-of-law-set-up-under-british-colonial-rule-in-palestine-heres-what-that-tells-us-210401

Isichie, Elizabeth, *A History of the Igbo People*, Macmillan, 1976

'Island Delight, and the Origins of the Jamaican Pattie', *Island Delight*, accessed 10/03/2023, https://www.island-delight.co.uk/history-of-the-jamaican-patty/

Jack, Ian, 'Britain took more out of India than it put in – could China do the same to Britain?', *Guardian*, 20/06/2014, https://www.theguardian.com/commentisfree/2014/jun/20/britain-took-more-out-of-india

Jain, Ravindra K., 'South Indian Labour in Malaya, 1840–1920: Asylum Stability and Involution', in Kay Saunders (ed.), *Indentured Labour in the British Empire: 1834–1920*, Routledge, 1984, pp. 158–82

James, C. L. R., *Beyond a Boundary: 50th Anniversary Edition*, Duke University Press, 2013

Jamieson, Roberta, 'Decolonizing philanthropy: Building new relations', in Peter R. Elson, Sylvain A. Lefèvre and Jean-Marc Fontan (eds.), *Philanthropic Foundations in Canada: Landscapes, Indigenous Perspectives and Pathways to Change*, PhiLab, 2020, pp. 157–72, https://decolonizingwealth.com/about/

*Jan Morris: Writing a Life*, Archive on 4, https://www.bbc.co.uk/programmes/m0011jxq

Jasanoff, Maya, 'Mourn the Queen, Not her Empire', *New York Times*, 08/09/2022, https://www.nytimes.com/2022/09/08/opinion/queen-empire-decolonization.html?smtyp=cur&smid=tw-nytimes

Jeffries, Sir Charles, *Proud Record: Britain's Colonial Achievement*, HMSO, 1962

Jewell, Lisa, and Robinson, Randall, *The Debt: What America Owes Blacks*, Penguin Books, 2000

Jhala, Kabir, 'Controversial $1.8bn redevelopment of Delhi's parliament complex enters second phase', *Art Newspaper*, 28/09/2022, https://www.theartnewspaper.com/2022/

09/28/first-phase-of-controversial-18bn-redevelopment-of-delhis-parliament-complex-is-complete

Johnson, David A., 'A British Empire for the twentieth century: the inauguration of New Delhi, 1931', *Urban History* 2008, 35:3, pp. 462–84

Johnson, David A., 'The Library: New Delhi: The Last Imperial City', *The British Empire*, accessed 20/03/2023, https://www.britishempire.co.uk/library/newdelhi.htm

Johnson, Sherry, *Climate and Catastrophe in Cuba and the Atlantic World in the Age of Revolution*, University of North Carolina Press, 2011

Johnson, Sherry, 'El Niño, Environmental Crisis, and the Emergence of Alternative Markets in the Hispanic Caribbean, 1760s–70s', *William and Mary Quarterly* 2005, 62:3, pp. 365–410

Johnston, Nicole, 'Offshore processing of asylum seekers: Is the UK copying Australia's hardline policy?', *Sky News*, 14/04/2022, https://news.sky.com/story/offshore-processing-of-asylum-seekers-is-the-uk-copying-australias-hardline-policy-12589728

Jones, Emily, 'Brexit: Opportunity or peril for trade with small and poor developing economies?', *GEG: Global Economic Governance Programme*, accessed 04/07/2023, https://www.geg.ox.ac.uk/publication/brexit-opportunity-or-peril-trade-small-and-poor-developing-economies

Judd, Denis, *Empire: The British Imperial Experience, from 1765 to the Present*, Fontana Press, 1997

Kahn, Jeremy, 'Lutyens' bungalows: Saving a slice of imperial New Delhi', *New York Times*, 08/01/2008, https://www.nytimes.com/2008/01/08/arts/08iht-30kahn.9075163.html

Kale, Madhavi, *Fragments of Empire: Capital, Slavery, and Indian Indentured Labor Migration in the British Caribbean*, University of Pennsylvania Press, 1998

Kalof, Linda, and Montgomery, Georgina M. (eds.), *Making Animal Meaning (The Animal Turn)*, Michigan State University Press, 2011

Kampfner, Constance, 'British Museum's Myanmar exhibition explores how colonial rule "set stage for genocide"', *The Times*, 18/07/2023, https://shorturl.at/zFMZ2

Kamran, Tahir, 'Pakistan's first decade: democracy and constitution – a historical appraisal of centralisation', in Harshan Kumarasingham (ed.), *Constitution-Making in Asia: Decolonisation and State-Building in the Aftermath of the British Empire*, Routledge, 2016, pp. 96–111

Karas, Serkan, and Arapostathis, Stathis, 'Electrical Colonialism: Techno-politics and British Engineering Expertise in the Making of the Electricity Supply Industry in Cyprus', in Alain Beltran, Léonard Laborie, Pierre Lanthier and Stéphanie Le Gallic (eds.), *Electric Worlds / Mondes électriques: Creations, Circulations, Tensions, Transitions (19th–21st Century)*, P.I.E. Peter Lang, 2017, pp. 201–20

Karmakar, Chandrima, 'V. S. Naipaul: From Memory en route to Roots', accessed 10/03/2023, https://ntm.org.in/download/ttvol/Contextualising_Migration_SpecialIssue/article%209.pdf

'Kashmir', *Britannica*, accessed 31/03/2023, https://www.britannica.com/place/Kashmir-region-Indian-subcontinent

'Kashmir: Why India and Pakistan fight over it', *BBC News*, 08/08/2019, https://www.bbc.co.uk/news/10537286

Katsha, Habiba, 'David Lammy is right to call out the "white saviour" narrative – if only Comic Relief understood that', *Independent*, 28/02/2019, https://www.independent.co.uk/voices/david-lammy-comic-relief-stacey-dooley-white-saviour-charity-africa-a8801676.html

Katwala, Sunder, 'Is the British Empire to blame?', *Guardian*, 17/11/2002, https://www.theguardian.com/politics/2002/nov/17/foreignpolicy.comment

Kaur, Brahmjot, 'Camilla swaps the Kohinoor diamond for another controversial stone on her coronation crown', *NBC News*, 17/02/2023, https://www.nbcnews.com/news/asian-america/camilla-swaps-kohinoor-diamond-another-controversial-stone-coronation-rcna71032

Kazmin, Amy, 'India gay sex court ruling sets stage for cultural battle', *Financial Times*, 12/09/2018, https://www.ft.com/content/8a8cbd02-b5c5-11e8-b3ef-799c8613f4a1

Keegan, Timothy J., *Colonial South Africa and the Origins of the Racial Order*, David Philip, 1996

Kempadoo, Kamala, ' "Bound Coolies" and Other Indentured Workers in the Caribbean: Implications for Debates about Human Trafficking and Modern Slavery', *Anti-Trafficking Review* 2017, 9, pp. 48–63, https://www.antitraffickingreview.org/index.php/atrjournal/article/view/263/252

Kennedy, Jonathan, *Pathogenesis: How Germs Made History*, Torva, 2023

'Kenyan group sues UK government over what it calls colonial-era land theft', *Reuters*, 23/08/2022, https://www.reuters.com/world/africa/kenyan-group-sues-uk-government-over-what-it-calls-colonial-era-land-theft-2022-08-23/

Keogh, Luke, *The Wardian Case: How a Simple Box Moved Plants and Changed the World*, University of Chicago Press, 2020

Khalidi, Walid Ahmed, Faris, Nabih Amin, Brice, William Charles, Foxwell Albright, William, Jones, Arnold Hugh Martin, Khalidi, Rashid Ismail, Bickerton, Ian J., Fraser, Peter Marshall, Kenyon, Kathleen Mary, and Bugh, Glenn Richard, 'Palestine: World War I and after', *Britannica*, accessed 22/03/2023, https://www.britannica.com/place/Palestine/World-War-I-and-after

Klein, Elise, and Mills, China, 'Islands of deterrence: Britain's long history of banishing "undesirables" ', *Open Democracy*, 01/04/2021, https://www.opendemocracy.net/en/opendemocracyuk/islands-of-deterrence-britains-long-history-of-banishing-undesirables/

Knight, Kyle, 'India's Transgender Rights Law Isn't Worth Celebrating', *Human Rights Watch*, 05/12/2019, https://www.hrw.org/news/2019/12/05/indias-transgender-rights-law-isnt-worth-celebrating

Koch, Dirk-Jan, Dreher, Axel, Nunnekamp, Peter, and Thiele, Rainer, 'Keeping a low profile: what determines allocation of aid by non-governmental organizations?', *World Development* 2009, 37:5, pp. 902–18, https://doi.org/10.1016/j.worlddev.2008.09.004

Kolsky, Elizabeth, *Colonial Justice in British India: White Violence and the Rule of Law*, Cambridge University Press, 2010

Koram, Kojo, 'Britain needs a truth and reconciliation commission, not another racism inquiry', *Guardian*, 16/06/2023, https://www.theguardian.com/commentis free/2020/jun/16/britain-truth-reconciliation-commission-racism-imperial

Krebs, Paula M., ' "The Last of the Gentlemen's Wars": Women in the Boer War Concentration Camp Controversy', *History Workshop* 1992, 33:1, pp. 38–56

Kuhn, Philip A., *Chinese among Others: Emigration in Modern Times*, Rowman & Littlefield, 2008

Kumar, Ashutosh, *Coolies of the Empire: Indentured Indians in the Sugar Colonies, 1830–1920*, Cambridge University Press, 2017

Kumarasingham, Harshan (ed.), *Constitution-Making in Asia: Decolonisation and State-Building in the Aftermath of the British Empire*, Routledge, 2016

Kwarteng, Kwasi, *Ghosts of Empire: Britain's Legacies in the Modern World*, Bloomsbury, 2012

Kwet, Michael, 'Digital colonialism: US empire and the new imperialism in the Global South', *Race & Class* 2019, 60:4, https://doi.org/10.1177/0306396818823172

Lagan, Bernard, 'Anti-monarchy protesters burn Australian flag on day of mourning', *The Times*, 22/09/2022, https://www.thetimes.co.uk/article/anti-monarchy-protesters-burn-australian-flag-on-day-of-mourning-pnkpbmtcd

Laidlaw, Zoë, *Protecting the Empire's Humanity: Thomas Hodgkin and British Colonial Activism 1830–1870*, Cambridge University Press, 2021

Laidlaw, Zoë, and Lester, Alan (eds.), *Indigenous Communities and Settler Colonialism: Land Holding, Loss and Survival in an Interconnected World*, Palgrave Macmillan, 2015

Lake, Marilyn, and Reynolds, Henry, *Drawing the Global Colour Line: White Men's Countries and the International Challenge of Racial Equality*, Cambridge University Press, 2008

Lal, Brij V., *Girmitiyas: The Origins of the Fiji Indians*, Journal of Pacific History, 1983

Lal, Brij V., 'Labouring Men and Nothing More: Some Problems of Indian Indenture in Fiji', in Kay Saunders (ed.), *Indentured Labour in the British Empire: 1834–1920*, Routledge, 1984, pp. 126–57

Lambdon, Phil, and Cronk, Quentin, 'Extinction Dynamics under Extreme Conservation Threat: The Flora of St Helena', *Front. Ecol. Evol.* 2020, 8:41, pp. 1–10, https://doi.org/10.3389/fevo.2020.00041

Lambert, David, and Lester, Alan (eds.), *Colonial Lives across the British Empire: Imperial Careering in the Long Nineteenth Century*, Cambridge University Press, 2006

Lambert, David, and Lester, Alan, 'Geographies of Colonial Philanthropy', *Progress in Human Geography* 2004, 28:3, pp. 320–41

Landes, David S., *The Wealth and Poverty of Nations: Why Some Are So Rich and Some So Poor*, W. W. Norton, 1999

Lange, Matthew, *Lineages of Despotism and Development: British Colonialism and State Power*, University of Chicago Press, 2009

Lange, Matthew, Mahoney, James, and vom Hau, Matthias, 'Colonialism and Development: A Comparative Analysis of Spanish and British Colonies', *American Journal of Sociology* 2006, 111:5, pp. 1412–62

Lanham, Andrew, 'When W. E. B. Du Bois Was Un-American', *Boston Review*, 13/01/2017, https://www.bostonreview.net/articles/when-civil-rights-were-un-american/

LaPorta, Rafael, Lopez-de-Silanes, Florencio, Pop-Eleches, Cristian, and Shleifer, Andrei, 'Judicial Checks and Balances', *Journal of Political Economy* 2004, 112:2, pp. 445–70

LaPorta, Rafael, Lopez-de-Silanes, Florencio, Shleifer, Andrei, and Vishny, Robert, 'The Quality of Government', *Journal of Law, Economics and Organization* 1999, 15:1, pp. 222–79

Lashmar, Paul, and Smith, Jonathan, 'He's the MP with the Downton Abbey lifestyle. But the shadow of slavery hangs over the gilded life of Richard Drax', *Observer*, 12/12/2020, www.theguardian.com/world/2020/dec/12/hes-the-mp-with-the-downton-abbey-lifestyle-but-the-shadow-of-slavery-hangs-over-the-gilded-life-of-richard-drax

'Law, Colonial Systems of, British Empire', *Encyclopedia.com*, accessed 31/01/2023, https://www.encyclopedia.com/history/encyclopedias-almanacs-transcripts-and-maps/law-colonial-systems-british-empire

Laycock, Stuart, and Laycock, Philip, *How Britain Brought Football to the World*, The History Press, 2022

Le Ferrand, Hortense, and Bacha, Abbas, 'Discovery and Rediscovery of Gutta Percha, a Natural Thermoplastic', *MRS Bulletin* 2021, 46, pp. 84–5

Lee, Alexander, and Paine, Jack, 'British colonialism and democracy: Divergent inheritances and diminishing legacies', *Journal of Comparative Economics* 2019, 47:3, pp. 487–503

Lee, Chermaine, 'Understanding Climate Colonialism', *Fair Planet*, 14/08/2022, https://www.fairplanet.org/story/understanding-climate-colonialism/

'The legacy of Indian migration to European colonies', *Economist*, 02/09/2017, https://www.economist.com/international/2017/09/02/the-legacy-of-indian-migration-to-european-colonies

'Legacies of British Slavery', UCL, accessed 04/07/2023, https://www.ucl.ac.uk/made-at-ucl/stories/legacies-british-slavery

Leonhardt, Megan, ' "Nigerian prince" email scams still rake in over $700,000 a year – here's how to protect yourself', *CNBC Make It*, 18/04/2019, https://www.cnbc. com/2019/04/18/nigerian-prince-scams-still-rake-in-over-700000-dollars-a-year. html

'Less money equals better care: Inquiries springing up: But where are the shears?', *Public*, 02/11/2006

Lester, Alan, 'The British Empire Rehabilitated?', *Bella Caledonia*, 07/03/2023, https:// bellacaledonia.org.uk/2023/03/07/the-british-empire-rehabilitated/

Lester, Alan, 'British Settler Discourse and the Circuits of Empire', *History Workshop Journal* 2002, 54:1, pp. 24–48, https://doi.org/10.1093/hwj/54.1.24

Lester, Alan, *Imperial Networks: Creating Identities in Nineteenth-Century South Africa and Britain*, Routledge, 2001

Lester, Alan, 'Race and Citizenship: Colonial Inclusions and Exclusions', in Martin Hewitt (ed.), *The Victorian World*, Routledge, 2012, pp. 381–97

Lester, Alan, 'Time to Throw Out the Balance Sheet', *University of Sussex: School of Global Studies Blog*, 21/03/2016, https://blogs.sussex.ac.uk/global/2016/03/21/time-to-throw-out-the-balance-sheet/

Lester, Alan, 'What are the British Empire's "Legacies"?', *University of Sussex: Snapshots of Empire*, 10/10/2022, https://blogs.sussex.ac.uk/snapshotsofempire/2022/10/10/what-are-the-british-empires-legacies/

Lester, Alan, Boehme, Kate, and Mitchell, Peter, *Ruling the World: Freedom, Civilisation and Liberalism in the Nineteenth-Century British Empire*, Cambridge University Press, 2021

Lester, Alan, and Dussart, Fae, 'Trajectories of Protection: Protectorates of Aborigines in Early 19th Century Australia and Aotearoa New Zealand', *New Zealand Geographer* 2008, 64:3, pp. 205–20

Lester, Alan, Nel, Etienne, and Binns, Tony, *South Africa Past, Present and Future: Gold at the End of the Rainbow?*, Routledge, 2000

Letzing, John, and Sung, Minji, 'What does colonialism have to do with climate change?', *World Economic Forum*, 09/09/2022, https://www.weforum.org/agenda/2022/09/colonialism-climate-change-pakistan-floods/

Levering Lewis, David, *W. E. B. Du Bois: A Biography*, Holt, 2009

Levine, Philippa, *Prostitution, Race and Politics: Policing Venereal Disease in the British Empire*, Routledge, 2003

'Lieutenant-General Sir Thomas Picton (1758–1815)', *Amgueddfa Cymru*, accessed 31/01/2023, https://museum.wales/collections/online/object/4adfdd41-6370-36bf-a907-c74f5ad7d4a5/Lieutenant-General-Sir-Thomas-Picton-1758-1815/

Lipset, S. M., Seong, K., and Torres, J. C., 'A Comparative Analysis of the Social Requisites of Democracy', *International Social Science Journal* 1993, 136, pp. 155–75

Long, Scott, 'Before the law: Criminalizing sexual conduct in colonial and post-colonial southern African societies', *More Than a Name: State-Sponsored Homophobia and its Consequences in Southern Africa*, Human Rights Watch, 2003, https://www. hrw.org/reports/2003/safrica/safriglhrc0303-07.htm

Look Lai, Walton, *Indentured Labor, Caribbean Sugar: Chinese and Indian Migrants to the British West Indies, 1838–1918*, Johns Hopkins University Press, 1993

Lotem, Itay, *The Memory of Colonialism in Britain and France: The Sins of Silence*, Palgrave Macmillan, 2021

Lotzof, Kerry, 'Joseph Banks: scientist, explorer and botanist', *Natural History Museum*, accessed20/01/2023,https://www.nhm.ac.uk/discover/joseph-banks-scientist-explorer-botanist.html

Lovell, Julia, *The Opium War: Drugs, Dreams and the Making of China*, Picador, 2011

Low, Valentine, 'Bob Geldof: I don't like criticism of so-called white saviours', *The Times*, 25/10/2022, https://www.thetimes.co.uk/article/bob-geldof-i-dont-like-criticism-of-so-called-white-saviours-lwz86jwtj

Low, Valentine, 'Camilla's crown for coronation avoids Koh-i-noor headache', *The Times*,14/02/2023,https://www.thetimes.co.uk/article/camillas-crown-shows-colonial-diamonds-arent-for-ever-z0vnkc3s7

Low, Valentine, 'Commonwealth Day service: King urges leaders to "unite for a global good"', *The Times*,13/03/2023,https://www.thetimes.co.uk/article/king-charles-first-commonwealth-day-service-speech-2023-qv8cspzk6

Low, Valentine, 'Crown Jewels exhibition at Tower of London to recognise British imperialism', *The Times*,15/03/2023,https://www.thetimes.co.uk/article/crown-jewels-exhibition-at-tower-of-london-to-recognise-british-imperialism-6wvhqlok8

Low, Valentine, 'William's poaching warning in first major speech as Prince of Wales', *The Times*, 04/10/2022, https://www.thetimes.co.uk/article/8910b764-43cc-11ed-8885-043c27446b97?shareToken=dd9a203997a3f7e2899efe057696a7fa

'Lutyens Bungalow Zone', *World Monuments Fund*, accessed 20/03/2023, https://www. wmf.org/project/lutyens-bungalow-zone

Lyndall, Ryan, 'List of multiple killings of Aborigines in Tasmania: 1804–1835', *SciencesPo*, 05/03/2008, https://www.sciencespo.fr/mass-violence-war-massacre-resistance/fr/document/list-multiple-killings-aborigines-tasmania-1804-1835. html

Lynn, Martin, *Commerce and Economic Change in West Africa: The Palm Oil Trade in the Nineteenth Century*, Cambridge University Press, 2002

McAllister, William B., *Drug Diplomacy in the Twentieth Century*, Routledge, 2000

Macaulay, Cecilia, 'Nigerian schools: Flogged for speaking my mother tongue', *BBC News*, 07/01/2023, https://www.bbc.co.uk/news/world-africa-63971991.amp

Macaulay, T. B., Speech delivered in the House of Commons, 10/07/1833, *The Miscellaneous Speeches and Writings of Lord Macaulay*, Longmans, Green, 1889

McBride, Keally, *Mr. Mothercountry: The Man Who Made the Rule of Law*, Oxford University Press, 2016

McBride, Keally, 'Mr. Mothercountry: The Rule of Law as Practice', *Law, Culture and the Humanities* 2017, 13:3, pp. 320–34

McClintock, Anne, *Imperial Leather: Race, Gender and Sexuality in the Colonial Contest*, Routledge, 1995

McCracken, Donal, *Gardens of Empire: Botanical Institutions of the Victorian British Empire*, Leicester University Press, 1997

Macintyre, Ben, 'The Crown and the Commonwealth face a perilous future', *The Times*, 25/03/2022, https://www.thetimes.co.uk/article/the-crown-and-the-common wealth-face-a-perilous-future-lx3vjlmrf

MacKenzie, John M., *The British Empire through Buildings: Structure, Function and Meaning*, Manchester University Press, 2020

MacKenzie, John M., *A Cultural History of the British Empire*, Yale University Press, 2022

MacKenzie, John M., *The Empire of Nature: Hunting, Conservation and British Imperialism (Studies in Imperialism)*, Manchester University Press, 1997

MacKenzie, John M., *Propaganda and Empire: The Manipulation of British Public Opinion, 1880–1960*, Manchester University Press, 1984

Mackillop, Andrew, *Human Capital and Empire: Scotland, Ireland, Wales and British Imperialism in Asia, c.1690–c.1820*, Manchester University Press, 2021

Mackintosh, Thomas, 'Canadian province Alberta cancels bid for 2030 Commonwealth Games', *BBC News*, 04/08/2023, https://www.bbc.co.uk/news/world-us-canada-66402140

McLisky, Claire, ' "Due Observance of Justice, and the Protection of their Rights": Philanthropy, Humanitarianism and Moral Purpose in the Aborigines Protection Society circa 1837 and its Portrayal in Australian Historiography, 1883–2003', *Limina: A Journal of Historical and Cultural Studies* 2005, 11, pp. 57–66

Macmillen Voskoboynik, Daniel, 'To fix the climate crisis, we must face up to our imperial past', *Open Democracy*, 8/10/2018, https://www.opendemocracy.net/en/opendemocracyuk/to-fix-climate-crisis-we-must-acknowledge-our-imperial-past/

MacRae, Penelope, 'Narendra Modi vows to make India a developed nation', *The Times*, 15/08/2022, https://www.thetimes.co.uk/article/a975ef56-1c7b-11ed-add4-d333562d46fb?shareToken=933058c5b78c4c10b4dcb10be35fd079

MacRae, Penelope, 'No justice, says India gang-rape victim after killers get early release', *The Times*, 18/08/2022, https://www.thetimes.co.uk/article/2045eb84-1efe-11ed-b7c3-8b288ab55a56?shareToken=40090cafd02b3b9872b41b53dca84e2f

Mahoney, Michael, 'A "new system of slavery"? The British West Indies and the origins of Indian indenture', *The National Archives*, 03/12/2020, https://blog.nationalarchives.gov.uk/a-new-system-of-slavery-the-british-west-indies-and-the-origins-of-indian-indenture/

Mahony, Martin, and Endfield, Georgina, 'Climate and Colonialism', *University of East Anglia Prints*, accessed 10/02/2023, https://ueaeprints.uea.ac.uk/id/eprint/65708/4/Climate_Colonialism_pre_print.pdf

Maizland, Lindsay, 'Myanmar's Troubled History: Coups, Military Rule, and Ethnic Conflict', *Council on Foreign Relations*, last updates 31/01/2022, https://www.cfr.org/backgrounder/myanmar-history-coup-military-rule-ethnic-conflict-rohingya

Makovsky, Michael, *Churchill's Promised Land: Zionism and Statecraft*, Yale University Press, 2007

Malagodi, Mara, 'Constitution drafting as Cold War realpolitik: Sir Ivor Jennings and Nepal's 1959 constitution', in Harshan Kumarasingham (ed.), *Constitution-Making in Asia: Decolonisation and State-Building in the Aftermath of the British Empire*, Routledge, 2016, pp. 154–72

'Malayan Emergency', National Army Museum, https://www.nam.ac.uk/explore/malayan-emergency

'Malaysia Population 1950–2023', *Macrotrends*, accessed 10/02/2023, https://www.macrotrends.net/countries/MYS/malaysia/population

Mamdani, Mahmood, *Citizen and Subject: Contemporary Africa and the Legacy of Late Colonialism*, Princeton University Press, 1996

Mander, Samuel S., *Our Opium Trade with China*, Simpkin, Marshall, 1877

Manjapra, Kris, *Black Ghost of Empire: The Long Death of Slavery and the Failure of Emancipation*, Scribner, 2022

Manji, Firoze, and O'Coill, Carl, 'The Missionary Position: NGOs and Development in Africa', *International Affairs (Royal Institute of International Affairs 1944– )* 2002, 78:3, pp. 567–83

Mankoff, Jeffrey, *Empires of Eurasia: How Imperial Legacies Shape International Security*, Yale University Press, 2022

Mann, Gregory, *From Empires to NGOs in the West African Sahel: The Road to Nongovernmentality*, Cambridge University Press, 2015

Mann, Kristin, and Roberts, Richard (eds.), *Law in Colonial Africa*, Heinemann, 1991

Mansfield, Nick, *Soldiers as Citizens: Popular Politics and the Nineteenth-Century British Military*, Oxford University Press, 2019

Mansour, Johnny, 'The Hijaz–Palestine Railway and the Development of Haifa', *Jerusalem Quarterly* 2006, 28, pp. 5–21

Manuel, Thomas, *Opium Inc: How a Global Drug Trade Funded the British Empire*, HarperCollins India, 2021

Marcus, Leah S., *How Shakespeare Became Colonial: Editorial Traditions and the British Empire*, Routledge, 2017

Margalit, Avishai, 'Palestine: How Bad, & Good, Was British Rule?', *New York Review*, 07/02/2013, https://www.nybooks.com/articles/2013/02/07/palestine-how-bad-and-good-was-british-rule/

'Marianne North Gallery', *Royal Botanic Gardens Kew*, accessed 20/01/2023, https://www.kew.org/kew-gardens/whats-in-the-gardens/marianne-north-gallery

'Mark Nesbitt', *Royal Botanic Gardens Kew*, accessed 20/01/2023, https://www.kew.org/science/our-science/people/mark-nesbitt

Martens, Jeremy, 'A transnational history of immigration restriction: Natal and New South Wales, 1896–97', *Journal of Imperial and Commonwealth History* 2006, 34:3, pp. 323–44

Martin, Laura C., *Tea: The Drink That Changed the World*, Tuttle Publishing, 2007

Martinez, Deniss, and Irfan, Ans, 'Colonialism, the climate crisis, and the need to center Indigenous voices', *Environmental Health News*, 04/11/2021, https://www.ehn.org/indigenous-people-and-climate-change-2655479728.html

Martinez, Jenny S., 'The Anti-Slavery Movement and the Rise of International Non-Governmental Organizations', in Dinah Shelton (ed.), *The Oxford Handbook of International Human Rights Law*, Oxford University Press, 2013, pp. 222–49

Mascarenhas, Hyacinth, 'How the British screwed up the Middle East, in 10 classic cartoons', *MIC*, 13/06/2023, https://www.mic.com/articles/91071/how-the-british-screwed-up-the-middle-east-in-10-classic-cartoons

'Mau Mau torture victims to receive compensation – Hague', *BBC News*, 06/06/2013, https://www.bbc.co.uk/news/uk-22790037

May, Melanie, 'Animal welfare is UK's favourite cause', *UK Fundraising*, 10/08/2022, https://shorturl.at/qJM58

Mazower, Mark, *Governing the World: The History of an Idea*, Penguin Books, 2012

Mazower, Mark, *No Enchanted Palace: The End of Empire and the Ideological Origins of the United Nations*, Princeton University Press, 2013

Mazzini, Giuseppe, *A Cosmopolitanism of Nations: Giuseppe Mazzini's Writings on Democracy, Nation Building, and International Relations*, Princeton University Press, 2009

Meade, Amanda, 'Sydney Morning Herald apologises for failing "dismally" on coverage of 1838 Myall Creek massacre', *Guardian*, 09/06/2023, https://www.theguardian.com/media/2023/jun/09/sydney-morning-herald-apologises-for-failing-dismally-on-coverage-of-1838-myall-creek-massacre

Meadows Taylor, Philip, *Confessions of a Thug*, ed. Kim A. Wagner, Oxford World's Classics, due to be published February 2024

Mégret, Frédéric, 'From "savages" to "unlawful combatants": a postcolonial look at international humanitarian law's "other"', in Anne Orford (ed.), *International Law and its Others*, Cambridge University Press, 2006, pp. 265–317

Mellino, Emiliano, and Das, Shanti, 'Seasonal fruit pickers left thousands in debt after being sent home early from UK farms', *Guardian*, 13/11/2022, https://www.theguardian.com/uk-news/2022/nov/13/seasonal-fruit-pickers-left-thousands-in-debt-after-being-sent-home-early-from-uk-farms

Mendick, Robert, 'A year after becoming a republic, Barbados pursues damages for sins of its colonial past', *Telegraph*, 25/11/2022, https://www.telegraph.co.uk/news/2022/11/25/year-becoming-republic-barbados-pursues-damages-sins-colonial/

Mercer, Harriet, 'Colonialism: why leading climate scientists have finally acknowledged its link with climate change', *The Conversation*, 22/04/2022, https://theconversation.com/colonialism-why-leading-climate-scientists-have-finally-acknowledged-its-link-with-climate-change-181642

Mercer, Harriet, 'The link between colonialism and climate change examined', *The Week*, 25/04/2022, https://www.theweek.co.uk/news/environment/956530/the-link-between-colonialism-and-climate-change-examined

Merchant, Preston, 'Fiji's Indian Cane Cutters', *Time*, 17 September 2007, https://content.time.com/time/photogallery/0,29307,1662439,00.html

Middleton, Alex, 'Review of *Rage for Order: The British Empire and the Origins of International Law, 1800–1850*', *Reviews in History*, March 2017, https://reviews.history.ac.uk/review/2084

Midgley, Clare, *Women against Slavery: The British Campaigns, 1780–1870*, Routledge, 1992

Miller, Robert J., Ruru, Jacinta, Behrendt, Larissa, and Lindberg, Tracey, *Discovering Indigenous Lands: The Doctrine of Discovery in the English Colonies*, Oxford University Press, 2010

Mills, James H., *Cannabis Britannica: Empire, Trade, and Prohibition, 1800–1928*, Oxford University Press, 2005

Mills, James, 'Decolonising drugs in Asia: the case of cocaine in colonial India', *Third World Quarterly* 2018, 39:2, pp. 218–31

Milne, Richard, *Rhododendron*, Reaktion Books, 2014, ch. 3, https://www.pure.ed.ac.uk/ws/portalfiles/portal/126022575/Rhododendron_ext_002_.pdf

Mitcham, Roderick E., *The Geographies of Global Humanitarianism: The Anti-Slavery Society and Aborigines Protection Society, 1884–1933*, Royal Holloway, University of London, 2002

Mitra, Durba, *Indian Sex Life: Sexuality and the Colonial Origins of Modern Social Thought*, Princeton University Press, 2020

Mody, Ashoka, 'India's Law-of-the-Jungle Raj', *Project Syndicate*, 12/05/2023, https://www.project-syndicate.org/onpoint/atiq-ahmed-murder-reveals-india-lawlessness-state-violence-by-ashoka-mody-2023-05

Mohdin, Aamna, 'Clive Lewis calls for UK to negotiate Caribbean slavery reparations', *Guardian*, 08/03/2023, https://www.theguardian.com/world/2023/mar/08/clive-lewis-calls-for-uk-to-negotiate-caribbean-slavery-reparations

Mohdin, Aamna, 'Guardian owner apologises for founders' links to transatlantic slavery', *Guardian*, 28/03/2023, https://www.theguardian.com/news/2023/mar/28/guardian-owner-apologises-founders-transatlantic-slavery-scott-trust

Mohdin, Aamna, 'Laura Trevelyan quits BBC to campaign for reparative justice for Caribbean', *Guardian*, 16/03/2023, https://www.theguardian.com/world/2023/mar/16/laura-trevelyan-quits-bbc-to-campaign-reparative-justice-slavery-caribbean

Mohdin, Aamna, 'UK government and royals called on to investigate slavery links after Guardian apology', *Guardian*, 29/03/2023, https://www.theguardian.com/news/2023/mar/29/uk-government-royals-called-on-investigate-slavery-links-after-guardian-apology

Moirt, José, *Gagner, ne suffit pas!*, trans. Eric Bahloo, Cathay Printing, 2019

Mommsen, Wolfgang J., and de Moor, Jaap A. (eds.), *European Expansion and Law: The Encounter of European and Indigenous Law in 19th- and 20th-Century Africa and Asia*, Berg Publishers, 1992

Mondon, Aurelien, and Winter, Aaron, *Reactionary Democracy: How Racism and the Populist Far Right Became Mainstream*, Verso Books, 2020

Monnais, Laurence, *The Colonial Life of Pharmaceuticals: Medicines and Modernity in Vietnam*, Cambridge University Press, 2019

Moody, Ann, 'The National Trust goes to war: is Tufton Street planning a land grab?', *Yorkshire Bylines*, 13/10/2022, https://yorkshirebylines.co.uk/politics/the-national-trust-goes-to-war-is-tufton-street-planning-a-land-grab/

Morgan, Ruth A., 'Climatology and Empire in the Nineteenth Century', in Sam White, Christian Pfister and Franz Mauelshagen (eds.), *The Palgrave Handbook of Climate History*, Palgrave Macmillan, 2018, pp. 589–603

Morton, Bill, Case Study 7: An Overview of International NGOs in Development Cooperation, *University of Athens*, 2013

'The most spoken languages worldwide in 2022', *Statista*, accessed 20/03/2023, https://shorturl.at/rzO18

Moyn, Samuel, 'Empathy in History, Empathizing with Humanity', *History and Theory* 2006, 45:3, pp. 397–415

Moyn, Samuel, *The Last Utopia: Human Rights in History*, Belknap Press of Harvard University Press, 2010

Mukherjee, Siddhartha, *The Gene: An Intimate History*, Vintage, 2017

Mukherjee, Sugato, 'Mahua: The Indian liquor the British banned', *BBC News*, 22/11/2022, https://www.bbc.com/travel/article/20221121-mahua-the-indian-liquor-the-british-banned

Müller-Wille, Staffan, 'Carolus Linnaeus', *Britannica*, updated 06/01/2023, https://www.britannica.com/biography/Carolus-Linnaeus

Mulligan, William, and Bric, Maurice (eds.), *A Global History of Anti-Slavery Politics in the Nineteenth Century*, Palgrave Macmillan UK, 2013

Munshi, Neil, 'Gun for hire: Nigeria security fears spark boom in private protection', *Financial Times*, 26/10/2021, https://www.ft.com/content/a12bb6b1-798d-4863-8b49-104a56ccc716

Murphy, Craig N., 'Imperial Legacies in the UN Development Programme and the UN Development System', in Sandra Halperin and Ronen Palan (eds.), *Legacies of Empire: Imperial Roots of the Contemporary Global Order*, Cambridge University Press, 2015

Murphy, Philip, *The Empire's New Clothes: The Myth of the Commonwealth*, Hurst, 2021

Muschik, Eva-Maria, 'The Art of Chameleon Politics: From Colonial Servant to International Development Expert', *Humanity: An International Journal of Human Rights, Humanitarianism, and Development* 2018, 9:2, pp. 219–44

Myers, Russell, 'William and Kate Middleton's open-top parade branded "awful" echo of colonialist past', *Mirror*, 24/03/2022, https://www.mirror.co.uk/news/uk-news/william-kate-middletons-open-top-26552102

Nakate, Vanessa, 'African nations can't "adapt" to the climate crisis. Here's what rich countries must do', *Guardian*, 08/11/2022, https://www.theguardian.com/commentisfree/2022/nov/08/rich-countries-climate-crisis-cop27-africa-loss-and-damage

Nashashibi, Sharif, 'Balfour: Britain's Original Sin', *Al Jazeera*, 04/11/2014, https://www.aljazeera.com/opinions/2014/11/4/balfour-britains-original-sin

'Natural Rubber Market – Growth, Trends, COVID-19 Impact, and Forecasts (2023–2028)', *Mordor Intelligence*, accessed 20/01/2023, https://www.mordorintelligence.com/industry-reports/natural-rubber-market

Ndebele, Lenin, 'What Nigerians think of their democracy ahead of elections', *News 24*, 04/02/2023, https://www.news24.com/news24/africa/news/what-nigerians-think-of-their-democracy-ahead-of-elections-20230204

Nesbitt, Mark, 'Botany in Victorian Jamaica', in Tim Barringer and Wayne Modest (eds.), *Victorian Jamaica*, Duke University Press, 2018, pp. 209–39

Nesbitt, Mark, 'Trade and Exploration', in David Mabberley (ed.), *A Cultural History of Plants in the Nineteenth Century*, Bloomsbury, 2022, pp. 67–84

Nesbitt, Mark, and Cornish, Caroline, 'Seeds of Industry and Empire: Economic Botany Collections between Nature and Culture', *Journal of Museum Ethnography* 2016, 29, pp. 53–70

Nettelbeck, Amanda, *Indigenous Rights and Colonial Subjecthood: Protection and Reform in the Nineteenth-Century British Empire*, Cambridge University Press, 2021

Nevett, Joshua, 'Richard Drax: Jamaica eyes slavery reparations from Tory MP', *BBC News*, 30/11/2022, https://www.bbc.co.uk/news/uk-politics-63799222

Nevett, Joshua, 'UK's £18tn slavery debt is an underestimation, UN judge says', *BBC News*, 23/08/2023, https://www.bbc.co.uk/news/uk-politics-66596790

Nevin, Andrew S., Kymal, Uma, Cameron, Peter Nigel, and Oseni, Rufai, 'Self-organizing Nigeria: The antifragile state', 2/03/2023, https://www.brookings.edu/blog/africa-in-focus/2023/03/02/self-organizing-nigeria-the-antifragile-state/

'New Delhi', *Britannica*, accessed 20/03/2023, https://www.britannica.com/place/New-Delhi

Newman, Brooke, 'The Royal Family should apologise for their links to slavery before they are embarrassed into doing so', *i News*, 29/07/2022, https://inews.co.uk/opinion/royal-family-apologise-links-slavery-before-embarassed-1677595

Newton, Melanie, ' "The Children of Africa in the Colonies": Free People of Colour in Barbados during the Emancipation Era, 1816–1854', DPhil. thesis, University of Oxford, 2001

Nicolson, L. F., *The Administration of Nigeria, 1900–1960: Men, Methods and Myths*, Clarendon Press, 1969

'Nigeria', *The World Factbook*, accessed 22/03/2023, https://www.cia.gov/the-world-factbook/countries/nigeria/#people-and-society

'Nigeria: Gunmen abduct more than 30 in train station attack', *DW*, 01/08/2023, https://www.dw.com/en/nigeria-gunmen-abduct-more-than-30-in-train-station-attack/a-64321012

'Nigeria–India: Learnings from two large democracies', *PWC*, accessed 22/03/2023, https://www.pwc.com/ng/en/publications/nigeria-india-learnings-from-two-democracies.html

'Nigeria: Steel factory will open after 40 years | Al Jazeera English', YouTube, 16/06/2018, https://www.youtube.com/watch?v=FqVyWiYdKQA

Nikkhah, Roya, 'Prince William casts doubt over future leadership of the Commonwealth', *The Times*, 26/03/2022, https://www.thetimes.co.uk/article/prince-william-casts-doubt-over-future-leadership-of-the-commonwealth-nd2wx2wn5

'1903: Maidens Hotel', *Historic Hotels of the World: Then & Now*, accessed 20/03/2023, https://www.historichotelsthenandnow.com/maidensdelhi.html

Norfield, Tony, *The City: London and the Global Power of Finance*, Verso, 2017

North-Coombes, M. D., 'From Slavery to Indenture: Forced Labour in the Political Economy of Mauritius 1834–1867', in Kay Saunders (ed.), *Indentured Labour in the British Empire: 1834–1920*, Routledge, 1984, pp. 78–125

Northrup, David, *Indentured Labor in the Age of Imperialism, 1834–1922*, Cambridge University Press, 1995

'Nostalgia for the British empire is no solution to the crisis in Hong Kong', *CGTN*, 26/07/2019,https://news.cgtn.com/news/2019-07-26/Nostalgia-for-British-empire-is-no-solution-for-Hong-Kong-IEfDhcX7fW/index.html

Notestein, Wallace, 'Jan Smuts', *The Atlantic*, July 1918, https://www.theatlantic.com/magazine/archive/1918/07/jan-smuts/645967/

Nugent, Ciara, 'Western Architecture is Making India's Heatwaves Worse', *Time*, 16/05/2022, https://time.com/6176998/india-heatwaves-western-architecture/

Nugent, Maria, 'The politics of memory and the memory of politics: Australian Aboriginal interpretations of Queen Victoria, 1881–2011', in Sarah Carter and Maria Nugent (eds.), *Mistress of Everything: Queen Victoria in Indigenous Worlds*, Manchester University Press, 2016, pp. 100–122

Nugent, Paul, 'Modernity, Tradition, and Intoxication: Comparative Lessons from South Africa and West Africa', *Past and Present* 2014, 222:9, pp. 126–45

Nwaubani, Adaobi Tricia, 'Remembering Nigeria's Biafra war that many prefer to forget', *BBC News*, 15/01/2020, https://www.bbc.co.uk/news/world-africa-51094093

Oba, Gufu, *Nomads in the Shadows of Empires: Contests, Conflicts and Legacies on the Southern Ethiopian–Northern Kenyan Frontier*, Brill, 2013

'Offshore processing', *Refugee Council of Australia*, accessed 04/07/2023, https://www.refugeecouncil.org.au/offshore-processing/

'Ogimaa Mikana: Reclaiming/Renaming', *Tumblr*, accessed 20/03/2023, https://ogimaamikana.tumblr.com/

Ogle, Vanessa, ' "Funk Money": The End of Empires, the Expansion of Tax Havens, and Decolonization as an Economic and Financial Event', *Past & Present* 2020, 249:1, pp. 213–49

Ogle, Vanessa, *The Global Transformation of Time, 1870–1950*, Harvard University Press, 2015

Ogundapo, Abdulqudus, 'Kidnappers abduct farmers, demand N10m ransom in Osun', *Premium Times*, 13/01/2023, https://www.premiumtimesng.com/regional/ssouth-west/575412-kidnappers-abduct-farmers-demand-n10m-ransom-in-osun.html

Okonjo, M., *British Administration in Nigeria, 1900–1950: A Nigerian View*, Nok Publishers, 1974

Olu-Ojegbeje, Lolade, 'Bolt Driver Connives with Abuja Police to "Kidnap", Rob Passenger of N1m', *Foundation of Investigative Journalism*, 31/03/2022, https://fij.ng/article/bolt-driver-connives-with-abuja-police-to-kidnap-rob-passenger-of-n1m/

Olusoga, David, 'Slavery and the Guardian: The Ties That Bind Us', *Guardian*, 28/03/2023, https://www.theguardian.com/news/ng-interactive/2023/mar/28/slavery-and-the-guardian-the-ties-that-bind-us

Olusoga, David, *The World's War: Forgotten Soldiers of Empire*, Apollo Publishers, 2014

O'Malley, Kate, *Ireland, India and Empire: Indo-Irish Radical Connections, 1919–64*, Manchester University Press, 2009

'100 years on – the unsolved mystery of the rubber boom slaves', *Survival International*, 01/08/2011, https://www.survivalinternational.org/news/7541

O'Neill, Sean, 'UN soldiers "fathered thousands" in Democratic Republic of Congo', *The Times*, 15/08/2022, https://www.thetimes.co.uk/article/27ea5846-1bf4-11ed-b7c3-8b288ab55a56?shareToken=88caebe977214dd51740b7970ee61172

Onuba, Ifeanyi, 'How Buhari's Govt Failed to Revive Ajaokuta Steel Company Despite N31bn Allocation', *The Whistler*, 18/05/2022, https://thewhistler.ng/how-buharis-govt-failed-to-revive-ajaokuta-steel-company-despite-n31bn-allocation/

Osori, Ayisha, 'Nigeria's elections have bigger problems than vote trading', *Al Jazeera*, 17/02/2023, https://www.aljazeera.com/opinions/2023/2/17/nigerias-elections-have-bigger-problems-than-vote-trading

Osseo-Asare, Abeno D., *Bitter Roots: The Search for Healing Plants in Africa*, University of Chicago Press, 2014

O'Sullivan, Kyle, 'Why Comic Relief stopped sending "white saviour" celebrities to Africa after scandal', *Mirror*, 18/03/2022, https://www.mirror.co.uk/tv/tv-news/comic-relief-stopped-sending-white-26491455

O'Toole, Fintan, *Hungry Eyes*, prod. Mary Price, BBC Radio 4, 01/11/1995

Ottaway, Marina, and El-Sadany, Mai, 'Sudan: From Conflict to Conflict', *Carnegie Endowment for International Peace*, 16/05/2012, https://carnegieendowment.org/2012/05/16/sudan-from-conflict-to-conflict-pub-48140

'Our Vision and Mission', *Royal Commonwealth Society*, accessed 22/03/2023, https://www.royalcwsociety.org/

Outley, Corliss, Bowen, Shamaya, and Pinckney, Harrison, 'Laughing While Black: Resistance, Coping and the Use of Humor as a Pandemic Pastime among Blacks', *Leisure Sciences* 2021, 43:1–2, pp. 305–14, https://doi.org/10.1080/01490400.2020.1774449

Owen, Gareth, 'The Rise of the Humanitarian Corporation: Save the Children and the Ordering of Emergency Response', in Juliano Fiori, Fernando Espada, Andrea Rigon, Bertrand Taithe and Rafia Zakaria (eds.), *Amidst the Debris: Humanitarianism and the End of Liberal Order*, Routledge, 2021, pp. 35–54

Owen, Nicholas, 'Democratisation and the British Empire', *Journal of Imperial and Commonwealth History* 2019, 47:5, pp. 974–98

Owolabi, Tife, 'Gunmen kidnap 32 people from southern Nigeria train station', *Reuters*, 09/01/2023, https://www.reuters.com/world/africa/gunmen-kidnap-32-people-southern-nigeria-train-station-2023-01-08/

PA Media, 'St Kitts and Nevis PM says country is not free while King Charles is head of state', *Guardian*, 08/05/2023, https://www.theguardian.com/world/2023/may/08/saint-kitts-and-nevis-pm-says-country-is-not-free-while-king-charles-is-head-of-state

Packard, Randall M., *The Making of a Tropical Disease: A Short History of Malaria*, Johns Hopkins University Press, 2007

Paisley, Fiona, and Reid, Kirsty (eds.), *Critical Perspectives on Colonialism: Writing the Empire from Below*, Routledge, 2014

Palan, Ronen, 'The Second British Empire and the Re-emergence of Global Finance', in Sandra Halperin and Ronen Palan (eds.), *Legacies of Empire: Imperial Roots of the Contemporary Global Order*, Cambridge University Press, 2015, pp. 46–68

Pankhurst, Richard, 'Post-World War II Ethiopia: British Military Policy and Action for the Dismantling and Acquisition of Italian Factories and Other Assets, 1941–2', *Journal of Ethiopian Studies* 1996, 29:1, pp. 35–77

Pant, Pushpesh, 'INDIA: Food and the Making of the Nation', *India International Centre Quarterly* 2013, 40:2, pp. 1–34

'Parakram Diwas', *National Today*, accessed 20/03/2023, https://nationaltoday.com/parakram-diwas/

Parker, Matthew, *The Sugar Barons: Family, Corruption, Empire and War*, Windmill Books, 2012

Parkin, Benjamin, and Hancock, Alice, 'Inside the mysterious downfall of India's Cox & Kings', *Financial Times*, 22/01/2022, https://www.ft.com/content/3f1448d5-d1c2-412b-b660-5264680d2a0b

Parry, Richard Lloyd, and Blet, Raphael, 'Colonial nostalgia rules in Hong Kong as young refuse to accept China's authority', *The Times*, 14/06/2019, https://www.the-times.co.uk/article/colonial-nostalgia-rules-as-young-refuse-to-accept-beijing-rule-gswccqovf

Parsons, L., Safra de Campos, R., Moncaster, A., Cook, I., Siddiqui, T., Abenayake, C., Jayasinghe, A., Mishra, P., Scungio, L., and Billah, T., *Disaster Trade: The Hidden Footprint of UK Production Overseas*, Royal Holloway, University of London, 2021

Parsons, Timothy, *The British Imperial Century, 1815–1914: A World History Perspective*, Rowman & Littlefield, 2019

Partridge, Matthew, '19 December 1932: BBC World Service begins', *Money Week*, 19/10/2020, https://moneyweek.com/365399/19-december-1932-bbc-world-service-begins

Parveen, Nazia, 'How Kenyans are seeking amends for British tea steeped in "stolen lands"', *Guardian*, 02/12/2019, https://www.theguardian.com/global-development/2019/dec/02/kenyas-dispossessed-seek-redress-for-britains-colonial-injustices

Parveen, Nazia, 'Kew Gardens director hits back at claims it is "growing woke"', *Guardian*, 18/03/2021, https://www.theguardian.com/science/2021/mar/18/kew-gardens-director-hits-back-at-claims-it-is-growing-woke

'Passage to India', *P&O Heritage*, 15/08/2017, https://www.poheritage.com/features/passage-to-india

Peck, Tom, 'The mystery of the missing Amazonian rubber slaves', *Independent*, 02/08/2011, https://www.independent.co.uk/news/world/americas/the-mystery-of-the-missing-amazonian-rubber-slaves-2330280.html

Pegg, David, and Evans, Rob, 'Buckingham Palace banned ethnic minorities from office roles, papers reveal', *Guardian*, 02/06/2021, https://www.theguardian.com/uk-news/2021/jun/02/buckingham-palace-banned-ethnic-minorities-from-office-roles-papers-reveal

Pegg, David, and Ganguly, Manisha, 'India archive reveals extent of "colonial loot" in royal jewellery collection', *Guardian*, 06/04/2023, https://www.theguardian.com/uk-news/2023/apr/06/indian-archive-reveals-extent-of-colonial-loot-in-royal-jewellery-collection?CMP=share_btn_tw

Peterson, Derek R. (ed.), *Abolitionism and Imperialism in Britain, Africa, and the Atlantic*, Ohio University Press, 2010

Phillips, Richard, *Sex, Politics and Empire: A Postcolonial Geography*, Manchester University Press, 2006

Pilling, David, 'How Nigeria's state lost the trust of its citizens', *Financial Times*, 19/09/2022, https://www.ft.com/content/bco86fd8-12c5-4a15-afc2-734be4443aac

'Plans for a Colony', *Australian Museum*, 03/09/2021, https://australian.museum/learn/first-nations/unsettled/recognising-invasions/plans-for-a-colony/

'PM Modi renames 3 Andaman & Nicobar islands as tribute to Netaji', *Economic Times*, 31/12/2018, https://economictimes.indiatimes.com/news/politics-and-nation/pm-modi-renames-3-islands-of-andaman-and-nicobar/articleshow/67311674.cms

'PM Narendra Modi renames 3 islands of Andaman Nicobar', *Times of India*, 30/12/2018, http://timesofindia.indiatimes.com/articleshow/67311660.cms?utm_source=contentofinterest&utm_medium=text&utm_campaign=cppst

Porter, Andrew, 'Trusteeship, Anti-Slavery and Humanitarianism', in Andrew Porter (ed.), *The Oxford History of the British Empire*, vol. 3: *The Nineteenth Century*, Oxford University Press, 1999, pp. 198–221

Porter, Bernard, *British Imperial: What the Empire Wasn't*, I.B. Tauris, 2016

Porter, Bernard, *Empire Ways: Aspects of British Imperialism*, I.B. Tauris, 2016

Porter, Bernard, *The Lion's Share: A History of British Imperialism 1850 to the Present*, Pearson Publishing, 2012

'Post Office admits "abhorrent" racist slur was used to describe suspects in Horizon scandal', *Sky News*, 27/05/2023, https://news.sky.com/story/post-office-admits-abhorrent-racist-slur-was-used-to-describe-suspects-in-horizon-scandal-12890411

Potter, Simon J., *Broadcasting Empire: The BBC and the British World, 1922–1970*, Oxford University Press, 2012

Prance, Ghillean, and Nesbitt, Mark (eds.), *The Cultural History of Plants*, Routledge, 2005

Prendergast, David K., and Adams, William M., 'Colonial Wildlife Conservation and the Origins of the Society for the Preservation of the Wild Fauna of the Empire (1903–1914)', *Oryx* 2003, 37:2, pp. 251–60

Press Association, 'Prince William "calls for Buckingham Palace ivory to be destroyed"', *Guardian*, 17/02/2014, https://www.theguardian.com/uk-news/2014/feb/17/prince-william-buckingham-palace-ivory-destroyed

Prevost, Elizabeth, 'Assessing Women, Gender, and Empire in Britain's Nineteenth-Century Protestant Missionary Movement', *History Compass* 2009 7:3, pp. 765–99, https://compass.onlinelibrary.wiley.com/doi/10.1111/j.1478-0542.2009.00593.x

'The prickly pear story', *The State of Queensland Department of Agriculture and Fisheries*, 2020, https://www.daf.qld.gov.au/__data/assets/pdf_file/0014/55301/prickly-pear-story.pdf

PTI, 'More than 19,500 mother tongues spoken in India: Census', *Indian Express*, 01/07/2018,https://indianexpress.com/article/india/more-than-19500-mother-tongues-spoken-in-india-census-5241056/

PTI, 'Queen Elizabeth calls for bold reforms in Commonwealth', *The Hindu*, 28/10/2011, https://www.thehindu.com/news/international/queen-elizabeth-calls-for-bold-reforms-in-commonwealth/article2577183.ece

'Qatar World Cup of Shame', *Amnesty International*, accessed 10/03/2023, https://www.amnesty.org/en/latest/campaigns/2016/03/qatar-world-cup-of-shame/

'Queen "must say sorry for Empire sins"', *Evening Standard*, 27/05/2002, https://www.standard.co.uk/hp/front/queen-must-say-sorry-for-empire-sins-6328283.html?amp

'Race, Prostitution and the British Empire', *Royal Historical Society*, 2021, https://blog.royalhistsoc.org/2021/05/24/race-prostitution-and-the-british-empire/

'Racial Justice Report 2022', *Royal Botanic Garden of Edinburgh*, accessed 17/03/2023, https://www.rbge.org.uk/media/9172/racial-justice-report-2022.pdf

Raghavan, R. K., 'World Factbook of Criminal Justice Systems', *Indian Police Service*, 1992, https://bjs.ojp.gov/content/pub/pdf/wfbcjsin.pdf

Rahn, Joan E., *Plants That Changed History*, Atheneum, 1985

Raj, Suhasini, 'The queen's death draws a more muted response in India, the largest of Britain's former colonies', 09/09/2022, https://www.nytimes.com/2022/09/09/world/europe/queen-elizabeth-death-india-empire.html

Raman, Bhavani, *Document Raj: Writing and Scribes in Early Colonial India*, University of Chicago Press, 2012

Ramesar, Marianne D., 'Indentured Labour in Trinidad 1880–1917', in Kay Saunders (ed.), *Indentured Labour in the British Empire: 1834–1920*, Routledge, 1974, pp. 57–77

Rappaport, Erika, *A Thirst for Empire: How Tea Shaped the Modern World*, Princeton University Press, 2017

Rathore, Aakash Singh, and Goswamy, Garima, *Rethinking Indian Jurisprudence: An Introduction to the Philosophy of Law*, Routledge, 2018

Raza, Shozab, 'Flooding has devastated Pakistan – and Britain's imperial legacy has made it worse', *Guardian*, 31/08/2022, https://www.theguardian.com/commentisfree/2022/aug/31/flooding-pakistan-britains-imperial-legacy

Reiff, David, 'The Wrong Moral Revolution: On Michael Barnett', *The Nation*, 24/10/2011, https://www.thenation.com/article/archive/wrong-moral-revolution-michael-barnett/

Renton, Alex, *Blood Legacy: Reckoning with a Family's Story of Slavery*, Canongate Books, 2021

'Research on the source of strength of Western NGOs – society or system?', *Ministry of Foreign Affairs of Japan*, accessed 02/02/2023, https://www.mofa.go.jp/mofaj/gaiko/oda/files/000073033.pdf

Reuters, 'Dutch King apologizes for Netherlands' historic role in slavery', *CNN World*, 01/07/2023, https://edition.cnn.com/2023/07/01/europe/dutch-king-apolo gizes-netherlands-slavery-intl/index.html

Rey, Matthieu, 'The British, the Hashemites and monarchies in the Middle East', in R. Aldrich and C. McCreery (eds.), *Crowns and Colonies: European Monarchies and Overseas Empires*, Manchester University Press, 2016, pp. 227–44

Rhodes, R. A. W., Wanna, John, and Weller, Patrick, *Comparing Westminster*, Oxford University Press, 2009

Richards, Thomas, *The Imperial Archive: Knowledge and the Fantasy of Empire*, Verso, 1993

Richardson, Peter, *Chinese Mine Labour in the Transvaal*, Macmillan, 1982

Riley, Charlotte Lydia, *Imperial Island: A History of Empire in Modern Britain*, Bodley Head, 2023

Ritschel, Chelsea, 'The reasons why palm oil is so controversial', *Independent*, 12/10/2020, https://www.independent.co.uk/life-style/palm-oil-health-impact-environment-animals-deforestation-heart-a8505521.html

Ritter, Caroline, *Imperial Encore: The Culture Project of the Late British Empire*, University of California Press, 2021

Roberts, M. J. D., *Making English Morals: Voluntary Association and Moral Reform in England, 1787–1886*, Cambridge University Press, 2004

Robins, James, 'Can Historians Be Traumatized by History?', *New Republic*, 16/02/2021, https://newrepublic.com/article/161127/can-historians-traumatized-history

Robins, Jonathan E., *Oil Palm: A Global History*, University of North Carolina Press, 2021

Robins, Nick, *The Corporation That Changed the World: How the East India Company Shaped the Modern Multinational*, 2nd edn, Pluto Press, 2012

Robins, Nick, 'The East India Company: The Future of the Past', *openDemocracy*, https://www.opendemocracy.net/en/east_india_company_3899jsp/

Rodney, Walter, *How Europe Underdeveloped Africa*, Verso, 2018

Rolandsen, Oystein H., and Daly, M. W., *A History of South Sudan*, Cambridge University Press, 2016

Roos, Dave, 'Was the Cullinan Diamond a Royal Gift or Stolen Gem?', *How Stuff Works*, 06/10/2022, https://science.howstuffworks.com/environmental/earth/geol ogy/cullinan-diamond.htm

Rose, Sarah, *For All the Tea in China: Espionage, Empire and the Secret Formula for the World's Favourite Drink*, Arrow, 2010

Rossing, J. P., 'Emancipatory Racial Humor as Critical Public Pedagogy: Subverting Hegemonic Racism', *Communication, Culture & Critique* 2016, 9:4, pp. 614–32, https://doi.org/10.1111/cccr.12126

Rough, Lisa, 'Jamaica's Cannabis Roots: The History of Ganja on the Island', *Leafly*, 14/05/2015, https://www.leafly.com/news/lifestyle/jamaicas-roots-the-history-of-ganja-on-the-island

Rowlatt, Justin, and Deith, Jane, 'The bitter story behind the UK's national drink', *BBC News*, 08/09/2015, https://www.bbc.co.uk/news/world-asia-india-34173532

Roy, Rohan Deb, 'White Ants, Empire, and Entomo-politics in South Asia', *Historical Journal* 2020, 63:2, pp. 411–36

Rudra, Pravina, 'Queen Elizabeth made us feel less embarrassed about Britishness and empire', *New Statesman*, 09/09/2022, https://www.newstatesman.com/quickfire/2022/09/queen-elizabeth-british-empire-embarrassed

Rudwick, Elliot, 'W. E. B. Du Bois', *Britannica*, 25/01/2023, https://www.britannica.com/biography/W-E-B-Du-Bois

Rueschemeyer, Dietrich, Huber, Evelyne, and Stevens, John D., *Capitalist Development and Democracy*, University of Chicago Press, 1992

Rukmini, S., 'World Bank Finds Evidence of Labour Abuse on Assam Tea Plantations It Owns with the Tatas', *Huffington Post*, 07/11/2016, https://www.huffpost.com/archive/in/entry/world-bank-finds-evidence-of-labour-abuse-on-assam-tea-plantatio_in_5c0fe358e4b051c73eabf82c

'Rule of law', *Merriam Webster*, accessed 31/01/2023, https://www.merriam-webster.com/dictionary/rule%20of%20law

'Rum: liquor', *Britannica*, updated 18/09/2022, https://www.britannica.com/topic/rum-liquor

'Rum Rebellion', *Britannica*, last updated 19/01/2023, https://www.britannica.com/event/Rum-Rebellion

Sabanathan, Dhana, 'What exactly is a non-dom?', *FT Adviser*, 25/04/2022, https://www.ftadviser.com/investments/2022/04/25/what-exactly-is-a-non-dom/

Sabaratnam, Meera, *Decolonising Intervention: International Statebuilding in Mozambique*, Rowman & Littlefield International, 2017

Safi, Michael, 'Campaigners celebrate as India decriminalises homosexuality', *Guardian*, 06/09/2018, https://www.theguardian.com/world/2018/sep/06/indian-supreme-court-decriminalises-homosexuality

Saillant, John, 'The Black Body Erotic and the Republican Body Politic', in Thomas A. Foster (ed.), *Long before Stonewall: Histories of Same-Sex Sexuality in Early America*, New York University Press, 2007, pp. 303–30

Saini, Angela, *Superior: The Return of Race Science*, Fourth Estate, 2019

Salick, Jan, Konchar, Katie, and Nesbitt, Mark (eds.), *Curating Biocultural Collections: A Handbook*, Kew Publishing in association with Missouri Botanical Garden Press, 2014

Salverda, Tijo, and Hay, Iain, 'Change, anxiety and exclusion in the post-colonial reconfiguration of Franco-Mauritian elite geographies', *Geographical Journal* 2014, 180:3, pp. 236–45

Samson, Jane, *Imperial Benevolence: Making British Authority in the Pacific Islands*, University of Hawai'i Press, 1998

Sanders, Douglas E., '377 and the Unnatural Afterlife of British Colonialism in Asia', *Asian Journal of Comparative Law* 2009, 4, pp. 1–49

Sanderson, David, 'Commonwealth Games to Open with Accent on Brummie Culture', *The Times*, 25/07/2022, https://www.thetimes.co.uk/article/commonwealth-games-to-open-with-accent-on-brummie-culture-2dn2hs07h

Sandiford, Keith Albert, *The Cultural Politics of Sugar: Caribbean Slavery and Narratives of Colonialism*, Cambridge University Press, 2000

Sands, Philippe, *The Last Colony: A Tale of Exile, Justice and Britain's Colonial Legacy*, Weidenfeld & Nicolson, 2022

Sanghera, Sathnam, 'Alex Renton on exposing transatlantic slave traders – in his own family', *The Times*, 30/04/2021, https://www.thetimes.co.uk/article/alex-renton-my-relatives-the-slave-owners-088cdgfnw

Sanghera, Sathnam, 'David Harewood on racism, prejudice and Covid's victims in ethnic communities', *The Times*, 26/02/2021, https://www.thetimes.co.uk/article/david-harewood-on-racism-prejudice-and-covid-s-victims-in-ethnic-communities-x55qns9gf

Sanghera, Sathnam, *Empireland: How Imperialism Has Shaped Modern Britain*, Penguin Books, 2021

Sapire, Hilary, 'African Loyalism and its Discontents', *Historical Journal* 2011, 54:1, pp. 215–40, https://doi.org/10.1017/S0018246X10000634

Satia, Priya, 'Drones: A History from the British Middle East', *Humanity* 2014, 5:1, pp. 1–31

Saunders, Nicholas J., *The Poppy: A Cultural History from Ancient Egypt to Flanders Fields to Afghanistan*, Oneworld Publications, 2013

Sawe, Benjamin E., 'Top Sisal Producing Countries in the World', *World Atlas*, 15/04/2017, https://www.worldatlas.com/articles/top-sisal-producing-countries-in-the-world.html

Searcy, Kim, 'Sudan in Crisis', *Origins: Current Events in Historical Perspective* June 2019, https://origins.osu.edu/article/sudan-darfur-al-bashir-colonial-protest?language_content_entity=en

Sears, Nell, and Hooper, Ryan, 'Beyond parody! Oxfam's new 92-page inclusivity guide calls English "the language of a colonising nation" and tells staff to avoid the words "mother", "headquarters" – and even "youth", in move slammed by critics', *Daily Mail*, 16/03/2023, https://www.dailymail.co.uk/news/article-11869961/Oxfams-new-92-page-inclusivity-guide-calls-English-language-colonising-nation.html

Segev, Tom, *One Palestine, Complete: Jews and Arabs under the British Mandate*, Abacus, 2001

Select Committee on Soft Power and the UK's Influence, *First Report: Persuasion and Power in the Modern World*, House of Lords, 11/03/2014, https://publications.parliament.uk/pa/ld201314/ldselect/ldsoftpower/150/15002.htm

Sen, Amartya, 'Illusions of empire: Amartya Sen on what British rule really did for India', *Guardian*, 29/062021, https://www.theguardian.com/world/2021/jun/29/british-empire-india-amartya-sen

Sen, Gautam, 'How Narendra Modi is decolonising India's colonial mindset', *Firstpost*, 17/09/2022, https://www.firstpost.com/opinion-news-expert-views-news-analysis-firstpost-viewpoint/how-narendra-modi-is-decolonising-indias-colonial-mindset-11275531.html

Sen, Indrani, *Gendered Transactions: The White Woman in Colonial India, c. 1820–1930*, Manchester University Press, 2017

Sengupta, T., 'Papered Spaces: Clerical Practices, Materialities and Spatial Cultures of Provincial Governance in Bengal, Colonial India, 1820s–60s', *Journal of Architecture* 2020, 25:2, pp. 111–37

Sentance, Nathan, 'Genocide in Australia', *Australian Museum*, 12/07/2022, https://australian.museum/learn/first-nations/genocide-in-australia/

Shankar, Shobana, 'Precolonial Christianity and Missionary Legacies', in Carl Levan and Patrick Ukata (eds.), *The Oxford Handbook of Nigerian Politics*, Oxford University Press, 2018, pp. 47–59

Sharma, Arvind, *Sati: Historical and Phenomenological Essays*, Motilal Banarsidass Publishers, 2001

Sharma, Jayeeta, 'British science, Chinese skill and Assam tea: making Empire's garden', *Indian Economic & Social History Review* 2006, 43:4, pp. 429–55, https://doi.org/10.1177/001946460604300402

Sharma, Jayeeta, *Empire's Garden: Assam and the Making of India*, Duke University Press, 2011

Sheena Sookrajowa, Sheetal, 'Legibility and the Politics of Ethnic Classification of the Population in the National Census of Mauritius: A Statist Perspective', *Nationalism and Ethnic Politics* 2021, 27:2, pp. 128–48

Sherman, Arnold A., 'Pressure from Leadenhall: The East India Company Lobby, 1660–1678', *Business History Review* 1976, 50:3, pp. 329–55, https://www.jstor.org/stable/3112999?mag=the-east-india-company-invented-corporate-lobbying#metadata_info_tab_contents

Sherman, Taylor C., *State Violence and Punishment in India*, Routledge, 2010

Sherwood, Harriet, 'C of E setting up £100m fund to "address past wrongs" of slave trade links', *Guardian*, 10/01/2023, https://www.theguardian.com/world/2023/jan/10/church-of-england-100m-fund-past-wrongs-slave-trade-links

'Shetland cut off from world after undersea cable breaks', *New York Times*, 21/10/2022, https://www.nytimes.com/2022/10/20/world/europe/shetland-scotland-outage.html

Shineberg, Dorothy, *The People Trade: Pacific Island Laborers and New Caledonia, 1865–1930*, University of Hawai'i Press, 1999

Ship, Chris, 'A new "Cambridge way" for future tours as William and Kate respond after Caribbean trip', *ITV News*, 28/03/2022, https://www.itv.com/news/2022-03-28/a-new-cambridge-way-for-future-tours-as-william-and-kate-respond

Shlomowitz Ralph, and McDonald, John, 'Mortality of Indian Labour on Ocean Voyages, 1843–1917', *Studies in History* 1990, 6:1, pp. 35–65

Siddique, Asheesh Kapur, 'Governance through Documents: The Board of Trade, its Archive, and the Imperial Constitution of the Eighteenth-Century British Atlantic World', *Journal of British Studies* 2020, 59:2, pp. 264–90

Silvestri, M., ' "Paddy Does Not Mind Who the Enemy Is": The Royal Irish Constabulary and Colonial Policing', in T. McMahon, M. de Nie and P. Townend (eds.), *Ireland in an Imperial World*, Palgrave Macmillan, 2017

Simms, Brendan, and Trim, David J. B. (eds.), *Humanitarian Intervention: A History*, Cambridge University Press, 2011

Simpson, Alfred William Brian, *Human Rights and the End of Empire: Britain and the Genesis of the European Convention*, Oxford University Press, 2001

Sinclair, Georgina, 'The "Irish" policeman and the Empire: influencing the policing of the British Empire–Commonwealth', *Irish Historical Studies* 2008, 36:142, pp. 173–87

Siollun, Max, *What Britain Did to Nigeria: A Short History of Conquest and Rule*, Hurst, 2021

'Sir Francis Drake facts', *Royal Museums Greenwich*, accessed 20/03/2023, https://www.rmg.co.uk/stories/topics/sir-francis-drake-facts

'Sir Joseph Banks', *Britannica*, accessed 31/01/2023, https://www.britannica.com/biography/Joseph-Banks

Sivaramakrishnan, Kavita, *Old Potions, New Bottles: Recasting Indigenous Medicine in Colonial Punjab, 1850–1945*, Longman, 2006

Skinner, Rob, *The Foundations of Anti-Apartheid: Liberal Humanitarianism and Transnational Activism in Britain and the United States, c. 1919–64*, Palgrave Macmillan, 2010

Skinner, Rob, 'The Moral Foundations of British Anti-Apartheid Activism, 1946–1960', *Journal of Southern African Studies* 2009, 35:2, pp. 399–416

Skinner, Rob, and Lester, Alan, 'Humanitarianism and Empire: Introduction', *Journal of Imperial and Commonwealth History* 2012, 40:5, pp. 729–47

'Slave Route Monument: Le Morne, Mauritius', *Atlas Obscura*, accessed 10/03/2023, https://www.atlasobscura.com/places/le-morne-slave-route-monument

Slow, Oliver, 'Trevor Noah: I never said entire UK racist, says comic after Rishi Sunak row', *BBC News*, 29/10/2022, https://www.bbc.co.uk/news/entertainment-arts-63437351

Smith, Jonathan, and Lashmar, Paul, 'William Gladstone: family of former British PM to apologise for links to slavery', *Guardian*, 19/08/2023, https://www.theguardian.com/world/2023/aug/19/william-gladstone-family-of-former-british-pm-to-apologise-for-links-to-slavery

Solomon, Feliz, 'Compromise Lies behind Singapore's New Approach to LGBT Rights', *Wall Street Journal*, 02/09/2022, https://www.wsj.com/articles/compromise-lies-behind-singapores-new-approach-to-lgbt-rights-11662110698

'South African city of Port Elizabeth becomes Gqeberha', *BBC News*, 24/02/2021, https://www.bbc.co.uk/news/world-africa-56182349

Spies, S. B., *Methods of Barbarism? Roberts and Kitchener and Civilians in the Boer Republics, January 1900–May 1902*, Human & Rousseau, 1977

Spurlin, William, *Imperialism within the Margins: Queer Representation and the Politics of Culture in Southern Africa*, Palgrave Macmillan, 2006

'Sri Lanka country profile', *BBC News*, 20/03/2023, https://www.bbc.co.uk/news/world-south-asia-11999611

Stables, W. Gordon, *The Practical Kennel Guide: With Plain Instructions How to Rear and Breed Dogs for Pleasure, Show, and Profit*, Cassell Petter & Galpin, 1877

Staunton, George, *An Authentic Account of an Embassy from the King of Great Britain to the Emperor of China*, W. Bulmer and Co. for G. Nicol, 1798

Stepan, Nancy, *The Idea of Race in Science: Great Britain, 1800–1960*, Macmillan, 1982

Stoddart, Brian, 'Sport, Cultural Imperialism, and Colonial Response in the British Empire', *Comparative Studies in Society and History* 1988, 30:4, pp. 649–73

Stoddart, Brian, *Sport, Culture and History: Region, Nation and Globe*, Taylor & Francis, 2013

Stokke, Olav, *The UN and Development: From Aid to Cooperation*, Indiana University Press, 2009

Storey, Xain, 'Ghosts of History: The Tasmanian Aborigines', *Ceasefire*, 03/09/2014, https://ceasefiremagazine.co.uk/part-i-tasmanian-aborigines/

Storrs, Ronald, *The Memoirs of Sir Ronald Storrs*, G. P. Putnam's, 1937

Stowe, Harriet Beecher, *The Key to 'Uncle Tom's Cabin'; Presenting the Original Facts and Documents upon Which the Story Is Founded, Together with Corroborative Statements Verifying the Truth of the Work*, John P. Jewett and Company, 1854, http://utc.iath.virginia.edu/uncletom/key/kyhp.html

Streets, Heather, *Martial Races: The Military, Race and Masculinity in British Imperial Culture, 1857–1914*, Manchester University Press, 2004

Stringer, Olivia, 'William and Kate's huge tour blow as "others set to follow Jamaica's republican demands"', *Express*, 25/03/2022, https://www.express.co.uk/news/royal/1586240/royal-news-republican-kate-middleton-prince-william-duke-duchess-cambridge-caribbean-jamai

Strings, Sabrina, *Fearing the Black Body: The Racial Origins of Fat Phobia*, New York University Press, 2019

Strobel, Margaret, *European Women and the Second British Empire*, Indiana University Press, 1991

Sturman, Rachel, 'Indian Indentured Labor and the History of International Rights Regimes', *American Historical Review* 2014, 119:5, pp. 1439–65

Styron, William, *The Confessions of Nat Turner*, Random House, 1968

Sullivan, Dylan, and Hickel, Jason, 'Capitalism and extreme poverty: A global analysis of real wages, human height, and mortality since the long 16th century', *World Development* 2023, 161, pp. 1–18

Sullivan, Dylan, and Hickel, Jason, 'How British colonialism killed 100 million Indians in 40 years', *Al Jazeera*, 02/12/2022, https://www.aljazeera.com/opinions/2022/12/2/how-british-colonial-policy-killed-100-million-indians

Sundaram, K. V., Lova Suraya Prakasa Rao, Vaddiparti, and Ram, Vernon, 'Delhi', *Britannica*, accessed 20/03/2023, https://www.britannica.com/place/Delhi

Sunday Mercury, 'The areas of Birmingham that are no-go areas for white people', *Birmingham Mail*, 03/01/2009, https://www.birminghammail.co.uk/news/local-news/the-area-of-birmingham-that-are-no-go-areas-for-white-237564

'Sykes–Picot Agreement', *Britannica*, accessed 31/03/2023, https://www.britannica.com/event/Sykes-Picot-Agreement

Tamuno, T. N., *The Evolution of the Nigerian State: The Southern Phase, 1898–1914*, Longman, 1972

Tapalaga, Andrei, 'Buck Breaking: The Worst Form of Punishment against Enslaved Men', *History of Yesterday*, 23/01/2023, https://historyofyesterday.com/buck-breaking-the-use-of-sexual-violence-against-enslaved-men-as-punishment-for-wrongdoing-897647489732

Taylor, Diane, 'Housing asylum seekers on barge may only save £10 a person daily, report says', *Guardian*, 11/07/2023, https://www.theguardian.com/uk-news/2023/jul/11/housing-asylum-seekers-on-barge-may-only-save-10-a-person-daily-report-says?CMP=Share_iOS App_Other

Taylor, Michael, 'The Manchester Guardian: The Limits of Liberalism in the Kingdom of Cotton', *Guardian*, 29/03/2023, https://shorturl.at/qyEFW

Taylor, Michael, 'Never forget that the British political and media elite endorsed slavery', *Guardian*, 30/01/2023, https://www.theguardian.com/commentisfree/2023/jan/30/britain-abolition-slavery-society-200-years-radical-

Taylor, Michael, 'Powers of Darkness', *London Review of Books*, 21 October 2021, 43:20, https://www.lrb.co.uk/the-paper/v43/n20/michael-taylor/powers-of-darkness

Taylor Vurpillat, J., *Empire, Industry and Globalization: Rethinking the Emergence of the Gold Standard in the 19th-Century World*, John Wiley, 2014

Team LHI, 'When New Delhi Became India's Capital', *Peepul Tree*, 30/06/2022, https://www.livehistoryindia.com/story/eras/new-delhi

Teltscher, Kate, *Palace of Palms: Tropical Dreams and the Making of Kew*, Picador, 2020

'10 films about the ugly face of the British Empire', 28/06/2018, *Dmovies.org*, https://www.dmovies.org/2018/06/28/top-10-films-atrocities-british-empire/

'Terra nullius', *Australian Museum*, 09/09/2021, https://australian.museum/learn/first-nations/unsettled/recognising-invasions/terra-nullius/, https://www.nma.gov.au/defining-moments/resources/mabo-decision

Tharoor, Shashi, 'Shashi Tharoor on why India is suited to a presidential system', *The News Minute*, 07/11/2016, https://www.thenewsminute.com/article/shashi-tharoor-why-india-suited-presidential-system-52516

'Thomas Babington Macaulay', *New World Encyclopedia*, accessed 31/01/2023, https://www.newworldencyclopedia.org/entry/Thomas_Babington_Macaulay

Thompson, Andrew S., *Living in the Past: Public Memories of Empire in the Twenty-first Century*, Menzies Centre for Australian Studies, 2008

Thompson, Gardner, *Legacy of Empire: Britain, Zionism and the Creation of Israel*, Saqi, 2019

Thornycroft, Peta, 'South Africa's Port Elizabeth changed for Xhosa "click language" name Gqeberha to cut colonial ties', *Telegraph*, 24/02/2021, https://www.telegraph.co.uk/news/2021/02/24/south-africas-port-elizabeth-changed-xhosa-click-language-name/

Thrush, Coll, *Indigenous London: Native Travelers at the Heart of Empire*, Yale University Press, 2016

Tinker, Hugh, *A New System of Slavery: The Export of Indian Labour Overseas, 1830–1920*, Hansib Publishing, 1993

'To the nations of the world, ca. 1900', Copy of address signed by Du Bois, Alexander Walters, Henry B. Brown, and H. Sylvester Williams, https://credo.library.umass.edu/view/full/mums312-b004-i321

*Tom Daley: Illegal to Be Me*, BBC, 15/08/2022, https://www.bbc.co.uk/programmes/m001boyv

Tomlins, Christopher L., and Mann, Bruce H. (eds.), *The Many Legalities of Early America*, University of North Carolina Press, 2001

Toner, Deborah, *Alcohol in the Age of Industry, Empire, and War*, Bloomsbury Academic, 2023

'Toni Morrison at Portland State, May 30, 1975', *Mackenzian*, accessed 09/02/2023, https://www.mackenzian.com/wp-content/uploads/2014/07/Transcript_Port landState_TMorrison.pdf

'Top 10 Tea Producing Countries in the World 2021', *Farrer's Tea & Coffee Merchants*, 10/09/2020, https://farrerscoffee.co.uk/blogs/blog/top-10-tea-producing-countries-in-the-world-2021

Topham, Gwyn, 'DP World's controversial history of P&O ownership', *Guardian*, 18/03/2022, https://www.theguardian.com/business/2022/mar/18/dp-world-p-and-o-ownership-dubai

Townsend, Mark, 'Revealed: how Britain tried to legitimise Batang Kali massacre', *Guardian*, 06/05/2012, https://www.theguardian.com/world/2012/may/06/britain-batang-kali-massacre-malaysia

'Trade opportunities for Commonwealth post-Brexit', *The Commonwealth*, 10/01/2017, https://thecommonwealth.org/news/trade-opportunities-commonwealth-post-brexit

Trevithick, Alan, 'Some Structural and Sequential Aspects of the British Imperial Assemblages at Delhi: 1877–1911', *Modern Asian Studies* 1990, 24:3, pp. 561–78

Trocki, Carl A., *Opium, Empire and the Global Political Economy: A Study of the Asian Opium Trade*, Routledge, 1999

Truth and Justice Commission, *Report of the Truth and Justice Commission*, vol. 1, Mauritius Government Printing, 2011, accessed 04/07/2023, https://shorturl.at/oAP05

Tully, John, *The Devil's Milk: A Social History of Rubber*, Monthly Review Press, 2011

Tully, John, 'A Victorian Ecological Disaster: Imperialism, the Telegraph, and Gutta-Percha', *Journal of World History* 2009, 20:4, pp. 559–79

Tunzelmann, Alex von, 'Who is to blame for partition? Britain', *New York Times*, 19/08/2017

Turnbull, Tiffanie, 'Commonwealth Games: 2026 event in doubt after Victoria cancels', *BBC News*, 19/07/2023, https://www.bbc.co.uk/news/world-australia-66229574

'Twitter User Accuses Uber Driver of Trying to Kidnap Her', *Bella Naija*, 11/01/2017, https://www.bellanaija.com/2017/01/twitter-user-accuses-uber-driver-of-trying-to-kidnap-her/

'Two centuries of forgetting', *Economist*, 19/08/2023

Twomey, Anne, 'Discretionary reserve powers of heads of state', in Harshan Kumarasingham (ed.), *Constitution-Making in Asia: Decolonisation and State-Building in the Aftermath of the British Empire*, Routledge, 2016, pp. 55–78

Uchendu, Victor C., *The Igbo of Southeastern Nigeria*, Holt, Rinehart & Winston, 1965

'UK's lead role in 1953 Iran coup d'état exposed', *Al Jazeera*, 18/08/2022, https://www.aljazeera.com/news/2020/8/18/uks-lead-role-in-1953-iran-coup-detat-exposed

*United Nations Charter*, United Nations, https://www.un.org/en/about-us/un-charter/full-text

*The University of Bristol: Our History and the Legacies of Slavery*, University of Bristol, 2022, pp. 15–19, https://www.bristol.ac.uk/media-library/sites/university/documents/university-of-bristol-legacies-of-slavery-report.pdf

Vahed, Goolam, ' "An evil thing": Gandhi and Indian Indentured Labour in South Africa, 1893–1914', *South Asia: Journal of South Asian Studies* 2019, 42:4, pp. 654–74

Vail, Leroy, 'The Making of an Imperial Slum: Nyasaland and its Railways, 1895–1935', *Journal of African History* 1975, 16:1, pp. 89–112

Van der Hoogte, Arjo R., and Pieters, Toine, 'Science in the Service of Colonial Agro-industrialism: The Case of Cinchona Cultivation in the Dutch and British East Indies, 1852–1900', *Studies in History and Philosophy of Science Part C: Studies in History and Philosophy of Biological and Biomedical Sciences* 2014, 47:A, pp. 12–22

Varanasi, Anuradha, 'How Colonialism Spawned and Continues to Exacerbate the Climate Crisis', *State of the Planet*, 21/09/2020, https://news.climate.columbia.edu/2022/09/21/how-colonialism-spawned-and-continues-to-exacerbate-the-climate-crisis/

Vaughan, Megan, *Curing their Ills: Colonial Power and African Illness*, Polity Press, 1991

Verghese, Ajay, *The Colonial Origins of Ethnic Violence in India*, Stanford University Press, 2016

Verma, Sanju, 'Decolonising Bharat: The Modi Factor', *Daily Guardian*, 19/09/2022, https://thedailyguardian.com/decolonising-bharat-the-modi-factor/

Vernon, James, *Hunger: A Modern History*, Harvard University Press, 2007

'Victoria', *Wikipedia*, accessed 20/03/2023, https://en.wikipedia.org/wiki/Victoria

Villanueva, Edgar, *Decolonizing Wealth: Indigenous Wisdom to Heal Divides and Restore Balance*, Berrett-Koehler, 2018

Villanueva, Edgar, 'Money as Medicine: Leveraging Philanthropy to Decolonize Wealth', 29/01/2019, *Non-Profit Quarterly*, https://nonprofitquarterly.org/money-as-medicine-leveraging-philanthropy-to-decolonize-wealth/

Viswanathan, Gauri, *Masks of Conquest: Literary Study and British Rule in India*, Columbia University Press, 1989

'The Waco Horror', *Brown University Library*, July 1916, https://library.brown.edu/pdfs/1292363091648500.pdf

Wagner, Kim A., 'Savage Warfare: Violence and the Rule of Colonial Difference in Early British Counterinsurgency', *History Workshop Journal* 2018, 85, pp. 217–37

Wahlquist, Calla, ' "The right thing to do": restoring Aboriginal place names key to recognising Indigenous histories', *Guardian*, 28/05/2021, https://www.theguardian.com/australia-news/2021/may/29/the-right-thing-to-do-restoring-aboriginal-place-names-key-to-recognising-indigenous-histories

Walcott, Derek, 'Nobel Lecture: The Antilles: Fragments of Epic Memory', *The Nobel Prize*, 07/12/1992, https://www.nobelprize.org/prizes/literature/1992/walcott/lecture/

Wald, Erica, 'Governing the Bottle: Alcohol, Race and Class in Nineteenth-Century India', *Journal of Imperial and Commonwealth History* 2018, 46:3, pp. 397–417

Walker, Kim, and Nesbitt, Mark, *Just the Tonic: A Natural History of Tonic Water*, Kew Publishing, 2019

Walker, Martin, 'The Making of Modern Iraq', *Wilson Quarterly* 2003, 27:2, pp. 29–40

Wallace, Tina, 'Trends in UK NGOs: A Research Note', *Development in Practice* 2003, 13:5, pp. 564–9, https://www.jstor.org/stable/4029945

Ward, Victoria, 'King Charles wants Britain's role in the slave trade "better highlighted and acknowledged" ', *Daily Telegraph*, 09/11/2022

Washbrook, David A., 'Law, State and Agrarian Society in Colonial India', *Modern Asian Studies* 1981, 15:3, pp. 649–721

Waterfield, Bruno, 'Belgium to return looted artefacts from colonial past', *The Times*, 17/03/2023, https://www.thetimes.co.uk/article/belgium-to-return-looted-artefacts-from-colonial-past-vjfwgvrp5

Waterfield, Bruno, 'Dutch royals pocketed €1bn from conquest and slavery', *The Times*, 18/06/2023, https://www.thetimes.co.uk/article/44c5de96-0e14-11ee-a92d-cf7c831c99b5?shareToken=fa161a27d99697b5b6327608110fc073

Waters, Simon, 'Cameron's F-word outburst at reporters over British empire "gaffe"', *Daily Mail*, 10/04/2011, https://www.dailymail.co.uk/news/article-1375341/David-Camerons-F-word-outburst-reporters-British-Empire-gaffe.html

Watson, Matthew, 'Michael Gove's war on professional historical expertise: conservative curriculum reform, extreme whig history and the place of imperial heroes in modern multicultural Britain', *British Politics* 2020, 15, pp. 271–90,

Weaver, John C., *The Great Land Rush and the Making of the Modern World, 1650–1900*, McGill-Queen's University Press, 2003

Webster, Anthony, 'Business and Empire: A Reassessment of the British Conquest of Burma in 1885', *Historical Journal* 2000, 43:4, pp. 1003–25

Weiner, Myron, 'Empirical Democratic Theory', in Myron Weiner and Ergun Ozbudun (eds.), *Competitive Elections in Developing Countries*, Duke University Press, 1987, pp. 3–34

Weingartner, Katharina, ' "The Fever": Questioning Malaria Management as a Colonial Legacy', *Development* 2020, 63, pp. 312–15

'Welcome to Rashtrapati Bhavan', *Rashtrapati Bhavan: The Office and Residence of the President of India*, accessed 20/03/2023, https://rashtrapatisachivalaya.gov.in/rbtour/

Welikala, Asanga, ' "Specialist in omniscience"? Nationalism, constitutionalism, and Sir Ivor Jennings' engagement with Ceylon', in Harshan Kumarasingham (ed.), *Constitution-Making in Asia: Decolonisation and State-Building in the Aftermath of the British Empire*, Routledge, 2016, pp. 112–36

Wells Bowman, Larry, 'Mauritius', *Britannica*, last updated 24/02/2023, https://www.britannica.com/place/Mauritius/The-arts-and-cultural-institutions

Wenzlhuemer, Roland, *From Coffee to Tea Cultivation in Ceylon, 1880–1900*, Brill, 2008

'West Indies Central Sugar Cane Breeding Station', *Cane Breeding Station*, accessed 20/01/2023, https://www.canebreedingstation.com/our-team/

Westcott, Nick, 'Oligarchs, Oil and Obi-dients: The Battle for the Soul of Nigeria', *African Arguments*, 03/02/2023, https://africanarguments.org/2023/02/oligarchs-oil-and-obi-dients-the-battle-for-the-soul-of-nigeria

'What caused Bligh's crew to lead a mutiny on his ship, the *Bounty*, in 1789?', *Royal Museums Greenwich*, accessed 16/02/2023, https://www.rmg.co.uk/stories/topics/william-bligh

White, Nadine, 'Jamaica: government "has already begun" process of removing Queen as head of state', *Independent*, 22/03/2022, https://www.independent.co.uk/world/jamaica-queen-head-of-state-b2041296.html

'White Australia policy', *National Museum Australia*, https://www.nma.gov.au/defining-moments/resources/white-australia-policy

'Who We Are', *Caricom*, accessed 19/01/2023, https://caricom.org/our-community/who-we-are/

'Why is cricket so popular in India?', *Wisden*, 10/03/2021, https://wisden.com/stories/why-is-cricket-so-popular-in-india

'Why is Sudan so unstable?' *Economist*, 04/01/2022, https://www.economist.com/the-economist-explains/2022/01/04/why-is-sudan-so-unstable

Wight, John, 'Band Aid Is Offensive', *Huffington Post*, 18/11/2014, https://www.huffingtonpost.co.uk/john-wight/band-aid-ebola_b_6176354.html

Willan, Brian, 'The Anti-Slavery and Aborigines' Protection Society and the South African Natives' Land Act of 1913', *Journal of African History* 1979, 20:1, pp. 83–102

Williams, Eric, *Capitalism and Slavery*, University of North Carolina Press, 1944

Wills, Matthew, 'The East India Company Invented Corporate Lobbying', *JSTOR Daily*, 02/11/2019, https://daily.jstor.org/the-east-india-company-invented-corporate-lobbying/

Wilson, Jon, *India Conquered: Britain's Raj and the Chaos of Empire*, Simon & Schuster, 2016

Wilson, Jon, and Dilley, Andrew, 'The Incoherence of Empire. Or, the Pitfalls of Ignoring Sovereignty in the History of the British Empire', *Transactions of the Royal Historical Society* 2023, pp. 1–27, https://doi.org/10.1017/S0080440123000063

Wilson, J. S., 'On the general and gradual desiccation of the earth and atmosphere', *Proceedings of the British Association for the Advancement of Science, Transactions* 1858

Wilson, Ninian, 'Anti-monarchy marchers in Dublin throw coffin marked "RIP British Empire" into river', *The National*, 19/09/2022, https://www.thenational.scot/news/22313008.anti-monarchy-marchers-dublin-throw-coffin-marked-rip-british-empire-river/

Winfield, Nicole, 'Pope Voices Willingness to Return Indigenous Artifacts', *Time.com*, 30/04/2023, https://time.com/6275864/pope-indigenous-artifacts/

Winseck, Dwayne, 'Submarine Telegraphs, Telegraph News, and the Global Financial Crisis of 1873', *Journal of Cultural Economy* 2012, 5:2, pp. 197–212

Wintour, Patrick, 'UN court rejects UK claim to Chagos Islands in favour of Mauritius', *Guardian*, 28/01/2021, https://www.theguardian.com/world/2021/jan/28/un-court-rejects-uk-claim-to-chagos-islands-in-favour-of-mauritius

Wood, Peter, *Black Majority: Negroes in Colonial South Carolina from 1670 through the Stono Rebellion*, Knopf, 1974

Woolcock, Nicola, 'British influence on wane as leaders are educated elsewhere', 24/08/2022, *The Times*, https://www.thetimes.co.uk/article/british-influence-wanes-as-world-leaders-are-educated-elsewhere-3hhwd538z

Workman, Daniel, 'Top 10 Exports from Mauritius', *World's Top Exports*, accessed 04/07/2023, https://www.worldstopexports.com/top-10-exports-from-mauritius/?utm_content=cmp-true

'The world's most, and least, democratic countries in 2022', *Economist*, 01/02/2023, https://www.economist.com/graphic-detail/2023/02/01/the-worlds-most-and-least-democratic-countries-in-2022?fsrc=core-app-economist

Wright, Robin, 'How the Curse of Sykes–Picot Still Haunts the Middle East', *New Yorker*, 30/04/2016, https://www.newyorker.com/news/news-desk/how-the-curse-of-sykes-picot-still-haunts-the-middle-east

Wrong, Michela, *I Didn't Do It for You: How the World Used and Abused a Small African Nation*, Harper Perennial, 2005

Wulf, Andrew, *The Brother Gardeners: Botany, Empire and the Birth of an Obsession*, Windmill Books, 2009

Yachot, Noa, ' "We want our land back": for descendants of the Elaine massacre, history is far from settled', *Guardian*, 18/06/2021, https://www.theguardian.com/us-news/2021/jun/18/elaine-massacre-red-summer-descendants-history

Yao, Souchou, *The Malayan Emergency: Essays on a Small, Distant War*, NIAS Press, 2016, https://www.diva-portal.org/smash/get/diva2:1379592/FULLTEXT01.pdf

Young, Crawford, *The African Colonial State in Comparative Perspective*, Yale University Press, 1997

Young, D. M., *The Colonial Office in the Early Nineteenth Century*, Longman, Green, 1961

Young, Robert, *Postcolonialism: A Very Short Introduction*, Oxford University Press, 2020

Younge, Gary, 'Lest We Remember: How Britain Buried its History of Slavery', *Guardian*, 29/03/2023, https://www.theguardian.com/news/ng-interactive/2023/mar/29/lest-we-remember-how-britain-buried-its-history-of-slavery

# Notes

## Introduction: Spot the Colonial Inheritance

1 'One of the most extraordinary of the urban manifestations of the British empire was the creation of new capitals,' writes John M. MacKenzie. 'The notion of their foundation (a historic phenomenon throughout the history of empires, not least in India) had been around in the British empire since the nineteenth century . . . Ottawa emerged from the tiny lumbering village of Bytown and became respectively the capital of Upper and Lower Canada in 1857 and of the Canadian Confederation after 1867 . . . Some capitals of planned new colonies, such as Adelaide in South Australia, were carefully laid out with environmental and social factors in mind.' Other examples include Rangoon, Canberra and Lusaka. John M. MacKenzie, *The British Empire through Buildings: Structure, Function and Meaning*, Manchester University Press, 2020, pp. 240–41.

David A. Johnson, 'A British empire for the twentieth century: the inauguration of New Delhi, 1931', *Urban History* 2008, 35:3; David A. Johnson, 'The Library: New Delhi: The Last Imperial City', *The British Empire*, https://www. britishempire.co.uk/library/newdelhi.htm; Team LHI, 'When New Delhi Became India's Capital', *Peepul Tree*, 30/06/2022, https://www.livehistoryindia. com/story/eras/new-delhi; K. V. Sundaram, Vaddiparti Lova Surya Prakasa Rao and Vernon Ram, 'Delhi', *Britannica*, https://www.britannica.com/place/Delhi; Gautam Sen, 'How Narendra Modi is decolonising India's colonial mindset', *Firstpost*, 17/09/2022, https://www.firstpost.com/opinion-news-expert-views-news-analysis-firstpost-viewpoint/how-narendra-modi-is-decolonising-indias-colonial-mindset-11275531.html; 'New Delhi', *Britannica*, https://www. britannica.com/place/New-Delhi;

2 Miki Desai and Madhavi Desai, 'The colonial bungalow in India', *The Newsletter: International Institute for Asian Studies*, Summer 2011, https://www.iias.asia/sites/ iias/files/nwl_article/2019-05/IIAS_NL57_2627.pdf; 'Lutyens Bungalow Zone', *World Monuments Fund*, https://www.wmf.org/project/lutyens-bungalow-zone.

3 According to one historian, the veranda was 'a nagging reminder of the frailty of white European occupation, its thinness on the ground, an almost defiant acknowledgment, signalling an unwillingness to be more deeply rooted in the country'. Cited by Robert Home, *Of Planting and Planning: The Making of British Colonial Cities*, E. & F. N. Spon, 1997, p. 95; Jeremy Kahn, 'Lutyens' bungalows:

Saving a slice of imperial New Delhi', *New York Times*, 08/01/2008, https://www.nytimes.com/2008/01/08/arts/08iht-30kahn.9075163.html.

4  'After the Mutiny in 1857, the British moved out of the Walled City and settled in the area just north of it and called it Civil Lines. By 1890 European residents comprising railway officials and mill managers moved into Civil Lines, and over 110 large colonial houses came up. 3 hotels, Maidens Hotel, Swiss Hotel and The Cecil, were also established during this time.' See '1903: Maidens Hotel', *Historic Hotels of the World: Then & Now*, https://www.historichotelsthenandnow.com/maidensdelhi.html.

5  https://www.maidenshotel.com/our-heritage.

6  Sen, 'How Narendra Modi is decolonising India's colonial mindset'; Sanju Verma, 'Decolonising Bharat: The Modi Factor', *Daily Guardian*, 19/09/2022, https://thedailyguardian.com/decolonising-bharat-the-modi-factor/; Kabir Jhala, 'Controversial $1.8bn redevelopment of Delhi's parliament complex enters second phase', *Art Newspaper*, 28/09/2022, https://www.theartnewspaper.com/2022/09/28/first-phase-of-controversial-18bn-redevelopment-of-delhis-parliament-complex-is-complete.

7  These durbars took place in 1877 when Queen Victoria was declared Empress of India; in 1903 to mark the accession of Edward VII; and in 1911 when George V announced the relocation of the capital from Calcutta to Delhi. John M. MacKenzie, *A Cultural History of the British Empire*, Yale University Press, 2022, pp. 57–63.

8  Statues became, according to John M. MacKenzie, 'an essential aspect of imperial propaganda' and then, in the post-colonial era, came under intense scrutiny by nationalists across the former empire. 'Throughout Africa, most British statues were either destroyed, put into storage, or repatriated. An example is the Sudan, which returned two notable statues to Britain in 1957 following the Suez crisis . . . The British themselves removed the statue of Lord Delamere from Nairobi in 1963 just ahead of independence. Other transfers included the highly sensitive one of the brutal John Nicholson. Although the Indian government has generally been sensitive about the survival of statues, particularly during the prime ministership of Nehru, both external and internal political relationships have ensured that they have been a source of controversy . . . Nevertheless, some were decapitated or otherwise damaged (arms and hands cut off for example) in the aftermath of independence or at key emotional moments, such as the hundredth anniversary of the Indian Revolt of 1857. It is an irony that statues, for example at the Victoria Memorial in Kolkata, may now be noticed more as an intriguing aspect of cultural heritage. It is also surprising that the Marxist government of West Bengal has been more sympathetic to British statues than the administrations of other states, partly in an attempt to encourage investors, partly to develop tourism. In the case of Pakistan, all statues were removed into

museums or storage in view of the Islamic ban on the representation of the human form.' See MacKenzie, *A Cultural History of the British Empire*, pp. 191–3, 318; 'Coronation Park: Where the Statues of the Raj Rest in Ruins', *Outlook India*, https://www.outlookindia.com/national/coronation-park-where-the-statues-of-the-raj-rest-in-ruins-photos-82480.

9   Rizwan Ahmad, 'Renaming India: Saffronisation of public spaces', 12/10/2018, https://www.aljazeera.com/opinions/2018/10/12/renaming-india-saffronisation-of-public-spaces.

10  Verma, 'Decolonising Bharat'.

11  'Parakram Diwas', *National Today*, https://nationaltoday.com/parakram-diwas/.

12  Havelock Island (named for General Henry Havelock), Neil Island (named for Brigadier General James Neill) and Ross Island (named after Sir Daniel Ross, Marine Surveyor General), are now respectively named Swaraj Dweep, Shaheed Dweep and Netaji Subhas Chandra Bose Dweep. See 'PM Modi renames 3 Andaman & Nicobar islands as tribute to Netaji', *Economic Times*, 31/12/2018, https://economictimes.indiatimes.com/news/politics-and-nation/pm-modi-renames-3-islands-of-andaman-and-nicobar/articleshow/67311674.cms.

13  See Peta Thornycroft, 'South Africa's Port Elizabeth changed for Xhosa "click language" name Gqeberha to cut colonial ties', *Telegraph*, 24/02/2021, https://www.telegraph.co.uk/news/2021/02/24/south-africas-port-elizabeth-changed-xhosa-click-language-name/; Ahmad, 'Renaming India'; Kaleigh Bradley, 'What's in a Name? Place Names, History, and Colonialism', *Active History*, 02/02/2015, http://activehistory.ca/2015/02/whats-in-a-name-place-names-history-and-colonialism/; Calla Wahlquist, ' "The right thing to do": restoring Aboriginal place names key to recognising Indigenous histories', *Guardian*, 28/05/2021, https://www.theguardian.com/australia-news/2021/may/29/the-right-thing-to-do-restoring-aboriginal-place-names-key-to-recognising-indigenous-histories; 'South African city of Port Elizabeth becomes Gqeberha', *BBC News*, 24/02/2021, https://www.bbc.co.uk/news/world-africa-56182349; Fernando Fong, 'Georgetown Won't Be Renamed Tanjong Penaga', *TRP*, 15/03/2022, https://www.therakyatpost.com/news/malaysia/2022/03/15/georgetown-wont-be-renamed-tanjong-penaga/; 'Ogimaa Mikana: Reclaiming/Renaming', *Tumblr*, https://ogimaamikana.tumblr.com/.

14  Man Aman Singh Chhina, 'PM Narendra Modi unveils new naval ensign, here's why it is significant', *Indian Express*, 02/09/2022, https://indianexpress.com/article/explained/explained-what-naval-ensign-why-indian-navy-set-new-8121252/.

15  Robert Young, *Postcolonialism: A Very Short Introduction*, Oxford University Press, 2020, p. 25. Young continues: 'In almost every case, colonial rule established the colonizer's language as the official language, of administration, law, and education, while the local languages which had previously fulfilled these functions were degraded to the status of "native" languages or dialects and ignored.'

16   Amrit Dhillon, 'Don't say hello, it's too western, Indian civil servants told', *The Times*, 03/10/2022, https://www.thetimes.co.uk/article/1df7bc02-4269-11ed-abc9-d0d53e948d21?shareToken=9cfc72be6c540ab1b0d8e8e2a9c5c69e.

17   Vande Mataram is also the title of India's national song, which has its own contentious political history. It is considered offensive to Muslims because the Motherland is identified with Hindu goddesses. Elsewhere, the colonial elements of Indian 'army uniforms, crests, military band instruments, names of regiments and buildings, mess rules and perhaps even bagpipes' are being Indianized. See André J. P. Elias, ' "Vande Mataram!": Constructions of Gender and Music in Indian Nationalism', *Asian Music* 2017, 48:2, pp. 90–110.

18   Amrit Dhillon, 'Modi employs new tool in India's war against the English language: Hindi medical degrees', *Guardian*, 22/10/2022, https://www.theguardian.com/world/2022/oct/22/modi-employs-new-tool-in-indias-war-against-the-english-language-hindi-medical-degrees.

19   'The most spoken languages worldwide in 2022', *Statista*, https://shorturl.at/rzO18.

20   'Instead of marginalizing English as an unwanted colonial legacy, India will be better off appropriating it as its own,' argued Nitin Pai in *Mint* recently. 'If there is [such] a thing as Australian English, there certainly is Indian English. There are far more English-speakers in India than there are people in Australia. It is the enduring failure of English departments at our universities that they have not asserted this claim. Words like "prepone" and "co-brother" might not exist in English (UK) but are part of English (India). With over 150 million people comfortable in it, English is an Indian language and we must proclaim it as one.' See 'The Intersection: English is an Indian language', *Mint*, 27/02/2023, https://www.nitinpai.in/2023/02/27/english-is-an-indian-language.

21   PTI, 'More than 19,500 mother tongues spoken in India: Census', *Indian Express*, 01/07/2018, https://indianexpress.com/article/india/more-than-19500-mother-tongues-spoken-in-india-census-5241056/.

22   MacKenzie, *A Cultural History of the British Empire*, pp. 235–7, 244–8.

23   https://www.statista.com/statistics/885417/india-most-read-english-publications/.

24   'The teaching of Shakespeare in India', Leah Marcus notes, 'goes as far back as the early eighteenth century, and by the mid-nineteenth, had become routine in British government schools.' She continues: 'the editing of Shakespeare in India . . . generated distinctive features that became models for later British editions'. Caroline Ritter adds: 'Three years after independence, one might expect Shakespeare plays and the BBC news would be rare in Nigeria. Yet, instead of disappearing, British plays, broadcasts, and books not only remained but drew large audiences . . . A cultural version of the British empire took root and sustained itself far beyond the formal end of political rule.' Leah S. Marcus, *How*

*Shakespeare Became Colonial: Editorial Traditions and the British Empire*, Routledge, 2017, pp. 132–3; Caroline Ritter, *Imperial Encore: The Culture Project of the Late British Empire*, University of California Press, 2021, p. 1.

25 'English literature appeared as a subject in the curriculum of the colonies long before it was institutionalized in the home country . . . As early as the 1820s, when the classical curriculum still reigned supreme in England despite the strenuous efforts of some concerned critics to loosen its hold, English as the study of culture and not simply the study of language had already found a secure place in the British Indian curriculum.' See Gauri Viswanathan, *Masks of Conquest: Literary Study and British Rule in India*, Columbia University Press, 1989, p. 3.

26 Ciara Nugent, 'Western Architecture is Making India's Heatwaves Worse', *Time*, 16/05/2022, https://time.com/6176998/india-heatwaves-western-architecture.

27 One of the first ever colonial agencies for urban development, in Dublin in the eighteenth century, was named the Wide Streets Commissioners. In 1878 a member of the New Zealand House of Representatives remarked: 'If they looked for crime, vice, destitution, and everything that was bad, they would go to the narrow slums and lanes, where these evils were actually engendered. If they made good wide streets, depend upon it they would greatly promote the virtue, morality, and health of the people, so that in the interests of every community, the Government should insist upon the laying out of wide streets.' See Home, *Of Planting and Planning*, pp. 14, 44, 59, 84.

28 Correspondents would sometimes just provide the name of the addressee, their trade and the bazaar they tended to frequent. Mark R. Frost, 'Pandora's Post Box: Empire and Information in India, 1854–1914', *English Historical Review* 2016, 131:552, p. 1057.

29 Brian Stoddart, 'Sport, Cultural Imperialism, and Colonial Response in the British Empire', *Comparative Studies in Society and History* 1988, 30:4, p. 658.

30 'Why is cricket so popular in India?', *Wisden*, 10/03/2021, https://wisden.com/stories/why-is-cricket-so-popular-in-india.

31 Stoddart, 'Sport, Cultural Imperialism, and Colonial Response in the British Empire', p. 656.

32 Matthew Parker, *The Sugar Barons: Family, Corruption, Empire and War*, Windmill Books, 2012, p. 269.

33 Stoddart, 'Sport, Cultural Imperialism, and Colonial Response in the British Empire', p. 654.

34 Ronald Storrs, Governor of Jerusalem, recalled the incident, which took place when Palestine was in the Occupied Enemy Territory Administration, in a diary entry. 'At tea afterwards with the Military Governor [of Hebron] we found tennis, and I was asked to play. An Arab handed me the balls for service and as he

turned to pick up more emitted a curious clank. Looking closer I discovered that both he and his colleague at the other end were long term criminals, heavily chained by the ankles, whom the local police officer had sent up from the gaol to act as ball boys. I could not believe that such a practice (convenient though it were) would favourably impress a Cabinet Minister, but Lord Milner seemed to endure it with fortitude.' See Ronald Storrs, *The Memoirs of Sir Ronald Storrs*, G. P. Putnam's, 1937, p. 454; Tom Segev, *One Palestine, Complete: Jews and Arabs Under the British Mandate*, Abacus, 2001, p. 8.

35  Brian Stoddart adds that 'one immediate problem for the imperial power was that, having encouraged the measurement of social progress by comparing colonial against British achievements in sport, there would always come the day of a colonial victory that might be interpreted as symbolic of general parity'. One came about in India in 1911 when the Mohan Bagan district squad defeated the East Yorks Regiment 2–1. The triumph, which occurred at a time of great political instability, was widely viewed as evidence of Indian advancement and even dominance. According to one newspaper published in Bengali: 'It fills every Indian with pride and joy to know that rice-eating, malaria-ridden, bare-footed Bengalis have got the better of beef-eating, Herculean, booted John Bull in that peculiarly English sport.' Stuart Laycock and Philip Laycock, *How Britain Brought Football to the World*, The History Press, 2022, pp. 18, 31–2, 60–61, 301–2; Brian Stoddart, *Sport, Culture and History: Region, Nation and Globe*, Taylor & Francis, 2013, pp. 129–30; Niall Ferguson, *Empire: How Britain Made the Modern World*, Penguin Books, 2003, p. 365.

36  Rashtrapati Bhavan's official website claims that it 'epitomizes India's strength, its democratic traditions and secular character. Rashtrapati Bhavan was the creation of architects of exceptional imagination and masterfulness, Sir Edwin Lutyens and Herbert Baker . . . Originally built as the residence for the Viceroy of India, Viceroy's House as it was then called has metamorphosed into today's Rashtrapati Bhavan. From being a symbol of imperial domination and power, it is today emblematic of Indian democracy and its secular, plural and inclusive traditions.' See 'Welcome to Rashtrapati Bhavan', *Rashtrapati Bhavan: The Office and Residence of the President of India*, https://rashtrapatisachivalaya.gov.in/rbtour/; G. A. Bremner, 'Stones of Empire: Monuments, Memorials, and Manifest Authority', in G. A. Bremner (ed.), *Architecture and Urbanism in the British Empire*, Oxford University Press, 2016, p. 86.

37  Mark Abadi and Shayanne Gal, 'Only about 30% of the world's population drives on the left side of the road', *Insider*, 19/10/2018, https://www.businessinsider.com/which-countries-drive-on-left-2018-10?r=US&IR=T.

38  Timothy Parsons, *The British Imperial Century, 1815–1914: A World History Perspective*, Rowman & Littlefield, 2019, pp. 151–2.

39 Ritter, *Imperial Encore*, p. 5: 'Confrontations such as Mau Mau and Suez were determinant in both how and when Britain gave up political rule in Africa. But . . . cultural initiatives did not relent – and were in fact strengthened – during the events that marked the waning and then formal end of empire. Throughout the state of emergency in Kenya, for example, British cultural work proceeded apace. British organizations published schoolbooks on East African oral histories, staged plays in the British Council's centre in Nairobi, and transmitted educational and cultural programs over the BBC.'

40 Matthew Partridge, '19 December 1932: BBC World Service begins', *Money Week*, 19/10/2020, https://moneyweek.com/365399/19-december-1932-bbc-world-service-begins.

41 'Much of this diaspora was located in the dominions of Canada, Australia, New Zealand, and South Africa,' Potter continues. 'These people, and these places, were perceived to be part of a white, English-speaking British world . . . Seeking to reflect and ensure the continued existence of a transnational community of Britons, the BBC inevitably assigned a secondary status to others . . . non-whites in Africa, Asia, and the Caribbean, and indigenous peoples in the dominions, were largely ignored . . . The white British world was perceived to be the most important part of the empire, from which most could be gained by strengthening imperial bonds, and in which the need to do such work seemed most pressing.' See Simon J. Potter, *Broadcasting Empire: The BBC and the British World, 1922–1970*, Oxford University Press, 2012, pp. 7, 14.

42 Benjamin Parkin and Alice Hancock, 'Inside the mysterious downfall of India's Cox & Kings', *Financial Times*, 22/01/2022, https://www.ft.com/content/3f1448d5-d1c2-412b-b660-5264680d2a0b.

43 Thomas Manuel, *Opium Inc: How a Global Drug Trade Funded the British Empire*, HarperCollins India, 2021. Cited in https://asianreviewofbooks.com/content/opium-inc-how-a-global-drug-trade-funded-the-british-empire-by-thomas-manuel/.

44 It was British empire's pushing of opium that eventually led to regulation. As James Mills explains, 'consumers of intoxicants and narcotics were certainly the reason for the establishment and early development of today's international drugs regulatory system, as the 1909 Shanghai Opium Conference led directly to the establishment of the Opium Advisory Committee and the Permanent Central Opium Board at the League of Nations. It was Asian consumption of local drugs, opium and to a lesser extent cannabis which drove these processes and historians have therefore focused on these.' The United Nations' Office on Drugs and Crime adds that the impetus for 1909's International Opium Commission came from US President Theodore Roosevelt's government, and the 'international ramifications of the Chinese opium problem were the primary motive

for convoking the Commission. In 1906 an imperial edict had been published prohibiting the cultivation and smoking of opium in the Chinese Empire over a period of ten years. This was being implemented with greater success than had been anticipated, and meanwhile the Indian Government, pressed by rising British public opinion, had agreed to a contemporaneous reduction in the export of Indian opium to China, the revenue alone from which had amounted to almost £3,000,000 sterling in 1907. While the regional aspect of opium smoking and of international trade in prepared opium constituted the primary concern of the Commission, its members were already well aware of the wider geographical scope of the narcotics problem in general, including addiction to manufactured opiates . . . Although the Commission was not intended to establish binding obligations, it nevertheless accelerated the efforts which only three years later led to the conclusion of The Hague Opium Convention of 1912, establishing narcotics control as an institution of international law on a multilateral basis.' See James Mills, 'Decolonising drugs in Asia: the case of cocaine in colonial India', *Third World Quarterly* 2018, 39:2, pp. 218–31; https://www.unodc.org/unodc/en/data-and-analysis/bulletin/bulletin_1959-01-01_1_page006.html.

45  James Mills argues that empire had an indirect influence over the development of the cocaine trade. 'It was suggested that by 1929 "somewhere between a quarter and a half a million individuals [were] taking cocaine in India" . . . Men and women used the drug, those that did so could be rich or poor, and Muslim and Hindu were numbered among those that sought it. It was consumed for a range of purposes, from the medicinal to the recreational.' Mills suggests that cocaine use was not the product of British colonial policy, but was a consequence of colonial migration and colonial trade. British authorities did not profit from exporting cocaine to India, but it was British and Indian people who smuggled it to sell it there: 'There is no well-organised supplier of the drug that might be accused of acting as the East India Company may have done with opium in China. Instead, what emerges from the records is a diverse and disparate range of opportunists who sourced batches of the drug to smuggle into India to take advantage of the prices inflated by British controls.' See Mills, 'Decolonising drugs in Asia', pp. 218–31.

46  See Christopher Bayly, *Empire and Information: Intelligence Gathering and Social Communication in India, 1780–1870*, Cambridge University Press, 2009; Bhavani Raman, *Document Raj: Writing and Scribes in Early Colonial India*, University of Chicago Press, 2012; Asheesh Kapur Siddique, 'Governance through Documents: The Board of Trade, its Archive, and the Imperial Constitution of the Eighteenth-Century British Atlantic World', *Journal of British Studies* 2020, 59:2, pp. 264–90; Matthew Hull, *Government of Paper: The Materiality of Bureaucracy in Urban Pakistan*, University of California Press, 2012.

47 Rohan Deb Roy, 'White Ants, Empire, and Entomo-politics in South Asia', *Historical Journal* 2020, 63:2, p. 3.

48 In the mid-1860s, the first diamonds to be unearthed in southern Africa were discovered on a farm belonging to Nicolaas and Diederik de Beer, located close to what is now the city of Kimberley. The arch-imperialist and unabashed white supremacist Cecil Rhodes soon got in on the action, acquiring a claim to the De Beers mine in 1871 before buying up the majority of diamond mines in the region, aiming for a monopoly of the world diamond market. See 'De Beers S.A.', *Britannica*, https://www.britannica.com/topic/De-Beers-SA.

49 Walter Rodney, *How Europe Underdeveloped Africa*, Verso, 2018, pp. 218–22.

50 Iain Gately, *Tobacco: A Cultural History of How an Exotic Plant Seduced Civilization*, Grove Books, 2007, p. 44.

51 See Phil Chamberlain, Nancy Karreman and Louis Laurence, 'Racism and the Tobacco Industry', *Tobacco Tactics*, 10/02/2021, https://tobaccotactics.org/wiki/racism-and-the-tobacco-industry/.

52 Emmanuel Akyeampong, 'What's in a Drink? Class Struggle, Popular Culture and the Politics of Akpeteshie (Local Gin) in Ghana, 1930–67', *Journal of African History* 1996, 37:2, pp. 215–36; Deborah Toner, *Alcohol in the Age of Industry, Empire, and War*, Bloomsbury Academic, 2023; Jason Gilbert, 'Empire and Excise: Drugs and Drink Revenue and the Fate of States in South Asia', in James Mills and Patricia Barton (eds.), *Drugs and Empire: Essays in Modern Imperialism and Intoxication, c. 1500–c. 1930*, Palgrave Macmillan, 2007, pp. 117–18; Erica Wald, 'Governing the Bottle: Alcohol, Race and Class in Nineteenth-Century India', *Journal of Imperial and Commonwealth History* 2018, 46:3, pp. 397–417; Paul Nugent, 'Modernity, Tradition, and Intoxication: Comparative Lessons from South Africa and West Africa', *Past and Present* 2014, 222:9, pp. 141–2; Emmanuel Akyeampong, 'Threats to Empire: Illicit Distillation, Venereal Diseases, and Colonial Disorder in British West Africa, 1930–1948', in Jessica Pliley, Robert Kramm and Harald Fischer-Tiné (eds.), *Global Anti-Vice Activism, 1890–1950: Fighting Drinks, Drugs, and 'Immorality'*, Cambridge University Press, 2016, pp. 162–5, 172; Sugato Mukherjee, 'Mahua: The Indian liquor the British banned', BBC, 22/11/2022, https://www.bbc.com/travel/article/20221121-mahua-the-indian-liquor-the-british-banned; MacKenzie, *A Cultural History of the British Empire*, p. 33.

53 John W. Frank, Roland S. Moore and Genevieve M. Ames, 'Public Health Then and Now: Historical and Cultural Roots of Drinking Problems among American Indians', *American Journal of Public Health* 2000, 90:3, pp. 344–51.

54 'Many travelogues and memoirs give us a fair idea of what happened in the kitchens during the Raj,' writes Pushpesh Pant. 'This was the time when the curry was invented. Although it shares its name with the native dish, *kari*, it was a pale

imitation of the considerably spicier *korma* and *salan* . . . curry powder thus reduced all to a common denominator – fish, chicken, mutton and eggs . . . Slowly but surely, and inevitably, the ruler's repast deviated from the original to the local, becoming tinted by Indian/regional elements. Conversely, the injection of the British/European elements subtly changed Indian recipes and encouraged creative chefs to experiment and innovate. This accelerated the evolution of classics such as *chilman main biryani*; *shahi tukrha*, as we know it; and *badam ki jali.*' See Pushpesh Pant, 'INDIA : Food and the Making of the Nation', *India International Centre Quarterly* 2013, 40:2, pp. 11–12.

55 Ferguson, *Empire*, p. xxiii.

56 https://www.visitsingapore.com/travel-guide-tips/about-singapore/.

57 Lizzie Collingham, *The Hungry Empire*, Penguin Books, 2017, p. 242.

58 The *Blackpast* website explains how Freetown was 'founded by British Naval Lieutenant John Clarkson and freed American slaves from Nova Scotia. Freetown was part of the larger colony of the Sierra Leone which was founded by the Sierra Leone Company (SLC) in 1787. The SLC, organized by British businessman and abolitionist William Wilberforce, sought to rehabilitate the black poor of London and former slaves of North America by bringing them to the settlement in Sierra Leone where they would stop the African slave trade by spreading Christianity through the continent. The first groups of blacks, about 400 Londoners, arrived in Sierra Leone in 1787 and established Granville Town, named after British abolitionist Granville Sharp. When the settlement was destroyed by the indigenous inhabitants in 1789, British abolitionists sent a second, larger party of 1,100 former American slaves who had been resettled in Nova Scotia at the end of the American Revolution. These settlers established Freetown in 1792. In 1800, 500 Jamaican Maroons were landed by the British. The surviving Londoners, the Nova Scotians, and Jamaican maroons intermarried to create the Creole population of Freetown.' 'Freetown, Sierra Leone, 1792–', *Blackpast*, 20/04/2011, https://www.blackpast.org/global-african-history/places-global-african-history/freetown-sierra-leone-1792/; 'Freetown', *Britannica*, https://www.britannica.com/place/Freetown.

59 Kwasi Kwarteng, *Ghosts of Empire: Britain's Legacies in the Modern World*, Bloomsbury, 2012, p. 273.

60 Michela Wrong, *I Didn't Do It for You: How the World Used and Abused a Small African Nation*, Harper Perennial, 2005, p. 7.

61 The disambiguation sections for town and city names on *Wikipedia* and geotarget.com.

62 'Birmingham (disambiguation)', *Wikipedia*, https://en.wikipedia.org/wiki/Birmingham_(disambiguation); 'How many places are named Birmingham?', *geotargit.com*, https://geotargit.com/called.php?qcity=Birmingham.

63 'Victoria', *Wikipedia*, https://en.wikipedia.org/wiki/Victoria.

64 @corinne_fowler, 09/08/2023, https://twitter.com/corinne_fowler/status/1545 851689994944514?t=1YXQ5bmi6ZybQRrUTKKDmg&s=03.

65 @andrewpopp6, 17/10/2022, https://twitter.com/andrewpopp6/status/1581968 843404021761.

66 Tony Norfield, *The City: London and the Global Power of Finance*, Verso, 2017, pp. 111–12.

67 Norman C. Baldwin, *Imperial Airways (and Subsidiary Companies): A History and Priced Check List of the Empire Air Mails*, Francis J. Field, 1950.

68 'Passage to India', *P&O Heritage*, 15/08/2017, https://www.poheritage.com/features/passage-to-india.

69 The *Guardian* recently explained the complex history: 'Bin Sulayem and DP World originally bought P&O – then a London listed company – in 2006 for £3.3bn. It paid a huge premium, about 70% over the market value, for a group that Margaret Thatcher had once described as "the fabric of the British empire". However, the ports were always its key target: Bin Sulayem admitted then that he had limited knowledge of the ferry business that came alongside, but denied he had plans to sell them off. They were however sold to a separate state-owned entity, Dubai World, around the time of the financial crisis, before DP World bought them back for $322m (£244m) in 2019. Among its 70 ports worldwide, the closest to home, as far as most sacked P & O workers see it, are the big container operations at London Gateway and Southampton. Both now are the central hubs of the first freeports, Thames and Solent, putting DP World firmly in the slipstream of post-Brexit government economic policy.' See Gwyn Topham, 'DP World's controversial history of P&O ownership', *Guardian*, 18/03/2022, https://www.theguardian.com/business/2022/mar/18/dp-world-p-and-o-ownership-dubai.

70 Daniel R. Headrick, *The Tools of Empire: Technology and European Imperialism in the Nineteenth Century*, Oxford University Press, 1981, pp. 138–9.

71 Serkan Karas and Stathis Arapostathis, 'Electrical Colonialism: Techno-politics and British Engineering Expertise in the Making of the Electricity Supply Industry in Cyprus', in Alain Beltran, Léonard Laborie, Pierre Lanthier and Stéphanie Le Gallic (eds.), *Electric Worlds / Mondes électriques: Creations, Circulations, Tensions, Transitions (19th–21st Century)*, P.I.E. Peter Lang, 2017; Moses Chikoweo, 'Sub-alternating Currents: Electrification and Power Politics in Bulawayo, Colonial Zimbabwe, 1894–1939', *Journal of Southern African Studies* 2007, 33:2, pp. 287–306.

72 Alberto Alesina, William Easterly and Janina Matuszeski, 'Artificial States', February 2006, Harvard University and New York University, https://williameasterly.files.wordpress.com/2010/08/59_easterly_alesina_matuszeski_artificialstates_prp.pdf.

73  Home, *Of Planting and Planning*, pp. 11–14.

74  Charles Currier, 'A Plan of the Town of New Haven with All the Buildings in 1748 Taken by the Hon Gen. Wadsworth of Durham to Which Are Added the Names and Professions of the Inhabitants at That Period – Also the Location of Lots to Many of the First Grantees . . .', *Rare Maps*, https://www.raremaps.com/gallery/detail/20308/a-plan-of-the-town-of-new-haven-with-all-the-buildings-in-1-currier.

75  Home, *Of Planting and Planning*, p. 15.

76  Ibid., p. 228.

77  William Easterly, *The White Man's Burden: Why the West's Efforts to Aid the Rest Have Done So Much Ill and So Little Good*, Oxford University Press, 2007, p. 246.

78  Daniel R. Headrick, *The Tentacles of Progress: Technology Transfer in the Age of Imperialism, 1850–1940*, Oxford University Press, 1988, p. 381.

79  Ibid., p. 380.

80  Headrick explains that 'in terms of railroads, the difference between Africa and India is astounding. India caught the railroad boom at its height and emerged from the colonial age with a complete and efficient railroad system. In contrast tropical Africa emerged from colonialism with only scattered unconnected lines, serving mainly Europe's need for raw materials.' See ibid., p. 196.

81  Victoria Falls Bridge (once known as the Zambezi Bridge) opened in 1935. Leroy Vail points out that the bridge, which was part of Cecil Rhodes' failed Cape-to-Cairo line, was an unsolicited project, initiated in part to create employment for British workers, and that Nyasaland was nevertheless required to pay for the bridge. See Leroy Vail, 'The Making of an Imperial Slum: Nyasaland and its Railways, 1895–1935', *Journal of African History* 1975, 16:1, pp. 89–112; Paul Cotterell, *The Railways of Palestine and Israel*, Tourret Publishing, 1984, p. 23.

82  In Johnny Mansour's 'The Hijaz–Palestine Railway and the Development of Haifa', *Jerusalem Quarterly* 2006, 28, p. 9, he explains that 'at the beginning of the British mandate period in Palestine, the British strategic decision to construct a modern port in Haifa stemmed from purely colonialist considerations without addressing any local interests in Palestine.'

83  MacKenzie, *The British Empire through Buildings*, p. 109.

84  Ibid., pp. 109–18.

85  Ibid., pp. 125–36.

86  'The general post offices of all the most significant colonial and imperial cities were often among the grandest buildings, as they were in British cities. They were freighted with all kinds of symbolic significance as well as the highly practical business of the imperial posts.' See ibid., p. 148.

87  'Churches and cathedrals . . . became more than religious statements. They also

laid down powerful ethnic, cultural and political markers that deeply embedded them in the whole business of imperial expansion and rule.' See ibid., p. 203.

88  Robert Home reports that 'the new town idea, which was being implemented in Britain under the New Towns Act of 1945, was applied in many colonies, not only in Hong Kong and Singapore, but also in India, Israel, Malaysia and elsewhere. These were all states struggling with large-scale population growth and political upheaval.' Some of this upheaval was caused by empire, of course. India housed around 5 million people in 118 new towns built between independence and the early 1980s, while the Brits built thirty railway towns by 1941, including the likes of Kharagpur. See Home, *Of Planting and Planning*, p. 214.

89  See Ritter, *Imperial Encore*, p. 1; MacKenzie, *The British Empire through Buildings*, pp. 35–40.

90  'The marketing of fairness technologies demonstrates an evolution from portrayals of civilising medicines and hygienic soaps between the 1890s and 1920s to more explicit messages about idealised beauty and fairness in the 1930s and 1940s,' writes Mobeen Hussain. 'During the 1920s, most advertisements focused on "clear" complexions and protecting the skin from the climate. However, terms such as "bleaching", "whitening" and "vanishing" became more prominent, initially targeting European women in the colonies.' See Mobeen Hussain, 'Combining Global Expertise with Local Knowledge in Colonial India: Selling Ideals of Beauty and Health in Commodity Advertising (c. 1900–1949)', *South Asia: Journal of South Asian Studies* 2021, 44:5, p. 940; Richard Assheton, 'Nigeria's advertising regulator recently banned the use of foreign models and voiceover artists', *The Times*, 26/08/2022, https://www.thetimes.co.uk/article/nigeria-becomes-first-country-to-ban-foreign-models-in-adverts-3xv8klvp7.

91  Sabrina Strings, *Fearing the Black Body: The Racial Origins of Fat Phobia*, New York University Press, 2019, pp. 84, 100.

92  Adam Edwards, 'In praise of the British baddie', *Daily Express*, 23/04/2010, https://www.express.co.uk/expressyourself/170852/In-praise-of-the-British-baddie; John Bleasdale, 'Things Britain Does Better than America | Top 5 Best British Baddies', *Hotcorn.com*, 18/10/2020, https://hotcorn.com/en/movies/news/top-5-best-british-villains-movies/; 'Evil Brit', *TVtropes.org*, https://tvtropes.org/pmwiki/pmwiki.php/Main/EvilBrit; '10 films about the ugly face of the British empire', 28/06/2018, *Dmovies.org*, https://www.dmovies.org/2018/06/28/top-10-films-atrocities-british-empire/; Vincent Flood, 'Hollywood, and the enduring British villain', *Screen Robot*, 09/07/2019, https://screenrobot.com/hollywood-enduring-british-villain/.

93  Home, *Of Planting and Planning*, p. 17.

94  Sarah Cheang takes up the theme, writing that 'in many respects, the nineteenth-century dog fancy represented a microcosm of the broader issues at stake in

Victorian society . . . Dogs were remade culturally with imagined pasts and assumed correlations between form and function, and the best dogs were thought to be those with high-class, purebred ancestries.' Victorian ideas of race, culture and hierarchy were built into dog breeding and dog shows. Cheang proffers the example of Pekingese dogs. 'The Pekingese was constructed as capable of race memory, with some aficionados claiming that Pekingese dogs reared in Britain disliked thunderstorms because they actually remembered tropical typhoons or that tawny pekes would not mate with pekes of other colors because the dogs themselves were conscious that yellow was the sacred color of the Chinese emperor and empress. This colonial nostalgia, projected onto the animals, enabled an array of incredible assertions to be indulged within an orientalist fantasy of exotic palaces and silk-clad mandarins . . . given the importance of notions of human selective breeding and racial purity, and the essentialist class and race hierarchies that underscored eugenicist projects at home and colonial projects abroad, it was considered only natural for a Chinese palace dog to exhibit what was thought to be aristocratic Chinese behavior as an innate or instinctive aspect of its breeding . . . Through the use of authenticating stories, objects, and people, fantasies of China were produced through the agency of upper-class women who were able to shape "China" in Britain, even as their male relatives – army officers, diplomats, and traders – were attempting to shape China abroad. In this process, possession of the most favored dog of a fading Chinese Imperial household was used to signify the victory of Western imperialism in China and also the high social and imperial status of Pekingese dog owners.' See Meg Daley Olmert, 'Genes unleashed: how the Victorians engineered our dogs', *Nature*, 16/10/2018, https://www.nature.com/articles/d41586-018-07039-z; Helen Cowie, 'Michael Worboys, Julie-Marie Strange, and Neil Pemberton, *The Invention of the Modern Dog: Breed and Blood in Victorian Britain*', *American Historical Review* 2021, 126:2, pp.855–6; Sarah Cheang, 'Women, Pets, and Imperialism: The British Pekingese Dog and Nostalgia for Old China', *Journal of British Studies*, 45:2, pp. 359–87, https://www.cambridge.org/core/journals/journal-of-british-studies/article/abs/women-pets-and-imperialism-the-british-pekingese-dog-and-nostalgia-for-old-china/DE527C14F5805999402ACC870519FE91; Linda Kalof and Georgina M. Montgomery (eds.), *Making Animal Meaning (The Animal Turn)*, Michigan State University Press, 2011, pp. 113–25; W. Gordon Stables, *The Practical Kennel Guide: With Plain Instructions How to Rear and Breed Dogs for Pleasure, Show, and Profit*, Cassell Petter & Galpin, 1877.

## Chapter 1: *The Civilized Island*

1 Matthew Parker, *The Sugar Barons: Family, Corruption, Empire and War*, Windmill Books, 2012, p. 259.

2 Hilary McD. Beckles, *The First Black Slave Society: Britain's 'Barbarity Time' in Barbados, 1636–1876*, University of the West Indies Press, 2016, p. xi.

3 Parker, *The Sugar Barons*, pp. 13, 62–3.

4 Peter Frankopan explains: 'Sugar plantations were created in the Atlantic on Madeira, the Canary Islands and São Tomé before being introduced by the Flemish and Dutch to Brazil and to one island of the Caribbean after another; it spread further, as production later took off in Louisiana and above all in Cuba, which by the nineteenth century was the most productive sugar island in the world.' See Beckles, *The First Black Slave Society*, p. xiii; Mark Cartwright, 'The Portuguese Colonization of São Tomé and Principe', *World History Encyclopedia*, 28/05/2021, https://www.worldhistory.org/article/1763/the-portuguese-colonization-of-sao-tome-and-princi/; Peter Frankopan, *The Earth Transformed: An Untold Story*, Bloomsbury, 2023, p. 341.

5 https://twitter.com/aljhlester/status/1671173980999368705 and this highly illuminating episode of William Dalrymple and Anita Anand's *Empire* podcast, 'Royal African Company: Slavery Inc', 06/06/2023, https://open.spotify.com/episode/3Ya8NXoDAXZkQ62dOyLRDM?si=0e0f295e32334b7c.

6 Frankopan, *The Earth Transformed*, p. 356; Beckles, *The First Black Slave Society*, p. 30.

7 Jonathan Kennedy, *Pathogenesis: How Germs Made History*, Torva, 2023, p. 159; Frankopan, *The Earth Transformed*, p. 353.

8 Parker, *The Sugar Barons*, p. 360.

9 Beckles, *The First Black Slave Society*, p. 5.

10 The phrase 'colony of a colony' seems to originate from Peter Wood, *Black Majority: Negroes in Colonial South Carolina from 1670 through the Stono Rebellion*, Knopf, 1974.

11 Beckles, *The First Black Slave Society*, p. 78.

12 'A professional soldier . . . reported being horrified in the West Indies in 1816 at the sight of a white woman in the slave market examining the genitals of male slaves "with all possible indelicacy".' Beckles, *The First Black Slave Society*, pp. 77, 81, 82.

13 Melanie Newton, ' "The Children of Africa in the Colonies": Free People of Colour in Barbados during the Emancipation Era, 1816–1854', University of Oxford, DPhil. thesis, 2001, p. 64.

14 Beckles, *The First Black Slave Society*, p. 145.

15  Hilary McD. Beckles, *Britain's Black Debt*, University of the West Indies Press, 2013, p. 110.

16  Parker, *The Sugar Barons*, p. 259.

17  Ibid., p. 260.

18  Ibid., pp. 259–60.

19  Beckles, *The First Black Slave Society*, p. 176.

20  Robert Mendick, 'A year after becoming a republic, Barbados pursues damages for sins of its colonial past', *Telegraph*, 25/11/2022, https://www.telegraph.co.uk/news/2022/11/25/year-becoming-republic-barbados-pursues-damages-sins-colonial/.

21  Parker, *The Sugar Barons*, pp. 263–4.

22  Ibid., p. 364.

23  Beckles, *Britain's Black Debt*, pp. 61–2.

24  Ibid., p. 63; Parker, *The Sugar Barons*, p. 159.

25  Parker, *The Sugar Barons*, p. 268.

26  Ibid., p. 267.

27  Ibid.

28  Ibid.

29  Beckles, *Britain's Black Debt*, p. 3.

30  James Robins, 'Can Historians Be Traumatized by History?', *New Republic*, 16/02/2021, https://newrepublic.com/article/161127/can-historians-traumatized-history.

31  Ibid.

32  Parker, *The Sugar Barons*, pp. 62, 269.

33  Mendick, 'A year after becoming a republic'.

34  Paul Lashmar and Jonathan Smith, 'He's the MP with the Downton Abbey lifestyle. But the shadow of slavery hangs over the gilded life of Richard Drax', *Observer*, 12/12/2020, www.theguardian.com/world/2020/dec/12/hes-the-mp-with-the-downton-abbey-lifestyle-but-the-shadow-of-slavery-hangs-over-the-gilded-life-of-richard-drax; Parker, *The Sugar Barons*, pp. 62–3, 123.

35  Beckles, *The First Black Slave Society*, p. xiv.

36  Parker, *The Sugar Barons*, p. 34.

37  Ibid., p. 359.

38  'Barbados – Home of Many Windmills', *Barbados.org*, https://barbados.org/windmill.htm#.YtlVjHbMKUk.

39  Jordan Buchanan Smith, 'The Invention of Rum', PhD thesis, Georgetown University, 2018, https://repository.library.georgetown.edu/handle/10822/1050790; 'Rum: liquor', *Britannica*, https://www.britannica.com/topic/rum-liquor; Beckles, *Britain's Black Debt*, p. 89.

40  Philip Whitehead, who has run the plantation for nearly four decades, was recently quoted in the *Daily Telegraph* remarking: 'To me it's crazy they have

vilified Richard Drax. It's not right. Of course no one can condone slavery in any form. But back in the 1600s slavery was not viewed as it is now. We know it's a crime now but it wasn't looked at like that then.' See Mendick, 'A year after becoming a republic'; Parker, *The Sugar Barons*, p. 361.

41 As Niall Ferguson points out, it often gets forgotten that the Caribbean was much more valuable to Britain than the American colonies were: in the seventeenth century, nearly 70 per cent of British emigrants headed for the West Indies to chase the cash, with British–Caribbean trade far outweighing British–American trade, and the sugar trade far outweighing the trade in tobacco. 'For most of the eighteenth century, the American colonies were little more than economic subsidiaries of the sugar islands, supplying them with the basic food-stuffs their monoculture could not produce . . . The problem was that mortality on these tropical islands was fearful, particularly during the summer "sickly season". In Virginia it took a total immigration of 116,000 to produce a settler community of 90,000. In Barbados, by contrast, it took immigration of 150,000 to produce a population of 20,000. People soon learned. After 1700 emigration to the Caribbean slumped as people opted for the more temperate climes (and more plentiful land) of America.' Ferguson, *Empire*, pp. 72–3.

42 Parker, *The Sugar Barons*, p. 123.

43 Richard Godwin, 'Roll with the rum punches in Barbados', *The Times*, 15/01/2022, https://www.thetimes.co.uk/article/roll-with-the-rum-punches-in-barbados-m333dxb6g.

44 Ibid.

45 Parker, *The Sugar Barons*, pp. 265–7, and 'George Washington House', *Barbados. org*, https://barbados.org/george_washington.htm#.Yt GJR 3bMKUk.

46 Thomas Harding, *White Debt: The Demerara Uprising and Britain's Legacy of Slavery*, Weidenfeld & Nicolson, 2022, pp. 115, 127–8, 135.

47 Sathnam Sanghera, 'Alex Renton on exposing transatlantic slave traders – in his own family', *The Times*, 30/04/2021, https://www.thetimes.co.uk/article/alex-renton-my-relatives-the-slave-owners-o88cdgfnw.

48 Alex Renton, *Blood Legacy: Reckoning with a Family's Story of Slavery*, Canongate Books, 2021, pp. 93–4, 316–18; Sanghera, 'Alex Renton on exposing transatlantic slave traders – in his own family'.

49 'Who We Are', *Caricom*, https://caricom.org/our-community/who-we-are/.

50 Will Pavia, 'Caribbean nations to seek $33trn in slavery reparations', *The Times*, 12 September 2023.

51 https://shorturl.at/epDE9.

52 Alison Flood, ' "Imperially nostalgic racists" target Empireland author with hate mail', *Guardian*, 12/03/2021, https://www.theguardian.com/books/2021/mar/12/imperially-nostalgic-racists-target-empireland-author-with-hate-mail.

53  'Toni Morrison at Portland State, May 30, 1975', *Mackenzian*, https://www.mac
kenzian.com/wp-content/uploads/2014/07/Transcript_PortlandState_TMorrison
.pdf, p. 7.

54  William Dalrymple and Anita Anand, 'Queen Elizabeth II & Empire (with David
Olusoga)', *Empire* podcast, 13/09/2022, https://open.spotify.com/episode/5fvid
V68X1ddQrNLfdJOaz?si=879ddc1fb23f4c18&nd=1.

55  Renton, *Blood Legacy*, pp. 88–92.

56  Ibid., p. 306.

57  Beckles, *Britain's Black Debt*, p. 4.

58  Maxine Berg and Pat Hudson, *Slavery, Capitalism and the Industrial Revolution*,
Polity, 2023; Stephan Heblich, Stephen J. Redding and Hans-Joachim Voth,
'Slavery and the British Industrial Revolution', Working Paper 30451, National
Bureau of Economic Research, Cambridge, Mass., 2022, http://www.nber.org/
papers/w30451.

59  Siddhartha Mukherjee, *The Gene: An Intimate History*, Vintage, 2017, pp. 392–4.

60  Lisa Jewell and Randall Robinson, *The Debt: What America Owes Blacks*, Penguin
Books, 2000; Joy DeGruy, a clinical psychologist, authored *Post Traumatic Slave
Syndrome: America's Legacy of Enduring Injury and Healing*, Joy DeGruy Publica-
tions, 2017; Jacquelyn Clemons, 'Black Families Have Inherited Trauma, But We
Can Change That', *Healthline*, 26/08/2020, https://www.healthline.com/health/
parenting/epigenetics-and-the-black-experience; GHFP, 'Trauma of slavery
and epigenetics', *Healing the Wounds of Slavery*, 15/10/2018, https://shorturl.at/
KMOS2.

61  Beckles, *Britain's Black Debt*, p. 169.

62  Yeo also put into context the increasingly common claim that the greater incidence
of Type 2 diabetes and obesity in South Asians can be explained as a response to
colonial famines. The *Huffington Post* recently claimed that millions of Indians died
as a result of famine during the Raj, and quoted Dr Mubin Syed, a radiologist from
Ohio who also works in vascular and obesity medicine, arguing that South Asians
have a tendency to generate and store fat and not burn it off because they are 'star-
vation-adapted'. The argument goes that surviving just one famine doubles the risk
of diabetes and obesity in the next generation, and the fact that some recent generations of Indians have survived thirty-one famines or more makes them particularly
prone to illness. 'Exposure to even one famine has a multi-generational effect of
causing metabolic disorders including diabetes, hyperglycemia and cardiovascular
diseases,' said Dr Syed. In response Yeo tells me: 'the argument that South Asians
are "starvation adapted" is an attempt to provide an explanation for a biological
phenomenon. The answer is we don't know, but the timeline looks a little short for
that to have happened. The most recent examples of such adaptations have probably come from the Polynesians, as they colonized the South Pacific. This happened

over a period of a couple of thousand years.' Giles Yeo adds: 'What *is* true is that colonialism, then latterly globalisation, brought about huge changes in diet, some for better, some for worse. This has resulted in an upward shift in bodyweight throughout the world. Those who can't store as much fat safely, such as south Asians, then bear the brunt of getting type 2 diabetes and other metabolic conditions.' Faima Bakar, 'How History Still Weighs Heavy on South Asian Bodies Today', *Huffington Post*, 14/03/2022, https://www.huffingtonpost.co.uk/entry/south-asian-health-colonial-history_uk_620e74fee4b055057aac0e9f.

63  Paul Lashmar and Jonathan Smith, 'Barbados plans to make Tory MP pay reparations for family's slave past', *Guardian*, 26/11/2022, https://www.theguardian.com/world/2022/nov/26/barbados-tory-mp-pay-reparations-family-slave-richard-drax-caribbean-sugar-plantation.

64  Joshua Nevett, 'Richard Drax: Jamaica eyes slavery reparations from Tory MP', *BBC News*, 30/11/2022, https://www.bbc.co.uk/news/uk-politics-63799222.

65  Mendick, 'A year after becoming a republic'.

66  Ibid.

67  Of the Slavery Abolition Act's sixty-six paragraphs, thirty-seven were devoted to the financial arrangements for compensating owners of the enslaved. See Kris Manjapra, *Black Ghost of Empire: The Long Death of Slavery and the Failure of Emancipation*, Scribner, 2022, pp. 98–9.

68  The duration of the apprenticeship scheme varied according to individual colonies. The Emancipation Bill came into force in August 1834. The Act set six years as a maximum length of apprenticeship, but allowed individual colonial governments to decide if they wanted to opt for a shorter term. Antigua gave immediate freedom. The problems with the apprenticeship scheme led to its early abandonment. The length of apprenticeship also depended on the status of the formerly enslaved: for those who had previously worked in the fields (praedials) it was six years, for skilled workers and domestics (non-praedials) it was four years. See https://shorturl.at/jnHLR; https://shorturl.at/MN248; Beckles, *The First Black Slave Society*, pp. 211–27.

69  Manjapra, *Black Ghost of Empire*, pp. 98–9, 109; Hugh Tinker, *A New System of Slavery: The Export of Indian Labour Overseas, 1830–1920*, Hansib Publishing, 1993, pp. 16–17; Beckles, *The First Black Slave Society*, pp. 211–27.

70  Manjapra, *Black Ghost of Empire*, pp. 100–101.

71  Beckles, *The First Black Slave Society*, pp. 217–18.

72  Ibid., p. 218.

73  Ibid., p. 219.

74  Jo N. Hays, *Epidemics and Pandemics: Their Impacts on Human History*, ABC Clio, 2005, p. 230.

75  The Ellis Castle, Ruby and Graeme Hall plantations were owned by non-whites. See Hilary Beckles, *Great House Rules: Landless Emancipation and Workers' Protest 1838–1938*, Ian Randle Publishers, 2004, p. 58.

76  Beckles, *The First Black Slave Society*, p. 219.

77  Beckles, *Great House Rules*, p. 137.

78  Renton, *Blood Legacy*, p. 306.

79  Ibid., pp. 5, 317.

80  Lucile H. Brockway, *Science and Colonial Expansion: The Role of the British Royal Botanic Gardens*, Yale University Press, 2002, p. 31.

81  Parker, *The Sugar Barons*, p. 363.

82  It's often forgotten that Britain repealed the Corn Laws in the same year as it abolished preferential sugar duties – the acts were passed by different governments (Peel's ministry collapsed in the summer) – but it was all part of the same movement, and West Indian workers were the ones who suffered most. See Keally McBride, *Mr. Mothercountry: The Man Who Made the Rule of Law*, Oxford University Press, 2016, pp. 94–5.

83  Erika Rappaport, *A Thirst for Empire: How Tea Shaped the Modern World*, Princeton University Press, 2017, p. 12.

84  Parker, *The Sugar Barons*, p. 363.

85  Beckles, *The First Black Slave Society*, p. 52.

86  Parker, *The Sugar Barons*, p. 363.

87  Frankopan, *The Earth Transformed*, pp. 383–4.

88  The acclaimed British economic historian Professor Sir Roderick Floud recently took on the claim made by a reader of the *Guardian* that his ancestors who 'worked in the mills and factories of Lancashire . . . in the most appalling conditions' did not benefit from black slavery. 'Everyone in Britain and the rest of the developed world has benefited from at least 200 years of cheap tobacco, coffee, chocolate and, above all, tea and sugar, produced by slaves or indentured labourers (or, today, low-paid workers) in conditions even worse than those his forebears experienced in Manchester and Salford in the 1840s,' he wrote in a letter published by the newspaper. 'In addition, they were probably paid to make clothes out of raw cotton grown by slaves in the southern United States. The direct responsibility for slavery certainly lies with the slavers and plantation owners, including the British royal family and most of the aristocracy and merchant classes who invested in the hateful trade. But the moral responsibility has to be borne much more widely and should be in our minds whenever we buy "cheap" goods today.' See https://www.theguardian.com/world/2023/mar/15/the-fair-way-to-pay-slavery-reparations; https://www.theguardian.com/world/2023/mar/20/like-it-or-not-we-all-bear-some-responsibility-for-slavery.

89  https://twitter.com/hyfreelance/status/1555987388383596546/photo/2.

90  https://twitter.com/hyfreelance/status/1555987388383596546?t=rWzrJKDuaJN djZGw9tj3CA&s=o3.

91  Theo Usherwood, 13/07/2022, 10:38am, https://twitter.com/theousherwood/ status/1547153369273454593.

92  Explaining memes is even more awkward than explaining jokes: @historyin memes, 17/07/2022, https://www.instagram.com/p/CgHyAsZLPGx/?igshid=Y mMyMTA2M2Y=; @NoContextBrits, 21/07/2022, 9:17pm, https://twitter. com/NoContextBrits/status/1550213282883067904?t=VNiv2rBcDFq9aUj5lujiE A&s=o3.

93  Chris Ship, 'A new "Cambridge way" for future tours as William and Kate respond after Caribbean trip', *ITV News*, 28/03/2022, https://www.itv.com/ news/2022-03-28/a-new-cambridge-way-for-future-tours-as-william-and-kate-respond; Russell Myers, 'William and Kate Middleton's open-top parade branded "awful" echo of colonialist past', *Mirror*, 24/03/2022, https://www.mirror. co.uk/news/uk-news/william-kate-middletons-open-top-26552102.

94  'Of all ceremonial events, it was perhaps royal tours which had the greatest public and press prominence in colonial territories,' writes John M. MacKenzie of attitudes at the height of empire. 'These promoted rituals of visibility supposedly reflecting the mystique, global diplomatic leverage, theatrical effects and imperial marketing power of the British royal family. They embraced an endless round of ceremony, featured in the illustrations of the many commemorative books published in their wake … The major climax of these tours comes with the extensive empire tour of the Duke and Duchess of York (future George V and Queen Mary) on HMS *Ophir* in 1901, when they visited Gibraltar, Malta, Ceylon, the Straits Settlements, New Zealand, Australia, South Africa and Canada. Between mid-March and early November they covered 50,000 miles, 38,000 of them by sea. As usual, the emphasis was on the unity and loyalty of the empire …' MacKenzie, *A Cultural History of the British Empire*, pp. 66–7.

95  'Jamaica … is a country that is very proud of our history, very proud of what we have achieved, and we are moving on and we intend to attain in short order our goals and fulfil our true ambitions as an independent, developed, prosperous country.' Nadine White, 'Jamaica: government "has already begun" process of removing Queen as head of state', *Independent,* 22/03/2022, https://www.independent.co.uk/ world/jamaica-queen-head-of-state-b2041296.html; Olivia Stringer, 'William and Kate's huge tour blow as "others set to follow Jamaica's republican demands"', *Express*, 25/03/2022, https://www.express.co.uk/news/royal/1586240/ royal-news-republican-kate-middleton-prince-william-duke-duchess-cambridge-caribbean-jamai.

96  @afuahirsch, 24/03/2022, https://www.instagram.com/p/CbfxG7GKEkB/.

97  Roya Nikkhah, 'Prince William casts doubt over future leadership of the Commonwealth', *The Times*, 26/03/2022, https://www.thetimes.co.uk/article/prince-william-casts-doubt-over-future-leadership-of-the-commonwealth-nd2wx2wn5.

98  Ship, 'A new "Cambridge way" for future tours as William and Kate respond after Caribbean trip'.

99  Not long afterwards in June, the then Prince Charles called for the history of trafficking by slave traders of African people to be taught as widely as the Holocaust in Britain. According to reports, he believed the gap in Britons' knowledge had to be bridged, and he said in a speech that he was on a 'personal journey of discovery' and was continuing to 'deepen his own understanding of slavery's enduring impact'. Emily Atkinson, 'Prince Charles "wants slave trade to be taught as widely as Holocaust"', *Independent*, 26/06/2022, https://www.independent.co.uk/news/uk/home-news/prince-charles-slave-trade-holocaust-b2109517.html.

100 Pravina Rudra, 'Queen Elizabeth made us feel less embarrassed about Britishness and empire', *New Statesman*, 09/09/2022, https://www.newstatesman.com/quickfire/2022/09/queen-elizabeth-british-empire-embarrassed.

101 Steven Erlanger, 'A Global Outpouring of Grief Mixes with Criticism of the Monarchy', *New York Times*, 8/9/2022, https://www.nytimes.com/2022/09/08/world/europe/queen-elizabeth-reaction.html.

102 Ninian Wilson, 'Anti-monarchy marchers in Dublin throw coffin marked "RIP British Empire" into river', *The National*, 19/09/2022, https://www.thenational.scot/news/22313008.anti-monarchy-marchers-dublin-throw-coffin-marked-rip-british-empire-river/.

103 Bernard Lagan, 'Anti-monarchy protesters burn Australian flag on day of mourning', *The Times*, 22/09/2022, https://www.thetimes.co.uk/article/anti-monarchy-protesters-burn-australian-flag-on-day-of-mourning-pnkpbmtcd.

104 Larry Madowo, 09/09/2022, 8:12am, https://t.co/1PyK2l6vqZ.

105 Hannah Ellis-Petersen, '"There hasn't been closure": India mourns Queen but awaits apology', *Guardian*, 14/09/2022, https://www.theguardian.com/world/2022/sep/14/india-mourns-queen-elizabeth-apology-commonwealth.

106 Maya Jasanoff, 'Mourn the Queen, Not her Empire', *New York Times*, 08/09/2022, https://www.nytimes.com/2022/09/08/opinion/queen-empire-decolonization.html?smtyp=cur&smid=tw-nytimes.

107 Nile Gardiner, 18/09/2022, 1:53pm, https://twitter.com/NileGardiner/status/1571482566942724096.

108 Ian Cobain, 'Revealed: the bonfire of papers at the end of Empire', *Guardian*, 29/11/2013, https://www.theguardian.com/uk-news/2013/nov/29/revealed-bonfire-papers-empire.

109 Manjapra, *Black Ghost of Empire*, p. 72.

110 Troy S. Floyd, *The Columbian Dynasty in the Caribbean, 1492–1526*, University of New Mexico Press, 1973, p. 97, cited by Beckles, *Britain's Black Debt*, p. 41.

111 Beckles, *Britain's Black Debt*, p. 42; Michael Taylor, 'The Manchester Guardian: The Limits of Liberalism in the Kingdom of Cotton', *Guardian*, 29/03/2023, https://shorturl.at/qyEFW.

112 When the contract was eventually sold to the South Sea Company for £7.5 million, Queen Anne retained over 20 per cent of the stock. Corinne Fowler, *Thread Reader*, https://threadreaderapp.com/thread/1505483656000946176.html.

113 Beckles, *Britain's Black Debt*, p. 44.

114 Trevor Burnard, 'As a historian of slavery, I know just how much the royal family has to answer for in Jamaica', *Guardian*, 25/03/2022, https://www.theguardian.com/commentisfree/2022/mar/25/slavery-royal-family-jamaica-ducke-duchess-cambridge-caribbean-slave-trade.

115 Corinne Fowler, *Green Unpleasant Land: Creative Responses to Rural England's Colonial Connections*, Peepal Tree, 2020, p. 33.

116 Beckles, *Britain's Black Debt*, pp. 122–3, and *The First Black Slave Society*, p. 199.

117 David Olusoga and Afua Hirsch spoke about the royal family's intense involvement in slavery on the *Harry & Meghan* documentary series aired by Netflix. 'Who dreamed that Britain would have a black princess?' asked Olusoga, connecting the couple's mixed-race relationship to the history of British empire. 'It was a conclusion to a history that was so improbable as to be astonishing.' Meanwhile, Hirsch observed that 'the first ever commercial slave voyage conducted by the British was financed by Queen Elizabeth I. It continued being financed by kings and queens right up to its abolition.' Olusoga added that he had hoped that the entry of a person of colour into the royal family would offer a way into confronting difficult questions about empire, but had been disappointed. https://www.netflix.com/gb/title/81439256, Episode 3. 4¢20²; Sathnam Sanghera, 'David Harewood on racism, prejudice and Covid's victims in ethnic communities', *The Times*, 26/02/2021, https://www.thetimes.co.uk/article/david-harewood-on-racism-prejudice-and-covid-s-victims-in-ethnic-communities-x55qns9gf.

118 *The Daily Show*, 17/09/2022, https://twitter.com/TheDailyShow/status/1570911281497915392?t=WzNIQCo-Zt4cdoGfk3EU9Q&s=03.

119 Dalrymple and Anand, 'Queen Elizabeth II & Empire (with David Olusoga)'.

120 Jenny S. Martinez, 'The Anti-Slavery Movement and the Rise of International Non-Governmental Organizations', in Dinah Shelton (ed.), *The Oxford Handbook of International Human Rights Law*, Oxford University Press, 2013, pp. 222–49.

121 Derek Peterson points out that 'reformers seeking to limit working hours, improve factory conditions, and magnify workers' political voice found in the

figure of the slave a useful means of illuminating the inhumanity that industrial capitalism was cultivating in Britain'. He continues: 'This political strategy was widely adopted in the early 1830s, when campaigners working for the Ten Hours Bill borrowed freely from abolitionist discourse . . . A banner commonly carried in working-class rallies depicted a deformed white man with the inscription Am I Not a Man and a Brother? Josiah Wedgwood's famous icon of the supplicant slave gave working-class men and women a means of highlighting the inhumanity of factory labor.' See Derek R. Peterson (ed.), *Abolitionism and Imperialism in Britain, Africa, and the Atlantic*, Ohio University Press, 2010, pp. 15–16.

122   Martinez, 'The Anti-Slavery Movement and the Rise of International Non-Governmental Organizations', pp. 225–6; Moira Ferguson, *Subject to Others: British Women Writers and Colonial Slavery, 1670–1834*, Routledge, 1992, pp. 3–6; Antoinette M. Burton, 'The White Woman's Burden: British Feminists and the Indian Woman, 1865–1915', *Women's Studies International Forum* 1990, 13:4, pp. 295–308; Antoinette M. Burton, *Burdens of History: British Feminists, Indian Women, and Imperial Culture, 1865–1915*, University of North Carolina Press, 1994; https://www.guernicamag.com/sara-ahmed-the-personal-is-institutional/; Lila Abu-Lughod, *Do Muslim Women Need Saving?*, Harvard University Press, 2013.

123   Anti-Slavery International is 'the organizational successor of early organizations that grew out of the British and Foreign Anti-Slavery Society that was formed in 1839 by British abolitionist Thomas Clarkson and others, and had ties to the 1823 Anti-Slavery Society'. See Martinez, 'The Anti-Slavery Movement and the Rise of International Non-Governmental Organizations', pp. 225–6.

124   Though this is an area of considerable debate, with Samuel Moyn dismissing the relationship between human rights and abolitionism and Michael Barnett, after distinguishing between human rights and humanitarianism, arguing that abolition only led to the latter. Martinez, 'The Anti-Slavery Movement and the Rise of International Non-Governmental Organizations', pp. 225, 248; William Mulligan and Maurice Bric (eds.), *A Global History of Anti-Slavery Politics in the Nineteenth Century*, Palgrave Macmillan UK, 2013, pp. 5–6.

125   In a seminal work on the subject, Wilhelm Grewe refers to the years 1815–1919 as the 'British Era' of international law. Others have seen Britain's efforts to uphold international restrictions, particularly a ban on piracy and the slave trade, as the forerunners of strong international norms, including the seeds of human rights law. In *Rage for Order* Benton and Ford note: 'Continuities with imperial law also show up in food policy debates before the World Trade Organization that echo arguments presented by British policy makers in the late nineteenth century to justify standing by while famines took the lives of millions of Indians . . . More broadly, when international actors engage in debates today about when and under what conditions humanitarian intervention is permissible, or when they dispute the legalities of "small wars", they do so using language and categories

elaborated within the British global order.' See Lauren Benton and Lisa Ford, *Rage for Order: The British Empire and the Origins of International Law, 1800–1850,* Harvard University Press, 2016, pp. 20, 191–2.

126 'For the architects of empire in the late nineteenth and in the twentieth centuries, it was the abolitionist project that made Britain uniquely qualified to govern its African subjects,' explains Derek Peterson. William Mulligan adds that 'the abolition of slavery was rooted in a civilizing mission that was bound up with and perhaps fatally compromised by its association with imperial expansion.' See Peterson (ed.), *Abolitionism and Imperialism in Britain, Africa, and the Atlantic,* p. 6; Mulligan and Bric (eds.), *A Global History of Anti-Slavery Politics in the Nineteenth Century,* pp. 5–6.

127 See Catherine Hall's essay 'Missionary Stories: Gender and Ethnicity in England in the 1830s and 1840s', in her collection *White, Male and Middle Class: Explorations in Feminism and History,* Polity Press, 2013, pp. 205–10; Michael Bundock, *The Fortunes of Francis Barber: The True Story of the Jamaican Slave Who Became Samuel Johnson's Heir,* Yale University Press, 2015, p. 109.

128 Richard Huzzey, *Freedom Burning: Anti-Slavery and Empire in Victorian Britain,* Cornell University Press, 2012, p. 175.

## Chapter 2: Useful Plants

1 Jayeeta Sharma, 'British science, Chinese skill and Assam tea: making empire's garden', *Indian Economic and Social History Review* 2006, 43:4, p. 453.

2 Needless to say, Kew Gardens has become yet another locus of tension in the imperial culture wars, with a public battle raging between those who want Kew to acknowledge its colonial role and those who would rather it didn't. As ever with these things, the warring parties, like squabbling children, blame one another for starting it, but from where I stand its roots lie in Kew Gardens releasing its new strategy – a ten-year manifesto for change – in the shadow of the Black Lives Matter protests. It declared an aim to engage in open dialogue about its imperial and colonial past, which might seem like a logical thing to do, given that it proudly advertised its colonial role while it was involved in colonialism and given the open imperial racism of some botanists at the time. Nevertheless, shortly after its release, Kew's Manifesto – which contained a pledge to 'decolonise' the garden's collections – caught the attention of Tory M P Sir John Hayes, who complained that it represented 'preposterous posturing by people who are so out of touch with the sentiment of patriotic Britain'. Initially, Kew's Director, Richard Deverell, seemed to defend the initiative, saying that staying silent on issues of race could be seen as complicity. But later he told the *Daily Telegraph* in

an interview that Kew had found the word 'decolonise' 'unhelpful' and that 'you're not going to read anything, I think, that is critical of Kew's, or indeed British history'. As I've argued many times, this is no way to approach history of any kind: we should seek to understand historical events through the prism of real evidence, not treat them like a beloved grandmother who needs to be shielded from insult or attack. But, with Kew reliant on the government for some of its funding, maybe he had no choice. Or perhaps the more generous take is that he realized it wasn't a battle he needed to embark on so publicly: Kew seems to be quietly continuing with its decolonizing efforts without making a fuss about them. Kew has since published its 'History, Equity and Inclusion' report by a working group formed to do this and which is on its website with a clear list of actions by sector. And I can't help noticing that Kew currently has strong relations with leading imperial historians in the UK and overseas, and has recently been associated with two acclaimed books that fully engage with its colonial history (*Just the Tonic*; *Palace of Palms*). It has more than a dozen PhD students hard at work mining primary sources on broadly historical topics, and hosted a conference on Botany, Trade and Empire in 2021. Just like the National Trust, Historic England and the Royal Botanic Garden of Edinburgh, which recently published its 'Racial Justice Report 2022', it's work they appear to take seriously. See Nazia Parveen, 'Kew Gardens director hits back at claims it is "growing woke"', *Guardian*, 18/03/2021, https://www.theguardian.com/science/2021/mar/18/kew-gardens-director-hits-back-at-claims-it-is-growing-woke; Daniel Capurro, 'We are not trashing history, says Kew chief', *Telegraph*, 14/01/2022, https://www.telegraph.co.uk/news/2022/01/14/kew-gardens-change-wont-decolonising/; Ursula Buchan, 'Has Kew Gardens Really Climbed Down after Criticism over its "Decolonisation of Science" Policy?', *History Reclaimed*, 03/02/2022, https://historyreclaimed.co.uk/has-kew-gardens-really-climbed-down-after-criticism-over-its-decolonisation-of-science-policy/; Luke Keogh, *The Wardian Case: How a Simple Box Moved Plants and Changed the World*, University of Chicago Press, 2020, p. 175.

3   Parker, *The Sugar Barons*, p. 10.

4   Robert S. Anderson, Richard H. Grove and Karis Hiebert, *Islands, Forests and Gardens in the Caribbean: Conservation and Conflict in Environmental History*, Macmillan Caribbean, 2006, p. 141.

5   Parker, *The Sugar Barons*, pp. 143, 259. 'According to one clergyman in Barbados in the 1730s, "the face of the earth appeared, as it were, a dry crust, burnt up and gaping", while a contemporary noted that "excessive drought, the number of people running off, and the miserable condition and poverty" of an island that had been the source of colossal fortunes only a century before now meant that famine and disaster seemed inevitable ... Plantation agriculture in the

Caribbean opened up other environmental hazards too. These included destructive landslides that were dangerous to workers and damaging to ecosystems. Rampant deforestation did not only have implications for soil run-off but magnified the threat posed by hurricanes because of the removal of trees that served as natural protection for animal and plant life alike.' Frankopan, *The Earth Transformed*, p. 377.

6    Brockway, *Science and Colonial Expansion*, pp. 31–2; J. H. Galloway, 'Botany in the Service of Empire: The Barbados Cane-Breeding Program and the Revival of the Caribbean Sugar Industry, 1880s–1930s', *Annals of the Association of American Geographers* 1996, 86:4, pp. 682–706.

7    Galloway, 'Botany in the Service of Empire', p. 682.

8    Ibid., p. 687.

9    Ibid., p. 692. Today, Barbados continues to supply the Caribbean with new varieties of sugar cane via the West Indies Central Sugar Cane Breeding Station, an institution which grew out of the imperial project and which is now financed by an array of governments in the Caribbean and Central and South America. 'West Indies Central Sugar Cane Breeding Station', *Cane Breeding Station*, https://www.canebreedingstation.com/our-team/. John Redman Bovell recently featured on one of Barbados' banknotes.

10    Mark Nesbitt, 'Trade and Exploration', in David Mabberley (ed.), *A Cultural History of Plants in the Nineteenth Century*, Bloomsbury, 2022, pp. 67–84.

11    Kate Teltscher, *Palace of Palms: Tropical Dreams and the Making of Kew*, Picador, 2020; Caroline Donald, 'Why the Palm House at Kew is still a palace of exotic wonders after all these years', *Telegraph*, 25/07/2020, https://www.telegraph.co.uk/gardening/gardens-to-visit/palm-house-kew-still-palace-exotic-wonders-years/.

12    Teltscher, *Palace of Palms*, pp. 230, 232.

13    https://www.kew.org/kew-gardens/whats-in-the-gardens/marianne-north-gallery.

14    Queen Victoria introduced the Kentia palm into many of her residences, which inspired many Brits to do the same, and the houseplant remains a mundane legacy of British empire in many homes today. In 1897 Rudyard Kipling wrote the poem 'Recessional' in honour of Queen Victoria's Diamond Jubilee. It would subsequently be set to music and sung as a hymn across empire, and opens with the lines: 'God of our fathers, known of old, / Lord of our far-flung battle-line, / Beneath whose awful hand we hold / Dominion over palm and pine.' See Teltscher, *Palace of Palms*, pp. 302–3.

15    Chelsea Ritschel, 'The reasons why palm oil is so controversial', *Independent*, 12/10/2020, https://www.independent.co.uk/life-style/palm-oil-health-impact-environment-animals-deforestation-heart-a8505521.html.

16    Jonathan E. Robins, *Oil Palm: A Global History*, University of North Carolina

Press, 2021; Martin Lynn, *Commerce and Economic Change in West Africa: The Palm Oil Trade in the Nineteenth Century*, Cambridge University Press, 2002; Janice Henderson and Daphne J. Osborne, 'The oil palm in all our lives: how this came about', *Endeavour* 2000, 24:2, pp. 63–8.

17  'Elites fretting about disease and the moral character of the urban poor made soap into a leading "Victorian Fetish",' writes Jonathan E. Robins. 'Advertisers often used racist caricatures of Africans to sell soap, depicting black children turning white after a good scrubbing. And soap figured prominently in accounts of Britain's "civilizing" work in Africa.' Robins, *Oil Palm*, p. 78.

18  Ibid., pp. 78, 83, 217–45, 254; Lynn, *Commerce and Economic Change in West Africa*, p. 83.

19  Max Siollun, *What Britain Did to Nigeria: A Short History of Conquest and Rule*, Hurst, 2021, p. 48.

20  Sharma, 'British science, Chinese skill and Assam tea', p. 430.

21  A history textbook from the 1930s talked about how the territories of empire depended on one another economically. 'We began by saying that once upon a time men in this country provided themselves with almost everything that they wanted. Nowadays we get much of what we want from overseas. A great many of the things come from different parts of the empire. There are, for instance, meat from New Zealand, wheat for flour from Canada, wool from Australia, tea from Ceylon, fruit from South Africa, and so on. We could easily make a long list of the things in our own homes which were sent to us by men living in the empire.' See John M. MacKenzie, *Propaganda and Empire: The Manipulation of British Public Opinion, 1880–1960*, Manchester University Press, 1984, pp. 188–9.

22  Kerry Lotzof, 'Joseph Banks: scientist, explorer and botanist', *Natural History Museum*, https://www.nhm.ac.uk/discover/joseph-banks-scientist-explorer-botanist.html.

23  It was a significantly greater fortune than North inherited. Banks was nothing less than one of the wealthiest men in England.

24  'There were . . . professional precedents predating Banks's involvement with the Cook voyage. The British Museum had taken on Daniel Solander (Banks's assistant on the *Endeavour*) as a paid naturalist and curator as early as 1763.' See Richard H. Grove, *Green Imperialism: Colonial Expansion, Tropical Island Edens and the Origins of Environmentalism, 1600–1860*, Cambridge University Press, 1995, p. 312.

25  Andrew Wulf, *The Brother Gardeners: Botany, Empire and the Birth of an Obsession*, Windmill Books, 2009, pp. 219–20; 'Sir Joseph Banks', *Britannica*, https://www.britannica.com/biography/Joseph-Banks.

26  As the National Museum Australia explains, 'Botany Bay wasn't James Cook's first choice of name for the bay. He first named it "Sting Ray Harbour". On 6 May

1770, Cook changed the name in his journal. First to "Botanist's Bay", before settling on "Botany Bay" because of the "great quantity of new plants . . . collected by Mr Banks and Dr Solander"': https://www.nma.gov.au/exhibitions/endeavour-voyage/kamay-botany-bay/settling-on-a-name#:~:text= Botany%20Bay%20 wasn't%20James,great%20quantity%20of%20new%20plants%20%E2%80%A6.

27  Wulf, *The Brother Gardeners*, p. 208.

28  https://australian.museum/learn/first-nations/unsettled/recognising-invasions/plans-for-a-colony/.

29  Fowler, *Green Unpleasant Land*, pp. 233–4.

30  https://www.rmg.co.uk/stories/topics/mutiny-on-bounty.

31  B. W. Higman, *Jamaican Food: History, Biology, Culture*, University of the West Indies Press, 2009, p. 149; Fowler, *Green Unpleasant Land*, p. 233.

32  On Hooker's expedition to the Himalayas, the imperial dimension becomes even more explicit when you take into account the fact that the Rajah of Sikkim imprisoned him and a companion because they had ventured into his territory without permission, setting in train a series of events which led to the annexation of Sikkim.

33  Hooker introduced some twenty-five species of rhododendrons and helped to create the Victorian craze for them. From Kew, seedlings were sent to Scotland, Wales, Ireland and Cornwall and the plant then spread to Europe and North America. They can still be seen at Kew, in the Lost Gardens of Heligan in Cornwall and at Castle Howard in Yorkshire. The new Sikkim rhododendrons were also hybridized with other species. See Richard Milne, *Rhododendron*, Reaktion, 2014, ch. 3, https://www.pure.ed.ac.uk/ws/portalfiles/portal/126022575/Rhododendron_ext_002_.pdf.

34  It was, for a brief period, called the Kew Museum of Vegetable Products.

35  Teltscher, *Palace of Palms*, pp. 240–41.

36  'Mark Nesbitt', *Royal Botanic Gardens Kew*, https://www.kew.org/science/our-science/people/mark-nesbitt.

37  Mark Nesbitt and Caroline Cornish, 'Seeds of Industry and Empire: Economic Botany Collections between Nature and Culture', *Journal of Museum Ethnography* 2016, 29, p. 61.

38  Ibid., p. 56.

39  'History and curation of economic botany collections', *Royal Botanic Gardens Kew*, https://www.kew.org/science/our-science/projects/history-curation-economic-botany-collections.

40  Keogh, *The Wardian Case*, p. 94; Brockway, *Science and Colonial Expansion*, pp. 103–33.

41  Katharina Weingartner, '"The Fever": Questioning Malaria Management as a Colonial Legacy', *Development* 2020, 63, p. 312.

42   Randall M. Packard, *The Making of a Tropical Disease: A Short History of Malaria*, Johns Hopkins University Press, 2007.

43   Ibid., p. 4.

44   Ibid., p. 54.

45   Ibid., p. 87.

46   Kennedy, *Pathogenesis*, pp. 178–87.

47   Kim Walker and Mark Nesbitt, *Just the Tonic: A Natural History of Tonic Water*, Kew Publishing, 2019, pp. 84–7, 91–3, 101–2.

48   Keogh, *The Wardian Case*, p. 95.

49   Cited in ibid., p. 146.

50   Brockway, *Science and Colonial Expansion*, p. 113.

51   Keogh, *The Wardian Case*, p. 96.

52   Walker and Nesbitt, *Just the Tonic*, pp. 52–3.

53   Keogh, *The Wardian Case*, pp. 101–2.

54   Arjo Roersch van der Hoogte and Toine Pieters, 'Science in the service of colonial agro-industrialism: The case of cinchona cultivation in the Dutch and British East Indies, 1852–1900', *Studies in History and Philosophy of Science Part C: Studies in History and Philosophy of Biological and Biomedical Sciences* 2014, 47:A, pp. 12–22; Walker and Nesbitt, *Just the Tonic*, pp. 52–3.

55   'Until the inter-war period and the advent of synthetic anti-malarials, the only cure was quinine,' writes Patricia Barton. 'Despite an increasing number of government schemes devised at both provincial and central level to distribute quinine in higher quantities to more people', it is estimated that in 1938, in the United Provinces, a historical area in India, now the state of Uttar Pradesh, the average treatment per patient was 22.5 grains at a time when the prescribed dose was 30 grains per day for at least one week. 'Even the combined Indian production and imports failed to meet the needs of malaria patients in India . . . only 10 per cent of malaria sufferers were being treated by the mid-1930s . . . even the combined annual world production of cinchona would [have been] insufficient to meet Indian demand.' See Patricia Barton, '"The Great Quinine Fraud": Legality Issues in the "Non-Narcotic" Drug Trade in British India', *Social History of Alcohol and Drugs* 2007, 22:1, pp. 8–10.

56   'In the nineteenth century many chemists attempted to synthesise quinine, which would enable its manufacture in factories without the need to harvest bark. In 1856, eighteen-year-old William Henry Perkin attempted it using coal tar. He failed, but noticed that the resulting mixture was a deep purple. He was astute enough to experiment with his failed sludge to see if it would dye fast to cloth. It did, and he became the accidental inventor of the first synthetic aniline dye, mauveine. Before this, purple dye was only obtainable from expensive natural sources. The results led to an explosion in demand for purple clothing,

previously only available to the highest classes in society, termed "mauve madness" or, in *Punch* magazine, "mauve measles".' See Walker and Nesbitt, *Just the Tonic*, p. 46.

57  'During the early nineteenth century the political situation in South America became unstable, as nations asserted their independence from Spain,' write Walker and Nesbitt. 'In 1844, Bolivia brought in measures to control cinchona harvesting but failed to pay workers proper wages and a black market in barks arose. European empires urgently desired better control over quantity, quality and price [of cinchona], and expressed concerns over sustainability that were perhaps an early form of "greenwash" to hide their desire for direct control of such an essential medical resource.' Walker and Nesbitt, *Just the Tonic*, p. 41.

58  Ibid., p. 57.

59  Brockway, *Science and Colonial Expansion*, pp. 141–65; Keogh, *The Wardian Case*, pp. 153–7; Ghillean Prance and Mark Nesbitt (eds.), *The Cultural History of Plants*, Routledge, 2005, pp. 338–9.

60  '100 years on – the unsolved mystery of the rubber boom slaves', *Survival International*, 01/08/2011, https://www.survivalinternational.org/news/7541; Tom Peck, 'The mystery of the missing Amazonian rubber slaves', *Independent*, 02/08/2011, https://www.independent.co.uk/news/world/americas/the-mystery-of-the-missing-amazonian-rubber-slaves-2330280.html.

61  Initially, it was not profitable to cultivate rubber in Ceylon; tea was the more profitable crop, and land was devoted to the cultivation of tea rather than rubber. The variety of rubber (Ceará) first cultivated was not best suited to soil and climatic conditions in Ceylon, and did not yield much latex. But towards the end of the century, tea prices fell and rubber prices rose. Also, a new variety of rubber (Pará) was introduced that was better suited to the environment and higher yielding. Rubber cultivation took off in Ceylon around 1904. See Roland Wenzlhuemer, *From Coffee to Tea Cultivation in Ceylon, 1880–1900*, Brill, 2008, pp. 96–8.

62  Lucile Brockway points out that 'nineteenth-century European colonial expansion was characterized by both competition and cooperation among the powers. The Dutch from their botanic garden on Java engaged in parallel activities of plant transfer and development . . . sometimes competing with the British, sometimes cooperating with them, and in the end, fixing the market through cartel agreements. The French copied British and Dutch plantation methods in their rubber industry in Indochina.' Brockway, *Science and Colonial Expansion*, p. 8.

63  Ibid., p. 142.

64  Natalie Aster, 'Natural vs. Synthetic Rubber: Key Market Trends & Statistics', *Market Publishers*, 31/07/2018, https://marketpublishers.com/lists/23821/news.html.

65   James Hagan and Andrew Wells, 'The British and rubber in Malaya, c1890–1940', *University of Wollongong Faculty of Arts*, 2005, https://ro.uow.edu.au/cgi/viewcontent.cgi?referer=&httpsredir=1&article=2648&context=artspapers.

66   See 'Malayan Emergency', National Army Museum, https://www.nam.ac.uk/explore/malayan-emergency. Souchou Yao, *The Malayan Emergency: Essays on a Small, Distant War*, N I A S Press, 2016, p. 42, https://www.diva-portal.org/smash/get/diva2:1379592/FULLTEXT01.pdf.

67   Caroline Elkins, *Legacy of Violence: A History of the British Empire*, Bodley Head, 2022, p. 501

68   Ibid., pp. 491–508.

69   Mark Townsend, 'Revealed: how Britain tried to legitimise Batang Kali massacre', *Guardian*, 06/05/2012, https://www.theguardian.com/world/2012/may/06/britain-batang-kali-massacre-malaysia.

70   Brockway, *Science and Colonial Expansion*, p. 143.

71   Data from the International Rubber Study Group based in Singapore shows that the Asia-Pacific region dominates both production and consumption of natural rubber. Total world production of natural rubber in 2022 was led by Thailand, followed by Indonesia and Vietnam. Other large producers include India, China and the Cambodia–Myanmar–Laos region. Malaysia is now the eighth largest producer in the world. Sir Henry Wickham's seeds, once germinated at Kew, were shipped to British territories overseas. As the International Rubber Study Group explains it, the first viable seedlings arrived in Sri Lanka in 1876. In 1876 and 1877 seedlings were shipped to other countries in South-east Asia that had suitable climates, including the modern countries of Malaysia, Singapore and Indonesia. From Malaysia, rubber plantations arrived in Thailand in the early 1900s. Singapore became a major centre of the rubber trade in the inter-war period. See W. G. Huff, 'The Development of the Rubber Market in Pre-World War II Singapore', *Journal of Southeast Asian Studies* 1993, 24:2, pp. 285–306; 'Natural Rubber Market – Growth, Trends, C O V I D-19 Impact, and Forecasts (2023–2028)', *Mordor Intelligence*; Global Industry Analysts, 'Global Industry Analysts Predicts the World Industrial Rubber Products Market to Reach $136.5 Billion by 2026', *C I S I O N PR Newswire*, 24/03/2022 https://shorturl.at/ovLQ2.

72   Fowler, *Green Unpleasant Land*, p. 257; Staffan Müller-Wille, 'Carolus Linnaeus', *Britannica*, https://www.britannica.com/biography/Carolus-Linnaeus; Subhadra Das and Miranda Lowe, 'Nature Read in Black and White: Decolonial Approaches to Interpreting Natural History Collections', *Journal of Natural Science Collections*, 6, pp. 4–14.

73   Keogh, *The Wardian Case*, pp. 86–94; Brockway, *Science and Colonial Expansion*, pp. 27–8.

74   Sharma, 'British science, Chinese skill and Assam tea', p. 432.

75  Luke Keogh, *The Wardian Case*, pp. 89–92.

76  Sharma, 'British science, Chinese skill and Assam tea', p. 434.

77  Ibid., pp. 441–2.

78  Nesbitt, 'Trade and Exploration', p. 82.

79  Sharma, 'British science, Chinese skill and Assam tea', p. 442.

80  Rappaport, *A Thirst for Empire*, pp. 86–8.

81  Ibid., pp. 86–7.

82  'It needs to be considered why an entire decade went by before a local discovery could be assimilated into the official tea quest,' writes Jayeeta Sharma. 'Apart from reporting on the jungles where the tea grew, these experts were already seeking means to "improve" the plant. In their view, Nature's bounty, bestowed upon these otherwise unproductive domains, could only be of full use once it was subjected to the civilising influence of China, the original home of tea. [A British expert] proclaimed that the indigenous plant in Assam was unacceptably savage. As he saw it, the most important measure for the new tea enterprise was the importation of Chinese seeds of unexceptional quality, and of small numbers of the finest sorts of tea plant . . . in England, tea, obtained from the awe-inspiring Celestial Empire . . . had come to signify refinement and luxury in the flourishing bourgeois world of consumption. But the "savage" native product of Assam, it was feared, would not suit the refined London palate, which, for the present, the East India Company saw as its best customer . . . [It was a Chinese] hybrid that served as the plant of choice for the plantations established by the Assam Company and other entrepreneurs. Only in the 1880s was this plant finally abandoned in favour of the indigenous [Indian] variety. It is tempting to see the growing discomfort with mixed race in British imperial discourses, or the opposition to white colonisation in the tropics, as mirrored in the distaste evinced by the later generation of English planter for the tea hybrid. In a fascinating turnaround, the Assam plant [eventually won] praise for its "robustness and vigour", so well suited for the cruder palate of the British working classes, while the hybrid was condemned for its effeminacy and artificiality.' Sharma, 'British science, Chinese skill and Assam tea', pp. 437–43.

83  Keogh, *The Wardian Case*, p. 92.

84  Sharma, 'British science, Chinese skill and Assam tea', pp. 429–30.

85  'Top 10 Tea Producing Countries in the World 2021', *Farrer's Tea & Coffee Merchants*, 02/06/2023, https://farrerscoffee.co.uk/blogs/blog/top-10-tea-producing-countries-in-the-world-2021.

86  Rappaport, *A Thirst for Empire*, pp. 207–13.

87  Matthew Adams, 'Book review: Erika Rappaport's *A Thirst for Empire: How Tea Shaped the Modern World*', *Arts & Culture*, 05/08/2017, https://shorturl.at/ghmr5.

88  The Young Queen Victoria gushed about the tea's 'quality and flavour', saying she was 'extremely pleased', and predicted that 'this Experiment' would 'have a major influence over the prosperity of the British empire in the East'. Rappaport, *A Thirst for Empire*, p. 85.

89  Ibid., p. 8.

90  'Decades before Coca-Cola refreshed the world or McDonald's served fast food to millions, tea growers combined propaganda, politics, and ideas derived from pre-existing consumer and commercial cultures to create tea drinkers in places as diverse as Glasgow, Cincinnati, and Calcutta.' Ibid., p. 9.

91  The development of the imperial press, explains John M. Mackenzie, 'was dependent on the development of agencies as the prime means for the collection and dissemination of news, a service ideally suited to the operations of the electric telegraph and international cables. The most celebrated was Reuters, founded by Paul Julius Reuter, a migrant from Germany via France after the European revolutionary activity of 1848. Arriving in Britain in 1851, Reuter started a telegram company and a news service for the banking and financial sector. In 1858 this attracted its first newspaper client and thereafter built up a major international network serving British colonial papers.' MacKenzie, *A Cultural History of the British Empire*, p. 251.

92  Daniel R. Headrick explains in *The Tools of Empire* that the art of sending electrical signals through networks of telegraph wires and submarine cables proved difficult to master. The ocean's depths were unknown until the 1860s, and the science of sending electrical impulses hundreds of miles away was in its infancy. The Hooghly River in Calcutta was crossed by a cable installed there in 1839, which appears to be the earliest instance of underwater telegraphy. But it wasn't until 1843 that a reliable insulating substance was found. This was gutta-percha, a natural plastic made from the sap of a Malayan tree. 'In 1850, John and Jacob Brett laid a cable across the English Channel. It was made of a single strand of copper wire coated with gutta-percha. A few hours after its debut, a fisherman's anchor broke it. The next year another cable was laid alongside the first. This one was made of four copper wires insulated with gutta-percha, sheathed with iron wire, and then wrapped in jute and coated again with pitch; thus protected, it worked well into the next century. Two years later, in 1852, a cable linked England and Ireland. Submarine telegraphy was born.' Investors became overly excited about how this technology might change the world and what followed echoed what would happen in the dot-com bubble of the 1990s: if a cable could span the Channel, the fevered thinking went, then cable could also span the Atlantic Ocean. Dwayne Winseck describes how submarine telegraph systems and telegraph news – the global media of their era – ended up being a feature of the global financial crisis of 1873. While new cables from Britain to South

America, and from Australia to New Zealand, opened in the mid-1870s, the bubble had burst, and the industry did little more than tick over for the next ten years. Nevertheless, the technology did, as Headrick tells it, eventually transform human communications. 'The first cable to India, which cost £800,000, never transmitted a single message . . . There followed a rush to install submarine cables . . . In the 1870s, after the triumph of the cables to America and India, there emerged a powerful submarine cable industry . . . By the 1890s there were several cables to Canada and Australia. The missing link was a cable from British Columbia to New Zealand . . . In 1902 this line was completed, and all parts of the British Empire could henceforth communicate by a cable network upon which the sun never set. Cables were an essential part of the new imperialism.' Headrick adds in *The Tentacles of Empire* that the effects were profound: in the early nineteenth century it could take eight months for a letter to make it from Britain to India, and the writer would not expect to receive a reply in less than two years; even with the emergence of steamships, letters would take six weeks to get to India, or to get from India to Britain. Incredibly, contemporary communication, in the digital age, still depends on a global network of physical cables lying under the sea. The Shetland Islands recently lost internet and telephone services after a cable that connected it to the mainland was cut, and news reports conveyed the fact that many modern cables follow the routes of cables laid down in the imperial age. As the *Sunday Times* explained, about 97 per cent of the world's internet traffic travels through 'a million-mile network of wires under the sea', and as 'every millisecond is money', 'sending signals across the ocean floor is done by the shortest route possible. For this reason, they tend to follow the paths first laid down a hundred years ago.' See Daniel R. Headrick, *The Tools of Empire: Technology and European Imperialism in the Nineteenth Century*, Oxford University Press, 1981, pp. 157–63; Daniel R. Headrick, *The Tentacles of Empire*, Oxford University Press, 1988, p. 97; Dwayne Winseck, 'Submarine Telegraphs, Telegraph News, and the Global Financial Crisis of 1873', *Journal of Cultural Economy* 2012, 5:2, pp. 197–212; Tom Calver, Jack Clover, Michael Keith and Venetia Menzies, 'The ties that bind: how we rely on a fragile network of undersea cables', *Sunday Times*, 30/10/2022.

93  John Tully, 'A Victorian Ecological Disaster: Imperialism, the Telegraph, and Gutta-Percha', *Journal of World History* 2009, 20:4, pp. 559–79.

94  A German agricultural scientist called Dr Hindorf, working for the German East African Company, thought that sisal might be successfully grown in the part of East Africa now known as Tanzania, which the Germans had controlled since the late nineteenth century, and his hunch was correct. Sisal was a big hit for the German East Africa Company, and came to supplant Ceará rubber, a dry-adapted rubber species, as their most profitable crop. Then, following the First World

War, the British were granted all of Germany's colonial sisal plantations; the colony was named Tanganyika, and subsequently renamed Tanzania. A few years ago Tanzania became the world's second largest producer of sisal, after Brazil. Benjamin E. Sawe, 'Top Sisal Producing Countries in the World', *WorldAtlas*, 15/04/2017, https://www.worldatlas.com/articles/top-sisal-producing-countries-in-the-world.html; Brockway, *Science and Colonial Expansion*, pp. 168–82.

95  Brockway, *Science and Colonial Expansion*, p. 58.

96  Ibid., pp. 144–5.

97  Some of this injustice is being confronted. In the summer of 2022, the descendants of the hunter-gatherers who discovered rooibos tea received their first share of the multimillion-pound profits. Long considered a local 'poor man's drink', the tea was first brewed for its health benefits thousands of years ago by the Khoi and San people in what is now South Africa. A payment of 12.2 million rand (£610,000) from South Africa's rooibos tea industry to the indigenous communities was the first tranche of a deal that took years to hammer out, and, in future, an annual levy of 1.5 per cent of the tea's 'farm-gate price' should be paid into a trust controlled by the Khoi and San. In a separate case in 2022, unresolved at the time of writing, Kenyan tribes sued the UK government over allegations of historic crimes including land theft, eviction and torture in the Kericho region of western Kenya, famous for its tea, between 1902 and 1962. The Talai and Kipsigis have gone to the European Court of Human Rights to ask for compensation of £168 billion along with an apology, while UN experts have expressed concern that there has been no accountability for the violation of the human rights of over half a million people from the area during British rule. Their allegations detail the forced expulsion of their people from favoured land in the Rift Valley in order to create tea plantations, and the subsequent detention of some tribe members in terrible conditions near Lake Victoria, resulting in many deaths. Following Kenya's independence in 1963, surviving tribe members returned to their homelands but never reclaimed them, instead residing in flimsy accommodation beside the tea estates. 'Today, some of the world's most prosperous tea companies, like Unilever, Williamson Tea, Finlay's and Lipton, occupy and farm these lands and continue to use them to generate considerable profits,' said the plaintiffs. Kenya exports more black tea than anywhere else in the world. See Jane Flanagan, 'Tribes win payout from South African tea industry over rights to rooibos', *The Times*, 14/07/2022, https://www.thetimes.co.uk/article/tribes-win-payout-from-south-african-tea-industry-over-rights-to-rooibos-2zlcsmw96; 'Kenyan group sues UK government over what it calls colonial-era land theft', *Reuters*, 23/08/2022, https://www.reuters.com/world/africa/kenyan-group-sues-uk-government-over-what-it-calls-colonial-era-land-theft-2022-08-23/; Nazia Parveen, 'How Kenyans are seeking amends for British

tea steeped in "stolen lands"', *Guardian*, 02/12/2019, https://www.theguardian.com/global-development/2019/dec/02/kenyas-dispossessed-seek-redress-for-britains-colonial-injustices; Brockway, *Science and Colonial Expansion*, p. 109; 'History of Indian Tea', *Indian Tea Association*, https://www.indiatea.org/history_of_indian_tea; Rappaport, *A Thirst for Empire*, pp. 3–7, 86–7, 92–3.

98  Alfred W. Crosby, *The Columbian Exchange: Biological and Cultural Consequences of 1492*, Praeger, 2003.

99  Judith A. Carney and Richard Rosomoff, *In the Shadow of Slavery: Africa's Botanical Legacy in the Atlantic World*, University of California Press, 2011.

100  Crosby, *The Columbian Exchange*, cited in Fowler, *Green Unpleasant Land*, p. 249. Fowler also points out an intriguing legacy of empire in Britain: the non-regimented approach taken by West Indian tenants in their allotment gardening, as opposed to the traditional British habit of planting vegetables in segregated rows. 'Mixed plantings were rooted in African gardening practices, and, as more recent expertise in raised-bed gardening has shown, these help to avoid insect-borne and other plant diseases' (p. 243).

101  The vital importance of indigenous knowledge and its exploitation by the West has recently been acknowledged by Alex Antonelli, Director of Science at Kew. In an opinion piece for *Nature*, Antonelli calls for scientists 'to re-evaluate their fundamental assumptions, and re-examine how they work with partners across cultures and power structures'. He argues that nothing less than the world's future food security depends on indigenous knowledge. Alexandre Antonelli, 'Indigenous knowledge is key to sustainable food systems', *Nature* 2023, 613, 239–42, https://www.nature.com/articles/d41586-023-00021-4.

102  For more, see Hortense Le Ferrand and Abbas Bacha, 'Discovery and Rediscovery of Gutta Percha, a Natural Thermoplastic', *MRS Bulletin* 2021, 46, pp. 84–5.

103  Mark Nesbitt, 'Botany in Victorian Jamaica', in Tim Barringer and Wayne Modest (eds.), *Victorian Jamaica*, Duke University Press, 2018, p. 236.

104  Ibid.

105  Roderick Floud, *An Economic History of the English Garden*, Penguin Books, 2020, p. 56.

106  The story is told beautifully by Wulf in *The Brother Gardeners*.

107  Converting prices to their 2019 equivalents, Floud found that in 1775 a nursery in York sold a rhododendron, either from the Appalachian Mountains or from Asia, for £1,142. Another nurseryman, William Thompson, sold a swamp magnolia imported from the American South for £736. Trees could fetch huge sums. In 1734 Frederick, the Prince of Wales, wanting to fill his new garden at Carlton House, bought a 25-foot-tall tulip tree (*Liriodendron tulipifera*) for the price of £38,120 – the most expensive tree in a list of plants sold by the nursery

of Robert Furber in London. See Floud, *An Economic History of the English Garden*, pp. 56–7; Nesbitt, 'Trade and Exploration', p. 82.

108  Keogh, *The Wardian Case*, p. 1.

109  Ibid., pp. 138–9.

110  Ibid., pp. 142–3.

111  Ibid., p. 143.

112  Ibid., pp. 142, 182.

113  Dunne, cited by ibid., p. 201.

114  Ibid., p. 208.

115  Ibid.

116  Clive Cookson, 'Biodiversity body warns of $423bn annual hit from "invasive alien species"', *Financial Times*, 04/09/2023, https://shorturl.at/fBM37.

117  'The prickly pear story', *The State of Queensland Department of Agriculture and Fisheries*, 2020, https://www.daf.qld.gov.au/__data/assets/pdf_file/0014/55301/prickly-pear-story.pdf.

118  Phil Lambdon and Quentin Cronk, 'Extinction Dynamics under Extreme Conservation Threat: The Flora of St Helena', *Front. Ecol. Evol.* 2020, 8:41, pp. 1–10, https://doi.org/10.3389/fevo.2020.00041; Quentin Cronk, 'The Past and Present Vegetation of St Helena', *Journal of Biogeography* 1989, 16:1, pp. 47–64; Grove, *Green Imperialism*, pp. 96–125.

119  Anuradha Varanasi, 'How Colonialism Spawned and Continues to Exacerbate the Climate Crisis', *State of the Planet*, 21/09/2020, https://news.climate.columbia.edu/2022/09/21/how-colonialism-spawned-and-continues-to-exacerbate-the-climate-crisis/.

120  Ibid.

121  Daniel Macmillen Voskoboynik, 'To fix the climate crisis, we must face up to our imperial past', *Open Democracy*, 8/10/2018, https://www.opendemocracy.net/en/opendemocracyuk/to-fix-climate-crisis-we-must-acknowledge-our-imperial-past/.

122  Fowler states that the Jamaican mahogany forests were so 'depleted' by the 1740s that 'the English had to import their timber from elsewhere in the Americas'. See Fowler, *Green Unpleasant Land*, p. 31; https://www.jstor.org/stable/23546503.

123  Grove, *Green Imperialism*, pp. 386, 388, 441, 388.

124  Ibid., p. 389.

125  'Back in the 19th century, the British Raj built alliances with local elites in order to secure its rule,' wrote Raza. 'In exchange for their loyalty, the Raj turned representative chiefs into unrepresentative aristocrats, granting them magisterial powers, a paramilitary apparatus and immense landed estates (jagirs) on newly irrigated land. The relationship set off a mutually beneficial pillaging of the region, whereby the British Raj and the now-landed aristocrats siphoned off rents, land revenues, and export cash crops like indigo, opium and cotton, all at

the expense of previously pastoral tribesmen now forced to settle and toil as local farmers. Combined with expanding canal irrigation, tribesmen's coerced settlement and exploitation – the British viewed seasonally migrating tribes as a security threat – left them further exposed to floods.' See Shozab Raza, 'Flooding has devastated Pakistan – and Britain's imperial legacy has made it worse', *Guardian*, 31/08/2022, https://www.theguardian.com/commentisfree/2022/aug/31/flooding-pakistan-britains-imperial-legacy.

126   L. Parsons, R. Safra de Campos, A. Moncaster, I. Cook, T. Siddiqui, C. Abenayake, A. Jayasinghe, P. Mishra, L. Scungio and T. Billah, *Disaster Trade: The Hidden Footprint of UK Production Overseas*, Royal Holloway, University of London, 2021, p. 22.

127   Ibid., p. 80. Parsons et al. continue: 'Although the relationship between landslides and tea plantations is widely noted . . . it is nowhere more in evidence than Sri Lanka . . . According to historical data, the "first eight decades of the 19th century recorded only six major landslide events in Sri Lanka, but the two decades since 1981 have registered five major occurrences of landslides": a trend which has accelerated in recent years. Whilst Sri Lanka experienced an average of less than 50 annual landslides up to 2002, this number has since rapidly increased . . . ever since British colonisers first introduced tea to the Sri Lankan highlands in 1839, the region's endemic hazards have been structured increasingly by the products that are grown and traded there.'

128   Damien Gayle, 'Climate emergency is a legacy of colonialism, says Greenpeace UK', *Guardian*, 21/07/2022, https://www.theguardian.com/environment/2022/jul/21/climate-emergency-is-a-legacy-of-colonialism-says-greenpeace-uk.

129   Amitav Ghosh, *The Nutmeg's Curse: Parables for a Planet in Crisis*, University of Chicago Press, 2021.

130   Hannah Ellis-Petersen, 'Amitav Ghosh: European colonialism helped create a planet in crisis, Indian author says', *Guardian*, 14/01/2022, https://www.theguardian.com/books/2022/jan/14/amitav-ghosh-european-colonialism-helped-create-a-planet-in-crisis. 'Why has this crisis come about?' Ghosh recently asked out loud. 'Because for two centuries, European colonists tore across the world, viewing nature and land as something inert to be conquered and consumed without limits and the indigenous people as savages whose knowledge of nature was worthless and who needed to be erased. It was this settler colonial worldview – of just accumulate, accumulate, accumulate, consume, consume, consume – that has got us where we are now.'

131   'Present development challenges causing high vulnerability are influenced by historical and ongoing patterns of inequity such as colonialism, especially for many Indigenous peoples and local communities,' the IPCC report said. 'Officials and scientists from around the globe now recognize the significant role colonialism

has played in heating our planet and destroying its many gifts.' See Varanasi, 'How Colonialism Spawned and Continues to Exacerbate the Climate Crisis'.

132    Grove, *Green Imperialism*, pp. 446–7. The Balfour paper was 'On the Influence Exercised by Trees on the Climate of a Country' in the *Madras Journal of Literature and Science*, 1840, reprinted in 1849.

133    Grove, *Green Imperialism*, pp. 469–70; J. S. Wilson, 'On the general and gradual desiccation of the earth and atmosphere', *Proceedings of the British Association for the Advancement of Science, Transactions*, 1858.

134    Frankopan, *The Earth Transformed*, p. 450.

135    Anil Agarwal and Sunita Narain, 'Global Warming in an Unequal World: A Case of Environmental Colonialism', in Navroz K. Dubash (ed.), *India in a Warming World: Integrating Climate Change and Development*, Oxford University Press, 2019, pp. 81–91; Gayle, 'Climate emergency is a legacy of colonialism, says Greenpeace UK'; Macmillen Voskoboynik, 'To fix the climate crisis, we must face up to our imperial past'; Chermaine Lee, 'Understanding Climate Colonialism', *Fair Planet*, 14/08/2022, https://www.fairplanet.org/story/understanding-climate-colonialism/; Harriet Mercer, 'The link between colonialism and climate change examined', *The Week*, 25/04/2022, https://www.theweek.co.uk/news/environment/956530/the-link-between-colonialism-and-climate-change-examined; Harriet Mercer, 'Colonialism: why leading climate scientists have finally acknowledged its link with climate change', *The Conversation*, 22/04/2022, https://theconversation.com/colonialism-why-leading-climate-scientists-have-finally-acknowledged-its-link-with-climate-change-181642; Martin Mahony and Georgina Endfield, 'Climate and Colonialism', *University of East Anglia Prints*, https://ueaeprints.uea.ac.uk/id/eprint/65708/4/Climate_Colonialism_pre_print.pdf; Deniss Martinez and Ans Irfan, 'Colonialism, the climate crisis, and the need to center Indigenous voices', *Environmental Health News*, 04/11/2021, https://www.ehn.org/indigenous-people-and-climate-change-2655479728.html; David M. Driesen, 'Review: Colonialism's Climate?', *International Studies Review* 2007, 9:3, pp. 484–6; Vanessa Nakate, 'African nations can't "adapt" to the climate crisis. Here's what rich countries must do', *Guardian*, 08/11/2022, https://www.theguardian.com/commentisfree/2022/nov/08/rich-countries-climate-crisis-cop27-africa-loss-and-damage; 'Barbados PM hails "loss and damage" addition to climate agenda at Cop27 – video', *Guardian*, 08/11/2022, https://www.theguardian.com/environment/video/2022/nov/08/barbados-pm-hails-loss-damage-addition-climate-agenda-cop27-video?utm_term=Autofeed&CMP=twt_b-gdnnews&utm_medium=Social&utm_source=Twitter#Echobox=1667931135; Varanasi, 'How Colonialism Spawned and Continues to Exacerbate the Climate Crisis'; Yessenia Funes, 'Yes, Colonialism Caused Climate Change, IPCC Reports', *Atmos*, 04/04/2022, https://atmos.earth/ipcc-report-colonialism-climate-change/; John Letzing and Minji Sung, 'What does colonialism have to do with

climate change?', *World Economic Forum*, 09/09/2022, https://www.weforum.org/agenda/2022/09/colonialism-climate-change-pakistan-floods/; '"A form of colonialism": Activists demand climate reparations', *Al Jazeera*, 25/09/2022, https://www.aljazeera.com/news/2022/9/25/why-are-climate-activists-calling-for-reparations; 'Climate Colonialism', *Oxford Talks*, 25/01/2021, https://talks.ox.ac.uk/talks/id/48b2c915-3965-496e-8dc0-ade137f218cb/.

136 Nakate, 'African nations can't "adapt" to the climate crisis'.

137 Parsons et al., *Disaster Trade*, pp. 98–100.

138 Grove, *Green Imperialism*, p. 486.

139 Ibid., pp. 474–5.

140 Ibid., p. 472.

141 Frankopan, *The Earth Transformed*, p. 466.

142 Guillaume Blanc continues: 'There are around 350 national parks in Africa, and in most of them, local populations have been driven out in favour of either animals, forests or savannas . . . Over the course of the twentieth century, at least a million people have been driven out of protected zones in Africa . . . These environmental policies were devised by Europeans during the period of colonization. And, since independence, they have been implemented by individual African states. The leaders of these states . . . systematically bow to any orders imposed by the international conservation institutions. Behind every incident of social injustice imposed on those living in natural environments throughout Africa, the presence of UNESCO, the WWF, the IUCN [International Union for Conservation of Nature] or Flora & Fauna International (FFI) is never far away.' Meanwhile, the 'Our Land, Our Nature' conferences have recently seen 'Indigenous and non-Indigenous activists, representatives and speakers from around 18 countries' share 'evidence and first-hand testimonies of racist conservation atrocities and land theft, as well as presented an alternative model that respects human rights and the environment'. Guillaume Blanc, *The Invention of Green Colonialism*, Wiley, 2022, pp. 1, 11–12; https://www.ourlandournature.org/; https://shop.survivalinternational.org/collections/books/products/decolonize-conservation-global-voices-for-indigenous-self-determination-land-and-a-world-in-common-book?s=03.

143 Keogh, *The Wardian Case*, p. 7.

144 Frankopan, *The Earth Transformed*, p. 486.

145 Brockway, *Science and Colonial Expansion*, p. 118.

146 Keogh, *The Wardian Case*, pp. 96–8.

147 Ibid., p. 100.

## Chapter 3: Phenomenal People Exporters

1   'The legacy of Indian migration to European colonies', *Economist*, 02/09/2017, https://www.economist.com/international/2017/09/02/the-legacy-of-indian-migration-to-european-colonies.

2   Franco-Mauritians own an estimated 36 per cent of the total land, which is mainly agricultural. See Tijo Salverda and Iain Hay, 'Change, anxiety and exclusion in the post-colonial reconfiguration of Franco-Mauritian elite geographies', *Geographical Journal* 2014, 180:3, pp. 236–45 at 244 n. 6.

3   Larry Wells Bowman, 'Mauritius', *Britannica*, https://www.britannica.com/place/Mauritius/The-arts-and-cultural-institutions.

4   'The legacy of Indian migration to European colonies'.

5   Joseph Cotterill, 'Reforms in Mauritius hint at discontent over ethnic representation', *Financial Times,* 30/10/2018, https://www.ft.com/content/cd36800a-cb1b-11e8-8d0b-a6539b949662.

6   Figure from Aapravasi Ghat.

7   Annick Lutchmeenaraidoo, 06/10/2021, https://www.facebook.com/photo.php?fbid=4588700667862125&set=p.4588700667862125&type=3.

8   'Very grand houses were also a characteristic of Indian colonial cities,' writes John M. MacKenzie. 'Calcutta famously became the "City of Palaces" with major residences in Chowringhee Road and elsewhere. Moreover, around Calcutta there were mansions which symbolised the interpenetration of the rural and the urban in the manner in which they were used as weekend retreats, as the residences of zamindars (the feudal landowners underpinned by the Permanent Settlement system in Bengal), Bengali elites and wealthy British businessmen and senior administrators.' See MacKenzie, *The British Empire through Buildings*, p. 173.

9   Gaiutra Bahadur, *Coolie Woman: The Odyssey of Indenture*, Hurst, 2013, p. xx.

10   Melvin Hunter, 'Racist Relics: An Ugly Blight on our Botanical Nomenclature', *Scientist,* 24/11/1991, https://www.the-scientist.com/opinion-old/racist-relics-an-ugly-blight-on-our-botanical-nomenclature-60358.

11   Bahadur, *Coolie Woman*, p. xx.

12   Horseracing being another legacy of British imperialism. 'Wherever the British went, the laying out of a racecourse was an immediate ambition and racing became an increasingly formalised activity.' MacKenzie, *A Cultural History of the British Empire*, p. 89.

13   Ashutosh Kumar, *Coolies of the Empire: Indentured Indians in the Sugar Colonies, 1830–1920*, Cambridge University Press, 2017, p. 24. There were often connections between territories that adopted indenture. As Reshaad Durgahee explains, Arthur Hamilton-Gordon was appointed Governor of Mauritius in 1871 and 'his transfer from Mauritius to become Governor of Fiji in 1875 connected the two

colonies. In Fiji he initiated the use of Indian indentured labour to support the colony's burgeoning sugar industry.' See Reshaad Durgahee, 'The Indentured Archipelago: Experiences of Indian Indentured Labour in Mauritius and Fiji, 1871–1916', PhD thesis, University of Nottingham, 2017, https://eprints.nottingham.ac.uk/44058/.

14  Kumar, *Coolies of the Empire*, p. 2.

15  Beckles, *The First Black Slave Society*, pp. 211–27; Tinker, *A New System of Slavery*, pp. 16–17.

16  Tinker, *A New System of Slavery*, p. 18.

17  Madhavi Kale, *Fragments of Empire: Capital, Slavery, and Indentured Labor Migration in the British Caribbean*, University of Pennsylvania Press, 1998, p. 61.

18  Bahadur, *Coolie Woman*, p. 179.

19  'In March 1837, John Gladstone, a representative of the West Indian Association (representing sugar planters), requested by letter a meeting with the Colonial Secretary Lord Glenelg, and Sir George Grey, his deputy,' explains an illuminating blog on the National Archives website. The letter stated: 'Unless a system of regular continuous labour is then adopted, the cultivation of the sugar cane cannot then be carried on to a productive result.' Gladstone was eager to acquire 'a supply of Hill Coolies from Bengal' on a five-year indentured labour contract. Nevertheless, less than three years later, Lord John Russell, the new Colonial Secretary, suspended the Indian indenture plan to British Guiana in response to criticism from the British and Foreign Anti-Slavery Society (BFASS), declaring 'I am not prepared to encounter the responsibility of a measure which may lead to a dreadful loss of life on the one hand, or, on the other, to a new system of slavery.' Thirty-eight of the 419 'coolies' that Gladstone's ship had landed in May 1838 had passed away, and seventy more were listed as unwell a few months later. By 1845 Gladstone was no longer involved in the Caribbean sugar business. Michael Mahoney, 'A "new system of slavery"? The British West Indies and the origins of Indian indenture', The National Archives, 03/12/2020, https://blog.nationalarchives.gov.uk/a-new-system-of-slavery-the-british-west-indies-and-the-origins-of-indian-indenture/; Kale, *Fragments of Empire*, p. 32. In Mauritius, indentured Indian workers proved cheaper than formerly enslaved people ('Creoles') as soon as the latter were 'apprenticed' in 1834. Even before they achieved full freedom from owners' control in 1838, they were being evicted from plantations and replaced by Indians. Alan Lester, Kate Boehme and Peter Mitchell, *Ruling the World: Freedom, Civilisation and Liberalism in the Nineteenth-Century British Empire*, Cambridge University Press, 2021, pp. 50–52; Kale, *Fragments of Empire*, p. 61.

20  Bahadur, *Coolie Woman*, p. 25.

21  Ibid.

22  Ibid., p. 137.

23  'The legacy of Indian migration to European colonies'.

24  Tinker, *A New System of Slavery*, p. 120.

25  M. D. North-Coombes, 'From Slavery to Indenture: Forced Labour in the Political Economy of Mauritius 1834–1867', in Kay Saunders (ed.), *Indentured Labour in the British Empire: 1834–1920*, Routledge, 1984, p. 93.

26  Daniel Workman, 'Top 10 Exports from Mauritius', *World's Top Exports*, https://www.worldstopexports.com/top-10-exports-from-mauritius/?utm_content=cmp-true.

27  Bahadur, *Coolie Woman*, p. 19.

28  Jerome S. Handler and Matthew C. Reilly, 'Contesting "White Slavery" in the Caribbean: Enslaved Africans and European Indentured Servants in Seventeenth-Century Barbados', *BRILL: New West Indian Guide*, 01/01/2017, https://brill.com/view/journals/nwig/91/1-2/article-p30_2.xml?language=en;    Richard B. Allen, 'Asian Indentured Labor in the 19th and Early 20th Century Colonial Plantation World', *Asian History*, 29/03/2017, https://oxfordre.com/asianhistory/display/10.1093/acrefore/9780190277727.001.0001/acrefore-9780190277727-e-33#acrefore-9780190277727-e-33-note-3. 'For [some] . . . early colonists in places such as Virginia and Barbados were "loose vagrant people" whose interests centred on "whoreing, thieving or other debauchery",' writes Peter Frankopan. 'Planters often saw little distinction between indentured servants who came from Europe and those shipped from Africa, with the former often being referred to as "white slaves". In some cases, enslaved African people were heavily outnumbered by indentured Europeans.' See Frankopan, *The Earth Transformed*, pp. 355–6.

29  Allen, 'Asian Indentured Labor in the 19th and Early 20th Century Colonial Plantation World'.

30  Ibid.

31  Elizabeth Kolsky, *Colonial Justice in British India: White Violence and the Rule of Law*, Cambridge University Press, 2009, pp. 142–84.

32  Clare Anderson (ed.), *A Global History of Convicts and Penal Colonies*, Bloomsbury, 2020, p. 7.

33  Until 1849, when the practice was abolished, those found guilty in Bengal and Madras were given a permanent tattoo on their forehead broadcasting their name, crime and date of sentence. See ibid., pp. 211, 216.

34  Clare Anderson explains in *A Global History of Convicts and Penal Colonies* that these transported convicts left a mark on the world in all sorts of ways. After the Anglo-Sikh Wars of the mid-nineteenth century, soldier convicts were shipped to the Straits Settlements and Burma, where they were used as prison guards in cities like Moulmein. These prisoners also constructed the Horsburgh Lighthouse, Government House (now the National Museum) and St Andrew's

Cathedral in Singapore, as well as dockyards, harbours and bunds. Indian prisoners of war in Mauritius worked on the island's citadel in Port Louis and constructed the road system to link the city to its sugar plantations. Ibid., pp. 222–5.

35  Home, *Of Planting and Planning*, p. 203; Elizabeth van Heyningen, *The Concentration Camps of the Anglo-Boer War: A Social History*, Jacana, 2013; Ferguson, *Empire*, p. 280.

36  Lester, Boehme and Mitchell, *Ruling the World*, p. 9.

37  Elkins, *Legacy of Violence*, p. 505.

38  'Malaysia Population 1950–2023', *Macrotrends*, https://www.macrotrends.net/countries/MYS/malaysia/population.

39  Elkins, *Legacy of Violence*, p. 505.

40  Ibid., p. 563.

41  Patrick Wintour, 'UN court rejects UK claim to Chagos Islands in favour of Mauritius', *Guardian*, 28/01/2021, https://www.theguardian.com/world/2021/jan/28/un-court-rejects-uk-claim-to-chagos-islands-in-favour-of-mauritius. For more, see Philippe Sands, *The Last Colony: A Tale of Exile, Justice and Britain's Colonial Legacy*, Weidenfeld & Nicolson, 2022.

42  Elkins, *Legacy of Violence*, pp. 410–41; 'Who is to blame for partition? Britain', Alex von Tunzelmann, 19/08/2017, *New York Times*.

43  'The commonly repeated statement that one-third of Bengal's population died – i.e. about 10m people – is barely credible,' writes Tim Dyson. 'Even a figure of 5m may well lie outside the plausible range. However, famine mortality and large-scale out-migration did cause significant depopulation in large parts of Bengal.' Tim Dyson, *A Population History of India: From the First Modern People to the Present Day*, Oxford University Press, 2018, pp. 79–81.

44  'Britain is responsible for deaths of 35 million Indians, says acclaimed author Shashi Tharoor', *Independent*, 13/03/2017, https://www.independent.co.uk/news/world/asia/india-35-million-deaths-britain-shashi-tharoor-british-empire-a7627041.html.

45  Dylan Sullivan and Jason Hickel, 'Capitalism and extreme poverty: A global analysis of real wages, human height, and mortality since the long 16th century', *World Development* 2023, 161. Dylan Sullivan and Jason Hickel's 'How British colonialism killed 100 million Indians in 40 years', *Al Jazeera*, 02/12/2022, claims that this 'is among the largest policy-induced mortality crises in human history. It is larger than the combined number of deaths that occurred during all famines in the Soviet Union, Maoist China, North Korea, Pol Pot's Cambodia, and Mengistu's Ethiopia.'

46  Nathan Sentance, 'Genocide in Australia', *Australian Museum*, 12/07/2022, https://australian.museum/learn/first-nations/genocide-in-australia/. The most verifiable source on massacres is the remarkable project by Lyndall Ryan to map all those for which documentary evidence can be found. You can expand the

map to get the details of every individual massacre. See 'Colonial Frontier Massacres, Australia, 1788 to 1930', The University of Newcastle, Australia, https://c21ch.newcastle.edu.au/colonialmassacres/map.php.

47 Amanda Meade, 'Sydney Morning Herald apologises for failing "dismally" on coverage of 1838 Myall Creek massacre', *Guardian,* 09/06/2023, https://www.theguardian.com/media/2023/jun/09/sydney-morning-herald-apologises-for-failing-dismally-on-coverage-of-1838-myall-creek-massacre; https://twitter.com/aljhlester/status/1667797627516207105; Sentance, 'Genocide in Australia'; Robert J. Miller, Jacinta Ruru, Larissa Behrendt and Tracey Lindberg, *Discovering Indigenous Lands: The Doctrine of Discovery in the English Colonies*, Oxford University Press, 2010, p. 175; Lorena Allam and Nick Evershed, 'Almost half the massacres of Aboriginal people were by police or other government forces, research finds', *Guardian*, 15/03/2022, https://www.theguardian.com/australia-news/2022/mar/16/almost-half-the-massacres-of-aboriginal-people-were-by-police-research-finds.

48 Ryan Lyndall, 'List of multiple killings of Aborigines in Tasmania: 1804–1835', *SciencesPo*, 05/03/2008, https://www.sciencespo.fr/mass-violence-war-massacre-resistance/fr/document/list-multiple-killings-aborigines-tasmania-1804-1835.html; Kristyn Harman, 'Explainer: the evidence for the Tasmanian genocide', *The Conversation*, 17/01/2018, https://theconversation.com/explainer-the-evidence-for-the-tasmanian-genocide-86828.

49 Beckles, *Britain's Black Debt*, pp. 24–5.

50 Jalil Sued-Badillo referenced by ibid., p. 24.

51 Ibid.

52 Ferguson, *Empire*, pp. 65–6.

53 Kennedy, *Pathogenesis*, pp. 173–4.

54 Ibid., pp. 175–6.

55 Naipaul captured the complexity of his experience in a letter in 1954: 'I certainly do not want to go back to Trinidad or any other island in the West Indies if I can help it. I very much want to go to India. However, there are many difficulties. I cannot be employed on the Indian side because I am British, and on the British side, I cannot be employed because I am not English. I think it is almost impossible for me to do anything worthwhile in this country, for reasons you doubtless know . . .' See Chandrima Karmakar, 'V. S. Naipaul: From Memory en route to Roots', https://ntm.org.in/download/ttvol/Contextualising_Migration_SpecialIssue/article%209.pdf.

56 Kale, *Fragments of Empire*, p. 2; Derek Walcott, 'Nobel Lecture: The Antilles: Fragments of Epic Memory', *The Nobel Prize*, 07/12/1992, https://www.nobelprize.org/prizes/literature/1992/walcott/lecture/.

57 Saunders, *Indentured Labour in the British Empire*.

58 'Island Delight, and the Origins of the Jamaican Pattie', *Island Delight*, https://
www.island-delight.co.uk/history-of-the-jamaican-patty/; Danny Friar, 'History of Jamaican Food', *Mas Media: Leeds Carnival Blog*, 28/02/2018, https://
leedsmasmedia.wordpress.com/2018/02/28/history-of-jamaican-food/; Lisa
Rough, 'Jamaica's Cannabis Roots: The History of Ganja on the Island', *Leafly*,
14/05/2015, https://www.leafly.com/news/lifestyle/jamaicas-roots-the-history-
of-ganja-on-the-island.

59 Kumar, *Coolies of the Empire*, pp. 27–8; Tinker, *A New System of Slavery*, p. 120.

60 'Between 1860 and 1911, 152,184 Indian indentured workers went to the then
British colony of Natal to work primarily on the sugar plantations. They were
followed by free Indian migrants. White settlers felt threatened by a settled
Indian population and passed legislation to curb their immigration, trading,
employment and residence rights. The struggle of Indians against this racist
legislation was spearheaded by Mohandas Karamchand Gandhi.' Goolam Vahed,
' "An evil thing": Gandhi and Indian Indentured Labour in South Africa, 1893–
1914', *South Asia: Journal of South Asian Studies* 2019, 42:4, pp. 654–74.

61 One of the pioneer investors in the new colony of Swan River in Western
Australia in the late 1830s was an East Indian Company trader who brought
indentured Indians with him to set up his 'run'. See Malcolm Allbrook, *Henry
Prinsep's Empire: Framing a Distant Colony*, Australian National University Press,
2014, https://www.jstor.org/stable/j.ctt13wwvzc.

62 Preston Merchant, 'Fiji's Indian Cane Cutters', *Time*, 17 September 2007, https://
content.time.com/time/photogallery/0,29307,1662439,00.html.

63 Rachel Sturman argues that 'many elements of modern attempts to establish
international labor rights and protections can be traced through . . . the official
British imperial system of Indian indentured labor . . . [it] occasioned new ideas,
among both supporters and opponents, about what constituted a legitimate and
humane labor system and about how to ensure that the humanity of such laborers would be protected. While the system remained exploitative and grounded in
both coercion and neglect, political pressure from anti-slavery activists coupled
with bureaucratic exigencies led to the institution of a modern (and in some cases
pioneering) regulatory regime that rendered the conditions of indentured life
and labor subject to a variety of new forms of scrutiny and intervention. Most
significantly, these efforts to create a legitimate system ultimately sought to protect the laborers' humanity not only by distinguishing indenture from slavery,
but by prompting a framework of laws and regulations that was oriented toward
welfare provisioning.' Rachel Sturman, 'Indian Indentured Labor and the History of International Rights Regimes', *American Historical Review* 2014, 119:5, pp.
1439–65. For an account of the ways that humanitarian attempts to protect indigenous peoples were related to those to safeguard indentured Indians see Amanda

Nettelbeck, *Indigenous Rights and Colonial Subjecthood: Protection and Reform in the Nineteenth-Century British Empire*, Cambridge University Press, 2021.

64  'The legacy of Indian migration to European colonies'.

65  Richard B. Allen, 'Re-conceptualizing the "new system of slavery"', *Man in India* 2012, 92:2, pp. 225–45; Tinker, *A New System of Slavery*, p. x.

66  Tinker, *A New System of Slavery*, pp. 121–4, 128; Kumar, *Coolies of the Empire*, p. 172.

67  Tinker, *A New System of Slavery*, p. 123.

68  The legal adviser to the Mauritius government recommended the man be sent home, and he returned to Bombay. Ibid., p. 125.

69  Ibid., pp. 130, 141, 134–5, 154.

70  Bahadur, *Coolie Woman*, p. 62.

71  Tinker, *A New System of Slavery*, p. 158.

72  Ibid., p. 197.

73  Bahadur, *Coolie Woman*, p. 83.

74  Brij V. Lal, 'Labouring Men and Nothing More: Some Problems of Indian Indenture in Fiji', in Saunders (ed.), *Indentured Labour in the British Empire*, p. 144.

75  Tinker, *A New System of Slavery*, p. 200.

76  Ibid., p. 204.

77  Ibid.

78  Bahadur, *Coolie Woman*, p. 109.

79  Ibid.

80  Tinker, *A New System of Slavery*, p. 190.

81  Kumar, *Coolies of the Empire*, p. 175.

82  Tinker, *A New System of Slavery*, p. 181.

83  Ibid., p. 183.

84  Bahadur, *Coolie Woman*, p. 26.

85  Tinker, *A New System of Slavery*, p. 191.

86  Lal, 'Labouring Men and Nothing More', p. 132.

87  Ravindra K. Jain, 'South Indian Labour in Malaya, 1840–1920: Asylum Stability and Involution', in Saunders (ed.), *Indentured Labour in the British Empire*, p. 165.

88  Alan H. Adamson, 'The Impact of Indentured Immigration on the Political Economy of British Guiana', in Saunders (ed.), *Indentured Labour in the British Empire*, p. 46.

89  Ibid.

90  Tinker, *A New System of Slavery*, pp. 191–2.

91  Harding, *White Debt*, p. 257.

92  Tinker, *A New System of Slavery*, p. 186.

93  Marianne D. Ramesar, 'Indentured Labour in Trinidad 1880–1917', in Saunders (ed.), *Indentured Labour in the British Empire*, p. 67.

94   Tinker, *A New System of Slavery*, p. 186.

95   North-Coombes, 'From Slavery to Indenture', p. 99.

96   Clare Anderson, 'The British Indian Empire', in Anderson (ed.), *A Global History of Convicts and Penal Colonies*, p. 229.

97   Tinker, *A New System of Slavery*, pp. 120–21.

98   Ibid., p. 178.

99   North-Coombes, 'From Slavery to Indenture', p. 99.

100  Ibid., p. 108.

101  Bahadur, *Coolie Woman*, p. 127.

102  Ibid., p. 163.

103  Tinker, *A New System of Slavery*, p. 5.

104  Kumar, *Coolies of the Empire*, p. 76.

105  David Eltis, 'Free and Coerced Transatlantic Migrations: Some Comparisons', *American Historical Review* 1983, 88:2, pp. 251–80; David Northrup, *Indentured Labor in the Age of Imperialism, 1834–1922*, Cambridge University Press, 1995, p. 84, cited in Kumar, *Coolies of the Empire*, p. 79.

106  Ralph Shlomowitz and John McDonald, 'Mortality of Indian Labour on Ocean Voyages, 1843–1917', *Studies in History* 1990, 6:1, pp. 35–65, cited in Kumar, *Coolies of the Empire*, p. 84.

107  Packard, *The Making of a Tropical Disease*, p. 89.

108  Tinker, *A New System of Slavery*, p. 139.

109  Ibid., p. 148.

110  Ibid., p. 150.

111  Bahadur, *Coolie Woman*, p. 57.

112  Kale, *Fragments of Empire*, pp. 90–91.

113  Lal, 'Labouring Men and Nothing More', p. 141.

114  Kale, *Fragments of Empire*, p. 7.

115  Tinker, *A New System of Slavery*, pp. 158, 165, 139.

116  Kale, *Fragments of Empire*, p. 147.

117  North-Coombes, 'From Slavery to Indenture', pp. 87–8.

118  Bahadur, *Coolie Woman*, p. 160.

119  Tinker, *A New System of Slavery*, p. 231.

120  Kumar, *Coolies of the Empire*, p. 113.

121  Bahadur, *Coolie Woman*, p. 172.

122  Kumar, *Coolies of the Empire*, p. 191.

123  Bahadur, *Coolie Woman*, pp. 68–9.

124  Kumar, *Coolies of the Empire*, p. 8.

125  Ibid., p. 11.

126  'Slave Route Monument: Le Morne, Mauritius', *Atlas Obscura*, https://www.atlasobscura.com/places/le-morne-slave-route-monument.

127   Some arrived after the British had actually officially abolished the slave trade. As the Truth and Justice Commission of Mauritius, established in 2009, explains, planters exploited the labour of so-called 'recaptives' or 'liberated slaves'. 'Following the abolition of the slave trade in the British empire in 1807, the British Government sent its Navy to seize enslaved peoples on board French and other ships. Those slaves were referred to as "liberated Africans", a misnomer as they were far from free. In effect, they were given to private employers or a Government Officer as apprentices or indentured labour for a period of up to fourteen years ... Some had been freed from slave ships illegally trading in slaves, hence the term "Liberated Africans" being applied to them. They did not benefit from the Act of Abolition of Slavery in 1833 and continued to work with their employers until their contract had expired ... In [the report of P. Salter, the Acting Collector of Customs] on Liberated Africans in Mauritius, in 1826 ... we learn that between 1813 and 1826, out of 2,998 Liberated Africans brought to Mauritius, some 291 had died even before being apprenticed. Women constituted only ¼ of them. More than 9% of the Liberated Africans died within less than a month after landing, dying of dysentery, cholera, and the small pox, as well as from severe cases of malnutrition and dehydration which prevailed on the slave vessels.' See Truth and Justice Commission, *Report of the Truth and Justice Commission*, vol. 1, Mauritius Government Printing, 2011, https://shorturl.at/oAPo5, pp. 69, 149.

128   Rosabelle Boswell, 'The Immeasurability of Racial and Mixed Identity in Mauritius', in Zarine L. Rocha and Peter J. Aspinall (eds.), *The Palgrave International Handbook of Mixed Racial and Ethnic Classification*, Palgrave Macmillan, 2020, pp. 457–78.

129   In 1838 there was a debate within the Colonial Office about whether planters should be discouraged from immediately ejecting Creoles and replacing them with indentured Indians. To do so seemed to be abandoning the former slaves whom humanitarians like Colonial Secretary James Stephen had spent so much energy trying to emancipate.

130   Cotterill, 'Reforms in Mauritius hint at discontent over ethnic representation'.

131   'People say that hundreds of slaves threw themselves off the cliff rather than face the horrors of dehumanization. There's another, even darker tale: some say that after the British passed the Slavery Abolition Act in 1834, a group of soldiers and police went to the Le Morne area to let runaway slaves know that they were finally free. But the slaves, seeing the authorities approaching, feared that they were being recaptured and returned to their masters, and climbed to the top of the mountain summit and threw themselves off committing suicide by landing in the ocean ... It should be noted that there is yet to be any archaeological evidence of the tragedy like bones found on the beach ... In 2009, Mauritius

established the Slave Route Monument as a symbol to recognize and commemo-
rate the impact and influence of slavery and the slave trade on Mauritian history. It
was part of a larger UNESCO effort officially launched in Benin in 1994 known
as the Slave Route Project, looking to have such monuments erected in countries
affected by the slave trade.' See 'Slave Route Monument: Le Morne, Mauritius'.

132 Larry Wells Bowman, 'Mauritius', *Britannica*, https://www.britannica.com/
place/Mauritius.

133 In a letter addressed to the Office of the High Commissioner for Human Rights,
the Prime Minister's Office asserted that 'it can safely be said that in Mauritius,
no person can be discriminated against by reason of his/her religion, race or
belief and if there is any attempt to do so, there are sufficient safeguards to enable
that person to denounce such discrimination and seek redress'. Affirmative
Action, *Alternative Report 2021*.

134 Adamson, 'The Impact of Indentured Immigration on the Political Economy of
British Guiana', p. 47.

135 Bahadur, *Coolie Woman*, p. 56.

136 Tinker, *A New System of Slavery*, p. 217.

137 Patrick French, *The World Is What It Is: The Authorized Biography of V. S. Naipaul*,
Picador, 2008, p. 5.

138 Adamson, 'The Impact of Indentured Immigration on the Political Economy of
British Guiana', pp. 48—9.

139 'The legacy of Indian migration to European colonies'.

140 José Moirt, *Gagner, ne suffit pas!*, trans. Eric Bahloo, Cathay Printing, 2019.

141 Lindsey Collen, 'Another Side of Paradise', *New Internationalist*, 02/05/2009,
https://newint.org/features/2009/05/01/mauritius-class.

142 Cotterill, 'Reforms in Mauritius hint at discontent over ethnic representation'.

143 Ibid.

144 Affirmative Action, *Alternative Report 2021*.

145 Leo Couacaud, Sheetal Sheena Sookrajowa and Jason Narsoo, 'The Vicious
Circle that is Mauritian Politics: The Legacy of Mauritius's Electoral Boundaries', *Ethnopolitics* 2022, 21:1, pp. 48—79.

146 The government has stated that 'stability is the pillar of socio-economic progress', and therefore it will not consent to a census based on communal affiliation.
It has been argued that the decision not to collect information on ethnicity is an
anti-colonial act: a rejection of imperial systems of racial classification. However,
it should be noted that, at independence, four parliamentary seats were reserved
for under-represented communities based on 'the latest official published census'.
Since the last census that collected this information was published in 1972, this
still determines the allocation of these seats. Sheetal Sheena Sookrajowa observes
that 'it remains a paradox that the main national political parties which are now

clamoring for national unity by refusing to perform an ethnic count of the population for electoral purposes, are themselves informally using the ethnic rationale to govern, from the nomination of candidates and coalition negotiations to the appointment of members of parliament.' See Cotterill, 'Reforms in Mauritius hint at discontent over ethnic representation'; Sheetal Sheena Sookrajowa, 'Legibility and the Politics of Ethnic Classification of the Population in the National Census of Mauritius: A Statist Perspective', *Nationalism and Ethnic Politics* 2021, 27:2, p. 140.

147  '. . . a majority of them live in housing estates, devoid of bare amenities and in over crowdedness . . .'. See Truth and Justice Commission, *Report of the Truth and Justice Commission*, vol. 1, p. 2.

148  '. . . due to their poor performance at school, few can get employed in Government services'. See ibid.

149  '. . . they have no real effective pressure groups to make their voices heard in higher and political quarters, most of their grievances remained unheard'. See ibid.

150  'Stigmatisation [has] prevailed for centuries in Mauritius . . . across all communities, including the Creole community.' See ibid., p. 226.

151  'Due to selective breeding, some slaves were deprived of the right to develop monogamous family relationships. Psychologically, selective breeding influenced slaves to believe that family relationships were of little value, and fostered insecurity.' See ibid., p. 227.

152  'It was found that Creoles, who are currently defined as slave descendants, routinely experienced racist attacks.' See ibid., p. 288.

153  'Examples of "racist" events include biased bureaucratic reports, hidden inquests, empty review procedures, the touting of equality policies never enforced, denial of earned recognition, exclusionary socialising, and covert maintenance of housing segregation.' See ibid.

154  'Indo-Fijians', *Minority Rights*, https://minorityrights.org/minorities/indo-fijians/.

155  Mangai Balasegaram, 'Special Report: Different Class: The Marginalisation of Indians in Malaysia', *Between the Lines*, https://betweenthelines.my/malaysias-indians-marginalised-over-a-century/.

156  Bahadur, *Coolie Woman*, pp. 194, 198, 200–201, 202, 204.

157  Truth and Justice Commission, *Report of the Truth and Justice Commission*, vol. 1, p. 3.

158  Crispin Bates and Marina Carter, 'Sirdars as Intermediaries in Nineteenth-Century Indian Ocean Indentured Labour Migration', *Modern Asian Studies* 2017, 51:2, pp. 462–84.

159 Kamala Kempadoo, '"Bound Coolies" and Other Indentured Workers in the Caribbean: Implications for Debates about Human Trafficking and Modern Slavery', *Anti-Trafficking Review* 2017, 9, pp. 48–63, https://www.antitrafficking-review.org/index.php/atrjournal/article/view/263/252.

160 Emiliano Mellino and Shanti Das, 'Seasonal fruit pickers left thousands in debt after being sent home early from UK farms', *Guardian*, 13/11/2022, https://www.theguardian.com/uk-news/2022/nov/13/seasonal-fruit-pickers-left-thousands-in-debt-after-being-sent-home-early-from-uk-farms.

161 'Qatar World Cup of Shame', *Amnesty International*, https://www.amnesty.org/en/latest/campaigns/2016/03/qatar-world-cup-of-shame/.

162 'Exploited and marginalized, Bangladeshi tea workers speak up for their rights', *UN News*, 21/03/2021, https://news.un.org/en/story/2021/03/1087622; 'The Exploitation of Tea Plantation Workers in Sri Lanka', *The Borgen Project*, 22/08/2021, https://borgenproject.org/tea-plantation-workers-in-sri-lanka/; Justin Rowlatt and Jane Deith, 'The bitter story behind the UK's national drink', *BBC News*, 08/09/2015, https://www.bbc.co.uk/news/world-asia-india-34173532. See Amy Huxtable, 'A cuppa reality: The truth behind your brew', *University of Sheffield*, https://www.sheffield.ac.uk/research/forced-labour.

163 Kolsky, *Colonial Justice in British India*, pp. 142–84.

164 S. Rukmini, 'World Bank Finds Evidence of Labour Abuse on Assam Tea Plantations It Owns with the Tatas', *Huffington Post*, 07/11/2016, https://www.huffpost.com/archive/in/entry/world-bank-finds-evidence-of-labour-abuse-on-assam-tea-plantatio_in_5c0fe358e4b051c73eabf82c.

165 'Between May 1863 and May 1866, about 84,915 labourers were imported into the Assam tea gardens,' writes Rana P. Behal. 'But the returns for 1866 showed only 49,750 as working on the gardens. The remaining 35,165 either died or deserted. A larger number of deserters also seemed to have died of hunger or exhaustion in the jungles. In the tea gardens inspected by the Commissioners in 1868, the average rate of mortality ranged from 137.6 per thousand to 556.6 per thousand.' See Kolsky, *Colonial Justice in British India*, p. 155;

166 Kolsky, *Colonial Justice in British India*, pp. 151, 167.

167 Rana P. Behal, 'Coolie Drivers or Benevolent Paternalists? British Tea Planters in Assam and the Indenture Labour System', *Modern Asian Studies* 2010, 44:1, pp. 29–51.

168 Rappaport, *A Thirst for Empire*, p. 208.

169 Kolsky, *Colonial Justice in British India*, pp. 167, 168, 159.

170 'Commonwealth countries can do much more to expand trade links with the UK, post-Brexit,' concluded a set of trade experts at the Commonwealth Secretariat soon after the Brexit vote. 'We already know there's a Commonwealth advantage in trading between member states,' claimed the Secretariat's head of

international trade policy, Dr Mohammad Razzaque. 'Where the UK is already a significant trading partner, Commonwealth members can mobilise pro-active policy support to relatively easily expand trade further. In some cases, bilateral trading arrangements could also be the way forward.' See 'Trade opportunities for Commonwealth post-Brexit', *The Commonwealth*, 10/01/2017, https://the commonwealth.org/news/trade-opportunities-commonwealth-post-brexit.

171  'Seven developing nations send over 10 percent of their world exports to the UK: Botswana, Belize, Seychelles, Mauritius, St Lucia, Sri Lanka and Bangladesh. 24 countries send more than 30 percent of their total EU trade exports to the UK. For example, the UK absorbs more than 70 percent of such exports from St Lucia and Tuvalu.' 'Trade opportunities for Commonwealth post-Brexit'. See Emily Jones, 'Brexit: Opportunity or peril for trade with small and poor developing economies?', *GEG: Global Economic Governance Programme*, https:// www.geg.ox.ac.uk/publication/brexit-opportunity-or-peril-trade-small-and-poor-developing-economies.

## Chapter 4: White Saviours

1  'Do They Know It's Christmas?', *Song Facts*, https://www.songfacts.com/facts/band-aid/do-they-know-its-christmas.

2  London's Kingsway International Christian Centre, founded by a Nigerian, is home to the largest church congregation in Western Europe. Siollun, *What Britain Did to Nigeria*, p. 334.

3  Frederick Cooper, *Africa since 1940: The Past of the Present*, Cambridge University Press, 2002, p. 36; Siollun, *What Britain Did to Nigeria*, pp. 253–5.

4  As expertly summarized by Jenny Edkins in *Whose Hunger? Concepts of Famine, Practices of Aid*, University of Minnesota Press, 2000, pp. xix, 6, 7, 103, 122, 109–10. See also Charlotte Lydia Riley, *Imperial Island: A History of Empire in Modern Britain*, Bodley Head, 2023, p. 199.

5  Jessica Howard-Johnston, 'Band Aid 30: A neo-colonial controversy?', *Pi Media*, 04/12/2014, https://uclpimedia.com/online/band-aid-30-a-neo-colonial-controversy.

6  Bim Adewunmi, 'Band Aid 30: clumsy, patronising and wrong in so many ways', *Guardian*, 11/11/2014, https://www.theguardian.com/world/2014/nov/11/band-aid-30-patronising-bob-geldof-ebola-do-they-know-its-christmas.

7  The fashion among certain white women on Instagram to pose with black children in Africa, 'without any indication as to whether they even had consent from their families to take as well as share their photos', has inspired the parody social

networking account 'Barbie Saviour'. Meanwhile, Kelsey Nielsen and Olivia Alaso have combined forces to launch the No White Saviours (NWS) campaign group, with the aim of challenging, in the words of the *Guardian*, 'underlying domination in development narratives and the relationship between white and black people. An issue that dates back to the first Europeans who raided Africa for slaves and raw materials.' See Habiba Katsha, 'David Lammy is right to call out the "white saviour" narrative – if only Comic Relief understood that', *Independent,* 28/02/2019, https://www.independent.co.uk/voices/david-lammy-comic-relief-stacey-dooley-white-saviour-charity-africa-a8801676.html; Patience Akumu, 'Charity at heart of "white saviour" row speaks out', *Guardian*, 03/03/2019, https://www.theguardian.com/tv-and-radio/2019/mar/03/we-need-to-talk-about-race-no-white-saviours-tells-stacey-dooley-comic-relief.

8  It came after TV presenter Stacey Dooley travelled to the continent for the charity, prompting Labour MP David Lammy, who is of Guyanese descent, to remark that films of white British celebrities going to Africa perpetuated 'an old idea from the colonial era' and that 'many black' Britons were 'deeply uncomfortable' with such 'poverty porn'. See Kyle O'Sullivan, 'Why Comic Relief stopped sending "white saviour" celebrities to Africa after scandal', *Mirror*, 18/03/2022, https://www.mirror.co.uk/tv/tv-news/comic-relief-stopped-sending-white-26491455.

9  https://www.worldwildlife.org/about/history.

10  https://shorturl.at/diMSY.

11  https://www.fauna-flora.org/news/raiders-lost-archive-episode-one/.

12  Nicola Banks and Dan Brockington, 'Mapping the UK's development NGOs: income, geography and contributions to international development: GDI Working Paper', GDI Working Paper 2019-035, University of Manchester, 2019, https://hummedia.manchester.ac.uk/institutes/gdi/publications/workingpapers/GDI/GDI-working-paper-2019035-banks-brockington.pdf, p. 8.

13  'Fast Forward', *Bond*, 01/07/2014, https://www.bond.org.uk/resources/fast-forward/.

14  Riley, *Imperial Island*, p. 199.

15  Written in response to the US taking over the Philippines after the Spanish–American War, it begins: 'Take up the White Man's burden / Send forth the best ye breed / Go bind your sons to exile / To serve your captives' need; / To wait in heavy harness / On fluttered folk and wild / Your new-caught, sullen peoples, / Half devil and half child.'

16  Ferguson, *Empire*, p. 140; Philip Meadows Taylor, *Confessions of a Thug*, ed. Kim A. Wagner, Oxford World's Classics, due to be published February 2024.

17  Ferguson, *Empire*, p. 139.

18  Arvind Sharma, *Sati: Historical and Phenomenological Essays*, Motilal Banarsidass Publishers, 2001, pp. ix–x, 3, 10–11, 16–17, 49; Kolsky, *Colonial Justice in British India*, p. 63.

19  According to a data scientist at the National Council for Voluntary Organisations, Save the Children International is the biggest of Britain's INGOs, with almost £1 billion of annual income, more than double the income of Oxfam, the INGO in second place. That's before you add the income generated by the Save the Children Fund, which is at number four.

20  Dorothy is a good example of the fact that in imperial times humanitarianism and philanthropy were often a family affair. Her husband was Charles Buxton, head of the Anti-Slavery Society, and her father-in-law Thomas Fowell Buxton, who was a founder of the Aborigines' Protection Society and successor to Wilberforce as leader of the Parliamentary anti-slavery lobby. Edward North Buxton, cited earlier as one of the founders of Britain's Fauna & Flora International (FFI), was Thomas Fowell Buxton's father.

21  See Elizabeth Prevost, 'Assessing Women, Gender, and Empire in Britain's Nineteenth-Century Protestant Missionary Movement', *History Compass* 2009 7:3, pp. 765–99, https://compass.onlinelibrary.wiley.com/doi/10.1111/j.1478-0542.2009.00593.x.

22  'Save the Children has become a global organization, comprising 29 national member organisations that work in 120 countries. Save the Children's UK branch has an annual income of over £300 million. It now employs over a thousand staff, its base a corporate office space in the City of London. Over its first century, Save the Children has moved from being a fringe protest movement to one of the world's largest and most influential humanitarian organisations.' Emily Baughan, 'Humanitarianism and History: A Century of Save the Children', in Juliano Fiori, Fernando Espada, Andrea Rigon, Bertrand Taithe and Rafia Zakaria (eds.), *Amidst the Debris: Humanitarianism and the End of Liberal Order*, Routledge, 2021, pp. 21–5.

23  Emily Baughan, *Saving the Children: Humanitarianism, Internationalism, and Empire*, University of California Press, 2021, p. 15.

24  Ibid., pp. 92–3.

25  Ibid., pp. 80, 87–8.

26  Ibid., p. 89.

27  Ibid., p. 93.

28  Ibid., p. 94.

29  Ibid., pp. 142–3.

30  Ibid., pp. 31, 68–9, 112, 159; Baughan, 'Humanitarianism and History', p. 28.

31  Baughan, *Saving the Children*, pp. 150–52.

32  Ibid., pp. 157–9.

33 'The British government recognises that Kenyans were subject to torture and other forms of ill-treatment at the hands of the colonial administration,' said Foreign Secretary William Hague at the time. 'The British government sincerely regrets that these abuses took place and that they marred Kenya's progress towards independence.' See 'Mau Mau torture victims to receive compensation – Hague', *BBC News*, 06/06/2013, https://www.bbc.co.uk/news/uk-22790037.

34 Baughan, *Saving the Children*, pp. 160, 163–5.

35 See Emily Baughan, 'Rehabilitating an empire: Humanitarian collusion with the colonial state during the Kenyan emergency, ca.1954–1960', *Journal of British Studies* 2020, 59:1, pp. 57–79, https://doi.org/10.1017/jbr.2019.243.

36 Baughan, *Saving the Children*, pp. 169–71.

37 Toyin O. Falola et al., 'Nigerian Civil War', *Britannica*, https://www.britannica. com/topic/Nigerian-civil-war; Kwarteng, *Ghosts of Empire*, pp. 313–18; Adaobi Tricia Nwaubani, 'Remembering Nigeria's Biafra war that many prefer to forget', *BBC News*, 15/01/2020, https://www.bbc.co.uk/news/world-africa-51094093.

38 Baughan, *Saving the Children*, pp. 173, 192–4, 194–5, 196.

39 The roots of contemporary 'crises' in early years care and maternity services in historical perspective: https://www.sheffield.ac.uk/history/people/academic/ emily-baughan.

40 Baughan, 'Humanitarianism and History', p. 27.

41 Eva-Maria Muschik, 'The Art of Chameleon Politics: From Colonial Servant to International Development Expert', *Humanity: An International Journal of Human Rights, Humanitarianism, and Development* 2018, 9:2, pp. 219–44; Olav Stokke, *The UN and Development: From Aid to Cooperation*, Indiana University Press, 2009, p. 74.

42 Riley, *Imperial Island*, pp. 127–9.

43 'As with the racist ideologies of the past, the discourse of development continued to define non-Western people in terms of their perceived divergence from the cultural standards of the West, and it reproduced the social hierarchies that had prevailed between both groups under colonialism. On this basis, the so-called "developing world" and its inhabitants were (and still are) described only in terms of what they are not. They are chaotic not ordered, traditional not modern, corrupt not honest, underdeveloped not developed, irrational not rational, lacking in all of those things the West presumes itself to be. White Westerners were still represented as the bearers of "civilization" and were to act as the exclusive agents of development, while black, post-colonial "others" were still seen as uncivilized and unenlightened, destined to be development's exclusive objects.' See Firoze Manji and Carl O'Coill, 'The Missionary Position: NGOs and Development in Africa', *International Affairs (Royal Institute of International Affairs 1944–)* 2002, 78:3, p. 574.

44  Ibid., pp. 567–83.

45  Gregory Mann, *From Empires to NGOs in the West African Sahel: The Road to Non-governmentality*, Cambridge University Press, 2015, pp. 2–3.

46  Gregory Mann, in ibid., pp. 213–14, states that '1960 is generally taken to be a signal year for African independence, witnessing national sovereignty for the Sahelian states and many others, the collapse of the Congo, and the ever-bloodier repression of the antiapartheid movement in South Africa, as marked by the shooting at Sharpeville. Amnesty International was founded in London the very next year. One of its first investigative missions was to Ghana, a pioneer in self-government, in the wake of Kwame Nkrumah's fall from power. In short, the period when Amnesty acquired "a virtual monopoly as a non-governmental authority speaking the language of universal Human Rights" coincided precisely with the years of African independence. The often tense relationship between human rights and African sovereignty is neither causal nor merely rhetorical. In the post-independence history of political discourse on the continent they are long-time companions, albeit with their backs often turned to each other.'

47  Lankelly Chase, the seventy-ninth biggest charitable foundation in 2021, declared it was going to abolish itself in 2023, after deciding it was not right to invest in international capital markets rooted in colonial and racial exploitation, and concluding that traditional philanthropy was a 'function of colonial capitalism'. Advocating for the cause in Canada, Roberta Jamieson has argued that 'despite some good intentions, history shows that the efforts of the philanthropic sector have often not been philanthropic – they have often advanced colonial enterprise at the expense of Indigenous peoples. There was, for example, the Residential School System, the appropriation of cultural artifacts for museums, and the "Sixties Scoop" that saw thousands of Indigenous children torn from their families and communities for adoption elsewhere.' She asks for philanthropic organizations to acknowledge that 'simply having money does not mean they know best what is needed for Indigenous communities'. Meanwhile, the author and activist Edgar Villanueva, who is from an indigenous American background and heads the Decolonizing Wealth Project in the US, has written in *Decolonizing Wealth* that 'the philanthropic industry has evolved to mirror colonial structures and reproduces hierarchy, ultimately doing more harm than good'. In a recent article, he described philanthropy as 'a sleepwalking sector, white zombies spewing the money of dead white people in the name of charity and benevolence', 'colonialism in the empire's newest clothes' and 'racism in institutional form'. He added: 'We need to put ALL our money where our values are.' Patrick Butler, 'UK charity foundation to abolish itself and give away £130m', 11/07/2023, *Guardian*, https://www.theguardian.com/society/2023/jul/11/uk-charity-foundation-to-abolish-

itself-and-give-away-130m?CMP=share_btn_tw; Edgar Villanueva, *Decolonizing Wealth: Indigenous Wisdom to Heal Divides and Restore Balance*, Berrett-Koehler, 2018; Peter R. Elson, Sylvain A. Lefèvre and Jean-Marc Fontan (eds.), *Philanthropic Foundations in Canada: Landscapes, Indigenous Perspectives and Pathways to Change*, PhiLab, 2020; Edgar Villanueva, 'Money as Medicine: Leveraging Philanthropy to Decolonize Wealth', *Non-Profit Quarterly*, 29/01/2019, https://nonprofitquar-terly.org/money-as-medicine-leveraging-philanthropy-to-decolonize-wealth/; Roberta Jamieson, 'Decolonizing Phil-anthropy: Building New Relations', in Elson et al. (eds.), *Philanthropic Foundations in Canada*, pp. 157–72 at p. 159; https://decolonizingwealth.com/about/.

48  Frederick Cooper points out that Fort Hare University in the Transkei, for instance, 'developed out of [British] mission schools, and through its doors around the 1940s passed future leaders of the struggle against apartheid, notably Nelson Mandela (who was expelled) and Oliver Tambo, as well as people who served the apartheid regime's system of homeland administration, such as Kaiser Matanzima (first President of the Transkei)'. Cooper, *Africa since 1940*, p. 75.

49  Anna Bocking-Welch, *British Civic Society at the End of the Empire: Decolonisation, Globalisation and International Responsibility*, Manchester University Press, 2018, pp. 155–6, 158.

50  'How did CAFOD begin: your questions answered', *CAFOD*, 25/07/2018, https://cafod.org.uk/About-us/Our-history-Q-A.

51  Manji and O'Coill, 'The Missionary Position', p. 572.

52  'Fast Forward'.

53  Bocking-Welch, *British Civic Society at the End of the Empire*, pp. 154–81.

54  Ibid., pp. 158–60.

55  Ibid., p. 177.

56  Ibid.

57  Ibid., p. 72.

58  Ibid., p. 10.

59  Ibid., p. 146.

60  Anna Bocking-Welch, 'The British Public in a Shrinking World: Civic Engage-ment with the Declining Empire, 1960-1970', PhD thesis, University of York, 2012, p. 185.

61  Matthew Hilton, 'Charity and the End of Empire: British Non-governmental Organizations, Africa, and International Development in the 1960s', *American Historical Review* 2018, 123:2, pp. 493–517 at p. 508.

62  Edkins, *Whose Hunger?*, p. 122.

63  Baughan, *Saving the Children*, p. 92.

64  Riley, *Imperial Island*, p. 129.

65    Barney Davis, 'Comic Relief to stop sending celebrities to Africa following "white saviour" criticism', *Evening Standard*, 28/10/2020, https://www.standard.co.uk/ showbiz/comic-relief-drops-white-savior-trips-africa-stacey-dooley-lenny-henry- a4573203.html; 'Comic Relief to stop sending celebrities to Africa after "white saviour" criticism', *Sky News*, 28/10/2020, https://news.sky.com/story/comic- relief-to-stop-sending-celebrities-to-africa-after-white-saviour-criticism-12116723.

66    Bill Morton, 'An Overview of International NGOs in Development Cooper- ation', *Working with Civil Society in Foreign Aid: Possibilities for South–South Cooperation?*, Case Study 7, UNDP China, 2013, pp. 325–52 at p. 336, https:// www.undp.org/sites/g/files/zskgke326/files/migration/cn/UNDP-CH11-An- Overview-of-International-NGOs-in-Development-Cooperation.pdf.

67    Among other things, Oxfam's guidance quite sensibly advised against using the phrases 'developed country, developing country, underdeveloped countries, third world' because 'talking about high/middle/low-income countries recognises that the economic status of a country is situational rather than definitive. Third vs first world implies that wealthier countries are better than poorer ones and erases the colonial history that led to the economic inequality of today.' See 'Inclusive Lan- guage Guide', *Oxfam*, 13/03/2023, https://policy-practice.oxfam.org/resources/ inclusive-language-guide-621487/; Nell Sears and Ryan Hooper, 'Beyond parody! Oxfam's new 92-page inclusivity guide calls English "the language of a colonising nation" and tells staff to avoid the words "mother", "headquarters" – and even "youth", in move slammed by critics', *Daily Mail*, 16/03/2023, https://www.daily- mail.co.uk/news/article-11869961/Oxfams-new-92-page-inclusivity-guide-calls- English-language-colonising-nation.html.

68    Baughan, *Saving the Children*, pp. 185–6, 212.

69    Matthew Hilton, 'Ken Loach and the Save the Children Film: Humanitarianism, Imperialism, and the Changing Role of Charity in Postwar Britain', *Journal of Modern History* 2015, 87:2, pp. 357–94 at pp. 357–63, 389–94.

70    James Vernon, *Hunger: A Modern History*, Harvard University Press, 2007, pp. 104–17, 277.

71    Ibid., pp. 106–8.

72    Ibid., p. 3.

73    Ibid., p. 17.

74    Michael Taylor, 'Never forget that the British political and media elite endorsed slavery', *Guardian*, 30/01/2023.

75    Fintan O'Toole, *Hungry Eyes*, prod. Mary Price, BBC Radio 4, 01/11/1995, cited in Edkins, *Whose Hunger?*, p. 3.

76    When Emily Hobhouse alerted the British public to the dreadful conditions inside British concentration camps in South Africa, built to imprison Boer and African civilians during the South African War, the suffering of 'native' African

women and children was not highlighted, even though they 'suffered from poorer rations, worse conditions, and greater numbers of deaths'. Vernon, *Hunger*, pp. 31–2.

77 Baughan, *Saving the Children*, p. 214.

78 Eleanor Davey, 'The conscience of the island? The NGO moment in Australian offshore detention', in Fiori et al. (eds.), *Amidst the Debris*, pp. 83–106.

79 https://www.nma.gov.au/defining-moments/resources/white-australia-policy.

80 The 1717 Transportation Act sent criminals and vagrants to penal colonies in what is now Australia. Australia then developed its own practice of 'far offshore processing' – using islands to warehouse indigenous people who got in the way of colonial expansion, including the forced removal of indigenous people from Tasmania to Flinders Island from 1829. Michael Collyer and Uttara Shahani see other precedents for this movement of people in the Atlantic slave trade, Indian Removal in the United States, the settlement of Scottish and English planters in Ulster plantations in the early 1600s, penal transportation and the relocation of 'criminal' and itinerant groups in British India. See Elise Klein and China Mills, 'Islands of deterrence: Britain's long history of banishing "undesirables"', *Open Democracy*, 01/04/2021, https://www.opendemocracy.net/en/opendemocracyuk/islands-of-deterrence-britains-long-history-of-banishing-undesirables/; Xain Storey, 'Ghosts of History: The Tasmanian Aborigines', *Ceasefire*, 03/09/2014, https://ceasefire-magazine.co.uk/part-i-tasmanian-aborigines/; Michael Collyer and Uttara Shahani, 'Offshoring Refugees: Colonial Echoes of the UK–Rwanda Migration and Economic Development Partnership', *Social Sciences* 2023, 12:8, p. 451.

81 'Offshore processing', *Refugee Council of Australia*, https://www.refugeecouncil.org.au/offshore-processing/; Nicole Johnston, 'Offshore processing of asylum seekers: Is the UK copying Australia's hardline policy?', *Sky News*, 14/04/2022, https://news.sky.com/story/offshore-processing-of-asylum-seekers-is-the-uk-copying-australias-hardline-policy-12589728; Klein and Mills, 'Islands of deterrence'; David Barrett, 'Channel migrants should be deported to processing centres on South Atlantic islands if an agreement with France fails, report suggests', *Daily Mail*, 16/02/2022, https://www.dailymail.co.uk/news/article-10517365/Channel-migrants-deported-processing-centres-South-Atlantic-islands.html; Agency, 'Archaeologists find graves containing bodies of 5,000 slaves on remote island', *Guardian*, 08/03/2012, https://www.theguardian.com/world/2012/mar/08/slave-mass-graves-st-helena-island; David Bolt, Independent Chief Inspector of Borders and Immigration, 'An inspection of the Home Office's approach to illegal working', August–December 2018, https://shorturl.at/jCJM6; Ben Doherty, '"Stop the Boats": Sunak's anti-asylum slogan echoes Australia's harsh policy', *Guardian*, 08/03/2023, https://www.theguardian.com/uk-news/2023/mar/08/stop-the-boats-sunaks-anti-asylum-slogan-echoes-australia-harsh-policy; Diane

Taylor, 'Housing asylum seekers on barge may only save £10 a person daily, report says', *Guardian*, 11/07/2023, https://www.theguardian.com/uk-news/2023/jul/11/housing-asylum-seekers-on-barge-may-only-save-10-a-person-daily-report-says?CMP=Share_iOSApp_Other.

82  Paul Farrell, Nick Evershed and Helen Davidson, 'The Nauru files: cache of 2,000 leaked reports reveal scale of abuse of children in Australian offshore detention', *Guardian*, 10/08/2016, https://www.theguardian.com/australia-news/2016/aug/10/the-nauru-files-2000-leaked-reports-reveal-scale-of-abuse-of-children-in-australian-offshore-detention.

83  On its website, Save the Children Australia talks about how 'from the furthest corners of Australia, to South-East and South Central Asia, Africa, the Middle East and the Pacific, Save the Children's programs always put children first . . . Where children are being exploited, neglected or abused, we protect them from harm.' https://www.savethechildren.org.au/our-work/our-programs.

84  'Fast Forward', p. 343.

85  'Uganda was once one of Africa's biggest producers of cotton, but is now drowning in tonnes of the cast-offs including designer fakes, fur, skiwear and bawdy hen-night T-shirts – some still marked with lipstick and sweat . . . more than eight out of ten garments bought in Uganda come from charity shops or donation bins in Britain and elsewhere.' See Jane Flanagan, 'Return to Sender: designer upcycles British hand-me-downs to reboot Ugandan textile industry', *The Times*, 29/04/2022, https://www.thetimes.co.uk/article/return-to-sender-designer-upcycles-british-hand-me-downs-to-reboot-ugandan-textile-industry-b8sdfkkzx.

86  Manji and O'Coill, 'The Missionary Position', p. 580.

87  Foreign, Commonwealth & Development Office and the Rt Hon. Dominic Raab MP, 'UK Official Development Assistance (ODA) allocations 2021 to 2022: written ministerial statement', *GOV. UK*, 21/04/2021, https://www.gov.uk/government/speeches/uk-official-development-assistance-oda-allocations-2021-to-2022-written-ministerial-statement.

88  Lizzy Davies, 'UK accused of abandoning world's poor as aid turned into "colonial" investment', *Guardian*, 21/12/2021, https://www.theguardian.com/global-development/2021/dec/21/uk-accused-of-abandoning-worlds-poor-as-aid-turned-into-colonial-investment.

89  In the years since the invasion of Iraq, the world's humanitarian sector has grown by four times in size to turn into a US$29 billion a year 'industry'. Some 50 per cent of this money is given by mainly Western nations, directly and indirectly, to 'non-governmental' aid agencies. Baughan notes that during this period humanitarian organizations also became 'service providers in "failed" states in the global South. What the world is left with, then, is aid organisations acting as intermediaries for Western states financing the functions of Southern, often postcolonial,

states, almost half a century after the era of decolonisation.' Writing in the same essay collection, Gareth Owen tells us that at the turn of the century Save the Children US (SCUS) 'was coming under state pressure from the US government which saw NGOs as "natural partners" in the management of the aftermath of war'. He quotes Secretary of State Colin Powell addressing NGOs in 2001, not long after the invasion of Afghanistan, with the words: 'Just as surely as our diplomats and military, American NGOs are out there serving and sacrificing on the front lines of freedom . . . I am serious about making sure we have the best relationship with NGOs who are such a force multiplier for us, such an important part of our combat team.' Baughan, 'Humanitarianism and History', pp. 26–7; Gareth Owen, 'The Rise of the Humanitarian Corporation: Save the Children and the Ordering of Emergency Response', in Fiori et al. (eds.), *Amidst the Debris*, p. 42.

90  Melanie May, 'Animal welfare is UK's favourite cause', *UK Fundraising*, 10/08/2022, https://shorturl.at/qJM58.

91  John M. MacKenzie, *The Empire of Nature: Hunting, Conservation and British Imperialism*, Manchester University Press, 1988, pp. 202, 271.

92  Ibid., pp. 38, 168.

93  Ibid., pp. 115, 116, 182–3, 207.

94  Frankopan, *The Earth Transformed*, pp. 378, 467–8; Fowler, *Green Unpleasant Land*, pp. 31–2.

95  FFI is open about this strange history, acknowledging on its website that 'paradoxically, FFI owes its existence to an assorted collection of big game hunters who realised that they were running out of things to shoot. Other founder members who shared Buxton's concern that hunting of African game had reached unsustainable levels included Colonel J. H. Patterson, whose lion-killing heroics inspired a bestselling book – *The Man-Eaters of Tsavo* – and a trio of Hollywood films; Frederick Selous, the archetypal great white hunter, inspiration for the fictional Allan Quatermain and First World War hero-in-waiting; and the brewing magnate, Samuel Whitbread, who was anxious to avert an African version of the free-for-all that had led to the near-total wipeout of the American bison. In its original guise, FFI operated first and foremost as a pressure group that drew on its collective aristocratic muscle in order to lean on the colonial authorities. With this in mind, Buxton and his co-founders wasted no time in recruiting heavyweight friends as honorary members. Among them was President Theodore Roosevelt, an ardent conservationist whose love of nature did not preclude him from mounting an African hunting expedition during which over 11,000 animals were trapped or killed in the name of science.' https://www.fauna-flora.org/news/raiders-lost-archive-episode-one/.

96  Frankopan, *The Earth Transformed*, p. 468.

97  MacKenzie, *The Empire of Nature*, pp. 39, 94–5.

98  Ibid., p. 201.

99  Of imperial big-game shooting, MacKenzie notes that 'no other sport went through such a rapid transition from an acceptable and central aspect of imperialism into an activity regarded as dubious, with the capacity to damage environments and seriously reduce the numbers of increasingly rare animals'. The speed was such that some imperialists changed their view within their lifetime, Baden-Powell among them. 'Formerly fierce in his extolling of pig sticking and shooting during his career, even incorporating the use of guns into the early editions of his *Scouting for Boys*, [he] changed his mind in the 1920s. It may be that for some like him, the experience of the carnage of the First World War made the substitution of camera for gun an attractive proposition.' See MacKenzie, *A Cultural History of the British Empire*, pp. 107–8.

100  One exception was H. A. Bryden, who became active in the preservationist lobby in Britain. 'In 1894 Bryden repeated his warnings with greater force in an article in the *Fortnightly Review*. He was quite clear about where the responsibility for destruction lay. It was with Europeans and the introduction of breech-loading firearms.' MacKenzie, *The Empire of Nature*, pp. 113–15.

101  Regional museums are beginning to look into how they built collections of hunting trophies and taxidermied animals. See recent *Guardian* article on exhibition at Scarborough Art Gallery: https://www.theguardian.com/culture/2023/jan/11/scarborough--museum-legacy-colonial-past-scarborough-art-gallery. And the research taking place at the Powell-Cotton Museum on hunting trophies and dioramas: https://pcmresearch.org/research/; https://powell-cottonmuseum.org/projects/colonial-critters/.

102  Corinne Fowler was the first writer I came across who pointed out that imperialists hunted exotic animals to the point of extinction. 'Tiger-hunting – always popular with Indian rulers – escalated under the British Raj and there is a direct link between colonialism and the decimation of tiger populations. By the 1930s, the Van Ingen taxidermy firm were processing 400 big cat skins a year. Elephant populations also diminished as European markets increasingly opened up for ivory products at the height of empire.' Fowler, *Green Unpleasant Land*, pp. 31–2.

103  The interior decor schemes of British stately homes like Blair Castle and Tatton Park have borne witness to the imperial hunting craze, with the heads and horns of exotic animals being placed alongside the more traditional sight of locally sourced stag heads. See Mackenzie, *The Empire of Nature*, pp. 29–31.

104  Valentine Low, 'William's poaching warning in first major speech as Prince of Wales', *The Times*, 04/10/2022, https://www.thetimes.co.uk/article/8910b764-43cc-11ed-8885-043c27446b97?shareToken=dd9a203997a3f7e28 99efe057696a7fa.

105 https://www.royal.uk/conservation.

106 Mackenzie, *The Empire of Nature*, pp. 115, 193, 309–10.

107 https://www.heirsofslavery.org/.

108 Press Association, 'Prince William "calls for Buckingham Palace ivory to be destroyed"', *Guardian*, 17/02/2014, https://www.theguardian.com/uk-news/2014/feb/17/prince-william-buckingham-palace-ivory-destroyed.

## Chapter 5: A Rational and Intelligible System of Law

1 Michael Safi, 'Campaigners celebrate as India decriminalises homosexuality', *Guardian*, 06/09/2018, https://www.theguardian.com/world/2018/sep/06/indian-supreme-court-decriminalises-homosexuality; Amy Kazmin, 'India gay sex court ruling sets stage for cultural battle', *Financial Times*, 12/09/2018, https://www.ft.com/content/8a8cbd02-b5c5-11e8-b3ef-799c8613f4a1.

2 Kyle Knight, 'India's Transgender Rights Law Isn't Worth Celebrating', *Human Rights Watch*, 05/12/2019, https://www.hrw.org/news/2019/12/05/indias-transgender-rights-law-isnt-worth-celebrating.

3 https://www.nazindia.org/.

4 The suicide of Arvey Malhotra, a sixteen-year-old pupil at the elite Delhi Public School in Greater Faridabad, made headlines across India in 2022. The Class 10 student jumped from the building where he lived with his mother, Aarti Malhotra, a teacher at the same school (who was away when it happened). The contents of the suicide note were widely published in Indian newspapers and he was clear about who was to blame: the school, which didn't challenge the relentless harassment and abuse he faced for being gay. Mrs Malhotra was fired as a teacher following her child's death. See Maitree Baral, '"The school has killed me": Arvey Malhotra's mother recalls his suicide note and elaborates on the bullying that led to her son's death; awaits justice even after 4 months', *Times of India*, 07/07/2022, https://timesofindia.indiatimes.com/life-style/parenting/moments/the-school-has-killed-me-arvey-malhotras-mother-recalls-his-suicide-note-and-elaborates-on-the-bullying-that-led-to-her-sons-death-awaits-justice-even-after-4-months/articleshow/92721354.cms.

5 'The Judicial Committee of the Privy Council is the highest court of appeal for many Commonwealth countries, as well as the United Kingdom's overseas territories, crown dependencies, and military sovereign base areas. It also hears very occasional appeals from a number of ancient and ecclesiastical courts. These include the Church Commissioners, the Arches Court of Canterbury, the Chancery Court of York, prize courts and the Court of Admiralty of the Cinque Ports.' https://www.jcpc.uk/about/role-of-the-jcpc.html.

6 'Law, Colonial Systems of, British Empire', *Encyclopedia.com*, https://www. encyclopedia.com/history/encyclopedias-almanacs-transcripts-and-maps/law-colonial-systems-british-empire.

7 Ferguson, *Empire*, pp. 64–5; 'Terra nullius', *Australian Museum*, 09/09/2021, https:// australian.museum/learn/first-nations/unsettled/recognising-invasions/ terra-nullius/https://www.nma.gov.au/defining-moments/resources/mabo-decision.

8 These include British Overseas Territories like Bermuda and the British Virgin Islands, Crown dependencies like the Channel Islands, and also, controversially, ten independent Commonwealth states, mostly in the Caribbean. Leslie Thomas QC, a prominent lawyer in London, recently suggested that British judges should cease sitting as the top court for Commonwealth countries, describing the Privy Council as one of the 'last vestiges of colonialism'. See Jonathan Ames and Catherine Baksi, 'Lawyer condemns British court as colonialist relic', *The Times*, 09/06/2022, https:// www.thetimes.co.uk/article/802fbe26-e74a-11ec-aa87-2eea7c6e5b01?shareToken= b7e9eb6df701848be465236d027a1dbb.

9 Amrit Dhillon, 'Indian minister calls for abolition of 1,500 laws dating back to Raj', *Guardian*, 25/10/2022, https://www.theguardian.com/world/2022/oct/25/ indian-minister-calls-for-abolition-of-1500-laws-dating-back-to-raj.

10 Enze Han and Joseph O'Mahoney, *British Colonialism and the Criminalization of Homosexuality: Queens, Crime and Empire*, Routledge, 2019, pp. 3–4, 11–13.

11 Ibid., pp. 10–13, 24, 34.

12 Ibid., pp. 2, 62; https://www.bbc.co.uk/news/world-latin-america-63970659; Feliz Solomon, 'Compromise Lies behind Singapore's New Approach to LGBT Rights', *Wall Street Journal*, 02/09/2022, https://www.wsj.com/articles/compromise-lies-behind-singapores-new-approach-to-lgbt-rights-11662110698.

13 Han and O'Mahoney, *British Colonialism and the Criminalization of Homosexuality*, p. 41.

14 Ibid., p. 4.

15 Douglas E. Sanders cited by Han and O'Mahoney, *British Colonialism and the Criminalization of Homosexuality*, p. 4; Douglas E. Sanders, '377 and the Unnatural Afterlife of British Colonialism in Asia', *Asian Journal of Comparative Law* 2009, 4, p. 1.

16 Han and O'Mahoney, *British Colonialism and the Criminalization of Homosexuality*, p. 59.

17 Chidera Ihejirika, 'Fuck your gender norms: how Western colonisation brought unwanted binaries to Igbo culture', *gal-dem*, 19/02/2020, https://gal-dem.com/ colonialism-nigeria-gender-norms-lgbtq-igbo/.

18 William Spurlin, *Imperialism within the Margins: Queer Representation and the Politics of Culture in Southern Africa*, Palgrave Macmillan, 2006, pp. 33–55.

19  Marc Epprecht, ' "Unnatural Vice" in South Africa: The 1907 Commission of Enquiry', *International Journal of African Historical Studies* 2001, 34:1, pp. 121–40.

20  Nilanjana Bhowmick, 'India's Opposition BJP Calls Homosexuality Unnatural', 16/12/2013, https://world.time.com/2013/12/16/indias-opposition-bjp-calls-homo sexuality-unnatural/.

21  Han and O'Mahoney, *British Colonialism and the Criminalization of Homosexuality*, p. 105.

22  Scott Long, 'Before the law: Criminalizing sexual conduct in colonial and post-colonial southern African societies', *More Than a Name: State-Sponsored Homophobia and its Consequences in Southern Africa*, Human Rights Watch, 2003, https://www.hrw.org/reports/2003/safrica/safriglhrc0303-07.htm.

23  Jessica Hinchy, *Governing Gender and Sexuality in Colonial India: The Hijra, c.1850–1900*, Cambridge University Press, 2019, p. 1.

24  The Act included section 61 on sodomy and bestiality: 'Whosoever shall be convicted of the abominable Crime of Buggery, committed either with Mankind or with any Animal, shall be liable, at the Discretion of the Court, to be kept in Penal Servitude for Life or for any Term not less than Ten Years.'

25  Han and O'Mahoney, *British Colonialism and the Criminalization of Homosexuality*, p. 31.

26  Ibid., pp. 10–11, 31.

27  Robert Aldrich, *Colonialism and Homosexuality*, Taylor & Francis, 2002, p. 276; Ronald Hyam, *Empire and Sexuality: The British Experience*, Manchester University Press, 1990.

28  Han and O'Mahoney, *British Colonialism and the Criminalization of Homosexuality*, pp. 6, 10–11, 41.

29  *Tom Daley: Illegal to Be Me*, BBC, 15/08/2022, https://www.bbc.co.uk/pro grammes/m001boyv; Andrei Tapalaga, 'Buck Breaking: The Worst Form of Punishment against Enslaved Men', *History of Yesterday*, 23/01/2023, https://histo ryofyesterday.com/buck-breaking-the-use-of-sexual-violence-against-enslaved-men-as-punishment-for-wrongdoing-897647489732;https://medium.com/black-history-month-365/buck-breaking-the-rape-and-beating-of-black-enslaved-men-to-make-them-compliant-75107aeaf2d6.

30  Thomas A. Foster, *Rethinking Rufus: Sexual Violations of Enslaved Men*, University of Georgia Press, 2019, p. 101.

31  John Saillant, 'The Black Body Erotic and the Republican Body Politic', in Thomas A. Foster (ed.), *Long before Stonewall: Histories of Same-Sex Sexuality in Early America*, New York University Press, 2007, p. 310.

32  Foster, *Rethinking Rufus*, p. 86.

33  William Styron, *The Confessions of Nat Turner*, Random House, 1968, pp. 226–40.

34   Foster, *Rethinking Rufus*, p. 86.

35   Benton and Ford, *Rage for Order*, p. 14.

36   Ibid., pp. 31–43; 'What caused Bligh's crew to lead a mutiny on his ship, the *Bounty*, in 1789?', *Royal Museums Greenwich*, https://www.rmg.co.uk/stories/topics/william-bligh; 'Rum Rebellion', *Britannica*, https://www.britannica.com/event/Rum-Rebellion.

37   Benton and Ford, *Rage for Order*, p. 28; Nathan Dorn, 'New Acquisition: *The Trial of Governor Picton* – A Case of Torture in Trinidad', *Library of Congress blog*, 10/03/2021, https://blogs.loc.gov/law/2021/03/new-acquisition-the-trial-of-governor-picton-a-case-of-torture-in-trinidad/; 'Lieutenant-General Sir Thomas Picton (1758–1815)', *Amgueddfa Cymru*, https://museum.wales/collections/online/object/4adfdd41-6370-36bf-a907-c74f5ad7d4a5/Lieutenant-General-Sir-Thomas-Picton-1758-1815/.

38   'Edward Huggins Sr.', *Centre for the Study of the Legacies of British Slavery* https://www.ucl.ac.uk/lbs/person/view/2146635234; Benton and Ford, *Rage for Order*, pp. 43–5; Josephine Humphreys, 'History and Mystery on Nevis', *New York Times*, 12/11/1995, https://www.nytimes.com/1995/11/12/t-magazine/history-and-mystery-on-nevis.html; https://rb.gy/xad6h.

39   Benton and Ford, *Rage for Order*, pp. 48–9; 'Arthur Hodge', *Centre for the Study of the Legacies of British Slavery*, https://www.ucl.ac.uk/lbs/person/view/2146650163; 'Arthur William Hodge', *National Portrait Gallery*, https://www.npg.org.uk/collections/search/portrait/mw14993/Arthur-William-Hodge?LinkID=mp14472&role=sit&rNo=0; Lauren Benton, 'This Melancholy Labyrinth: The Trial of Arthur Hodge and the Boundaries of Imperial Law', *Alabama Law Review* 2012, 64:1, pp. 91–122.

40   Benton and Ford, *Rage for Order*, p. 14.

41   Ibid., pp. 191–2.

42   Zoë Laidlaw, *Protecting the Empire's Humanity: Thomas Hodgkin and British Colonial Activism, 1830–1870*, Cambridge University Press, 2021, is very good on this theme. On the topic of colonized people themselves appealing to the Crown, there is Maria Nugent's insightful essay, 'The politics of memory and the memory of politics: Australian Aboriginal interpretations of Queen Victoria, 1881–2011', in Sarah Carter and Maria Nugent (eds.), *Mistress of Everything: Queen Victoria in Indigenous Worlds*, Manchester University Press, 2016, pp. 100–122.

43   Benton and Ford, *Rage for Order*, pp. 91, 102; Lee C. Godden and Niranjan Casinader, 'The Kandyan Convention 1815: Consolidating the British Empire in Colonial Ceylon', *Comparative Legal History* 2013, 1:2, pp. 179–210.

44   https://committees.parliament.uk/inquiries/.

45   'Less money equals better care: Inquiries springing up: But where are the shears?', *Public* magazine, 02/11/2006.

46  Benton and Ford, *Rage for Order*, p. 60.

47  Ibid., p. 57.

48  Ibid., p. 58.

49  In a recent article historians Jon Wilson and Andrew Dilley talk up the essential incoherence of the British empire. 'British assertions of sovereignty were multiple, mutually contradictory and thus, taken together, incoherent,' they maintain. 'Idioms of sovereignty varied; there was no single British way of claiming territory. The "British empire" was a jumble of different lands and societies, all ruled through different forms of government with differing claims to political power, ultimately unified by their common existence under the sovereignty of the Crown, as the 1911 edition of the *Encyclopædia Britannica* recognised. Claims to sovereignty were articulated through an extraordinary range of idioms and practices, from violent conquest through treaties and concessions to the right of settler communities to govern themselves. The plurality of imperial sovereignty meant "the empire" could never be a single power or space. It was not even a single "project". Incoherence was the essence of empire. Plural sovereignty is not just a helpful perspective for understanding empire. It was what Britain's empire actually was.' Jon Wilson and Andrew Dilley, 'The Incoherence of Empire. Or, the Pitfalls of Ignoring Sovereignty in the History of the British Empire', *Transactions of the Royal Historical Society* 2023, pp. 1–27, https://doi.org/10.1017/S0080440123000063.

50  Benton and Ford, *Rage for Order*, pp. 195, 197, 180.

51  Ferguson, *Empire*, p. xxii.

52  Kwarteng, *Ghosts of Empire*, pp. 5–6.

53  Richard Lloyd Parry and Raphael Blet, 'Colonial nostalgia rules in Hong Kong as young refuse to accept China's authority', *The Times*, 14/06/2019, https://www.thetimes.co.uk/article/colonial-nostalgia-rules-as-young-refuse-to-accept-beijing-rule-gswccqovf.

54  Winston Churchill, *The River War: An Historical Account of the Reconquest of the Soudan*, Dover Publications, 2007; Ferguson, *Empire*, p. xxvii.

55  MacKenzie continues: 'If any building should have been emblematic of the British empire, it should have been law courts. A central aspect of the ideology of empire was its alleged basis in law and its dissemination of distinctively English legal practices to the rest of the world: English because the common law, rooted in the Middle Ages, was so different from the Roman Dutch law of parts of continental practice, as well as of Scotland (the British encountered Roman Dutch law in Ceylon and in South Africa and often turned to Scots to operate what they had inherited).' See MacKenzie, *The British Empire through Buildings*, pp. 90 and 101.

56  Kolsky, *Colonial Justice in British India*, p. 230.

57   Many Western legal conventions arguably existed in various forms in pre-colonial India, which was governed by a mixture of regional laws, Hindu and Muslim personal law and Islamic criminal law before the British turned up. The Mughals had sharia law, which stood apart (formally, at least, as was the case with the British) from the executive. The Hindu concept of 'dharma' could be seen as a version of the rule of law ('Law is the king of kings, far more rigid and powerful than they; there is nothing higher than law; by its prowess as by that of highest monarch, the weak shall prevail over the strong': *The Brihadaranyaka Upanishad*). Meanwhile, Nandini Chatterjee reports that the Mughals ruled over largely non-Muslim multilingual populations, and that the sources of Mughal legal traditions were multilayered: 'I propose that "law in Mughal India" consisted of rules derived from a number of sources – royal and sub-royal orders, administrative conventions and rules, Islamic jurisprudence and local custom – "Islam" providing a general sense of order, together with royal grace.' See Aakash Singh Rathore and Garima Goswamy, *Rethinking Indian Jurisprudence: An Introduction to the Philosophy of Law*, Routledge, 2018, p. 74; Nandini Chatterjee, *Negotiating Mughal Law: A Family of Landlords across Three Indian Empires*, Cambridge University Press, 2020; Han and O'Mahoney, *British Colonialism and the Criminalization of Homosexuality*, pp. 11–12; Nandini Chatterjee, 'Reflections on Religious Difference and Permissive Inclusion in Mughal Law', *Journal of Law and Religion* 2014, 29:3, pp. 396–415.

58   Keally McBride, 'Mr. Mothercountry: The Rule of Law as Practice', *Law, Culture and the Humanities* 2017, 13:3, pp. 320–34, and McBride, *Mr. Mothercountry*.

59   McBride, *Mr. Mothercountry*, pp. 43, 48.

60   Ibid., pp. 50–51, 327.

61   Ibid., p. 321.

62   D. M. Young, *The Colonial Office in the Early Nineteenth Century*, Longman, Green, 1961, p. 12; McBride, *Mr. Mothercountry*, p. 47.

63   McBride, 'Mr. Mothercountry', pp. 321, 327.

64   McBride, *Mr. Mothercountry*, p. 157.

65   Ibid.

66   Severin Carrell, Rob Evans, David Pegg and Mario Savarese, 'Revealed: Queen's sweeping immunity from more than 160 laws', *Guardian*, 14/07/2022, https://www.theguardian.com/uk-news/2022/jul/14/queen-immunity-british-laws-private-property.

67   McBride, *Mr. Mothercountry*, pp. 63, 5, 11, 30.

68   'British law and order existed mainly to maintain White dominance in the colonies where British colonists dwelt,' writes Alan Lester. 'When the Colonial Office or India Office (after 1858) in London prescribed that colonial law be

non-racial, that intent was generally undermined by local colonial interests.' See Alan Lester, 'What are the British Empire's "Legacies"?', *University of Sussex: Snapshots of Empire*, 10/10/2022, https://blogs.sussex.ac.uk/snapshotsofempire/2022/10/10/what-are-the-british-empires-legacies/.

69  David Anderson and David Killingray, *Policing the Empire: Government, Authority, and Control, 1830–1940*, Manchester University Press, 1991, p. 7.

70  Ibid., passim; Georgina Sinclair, 'The "Irish" policeman and the Empire: influencing the policing of the British Empire–Commonwealth', *Irish Historical Studies* 2008, 36:142, pp. 173–87; M. Silvestri, ' "Paddy Does Not Mind Who the Enemy Is": The Royal Irish Constabulary and Colonial Policing', in T. McMahon, M. de Nie and P. Townend (eds.), *Ireland in an Imperial World*, Palgrave Macmillan, 2017; Richard Hill, 'Policing Ireland, Policing Colonies: The Royal Irish Constabulary "Model" ', in Angela McCarthy (ed.), *Ireland in the World: Comparative, Transnational and Personal Perspectives*, Routledge, 2015, pp. 61–80.

71  Anderson and Killingray, *Policing the Empire*, p. 7.

72  Jon Wilson, *India Conquered: Britain's Raj and the Chaos of Empire*, Simon & Schuster, 2016, pp. 209–11.

73  'Thomas Babington Macaulay', *New World Encyclopedia*, https://www.new worldencyclopedia.org/entry/Thomas_Babington_Macaulay.

74  T. B. Macaulay, Speech delivered in the House of Commons, 10/07/1833, *The Miscellaneous Speeches and Writings of Lord Macaulay*, Longmans, Green, 1889, p. 570.

75  Wilson, *India Conquered*, pp. 213, 214.

76  Kolsky, *Colonial Justice in British India*, p. 70.

77  James Fitzjames Stephen, the son of the James Stephen we came across earlier, served in India as law member of the Governor General's Council from 1869 to 1872, and was one of the architects of the code. He famously proclaimed: 'If it be asked how the system works in practice, I can only say that it enables a handful of unsympathetic foreigners . . . to rule justly and firmly about 200,000,000 persons of many races . . . The Penal Code, the Code of Criminal Procedure, and the institutions which they regulate, are somewhat grim presents for one people to make to another, and are little calculated to excite affection; but they are eminently well-calculated to protect peaceable men and to beat down wrongdoers, to extort respect, and to enforce obedience . . . If, however, the authority of the Government is once materially relaxed, if the essential character of the enterprise is misunderstood and the delusion that it can be carried out by assemblies representing the opinions of the natives is admitted, nothing but anarchy and ruin can be the result.' See https://blogs.sussex.ac.uk/snapshotsofempire/2022/10/10/what-are-the-british-empires-legacies/.

78  Kolsky, *Colonial Justice in British India*, p. 78.

79  Ibid., pp. 97–103; Ferguson, *Empire*, pp. 199–205; 'Ilbert Bill', *Britannica*, 18/01/2023, https://www.britannica.com/event/Ilbert-Bill.

80  Arthur Herman, *Gandhi and Churchill: The Rivalry That Destroyed an Empire and Forged our Age*, Random House, 2010, p. 34.

81  Ferguson, *Empire*, pp. 202–5.

82  Kolsky, *Colonial Justice in British India*, pp. 11, 210.

83  Ibid., pp. 190–91.

84  Ibid., p. 191.

85  Her mother, Ying-Ying Chang, remarked on her daughter's despair: 'Iris told us that the most difficult thing was to read one case after another of the atrocities . . . She read hundreds of such cases. She felt numb after a while. She told me she sometimes had to get up and away from the documents to take a deep breath. She felt suffocated and in pain.' See Robins, 'Can Historians Be Traumatized by History?'

86  Kolsky, *Colonial Justice in British India*, pp. 199–201.

87  Ibid., pp. 194, 203–4.

88  Ibid., p. 204.

89  Fae Dussart, ' "Strictly Legal Means": Assault, Abuse and the Limits of Acceptable Behaviour in the Servant–Employer Relationship in Metropole and Colony 1850– 1890', in Claire Lowrie and Victoria K. Haskins (eds.), *Colonization and Domestic Service: Historical and Contemporary Perspectives*, Taylor & Francis, 2014, p. 167; Christopher J. Fettweis, *The Pursuit of Dominance: 2000 Years of Superpower Grand Strategy*, Oxford University Press, 2022, pp. 173–207; Fae Dussart, *In the Service of Empire: Domestic Service and Mastery in Metropole and Colony*, Bloomsbury, 2022.

90  Nick Mansfield, *Soldiers as Citizens: Popular Politics and the Nineteenth-Century British Military*, Oxford University Press, 2019, p. 179.

91  Kolsky, *Colonial Justice in British India*, pp. 78, 108, 110.

92  Ibid., pp. 107, 4, 203, 18, 187.

93  Ibid., pp. 186, 194–5.

94  Rana P. Behal, 'Coolie Drivers or Benevolent Paternalists? British Tea Planters in Assam and the Indenture Labour System', *Modern Asian Studies* 2010, 44:1, pp. 29–51.

95  Kolsky, *Colonial Justice in British India*, pp. 195–6, 9–10, 195, 187.

96  Taylor C. Sherman, *State Violence and Punishment in India*, Routledge, 2010, pp. 174–5. Around 2016, the Indian court system had a backlog of over 30 million cases, and roughly 70 per cent of inmates in the nation's jails had never been put on trial for a crime. Meanwhile, Ashoka Mody, Visiting Professor of International Economic Policy at Princeton University, recently observed that 'the police kill suspects so often that Indians do not bother to spell out "killed in an encounter"; alleged criminals are simply "encountered". Indian elites, anxious to

protect their gated lives, celebrate police officers described as "encounter special-ists".' McBride, *Mr. Mothercountry*, pp. 33, 123; Ashoka Mody, 'India's Law-of-the-Jungle Raj', *Project Syndicate*, 12/05/2023, https://www.project-syndicate. org/onpoint/atiq-ahmed-murder-reveals-india-lawlessness-state-violence-by-ashoka-mody-2023-05.

97   Elkins, *Legacy of Violence*, p. 582.

98   David M. Anderson and David Killingray, *Policing and Decolonisation: Politics, Nationalism, and the Police, 1917–65*, Manchester University Press, 1992, p. 58.

99   McBride, *Mr. Mothercountry*, pp. 134–5.

100  As Alan Lester puts it: 'Since the demise of colonial regimes, of course law and order has often worked partially . . . in favour of other minorities defined ethnic-ally, regionally, by kinship or clientelism. In these instances, conservatives use phrases such as corruption that they tend not to apply to equivalent British colo-nial practices that favoured White people.' See Lester, 'What are the British Empire's "Legacies"?'

101  Han and O'Mahoney, *British Colonialism and the Criminalization of Homosexuality*, pp. 59–61.

102  Safi, 'Campaigners celebrate as India decriminalises homosexuality'.

103  See Penelope MacRae, 'No justice, says India gang-rape victim after killers get early release', *The Times*, 18/08/2022, https://www.thetimes.co.uk/article/ 2045eb84-1efe-11ed-b7c3-8b288ab55a56?shareToken=40090cafd02b3b9872b41b5 3dca84e2f.

## *Chapter 6: The Colour Line*

1   Bundock, *The Fortunes of Francis Barber*.

2   Ibid., p. 192.

3   Elliot Rudwick, 'W. E. B. Du Bois', *Britannica*, 25/01/2023, https://www.britan nica.com/biography/W-E-B-Du-Bois.

4   Marilyn Lake and Henry Reynolds, *Drawing the Global Colour Line: White Men's Countries and the International Challenge of Racial Equality*, Cambridge University Press, 2008, p. 247; David Levering Lewis, *W. E. B. Du Bois: A Biography*, Holt, 2009, pp. 279–80, 335.

5   Lake and Reynolds, *Drawing the Global Colour Line*, pp. 1–4; Duncan Bell, *Dream-worlds of Race: Empire and the Utopian Destiny of Anglo-America*, Princeton University Press, 2020, pp. 380–85; J. R. Hooker, 'The Pan-African Conference 1900', *Transition* 1974, 46, pp. 20–24.

6   Coleridge-Taylor organized the musical entertainment for the Conference, composing the music for five songs.

7   'To the nations of the world, ca. 1900', Copy of address signed by Du Bois, Alexander Walters, Henry B. Brown and H. Sylvester Williams, https://credo.library. umass.edu/view/full/mums312-b004-i321.

8   W. E. B. Du Bois, 'Strivings of the Negro People', *The Atlantic*, August 1897, https://www.theatlantic.com/magazine/archive/1897/08/strivings-of-the-negro-people/305446/

9   Bell, *Dreamworlds of Race*, pp. 380–81.

10  Lake and Reynolds, *Drawing the Global Colour Line*, pp. 1–2, 247; Bell, *Dreamworlds of Race*, pp. 32, 381; W. E. B. Du Bois, 'The Souls of White Folk', *Library of America*, pp. 923–4.

11  Levering Lewis, *W. E. B. Du Bois*, pp. 192–3.

12  Bell, *Dreamworlds of Race*, pp. 381–2, and https://twitter.com/DrKevinGray/status/1579391884577103872?lang=en.

13  Alan Lester explains how the narrative that abolition had failed took root. 'Anti-slavery proponents . . . had promised their fellow Britons that, in line with the new principles of political economy, freed black men and women would work harder on the West Indian plantations than they had as enslaved labourers, that they would practise a sober and diligent Christianity, and that they would receive gratefully the blessing of instruction in the art of civilised, British, conduct in church, in the home and in the workplace. When, in the early 1840s, most former slaves in Jamaica, Britain's main focal point for the discursive contest over slavery, chose to leave the plantations on which they had been held captive, to work for themselves and their reconstituted families rather than for their former owners, and to define their own syncretic take on Christianity rather than reproduce the dour forms of worship that their missionaries taught, plantations were left short of labour, sugar production plummeted and the Jamaican economy collapsed. By 1857, *The Times* was proclaiming the failure of the emancipation experiment: "it destroyed an immense property, ruined thousands of good families, degraded the Negroes still lower than they were, and, after all, increased the mass of Slavery in less scrupulous hands".' Alan Lester, 'Race and Citizenship: Colonial Inclusions and Exclusions', in Martin Hewitt (ed.), *The Victorian World*, Routledge, 2012, p. 383.

14  'In every single colony, White colonists had rights that were denied to colonised people of colour,' writes Alan Lester. 'Even in India where the accommodations and alliances between elite Indians and British rulers were perhaps most evident, Indians were allowed to participate in governance only in an advisory role, only very late in the era of colonial governance, and only in response to nationalist agitation. Judicial systems systematically punished people of colour and White colonists differentially for the same crimes in every colony throughout the colonial period. On a quotidian level, people of colour were generally expected to

show deference to White colonists no matter what their respective class status. Only Black people were enslaved within the British empire, and they were "owned" overwhelmingly by White people, with a relatively few free people of colour also slave-owners. White colonists generally had Black servants, never the other way around. White colonists could use violence against colonised people of colour relatively freely, with punishment quite exceptional. Never the other way around. The everyday discourse of colonial governance was predicated on racial distinctions, as you will appreciate if you work in any colonial archive.' https://twitter.com/aljhlester/status/1671099643726295043?t=oJnfyuVUntNb7_Eh-hgODw&s=03.

15  Titles including Lake and Reynolds, *Drawing the Global Colour Line*; Bell, *Dreamworlds of Race*; Paul Gilroy, *The Black Atlantic*, Harvard University Press, 1995.

16  https://twitter.com/aljhlester/status/1647856752254132225.

17  The full quotation from Beckles is worth reading: 'First, they globalized the trade so that, by the eighteenth century, they were the largest shippers; second, they produced the most abundant body of writing that established, within the intellectual and social consciousness of the world, the racist philosophy that African people were not entitled to the freedom they cherished. During the seventeenth century, the English generally believed that black Africans were an inferior people. This view was expressed in the laws and customs used to govern them as enslaved persons. It was also stimulated by writing about the slave trade. Together these texts constituted a source of cultural authority used to justify slavery and the slave trade as entrepreneurial activity. The English justification of slave trading was a large-scale literary and intellectual project. The notion that Africans were non-human, or subhuman at best, and that their right to humanity could be denied and ignored was an intellectual construct that required considerable literary focus and sustained articulation. A mountain of published materials was produced supporting this justification of slavery. As a body of writing, it represents the moral descent of the British mind into the darkest pit of racial hatred. Seeking to deny the human status of Africans also required the theological support of the church. The English public would support the crime only if it was presented to them as "right" and in the national interest.' Beckles, *Britain's Black Debt*, p. 39.

18  Surodya Prakasika quoted by Kolsky, *Colonial Justice in British India*, p. 16.

19  Hall quoted by ibid.

20  Ibid., p. 18.

21  Michael Makovsky, *Churchill's Promised Land: Zionism and Statecraft*, Yale University Press, 2007, pp. 156–7.

22  'While I should have no scruple whatever in entrusting to natives properly trained the care of the lighthouses at Colombo, Galle, and Trincomalie,' the

Governor of Ceylon declared in 1879, 'I think that the entrusting to natives the care of such important and at the same time such isolated lighthouses as the Great and Little Basses, requires grave consideration. I find upon inquiry in India and Singapore that in the Madras Presidency natives (Asiatics) have not been placed in sole or partial charge of any lighthouses. And the lighthouses throughout the Straits have a European or Eurasian in charge. In Hong Kong a Light . . . is said to be in charge of Chinese only, under frequent supervision. But Chinese are so far superior to the bulk of other Orientals in steadiness and intelligence that the successful employment of Chinese in any pursuit is by no means a guarantee that the employment of other Orientals in the same pursuit would be equally successful.' Lester, Boehme and Mitchell, *Ruling the World*, p. 10.

23    The South African comedian Noah became the focus of intense criticism, involving public figures and government ministers, when he dared to observe the simple fact that Rishi Sunak's appointment as Prime Minister had provoked racism among some Brits. See Oliver Slow, 'Trevor Noah: I never said entire U K racist, says comic after Rishi Sunak row', *BBC News*, 29/10/2022, https://www.bbc.co.uk/news/entertainment-arts-63437351.

24    Levering Lewis, *W. E. B. Du Bois*, p. 328.

25    Sean Elias, 'Colour Line', *The Wiley Blackwell Encyclopedia of Race, Ethnicity, and Nationalism*, Wiley Blackwell, 2015, https://www.researchgate.net/publication/315772103_Colour_Line/link/6079cf6a907dcf667ba44372/download.

26    Arnold, cited by Daniel Gorman, *Imperial Citizenship: Empire and the Question of Belonging*, Manchester University Press, 2006, p. 8.

27    Cited by Nancy Stepan in *The Idea of Race in Science: Great Britain, 1800–1960*, Macmillan, 1982, p. xvii.

28    Even though they spent their careers in Jamaica criticizing the cruel treatment of slaves, British missionaries did not consider them equals: they saw themselves as the teachers of these 'children' within the 'universal family of man'. The missionaries' concern for the underprivileged was often combined with the conviction that white people were their only hope. See Kolsky, *Colonial Justice in British India*, p. 15.

29    I'm thinking of biographer James Boswell, who was notably kind and generous towards Francis Barber, Samuel Johnson's black servant, even as he expressed enthusiastic support for West Indian planters.

30    Gorman, *Imperial Citizenship*, pp. 51–2.

31    'The Waco Horror', *Brown University Library*, July 1916, https://library.brown.edu/pdfs/1292363091648500.pdf.

32    'A young black laborer on a farm outside Atlanta, Hose got into a dispute with his employer and killed him in self-defense,' explains a blog on the website of the Library of America. 'During the ensuing ten-day manhunt, the rival Atlanta

newspapers excited their readers by competing on lurid details. As days went by, rape, infanticide, and other "unnatural acts" were added to descriptions of the crime. When Hose was finally apprehended, the surrounding hysteria led to excursion trains being arranged to transport hundreds of Georgians from Atlanta to the site of his execution. On Sunday, 23 April 1899, the day after his capture, Hose was brought before an estimated crowd of 2,000 in the town square of Newman, Georgia. There he was stripped; his ears, fingers, and genitals cut off; his face skinned, and his body burned on a pyre. Souvenir hunters fought over his organs and bones. For W. E. B. Du Bois the lynching was an awakening. Having arrived at Atlanta University two years before, the pleasantries of his studies were shattered.' See 'How Sam Hose's lynching became an awakening for W. E. B. Du Bois', *The official blog of The Library of America*, 18/03/2011, http://blog. loa.org/2011/03/how-sam-hose-lynching-became-awakening.html. Also: Edwin T. Arnold, 'Across the Road from the Barbecue House', *Mississippi Quarterly* 2008, 61:1/2, Special Issue on Lynching and American Culture, pp. 267–92.

33 'Immigration policy during this period was discriminatory and heavily Eurocentric,' writes Salih Omar Eissa. 'Even when the McCarran–Walter Act of 1952 eliminated all racially specific language from the Immigration and Nationality Act (INA), national quotas remained and migration from the African continent was set at the lowest quota of 1,400 annually.' This changed with the 1965 Hart–Cellar Immigration Act: 'Voluntary immigration of peoples of African descent did not begin in earnest until passage of the Hart–Cellar Immigration Act of 1965, which revolutionized the criteria for immigration to the United States. The Act called for the admission of immigrants based on their skills, profession, or relationship to families in the United States.' Salih Omar Eissa, 'Diversity and Transformation: African Americans and African Immigration to the United States', Immigration Policy Center, https://www.americanimmigrationcouncil. org/sites/default/files/research/Diversity and Transformation March 2005.pdf.

34 Noa Yachot, ' "We want our land back": for descendants of the Elaine massacre, history is far from settled', *Guardian*, 18/06/2021, https://www.theguardian. com/us-news/2021/jun/18/elaine-massacre-red-summer-descendants-history.

35 For a discussion of the reliability of the quotation see Mark E. Benbow, 'Birth of a Quotation: Woodrow Wilson and "Like Writing History with Lightning" ', *Journal of the Gilded Age and Progressive Era* 2010, 9:4, pp. 509–33.

36 Gary Younge, 'Lest We Remember: How Britain Buried its History of Slavery', *Guardian*, 29/03/2023, https://www.theguardian.com/news/ng-interactive/2023/ mar/29/lest-we-remember-how-britain-buried-its-history-of-slavery; Aurelien Mondon and Aaron Winter, *Reactionary Democracy: How Racism and the Populist Far Right Became Mainstream*, Verso Books, 2020, p. 55; Riley, *Imperial Island*, pp. 44–5.

37  Tom Holland and Dominic Sandbrook, 'USA vs England: The 200-Year Rivalry', *The Rest Is History* podcast, episode 263, 25/11/ 2022, ten minutes in, https://open.spotify.com/episode/1fmP92v1fZeUWdXVFZTDFB?si=e21ee d1527e54a6b. 'The greatest shortcoming of much of the historical work being done in the United States is not its lack of the methodological or theoretical rigor that is found in the "hard" social sciences – history has its own quite defensible methods and theoretical assumptions – but rather its parochial vision,' writes George M. Fredrickson. 'Historians of the United States in particular characteristically know little in depth about the history of other societies, unless, like Early Modern England, they can be directly linked to the American experience.' See George M. Fredrickson, *White Supremacy: A Comparative Study*, Oxford University Press, 1981, p. xiv.

38  For more, see Zoë Laidlaw and Alan Lester (eds.), *Indigenous Communities and Settler Colonialism: Land Holding, Loss and Survival in an Interconnected World*, Palgrave Macmillan, 2015; James Belich, *Replenishing the Earth: The Settler Revolution and the Rise of the Anglo-World, 1783–1939*, Oxford University Press, 2011; Fredrickson, *White Supremacy*, p. 45.

39  Ibid., p. 241.

40  Ibid.

41  Ibid., pp. xviii–xix.

42  The intellectual age of supposed reason that dominated the West between the seventeenth and nineteenth centuries developed differently on the east side of America and, for example, in Scotland. Also, it had varying degrees of influence on how countries developed. But the international book trade allowed for the worldwide reach of Enlightenment thinkers, and what the major personalities had to say about race shows that white supremacy developed at roughly the same time, and in roughly the same way, on both sides of the Atlantic. David Hume, the revered Scottish thinker of the Enlightenment, said in 1753, 'I am apt to suspect the negroes to be naturally inferior to whites,' while the German philosopher Immanuel Kant included in his Lectures on Physical Geography (published in 1802) his opinion that 'the yellow [Asian] Indians do have a meagre talent' but that 'Negroes are far below them and at the lowest point are a part of the American peoples.' In the seventeenth century, the English philosopher John Locke maintained that 'Negroes' were the result of African women mating with apes, and as a consequence should be viewed as subhuman. And then there was the Founding Father Thomas Jefferson, who noted in 1785 that 'the blacks, whether originally a distinct race, or made distinct by time and circumstances, are inferior to the whites in the endowments both of body and mind'. Despite this, Jefferson was still able to have several children with Sally Hemings, a black slave he had been abusing sexually since she was fourteen. 'When European thinkers set the

standard for what they considered a modern human, many built it around their own experiences and what they happened to value at that time,' writes Angela Saini. 'While a few Enlightenment thinkers did resist the idea of a racial hierarchy, many . . . saw no contradiction between the values of liberty and fraternity and their belief that non-whites were innately inferior to whites.' Angela Saini, *Superior: The Return of Race Science*, Fourth Estate, 2019, pp. 23–5; Kehinde Andrews, *The New Age of Empire: How Racism and Colonialism Still Rule the World*, Allen Lane, 2021, pp. 2, 8, 17; https://blackcentraleurope.com/sources/1750-1850/kant-on-the-different-human-races-1777/; Tom Holland and Dominic Sandbrook, 'The Enlightenment', *The Rest is History* podcast, episode 86, 16/08/2021, 7 mins, 10 seconds, https://open.spotify.com/episode/3Lu92A3BR BL3uYQ15wwmSS?si=OSGGDLDITA2OnPzMCUl5Cg&dl_branch=1.

43  'Cotton Capital: How slavery changed the Guardian, Britain and the world', *Guardian* [no date], https://www.theguardian.com/news/series/cotton-capital.

44  Andrews, *The New Age of Empire*, p. 104.

45  Ibid.

46  Younge, 'Lest We Remember'.

47  David Olusoga, 'Slavery and the Guardian: The Ties That Bind Us', *Guardian*, 28/03/2023, https://www.theguardian.com/news/ng-interactive/2023/mar/28/ slavery-and-the-guardian-the-ties-that-bind-us.

48  Ibid.

49  Lake and Reynolds, *Drawing the Global Colour Line*, p. 109.

50  Andrews, *The New Age of Empire*, p. xiv.

51  Bell, *Dreamworlds of Race*, p. 30; the theme is expanded upon at p. 373.

52  Lake and Reynolds, *Drawing the Global Colour Line*, p. 131.

53  The official justification for intervention was on behalf of the 'uitlanders' – white immigrants, mainly of British origin, living on the goldfields controlled by the Afrikaner Transvaal government, who were denied the same voting rights as Afrikaner citizens. The British wanted to gain control of gold and diamond mines and there was little attention paid to the rights of Indians or Africans in the Transvaal. However, the British did promise that the 'non-racial' constitution of the Cape and Natal (both of which excluded the vast majority of Africans from the vote in practice) would be extended to the Afrikaner republics after their defeat. This persuaded many Africans and Indians (like Gandhi) to side with the British in the war. That promise was betrayed at the Treaty of Vereeniging which finally brought the war to an end. The British thus abandoned their new Black subjects to explicitly racial exclusion from the franchise in the two former republics because the guerrilla war being fought by the Boers was proving enormously costly in British lives and in damage to Britain's reputation. The use of scorched-earth tactics and concentration camps against white colonists was causing

considerable opposition at home and in Europe (of course these tactics were far less controversial when used against Black people resisting colonization; Black concentration camps resulted in at least 14,000 deaths). So the British compromised, forsaking promises of non-racialism in order to secure peace and achieve the objective of unifying the region under British rule.

54  'Apartheid' is an Afrikaans word (literally 'apartness') specifically associated with the Afrikaner nationalist government elected from 1948. Essentially what it did was reinforce the British policies that maintained white supremacy and added positive discrimination for Afrikaners relative to English-speaking whites. At the time more than 80 per cent of the land was owned by the white minority, and only 13 per cent of land had been designated Bantu Homelands for the black African majority. Apartheid extended segregationist racist policies into more personal domains – marriage, 'intimacy' and so on – and made them easier to enforce with mandatory racial classification; it also created a vast sector of state employment for Afrikaners and promoted the Afrikaans language so that Afrikaners ceased to be the 'poor whites' and, by the 1980s, were as privileged as English-speakers. For an overview see Alan Lester, Etienne Nel and Tony Binns, *South Africa Past, Present and Future: Gold at the End of the Rainbow?*, Routledge, 2000.

55  Lake and Reynolds, *Drawing the Global Colour Line*, p. 230; House of Commons Debates 1909, vol. IX, col. 998.

56  Lake and Reynolds, *Drawing the Global Colour Line*, p. 121.

57  Ibid., p. 124.

58  Ibid., pp. 210–13; Saul Dubow, *Racial Segregation and the Origins of Apartheid in South Africa, 1919–36*, Palgrave Macmillan, 1989.

59  Viceroy of India 1894–9; Colonial Secretary 1905–8. Grandson of the man famously associated with the Marbles from the Parthenon.

60  Lake and Reynolds, *Drawing the Global Colour Line*, p. 232.

61  Ibid., p. 9. I looked up the source material at the National Archives, which directed me to surreal correspondence between imperial civil servants on the topic, one Morgan Evans in the Attorney General's Office in Cape Town informing colleagues in 1903 that in the case of South Africa 'Japanese subjects are in exactly the same plight as other Asiatics. They being, however, more Anglicized than many other Asiatics, they, and the better class Indians, are much more likely to come in than, e.g., Chinese.' The request was made by M. Cambon to Lansdowne on 24/09/1902. See Foreign Office to Colonial Office, Enclosure, CO 885/8/1.

62  Nigel Biggar, *Colonialism: A Moral Reckoning*, William Collins, 2023. For a forensic review of the book by a historian who has studied the British empire for decades, see Alan Lester, 'The British Empire Rehabilitated?', *Bella Cale-*

*donia*, 07/03/2023, https://bellacaledonia.org.uk/2023/03/07/the-british-empire-rehabilitated/.

63  Alan Lester, 'Race and Citizenship: Colonial Inclusions and Exclusions', in Hewitt (ed.), *The Victorian World*, p. 383.

64  The legislative assembly of British Columbia passed an act designed to limit Asian immigration, but it was blocked by Earl Minto who, as the Governor General of Canada (based in Ottawa), had the power to overrule the provincial assembly.

65  Lake and Reynolds, *Drawing the Global Colour Line*, p. 165.

66  Ibid., p. 61.

67  James Belich, *The New Zealand Wars and the Victorian Interpretation of Racial Conflict*, Auckland University Press, 1986, p. 328; Alan Lester, 'British Settler Discourse and the Circuits of Empire', *History Workshop Journal* 2002, 54:1, pp. 24–48, https://doi.org/10.1093/hwj/54.1.24.

68  Lake and Reynolds, *Drawing the Global Colour Line*, pp. 50–51, 56–7.

69  Ibid., pp. 49–50, 58–9.

70  Ibid., pp. 49–50, 59.

71  Ibid., p. 64.

72  Ibid., p. 61.

73  Ibid., pp. 61, 69.

74  Ibid., p. 64.

75  Ibid., pp. 3, 75–6.

76  Ibid., p. 92.

77  Duncan Bell, 'The Anglosphere: new enthusiasm for an old dream', *Prospect Magazine*, 19/01/2017, https://www.prospectmagazine.co.uk/magazine/anglosphere-old-dream-brexit-role-in-the-world.

78  Bell, *Dreamworlds of Race*, p. 294.

79  Ibid., p. 203.

80  Ibid., p. 287.

81  Ibid., pp. 212, 213.

82  Ibid., p. 159.

83  Ibid., pp. 177–80, 184.

84  Ibid., pp. 185–6.

85  Lake and Reynolds, *Drawing the Global Colour Line*, pp. 5, 62–7, 128–9. For a good article on the topic see Jeremy Martens, 'A transnational history of immigration restriction: Natal and New South Wales, 1896–97', *Journal of Imperial and Commonwealth History* 2006, 34:3, pp. 323–44.

86  Lake and Reynolds, *Drawing the Global Colour Line*, pp. 5, 63, 147, 300–301.

87  Ibid., p. 18.

88  Ibid., pp. 125–6.

89  Ibid., pp. 293–7, 316–17.

90  Josh Axelrod, 'A Century Later: The Treaty of Versailles and its Rejection of Racial Equality', *NPR*, 11/08/2019, https://www.npr.org/sections/codeswitch/2019/08/11/742293305/a-century-later-the-treaty-of-versailles-and-its-rejection-of-racial-equality?t=1654014119173; Lake and Reynolds, *Drawing the Global Colour Line*, p. 293.

91  In 1919 Balfour stated that 'he believed it was true in a certain sense that all men of a particular nation were created equal, but not that a man in Central Africa was created equal to a European'. See Lake and Reynolds, *Drawing the Global Colour Line*, p. 11.

92  Ibid., p. 308.

93  https://www.nytimes.com/2023/05/13/us/politics/biden-howard-commencement-black-voters.html.

94  See 'Post Office admits "abhorrent" racist slur was used to describe suspects in Horizon scandal', *Sky News*, 27/05/2023, https://news.sky.com/story/post-office-admits-abhorrent-racist-slur-was-used-to-describe-suspects-in-horizon-scandal-12890411.

95  Lake and Reynolds, *Drawing the Global Colour Line*, pp. 1–3.

96  See ibid., p. 185.

97  Ibid., p. 203.

98  The historian Heather Streets has written about how the British decided after the Mutiny of 1857 that the Sikhs, Highlanders and Gurkhas were inherently 'martial' people. Other 'racial' groups to be fetishized by British imperialists included the Zulus and Hausas of Africa. Heather Streets, *Martial Races: The Military, Race and Masculinity in British Imperial Culture, 1857–1914*, Manchester University Press, 2004.

99  Lake and Reynolds, *Drawing the Global Colour Line*, pp. 312–15.

100  Stepan, *The Idea of Race in Science*, p. xix.

101  Lake and Reynolds, *Drawing the Global Colour Line*, pp. 159–62.

102  Ibid., p. 68.

103  https://www.lib.washington.edu/specialcollections/collections/exhibits/south-asianstudents/das.

104  Lake and Reynolds, *Drawing the Global Colour Line*, p. 187.

105  Ibid., p. 280.

106  Ibid., p. 325.

107  Lester, 'Race and Citizenship', p. 381.

108  Report of the Parliamentary Select Committee on Aborigines, British Parliamentary Papers (1837), vol. 7, p. 5.

109  Bell, *Dreamworlds of Race*, p. 8.

110  Ibid., p. 374.

111 Manan Desai, 'What B. R. Ambedkar Wrote to W. E. B. Du Bois', *SAADA*, 22/04/2014, https://www.saada.org/tides/article/ambedkar-du-bois.

112 There is a long tradition in Britain of attempting to teach imperial history through the stories of individuals. In 1927, the HMSO *Handbook for Teachers* advised that teachers could bring the history alive through human examples. '[Pupils] will learn naturally in how many different ways the patriot has helped his country, and by what sort of actions nations and individuals have earned the gratitude of posterity. Without any laboured exhortations they will feel the splendour of heroism, the worth of unselfishness and loyalty, and the meanness of cruelty and cowardice.' Numerous texts and teachers' manuals commended 'books of heroes' as teaching aids in the early to mid-twentieth century. More recently, when he was Secretary of State for Education in 2013, Michael Gove announced plans, subsequently withdrawn, to enforce a curriculum for English schools based on a chronological timeline of British national heroes' achievements. See MacKenzie, *Propaganda and Empire*, pp. 178, 180–81; Matthew Watson, 'Michael Gove's war on professional historical expertise: conservative curriculum reform, extreme whig history and the place of imperial heroes in modern multicultural Britain', *British Politics* 2020, 15, pp. 271–90, https://link.springer.com/article/10.1057/s41293-019-00118-3.

## Chapter 7: Reaping the Chaos

1 T. G. O. Gbadamosi, Olugbolahan Abisogun Alo and Wale Osisanya-Olumuyiwa (eds.), *Floreat Collegium: 100 Years of King's College, Lagos*, Third Millennium Publishing, 2014, p. 57.

2 Ibid., p. 45.

3 King's College was opened nearly seventy years after missionaries opened Nigeria's first primary school and five decades after they opened Nigeria's first secondary school. Siollun, *What Britain Did to Nigeria*, pp. 265–80.

4 The administrator George Goldie was responsible 'more than anyone else', according to Kwasi Kwarteng, for the 'aggressive imperialism' that Nigeria witnessed. His involvement began in 1879 with the takeover of a modest trading company that operated in the region around the River Niger, which he refashioned first as the United Africa Trading Company and then as the National African Company, before obtaining a Royal Charter in 1886 and creating the Royal Niger Company. In a series of treaties that, it appears, the chiefs themselves did not always fully understand, he persuaded indigenous leaders to sign away much of their powers over their nations in order to further his objectives. The company was essentially 'doing the job of the British government at a much

less burdensome cost to the British taxpayer'. Kwarteng, *Ghosts of Empire*, pp. 276–82.

5 King's College is probably not Nigeria's most exclusive school – that accolade goes to Katsina College (later Barewa College), which was founded in 1921 to educate the sons of emirs in the tradition of similar institutions in British India and has produced more political leaders than any other school in Nigeria. Approximately 42 per cent of the nation's heads of government during the post-independence era received their education there. See Siollun, *What Britain Did to Nigeria*, pp. 265–80.

6 Gbadamosi, Abisogun Alo and Osisanya-Olumuyiwa, *Floreat Collegium*, pp. 14–15.

7 Ibid., p. 101.

8 Lugard was the second most important Briton in the history of Nigeria and also made a key contribution to the intellectual development of British empire in his espousal of 'indirect rule'. As an unofficial policy in Nigeria this had originated with George Goldie who, back in the 1880s, was happy to let local chiefs remain in charge of their areas on the condition they let him trade as he wished, though the princely states in India were the earliest model of indirect governance. Driven by the recognition that the British could not afford to govern Nigeria entirely themselves, Lugard turned this practice of indirect rule into an official policy, meaning that 'fifty or a hundred different Native administrations' in Nigeria were free to develop in their own way, 'subject only to a general scheme of policy'. Kwarteng, *Ghosts of Empire*, p. 290.

9 Siollun, *What Britain Did to Nigeria*, p. 272.

10 Ibid., p. 2.

11 'I think my upbringing and schooling in another country has really influenced the way that I look at these things,' Kemi Badenoch told Times Radio. 'There wasn't any sort of attempt to describe the British empire as this awful, terrible thing that oppressed and victimised us.' See Zaina Alibhai, 'Equalities minister Kemi Badenoch says British empire achieved "good things" throughout rule', *Independent*, 21/03/2022, https://www.independent.co.uk/news/uk/politics/kemi-badenoch-british-empire-colonialism-b2040002.html.

12 Philip Murphy, *The Empire's New Clothes: The Myth of the Commonwealth*, Hurst, 2021, pp. 56–60; Penelope MacRae, 'Narendra Modi vows to make India a developed nation', *The Times*, 15/08/2022, https://www.thetimes.co.uk/article/a975ef56-1c7b-11ed-add4-d333562d46fb?shareToken=933058c5b78c4c10b4dcb10be35fd079.

13 A 2017 'soft power index' found that fifty-eight of the world's leaders at the time had been educated in the UK, a tally not rivalled by any other country. In 2023, the US was found to have provided tertiary education for one or more leaders in

fifty-four countries, compared to Britain's tally of fifty-three. Meanwhile, a recent investigation by *The Times* found that Russian oligarchs convicted of embezzling hundreds of millions of pounds were sending their children to Britain's private schools. Transparency International, an anti-corruption organization, said schools were not just providing education but 'conveying legitimacy'. There are, however, signs that the prestige of British education, established during the British empire, might finally be fading. The USA took the top position in the 'soft power index' produced in 2018 – with fifty-eight world leaders compared with the UK's fifty-seven – and widened its lead in 2022, having educated sixty-seven world presidents and prime ministers compared with fifty-five who studied at British institutions. *The Times* reported mournfully that several UK-educated leaders had lost office in the past year, including Costa Rica's Carlos Quesada (alumnus of the University of Sussex), Armenia's Armen Sarkissan (University of Cambridge) and Pakistan's Imran Khan (University of Oxford). See Shayma Bakht and Anna Dowell, 'Britain vies with America to educate the world's leaders', *The Times*, 22/08/2023, https://www.thetimes.co.uk/article/0527fd6e-4069-11ee-8b31-3c9c533abb75?shareToken=28cf9540f551a71741dac13146d854a5; Nicola Woolcock, 'British influence on wane as leaders are educated elsewhere', 24/08/2022,https://www.thetimes.co.uk/article/british-influence-wanes-as-world-leaders-are-educated-elsewhere-3hhwd538z.

14  Siollun, *What Britain Did to Nigeria*, pp. 267–78.

15  In defence of the aforementioned imperially nostalgic book produced by King's College for its centenary, it does take time to recall that the proposed syllabus at King's was initially rejected by the school's board in London because it was not vocational enough. Rather than languages and classics, the board said the school should concentrate on technical, practical subjects, presumably in order to produce the railway engineers and so forth that the country needed. 'The board also recommended agricultural and industrial training for the project and objected to the use of the words "college" and "professor".' Siollun, *What Britain Did to Nigeria*, pp. 272–3; Gbadamosi, Abisogun Alo and Osisanya-Olumuyiwa, *Floreat Collegium*, p. 39.

16  Siollun, *What Britain Did to Nigeria*, p. 268.

17  At least, north vs south was how many British imperialists saw the country. Following their initial takeover of Lagos, the British pushed to annex much of Yorubaland: these lands were consolidated first as the Niger Coast Protectorate, then as the Southern Nigerian Protectorate. The British takeover of the north occurred in 1900, resulting in the Northern Nigerian Protectorate. The whole country was then under Britain's control. But many scholars stress that the ethnic demography of Nigeria is much more complex than this basic division between north and south suggests – the south, for instance, is also home to other

394 Notes to pp. 200–201

long-established groups, such as the Ijaw and the Tiv. Kwarteng, for his part, describes the country as being split in three. 'In simple terms the British understood, there was a northern region, which was predominantly Muslim, a western region, which was dominated by the Yoruba tribe, and an eastern region, where the Igbo were the predominant ethnic group . . . For the British, the division of Nigeria into three parts was a crucially important fact in its short history. The north was dominated by feudal, Islamic lords known as emirs. In the west, the Yorubas had a society in which chiefs were powerful. In the east, the Igbos were widely known to be less feudal.' Kwarteng adds that even 'this was an oversimplified view'. Ajay Verghese, *The Colonial Origins of Ethnic Violence in India*, Stanford University Press, 2016, pp. 195–6; Kwarteng, *Ghosts of Empire*, p. 284.

18 Siollun, *What Britain Did to Nigeria*, pp. 278–9.

19 In 1912, the French-born British journalist E. D. Morel maintained that the 'Southern Nigerian system is turning out every year hundreds of Europeanized Africans', but the 'Northern Nigerian system aims at the establishment of an educational system based upon a totally different ideal'. Kwarteng, *Ghosts of Empire*, p. 305; Siollun, *What Britain Did to Nigeria*, pp. 323–4.

20 'Nigeria', *The World Factbook*, https://www.cia.gov/the-world-factbook/countries/nigeria/#people-and-society; Verghese, *The Colonial Origins of Ethnic Violence in India*, pp. 195–9; John Burger, 'Backgrounder: Why is there so much Christian persecution in Nigeria?', *Aleteia*, 24/01/2023, https://aleteia.org/2023/01/24/backgrounder-why-is-there-so-much-christian-persecution-in-nigeria/; Justine John Dyikuk, '"Scores of Christians killed, others displaced" – Nigerian think tank builds "atrocities database"', *The Pillar*, 14/02/2023, https://www.pillarcatholic.com/scores-of-christians-killed-others-displaced-nigerian-think-tank-builds-atrocities-database/; Kwarteng, *Ghosts of Empire*, p. 321; Siollun, *What Britain Did to Nigeria*, pp. 256–7; Shobana Shankar, 'Precolonial Christianity and Missionary Legacies', in Carl Levan and Patrick Ukata (eds.), *The Oxford Handbook of Nigerian Politics*, Oxford University Press, 2018, pp. 47–59.

21 Siollun, *What Britain Did to Nigeria*, p. 324.

22 Jack Straw said: 'I'm not a liberal imperialist. There's a lot wrong with liberalism, with a capital L, although I am a liberal with a small L. And there's a lot wrong with imperialism. A lot of the problems we are having to deal with now are a consequence of our colonial past. India, Pakistan – we made some quite serious mistakes. We were complacent about what happened in Kashmir, the boundaries weren't published until two days after independence. Bad story for us, the consequences are still there. Afghanistan – where we played a less than glorious role over a century and a half . . . The odd lines for Iraq's borders were drawn by Brits. The Balfour declaration and the contradictory assurances which were being given to Palestinians in private at the same time as they were being given

to Israelis – again, an interesting history for us but not an entirely honourable one.' Sunder Katwala, 'Is the British empire to blame?', *Guardian*, 17/11/2002, https://www.theguardian.com/politics/2002/nov/17/foreignpolicy.comment.

23 Kwarteng, *Ghosts of Empire*, p. 3.

24 Richard Assheton, 'Peter Obi, the 61-year-old "youngster" who wants to clean up Nigeria', *Sunday Times*, 07/01/2023, https://www.thetimes.co.uk/article/538d8d6e-8e00-11ed-a303-61858d68dcd6?shareToken=d9715f67849647111dc08285cf02161c.

25 David Pilling, 'How Nigeria's state lost the trust of its citizens', *Financial Times*, 19/09/2022, https://www.ft.com/content/bc086fd8-12c5-4a15-afc2-734be4443aac.

26 Lolade Olu-Ojegbeje, 'Bolt Driver Connives with Abuja Police to "Kidnap", Rob Passenger of N1m', *Foundation of Investigative Journalism*, 31/03/2022, https://fij.ng/article/bolt-driver-connives-with-abuja-police-to-kidnap-rob-passenger-of-n1m/; 'Twitter User Accuses Uber Driver of Trying to Kidnap Her', *Bella Naija*, 11/01/2017, https://www.bellanaija.com/2017/01/twitter-user-accuses-uber-driver-of-trying-to-kidnap-her/.

27 'Nigeria: Gunmen abduct more than 30 in train station attack', *DW*, 01/08/2023, https://www.dw.com/en/nigeria-gunmen-abduct-more-than-30-in-train-station-attack/a-64321012.

28 Uduegbunam Chukwujama, 'Violent Attacks: Nigeria's 10 Most Dangerous Highways This Season', *Prime Business Africa*, https://www.primebusiness.africa/violent-attacks-nigerias-10-most-dangerous-highways-this-season/.

29 'The reconfiguring of buildings was a key aspect of imperialism,' observes John M. MacKenzie. 'In the British imperial period in India, Mughal buildings were adapted as residences for the British (as in the case of the tomb at Lahore). Indigenous forts were taken over as redoubts and barracks for the British military. It is not surprising then that postcolonial nationalists have similarly taken over buildings and developed them. Some buildings have been demolished, certainly, and many statues have been destroyed or removed, but much else has been retained and provided with new meanings . . . The church in Fort William, Calcutta is now a library. Decline of Christian observance has led to the reuse of churches elsewhere too. In Quebec City, the former Anglican St Matthew's Church is also now a library. Elsewhere, churches have been taken over by indigenous worshippers and often converted to new forms of communal and demonstrative worship.' MacKenzie, *The British Empire through Buildings*, pp. 269–70.

30 As the Brookings Institution puts it, Nigeria is 'not yet a failed state' despite many predictions, because of Nigerians' incredible 'self-organizing impulse'. 'Despite the chaos and disorder in the nation's public sector, the volatile nature of the economy, and societal stressors of various dimensions, Nigerians find impetus to organize life by themselves and for themselves.' See Andrew S. Nevin, Uma Kymal, Peter Nigel Cameron and Rufai Oseni,

'Self-organizing Nigeria: The antifragile state', 2/03/2023, https://www.brookings.edu/blog/africa-in-focus/2023/03/02/self-organizing-nigeria-the-antifragile-state/.

31    Siollun, *What Britain Did to Nigeria*, pp. 300–301.

32    Kwarteng, *Ghosts of Empire*, pp. 301–3.

33    Siollun, *What Britain Did to Nigeria*, pp. 40–41.

34    Ibid., p. 40.

35    Elliott Green, 'On the Size and Shape of African States', *International Studies Quarterly* 2012, 56:2, p. 2; Ieuan Griffiths, 'The Scramble for Africa: Inherited Political Boundaries', *Geographical Journal* 1986, 152:2, pp. 204–16; Alberto Alesina and Enrico Spolaore, *The Size of Nations*, The MIT Press, 2005; Alberto Alesina and Enrico Spolaore, 'Conflict, Defense Spending, and the Number of Nations', *European Economic Review* 2006, 50:1, pp. 91–120.

36    Kwarteng, *Ghosts of Empire*, p. 294.

37    Siollun adds that 'the introduction of Christian missionaries in the south had caused a revolutionary change to the region's religious life and created a Western-educated cadre that was anxious for independence, while the north had little interest in rushing into a union with a southern region that was so radically different in religious and social ethos. British rule had also changed the north by introducing a Christian convert population into the region on the outskirts of the Muslim emirates.' Siollun, *What Britain Did to Nigeria*, pp. 323–4.

38    Ibid., p. 151.

39    Ibid., p. 326.

40    Ibid., pp. 11–12; Michael Taylor, 'Powers of Darkness', *London Review of Books*, 21 October 2021, 43:20, https://www.lrb.co.uk/the-paper/v43/n20/michael-taylor/powers-of-darkness.

41    Daron Acemoglu and James A. Robinson, *Why Nations Fail: The Origins of Power, Prosperity and Poverty*, Profile Books, 2012, pp. 252–5. Peter Frankopan argues that this enslavement explains a lot of instability across West Africa today. 'Supplying captives to traders on the coast demanded constant raiding to secure near endless numbers of captives – which created a vicious and circular world of enslaving or being enslaved. That in itself had other consequences, not least demand for weapons and above all guns – areas in which Europeans had an advantage by the time of enhanced contact with Africa, an advantage maintained and furthered thanks in part to the sheer number of conflicts in Europe and between Europeans that incentivised the development of improvements in reliability of firearms. The demand for guns, itself in part a function of the need both to defend against raiding and to use in raids, became a motor of intensification of the slave trade in its own right, as well as propelling the emergence of highly centralised states dominated by military elites such as Oyo, Dahomey and Asante, each of whose fortunes were closely connected to the European expansion . . . In this age of

mounting violence and insecurity, it was perhaps not surprising that ties between villages weakened, communities became introverted and levels of trust plummeted dramatically . . . Research has suggested that these breakdowns developed into long-term issues which are still prevalent today in many parts of West Africa, and explain low levels of co-operation, low levels of trust and poor economic performance. Regions that provided large numbers of captives to be shipped across the Atlantic are worse off now thanks to the historical effects of slavery. In other words, it is not just that peoples and places in Africa paid a heavy price centuries ago; they continue to do so to this day.' See Frankopan, *The Earth Transformed*, pp. 384–5.

42  Siollun, *What Britain Did to Nigeria*, p. 48.

43  Ibid., p. 92.

44  Ibid.

45  Ibid., p. 82.

46  Ibid., pp. 83–4.

47  Ibid., p. 83.

48  Ibid., p. 188.

49  Ibid., pp. 191–2.

50  Falola continues: 'The linkage between parties and violence began early. The post-1940 political parties were formed in an atmosphere of distrust and ethnic competition. Each major political party represented a region: the Nigerian People's Congress in the North, the National Council of Nigeria and the Cameroons in the East, and the Action Group in the West. Each successfully kept control of its region and all struggled bitterly to control the center. The task of national integration was complicated.' Toyin Falola, *Colonialism and Violence in Nigeria*, Indiana University Press, 2009, pp. 172, 173, 181.

51  Pilling, 'How Nigeria's state lost the trust of its citizens'.

52  Adam Forrest, 'End SARS protests: UK government admits it did train and supply equipment to Nigeria's "brutal" police unit', *Independent*, 30/10/20, https://www.independent.co.uk/news/uk/politics/sars-nigeria-police-protests-uk-government-training-equipment-b1424447.html.

53  Neil Munshi, 'Gun for hire: Nigeria security fears spark boom in private protection', *Financial Times*, 26/10/2021, https://www.ft.com/content/a12bb6b1-798d-4863-8b49-104a56ccc716.

54  Siollun, *What Britain Did to Nigeria*, pp. 106–8; Falola, *Colonialism and Violence in Nigeria*, pp. 178–9.

55  Micah Damilola John, 'Public Perception of Police Activities in Okada, Edo State Nigeria', *Covenant Journal of Business & Social Sciences* 2017, 8:1, p. 31.

56  Siollun, *What Britain Did to Nigeria*, pp. 116–17. He continues: 'The ethnic composition of the army remains a controversial and difficult problem with which Nigeria still grapples in the 21st century. Its effect on national stability is so

serious that to make military recruitment more balanced, Nigeria still applies an ethnic quota to military recruitment and promotions.'

57  It's a problem that afflicts other armies and police forces in other parts of the former empire. 'Decolonisation marked an uneasy political transition for the colonial police,' write David Anderson and David Killingray. 'Officers and constables who one month carried out the surveillance of nationalist leaders and anti-colonial protesters, in the next month found these same "suspects" transformed into their paymasters and political overlords. It is therefore not difficult to appreciate why the history of policing in the transfer of powers remains a matter of some political sensitivity and one upon which documentary sources are still commonly withheld from public scrutiny.' See Anderson and Killingray, *Policing and Decolonisation*, p. 10; Siollun, *What Britain Did to Nigeria*, pp. 116–17.

58  Kwarteng, *Ghosts of Empire*, p. 320; 'Nigeria: Steel factory will open after 40 years | Al Jazeera English', YouTube, 16/06/2018, https://www.youtube.com/watch?v=FqVyWiYdKQA ; Ifeanyi Onuba, 'How Buhari's Govt Failed to Revive Ajaokuta Steel Company Despite N31bn Allocation', *The Whistler*, 18/05/2022, https://thewhistler.ng/how-buharis-govt-failed-to-revive-ajaokuta-steel-company-despite-n31bn-allocation/.

59  Siollun, *What Britain Did to Nigeria*, p. 49.

60  Ibid., pp. 316–17.

61  Megan Leonhardt, ' "Nigerian prince" email scams still rake in over $700,000 a year – here's how to protect yourself,' *CNBC Make It*, 18/04/2019, https://www.cnbc.com/2019/04/18/nigerian-prince-scams-still-rake-in-over-700000-dollars-a-year.html.

62  Femi Aribisala, 'Bigmanism in Nigeria', *Vanguard*, 01/10/2013, https://www.vanguardngr.com/2013/10/bigmanism-nigeria/; Farah Bakaari, Vincent Benlloch and Barry Driscoll, 'Political scientists talk about African "Big Men" inconsistently', *London School of Economics*, 22/03/2021, https://blogs.lse.ac.uk/africaatlse/2021/03/22/political-science-talk-about-african-big-men-governance-patronage-inconsistently/.

63  Ihejirika, 'Fuck your gender norms'.

64  Under the colonial administration, the red cap was a symbol of authority, used as a means of social control. 'The practice of giving caps was started at Ikot Ekpene by the district commissioner, Mr Reginald Hargrove,' reports Adiele Eberechukwu Afigbo. 'He gave fez caps bearing metal engravings of the crown to all Warrant Chiefs and satisfactory headmen, and special staffs with decorated heads to chiefs who were considered more influential than others. This created a new hierarchy of status in society. An ambitious and successful young man could become a "capped" headman, then a Warrant Chief and perhaps earn a staff. The "cap and staff" system proved very popular and spread from Ikot Ekpene to

other divisions. It gave political officers a firmer control over the headmen and the chiefs. To be deprived of one's cap or staff was an obvious disgrace, a proof that the victim had been found wanting in certain respects.' The red cap continues to be used (and abused) as an emblem of authority in contemporary Nigeria. See Adiele Eberechukwu Afigbo, *The Warrant Chiefs: Indirect Rule in Southeastern Nigeria, 1891–1929*, Longman, 1972, p. 105.

65 Siollun, *What Britain Did to Nigeria*, pp. 287–8, 290.

66 Femi Adegbulu, 'From Warrant Chiefs to Ezeship: A Distortion of Traditional Institutions in Igboland?', *Afro Asian Journal of Social Sciences* Quarter II 2011, 2:2.2, pp. 1–25.

67 Siollun, *What Britain Did to Nigeria*, pp. 294–5.

68 Victor C. Uchendu has described traditional local Igbo political village culture as 'an exercise in direct democracy', but Femi Adegbulu points out that 'their history was more complex and changing than is often assumed' and that 'there were exceptions to this general picture: some Igbo communities, especially trading cities along the Niger, like Onitsha, Oguta, Arochukwu, Ossomari and the "holy city" of Nri had elaborated chieftaincy institutions in pre-colonial times'. Also, 'However "democratic", some believe that inner structures of pre-colonial Igbo communities were anything but egalitarian. Igbo society, they argue, had its "slaves" (ohu) and "cult slaves" (osu) on the one hand, and it had leaders on the other. Depending on what sub-cultural area of Igboland we are discussing, there were lineage headships, influential age groups, and powerful titled and secret societies. There were also individuals carrying the title eze or obi, indicating a special degree of influence and power, though not independent of the person and, especially, the wealth it could mobilise.' See Victor C. Uchendu, *The Igbo of Southeastern Nigeria*, Holt, Rinehart & Winston, 1965. Cited by Adegbulu, 'From Warrant Chiefs to Ezeship', p. 3.

69 Cecilia Macaulay, 'Nigerian schools: Flogged for speaking my mother tongue', *BBC News*, 07/01/2023, https://www.bbc.co.uk/news/world-africa-63971991. amp.

70 Siollun, *What Britain Did to Nigeria*, p. 280.

71 Ibid., pp. 259–60.

72 Siollun notes that King Eyo Honesty of Creek Town issued an edict to forbid twin infanticide when Slessor was still a child. Ibid., pp. 262–3.

73 Ibid.

74 British empire is commemorated in a huge number of place and street names in Nigeria. Port Harcourt, the fifth most heavily populated city in Nigeria, is named in honour of Lord Harcourt, an infamous paedophile who committed suicide when his sexual assault of a young boy was reported to the boy's mother. In the town of Owerri we find Douglas Road, commemorating another

notorious colonial officer, Harold Morday Douglas, labelled by one historian as
'the worst D.O. [District Officer] to ever serve in the region'. See ibid., pp. 322–
3, 307.

75    After all, the threat of kidnapping is a massive problem in modern Nigeria, just
as kidnapping has, historically, been an enormous problem for this part of Africa.
I'm not just thinking of those people who were kidnapped for the transatlantic
slave trade, or of Britain's tradition of kidnapping local rulers to replace them
with more compliant ones (e.g. Jaja of Opobo), but of the slavery that persisted,
despite what Britain tells itself, long after abolition. As Daron Acemoglu and
James A. Robinson explain, 'legitimate commerce' in produce such as palm oil
still used the enslaved. 'What were all these slaves to do now that they could not
be sold to Europeans? The answer was simple: they could be profitably put to
work, under coercion, in Africa, producing the new items of legitimate
commerce . . . slavery, rather than contracting, appears to have expanded in
Africa throughout the nineteenth century.' Also, Africans continued being
essentially enslaved by Britons in Nigeria even as the empire claimed to be wiping
out slavery elsewhere, through the forced labour that was widespread in the early
colonial era. Forced labour was used by the British government for everything
from building roads to carrying the luggage (the latter was not necessarily the
cushier option: carriers were known to drop dead from thirst, hunger and strain).
Conscripts would often have to leave their families and communities to work far
away, and sometimes made to act against their own interests, such as razing their
own agricultural land in order to make way for a colonial infrastructure project.
All this without any form of wage or compensation. The colonialists did not
seem to be aware of their hypocrisy. 'To the natives, it appeared as if Britain had
abolished indigenous slavery so it could replace it with its own system of slave
labour,' writes Siollun. 'Yet Britain defended forced labour as an unavoidable
instrument of colonial rule. In 1906 Winston Churchill defended the practice in
Parliament by stating: "In West African Colonies and Protectorates in which
there is legal power to demand labour on roads and waterways, the Governor or
High Commissioner alone can make an order that such work shall be done."' See
Siollun, *What Britain Did to Nigeria*, pp. 312–16; Tife Owolabi, 'Gunmen kidnap
32 people from southern Nigeria train station', *Reuters*, 09/01/2023, https://
www.reuters.com/world/africa/gunmen-kidnap-32-people-southern-nigeria-
train-station-2023-01-08/; 'Twitter User Accuses Uber Driver of Trying to
Kidnap Her'; Abdulqudus Ogundapo, 'Kidnappers abduct farmers, demand
N10m ransom in Osun', *Premium Times*, 13/01/2023, https://www.premiumti-
mesng.com/regional/ssouth-west/575412-kidnappers-abduct-farmers-demand-
n10m-ransom-in-osun.html; Oludamola Adebowale, 'Jaja of Opobo: The Slave
Boy Who Became King', *Guardian: Life*, 25/08/2019, https://guardian.ng/life/

jaja-of-opobo-the-slave-boy-who-became-king/; Acemoglu and Robinson, *Why Nations Fail*, pp. 256–7.

76 Simon Waters, 'Cameron's F-word outburst at reporters over British empire "gaffe"', *Daily Mail*, 10/04/2011, https://www.dailymail.co.uk/news/article-1375341/David-Camerons-F-word-outburst-reporters-British-Empire-gaffe.html; Kwarteng, *Ghosts of Empire*, pp. 89–141; Kyle J. Gardner, *The Frontier Complex: Geopolitics and the Making of the India–China Border, 1846–1962*, Cambridge University Press, 2021.

77 'Maharajah Gulab Singh acknowledges the supremacy of the British Government and will in token of such supremacy present annually to the British Government one horse, twelve shawl goats of approved breed (six male and six female) and three pairs of Cashmere shawls.' The clause acknowledged the British interest in the luxury pashm 'shawl wool' trade used to produce the famed pashmina or Cashmere shawls. The actual tribute shawls were presented to the British monarch. See Gardner, *The Frontier Complex*, p. 166.

78 'Conference of San Remo', *Britannica*, https://www.britannica.com/event/Conference-of-San-Remo; Kwarteng, *Ghosts of Empire*, pp. 89–141; Matthieu Rey, 'The British, the Hashemites and monarchies in the Middle East', in R. Aldrich and C. McCreery (eds.), *Crowns and Colonies: European Monarchies and Overseas Empires*, Manchester University Press, 2016, pp. 227–44; Martin Walker, 'The Making of Modern Iraq', *Wilson Quarterly* 2003, 27:2, pp. 29–40, https://www.jstor.org/stable/40261182; 'Kashmir', *Britannica*, https://www.britannica.com/place/Kashmir-region-Indian-subcontinent; Christopher Clary, *The Difficult Politics of Peace: Rivalry in Modern South Asia*, Oxford University Press, 2022, pp. 43ff.; 'Kashmir: Why India and Pakistan fight over it', https://www.bbc.co.uk/news/10537286; Hyacinth Mascarenhas, 'How the British screwed up the Middle East, in 10 classic cartoons', *MIC*, 13/06/2023, https://www.mic.com/articles/91071/how-the-british-screwed-up-the-middle-east-in-10-classic-cartoons. 'The British, under the strains of war, recession, and dependence on oil, were never quite able to surrender their remaining control over Iraq's independence until they were forced to do so,' writes Martin Walker. 'And by maintaining that control, the British precluded the development of a political system that might have produced a non-authoritarian regime capable of governing the unstable, improbable country they had created.' See Walker, 'The Making of Modern Iraq', p. 40.

79 Kwarteng, *Ghosts of Empire*, pp. 145–208; 'Myanmar: The initial impact of colonialism', *Britannica*, https://www.britannica.com/place/Myanmar/The-initial-impact-of-colonialism; 'A Short History of Burma', *New Internationalist*, 18/04/2008, https://newint.org/features/2008/04/18/history; Anthony Webster, 'Business and Empire: A Reassessment of the British Conquest of Burma in 1885', *Historical Journal* 2000, 43:4, pp. 1003–25; Lindsay Maizland, 'Myanmar's

Troubled History: Coups, Military Rule, and Ethnic Conflict', *Council on Foreign Relations*, 31/01/2022, https://www.cfr.org/backgrounder/myanmar-history-coup-military-rule-ethnic-conflict-rohingya.

80  https://api.parliament.uk/historic-hansard/commons/1886/feb/22/resolution, cited by Kwarteng in *Ghosts of Empire*, p. 170.

81  Constance Kampfner, 'British Museum's Myanmar exhibition explores how colonial rule "set stage for genocide"', *The Times*, 01/07/2023, https://shorturl.at/zFMZ2.

82  Heikkilä-Horn continues, explaining that this simplifying has proved particularly problematic for the 'Rohingyas': 'There is a heated discussion going on among academics and activists concerning who the Rohingyas are, whether they are Burmese or Bengali/Chittagonians with deep roots in Burma, or possibly more recent Bengali/Chittagonian immigrants escaping the economic and political instability of East Pakistan/Bangladesh as the military government claims . . . The [imperial] statistics gave an impression of accuracy, yet many of the categories were artificial and simplistic . . . The group known as "Rohingyas" is still fighting to be regarded as citizens of Burma.' Jane M. Ferguson echoes the assessment, observing that 'British colonial censuses introduced in India in the nineteenth and twentieth centuries effectively re-arranged local difference into figures that were legible to the colonial empire, providing an "essential abstraction from social reality", and later serving to frame ethnic problems and issues . . . When they carried out the census, the British-trained enumerators required that respondents give single, discrete, unqualified answers for their race, and these would be fit into a prescribed categorical scheme. The Burmese term for race/ethnicity used in the census is *luumyo*, literally, "type of person". *Amyo*, type, or sort, in reference to people is often translated as "race", though the understanding of it being biologically immutable (ascribed), or socially constructed (achieved), is ambiguous, and thus situational.' Marja-Leena Heikkilä-Horn, 'Imagining "Burma": a historical overview', *Asian Ethnicity* 2009, 10:2, pp. 145–54, https://doi.org/10.1080/14631360902906839; Jane M. Ferguson, 'Who's Counting? Ethnicity, Belonging, and the National Census in Burma/Myanmar', *Bijdragen tot de Taal-, Land- en Volkenkunde* 2015, 171:1, pp. 1–28, https://www.jstor.org/stable/43819166.

83  Jeffrey Mankoff, *Empires of Eurasia: How Imperial Legacies Shape International Security*, Yale University Press, 2022.

84  The British-Sudanese journalist Nesrine Malik stresses that Sudan's most recent conflict, which has seen fighting between rival military factions turn Khartoum and other urban areas into battlefields, has little to do with colonial history. 'Colonialism in Sudan had one big legacy, civil war between the South and North, which should have been two different countries,' she tells me. 'But they

have separated. And what is happening now is a much more localised conflict between the centre and the periphery, which falls along the lines of ethnicity and class.'

85 'Why is Sudan so unstable?' *Economist*, 04/01/2022, https://www.economist. com/the-economist-explains/2022/01/04/why-is-sudan-so-unstable; Kim Searcy, 'Sudan in Crisis', *Origins: Current Events in Historical Perspective* June 2019, https:// origins.osu.edu/article/sudan-darfur-al-bashir-colonial-protest?language_con tent_entity=en; Marina Ottaway and Mai El-Sadany, 'Sudan: From Conflict to Conflict', *Carnegie Endowment for International Peace*, 16/05/2012, https://carne gieendowment.org/2012/05/16/sudan-from-conflict-to-conflict-pub-48140; Oystein H. Rolandsen and M. W. Daly, *A History of South Sudan*, Cambridge University Press, 2016.

86 Searcy, 'Sudan in Crisis'.

87 Wrong, *I Didn't Do It for You*, p. 144; Richard Pankhurst, 'Post-World War II Ethiopia: British Military Policy and Action for the Dismantling and Acquisition of Italian Factories and Other Assets, 1941–2', *Journal of Ethiopian Studies* 1996, 29:1, pp. 35–77; Gufu Oba, *Nomads in the Shadows of Empires: Contests, Conflicts and Legacies on the Southern Ethiopian–Northern Kenyan Frontier*, Brill, 2013.

88 'In the Ethiopian case too, victors invoked economic, political, racial and emotional arguments to rationalize the unlawful embezzlement of enemy property, both state and private. Victors also cooperated on the international stage to avoid responsibility by sponsoring self-serving clauses in the 1947 Paris Peace Treaty. What Ethiopia, Britain and Italy did with regard to the property of their defeated enemy had much in common with the long tradition of the appropriation of plunder. Hence, the war caused the unexpected downward and upward economic mobility of Italians and Ethiopians respectively, while enabling Britain and Ethiopia to finance state expenses using proceeds from enemy property.' Haile Muluken Akalu, 'The British and Ethiopian Disposal of Italian Property in Ethiopia, 1941–1956: A Historical Review of the Theory and Practice of the Custodianship of Enemy Property', *Canadian Social Science* 2019, 15:2, pp. 22–33 at p. 32.

89 Wrong, *I Didn't Do It for You*, pp. 135–6.

90 Noura Erakat, *Justice for Some: Law and the Question of Palestine*, Stanford University Press, 2019; Gardner Thompson, *Legacy of Empire: Britain, Zionism and the Creation of Israel*, Saqi, 2019; Segev, *One Palestine, Complete*; Avishai Margalit, 'Palestine: How Bad, & Good, Was British Rule?', *New York Review*, 07/02/2013, https://www.nybooks.com/articles/2013/02/07/palestine-how-bad-and-good-was-british-rule/; Walid Ahmed Khalidi, Nabih Amin Faris, William Charles Brice, William Foxwell Albright, Arnold Hugh Martin Jones, Rashid Ismail Khalidi, Ian J. Bickerton, Peter Marshall Fraser, Kathleen Mary Kenyon, Glenn

Richard Bugh, 'Palestine: World War I and after', *Britannica*, https://www.bri
tannica.com/place/Palestine/World-War-I-and-after.

91    The most important component of this double-dealing was the secret Sykes–Picot
Agreement, also known as the Asia Minor Agreement, which was formed in May
1916 between Great Britain and France (with the approval of imperial Russia) for
the break-up of the Ottoman Empire. The agreement resulted in the theoretical
division of Palestine, Syria, Lebanon, Iraq and other countries held by Turkey into
separate French- and British-administered regions. The borders of the mandates
were not decided upon for years after the secret agreement. Nonetheless, in the
words of the *New Yorker*, 'the Sykes–Picot Agreement launched a nine-year
process – and other deals, declarations, and treaties – that created the modern
Middle East states out of the Ottoman carcass'. And the fact that the agreement
established the foundation for these borders inspired intense animosity. Declarations of 'the end of Sykes–Picot' have frequently been pronounced in response to
political unrest in the modern age, not least the 2014 advent of the Islamic State in
Iraq and the Levant (ISIL). See 'Sykes–Picot Agreement', *Britannica*, https://
www.britannica.com/event/Sykes-Picot-Agreement; Robin Wright, 'How the
Curse of Sykes–Picot Still Haunts the Middle East', *New Yorker*, 30/04/2016,
https://www.newyorker.com/news/news-desk/how-the-curse-of-sykes-picot-still-
haunts-the-middle-east.

92    Segev, *One Palestine, Complete*, pp. 5–6; Sharif Nashashibi, 'Balfour: Britain's
Original Sin', *Al Jazeera*, 04/11/2014, https://www.aljazeera.com/opinions/
2014/11/4/balfour-britains-original-sin. The recent controversial move by Israel's
far-right, ultra-religious government to reduce the power and influence of the
nation's Supreme Court, and to push forward extreme policies, has an imperial
element. As the academic Anne Irfan has explained, the 'rule of reasonableness'
which has been withdrawn, and which has in the past entitled the Supreme
Court to overrule government decisions, was a British colonial creation. 'The
law that was struck down actually predates the state of Israel and is rooted in its
antecedent: the British Mandate of Palestine (1922–48). The British army entered
Palestine in late 1917 and occupied the whole country the following year . . . In
1922, the newly created League of Nations added a veneer of international legitimacy to the British occupation when it granted the Mandate for Palestine. The
mandate system was ostensibly designed to prepare colonised territories for self-
governance. In practice, it facilitated another form of colonial rule by Britain and
France – by no coincidence, the same powers that dominated the League . . . The
British system of rule in Palestine provided much of the basis for the subsequent
Israeli state. This included the "test of reasonableness", which dates back to 16th-
century English public law and means that laws must be properly considered and
not arbitrary. After 1948, Israeli jurists adopted and developed the principle of

"reasonableness" as part of the supreme court's system of checks and balances over the Knesset. In overturning it this week, the Knesset removed one plank of Mandate Palestine's lasting legal infrastructure.' Anne Irfan, 'Israel: unpopular judicial reform involves repeal of law set up under British colonial rule in Palestine – here's what that tells us', 26/07/2023, *The Conversation*, https://the-conversation.com/israel-unpopular-judicial-reform-involves-repeal-of-law-set-up-under-british-colonial-rule-in-palestine-heres-what-that-tells-us-210401.

93   Julia Lovell, *The Opium War: Drugs, Dreams and the Making of China*, Picador, 2011.

94   Ibid., p. 8.

95   Ibid., p. 277.

96   Ibid., p. 12; Peter Frankopan, 'West's reckless lack of expertise on China will cost us dear', *The Times*, 18/02/2023, https://www.thetimes.co.uk/article/d006ad54-af9c-11ed-bde0-64a2ad0fcf88?shareToken=bb15e644b80e5368ab5e24c708ae1a78.

97   Kim A. Wagner, 'Savage Warfare: Violence and the Rule of Colonial Difference in Early British Counterinsurgency', *History Workshop Journal* 2018, 85, pp. 217–37.

98   Ibid., p. 229; Frédéric Mégret, 'From "savages" to "unlawful combatants": a postcolonial look at international humanitarian law's "other" ', in Anne Orford (ed.), *International Law and its Others*, Cambridge University Press, 2006, p. 293.

99   Wrong, *I Didn't Do It for You*, p. 101.

100   Siollun, *What Britain Did to Nigeria*, p. 327.

101   Ferguson, *Empire*, pp. 357–8.

102   Ibid., p. 366.

103   As summarized in Michael Bernhard, Christopher Reenock and Timothy Nordstrom, 'The Legacy of Western Overseas Colonialism on Democratic Survival', *International Studies Quarterly* 2004, 48:1, pp. 229–30.

104   Nicholas Owen, 'Democratisation and the British Empire', *Journal of Imperial and Commonwealth History* 2019, 47:5, p. 974.

105   Alexander Lee and Jack Paine, 'British colonialism and democracy: Divergent inheritances and diminishing legacies', *Journal of Comparative Economics* 2019, 47:3, pp. 487–503; Myron Weiner, 'Empirical Democratic Theory', in Myron Weiner and Ergun Ozbudun (eds.), *Competitive Elections in Developing Countries*, Duke University Press, 1987, pp. 3–34; K. A. Bollen and R. W. Jackman, 'Economic and Noneconomic Determinants of Political Democracy in the 1960s', *Research in Political Sociology* 1985, 1, pp. 27–48; S. M. Lipset, K. Seong and J. C. Torres, 'A Comparative Analysis of the Social Requisites of Democracy', *International Social Science Journal* 1993, 136, pp. 155–75; Axel Hadenius, *Development and Democracy*, Cambridge University Press, 2009; Dietrich Rueschemeyer, Evelyne Huber and John D. Stevens, *Capitalist Development and Democracy*, University of Chicago

Press, 1992; Jean Blondel, *Comparing Political Systems*, Praeger, 1972; S. Huntington, 'Will More Countries Become Democratic?', *Political Science Quarterly* 1984, 99, pp. 192–218; S. Huntington, *The Third Wave: Democratization in the Late Twentieth Century*, Oklahoma University Press, 1991; Larry Diamond, 'Introduction', in Larry Diamond, Juan Linz and Seymour Martin Lipset (eds.), *Democracy in Developing Countries*, vol. 2: *Africa*, Lynne Rienner, 1988, pp. 1–32.

106 Bernhard, Reenock and Nordstrom, 'The Legacy of Western Overseas Colonialism on Democratic Survival', pp. 245–6.

107 Owen, 'Democratisation and the British Empire', pp. 976–7.

108 Ibid.

109 Harshan Kumarasingham (ed.), *Constitution-Making in Asia: Decolonisation and State-Building in the Aftermath of the British Empire*, Routledge, 2016, pp. 2–3.

110 R. A. W. Rhodes, John Wanna and Patrick Weller, *Comparing Westminster*, Oxford University Press, 2009, pp. 12–16; Wilson and Dilley, 'The Incoherence of Empire', pp. 1–27.

111 Rhodes, Wanna and Weller, *Comparing Westminster*, p. 16.

112 Ibid., p. 57.

113 Kumarasingham (ed.), *Constitution-Making in Asia*, p. 27.

114 Other essays in Kumarasingham's collection provide accounts of how Asian countries adapted the Westminster model to suit them. For example, bills of rights, which have long been seen in Britain 'as at best useless and at worst dangerous' appeared in the constitutions of Burma (1947), India (1950), Pakistan (1956) and Malaya (1957). Asian former colonies also tended to be more prescriptive in their constitutions regarding the powers granted to their leaders. These so-called Eastminsters (a term coined by the editor) also contained provisions for emergency powers of the kind that Caroline Elkins has cited as a prominent imperial legacy. In contrast, the constitutions of early former colonies such as Australia, New Zealand and Canada did not explicitly address the issue of emergency powers, explains Anne Twomey. 'Asian colonies, however, had a different background. First, the need for some kind of emergency power to deal with internal violence or insurrection has proved much greater in Asia than the older realms. Second, there is an historical basis for the use of such powers in Asia. Emergency powers were conferred upon British governors and governors-general as a means of asserting colonial power and suppressing insurrection and independence movements.' See Charles Parkinson, 'British constitutional thought and the emergence of bills of rights in Britain's overseas territories in Asia at decolonisation', in Kumarasingham (ed.), *Constitution-Making in Asia*, p. 36; Anne Twomey, 'Discretionary reserve powers of heads of state', in Kumarasingham (ed.), *Constitution-Making in Asia*, pp. 55, 70.

115 Kumarasingham (ed.), *Constitution-Making in Asia*, pp. 6, 23.

116 Ibid., p. 7.

117 Ibid., p. ix.

118 Asanga Welikala, ' "Specialist in omniscience"? Nationalism, constitutionalism, and Sir Ivor Jennings' engagement with Ceylon', in ibid., p. 112.

119 Kumarasingham (ed.), *Constitution-Making in Asia*, p. 10.

120 Ibid., p. 13.

121 Mara Malagodi, 'Constitution drafting as Cold War realpolitik: Sir Ivor Jennings and Nepal's 1959 constitution', in ibid., pp. 169–70.

122 Chandra D. Bhatta, 'Nepal's political and economic transition', *Observer Research Foundation*, 15/06/2022, https://www.orfonline.org/expert-speak/nepals-political-and-economic-transition/.

123 Welikala, ' "Specialist in omniscience"?', p. 130.

124 Neil DeVotta, 'Behind the crisis in Sri Lanka – how political and economic mismanagement combined to plunge nation into turmoil', *The Conversation*, 18/07/2022, https://theconversation.com/behind-the-crisis-in-sri-lanka-how-political-and-economic-mismanagement-combined-to-plunge-nation-into-turmoil-187137 https://www.bbc.co.uk/news/world-south-asia-11999611.

125 Tahir Kamran, 'Pakistan's first decade: democracy and constitution – a historical appraisal of centralisation', in Kumarasingham (ed.), *Constitution-Making in Asia*, p. 96.

126 Kwarteng, *Ghosts of Empire*, p. 140.

127 'The result was an inherent political instability. In the seven years after 1932, Iraq went through 12 different cabinets, and frustration with parliament's weaknesses helped provoke a military coup in 1936.' See Walker, 'The Making of Modern Iraq', p. 34.

128 Thomas C. Holt, *The Problem of Freedom: Race, Labor and Politics in Jamaica and Britain, 1832–1938*, Johns Hopkins University Press, 1992.

129 Kwarteng, *Ghosts of Empire*, p. 187.

130 Under the headline 'Colonial nostalgia rules in Hong Kong as young refuse to accept China's authority', *The Times* reported in 2019 that Union Jacks were appearing 'on T-shirts, on tiny flag poles' and 'even draped over a war memorial'. See Richard Lloyd Parry and Raphael Blet, 'Colonial nostalgia rules in Hong Kong as young refuse to accept China's authority', *The Times*, 14/06/2019, https://www.thetimes.co.uk/article/colonial-nostalgia-rules-as-young-refuse-to-accept-beijing-rule-gswccqovf; 'Nostalgia for the British empire is no solution to the crisis in Hong Kong', CGTN, 26/07/2019, https://news.cgtn.com/news/2019-07-26/Nostalgia-for-British-empire-is-no-solution-for-Hong-Kong-IEfDhcX7fW/index.html.

131 Kwarteng, *Ghosts of Empire*, p. 387.

132 Ibid., p. 381.

133 Ibid., p. 368.

134   Ibid., p. 390.

135   Owen, 'Democratisation and the British Empire', p. 987.

136   Ibid., p. 984.

137   In 2021 he wrote that 'the British claimed a huge set of achievements, including democracy . . . but often enough these were not gifts that could be exercised under the British administration during imperial days. They became realisable only when the British left – they were the fruits of learning from Britain's own experience, which India could use freely only after the period of empire had ended. Imperial rule tends to require some degree of tyranny: asymmetrical power is not usually associated with a free press or with a vote-counting democracy, since neither of them is compatible with the need to keep colonial subjects in check.' Meanwhile the politician and writer Shashi Tharoor argues in *What the British Did to India* that democratic processes of *anti*-colonial struggle led to the establishment of democracy in India. 'The Indian nationalist struggle and its evolution through various stages – decorous liberals seeking legislative rights, "extremists" clamouring for swaraj, Gandhi and his followers advocating non-violent struggle, the Congress, the Muslim League and other parties contending for votes even with limited franchise: all these pre-Independence experiences served as a kind of socialization process into democracy and helped to ease the country's transition to independence.' Amartya Sen, 'Illusions of empire: Amartya Sen on what British rule really did for India', *Guardian*, 29/06/2021, https://www.theguardian.com/world/2021/jun/29/british-empire-india-amartya-sen; Shashi Tharoor, 'Shashi Tharoor on why India is suited to a presidential system', *The News Minute*, 07/11/2016, https://www.thenewsminute.com/article/shashi-tharoor-why-india-suited-presidential-system-52516.

138   The *Economist* noted 'a serious deterioration in the quality of democracy under leader Narendra Modi, whose Hindu-nationalist Bharatiya Janata Party (BJP) has presided over increased intolerance and sectarianism towards Muslims and other religious minorities'. 'The world's most, and least, democratic countries in 2022', *Economist*, 01/02/2023, https://www.economist.com/graphic-detail/2023/02/01/the-worlds-most-and-least-democratic-countries-in-2022?fsrc=core-app-economist.

139   Nick Westcott, 'Oligarchs, Oil and Obi-dients: The Battle for the Soul of Nigeria', *African Arguments*, 03/02/2023, https://africanarguments.org/2023/02/oligarchs-oil-and-obi-dients-the-battle-for-the-soul-of-nigeria/; 'Nigeria–India: Learnings from two large democracies', *PWC*, https://www.pwc.com/ng/en/publications/nigeria-india-learnings-from-two-democracies.html.

140   Kwarteng, *Ghosts of Empire*, pp. 322–3.

141   Lenin Ndebele, 'What Nigerians think of their democracy ahead of elections', 04/02/2023, https://www.news24.com/news24/africa/news/what-nigerians-think-of-their-democracy-ahead-of-elections-20230204.

142   Ayisha Osori, 'Nigeria's elections have bigger problems than vote trading', *Al Jazeera*, 17/02/2023, https://www.aljazeera.com/opinions/2023/2/17/nigerias-elections-have-bigger-problems-than-vote-trading.

143   William Clowes and Ruth Olurounbi, 'Bright Side of Nigeria's Cash Shortage: Vote Buying Declines', *Yahoo Movies*, https://uk.movies.yahoo.com/bright-side-nigeria-cash-shortage-131553672.html?guccounter=1&guce_referrer=aHR0cHM6Ly93d3cuZ29vZ2xlLmNvbS88&guce_referrer_sig=AQAAADUf1GBGkvmo3pn8SQJhoGhDfRWBziayj8NUFHvRf6hCPulCtCin5JcwLhJpgUCeev_HkuFGfqKmx9ourlfblGHBkK8WwhVFE2jbjzSecxGPGwuwVi63fJGrsEFWHRtokqbPFMzRcx2A8DfNPndJSiDm5OQCskJqmmoCqoKiQQKh.

144   Emmanuel Akinwotu, 'Gunmen destroy 800 ballot boxes in Nigeria, the latest in a series of attacks', *NPR*, 02/02/2023, https://www.npr.org/2023/02/02/1153753025/nigeria-election-ballot-boxes-destroyed.

145   Incredibly, Nigeria imports much of its fuel: 'One of Africa's top oil producers, Nigeria often struggles with fuel shortages as it imports most of its petrol and diesel because its refineries are not working.' See AFP, 'Cash and fuel shortages crank up Nigeria election tensions', *Eyewitness News*, 03/02/2023, https://ewn.co.za/2023/02/03/cash-and-fuel-shortages-cranks-up-nigeria-election-tensions.

146   Richard Assheton, 'Nigeria election 2023: opposition demands cancellation of "sham" vote', *The Times*, 27/02/2023, https://www.thetimes.co.uk/article/f53d0046-b5fa-11ed-a513-158bcb2665eb?shareToken=9f85359135067ab84c4a37aea6662aab.

147   Richard Assheton, 'Nigeria presidential election: Bola Tinubu claims victory as rivals demand rerun', *The Times*, 01/03/2023, https://www.thetimes.co.uk/article/nigeria-presidential-election-bola-tinubu-claims-victory-as-rivals-demand-rerun-n07228v57; Aanu Adeoye, 'Bola Tinubu leads disputed Nigerian vote as opposition calls for election rerun', *Financial Times*, 28/02/2023, https://www.ft.com/content/64724f5c-a6b5-45cb-8fa6-96e1531a98f8.

148   Kwarteng, *Ghosts of Empire*, p. 7.

149   *The University of Bristol: Our History and the Legacies of Slavery*, University of Bristol, 2022, pp. 15–19, https://www.bristol.ac.uk/media-library/sites/university/documents/university-of-bristol-legacies-of-slavery-report.pdf.

150   Alan Lester, 'Time to Throw Out the Balance Sheet', *University of Sussex: School of Global Studies Blog*, 21/03/2016, https://blogs.sussex.ac.uk/global/2016/03/21/time-to-throw-out-the-balance-sheet/; Tristan Boyle, 'The Modern Myth of the British Empire with Kim A. Wagner – Modern Myth – Episode 20', *Archaeology Podcast Network*, 05/05/2021, https://www.archaeologypodcastnetwork.com/anarchaeologist/mm20-empire.

151   Not including the subsequent generations born into slavery between 1600 and 1833.

152   'Legacies of British Slavery', UCL, https://www.ucl.ac.uk/made-at-ucl/stories/legacies-british-slavery.

153  *Jan Morris: Writing a Life*, Archive on 4, https://www.bbc.co.uk/programmes/moo11jxq.

## Conclusion: An Evolutionary Outgrowth

1  Andy Bull, 'Can radical changes restore sagging prestige of Commonwealth Games?', *Guardian*, 23/07/2022, https://www.theguardian.com/sport/blog/2022/jul/23/can-radical-changes-restore-sagging-prestige-of-commonwealth-games.

2  https://twitter.com/joelycett/status/1552637751803236355.

3  Agency staff, '"Leftie multicultural crap": Blundering Tory MP Aidan Burley insists London 2012 opening ceremony swipe was "misunderstood"', *Mirror*, 28/07/2012,https://www.mirror.co.uk/news/uk-news/london-2012-tory-mp-aidan-1178770.

4  Originally slated to host the 2022 Games, the South African city of Durban lost its hosting rights in 2017 as a result of financial difficulties and missed deadlines. Nine months later, Birmingham agreed to serve as host. At the time of writing, as a result of the Australian state of Victoria cancelling its plans to host due to budget overruns, the 2026 Commonwealth Games are in doubt. Before Victoria offered to host in April 2022, the Commonwealth Games Federation (CGF) had difficulty finding a candidate. But Victoria's cost projections subsequently tripled. Meanwhile, the government of Alberta has recently withdrawn its support for a bid to host the 2030 Commonwealth Games due to rising costs. Tiffanie Turnbull, 'Commonwealth Games: 2026 event in doubt after Victoria cancels', *BBC News*, 19/07/2023, https://www.bbc.co.uk/news/world-australia-66229574; Thomas Mackintosh, 'Canadian province Alberta cancels bid for 2030 Commonwealth Games', *BBC News*, 04/08/2023, https://www.bbc.co.uk/news/world-us-canada-66402140

5  *Last Week Tonight*, 20/07/2014, https://www.youtube.com/watch?v=-Aj3KZa1ZCM.

6  In 1931 what emerged was the British Commonwealth of Nations. The modern Commonwealth, conceived as an organization of 'free and equal members', came into being in 1949 when it was renamed the Commonwealth of Nations.

7  In the Queen's Christmas Day 1953 broadcast. See Ben Macintyre, 'The Crown and the Commonwealth face a perilous future', *The Times*, 25/03/2022, https://www.thetimes.co.uk/article/the-crown-and-the-commonwealth-face-a-perilous-future-lx3vjlmrf.

8  Ibid.

9  PTI, 'Queen Elizabeth calls for bold reforms in Commonwealth', *The Hindu*, 28/10/2011,https://www.thehindu.com/news/international/queen-elizabeth-calls-for-bold-reforms-in-commonwealth/article2577183.ece.

10 'Our Vision and Mission', *Royal Commonwealth Society*, https://www.royalcwso ciety.org/.

11 Anna Bocking-Welch, *British Civic Society at the End of Empire: Decolonisation, Globalisation, and International Responsibility*, Manchester University Press, 2018, p. 30.

12 'Commonwealth: association of sovereign states', *Britannica*, https://www.bri tannica.com/topic/Commonwealth-association-of-states.

13 https://thecommonwealth.org/about-us.

14 'Up to 1949, the basic definition of the Commonwealth was of a group of countries under a common sovereign. Since then, with India allowed to remain in the organization as a republic, the monarch has had a separate, personal role as head of the Commonwealth. The organization now consists overwhelmingly of states of which she is not sovereign.' Murphy, *The Empire's New Clothes*, p. 82.

15 Ibid., p. 26.

16 'Commonwealth: association of sovereign states'.

17 Murphy, *The Empire's New Clothes*, pp. 21–2.

18 Bocking-Welch, *British Civic Society at the End of Empire*, p. 38.

19 The Design Museum now occupies the building once occupied by the Commonwealth Institute. Ibid. https://designmuseum.org/building.

20 Roger Boyes and Jane Flanagan, 'How revitalised Commonwealth can be a bulwark against Beijing', *The Times*, 17/06/2022, https://www.thetimes.co.uk/ article/533d9990-ee4f-11ec-b47a-cf598c451bbb?shareToken=0e59d173a4c585bb-77fb23be06cff025.

21 Murphy, *The Empire's New Clothes*, p. 203.

22 Bocking-Welch, *British Civic Society at the End of Empire*, pp. 29, 30, 24.

23 Murphy, *The Empire's New Clothes*, pp. 24–5.

24 Bocking-Welch, *British Civic Society at the End of Empire*, p. 30.

25 Ibid., p. 37.

26 Ibid., p. 38.

27 Anna Bocking-Welch, 'Whose Commonwealth? Negotiating Commonwealth Day in the 1950s and 1960s', in Saul Dubow and Richard Drayton (eds.), *Commonwealth History in the Twenty-First Century*, Palgrave Macmillan, 2020, p. 297.

28 Ferguson, *Empire*, p. 362.

29 Macintyre, 'The Crown and the Commonwealth face a perilous future'.

30 Murphy, *The Empire's New Clothes*, p. xi.

31 Ibid., p. 2.

32 Ibid., p. 16.

33 Tumaini Carayol, 'Athletic feats at Commonwealth Games cannot distract from Britain's colonial sins', *Guardian*, 28/07/2022, https://www.theguardian.com/ sport/2022/jul/28/athletic-feats-at-commonwealth-games-cannot-distract-from-britains-colonial-sins.

34    Sure, Amazon and Microsoft are not what the philosopher-politician Edmund
Burke called 'a state in the guise of a merchant' and they don't have armies
twice the size of Britain's like the East India Company did, but the historian
William Dalrymple, the author Nick Robins and others consider the EIC to
be a precursor of the modern corporation. Indeed, in 2002, the chief executive
of the Standard Chartered Bank declared that his aim was to 'build on the cou-
rageous, creative and truly international legacy of the East India Company'.
Meanwhile, the former executive of British Airways, Rod Eddington, saw the
EIC as an example of how corporations succeed 'by dint of hard work,
shrewdness and charm', which makes you wonder which history books he had
been reading. Just as the East India Company monopolized the tea trade and
Indian textile production, Nick Robins argues, its modern counterparts seek
to concentrate power and influence wherever they can, whether that is in
places such as commodity chains ('generating powerful downward pressure on
the prices of goods exported by developing countries'), companies managing
infrastructure utilities ('such as energy, telecoms, transport and water'), the
European power sector ('market concentration in the field of power generation
has to be seen as endangering fair, competitive and sustainable energy markets')
or the global media industry. Nick Robins, *The Corporation That Changed the
World: How the East India Company Shaped the Modern Multinational*, 2nd edn,
Pluto Press, 2012, pp. 212–13; Nick Robins, 'The East India Company: The
Future of the Past', *openDemocracy*, https://www.opendemocracy.net/en/
east_india_company_3899jsp/.

35    It has been suggested that the trade monopolies pursued by big tech are similar to
those that the East India Company pursued – though the monopolies today are not
in tea and spices, but in data and the minerals needed to make electronic parts and
technology. When it comes to data, tech behemoths press for the flow of unre-
stricted e-commerce and data across borders, to the annoyance of India, various
African countries and other states which are home to mounds of unprocessed data,
but lack the digital infrastructure to make use of it. See paper by Pallavi Arora and
Sukanya Thapliyal, 'Digital Colonialism and the World Trade Organization',
https://twailr.com/digital-colonialism-and-the-world-trade-organization/; Ian
Jack, 'Britain took more out of India than it put in – could China do the same
to Britain?', *Guardian*, 20/06/2014, https://www.theguardian.com/commentis
free/2014/jun/20/britain-took-more-out-of-india; Michael Kwet, 'Digital
colonialism: US empire and the new imperialism in the Global South', *Race &
Class* 2019, 60:4, https://doi.org/10.1177/0306396818823172.

36    The gold standard was a system where the standard economic unit of account was
based on a fixed quantity of gold. The historian J. Taylor Vurpillat writes that
'British pre-eminence played a crucial role in the emergence of the international

gold standard in the 1870s,' and Barry Eichengreen, author of *Globalizing Capital*, concurs. 'With Britain's industrial revolution and its emergence in the nineteenth century as the world's leading financial and commercial power, Britain's monetary practices became an increasingly logical and attractive alternative to silver-based money for countries seeking to trade with and borrow from the British Isles. Out of these autonomous decisions of national government an international system of fixed exchange rates was born.' See J. Taylor Vurpillat, *Empire, Industry and Globalization: Rethinking the Emergence of the Gold Standard in the 19th-Century World*, John Wiley, 2014; Barry Eichengreen, *Globalizing Capital: A History of the International Monetary System*, Princeton University Press, 2019, pp. 5–6.

37  Vanessa Ogle reports on how the British exported their own time standards: British Rhodesia was the first country to introduce standardized time on 1 August 1899 under British rule; in 1903, the British colonial administration adapted the time of UTC-8 as the official time for Hong Kong (UTC, Coordinated Universal Time, is a name adopted in 1972 for Greenwich Mean Time), a time zone subsequently embraced by numerous Chinese coastal cities; British North Borneo embraced UTC-8 in 1905, mainly because Hong Kong, the Philippines and Formosa had done so; South Africa's numerous time zones were merged into one in 1902; and empire played an important role in the subcontinent's adoption of Indian Standard Time (IST), five and a half hours ahead of UTC. According to Ogle, the name 'Indian Standard Time' came about to avoid drawing attention to its contentious 'British' origin, and arose out of initial correspondence discussing the time zones of America. Bombay resisted, as Indians 'perceived the change in official mean times as yet another in a long series of attempts by the colonial state to meddle with local and personal affairs'. Residents of the city complained, petitioned and insisted Indian Standard Time be revoked, but by the 1930s most of the city's institutions had complied. It still took another fifteen years, a combined period referred to in the press as the '44-Year-Old Battle of Clocks', for the city's municipal corporation to get on board. See Vanessa Ogle, *The Global Transformation of Time, 1870–1950*, Harvard University Press, 2015, pp. 99–119.

38  As Ruth A. Morgan explains, the 'quantitative approach to weather recording' in the colonies, and 'the systematic collection of meteorological statistics in colonial territories . . . fostered imperial understandings of climate in statistical terms'. In the middle of the nineteenth century, the East India Company built observatories in cities like Madras and Bombay, and these observatories evolved into hubs for the collection of climate data. The gathering of this meteorological data over time allowed colonial meteorologists to analyse local climatic patterns in the colonies. These interpretations were key to the development of weather

forecasting, a branch of predictive science vital to empire's maritime and agricultural endeavours. Also, the imperial gathering of meteorological data provided the statistics needed to progress the emerging field of climatology. Today, this archival data is essential for scientists in getting a sense of how the world's climate has changed. See Ruth A. Morgan, 'Climatology and Empire in the Nineteenth Century', in Sam White, Christian Pfister and Franz Mauelshagen (eds.), *The Palgrave Handbook of Climate History*, Palgrave Macmillan, 2018, pp. 589–603; Sherry Johnson, 'El Niño, Environmental Crisis, and the Emergence of Alternative Markets in the Hispanic Caribbean, 1760s–70s', *William and Mary Quarterly* 2005, 62:3, pp. 365–410; Sherry Johnson, *Climate and Catastrophe in Cuba and the Atlantic World in the Age of Revolution*, University of North Carolina Press, 2011.

39  The UN evolved from the League of Nations, which was founded in 1920 after the First World War to promote world peace. Jan Smuts, the South African statesman who was a key architect of the League of Nations, made no secret of the fact that British empire had been an inspiration, saying that the international cooperation involved was already evident in 'the British empire, which I prefer to call . . . the British Commonwealth of Nations'. At another time he declared that 'the British empire is the only League of Nations that has ever existed'. The argument that the United Nations inherited such imperial attitudes is not rare. The organization was founded in 1945, in the aftermath of the Second World War, with the stated aims of maintaining international peace and security, developing relationships between nations, promoting respect for human rights and achieving international cooperation for solving the world's problems. However, according to the historian Craig N. Murphy, the true aims of the UN were imperial in nature: 'When the UN Charter was negotiated, the European colonial powers wanted it to buttress and preserve empire.' Amrita Chhachhi and Linda Herrera argue that 'the UN presents an example of imperial sovereignty, which legitimizes a set of global hegemonic norms regarding biopolitical life, rights and codes of conduct'. Kehinde Andrews puts it more strongly: 'Western imperialism did not end after the Second World War, it merely evolved . . . The UN, IMF and World Bank pose as friends to the underdeveloped world, all whilst creating a framework that continues to allow the West to leach from the Rest.' This 'new age of empire', he writes, 'maintains colonial logic but has clothed itself in the legitimacy of democracy, human rights and universal values'. See Mark Mazower, *Governing the World: The History of an Idea*, Penguin Books, 2012, pp. 132–3, 128; Wallace Notestein, 'Jan Smuts', *The Atlantic*, July 1918, https://www.theatlantic.com/magazine/archive/1918/07/jan-smuts/645967/; *United Nations Charter*, United Nations, https://www.un.org/en/about-us/un-charter/full-text; Craig N. Murphy, 'Imperial Legacies in the UN Development

Programme and the UN Development System', in Sandra Halperin and Ronen Palan (eds.), *Legacies of Empire: Imperial Roots of the Contemporary Global Order*, Cambridge University Press, 2015, p. 152; Amrita Chhachhi and Linda Herrera, 'Empire, Geopolitics and Development', *Development and Change* 2007, 38:6, pp. 1021–40.

40  The historian Ronen Palan observes that, as empire dissolved, fourteen small island states chose to remain as British Overseas Territories, including Bermuda, the British Virgin Islands and the Cayman Islands, and financial specialists soon learned that one could use these territories to avoid British tax and take advantage of a lack of regulation. The British Virgin Islands was a pioneer in making a law allowing for the existence of companies which did not need records to be kept – so-called shell companies, which are now a primary means by which people hide their wealth and avoid the payment of taxes. Meanwhile, Vanessa Ogle writes, settlers escaping 'hostile non-white rule' across the decolonizing empire were lured to 'some of the newly expanding tax havens still safely within the fold of the British empire'. She continues: 'Jersey and, to a lesser degree, Guernsey soon attracted not only the money of former imperial dwellers but also empire's returnees themselves. For those accustomed to life in the empire, moving from one colony to another or a place like the Channel Islands was often the more natural choice than returning "home" to a Britain they had left long since or possibly never set foot in at all.' The developing tax-haven sector in the Channel Islands purposefully started to target empire returnees at the beginning of the 1960s. Similar steps were taken by Malta. The author Oliver Bullough goes deeper in the compelling *Butler to the World*, where he argues that it was the end of colonialism itself that triggered another international flow of cash offshore, this time into the so-called Eurodollar market. The pivotal moment, he says, was the Suez Crisis in 1956, which is seen by many as the point when it became clear that Britain's imperial age was at an end. Ronen Palan, 'The Second British Empire and the Re-emergence of Global Finance', in Halperin and Palan (eds.), *Legacies of Empire*, pp. 46–68; Vanessa Ogle, ' "Funk Money": The End of Empires, the Expansion of Tax Havens, and Decolonization as an Economic and Financial Event', *Past & Present* 2020, 249:1, pp. 213–49; Oliver Bullough, *Butler to the World*, Profile Books, 2022.

41  Just as British politicians today worry about these vital cables being cut by Britain's enemies (recently there were fears that a Russian 'scientific research vessel' might have been involved in the severing of cables linking the Shetlands to the mainland), imperial administrators fretted about their telegraph cables being cut. As Daniel R. Headrick explains, America and France had initially proposed that cables be treated as neutral in times of war, but Britain objected. A clause acknowledging the right of belligerents to cut one another's cables was

incorporated into the International Cable Agreement of 1885 at Britain's urging. The Royal Navy had a huge advantage in this field since British companies had placed all British and the majority of non-British cables throughout the world and possessed twenty-four of the thirty cable ships in existence. Headrick, *The Tentacles of Empire*; Alexander Downer, 'The threat to Britain's undersea cables', *Spectator*, 29/10/2022, https://www.spectator.co.uk/article/the-threat-to-britains-undersea-cables; 'Fibre optic cable sabotage causes global internet slowdown', *Brussels Times*, 25/10/2022, https://www.brusselstimes.com/311704/fibre-optic-cable-sabotage-causes-global-internet-slowdown; 'Shetland cut off from world after undersea cable breaks', *New York Times*, 21/10/2022, https://www.nytimes.com/2022/10/20/world/europe/shetland-scotland-outage.html; 'About International Telecommunication Union (ITU)', ITU, https://www.itu.int/en/about/Pages/default.aspx.

42   The term 'lobbying' in the context of politics may have originated in the United States in the nineteenth century, but the East India Company had been exerting 'pressure from Leadenhall Street', its London headquarters, from the seventeenth century. According to Arnold A. Sherman, the Company's political clout increased as a result of riches from Asian commerce, and in the seventeenth century it loaned and gifted large amounts of money to the King. 'These grants became a kind of business expense, needed to help the Company maintain its powers and privileges,' writes Sherman. This 'fiscal symbiosis' continued with successive royals. For those without blue blood, the Company had 'financial inducements and personal influence' to offer. Some Members of Parliament were Company investors. A number of these MPs subsequently took up important positions in the Company. At the same time, Company officers sat as Members of Parliament. As a consequence, 'the improvement in the Company's fortunes and the content of England's commercial and foreign policy came to be closely interwoven', and by the 1770s the EIC had become a company that was too big to fail. The amount of money involved and the influence of the people involved were so great that when the EIC found itself in crisis, flailing as a result of a famine in Bengal and a financial collapse in Europe, among other crises, it was subject to an unprecedented state bail-out. Edmund Burke's dramatic warning that 'this cursed Company would, at last, like a viper, be the destruction of the country which fostered it at its bosom' is one that could be applied to the banks that governments bailed out during the 2007–9 financial crisis. See Matthew Wills, 'The East India Company Invented Corporate Lobbying', *JSTOR Daily*, https://daily.jstor.org/the-east-india-company-invented-corporate-lobbying/; Arnold A. Sherman, 'Pressure from Leadenhall: The East India Company Lobby, 1660–1678', *Business History Review* 1976, 50:3, pp. 329–55, https://www.jstor.org/stable/3112999?mag=the-east-india-company-invented-corporate-lobbying#metadata_info_tab_contents.

43   Anna Greenwood prefaces the claim by pointing out that other specialities, such as epidemiology and public health, were also 'mobilised to serve in the colonial context'. Meanwhile, it should be noted that the development of gynaecology had an imperial element, with pioneering surgery often conducted on enslaved women and, later, on impoverished immigrant women, many from Ireland. But it was only tropical medicine that was developed with 'the explicit intent of facilitating and extending colonisation'. When the Secretary of State for the Colonies, Joseph Chamberlain, called for the founding of the London School of Hygiene and Tropical Medicine at the end of the nineteenth century, he did so out of national self-interest: the British empire needed fit and healthy men to run it. Its prominence owed quite a lot to Patrick Manson, who was a leading researcher in the field through his research on filariasis, a tropical disease caused by parasitical worms, commonly known as elephantiasis. 'Since 1895, Manson had been delivering lectures on the topic at St George's Hospital, London, UK, and he soon gained Chamberlain's ear – and an appointment as the Consulting Physician to the Colonial Office – persuading him that "constructive imperialism" involved establishing a training school for doctors about to embark on careers in colonised countries . . . The tropical medical career did not typically recruit top-flight physicians but was attractive to middle-class, masculine, sporty types, with less cerebral propensities.' Havelock Charles, a prominent doctor in the Indian Medical Service, put it thus: 'The best kind of man to go to the tropics is the good ordinary type of Britisher, with a clear head "well screwed on", an even temper, not over intellectual.' The colonies, bursting with 'new' diseases, illnesses and parasites, became, as Greenwood puts it, 'a living laboratory for research', and the imperial scientists didn't even have to worry about pesky issues such as participant consent. Anna Greenwood, 'The Art of Medicine: Diagnosing the Medical History of British Imperialism', *Lancet*, 03/09/2022, 400, pp. 726–7. See also Deirdre Cooper Owens, *Medical Bondage: Race, Gender, and the Origins of American Gynecology*, University of Georgia Press, 2017, p. 5.

44   As *The Times* explained recently, after it transpired that the wife of the then Chancellor, and eventual Prime Minister, was a 'non-dom', the policy was introduced in 1799 by William Pitt the Younger, with the aim of keeping 'the new class of colonial rich, who were financing and propping up the burgeoning Empire, happy by exempting all of their foreign earnings from British tax. At a time when some of the richest and most powerful of these British colonialists had acquired much of their wealth from abroad by farming sugar cane in Jamaica or tobacco plantations in Virginia, they would otherwise have faced eye-popping tax bills in Britain on their overseas earnings.' Of course, the non-doms of today are not citizens of British empire, but citizens of the planet. The tax break nowadays attracts the mega-rich from former Soviet republics, from Asia and from the fields of finance and entertainment, some 120,000 people according to a recent estimate. See David

Byers, 'What is non-domicile status? How it's earned and why it cuts tax', *The Times*, 08/04/2022, https://www.thetimes.co.uk/article/what-is-non-domicile-status-how-its-earned-and-why-it-cuts-tax-7tlx5g538; Richard Brooks, 'A relic of empire that created a tax economy', *Financial Times*, 20/02/2015, https://www.ft.com/content/6b83be28-b863-11e4-b6a5-00144feab7de; Dhana Sabanathan, 'What exactly is a non-dom?', *FT Adviser*, 25/04/2022, https://www.ftadviser.com/investments/2022/04/25/what-exactly-is-a-non-dom/; https://shorturl.at/bpyK1.

45   'Nuclear historians have neglected the imperial dimensions of the British nuclear programme, preferring instead to focus on the more instrumental role played by the USA,' explained the modern historian Christopher Hill to me over email. 'Yet one only needs to glance at the basic characteristics of the British nuclear programme to see it was highly entangled in imperial politics as well. We tested in Australia with the support of the Australian Prime Minister, Robert Menzies; we used the Gilbert and Ellice Island Colony (Christmas and Malden Island in present-day Kiribati) to test atomic and thermonuclear weapons. We procured our uranium by colluding with the Belgians in the Congo. We later sourced supplies from Namibia, illegally occupied at the time by Apartheid South Africa . . . Imperial politics of knowledge were reflected not only in the choice of test sites, but also in human radiation tests on the femurs of babies from Australia and Hong Kong. The Commonwealth was used as a global source of knowledge about radiation. British mining politics were a huge factor in the expansion and re-making of empire. Uranium and thorium were a significant part of this story when it was discovered that uranium was a fissile material that could be weaponised from the late 1930s. The sites of tests were usually places that had an entire history of colonial violence. Ironically, the colonisers often used indigenous knowledge to gain mastery of these environments. Take, for example, the role of Len Beadell in the creation of British test sites in South Australia.' Hill is lead researcher on a funded project entitled 'The New Nuclear Imperialism: Science, Diplomacy and Power in the British Empire'. The politics of non-proliferation and nuclear deterrence have also been shaped by decolonisation, with Shampa Biswas' book, *Nuclear Desire: Power and the Postcolonial Nuclear Order*, University of Minnesota Press, 2014, being illuminating on the theme.

46   In *Empireland* I talked about how current caste-based hierarchies in India can be traced back to the British, who oversimplified an elaborate system of religious and social identities to create new, rigid systems that still shape Indian life today. But Ajay Verghese, tracing the different patterns of violence in two different parts of modern India (the 75 per cent of Indians who were under the thumb of British colonial administrators vs the remainder of the country which was ruled by mostly autonomous local kings with the implementation of the aforementioned

post-Mutiny policy), comes to a more nuanced conclusion: in contemporary India, those provinces which had been directly ruled by the British see intensified *caste and tribal* conflict, while *religion* is more likely to be cause of violence in the former princely states, where the British had less influence. Sanjoy Chakravorty, 'Viewpoint: How the British reshaped India's caste system', *BBC News*, https://www.bbc.co.uk/news/world-asia-india-48619734; Ajay Verghese, *The Colonial Origins of Ethnic Violence in India*, Stanford University Press, 2016, pp. 3–4.

47   I do recommend this book, however: Gurminder K. Bhambra and Julia McClure (eds.), *Imperial Inequalities: The Politics of Economic Governance across European Empires*, Manchester University Press, 2022.

48   Danielle Heard, 'Comedy', *Oxford African American Studies Center*, https://doi.org/10.1093/acref/9780195301731.013.50279; J. P. Rossing, 'Emancipatory Racial Humor as Critical Public Pedagogy: Subverting Hegemonic Racism', *Communication, Culture & Critique* 2016, 9:4, pp. 614–32, https://doi.org/10.1111/cccr.12126; Corliss Outley, Shamaya Bowen and Harrison Pinckney, 'Laughing While Black: Resistance, Coping and the Use of Humor as a Pandemic Pastime among Blacks', *Leisure Sciences* 2021, 43:1–2, pp. 305–14, https://doi.org/10.1080/01490400.2020.1774449; https://www.usip.org/sites/default/files/ROL/TJC_Vol1.pdf.

49   *Sunday Mercury*, 'The areas of Birmingham that are no-go areas for white people', *Birmingham Mail*, 03/01/2009, https://www.birminghammail.co.uk/news/local-news/the-area-of-birmingham-that-are-no-go-areas-for-white-237564.

50   Murphy, *The Empire's New Clothes*, pp. 12, 68–9.

51   Bocking-Welch, *British Civic Society at the End of Empire*, p. 31.

52   The Demos report said: 'Britain's traditional connections with the rest of the world provide an opportunity to reinvent the role of the Commonwealth and forge new approaches to reconciliation, conflict prevention and poverty reduction. This could begin with a world tour which apologised for Imperial wrongs, combined with a new effort to make the Commonwealth effective and relevant to the new challenges of globalisation. These measures would help to transform perceptions of both the UK and its monarchy.' See Tom Bentley and James Wilsdon, 'The new monarchists', in Tom Bentley and James Wilsdon (eds.), *Monarchies*, Demos Collection 17, 2002, p. 15, https://demos.co.uk/wp-content/uploads/files/monarchies.pdf.

53   Ferguson, *Empire*, pp. xii–xiii; 'Queen "must say sorry for Empire sins" ', *Evening Standard*, 27/05/2002, https://www.standard.co.uk/hp/front/queen-must-say-sorry-for-empire-sins-6328283.html?amp.

54   Boyes and Flanagan, 'How revitalised Commonwealth can be a bulwark against Beijing'.

55   Murphy, *The Empire's New Clothes*, p. 134.

56    Victoria Ward, 'King Charles wants Britain's role in the slave trade "better highlighted and acknowledged" ', *Daily Telegraph*, 09/11/2022.

57    Valentine Low, 'Commonwealth Day service: King urges leaders to "unite for a global good" ', *The Times*, 13/03/2023, https://www.thetimes.co.uk/article/king-charles-first-commonwealth-day-service-speech-2023-qv8cspzk6.

58    Bocking-Welch, *British Civic Society at the End of Empire*, p. 28.

59    Murphy, *The Empire's New Clothes*, pp. 7–8.

60    Ibid., pp. 129, 133.

61    Brooke Newman, 'The Royal Family should apologise for their links to slavery before they are embarrassed into doing so', *I News*, 29/07/2022, https://inews.co.uk/opinion/royal-family-apologise-links-slavery-before-embarassed-1677595.

62    James II made £6,210 from his investment, equivalent to £1 million today (according to the historian K. G. Davies) and in the sixty years the Company lasted, 38,000 of its victims died during the process of trafficking. See Michael Taylor, 'The Manchester Guardian: The Limits of Liberalism in the Kingdom of Cotton', *Guardian*, 29/03/2023, https://shorturl.at/qyEFW.

63    Wills, 'The East India Company Invented Corporate Lobbying'; Sherman, 'Pressure from Leadenhall', pp. 329–55.

64    Newman, 'The Royal Family should apologise for their links to slavery before they are embarrassed into doing so'.

65    Newman, 'The Royal Family should apologise for their links to slavery before they are embarrassed into doing so'.

66    Ibid.

67    Upper Burma was offered as a present for Queen Victoria on New Year's Day, 1886. Kwarteng, *Ghosts of Empire*, p. 167, and Adam Gopnik, 'Finest hours: The making of Winston Churchill', *New Yorker*, 23/08/2010, https://www.newyorker.com/magazine/2010/08/30/finest-hours.

68    Gardner, *The Frontier Complex*, p. 166.

69    'Since [Queen Victoria] strongly opposed home rule for Ireland and approved of the war in South Africa, she was prepared to do as much as she could to ensure the survival of the Unionist government,' writes Phillip Buckner. 'Royal tours were one means of showing her approval' and she made a visit to Ireland in 1900 'partly to indicate her opposition to home rule and partly to show her gratitude to those of her Irish subjects who had served in the South African War'. Hilary Sapire adds that, more generally, 'royal tours to the empire, which originated in the visit of Queen Victoria's son Prince Alfred to the Cape and Natal in 1860, were the direct descendants of the great domestic progresses of Queen Elizabeth I. They had evolved to provide a means of associating successive generations of the royal family with the empire, to parade the symbols of imperial hierarchy before the subjects of empire, and allow them the chance to display their loyalty.

In its modern incarnation, the royal tour drew on the vision of George V who, in 1901 [shortly before becoming Prince of Wales], had visited South Africa as part of one of the longest world-wide tours. This visit in turn paved the way for his Christmas radio broadcasts to the empire in the thirties, and Edward VIII made his name with a series of empire tours including his successful visit to South Africa in 1925.' See Phillip Buckner, 'The Royal Tour of 1901 and the Construction of an Imperial Identity in South Africa', *South African Historical Journal* 1999, 41:1, pp. 324–48 at p. 325, https://doi.org/10.1080/02582479908671897; Hilary Sapire, 'African Loyalism and its Discontents', *Historical Journal* 2011, 54:1, pp. 215–40, https://doi.org/10.1017/S0018246X10000634.

70  Max Siollun tells us that '[After Benin city had been captured, Ralph Moor] supervised the looting of the artefacts, which he ordered to be collected at one location. He selected some as gifts for Queen Victoria and the Prince of Wales, and for officials at the Foreign Office. Moor later recalled: "I may mention that Her Majesty the Queen was graciously pleased to accept some trophies of the operations sent through Lord Salisbury – and I believe that His Royal Highness the Prince of Wales and the First Lord of the Admiralty also accepted trophies."' See Siollun, *What Britain Did to Nigeria*, p. 141.

71  'Friedrich Wilhelm Keyl, *Looty*', *Royal Collection Trust*, https://www.rct.uk/col lection/406974/looty.

72  Sapire, 'African Loyalism and its Discontents', p. 226.

73  David Pegg and Rob Evans, 'Buckingham Palace banned ethnic minorities from office roles, papers reveal', *Guardian*, 02/06/2021, https://www.theguardian. com/uk-news/2021/jun/02/buckingham-palace-banned-ethnic-minorities-from- office-roles-papers-reveal.

74  Bocking-Welch, *British Civic Society at the End of Empire*, p. 36.

75  Kojo Koram has proposed a British truth and reconciliation commission for colo- nialism, based on a Belgian model. See Kojo Koram, 'Britain needs a truth and reconciliation commission, not another racism inquiry', *Guardian*, 16/06/2023, https://www.theguardian.com/commentisfree/2020/jun/16/britain-truth-reconciliation- commission-racism-imperial.

76  David Barber Wellington, 'The Queen says sorry to wronged Maoris', *Independent*, 02/11/1995, https://www.independent.co.uk/news/world/the-queen-says-sorry- to-wronged-maoris-1536901.html.

77  Suhasini Raj, 'The queen's death draws a more muted response in India, the largest of Britain's former colonies', 09/09/2022, https://www.nytimes.com/2022/09/09/ world/europe/queen-elizabeth-death-india-empire.html.

78  Empire heightened the expectations for British coronation ceremonies. 'Osten- tatious spectacles and pageantry were central to imperialism,' explains John M. MacKenzie. 'Since empires cannot be self-effacing, repeated processions and

ritualised events were partly designed as acts of self-regard, to fortify and offer reassurance for the participants . . . Ceremonies also accompanied the arrival and departure of viceroys, governors general, governors and other imperial officials . . . The most elaborate of all ceremonial came to surround the royal visits to colonies that began in the 1860s.' Adopting the word used for Indian rulers' courts, and going on for up to a month, these 'durbars' made King Charles III's ceremony feel low key. In 1877, there were 84,000 spectators present, and by 1911 there were 250,000. In 1911, a total of 50,000 soldiers and military personnel were reviewed, the new Emperor and Empress appeared on thrones on the roof of the Red Fort, and a crown with 6,002 jewels was made for the occasion. In 1877, some 16,000 prisoners were let out of jails in celebration. In 1903 Lord Northcote, the Governor of Bombay, reportedly had glass doors on his tent and English fireplaces inside. Numerous objectives were served by the pageantry, including the establishment of hierarchies and the promotion of the idea that the British monarchy was a legitimate institution. These coronations-on-tour were also global media events, with newspapers, newsreels, Reuters, the Press Association, all publishing excitable coverage of the durbars of 1903 and 1911. MacKenzie continues: 'It is intriguing that in early [East India] Company days it was the Indian princely states that were more eager to impress the British with ceremonial than the other way round. Thus the princes sought to overawe them to turn aside their apparent threat to the existing order. But the British developed their own responses later in the century, seeking to make themselves appear "more Indian" by adopting what they conceived to be powerful resonances of Indian splendour.' MacKenzie, *A Cultural History of the British Empire*, pp. 39–41, 51; Alan Trevithick, 'Some Structural and Sequential Aspects of the British Imperial Assemblages at Delhi: 1877–1911', *Modern Asian Studies* 1990, 24:3, pp. 561–78.

79  Furthermore, it was reported that the Koh-i-Noor diamond would, in a new exhibition of the crown jewels at the Tower of London, be referred to as a 'symbol of conquest', alongside an explanation of how a ten-year-old Sikh maharaja was made to give up the Koh-i-Noor after the British conquest of the Punjab. See Valentine Low, 'Crown Jewels exhibition at Tower of London to recognise British imperialism', *The Times*, 15/03/2023, https://www.thetimes.co.uk/article/crown-jewels-exhibition-at-tower-of-london-to-recognise-british-imperialism-6wvhqlok8.

80  Described by one South African academic as 'a blood diamond' and 'stolen', the diamond is wrapped up in dark imperial history which saw Britain colonize South Africa. See Brahmjot Kaur, 'Camilla swaps the Kohinoor diamond for another controversial stone on her coronation crown', *NBC News*, 17/02/2023, https://www.nbcnews.com/news/asian-america/camilla-swaps-kohinoor-diamond-

another-controversial-stone-coronation-rcna71032; Dave Roos, 'Was the Cullinan Diamond a Royal Gift or Stolen Gem?', *How Stuff Works*, 06/10/2022, https://science.howstuffworks.com/environmental/earth/geology/cullinan-diamond.htm.

81   Valentine Low, 'Camilla's crown for coronation avoids Koh-i-noor headache', *The Times*, 14/02/2023, https://www.thetimes.co.uk/article/camillas-crown-shows-colonial-diamonds-arent-for-ever-z0vnkc3s7.

82   David Pegg and Manisha Ganguly, 'India archive reveals extent of "colonial loot" in royal jewellery collection', *Guardian*, 06/04/2023, https://www.theguardian.com/uk-news/2023/apr/06/indian-archive-reveals-extent-of-colonial-loot-in-royal-jewellery-collection?CMP=share_btn_tw.

83   Josh Butler, 'Commonwealth Indigenous leaders demand apology from the king for effects of colonisation', *Guardian*, 04/05/2023, https://www.theguardian.com/uk-news/2023/may/04/commonwealth-indigenous-leaders-demand-apology-from-the-king-for-effects-of-colonisation.

84   PA Media, 'St Kitts and Nevis PM says country is not free while King Charles is head of state', *Guardian*, 08/05/2023, https://www.theguardian.com/world/2023/may/08/saint-kitts-and-nevis-pm-says-country-is-not-free-while-king-charles-is-head-of-state.

85   Sabah Choudhry, 'Jamaica: King's coronation accelerates plans for Jamaican republic – with referendum "as early as 2024"', *Sky News*, 04/05/2023, https://news.sky.com/story/jamaica-kings-coronation-accelerates-plans-for-jamaican-republic-with-referendum-as-early-as-2024-12872453.

86   David Conn, Aamna Mohdin and Maya Wolfe-Robinson, 'King Charles signals first explicit support for research into monarchy's slavery ties', *Guardian*, 06/04/2023, https://www.theguardian.com/world/2023/apr/06/king-charles-signals-first-explicit-support-for-research-into-monarchys-slavery-ties.

87   Becky Grey, 'Commonwealth Games: Birmingham puts on captivating opening ceremony', *BBC Sport*, 28/07/2022, https://www.bbc.co.uk/sport/commonwealth-games/62340186; Ariana Baio, 'Tom Daley enters Commonwealth Games surrounded by Pride Flags to make powerful statement', *indy100*, 28/07/2022, https://www.indy100.com/sport/commonwealth-games-tom-daley-opening-ceremony.

88   Grey, 'Commonwealth Games'.

89   Bull, 'Can radical changes restore sagging prestige of Commonwealth Games?'; https://thecgf.com/news/commonwealth-sport-foundation-launches-ambition-lead-world-sport-and-social-change.

90   Siollun, *What Britain Did to Nigeria*, p. 81.

91   Reuters, 'Dutch King apologizes for Netherlands' historic role in slavery', *CNN World*, 01/07/2023, https://edition.cnn.com/2023/07/01/europe/dutch-king-apologizes-netherlands-slavery-intl/index.html.

92  Anna Holligan, 'Netherlands slavery: Saying sorry leaves Dutch divided', *BBC News*, 19/12/2022, https://www.bbc.co.uk/news/world-europe-63993283.amp. The research showed that the royal House of Orange earned the equivalent of €1 billion in today's money from the trade and colonial military conquest. The Princes of Orange, including William III who was also the King of England, played an important role in establishing a policy of robbery, exploitation, slavery and forced labour in Asia and the Caribbean. See Bruno Waterfield, 'Dutch royals pocketed €1bn from conquest and slavery', *The Times*, 18/06/2023, https://www.thetimes.co.uk/article/44c5de96-0e14-11ee-a92d-cf7c831c99b5?shareToken=fa161a27d99697b5b6327608110fc073.

93  Tine Destrooper, 'Belgium's "Truth Commission" on its overseas colonial legacy: An expressivist analysis of transitional justice in consolidated democracies', *Journal of Human Rights* 2023, 22:2, pp.158–73.

94  Bruno Waterfield, 'Belgium to return looted artefacts from colonial past', *The Times*, 17/03/2023, https://www.thetimes.co.uk/article/belgium-to-return-looted-artefacts-from-colonial-past-vjfwgvrp5.

95  Catarina Demony, 'Portugal Should Apologise, Confront Past Role in Slavery, Says President', Reuters, 25/04/2023, https://www.usnews.com/news/world/articles/2023-04-25/portugal-should-apologise-confront-past-role-in-slavery-says-president.

96  Catarina Demony and Belén Carreño, 'EU says slavery inflicted "untold suffering", hints at reparations', 18/07/2023, https://shorturl.at/dgHL7.

97  Nicole Winfield, 'Pope Voices Willingness to Return Indigenous Artifacts', *Time.com*, 30/04/2023, https://time.com/6275864/pope-indigenous-artifacts/.

98  'African royalty touchdown in Jamaica to discuss reparations', *The Voice*, 02/03/2023, https://www.voice-online.co.uk/news/world-news/2023/03/02/african-royalty-touchdown-in-jamaica-to-discuss-reparations/.

99  'Two centuries of forgetting', *Economist*, 19/08/2023.

100  Joshua Nevett, 'UK's £18tn slavery debt is an underestimation, UN judge says', *BBC News*, 23/08/2023, https://www.bbc.co.uk/news/uk-politics-66596790.

101  'Two centuries of forgetting'.

102  Harriet Sherwood, 'C of E setting up £100m fund to "address past wrongs" of slave trade links', *Guardian*, 10/01/2023, https://www.theguardian.com/world/2023/jan/10/church-of-england-100m-fund-past-wrongs-slave-trade-links.

103  Matilda Head, 'Cambridge's Trinity College to examine its links to slavery', *Independent*, 18/03/2023, https://www.independent.co.uk/news/uk/trinity-college-university-of-cambridge-africa-b2303546.html.

104  Jonathan Smith and Paul Lashmar, 'William Gladstone: family of former British PM to apologise for links to slavery', *Guardian*, 19/08/2023, https://www.theguardian.com/world/2023/aug/19/william-gladstone-family-of-former-british-pm-to-apologise-for-links-to-slavery.

105  Aamna Mohdin, 'Clive Lewis calls for UK to negotiate Caribbean slavery repar-
     ations', *Guardian*, 08/03/2023, https://www.theguardian.com/world/2023/mar/
     08/clive-lewis-calls-for-uk-to-negotiate-caribbean-slavery-reparations.

106  Aamna Mohdin, 'Guardian owner apologises for founders' links to transatlantic
     slavery', *Guardian*, 28/03/2023, https://www.theguardian.com/news/2023/mar/
     28/guardian-owner-apologises-founders-transatlantic-slavery-scott-trust.

107  Aamna Mohdin, 'UK government and royals called on to investigate slavery
     links after Guardian apology', *Guardian*, 29/03/2023, https://www.theguardian.
     com/news/2023/mar/29/uk-government-royals-called-on-investigate-slavery-links-
     after-guardian-apology.

108  Rob Harris, 'Penny Wong tells Britain to confront its colonial past', *The Age*,
     01/02/2023,https://www.theage.com.au/politics/federal/penny-wong-tells-britain-
     to-confront-its-colonial-past-20230131-p5cgvw.html?ref=rss.

# Index

Hawkins, Sir John, 10, 45, 241
Hayes, Sir John, 333
Headrick, Daniel R., 320, 342–3, 415
health and medicine: British empire's
    developments, 236, 417; in colonial-
    era Caribbean, 324; dental hygiene,
    58; diabetes, 29, 34, 326; effects of
    Old World diseases on New World,
    22, 89–90; freed slaves, 40;
    indentured labourers, 94, 98–9; India,
    4, 326; malaria, 57–62, 70, 338;
    mental health, 33–4; in modern
    Caribbean, 32, 33, 34; obesity, 326;
    and slavery's legacies, 37–8
Heblich, Stephan, 36–7
Heikkilä-Horn, Marja Leena,
    213, 402
Heirs of Slavery, 140
Hemings, Sally, 386
Herrera, Linda, 414
Hewitt, James, 164
Hickel, Jason, 353
Hickling, Professor Frederick, 34
Higman, B. W., 56
*hijra*, 146, 147
Hill, Christopher, 418
Hillary, William, 23
Hindorf, Dr, 343
Hinduism, 86, 100, 105–6, 116–17, 377
Hirsch, Afua, 331
Hispaniola, 22
Historic England, 334
Hobhouse, Emily, 368–9
Hodge, Arthur, 153
Hodgkin, Thomas, 154
Holland, Tom, 180
Holness, Andrew, 43
Home, Alec Douglas, 139
Home, Robert, 87, 321
homosexuality *see* LGBT issues
Hong Kong: and democracy, 221, 407;
    imperialism's legacy, 11, 201; law and
    legal system, 156, 157; LGBT issues,

147; lighthouses, 383; nuclear tests,
    418; police forces, 160; and time
    zones, 413
Hoogte, Arjo Roersch van der, 61
Hooker, Joseph, 53, 56, 337
Hooker, William, 56, 62
Hope, John, 239
Horricks, Benjamin Edward, 164
horse racing, 6, 83, 350
Hose, Sam, 179, 385
Howard-Johnston, Jessica, 113
Howell, Lord, 234
HSBC, 13
Hudson, Pat, 36–7
Huggins, Edward, 153
Hughes, William 'Billy', 192
human rights law, 48, 332, 344, 366
humanitarianism *see* charities; non-
    governmental organizations
Hume, David, 386
Humsafar Trust, 169
hunger and famine: British empire and
    nutrition, 130–31; Ethiopia, 113;
    Freedom from Hunger Campaign,
    127–8; historical attitudes to, 131;
    India, 76, 85, 88, 353; Ireland, 86, 132;
    legacy for health, 37, 38, 326
hunting, 135–41
Hussain, Mobeen, 15, 321
Huzzey, Richard, 48–9
Hyam, Ronald, 148

Igbo people, 200, 205, 209–10,
    394
Ijaw people, 394
Ilbert, Sir Courtenay Peregrine,
    161–2
IMF *see* International Monetary Fund
immigration *see* migration
imperial commissions, 154–6,
    160–61
indenture: on Barbados, 22; compared to
    slavery, 90–91, 92–102, 106–8; crime

Unilever, 9, 344
United Arab Emirates, 148
United Nations, 124, 127, 236,
    414–15
uranium, 418
urban planning *see* towns
USA: anti-racism, 194; attitude to
    British monarchy, 45; black resistance
    to white supremacy, 194; as British
    imperial creation, 11–12; charities and
    NGOs, 370; and concentration
    camps, 87; creation of, 90; and Diego
    Garcia, 88; education of world
    leaders, 392; eminent blacks, 195;
    environmental issues, 78; genocide of
    indigenous peoples, 89–90;
    immigration policies, 179, 187, 191,
    385; Native Americans, 10–11, 89;
    place names, 13; plant transportation's
    effects on ecology, 73; proposed
    formal union with Britain, 188–90;
    racism, 171, 179–83, 185–93; slavery's
    legacies, 37–8; South Carolina's
    establishment, 22; and tea industry,
    67–8; and telegraph cables, 415; urban
    planning, 17; value to Britain of early
    colonies, 325

Vail, Leroy, 320
Vavi, Zwelinzima, 243
Veerapen, Arvind, 81, 82–4, 100, 104,
    106, 107
Veerapen, Jaya, 81, 106, 107
verandas, 1, 309–10
Verghese, Ajay, 418–19
Vernon, James, 130–31, 368
Versailles, Treaty of (1919),
    176, 192
Victoria, Queen, 50, 242, 310, 335,
    342, 420
Victoria Falls Bridge, 320
Vietnam, 77
Villanueva, Edgar, 366

violence: abuse of indentured labourers,
    164, 168; abuse of servants, 165–7;
    abuse of slaves, 25–7, 97–8, 149–50,
    152–3; atrocities prompting legal
    reform, 152–3; effect of study on
    historians, 26–7; inflicted by British,
    65–6, 87–8, 121, 162–8, 344, 353, 365,
    380; as legacy of imperialism, 201–2,
    205–7, 236, 418; as legacy of
    indenture, 107; lynching, 179; in
    Malayan Emergency, 65–6; rape and
    sexual abuse, 47, 98, 132, 149–50, 162,
    164–5; *see also* crime and punishment
Viswanathan, Gauri, 5
Voth, Hans-Joachim, 36–7
Vurpillat, J. Taylor, 412–13

Wagner, Kim, 26, 116, 215, 225–6
Walcott, Derek, 91, 171
Wales, Frederick, Prince of, 345
Wales, Kate, Princess of, 43–4
Wales, William, Prince of, 43–4, 139,
    140
Walker, Kim, 58, 339
Walker, Martin, 221, 401, 407
Wanna, John, 218
Ward, Nathaniel Bagshaw, 59
Wardian cases, 59–60, 66–7, 73
Warr, Earl De La, 128
warrant chiefs, 209, 398
Warren, Larry and Anna, 29–30
Washington, George, 31
Washington, Lawrence, 31
Waterloo, Stanley, 189
Watling, John, 121
weather *see* climate change;
    meteorology
Webb, Alfred, 164
Wedgwood, Josiah, 331
weight, body, 16, 326
Welikala, Asanga, 220
Weller, Patrick, 218
Weller, Paul, 112